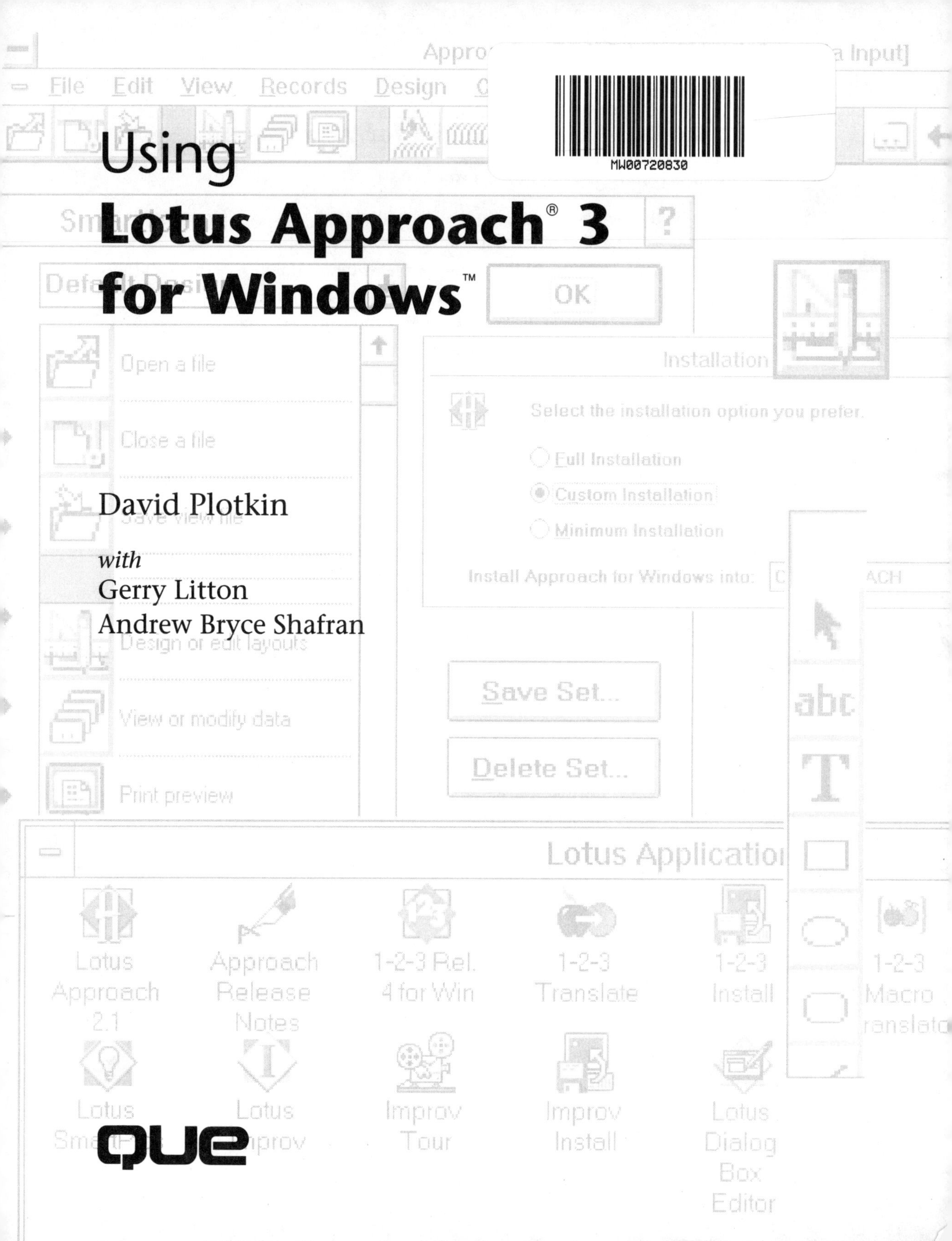

Using Lotus Approach® 3 for Windows™

David Plotkin

with
Gerry Litton
Andrew Bryce Shafran

QUE

Using Lotus Approach 3 for Windows

Library of Congress Catalog Number: 93-84121

ISBN: 1-56529-177-8

96 95 94 6 5 4 3 2 1

Interpretation of the printing code: The rightmost double-digit number is the year of the book's printing; the rightmost single-digit number, the number of the book's printing. For example, a printing code of 94-1 shows that the first printing of the book occurred in 1994.

Publisher: David P. Ewing

Associate Publisher: Don Roche, Jr.

Managing Editor: Michael Cunningham

Product Marketing Manager: Greg Wiegand

Associate Product Marketing Manager: Stacy Collins

Dedication

This book is dedicated to the most important editor in my life: my wife Marisa. Her constant support and editorial consulting enabled me to finish this, my first book. She is the most extraordinary event in my life.

Credits

Publishing Manager
Nancy Stevenson

Acquisitions Editor
Jenny Watson

Product Director
Kathie-Jo Arnoff

Product Development Specialist
Keith Aleshire

Production Editor
Lynn Northrup

Copy Editors
Kelli Brooks
Lisa Gebken
Jeff Riley
Nicole Rodandello

Technical Editors
Melanie Rowe
Glen Sprague

Technical Specialist
Cari Ohm

Acquisitions Coordinator
Debbie Abshier

Editorial Assistants
Jill Byus
Jill Stanley

Book Designer
Paula Carroll

Cover Designer
Dan Armstrong

Imprint Manager
Kelli Widdifield

Production Team
Steve Adams
Angela Bannan
Don Brown
Cheryl Cameron
Stephen Carlin
Kim Cofer
Amy Cornwell
Elaine Crabtree
Chad Dressler
Terri Edwards
DiMonique Ford
Teresa Forrester
Dennis Clay Hager
Aren Howell
Bob LaRoche
Malinda Lowder
Erika Millen
Stephanie Mineart
Wendy Ott
Beth Rago
Clair Schweinler
Dennis Sheehan
Kris Simmons
Mike Thomas
Tina Trettin
Mary Beth Wakefield

Composed in *Stone Serif* and *MCPdigital* by Que Corporation

About the Authors

David Plotkin is a Business Area Analyst with Integral Systems in Walnut Creek, California. He has extensive experience in designing and implementing databases, both at the desktop and on Client Server systems. He writes extensively for various computer periodicals, and his favorite editor is his wife, Marisa.

Gerry Litton is the author of numerous books on microcomputer software. With more than 30 years in the computer industry to his credit, he now works as a professional consultant. A former professor of computer science at the University of San Francisco, Litton resides in Oakland, California.

Andrew Bryce Shafran is a student at Ohio State University in Columbus, Ohio. He is a senior studying Computer Science Engineering. Born in Columbus, Andy has worked with Lotus Notes and the Lotus SmartSuite extensively. He currently works at CompuServe doing Lotus Notes development. His interests include computer networking, desktop publishing, software training, and Broadway musicals. This is his second project for Que Corporation.

Acknowledgments

Quite a few people helped make this book a reality. My good friends Marcus Aiu and Susan Clark at Lotus Approach provided timely information and advice. Nancy Stevenson at Que provided ongoing support and encouragement in the face of almost impossible deadlines. Finally, I would like to single out Production Editor Lynn Northrup, who did such a fine job that I need to figure out how to "persuade" Que to let her work on my next book.

Trademarks

Screen reproductions in this book were created using Collage Complete from Inner Media, Inc., Hollis, New Hampshire.

Contents at a Glance

Table of Contents

13 Automating Your Work 459

III Getting the Most from Approach 495

14 Using Worksheets and Crosstabs 497

Introduction

Welcome to *Using Lotus Approach 3 for Windows*. Approach for Windows was one of the first truly easy-to-learn and easy-to-use relational database products available for Windows. Originally produced by Approach Software, a small company based in Redwood City, California, the product went through two major revisions. Although it sold fairly well, Approach didn't have the marketing muscle to go up against the likes of Microsoft Access and Borland's Paradox for Windows. These competing products are more powerful than Approach, but are also harder to learn and use. Thus, Approach is a more satisfactory product for business persons, consultants, and even developers who do not require the complexity of a programming language.

In mid-1993, Lotus Development Corporation purchased Approach Software. You probably know Lotus from their high-profile line of products, including 1-2-3, Ami Pro, Organizer, and Notes. With Lotus' marketing savvy and budget, Approach began to gain popularity rapidly. Almost immediately after the acquisition, Lotus produced version 2.1 of Approach. This revision gave Approach the same look and feel as other Lotus products, including a SmartIcon bar, the use of the second mouse button, and an active status bar. However, many of the other limitations of Approach were not addressed. For example, the stringent limitation of opening only ten database tables at a time was not handled, nor was the restrictive design of macros addressed. These limitations have been removed in version 3.0.

What's New in Approach 3.0?

With version 3.0, Lotus has made significant improvements to Approach. The product can now directly open many new database types, and can use more than 30 tables in an application. Macro facilities have been greatly enhanced for automating repetitive tasks, and limitations on joining tables have been largely removed. Lotus added crosstabs and charting capabilities; "assistants" to aid in building forms, reports, form letters, and mailing labels; and even a spell checker. Dialog boxes and menu options are more logically arranged, and Approach can finally maintain records in a sort order that you define. There are very few database chores you can't accomplish with this new, more powerful version of Approach!

Who Should Read This Book?

Using Lotus Approach 3 for Windows is designed for anyone interested in building a database application in Approach. This book doesn't assume that you are a database expert—or even a computer expert. Even if you've never used a database management system before, you'll be able to design complex, powerful applications by the time you reach the end of the book.

This book assumes you know how to perform the common tasks that the Windows operating environment requires, such as selecting an item by clicking it, pulling down a menu, opening and closing files and windows, and using click-and-drag to move windows and other objects on-screen.

Note

The version of Approach described here is 3.0, the most current version available as of the publication date of this book. If you have chosen not to upgrade to 3.0, certain features won't work as described or won't be available at all. If your version of Approach doesn't perform as described in the text, you may want to upgrade to the most recent version.

Examples are presented throughout this book to help you understand various Approach concepts. For consistency, the examples all revolve around a single fictitious business—a publishing company that supplies legal newsletters to its customers. This company, called Owl Publishing, not only needs to keep track of its customers, it needs to know which customers ordered which newsletters, when their subscriptions expire, and so on. Trying out the examples as you progress through the book will help you become more familiar with how Approach works.

What Is Covered in This Book?

Using Lotus Approach 3 for Windows covers all the features of Approach. Besides detailed explanations of these features, it presents examples based on a sample database application for our fictitious company, Owl Publishing. These examples help illustrate important points about designing and using Approach. The book also includes tips for using Approach more effectively.

This book is divided into four major parts. Part I, "Getting Started with Approach," covers the basics, and gets you started using simple tables, forms, and queries. Part II, "Using Forms, Queries, and Reports," covers more advanced features, such as relational databases, calculated fields, and summary reports. Part III, "Getting the Most from Approach," describes Approach's worksheets, crosstab reports, charts, and advanced database relationships. It also describes how to customize Approach for your special needs. Part IV, "Integrating Approach with Other Applications," describes importing and exporting database, text, and spreadsheet files. It also describes how to use Approach with the workgroup software Lotus Notes as well as with the other software programs provided in the Lotus SmartSuite.

If your needs are simple, you may want to read just Part I and come back to Parts II, III, and IV later as your applications become more sophisticated.

Part I: Getting Started with Approach

Chapter 1, "Learning Approach Basics," familiarizes you with the objects onscreen, such as the SmartIcon bar and the status bar. It also shows you how to work with the various kinds of files that Approach creates and how to save your work.

Chapter 2, "Creating Database Tables," shows you how to create and modify the structure of an Approach database table. You can create databases by directly defining the database structure, or by converting a spreadsheet or text file into a database. This chapter discusses validation and data entry options, and how to protect your work with passwords. It also discusses some of the kinds of database files that Approach can use.

Chapter 3, "Building Data Input Forms," teaches you how to create forms in which to type your data. Approach's "Form Assistant" is available to help with the form-building process. This chapter also discusses the various layout tools available in the form builder.

Chapter 4, "Enhancing Data Input Forms," shows you how to modify forms and describes the various objects that you can place on a form. Approach supports many different formats of fields for holding your data, and can display the field data you enter in many different formats. You can also change color, add drop shadows, and adjust font, size, and effects for text.

Chapter 5, "Working with Your Data," shows you how to enter data on a form and then how to sort, delete, and edit the information. Approach can display your data in a default sort order, so that you always see your records in the order you expect.

Chapter 6, "Finding Records," discusses the basics of using an input form to build a query for finding records that meet the criteria you set. You may enter query criteria in any field, including radio buttons, check boxes, and drop-down lists. You can find exact values, ranges of values, and combine multiple criteria into a Find.

Chapter 7, "Creating Reports and Mailing Labels," explores different kinds of reports, how to create and modify the reports, and how to build mailing labels. Approach offers standard and columnar reports. You may customize reports using virtually all the same tools and objects as you use for forms. You can even enter and edit data on a report or a mailing label. Approach offers easy mailing label support, including pre-built templates for popular sizes of Avery mailing labels.

Part II: Using Forms, Queries, and Reports

Chapter 8, "Understanding Relational Databases," describes how to create and link multiple tables that have related information. Virtually all powerful database applications use relational databases. By properly using Approach's relational properties, you can minimize or eliminate the entry of redundant data.

Chapter 9, "Designing Advanced Forms," shows how to design forms that use related tables for lookups and how to display multiple lines of information about a related table. It also shows how to build list boxes whose contents are given by another table.

Chapter 10, "Using Advanced Field Types," details some of the more powerful fields that Approach can handle. These include fields for importing pictures and performing calculations. This chapter discusses some of the more popular functions for creating calculated fields.

Chapter 11, "Performing Advanced Finds," discusses advanced query techniques, such as combining criterion in a query and performing queries based on the result of a calculation.

Chapter 12, "Creating Advanced Reports," shows how to set up reports that use related tables, create form letters using your data, and create summaries in reports. Summary reports are useful because they enable you to total or count up your data.

Chapter 13, "Automating Your Work," explains how to use Approach's macro functions to perform a series of actions automatically whenever you choose. The macro functions enable you to build custom applications without doing any programming. You can attach macros to buttons, fields, and even pictures. You can instruct Approach to run a macro when you click a button, change the value in a field, or even run the macro automatically when you open a file in Approach.

Part III: Getting the Most from Approach

Chapter 14, "Using Worksheets and Crosstabs," details how to customize and use a spreadsheet-like worksheet to enter and edit data in your Approach database. A crosstab enables you to create tables that summarize your data in meaningful ways.

Chapter 15, "Creating Charts," shows you how to turn your data into colorful charts. Approach's "Chart Assistant" leads you through creating charts easily. Approach supports 20 different styles of charts. Several of these chart styles are available in three-dimensional versions as well.

Chapter 16, "Exploring Advanced Database Relationships," gives tips and hints on handling difficult relational database problems.

Chapter 17, "Customizing Approach," leads you through setting preferences for your application, including default styles (color, fonts, borders, and so on), the display of on-screen items, and customizing your own set of SmartIcons.

Part IV: Integrating Approach with Other Applications

Chapter 18, "Importing and Exporting Files," shows you how to exchange information between your Approach database and other common applications using various file formats. These formats include dBASE III+ and IV, Paradox 3.5 and 4.0, Excel, and Lotus.

Chapter 19, "Using Lotus Notes with Approach," demonstrates how Approach can be used with Lotus Notes, a network office automation application. This "groupware" program allows people to access, track, share, and organize information in numerous ways. For example, using Lotus Notes' electronic mail feature, you can send the current view of an Approach worksheet to someone else.

Chapter 20, "Using Approach with the Lotus SmartSuite," discusses how Approach can share data with the other members of the Lotus SmartSuite, such as Lotus 1-2-3 for Windows or Ami Pro. Using Object Linking and Embedding (OLE), Approach gives you access to up-to-date information in other files. For example, if cells in a spreadsheet are OLE-linked to a record in a database, any changes in the spreadsheet cells will appear in the database record.

You may find it useful to have the data files used to create the examples in this book. To download these files, go to the Electronic Publishing section of CompuServe and select the Macmillan Computer Publishing Forum.

Conventions Used in This Book

A number of conventions appear in *Using Lotus Approach 3 for Windows* to help you learn the program and distinguish the different elements. These conventions are explained in the following section.

The following special typefaces are used in this book:

Type	Used to Indicate
italics	New terms or phrases when initially defined
boldface	Information you are asked to type, and letters that appear underlined on-screen in the Approach menu and dialog box options
`special type`	Direct quotations of words that appear on-screen or in a figure, and formats such as text strings

In most cases, keys are represented as they appear on the keyboard. The arrow keys are usually represented by name (for example, the up-arrow key). The Print Screen key is abbreviated PrtSc, Page Up is PgUp, Insert is Ins, and so on; on your keyboard, these key names may be spelled out or abbreviated differently.

When two keys appear together with a plus sign, such as Ctrl+Home, press and hold down the first key while you press the second key. When two keys appear together, such as End Home, press and release the first key before you press the second key.

Tip
This paragraph format suggests easier or alternative methods of executing a procedure, or discusses advanced techniques related to the topic described in the text.

Note

This paragraph format indicates additional information that may help you avoid problems, or that should be considered in using the described features.

Caution

This paragraph format cautions you of hazardous procedures (such as activities that delete files).

Icons that appear in the margin indicate that the procedure described in the text includes instructions for using the appropriate SmartIcons.

Part I

Getting Started with Approach

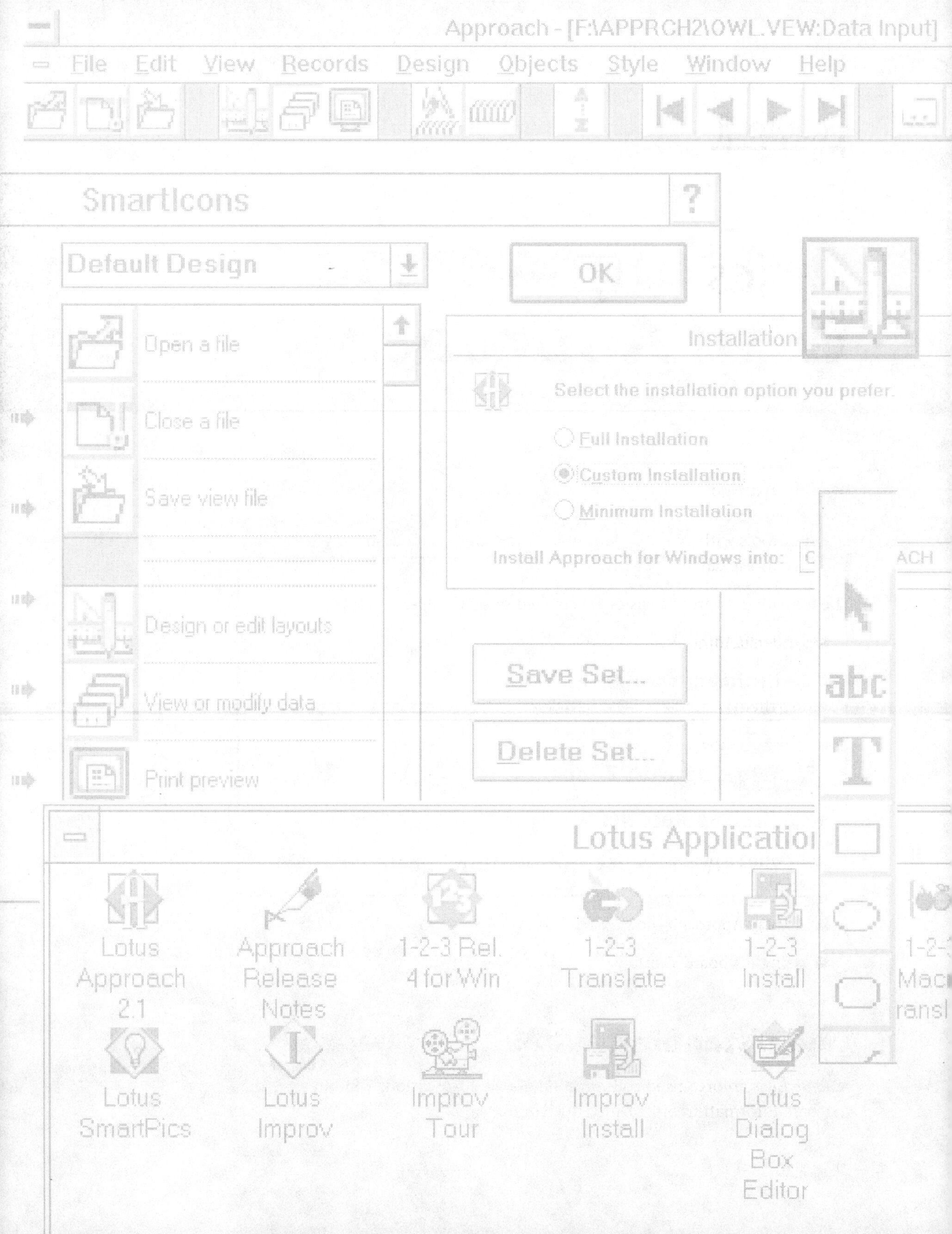

Approach - [F:\APPRCH2\OWL.VEW:Data Input]
File Edit View Records Design Objects Style Window Help
SmartIcons
Default Design
OK
Open a file
Close a file
Save view file
Design or edit layouts
View or modify data
Print preview
Installation
Select the installation option you prefer.
Full Installation
Custom Installation
Minimum Installation
Install Approach for Windows into:
Save Set...
Delete Set...
abc
Lotus Applicatio
Lotus Approach 2.1
Approach Release Notes
1-2-3 Rel. 4 for Win
1-2-3 Translate
1-2-3 Install
Lotus SmartPics
Lotus Improv
Improv Tour
Improv Install
Lotus Dialog Box Editor

Chapter 1

Learning Approach Basics

Until now, designing and building your own database application was a task few people were willing to try. But Approach for Windows combines a powerful set of tools with Windows' intuitive interface to provide an easy-to-learn and easy-to-use database program.

The following Approach basics are covered in this chapter:

- Understanding the definition and uses of a computerized database
- Recognizing the screen elements that make up Approach and how to use them
- Learning how to open, save, copy, and delete Approach files
- Setting and changing Approach file passwords
- Learning how to add Approach file information
- Creating a program item icon for opening an Approach file in a single step
- Adding Approach file information
- Using keyboard shortcuts

Understanding What a Database Is

A *database* is an organized collection of related information. You can store database information on paper or in a computer.

An example of a database stored on paper is an address book—certainly one of the more common databases in your life. Of course, you can also keep an address-book type database on a computer.

The information in a computerized database is usually stored in the form of tables, with rows and columns comprising each table. Table 1.1 shows the rows and columns in an address-book type database. Each row in Table 1.1 contains a set of columns, labeled Name, Address, City, State, Zip, and Phone. Rows in such a table are called *records*. The second row in Table 1.1, for example, containing the name Mary Smith and her address and phone number, is a record. The columns represent categories of related information in each record (row). Each category is called a *field*. City, for example, is one field in Table 1.1.

Table 1.1 Records and Fields in a Simple Database

Name	Address	City	State	Zip	Phone
Joe Chung	23 West 14th	New York	NY	10034	232-1234
Mary Smith	44 Gulf Ct.	Concord	NH	02457	334-5908
Mike Carter	98 Tone Ave.	Myers	AZ	88907	589-4689

Your address book is probably similar to Table 1.1. The information that pertains to one person is a single record. (However, you may have additional fields for other information you wish to track, such as birthdays and anniversaries.) An address-book database thus contains many records—one for each person you have noted. Each record contains many fields, such as the person's name, address, phone number, and so on.

The address-book example represents a simple type of database called a *flat-file database*. In a flat-file database, all the information about a particular subject is stored in a single table. A more sophisticated type of database is a *relational database*, which enables you to store related information in multiple tables and link the information in those tables. A relational database gives you considerably more flexibility in working with your data and creating reports than a flat-file database.

Approach is a relational database. Although this book initially discusses using Approach as a flat-file database, you will learn about its relational capabilities in Chapter 8.

Why Use a Computerized Database?

Chances are, you frequently need to revise your address-book database—add new names, change addresses and phone numbers when people move, and so on. Although keeping a simple database (such as an address book) in printed form makes sense, large databases quickly become unwieldy when you try to maintain them on paper.

Keeping your database on a computer has some significant advantages over the manual method:

- You can store a large amount of information in a relatively small amount of space.
- The computer can search for particular information quickly and efficiently.
- You can tell the computer to print reports, mailing labels, and form letters from the results of a search.
- You can sort the database based on a different piece of information (field).
- You can easily change the type of information you want to store in the database.
- You can tell the computer to perform complex calculations and summarize the data contained in the database.

If you want to reorganize the database based on a different piece of information, you can sort your address-book database by phone number instead of by last name. This way, you can group all the people with the same area codes. At any time, you can also add another category of information to the database—such as a fax number or a checkbox for whether someone sent you a Christmas card last year. Although all these items are certainly possible with a paper-based database, managing that database would require much more manual labor. A computer-based database enables you to work more efficiently and frees you to pursue more enjoyable interests.

Why Design Your Own Database?

Databases in one form or another are critical applications for individuals and businesses. Databases can improve your life and influence how your business operates. You can keep your financial data in a database, for example, and make decisions about how to manage your money based on that data. A business may keep virtually all the information it needs to operate in a database. This information can include data about employees, salaries, the products the business sells, and customers. But how do you get the database applications you need?

A variety of programs for building database applications have been available for years. Paradox, dBASE, FoxPro, Access, and other database programs enable people to design their own applications. Unfortunately, despite advances in user-friendliness, designing applications with these programs is still beyond the reach of most people because it's necessary to learn a programming language to use the programs effectively.

The tendency, therefore, is to hire a consultant to build a database application for you with one of these tools. Hiring a consultant has several disadvantages:

- *Cost.* Hiring a consultant can be expensive. The price varies widely, depending on the programmer's experience and the location of your business, but it can range from as little as $35 per hour to as much as $125 per hour.

- *Inaccuracy.* The finished application often doesn't quite reflect what you had in mind. Because describing your requirements to a consultant can be difficult, the finished application may not do everything you need.

- *Inappropriateness.* You are bound to find many annoying little things that you don't like about the finished application—perhaps the labeling on a menu is confusing, or the color scheme is jarring. Unfortunately, getting such problems fixed means having the consultant return—and paying for that time. As a result, all too often these unsatisfactory aspects of the application never get fixed.

- *Short Life Span.* The original consultant may be unavailable, meaning that a new consultant would have to become familiar enough with the application to make the changes for you. Not only might it be difficult to find another consultant, but it would probably be more expensive to bring in a new person.

With Approach, you can create your own databases without becoming a programming expert. You can design attractive forms for data input, print out reports and mailing labels, and make corrections to fine-tune the application as you see fit. As your needs or your company's needs change, you can change the database to match—all without incurring huge programming bills. Also, because Approach is a Windows program, training someone to enter the data takes much less time than if the application were built using a DOS database program. Training someone to enter data is even easier if the person has used other Windows programs.

Starting Approach

Approach can be launched just like any other Windows application. Follow these steps:

1. If the Program Manager window is not open, double-click the Program Manager icon to open it.

2. Double-click the group icon that contains Approach (for example, the Lotus Applications icon).

3. Double-click the Approach 3.0 icon to run Approach.

Introducing Approach

Approach is a very flexible product. As you perform tasks in Approach, you will use several different modes: Browse, Design, Preview, and Find. *Browse* mode enables you to enter data on a form or report. *Design* mode enables you to create your own forms, reports, form letters, and mailing labels. *Preview* mode shows you what your output will look like when you send it to the printer. Finally, you can locate records that match special criteria by using the *Find* mode. You can switch between the modes using the status line at the bottom of the screen, or by selecting a SmartIcon from the SmartIcon bar at the top of the screen.

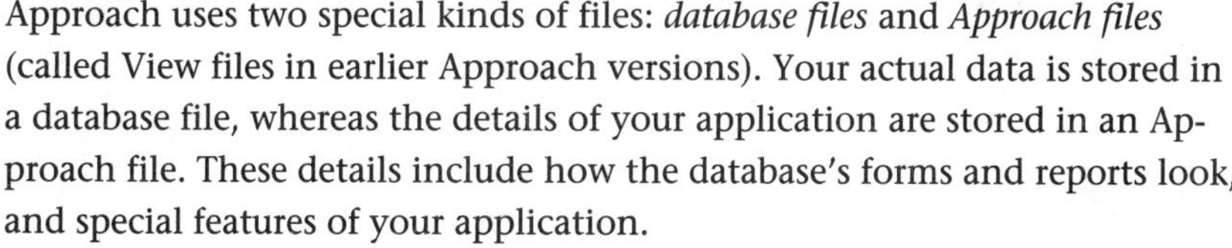

Approach uses two special kinds of files: *database files* and *Approach files* (called View files in earlier Approach versions). Your actual data is stored in a database file, whereas the details of your application are stored in an Approach file. These details include how the database's forms and reports look, and special features of your application.

Although Approach is designed to be used primarily with a mouse, you can use the keyboard to perform some operations, such as selecting items from menus and making selections from dialog boxes. However, only the mouse can be used for some actions, such as placing and sizing objects on a form.

Understanding the Screen Elements

The first step in beginning to use Approach is to learn the various screen elements. Figure 1.1 shows the data input form of the example scenario, a legal publishing company called Owl Publishing. The form is displayed in Design mode. Study this figure carefully as we discuss the various items that are visible on-screen.

> **Note**
>
> You can use the View menu selections to display or hide many of the on-screen items discussed below. For example, you can hide the SmartIcons, status bar, and view tabs.

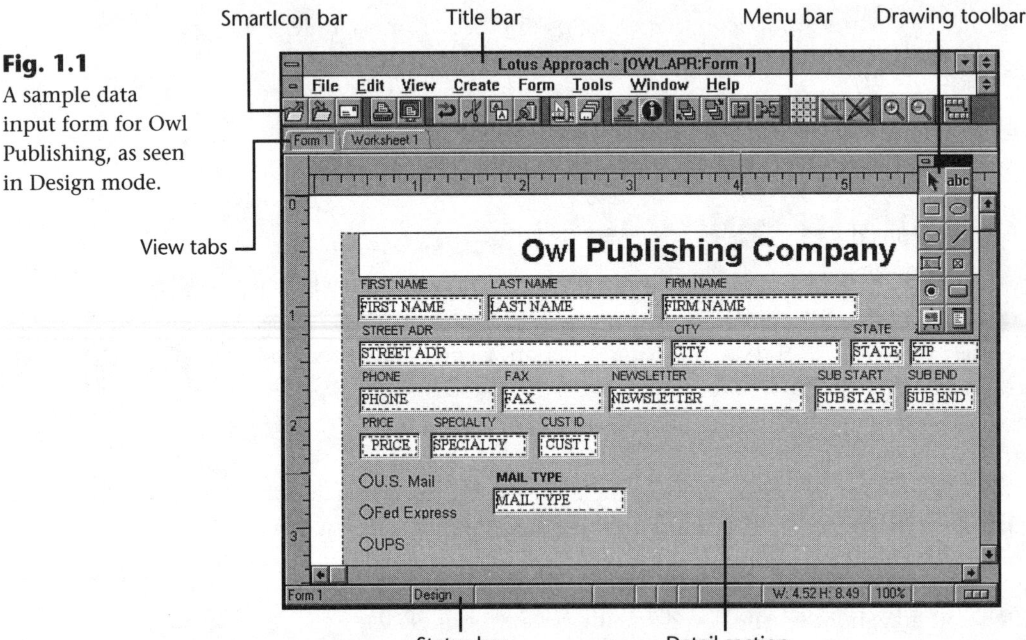

Fig. 1.1
A sample data input form for Owl Publishing, as seen in Design mode.

The Title Bar

Across the top of the Approach window is the *title bar*. The text in the title bar normally specifies the name of the file that is currently in use, as well as the name of the current view (form or report). The title bar also gives a quick explanation of the function of any menu item that you select.

The Menu Bar

Below the title bar is the *menu bar*, which contains the standard drop-down menus present in virtually all Windows applications.

To use the mouse to make a selection from a menu, move the pointer to a menu name on the menu bar and then click the menu name. The menu "drops down," showing the choices (items) available. You can choose one of these items by clicking it. For example, to quit Approach, open the **F**ile menu and choose E**x**it.

You can also access the menus from the keyboard. For more information, see "Using Keyboard Shortcuts" later in this chapter.

The SmartIcon Bar

Below the menu bar is the *SmartIcon bar*. The SmartIcon bar contains icons that make calling up the most common commands easy. SmartIcons duplicate commands available from the pull-down menus. To use a SmartIcon, click it with the mouse.

Tip
To display the SmartIcon bar by default, click the Smart**I**cons checkbox in the Show section of the Display panel in the Preferences dialog box, located in the Tools menu.

Approach offers help with the function of a SmartIcon in two ways. You can right-click a SmartIcon to display a balloon that describes the function of the SmartIcon. Or, if you have checked the Show Icon Descriptions checkbox in the SmartIcons dialog box, you can position the mouse pointer over a SmartIcon and the description balloon will appear. The balloon disappears when you move the mouse pointer away from the SmartIcon bar.

The SmartIcon bar varies with the mode (Browse, Design, Find, or Preview) that you are currently using. You can also customize the SmartIcon bar, hide the SmartIcon bar, or create an entirely new SmartIcon bar, as detailed in Chapter 17.

Tip
To open the SmartIcons dialog box, open the **T**ools menu and choose **T**ools Smart**I**cons.

You can position the SmartIcon bar along the top, bottom, left, or right sides of the screen. You can also create a "floating" window containing the SmartIcons (see fig. 1.2). You can reposition this window on the screen by clicking and dragging the window. To change the position of the SmartIcon bar, open the **T**ools menu and choose Smart**I**cons. Select the position you want for the SmartIcon bar from the **P**osition drop-down list.

You can display or hide the SmartIcon bar by opening the **V**iew menu and choosing Show **S**martIcons.

Chapter 5 discusses using the Browse mode SmartIcon bar. Using the Design mode SmartIcon bar is discussed in Chapters 4, 7, and 9. Using the Find mode SmartIcon bar is discussed in Chapters 6 and 11. Chapter 7 discusses using the Preview mode SmartIcon bar.

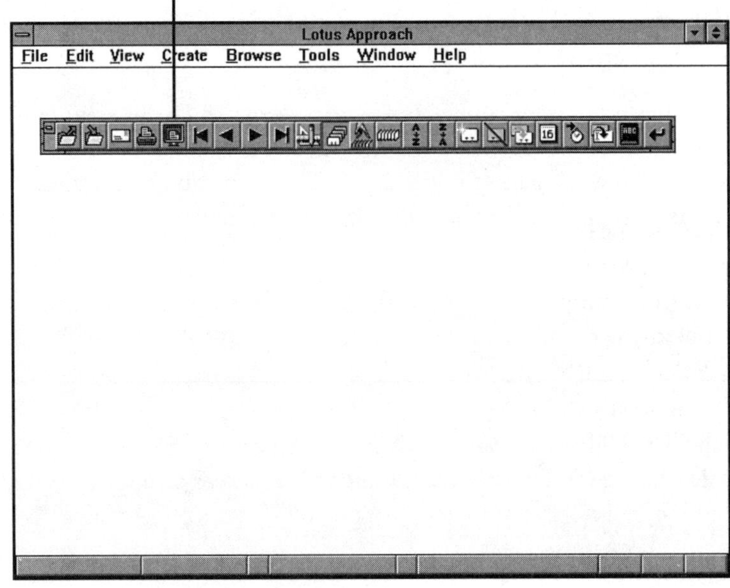

Fig. 1.2
A "floating" SmartIcon bar can be moved to different positions around the screen.

The Drawing Toolbar

Tip
To display the Drawing toolbar by default, click the Drawing Tools checkbox in the Show in Design section of the Display panel in the Preferences dialog box.

The *drawing toolbar* provides a set of tools for designing views. These tools include:

- Graphic shapes (rectangles, ovals, and so on)
- Various field formats such as checkboxes, radio buttons, and drop-down lists
- Text block tool
- Button tool
- Picture tool

The Drawing toolbar is available only in Design mode. You can toggle the display of the Drawing toolbar on and off using the Show Drawing Toolbar SmartIcon, or by opening the **V**iew menu and choosing Show Dra**w**ing Tools.

The Detail Section

The *detail section*—the largest portion of the screen—contains the data from your database. The detail section is where you enter or modify your data.

Besides the database fields, you can place other objects in the detail section. These objects can be text labels (perhaps to indicate what information is expected in a particular field), pictures, and graphics. You can also place buttons in this section and then click those buttons to execute certain tasks. (See Chapter 13 for more information on how you can add buttons to the detail section.)

The View Tabs

Just under the SmartIcon Bar are the *view tabs*. Approach displays a tab for each view (for example, form, report, form letter, and mailing label) that you create. The name of the view is displayed on the tab. You can switch to the view by clicking the tab for that view. If there are more tabs than Approach can fit on the screen, a pair of triangular arrow buttons appear at the far-right end of the view tabs. You can scroll the list of tabs left or right by clicking the left- or right-arrow button, respectively.

Tip
To display the view tabs by default, click the View **T**abs checkbox in the Show section of the Display panel in the Preferences dialog box.

To display or hide the view tabs, open the **V**iew menu and choose Show View **T**abs, or click the Show View Tabs SmartIcon. You rearrange the view tabs from within Design mode. Simply click a tab and drag it to a new location in relation to the other tabs.

The Status Bar

At the very bottom of the screen is the *status bar*. This line contains additional information about the current application and provides a place to make selections. You can display or hide the status bar by opening the **V**iew menu and choosing Show Stat**u**s Bar.

Tip
To display the status bar by default, click the Status Ba**r** checkbox in the Show section of the Display panel in the Preferences dialog box.

Many areas of the status bar are "live"—that is, when you click an area, Approach presents you with a list of choices. The contents of the status bar vary depending on whether you are in Design mode, Browse mode, or Preview mode.

In Browse mode, the status bar contains the following items:

- *The form or report currently in use.* If you click this indicator, Approach "pops up" a list of forms and reports included in the file you are using. You can switch to another form or report by selecting it from this list.

- *The current mode.* If you click this indicator, Approach presents a list of modes: Browse, Design, Preview, and Find. You can switch to another mode by choosing the mode from this list. If you select Preview while Approach is already in a Preview mode, the Preview mode is turned off and the mode returns to the last-used mode—Browse or Design.

- *The previous record button.* Click this button to move to the preceding record.

Note

This button moves to the previous page if Approach is in Preview mode and you are viewing a report or mailing labels.

- *The current record number.* Click this indicator to open the Go to Record dialog box, in which you can type the record number that you want to view. When you click OK, Approach places that record on-screen.

Note

This button displays the current page number if Approach is in Preview mode. Clicking this indicator under these circumstances opens the Go to Page dialog box, in which you can type the page number you want to look at. When you click OK, Approach places that page on-screen.

- *The next record button.* Click this button to move to the next record.

Note

This button moves to the next page if Approach is in Preview mode and you are viewing a report or mailing labels.

- *The active records indicator.* This part of the status bar displays the total number of records in the database and how many of those records are currently available for editing. Normally, all records are available. If you execute a query, however, only those records that match the criteria of the query are available for editing.

Note

To return to working with all the records in the database, open the **B**rowse menu and choose Show **A**ll, or select the Show All SmartIcon.

- *The SmartIcons button.* Click this button to display a list of available SmartIcon bars. The list includes only SmartIcon bars that are appropriate for the mode you are in. For example, if you are in Browse mode, the list includes only Browse mode SmartIcon bars (see Chapter 17 for more information on customizing SmartIcon bars). You can switch to any available SmartIcon bar by clicking it in the list. You can also hide the SmartIcon bar by selecting Hide SmartIcons from the list.

In Design mode, the status bar contains the following items:

- *The form or report currently in use.* If you click this indicator, Approach "pops up" a list of forms and reports included in the file you are using. You can switch to another form or report by selecting it from this list.

- *The current mode.* Click this indicator to see a list of modes. You can switch to another mode by selecting the mode from this list.

- *The text font.* This indicator displays the font (for example, Arial or Times New Roman) of the currently selected object. To change the font, click the font indicator and select a new font from the pop-up list. If the object does not contain any text, this indicator is blank.

- *The text size.* This indicator displays the size of the text in the selected object. To change the size, click the size indicator and select a new size from the pop-up list. If the object does not have a size, this indicator is blank.

Note

Text sizes are measured in a unit of measurement called *points.* There are 72 points in an inch.

- *The effects buttons.* The next three indicators on the status bar display the text effects for the selected object. The three indicators show whether the selected object's text is currently bold (**B**), italic (*I*), or Underlined (U). If the object does not have a font, these indicators are blank.

- *The style name indicator.* Approach enables you to define a set of properties that you can attach to an object. These properties include font, size, effects, colors, borders, drop shadows, and many others. When you attach a style to an object, that object takes on the properties defined by the style. The style name indicator on the status bar displays the style attached to the selected object. If the object does not have a style, this indicator is blank.

- *X- and y-coordinates/dimensions.* This section of the status bar displays the x- and y-coordinates of the mouse pointer if no object is selected. If an object is selected, this section of the status bar displays either the Left and Top coordinates of the selected object (the status bar shows "L:" and "T:") or the width and height of the selected object (the status bar shows "W:" and "H:"). You can toggle between the coordinates and dimensions by clicking this section of the status bar.
- *The magnification indicator.* This indicator is available in Design and Preview modes. Click this indicator for a list of available magnifications (from 25 to 200 percent) from which you can choose. Selecting a magnification smaller than 100 percent enables you to see more of your data or your design on-screen. Selecting a magnification greater than 100 percent enables you to enlarge a portion of the screen, making it easier to do detailed design work.

Note

In Preview mode, the mouse pointer turns into an outline of a mouse and magnifying glass. Press the left mouse button to increase the magnification one step (for example, from 50 to 75 percent) and press the right mouse button to decrease the magnification one step.

In Design mode, you can also increase and decrease the magnification one step at a time by clicking the Zoom In icon or the Zoom Out icon, respectively.

- *The SmartIcons button.* Click this button to display a list of available SmartIcon bars. The list only includes SmartIcon bars that are appropriate for the mode you are in. Click the option you want to use from this list. You can also hide the SmartIcon bar by selecting Hide SmartIcons from the list.

The Info Box

The *Info Box* is a special dialog box that is available in Design mode (see fig. 1.3). To display the Info Box, choose **S**tyles and Properties from the **O**bject menu, **F**orm menu, or the pop-up menu that appears when you right-click a screen object.

The Info Box provides a set of "panels" for customizing the look of a screen object. For example, you can set the font, size, and effects of text in a text box or field. You can also set the background color, borders, frame style, and shadow color for most types of objects. You can even change the size and position of a screen object using the Info Box. The Info Box panels are accessed by clicking the tabs near the top of the Info Box. You can leave the

Info Box visible on the screen, and the Info Box will change as you click different objects. To get help with an Info Box, click the question mark in the upper-right corner. To close the Info Box, click the close box in the upper-left corner.

You can shrink the Info Box to a smaller size—this way it'll still be handy on the screen, but it won't hide as much of the form. To shrink the Info Box, double-click on its title bar; to return the Info Box to its full size, double-click on the title bar again.

The various properties that you can set from the Info Box are discussed throughout this book.

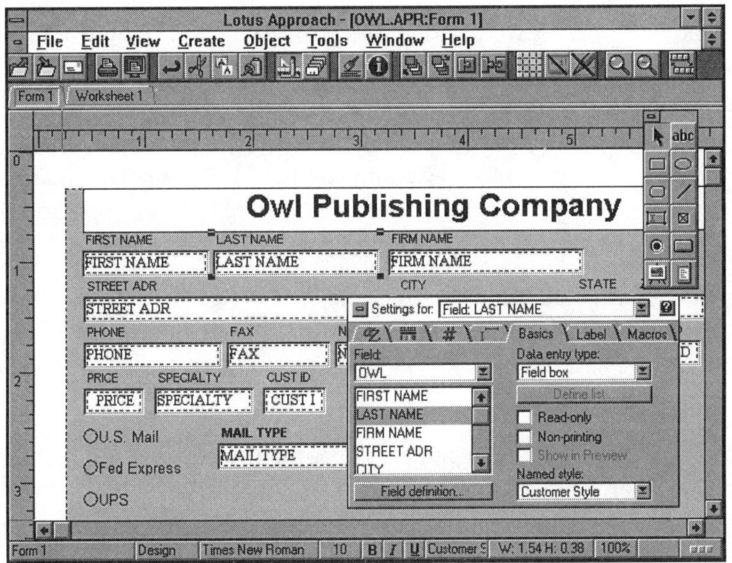

Fig. 1.3
The Info Box allows you to assign properties to an object.

Working with Files

An application that you build with Approach has two major kinds of files:

- The *database file* contains the data that you enter on a form or report.
- The *Approach file* contains the details of the application. These details include the layout of forms and reports, any macros you have defined, and the names of all databases that your application must access.

You never need to worry about saving a database file, because the data is saved automatically as you enter it. An Approach file, on the other hand, needs to be saved any time you make changes to any items on-screen (for example, when you move fields around on a form, add a new report, use a new database in your application, or build a new form). If you make changes that affect the Approach file and try to quit Approach or close the Approach file without saving the changes, Approach reminds you to save your Approach file changes.

The Approach file defines everything you have designed in your Approach application, including the relationships between databases (see Chapter 8), and the details of input forms (see Chapter 4) and reports (see Chapter 7). Thus, your application's Approach file is a very important file. In fact, after you define the database tables to hold your data (see Chapter 2), you likely will never work with any file except the Approach file. The next sections discuss how to work with Approach files in more detail.

Opening an Approach File

When you need to use your application, you simply open the Approach file. Approach then has access to everything you have built as part of that application. Creating an Approach file is covered under "Saving an Approach File" later in this chapter.

If you have configured Approach to display the Welcome to Lotus Approach dialog box, you can open an existing file using the **O**pen drop-down list. This list contains the last five Approach files you have used. Select the file you want to open and click OK.

You can also open an Approach file by opening the **F**ile menu and choosing **O**pen. The Open dialog box appears (see fig. 1.4). The Open dialog box is similar to other Open dialog boxes in Windows. By using this dialog box, you can open files, change directories and drives, and specify the file type you want to see.

Fig. 1.4
Use the Open dialog box to open your files.

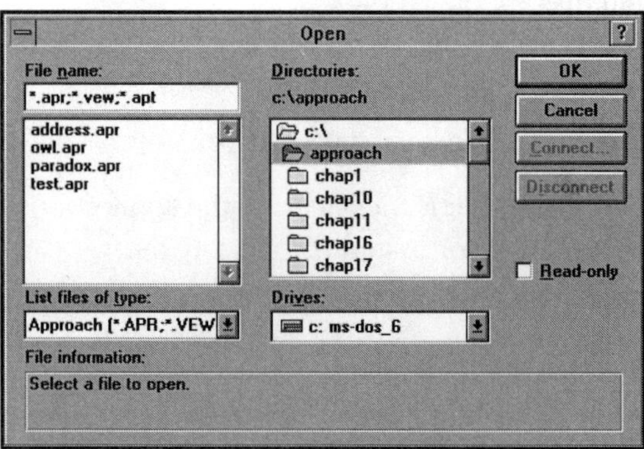

The list box on the left side of the dialog box displays files that match the current file selection criteria. To select one of these files, click the file name. The name appears in the File **N**ame text box.

In the center of the Open dialog box is an area from which you can set the directory and drive that contain the file you want to load. To move to a new directory, double-click its name in the **D**irectories list. To change drives, use the drop-down Dri**v**es list just below the **D**irectories box.

Below the file list is a drop-down list box of file types that Approach can open. By default, this list has Approach files (*.apr, *.vew, *.apt) selected; if they are not selected, click the down arrow at the right side of this line to access a list of file types. Click the Approach files (*.apr, *.vew, *.apt) line and all available Approach files appear in the list box.

On the right side of the Open dialog box is a checkbox for opening a file in **R**ead-only mode. This mode enables you to view the contents of the file but not to modify those contents. After you select the desired file, click OK to load the file.

Caution

The Approach file and the databases can get out of synch if you make changes to the database structure (for example, if you change a field name or delete a field from the database) and don't save the Approach file after the change. The next time you open the Approach file, Approach will automatically display the Field Mapping dialog box. You must use this dialog box to map the fields in the Approach file to the fields in the database. To avoid this problem, always save the Approach file after making changes to the database structure.

Tip

The read-only checkbox must be selected any time you want to open the file in Read-only mode; however, Approach doesn't remember the mode from the last time you opened the Approach file.

Saving an Approach File

The first time you need to save an Approach file, open the **F**ile menu and choose **S**ave Approach File. The Save Approach File dialog box appears (see fig. 1.5). In the File **N**ame text box (in the upper-left corner of the dialog box), type a name for the file. You can also accept the default name, which is the same as the database name. You don't need to include a file extension; Approach appends an APR extension by default. The first time you save an Approach file, the file automatically saves the information on the name of the open database and the default form created from that database.

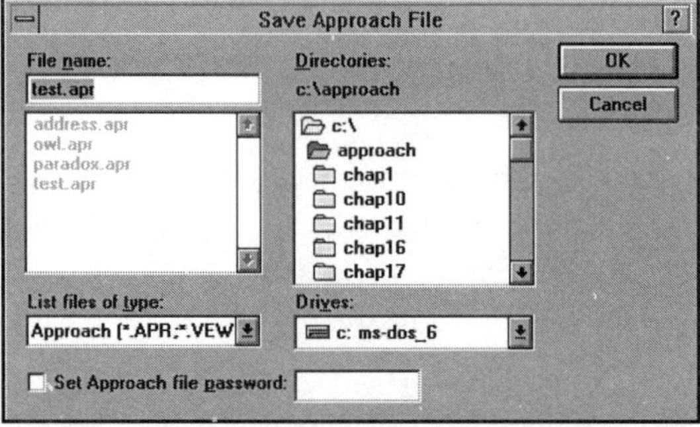

Fig. 1.5
Use the Save Approach File dialog box to save an Approach file.

Note

After you create and save an Approach file for the first time, Approach saves the Approach file to the same file name each time you open the **F**ile menu and choose **S**ave Approach File.

By default, Approach saves the Approach file to the directory selected in the **D**irectories list box. If you need to save the file to a different drive or directory, change the drive with the Dri**v**es drop-down list box and the directory through the **D**irectories list box.

Setting the Approach File Password

If you need to protect an Approach file, you can use a password. Although users can still enter data into a password-protected Approach file, they can't modify the Approach file in Design mode. If someone tries to enter Design mode, that person is prompted for the password before proceeding.

Caution

Consider very carefully whether you want to assign a password to an Approach file. If you forget the password, you cannot access the file in Design mode and must rebuild the Approach file to modify it.

To set an Approach file password, follow these steps:

1. Choose Set Approach File **P**assword at the bottom of the Save Approach File dialog box.

2. Enter the password you want to use in the text box. The typed text appears as asterisks so that someone watching you enter the password won't be able to read your password.

3. Click OK. The Confirm Approach File Password dialog box appears, asking you to retype your password to ensure that you typed it correctly the first time.

4. Retype the password in the **R**etype Approach File Password text box.

Tip
Pick a password that is easy to remember but difficult for someone else to guess. Adding a non-alphanumeric character to the password, such as an asterisk (*) or comma, can foil an intruder.

Changing or Deleting the Approach File Password

To change the Approach file password (or delete the Approach file password altogether), follow these steps:

1. Open the password-protected Approach file.

2. Open the **F**ile menu and choose Save **A**s. At the prompt, enter the password.

3. When the Save Approach File As dialog box opens, choose the .APR File Only radio button in the Databases section in the bottom-right corner.

4. If you want to change the password, choose Set Approach File **P**assword and enter the new password. If you don't want a password, uncheck the Set Approach File **P**assword.

5. Click OK to resave the Approach file under the same file name. Confirm that you want to do this when Approach queries you.

The Approach file is saved under the same file name with a different password or without password protection, depending on whether you selected a new password.

Copying an Approach File

An Approach file comprises the information about your entire application. Because you can spend a considerable amount of effort building an Approach file and getting it just right, Approach enables you to copy an Approach file so that you can create a similar file without rebuilding it from scratch. For example, you may want to build a contact database for your personal life and not just for business associates. Remember, however, that an Approach file cannot be created unless it is associated with at least one database. Thus, when you copy an Approach file, you must also link the new Approach file to existing databases or have Approach create new databases to link to the new Approach file.

To create a new Approach file from an existing one, follow these steps:

1. Open the existing Approach file.

2. Open the **F**ile menu and choose Save **A**s. The Save Approach File As dialog box appears.
3. In the File **N**ame text box, type the name of the new Approach file.
4. Set a password (as described earlier), if you want one.
5. Set the directory and drive where you want the Approach file saved using the other areas of the dialog box.
6. In the Databases section in the bottom-right corner of the Save Approach File As dialog box, choose one of three options. These options enable you also to copy the databases associated with an Approach file. You can choose only one option. (These options are discussed in the following sections.)
7. Click OK to save the new Approach file.

Using the Exact Copy Option

The **E**xact Copy option duplicates the databases and the Approach file. The newly created Approach file is linked to the copied databases rather than the original databases. Thus, you get a complete copy of your application, including the Approach file and databases. You can then make any changes to this copy without affecting the original application.

If you choose this option, you see a new dialog box after you click OK in the Save Approach File As dialog box . You use the Save Database As dialog box (see fig. 1.6) to specify the new name for the copy of the database. The name of the current database appears in the File **N**ame text box. You must specify either a new name for the database(s) or a new directory for the database(s).

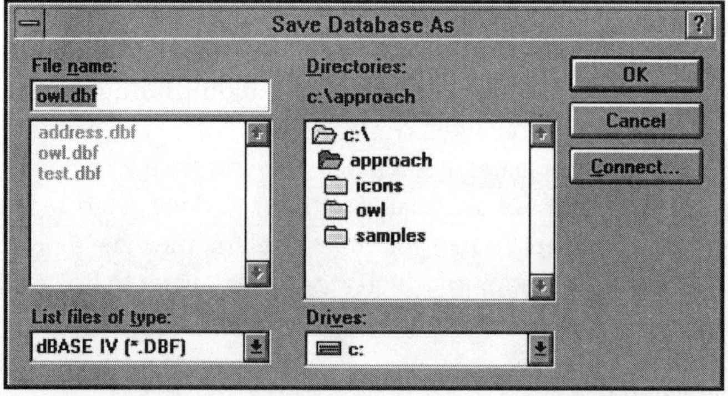

Fig. 1.6
The Save Database As dialog box enables you to save a database under a new name.

To save the new database under a different name, follow these steps:

1. In the File **N**ame text box, type the new name for the file.
2. If you want to change the type of database—for example, from dBASE III+ to FoxPro—choose List Files of **T**ype. From the drop-down list that appears, choose the type of database you want for the copy.
3. Specify where you want the database to be stored by using the **D**irectories and Dri**v**es options.
4. Click OK to create the copy of the database.

Note

If your Approach file is linked to multiple databases, the Save Database As dialog box appears once for each database. This way you can create a name for each copy. Clicking Cancel in any of these dialog boxes cancels the entire operation and returns you to the original Approach file.

Using the Blank Copy Option

The **B**lank Copy option duplicates the database structure (see Chapter 2 for information on how to create a database structure). The new databases have the same fields as the old databases, but no actual records are in them. This way, you can fill the new databases with new data. When you click OK in the Save Approach File As dialog box, the Save Database As dialog box appears (once for each database in the view) so that you can specify names for the new empty databases. Selecting Cancel in any Save Database As dialog box cancels the entire operation and returns you to the original Approach file.

Using the .APR File-Only Option

The .**A**PR File-Only option doesn't copy the databases at all. Instead, it links the new Approach file to the same databases as the old Approach file. You can then modify the new Approach file to change your application or to create an entirely new application (with new forms, reports, validation criteria, and so on) linked to the same databases as your original application. Creating a new .APR file is useful if you want two different sets of people (perhaps with access to different subsets of the database information) to use the same database.

Because you aren't creating any new copies of the databases, the Save Database As dialog box does not appear.

Deleting an Approach File or Database File

Tip

Approach files and database files must be closed before you can delete them.

You can delete an Approach file or database file from within Approach. If you delete a database file, Approach will delete all related files, such as the accompanying indexes. If you delete an Approach file, Approach will delete the associated database file(s) and all their associated files (see fig. 1.7).

Fig. 1.7
You will be asked if you want to delete each associated Approach database.

To delete a database or Approach file, follow these steps:

1. Open the **F**ile menu and choose **D**elete File. The Delete File dialog box appears.

2. To delete a database file, select the database file type in the List Files of **T**ype drop-down list.

   The file type is preset to show Approach's .APR, .VEW, or .APT files, so if you want to delete an Approach file, you don't need to change the file type in the List Files of **T**ype drop-down list.

3. Select the file you want to delete in the File **N**ame list and click OK. Approach asks if you're sure you want to delete the file.

4. Click **Y**es to delete the file. If deleting an Approach file, Approach asks if you're sure you want to delete each associated database file. You can click **N**o in any of these alert boxes to keep a particular database file. If you click **Y**es, the database file is deleted.

Caution

Be careful when deleting database files! Once a database file is deleted, it is no longer available for any use—including use by another Approach file.

Creating a Program Item Icon to Open an Approach File

You can create an icon in the Windows Program Manager that serves as a shortcut for running Approach and for loading a specific Approach file.

When the user double-clicks the icon, Approach runs and the Approach file loads automatically. Follow these steps:

1. Open the Program Manager window, if it is minimized.
2. Open the program group where you want the icon to be (such as the Lotus Applications group).
3. Open the **F**ile menu and choose **N**ew.
4. Make sure that the Program **I**tem option is selected, and then click OK. The Program Item Properties dialog box appears (see fig. 1.8).

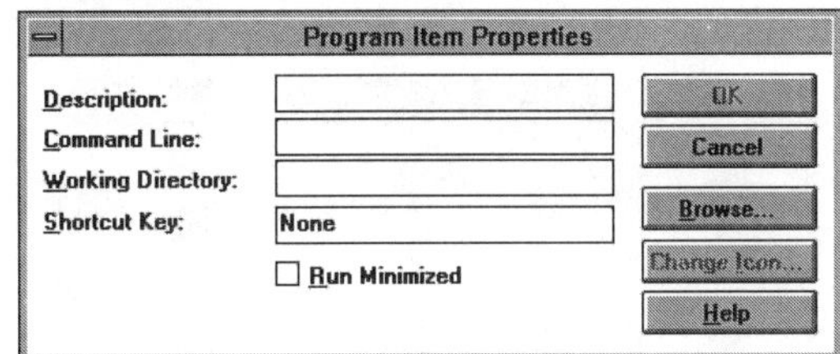

Fig. 1.8
Load a specific database using the Program Item Properties dialog box.

5. In the **D**escription text box, type the text that you want to appear below your icon (for example, **Owl Publishing**).
6. In the **C**ommand Line text box, type the full pathname of the Approach File (for example, **c:\approach\owl.apr**).
7. In the **W**orking Directory text box, type the directory where you want your files to be stored (for example, **c:\approach**).
8. Click OK to create an icon that looks just like the Approach icon.
9. To change the icon, choose Change **I**con. The Change Icon dialog box appears (see fig. 1.9).

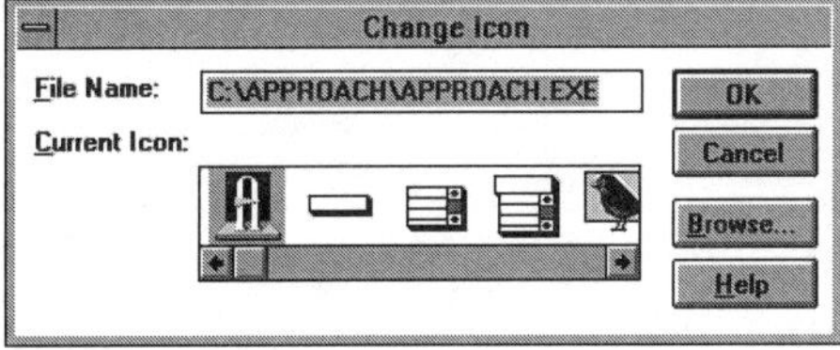

Fig. 1.9
Change the icon for the new Program Item using the Change Icon dialog box.

10. Choose an icon from the **C**urrent Icon list.

> **Note**
>
> If you want a different set of icons from which to choose, type another file name in the **F**ile **N**ame text box. Good files to use are the PROGMAN.EXE and MORICONS.DLL files in your Windows directory, which both contain a large assortment of icons. To see a list of files from which you can pick, choose **B**rowse. After you choose the file you want, choose the icon you like from the **C**urrent Icon list.

11. Click OK in the Change Icon and Program Item Properties dialog boxes. Your desktop now shows the new icon for your view (see fig. 1.10).

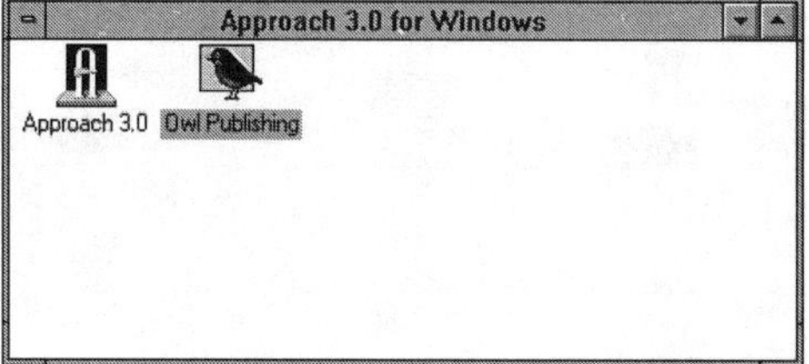

Fig. 1.10
The new icon appears for your Approach file.

Opening Database Files

Besides loading Approach files, as described earlier, Approach can load different types of external database files directly. These file types include dBASE III+ and IV, FoxPro, and Paradox.

Always open the Approach file (the .APR, .VEW, or .APT file) to open a database created in Approach. (Opening the Approach file automatically opens the database file.) If the database was created in an application other than Approach, however, you must open the database file directly because that file does not yet have an Approach file attached to it.

To open a database file, follow these steps:

1. Open the **F**ile menu and choose **O**pen. The Open dialog box appears (see fig. 1.11).

2. From the List Files of **T**ype drop-down list, choose the type of database file you want to open.

3. In the **D**irectories and Dri**v**es boxes, specify where the database is located.

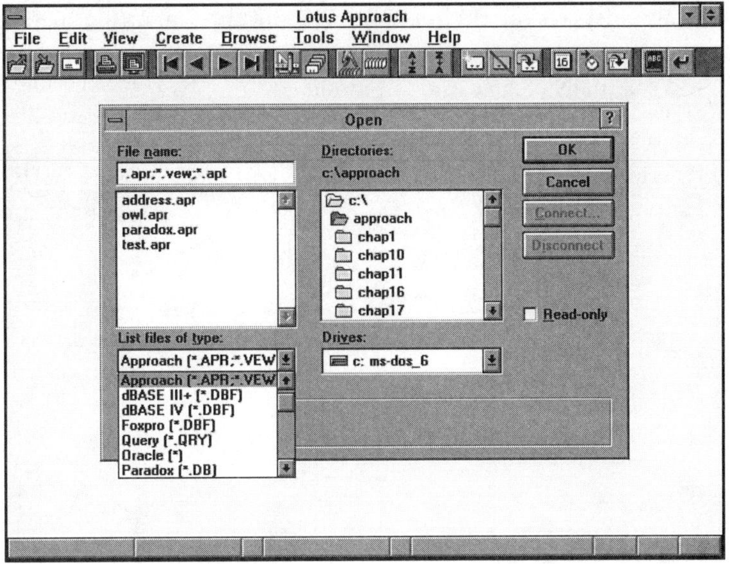

Fig. 1.11
Open other database files using the Open dialog box.

4. In the list box below the File **N**ame text box, select one of the file names. The file name appears in the File **N**ame text box.

5. After you select the file you want, click OK to load the file.

Adding Approach File Information

Approach can store general information about an Approach file. This information includes the name of the author, a description of the Approach file, and descriptive keywords. The author and description appear in the Open dialog box when you click an Approach file in the File **N**ame list. This information can help you determine which Approach file you want to use.

To add information to an Approach file, first open the proper Approach file, and then open the **F**ile menu and choose Approach **F**ile Info. The Approach File Info dialog box opens (see fig. 1.12). You can enter the following information:

- The name of the author of the file. Type the name into the **A**uthor text box. The default entry is the name of the person to whom the copy of Approach is registered.
- A description of the file. Type the description into the **D**escription text box.
- Descriptive keywords for the file. Type the keywords into the **K**eywords text box.

Approach also displays certain information about the file, including the associated databases, views, macros, variable fields, and the date and time that the file was originally created and last modified.

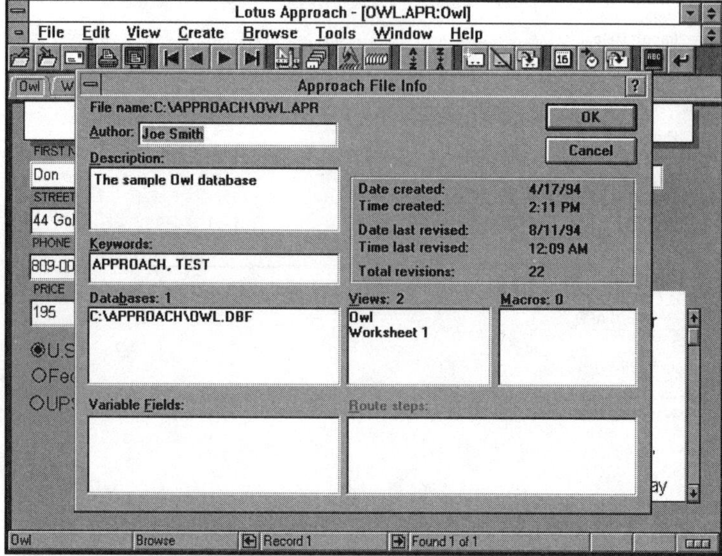

Fig. 1.12
The Approach File Info dialog box provides basic information about your database application.

Using Keyboard Shortcuts

The menu bar at the top of the screen is one way to choose commands in Approach. Sometimes, however, taking your hands off the keyboard to use the mouse is inconvenient. Approach offers some keyboard shortcuts so that you can give commands without having to use the mouse.

As with any Windows application, you can press the Alt key with another key to access a menu, and then press a third key to activate a command on that menu. Pressing Alt+F, for example, accesses the **F**ile menu. You can then press the letter O to access the **O**pen command and open a new file.

The letters that you use to activate commands are underlined. These underlined letters are called *hot keys* and are shown in **bold** throughout this book. On the **F**ile menu, for example, the **F** is underlined. After you pull down the menu, notice that the **O** in **O**pen is also underlined (see fig. 1.13).

Approach also enables you to use even more efficient keyboard shortcuts to access some common commands. Shortcut keystrokes consist of the Alt or Ctrl key and a single letter. (You press these two keys at the same time.) Pressing Ctrl+N, for example, brings up a new record.

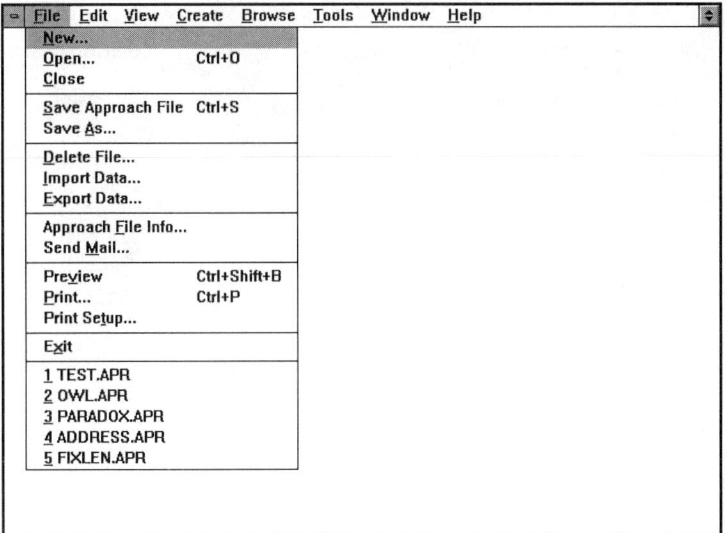

Fig. 1.13
Shortcut keyboard commands are shown to the right of menu choices.

The keyboard shortcuts, listed at the end of the Approach User's Guide, are shown on the menus. As you use the menus, note these keyboard shortcuts—they make navigating through Approach much quicker and easier.

From Here...

In this chapter, you learned what a database is and the advantages of using a computerized database. You also learned about Approach's screen layout and the Browse, Design, Preview, and Find modes, as well as the different types of files that Approach uses.

Giving commands to Approach is another important concept covered in this chapter. Using the mouse and menus, keyboard shortcuts, the status bar, and the SmartIcon bar were also discussed. You also discovered how to save, copy, and delete Approach files, how to protect them with file passwords, and how to add descriptive information to an Approach file.

For more information about working with database files and Approach files, refer to the following chapters in this book:

- Chapter 2, "Creating Database Tables," leads you through the process of creating databases.

- Chapter 3, "Building Data Input Forms," shows you how to build a form for data input and then save the form.

Chapter 2

Creating Database Tables

This chapter covers some of the theory of designing a database. It also discusses how to select a file type, how to specify fields to hold your data, and how to choose special options to ensure that the fields behave the way you want. You'll also learn how to modify your database structure if you need to. At the end of this chapter, you'll also learn how to build an example database file to illustrate these concepts.

In this chapter, you learn how to:

- Create a database from scratch
- Create a database by converting spreadsheet and text files
- Select the best file type for your database format
- Define new fields and their types
- Rearrange fields in your table structure
- Simplify data entry with default and calculated values
- Add formulas to your database fields
- Add passwords to your files
- Modify the table structure and fields
- View your data in an Approach worksheet

Designing a Database

As mentioned in Chapter 1, you can think of a database as an organized collection of data. The data is arranged in tables; each column in the table is a field in the database.

The first task in setting up a new database is to plan what the table will look like. Although leaping in and creating your new table immediately may tempt you greatly, this method isn't the best way to proceed. You should carefully plan the table's appearance. All too often, a user creates a database and starts entering his data, only to find that the database doesn't provide all the necessary information or the information isn't stored in the format he wanted.

Although Approach is powerful enough to enable you to correct these kinds of errors, the process of repairing your mistakes can be tedious and time-consuming, and may require you to reenter some of the data. By spending a little time planning the database early on, you can save time later.

The process of designing a database can be divided roughly into two steps. The first step is *data definition*, in which you list the fields of the database. The second step is *data refinement*, in which you use several techniques to answer these questions:

- Has all necessary data been included in the database?
- Is any unnecessary data being stored in the database?
- Is the data in the database being stored in the correct format?
- Can you use the database for all the purposes you want?

In the following sections, read through the two steps involved in designing a database using a fictional publishing company, Owl Publishing, as an example.

Step 1: Defining Data

The first step is to list on a sheet of paper as many pieces of data as you can think of that you need to store in the database.

Keep in mind how you plan to use the data. The usage directly affects how the data is stored. If you want to create mailings to people in specific zip codes, for example, ZIP CODE must be a separate field in the database—as opposed to being combined with the rest of the address information.

Note

You should list all the possible fields of the database. You can eliminate unwanted fields in Step 2.

In this example, the Owl Publishing Company has decided to create a database to keep track of its newsletter customers. The necessary information includes:

Customer name

Address

Phone number

Birth date

Newsletter name

Date when subscription started

Length of subscription

Step 2: Refining Data

Next comes the all-important step of refining the data. You should carry out this step with as many of the people who will use the database as possible—the more people involved in this process, the closer your final product is to being right.

During the data refinement process, you need to ask yourself what each piece of data is to be used for and what kinds of questions you expect the database to answer. By considering these things, you can decide whether the data in the database can provide the information you need to do your business.

Ask yourself these questions:

- For what reason will I use each piece of data? Can I efficiently use the data for that purpose?
- Can I get the type of information I need from the database? If not, what missing data will enable me to fulfill my business needs?

Keep in mind that even after you design the database, your design isn't permanent. You can always make changes later, if necessary. However, even something as simple as adding a new field involves a great deal of extra work that would have been unnecessary if you had included the field in the first place. At a minimum, you must go through and type the information in the new field of every record in the database. Adding the information in this field as you enter each new record is, of course, much more efficient.

Careful planning and time spent designing the database can help you avoid such problems. If you follow the systematic approach to database design outlined in this chapter, the chances are much better that you won't create a database that you later must redesign extensively.

Owl Publishing needs to target its customers by state or zip code for mailings regarding new newsletters. You could create a field called ADDRESS for this information, but then you couldn't sort the field by just state or zip code. Breaking the address line into STREET ADDRESS, CITY, STATE, and ZIP CODE fields would be more helpful. Also, because many prospective customers belong to firms, you need to record the firm name. Because Owl Publishing doesn't plan to send out birthday cards, the birth date of the customer is not important.

Next you need to ask, "What is the purpose of the Length of Subscription field?" Because Owl Publishing sends out renewal notices just before a subscription expires, a report of all customers whose newsletter subscriptions expire in the next three months would be helpful. Given this usage, the expiration date of the subscription should replace the LENGTH OF SUBSCRIPTION field. An expiration date field lends itself much more effectively to determining who needs to get a renewal notice. Also, if Owl Publishing is sending out renewal notices, you may want to record how many notices have been sent to a particular customer so that you can use different form letters for the second and subsequent notices. You will also want to record whether a flyer has been mailed and how it was sent.

The customer database should also contain all the information necessary to create and send out an invoice—except the newsletter price. Therefore, you need to add pricing information as well.

Finally, because lawyers specialize in various kinds of law, recording their specialties is important so that you can target the correct potential customers for subscription drives.

Given all these considerations, Owl Publishing came up with this list of fields for its customer database:

FIRST NAME

LAST NAME

FIRM NAME

STREET ADDRESS

CITY

STATE

ZIP

SPECIALTY OF LAW

NEWSLETTER NAME

SUBSCRIPTION START DATE

SUBSCRIPTION END DATE

NUMBER OF RENEWAL NOTICES SENT

PRICE OF NEWSLETTER

FLYER MAILED?

MAIL METHOD

Creating a Database File

After you figure out the fields you're going to need in your database, you're ready to create the new database file. You can convert an existing spreadsheet or text file to a database file, or create an entirely new database file.

Creating an Entirely New File

You may create a new database file using the Welcome to Lotus Approach dialog box or the **F**ile menu.

> **Note**
>
> The Welcome to Lotus Approach dialog box appears when you first start Approach and when you close all Approach files. If the Welcome to Lotus Approach dialog box does not appear under these circumstances, open the **T**ools menu and choose **P**references. In the Display tab, check We**l**come dialog.

To create a new file using the Welcome to Lotus Approach dialog box, select Create a **N**ew File from the Welcome dialog box and choose an option from the list of files. You can create a Blank Database, or choose one of the commonly used templates provided, such as Address Book, Contact Database, Customer, Employee, and so on. If you select a database template, Approach automatically includes the appropriate database fields in the new file.

Approach opens the New dialog box (see fig. 2.1). Follow these steps to create a new file:

1. In the File **N**ame text box, type a name for the file. You don't need to type a file extension—Approach automatically assigns the proper extension for you after you choose a file type.
2. Choose the file type you want from the List Files of **T**ype drop-down list. (The available file types are explained in "Understanding the File Types" later in this chapter.)
3. Click OK.

To create a new file using the **F**ile menu, open the **F**ile menu and choose **F**ile **N**ew. The New dialog box appears. Follow steps 1–3 above.

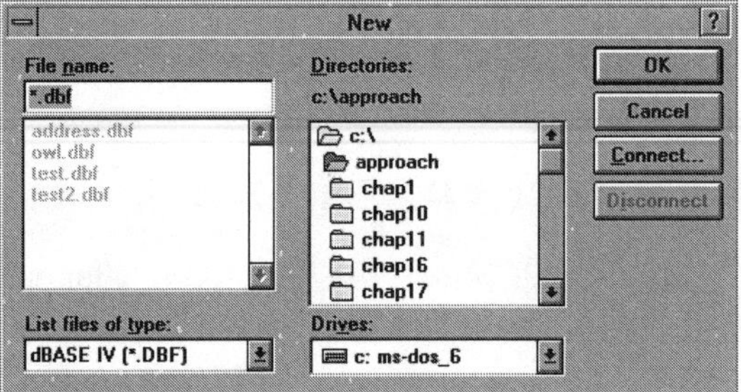

Fig. 2.1
The New dialog box indicates the types of files Approach can create.

Converting a Database from a Spreadsheet

You can import a spreadsheet in Lotus 1-2-3 or Excel format, and Approach creates a new database and Approach file using the information in the spreadsheet. When you create a new database using a spreadsheet, the columns in the spreadsheet become fields in the database, and the rows become records.

If the first row in the spreadsheet contains information (headings, for example) that identifies the rest of the contents, you can use the first row to provide the field names. Otherwise, the fields are initially named A, B, C, and so on. You can use the Field Definition dialog box to change the field names. (See "Modifying the Table Structure" later in this chapter.)

To create a new database from a spreadsheet, follow these steps:

1. Click the Open File icon, or open the **F**ile menu and choose **O**pen. If the Welcome to Lotus Approach dialog box is displayed, select **O**pen an Existing File, and then click OK.

2. Select Lotus 1-2-3 (*.WK*) or Excel (*.XL*) in the List Files of **T**ype drop-down list. Choose the file you want to open in the File **N**ame list. You can change the directory and disk to locate the spreadsheet file.

3. Click OK. The Field Names dialog box appears. To use the first row in the spreadsheet for the field names, make sure the First Row Contains Field Names checkbox is checked. Otherwise, uncheck this box. Click OK.

4. The Convert To dialog box appears. Type a name for your new database file into the File **N**ame text box. You don't need to specify a file extension because Approach will provide the extension for you. You can change the directory and disk if you want to specify a different location for the new file.

   Choose a file type in the List Files of **T**ype drop-down list. For more information on file types, see "Understanding the File Types" later in this chapter.

5. Click OK in the Convert To dialog box. Approach creates the new file for you and displays the contents of the database on a standard form. Be sure to save the new Approach file by opening the **F**ile menu and choosing S**a**ve Approach File.

Converting a Database from a Delimited Text File

You can open an ASCII text file with delimited text, and Approach will create a new database and Approach file using the information in the text file.

A *delimited text file* is a file that contains text separated into discrete units using delimiters such as commas, spaces, or tabs. The delimiters mark where one field, such as city name, ends and another field, such as state name, begins. You can specify the delimiter when you convert the text file into a database. Each line from the text file is a record in the database.

If the first row in the text file contains information that identifies the rest of the contents (for example, headings), you can use the first row to provide the field names. Otherwise, the fields are initially named Field1, Field2, Field3, and so on. You can use the Field Definition dialog box to change the field names. (See "Modifying the Table Structure" later in this chapter.)

To create a new database from a delimited text file, follow these steps:

1. Click the Open File icon, or open the **F**ile menu and choose **O**pen. If the Welcome to Lotus Approach dialog box is displayed, select **O**pen an Existing File, and then click OK.

2. Select Text—Delimited (*.TXT) in the List Files of **T**ype drop-down list. Choose the file you want to open in the File **N**ame list. You can change the directory and disk to locate the text file.

3. Click OK. The Text File Options dialog box appears. Select the delimiter from the Separate Fields With group box. To select a delimiter, click one of the radio buttons to select **C**ommas, **S**emicolons, S**p**aces, or **T**abs.

   Note

   If the text in the file is separated using a different delimiter, click the **O**ther radio button and then type the delimiter into the adjacent text box.

   To use the first row in the text file for the field names, make sure the First Row Contains Field Names checkbox is checked. Otherwise, uncheck this box.

4. Click OK. The Convert To dialog box appears. Type a name for your new database file into the File **N**ame text box. You don't need to specify a file extension because Approach will provide the extension for you. You can change the directory and disk if you want to specify a different location for the new file.

   Choose a file type in the List Files of **T**ype drop-down list. For more information on file types, see "Understanding the File Types" later in this chapter.

5. Click OK in the Convert To dialog box. Approach creates the new file for you and displays the contents of the database on a standard form. Be sure to save the new Approach file by opening the **F**ile menu and choosing S**a**ve Approach File.

Converting a Database from a Fixed-Length Text File

You can open an ASCII text file with fixed-length text, and Approach will create a new database and Approach file using the information in the text file.

A *fixed-length text file* is a file that contains text separated into discrete blocks of a fixed length. If the text in a block doesn't fill the entire length, the text has spaces after it until the next block begins. When you create a database from a fixed-length text file, you must tell Approach how long each block of text is. Each fixed-length block becomes a field in the database, and each row becomes a record. If the first row in the text file contains information that identifies the rest of the contents, you can use the first row to provide the field names. Otherwise, you must name the fields when you create the database. You can use the Field Definition dialog box to change the field names. (See "Modifying the Table Structure" later in this chapter.)

To create a new database from a fixed-length text file, follow these steps:

1. Click the Open File icon or open the **F**ile menu and choose **O**pen. If the Welcome to Lotus Approach dialog box is displayed, select **O**pen an Existing File, and then click OK.

2. Select Text—Fixed-Length (*.TXT) in the List Files of **T**ype drop-down list. Choose the file you want to open in the File **N**ame list. You can change the directory and disk to locate the spreadsheet file.

3. Click OK. The Fixed Length Text File Setup dialog box appears (see fig. 2.2). If the first row of the text file contains the field names, check the **F**irst Row Contains Field Names checkbox. Otherwise, type in the name of the first field name in the Field Name column.

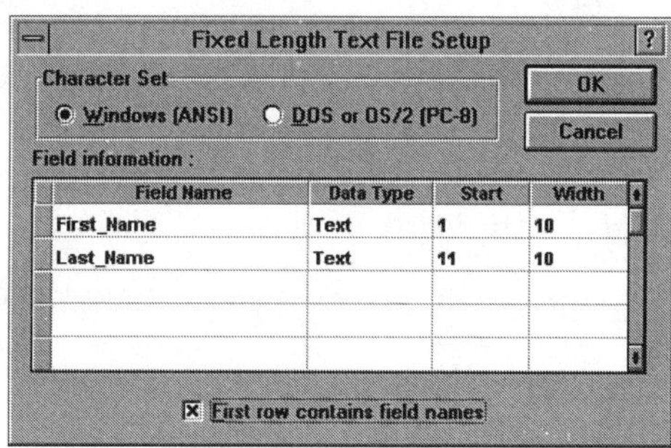

Fig. 2.2 Import fixed-length text files from the Fixed Length Text File Setup dialog box.

4. Choose the Data Type of the field. For more information on data types, see "Defining New Fields" later in this chapter.

5. Type the column number for the first block in the Start column. For example, if the first block starts in column 2, type "**2**" in the Start column. Type the width of the block in the Width column.

6. Click the next line in the Fixed Length Text File Setup dialog box. Approach automatically inserts the starting column for the next field in the Start column. Enter the width of the next block. Repeat this step for all blocks in the text file.

7. Click OK. The Convert To dialog box appears. Type a name for your new database file into the File **N**ame text box. You don't need to specify a file extension because Approach will provide the extension for you. You can change the directory and disk if you want to specify a different location for the new file.

   Choose a file type in the List Files of **T**ype drop-down list. For more information on file types, see the following section, "Understanding the File Types."

8. Click OK in the Convert To dialog box. Approach creates the new file for you and displays the contents of the database on a standard form. Be sure to save the new Approach file by opening the **F**ile menu and choosing S**a**ve Approach File.

Understanding the File Types

As stated earlier, Approach doesn't have its own file format. Instead, Approach can create, open, and use the most common of the existing database file formats. These include dBASE III+, dBASE IV, FoxPro, and Paradox. The one you choose depends on the file format that is most popular in your working environment. You don't need to have access to these database programs to use their file formats in Approach.

The following sections discuss some things you need to remember when choosing a file type.

Choosing dBASE Files

Two "flavors" of dBASE files exist: dBASE III+ and dBASE IV. The two file types are very similar, but some differences exist, such as the way indexes are handled. You may want to choose the older dBASE III+ format for compatibility with older applications built into that popular program.

If you choose dBASE III+ or dBASE IV as the file type, you can use Boolean (yes/no or true/false), date, time, text, numeric, and memo (free-form text) fields. (For a description of these field types, see the section, "Defining New Fields" later in this chapter.) Field names can contain up to 32 characters in Approach; if you open the dBASE file in another dBASE application, however, you'll see modified field names (dBASE normally allows only 10 characters). A dBASE text field length must be between 1 and 254 characters. If you need more characters for text, you must use a memo field (which has unlimited length). Numeric fields in dBASE can contain a maximum of 19 digits and display up to 15 decimal places.

You can use any character to name a field. However, since dBASE normally allows only letters A to Z, whole numbers, and the underscore character, the field names will appear differently if you open the dBASE file in another application.

Note

Although you can create memo fields of unlimited length in Approach, you can't open a memo field greater than 5,000 characters in dBASE III+, or greater than 64,000 characters in dBASE IV.

If you choose a dBASE file, you can use Approach PicturePlus fields (which hold graphics and linked or embedded objects), but you can't view the PicturePlus fields in dBASE. PicturePlus fields are very handy for storing non-textual data (such as pictures) in each record of the database.

One special feature of dBASE files is when you "delete" a record, the record is not actually removed from the database. Instead, the record is marked as deleted and does not appear on forms, or in reports. However, the deleted record continues to take up space in the database. Approach provides a way to remove these deleted records permanently, decreasing the size of the file. To removed deleted records (a process that dBASE calls "packing"), follow these steps:

1. Open the **T**ools menu and choose Select **P**references. The Preferences dialog box opens.

2. Click the Database tab, click the Compress button, and then click OK from Preferences. Approach removes all deleted records from the database file.

Choosing FoxPro Files

FoxPro (DOS) files work exactly the same way dBASE files do. FoxPro files are identical to dBASE files except for the format of the memo field. Approach can open and read FoxPro memo fields as well as dBASE memo fields, but cannot share FoxPro files across a network.

Choosing Paradox 3.5 Files

If you choose a Paradox 3.5 file type, you can select from date, numeric, text, Boolean, and time fields. The date, numeric, and text field names can contain up to 25 characters each, and the Boolean and time fields can contain up to 18 characters each. A Paradox text field can be between 1 and 255 characters long. Approach—and Paradox, for that matter—automatically sets the field length of all other field types.

To name a field, you can use letters A to Z, whole numbers, symbols, and spaces. The field name cannot begin with a space or contain square brackets ([ ]), braces ({ }), or parentheses. The field name also cannot contain the number (pound) sign (#) by itself, although the # can be combined with other symbols (for example, Customer #).

If you choose a Paradox 3.5 file, you also can use memo fields and Approach PicturePlus fields, but you can't view these fields in Paradox. The field names for memo and PicturePlus fields can contain up to 18 characters.

As discussed later in "Saving the Database," when you use a Paradox file, you also must identify a field (or combination of fields) that uniquely identifies each record in the database. This field is called a *key field*. If for some reason your database doesn't have a key field, Approach can create one for you.

Choosing a Paradox 4 or Paradox for Windows File

All the limitations mentioned above for Paradox 3.5 also apply to Paradox 4 and Paradox for Windows, except you can open both memo fields and PicturePlus fields in Paradox 4 and Paradox for Windows.

Defining the Database Structure

What happens after you enter the file name and file type in the New dialog box depends on how you chose the new database. If you used the Welcome to Lotus Approach dialog box and picked a template, Approach creates the new database automatically and displays the default data-entry form.

However, if you opened the **F**ile menu and chose **N**ew, or selected a Blank Database from the Welcome to Lotus Approach dialog box, the Creating New Database dialog box appears (see fig. 2.3). In this dialog box you can assign names, types, number of decimal places, and lengths to your fields. You can select a template from the Creating New Database dialog box by choosing a template in the **T**emplate drop-down list. Approach populates the dialog box with the appropriate fields from the template. You can add additional fields or remove any of the existing fields.

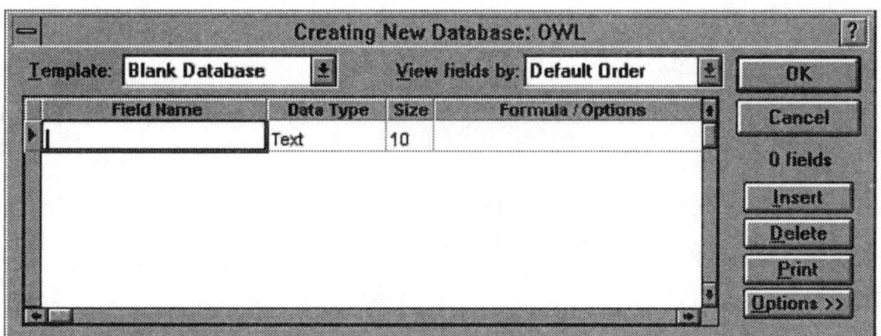

Fig. 2.3
Select Blank Database to display the Creating New Database dialog box.

You don't need to specify every quantity for every field. Approach makes available only the boxes needed for a given field type. The Size column, for example, is available for text fields because you must set the length of a text field. For a date field, however, the length is set automatically, so the Size column shows the word "fixed." For numeric fields, the size is displayed as a decimal number (for example, 10.2). The digits indicate the number of places to the left of the decimal point (10) and to the right of the decimal point (2). If you enter a whole number such as 8 in the Size column, Approach permits you to enter only the whole number—no decimal places are allowed.

Defining New Fields

The first step in defining new fields (the columns in the database table) is to type a field name in the Field Name column at the left side of the Creating New Database dialog box. Remember to follow the rules as noted earlier for length of field names and allowable characters; otherwise, Approach will not create the new field in the database.

The next step is to specify the type of field you want by using the drop-down list box in the Data Type column. Type the length of the field in the Size column. A size is required for text-type fields in all types of databases, and numeric fields in dBASE and FoxPro files. For numeric fields that contain a decimal point, type the whole portion of the field length, a decimal point, and the number of places to the right of the decimal point. For numeric fields in dBASE and FoxPro files, you can specify up to 15 decimal places.

Note

Not all field types that appear in the Data Type drop-down list are explained here. Refer to Chapter 10 for an explanation of Calculated, PicturePlus, and variable fields.

To define all your fields, simply type the required quantities in the rows of the Field Definition dialog box. When you are finished defining the fields, click OK to create the database.

Using Boolean Fields

Boolean fields can contain only one of two possible values. These values may be represented as yes/no or true/false. A Boolean field is often represented on a form as a checkbox, which also can have only two possible states: checked and unchecked.

Using Date Fields

Date fields contain only dates. The date must be entered in the Windows short format specified in the Control Panel (that is, mm/dd/yy). Although the date can only be entered this way, Approach can display the date in a wide variety of on-screen formats.

Using Memo Fields

Memo fields can contain an unlimited amount of text. Such fields are ideal for recording comments, giving the ongoing status of a project or situation, and so on.

Using Numeric Fields

Numeric fields contain numbers such as dollar amounts and other quantities.

Using Text Fields

Text fields hold text strings up to 255 character long (254 in dBASE III+, dBASE IV, and FoxPro). You can enter any kind of text or symbol in text fields, even numbers (such as zip codes). The text field is the most useful field because you can type virtually anything into it.

Using Time Fields

Time fields are used to hold times. Approach lets you record time to the nearest 1/100 of a second. You can enter any portion of the time (such as hours, or hours and minutes), or you can separate the numbers with colons or other non-numeric symbols. Times can be entered using a 24-hour clock or an AM/PM designation.

Rearranging Fields in the Creating New Database Dialog Box

You can insert, delete, and rearrange the order of the rows in the Creating New Database dialog box. You can also print out a list of rows by clicking the **P**rint button.

To insert a new field row, click anywhere on the row above which you want to insert a blank row and click the **I**nsert button. To delete a row, click anywhere on the row that you want to delete and click the **D**elete button. Confirm that you want to delete the row in the alert box that appears.

The Creating New Database dialog box normally displays the fields in the order you enter them. This is the default order, and also the order in which Approach creates the fields in the database.

> **Note**
>
> Approach creates the fields in the database in the default order, regardless of the order in which you view the fields in the Creating New Database dialog box. Approach also uses the default order when it creates the Default form.

You can change the order in which the Creating New Database dialog box displays the fields using the **V**iew Fields By drop-down list. The fields can be sorted by Field Name, Data Type, or Custom Order. If you select Custom Order, you can drag rows in the Creating New Database dialog box to rearrange the order in which the fields are displayed. To rearrange the viewed field order, follow these steps:

Tip
To deselect a row or a collection of rows, click anywhere except on the row-select button in a selected row.

1. Move the mouse pointer over the button at the left end of the row that you want to drag to a new location. For the row you are currently editing, this button contains a small arrowhead.

2. Click the button to highlight the row. If you want to highlight multiple rows, Shift+click the first row you want to select and drag the mouse pointer up or down to highlight additional rows. Alternatively, you can

click the first row, and then hold down the Shift key and click the last row. All rows in between these two rows are selected to be moved.

3. Drag the mouse to reposition the selected row(s). The mouse pointer becomes an open hand to indicate that the move operation is taking place. A dark bar appears between field rows in the Creating New Database dialog box to indicate where the row(s) will be located when you release the mouse button (see fig. 2.4).

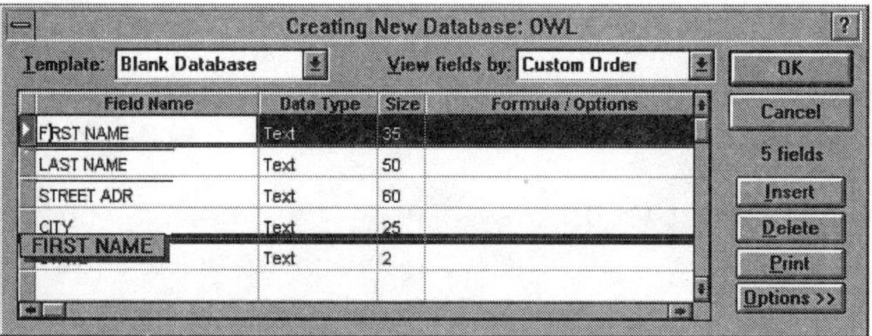

Fig. 2.4
Change the order of fields by dragging rows to a new location.

Modifying a Field Specification

As you're working, you can modify or delete the fields you have entered.

To modify a field, click its row in the Creating New Database dialog box. Make any necessary changes to the field name, data type, or size.

Tip
If you click and drag a field row button without switching the **V**iew Fields By List to Custom Order, Approach switches to Custom Order automatically.

Setting Up Field Options

Approach enables you to customize the fields you define for a database in two ways:

- You can set up a field so that Approach automatically enters default data into it.
- You can have Approach ensure that the data entered into a field is valid by meeting certain criteria.

To customize a field either of these ways, the bottom portion of the Creating New Database dialog box, which displays the Default Value and Validation information, must be visible (see fig. 2.5). If the lower portion of the Creating New Database dialog box is not visible, click the **O**ptions button. Select the field for which you want to set the Default Value or Validation information in the rows that display the database fields. You can switch fields and set the Default Value or Validation values for any field. To set the Default Value or Validation options for a field, click the tab for the panel you want.

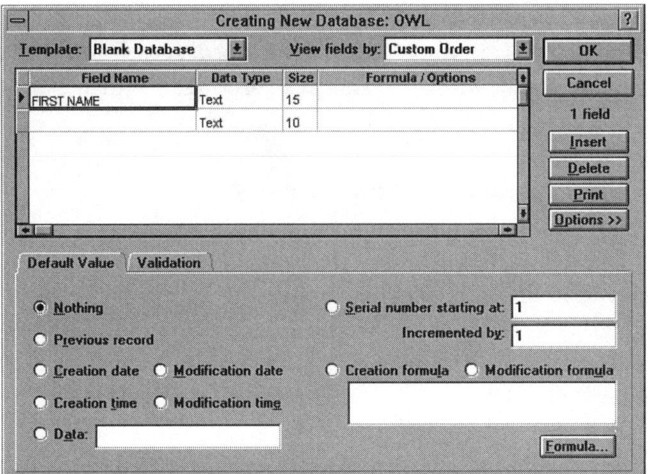

Fig. 2.5
Click the **O**ptions button to have Approach set default values or validate your data entry.

Note

The best approach for saving your table is to set the Default Value and Validation options before choosing OK in the Creating New Database dialog box. If you need to add these options to an existing table, see "Modifying the Table Structure" later in this chapter.

Using Automatic Data Entry

The first panel enables you to set the default values. This option tells Approach that you want specific information entered into a field every time a new record is created. The Default Value options are described in the following sections.

Note

Although Approach automatically enters information in fields for which you have set the Default Value options, you still can modify the information in the field.

The Nothing Option

The **N**othing option is the default. If this button is highlighted, Approach enters nothing in the field when you create a new record. This option is helpful when you are modifying the Default Value options. Choosing the **N**othing option turns off any previous choice.

The Previous Record Option

Choosing the P**r**evious Record option enters the data from the same field that was entered into the previous new record. This option is helpful if you are creating many new records with the same data in a field.

The Creation Date and Modification Date Options

The next two options, **C**reation Date and **M**odification Date, are available only if the selected field is a date field or a text field long enough to hold the date. The creation date is the date on which the record was created. The modification date is the date on which the record was last modified. You can attach these options to fields for databases in which keeping track of these dates is important.

The Creation Time and Modification Time Options

The next two options, Creation **T**ime and Modification Tim**e**, are available only if the field is a time field or a text field that is long enough to hold the time. The creation time is the time at which the record was created. The modification time is the time at which the record was last modified. You can attach these options to fields for databases in which keeping track of these times is important. These time fields are often used with the **C**reation Date and **M**odification Date options.

The Data Option

If you want the same data entered in a field each time a record is created, enter this data in the text box next to the D**a**ta option. Suppose you are specifying options for a state field, and you know that most of your customers live in a certain state. You can enter that state name in the D**a**ta text box as you customize the STATE field. When you enter records later, you can edit those fields in which the value entered by D**a**ta isn't accurate.

The Serial Number Option

Approach enters a sequential number into a serial number field whenever you create a new record. This type of field works well for arbitrary numbers such as Customer ID. You can specify the starting number by typing the number in the **S**erial Number Starting At text box. You can also specify the increment to the next number by typing the number in the Incremented **B**y text box. If you specify that the number starts at 10 and is incremented by 5, for example, the numbers Approach uses are 10, 15, 20, 25, and so on.

The Creation Formula Option

The Creation Formu**l**a option instructs Approach to enter the result of a formula into the field when you first create a record. For example, you could have a formula generate a date seven days from when the record was created so you can contact a person listed in that record. The formula is only evaluated when the record is first created, not when the record is later changed. To enter a formula, click the Creation Formula radio button. You can enter a formula in two ways:

1. Type the formula into the text box below the Creation Formula radio button.

2. Click the Formula button to open the Formula dialog box. When you are finished entering the formula in the Formula dialog box, click OK. The new formula appears in the text box below the Creation formula radio button. To modify the formula, click the Formula button to re-open the Formula dialog box. For more information on using formulas, see "Using Formulas" later in this chapter.

The Modification Formula Option

The Modification Formula option instructs Approach to enter the result of a formula when you first create a record and whenever you modify the value of any field in that record. The value of the field will change if any of the values that the formula depends on are changed. For example, you might want to keep a running record of when you next need to contact a client. If you have a field that records the last time you contacted that client, the Modification Formula field could calculate a date one month later. When you call the client again (and record the new contact date), the Modification Formula field automatically updates to show the *next* contact date. You can override the value Approach places in the field, but the next time you change the value of any field in that record, Approach will replace the value in the field with the results of the formula. To enter a formula, click the Modification Formula radio button. Enter the formula exactly the same way you would for Creation formulas.

Validating Entered Data

You use the second tab in the lower portion of the Field Definition dialog box for setting up data validation criteria (see fig. 2.6). Use the Validation area to tell Approach that the data entered into a field must meet certain tests or it can't be accepted. If, when entering a record, you enter data that doesn't meet the criteria, Approach displays an error message notifying you that the data can't be accepted because it doesn't meet the data validation. Since you can't override the validation criteria, you must carefully define your criteria.

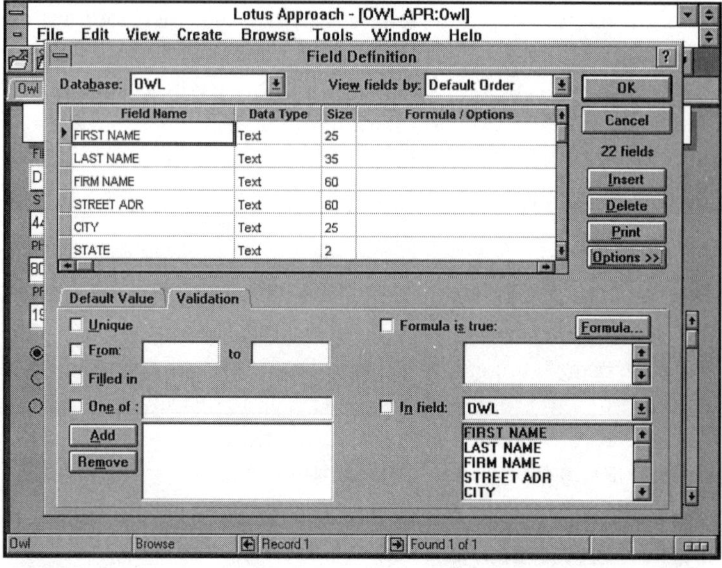

Fig. 2.6
Validate entered values using the Validation tab of the Field Definition dialog box.

The Unique Option

The value entered into a field using the **U**nique option can't be duplicated in this field when it appears in any other record. This option is handy for fields such as CUSTOMER NUMBER, where each number should be different.

The From Option

When you choose the F**r**om option, Approach ensures that the value entered into the field falls between the values specified. Next to this option is a pair of text boxes with the word `to` between them. The left text box is for the lowest acceptable value in the range; the right text box is for the highest acceptable value in the range. If the value falls between 1 and 100, for example, enter the value **1** in the left box, and **100** in the right box. You can also use alphabetic characters (such as a range from ab to xz). An alphabetic range is useful to ensure that the entered data are letters rather than numbers.

When entering records, if you try to enter a value outside the acceptable range, an error message appears (see fig. 2.7). The error message reminds you of the acceptable range.

The Filled In Option

When you choose the Fi**l**led In option, Approach requires you to enter a value into the field. If you leave the field blank when entering records, Approach doesn't proceed until a value is filled in. This option is handy if you must be certain that a field is not left blank.

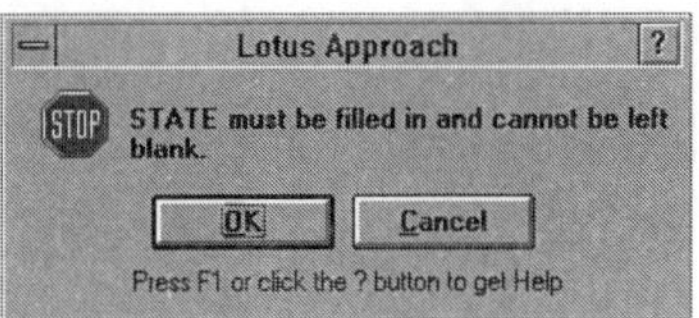

Fig. 2.7
An error message appears if your data entry falls outside the validation criteria.

The One Of Option

When you choose the On**e** Of option, Approach ensures that the value entered into a field is one of those in the list available to the right of this option. This option is handy to limit the values entered to a predetermined list.

To add values to the list, type them into the text box next to the On**e** Of option and click **A**dd.

To remove an item from the list, click the item you want to remove and then click Re**m**ove.

Tip
You can't edit an item on the list. Instead, you must remove the item and add a new one.

> **Note**
>
> When you use the On**e** Of data validation option, Approach automatically generates a drop-down list that provides the valid values for you to choose (see fig. 2.8). Another way to limit values to a valid list is to use the drop-down list format for a field and provide the valid values for the list. (See Chapter 4 for more information on data input forms.)

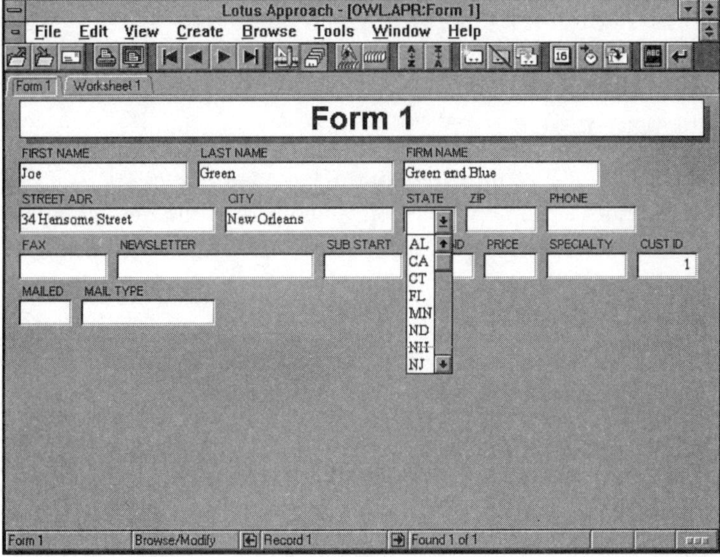

Fig. 2.8
The On**e** Of option automatically generates a drop-down list of acceptable values.

The Formula Is True Option

When you choose the Formula **Is** True option, Approach accepts a value typed into the field only if that value causes the formula you enter in the Formula **Is** True text box to evaluate true. You can design highly complex validations by building a formula. An example of a valid formula is

NAME>'A'

This formula ensures that the NAME field starts with a letter greater than A.

To enter a formula, click the Formula **I**s True checkbox. You can enter a formula in two ways:

1. Type the formula into the text box below the Formula **I**s True checkbox.

2. Click the **F**ormula button to open the Formula dialog box. When you are finished entering the formula in the Formula dialog box, click OK. The new formula appears in the text box below the Formula **I**s True checkbox. To modify the formula, click the **F**ormula button to reopen the Formula dialog box. For more information on using formulas, see "Using Formulas" later in this chapter.

Using the In Field Option

The I**n** Field option ensures that the value you enter into a field is a value that's already entered into another field (called a validation field) in the same or in a different database. If the value you type into the field is NOT contained in the validation field, Approach doesn't accept the value. Choose I**n** Field and then select the validation field from the list of fields that appears beside this option.

When you use the data validation option described above, Approach automatically provides a drop-down list of values in the validation field. You can also create your own drop-down field on the form and attach the list to the validation field. See Chapter 4 for information on how to set up such a drop-down list.

Note

The normal use of the I**n** Field option is to make sure that the value entered into a field in one database is a value that already has been entered into a field in another database. Before you can access other databases, however, you must link them to the current database. These relational links are covered in Chapter 8, which also tells you how to use the I**n** Field option with relationally linked databases.

Using Formulas

Three of the options available for setting up Default Values and Validations involve using formulas. As you'll see in the later chapters of this book, formulas play an important part in tapping the power of Approach. For example, in Chapter 10, we will use fields that get their values from the evaluation of a formula ("calculated fields"). To use the Default Value and Validation options, and to use calculated fields later, you must understand how to build formulas.

Examining the Parts of a Validation Formula

Validation formulas are constructed from four kinds of building blocks:

- References to field values
- References to constant values
- Operators (arithmetic, comparison, and Boolean)
- Functions

References to Field Values

To include a field value in a formula, type the name of the field. If the field name contains spaces, you must enclose the field name in double quotes (" ").

To refer to the value in the field NAME, for example, type **NAME** in the formula.

In the formula, you must refer to the value of the field that you are trying to validate. You can also refer to the values in other fields.

References to Constant Values

Constant values are values you type into the formula that don't change from record to record. You must follow certain rules when typing constant values into a formula:

- Enclose text string constants in single quotes (for example, **'Approach'**).
- Type date constants in the order of month, date, and year, separated by slashes and enclosed in single quotation marks (for example, **'03/12/56'**).

- Type time constants in the order of hours, minutes, seconds, and hundredths of seconds. Separate hours, minutes, and seconds with a colon (**:**). Separate seconds and hundredths of seconds with a decimal point. Enclose time constants in single quotes (for example, **'12:25:00.45'**).
- Type Boolean constants as **'Yes'** or **'No'** and enclose them in single quotes. You can also use **1** for yes and **0** for no.
- Don't type numeric constants in scientific notation (for example, 4.5E4).

To refer to the value A in a formula, for example, type the value in the formula as **'A'**.

Arithmetic Operators

You can use arithmetic operators to build arithmetic equations in the formula. These arithmetic operators are:

+	addition
–	subtraction
/	division
*	multiplication
%	percentage
NOT	negation operator

Approach evaluates arithmetic operations in a specific order:

- Multiplication (*) and division (/) operations are evaluated first.
- Addition (+) and subtraction (–) operations are evaluated second.
- The % operation is third, followed by the NOT operation.
- If any operations are on the same evaluation level (such as multiplication and division), they are evaluated from left to right in the formula.

The following examples show how arithmetic operations work:

5*6/2 = 15, because 5*6 = 30 and 30/2 = 15

4+3*2 = 10, because 3*2 = 6 and 6+4 = 10

You can use parentheses to modify the evaluation order of arithmetic operators. Approach always evaluates the contents of parentheses before evaluating other parts of the formula. Within a set of parentheses, the evaluation order is the same as outside the parentheses. The following example shows how parentheses are used:

(2+4)*3 = 18, because 2+4 = 6, and 6*3 = 18

Comparison Operators

You use comparison operators to compare two values or fields. The comparison operators consist of the following:

=	equal
>	greater than
<	less than
<>	not equal to
>=	greater than or equal to
<=	less than or equal to

To ensure that the value in the NAME field starts with a letter greater than or equal to A, for example, use

NAME>='A'

Alternatively, to ensure that the number in the NEWNUM field is greater than twice the value in the OLDNUM field, use

NEWNUM>OLDNUM*2

To make sure that the date in the field SUB DATE is at least five days later than the date in the MOD DATE field, use

SUB DATE>=MOD DATE+5

Boolean Operators

You can use the Boolean operators AND and OR to connect parts or clauses of the formula.

A clause containing the AND operator evaluates true only if both parts connected by the AND operator are true. The formula 5>6 AND 'A'<'B' is false, for example, even though 'A' is less than 'B', because 5 isn't greater than 6. The formula 5<6 AND 'A'<'B' is true, however, because both parts of the equation are true.

A clause containing the OR operator evaluates true if either part connected by the OR is true. The formula 5>6 OR 'A'<'B' is true, for example, because 'A' is less than 'B'. The formula 5>6 OR 'A'>'B' is false, however, because both sides are false.

You can connect multiple clauses with combinations of ANDs and ORs. Approach normally evaluates clauses from left to right (AND and OR have the same evaluation level). You can use parentheses to modify this order. Approach then uses the result of each clause (true or false) to evaluate the next clause. The formula 5>6 AND 'A'<'B' OR 10<12, for example, evaluates true. The first clause is 5>6 AND 'A'<'B'. Because 5 is not greater than 6, the entire clause evaluates as false. Approach then uses the result (false) with OR 10<12. The entire clause evaluates as false OR true, which results in a true value.

To ensure that the value in the NAME field begins with an alphabetic character, for example, use

NAME>='A' AND NAME<='Z'

Functions

Approach supports 84 functions that can perform various operations on text and numeric values. The details of these functions are discussed in Appendix A of the *Approach User Guide*.

The value by which a function operates (called an *argument*) can be a field value or a constant value. If a function uses multiple arguments, you must separate the arguments with commas.

> **Note**
>
> The delimiter is determined by the International settings in the Windows Control Panel. In the United States, the comma serves as the delimiter. Most European countries use the semicolon (;).

The MIDDLE function returns a text string of a certain size from a specified position in another text string. It has the following syntax:

MIDDLE(Text, Position, Size)

MIDDLE and LENGTH, which return the length of the argument, are especially useful when writing validation formulas.

The following paragraphs contain examples illustrating the use of the MIDDLE and LENGTH functions.

To make sure that the length of the value typed into the ZIP field is 5, use

LENGTH(ZIP)=5

To make sure that the length of the value typed into the ZIP field is 5 or 10, use

LENGTH(ZIP)=5 OR LENGTH(ZIP)=10

To make sure that the length of the value typed into the ZIP field is 5 or 10, and that the sixth character is a hyphen (using the ZIP+4 formatting), use

LENGTH(ZIP)=5 OR (LENGTH(ZIP)=10 AND MIDDLE(ZIP,6,1)='-')

Approach evaluates the preceding formula as follows:

- If the length of ZIP is 5, the formula is true because true OR false evaluates true.
- If the length of ZIP is 10 and the sixth character is a hyphen (-), this formula is true because the AND clause is true (false OR true evaluates true).
- If the length of ZIP is 10 but the sixth character is not a hyphen, the formula evaluates false. The reason is that the AND clause is false, and both sides of the OR clause are also false.

Entering Invalid Values

If you attach a validation formula to a field using the Validation tab in the Creating New Database dialog box, Approach doesn't accept any values that don't make the formula evaluate true. If you enter an invalid value, Approach places an on-screen error message and doesn't let you exit the field until you enter a valid value.

If a formula refers to values in more than one field, Approach checks that the formula is true after you enter a value in any field referenced in the formula. If the value you enter is invalid, Approach lets you modify it in any of the referenced fields. However, Approach doesn't give you access to any other fields. To ensure that a field called SUB DATE is at least five days after a field called MOD DATE, for example, you can use the following formula:

SUB DATE>=MOD DATE+5

On a form, the `Invalid value` error message appears if you modify the value in either field (SUB DATE or MOD DATE) so that the formula is no longer true. At that point, Approach lets you access either field to modify the values so that the formula is true. But you can't access any other fields until you fix this problem.

Entering References to Different Fields

For a validation formula, you can't separate references to values in different fields with Boolean operators (AND and OR). If you do, any portion of the formula (clause) that doesn't include the field being validated is ignored. If you try to write a formula for the NAME field such as

NAME>'A' AND SUB DATE>12/21/92

the reference to SUB DATE is ignored.

Entering the Formula into Approach

To enter formulas into Approach, choose the **F**ormula button to call up the Formula dialog box (see fig. 2.9). The Formula dialog box is handy because it ensures that the syntax for the formula is correct before it makes the OK button available.

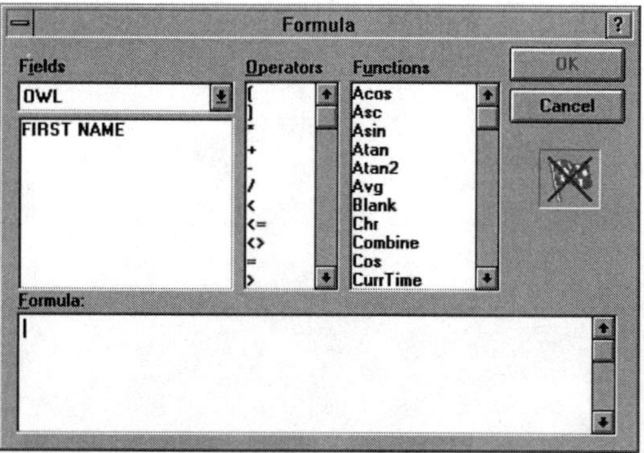

Fig. 2.9
Use the Formula dialog box to build formulas.

The Formula dialog box has four major sections you can use when setting up a validation formula:

- The F**i**elds list box lists all the fields available in your database.
- The **O**perators list box lists all the available operators—arithmetic, comparison, and Boolean.
- The F**u**nctions list box lists all the available functions, including summary, trigonometric, logarithmic, and statistical functions.
- The **F**ormula text box is where you build your formula.

To build a formula in the Formula dialog box, follow these steps:

1. Select an entry in the F**i**elds, **O**perators, or F**u**nctions list box. Approach transfers your selection into the **F**ormula text box.
2. Type any constant values (such as **'A'** or **'01/01/93'**) in the **F**ormula text box.
3. Continue entering the other parts of the formula by choosing from the text boxes or by typing information.
4. After you finish building the formula, click OK to return to the Creating New Database dialog box. If the OK button is not available in the Formula dialog box, the formula was not entered correctly or completely. Correct this syntax error and click OK. The formula you built appears in the box next to the formula option (Creation Formula, Modification Formula, or Formula Is True).

Saving the Database

After you finish defining the fields in your newly created database, click OK in the Creating New Database dialog box. Approach builds the database in the file format you chose (dBASE, Paradox, or FoxPro). If you chose a Paradox file format, you see the Choose Key Field dialog box so that you can select the key field(s) that make each record in the Paradox database unique (see fig. 2.10). Using the Choose Key Field dialog box, you must select the field or combination of fields that uniquely identifies each record in the database. For example, you might choose a CUSTOMER ID field that must be unique, or perhaps the combination of PHONE NUMBER and LAST NAME.

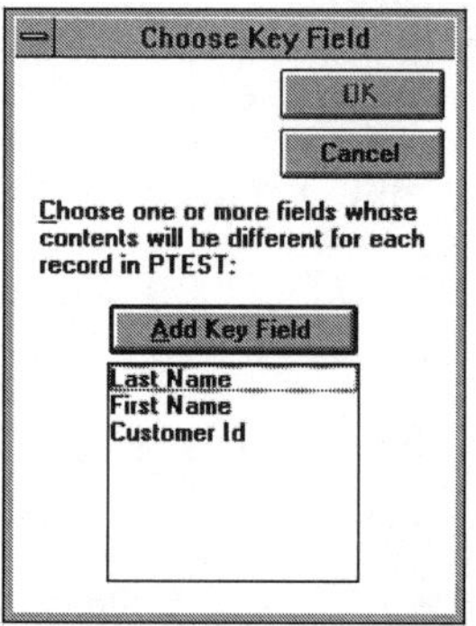

Fig. 2.10
Use the Choose Key Field dialog box to choose key field(s) for a Paradox database, or to create a new field to use as a key.

The list of fields in the database appears in a list box at the bottom of the Choose Key Field dialog box. To select a key field, click any fields in this list. If the key field is a combination of fields (such as LAST NAME and FIRST NAME), click the first field, press Ctrl, and then click any additional fields.

Tip
After you create and save the database, Approach displays a default form for data entry. You can use this form to begin entering data.

If no fields are unique, choose **A**dd Key Field to tell Approach to create a key field for you. The key field created in this manner is numeric, and Approach automatically fills in a sequential number in this key field each time you create a new record.

Adding a Password to the Database

You already have seen how you can add a password to an Approach file to keep others from modifying the design of the database application or changing the structure of the underlying database. You can also attach passwords to the database itself to limit access to the data.

You can attach two kinds of passwords to a database: *read/write* and *read-only*.

- With a read/write password, the user must enter the correct password before gaining ANY access to the database or the Approach file. If the user enters an incorrect password, the user won't be able to see (read) the values in the database or enter (write) new values. The user also won't be able to change the database structure (change or add fields).
- With a read-only password, the user can view the data in the database but can't modify the data or the structure.

You can attach both password types to a database. In this case, if the user enters the read-only password, the user can view the database. If the user enters the read/write password, full access to the database is available. If neither password is entered correctly, the user is denied access to the database.

To set the passwords, follow these steps:

1. Open the **F**ile menu and choose **O**pen to open the database for which you want to set the password(s).

2. Open the **T**ools menu and choose **P**references.

3. Select the Password tab to open the Password tab of the Preferences dialog box (see fig. 2.11).

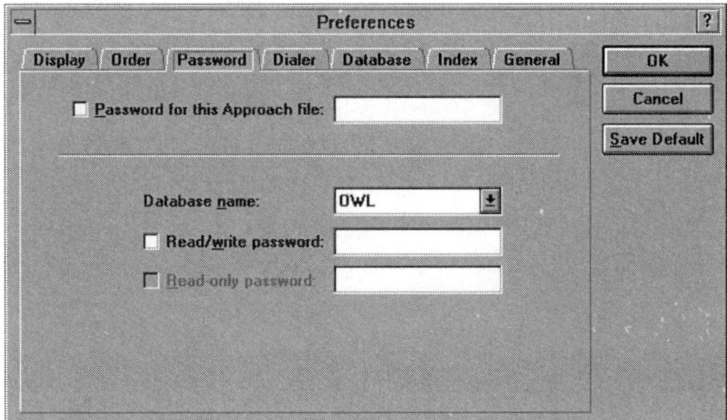

Fig. 2.11
You can limit access to your data with passwords from the Password tab of the Preferences dialog box.

4. To set a read/write password, choose Read/**w**rite Password and type the password in the text box. The password appears as asterisks in the box to prevent anyone from reading the password as you type it.

5. Press Tab, Enter, or click OK. Approach displays the Confirm Password dialog box. Retype your password and click OK to close the dialog box and set the read/write password.

When you have set a read/write password, you can set the read-only password. (Note that you can set a read-only password only if you have first set a read/write password.) To set the read-only password, follow these steps:

1. Choose the **R**ead-only Password option.

2. Type the read-only password. This password also appears as asterisks in the box.

3. Press Tab, Enter, or click OK. Approach displays the Confirm Password dialog box. Retype the password and click OK to close the dialog box and set the read-only password.

The next time someone tries to open this database, that user must enter either password before access to the database is granted.

Restricting Access Without a Password

You have the option of making a database's fields read-only without using a password. To do so, open the **T**ools menu and choose **P**references to open the Preferences dialog box. Select the Database tab. Check the **M**ake All Fields in Database Read-Only checkbox and click OK.

> **Note**
>
> Checking the **M**ake All Fields in Database Read-Only checkbox in the Preferences dialog box doesn't prevent someone from changing the database. If a database has no password protection, any user can open the Preferences dialog box and disable this option.

Enabling Approach to Update dBASE and FoxPro Indexes

Indexes give a database speed when searching for specific records. Although Approach doesn't use dBASE- or FoxPro-type indexes, the program can update existing indexes as you add new records. If you update existing indexes when using Approach, you can open the database by using dBASE (III+ or IV) or FoxPro, and the indexes will be current and usable.

> **Note**
>
> Approach cannot create dBASE and FoxPro indexes; it can only update them.

To have Approach update these indexes, follow these steps:

1. Open the **F**ile menu and choose **O**pen to open the dBASE or FoxPro database you want to work with.

2. Open the **T**ools menu and choose **P**references to open the Preferences dialog box.

3. Select the Index tab. The dBASE and FoxPro Indexes list contains the indexes that Approach will update (the box is empty if you haven't identified any indexes yet).

4. To add an index to this list, choose **A**dd Index. The Add Index dialog box appears (see fig. 2.12).

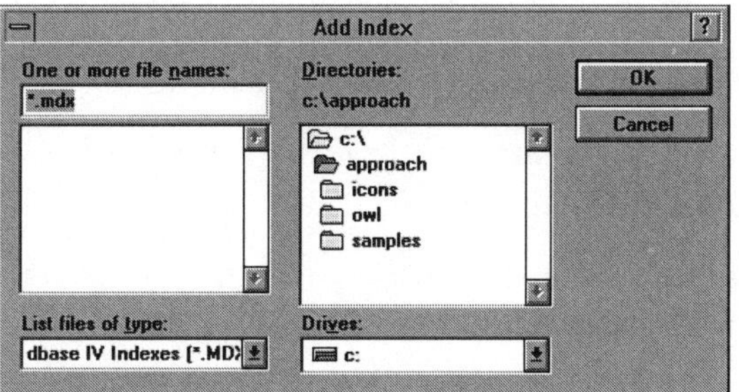

Fig. 2.12
Update your FoxPro and dBASE indexes by using the Add Index dialog box to indicate the indexes you want to keep updated.

The List Files of **T**ype drop-down list in the Add Index dialog box identifies the types of index files that Approach can open. These types include dBASE IV (*.MDX), dBASE III+ (*.NDX), FoxPro (*.IDX), and FoxPro compound indexes (*.CDX).

5. Select the type of index you want to add from the List Files of **T**ype drop-down list box. A list of index files appears in the list box above the List Files of **T**ype option.

6. Select the file you want. The file name appears in the One or More File **N**ames text box.

7. Click OK to add the index to the list of indexes that Approach updates.

If you decide that you no longer want Approach to update particular indexes, you can remove them from the list. Follow steps 1–3 above, and then do the following:

1. Select the index you no longer need to have updated.

2. Choose C**l**ose Index.

3. Click OK to close the dialog box.

Enabling Approach to Update Paradox Indexes

In a Paradox database file, a primary index is built on the key field specified when the file is created. However, you can create additional secondary indexes for the file in Approach. Approach automatically maintains all secondary indexes for Paradox files.

To create a Paradox secondary index, follow these steps:

1. Open the **F**ile menu and choose **O**pen to open the Paradox database you want to work with.

2. Open the **T**ools menu and choose **P**references to open the Preferences dialog box.

3. Select the Index tab (see fig. 2.13).

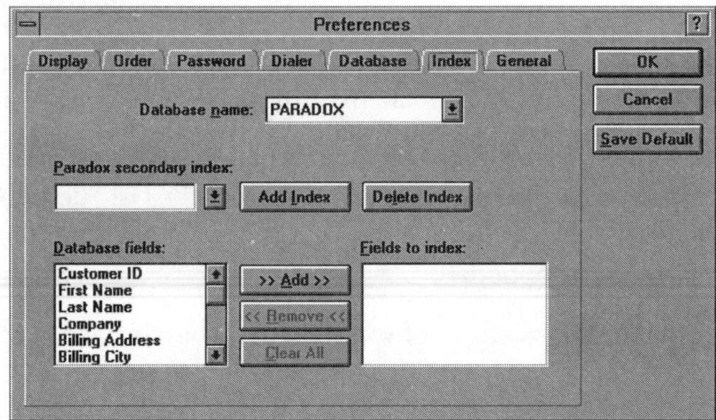

Fig. 2.13
Use the Index tab for Paradox databases in the Preferences dialog box to identify secondary indexes.

4. Click Add **I**ndex, type the name of the index in the **P**aradox Secondary Index list box, and add database fields to the index list.

   To move a field from the **D**atabase Fields list to the **F**ields to Index list, click the field and then click **A**dd, or double-click the field.

   To remove a field from the **F**ields to Index list and place it back in the **D**atabase Fields list, click the field in the **F**ields to Index list and then click **R**emove. To move all fields back to the **D**atabase Fields list, click **C**lear All.

5. To delete a secondary index, select the index in the **P**aradox Secondary Index list and click De**l**ete Index.

Modifying the Table Structure

You can modify the structure of a database at any time. For example, you can do any of the following:

- Add fields to the database
- Delete fields (which deletes all the data in those fields)
- Make fields longer or shorter
- Change the field type
- Change the field name
- Change the field options (Default Value or Validation)

The following sections discuss how to make specific changes to a database and the consequences of making certain changes.

Adding a New Field

To add a new field to the database, follow these steps:

1. Open the **F**ile menu and choose **O**pen to open the database.
2. Open the **C**reate menu and choose Field **D**efinition. The Field Definition dialog box appears.

> **Note**
>
> The Field Definition dialog box works exactly like the Creating New Database dialog box—it even looks the same. The only difference between the two is that the Template drop-down list found in the Creating New Database dialog box is unavailable. Instead, the Template drop-down list is replaced by a drop-down list that displays all joined or "linked" databases.

3. If necessary, scroll down to locate an empty line in the Field Definition dialog box. Type the new Field Name, Data Type, or the size and number of decimal places (if applicable).
4. If you prefer, choose **O**ptions and use the tabs to define the Default Value and Validation options. If you need to modify an existing formula (Creation Formu**l**a, Modification Form**u**la, or Formula **I**s True), click the **F**ormula button to open the Formula dialog box.

5. After you finish defining all new fields, click OK to add the new fields to the database.

> **Note**
>
> After you create new fields, if the Show **A**dd Field Dialog checkbox is checked in the General tab of the Preferences dialog box, the Add Field dialog box appears on the default form. The Add Field dialog box displays only the fields you added to the database.

Modifying an Existing Field

To modify an existing field in a database, follow these steps:

1. Open the **F**ile menu and choose **O**pen to open the database.
2. Open the **C**reate menu and choose Field **D**efinition. The Field Definition dialog box appears.
3. If necessary, scroll down to the line in the Field Definition dialog box that displays the field you want to modify, and then click that line.
4. Change the name of the field (edit the Field Name column), the Data Type, or the size or number of decimal places (if applicable).
5. If you prefer, choose **O**ptions and use the tabs to define the Default Value and Validation options.

When making changes to database fields that have data already in them, be aware of the following:

- If you shorten the size of a text or numeric field, the data that doesn't fit into the new length may be truncated and lost.
- If you decrease the number of decimal places for a numeric field, the data in the corresponding number of decimal places is lost.
- If you change the field type from numeric to text, no data is lost.
- If you change the type from text to numeric, no data is lost—*if* the field contains only numbers. If any non-numeric characters are present in the field, however, those characters—and any characters after the first non-numeric character in the field—are lost.
- If you change any data-entry options, existing records are not affected. For example, if you tell Approach to enter a value in a field automatically,

only records created after you modify the field have the value entered. The existing records remain as they were.

- If you change or add a validation option, the validation is applied to new records only. Existing records are validated only if you bring them up on-screen one at a time and move the cursor to the validated field.

> **Caution**
>
> Remember, if you change the type of data in any field except a text or number field, *all* the data in that field is lost.

Viewing Your Data in a Worksheet

Approach creates and displays a default form (entitled Form 1) when you create a new database. This form displays all the information for a single record on a screen.

Besides the default form, you can view the database data in a *worksheet*. A worksheet displays the database data in a spreadsheet-like table (see fig. 2.14). Each field in the database is one column in the worksheet, and each record is one row. Approach automatically creates a worksheet entitled Worksheet 1 when you create a new database. (For more information about using worksheets, see Chapter 14.)

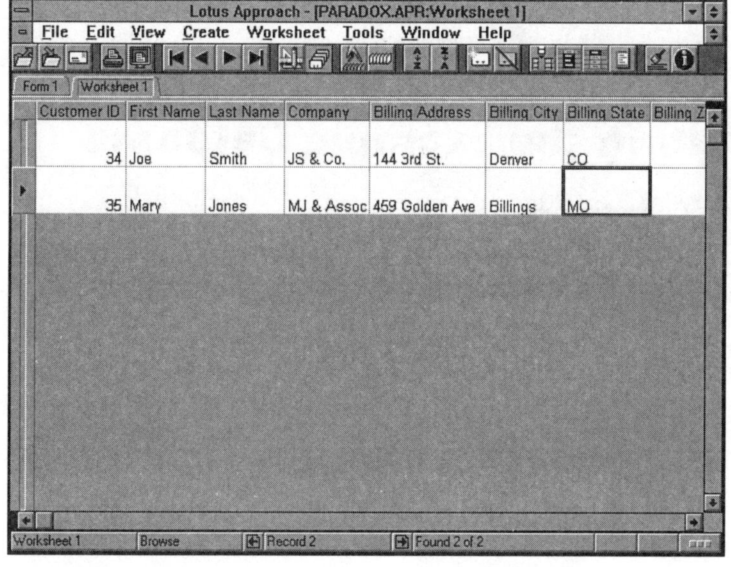

Fig. 2.14
Approach creates a default worksheet when you create a new database.

To switch from the default form to Worksheet 1, click the tab called Worksheet 1. Using a worksheet, you can do the following:

- *Edit the database data.* Simply double-click the data item that you want to modify and then type in your changes. When you move off the current row, Approach automatically saves the change to the database.
- *Add new records to the database.* Click the New Record icon and then type in the data for the new record. When you move off the current row, Approach automatically saves the change to the database.
- *Change the width of a column in the worksheet.* Move the mouse pointer to the border between two columns. The mouse pointer turns into a double-headed arrow. Click and drag the border to change the column width.
- *Change the height of a row in the worksheet.* Move the mouse pointer over a row border. The mouse pointer becomes a double-headed arrow. Click and drag the border row to set the new height of the row.
- *Rearrange the order of the fields (columns) in the worksheet.* Click a field name at the top of a column. The column is highlighted and the mouse pointer becomes an open hand. Click and drag the column left or right to the new location.
- *Rearrange the order of records (rows) in the worksheet.* Click the button at the left end of the row you want to move. The row is highlighted and the mouse pointer becomes an open hand. Click and drag the row up or down to its new location.

Creating the Example Database

In this section, you create a database using the Owl Publishing example illustrated throughout this book. Follow these steps:

1. Open the **F**ile menu and choose **N**ew. The New dialog box appears. You want to use a dBASE IV-type file, so leave the List Files of **T**ype option as is.
2. Type **owl** in the File **N**ame text box.
3. Click OK. The Field Definition dialog box appears.

4. Refer to Table 2.1 at the end of this list to enter the fields into the OWL.DBF database. Enter the information from each row of the table into a row in the Creating New Database dialog box.

   For example, type **first name** into the Field Name column on the first row. Because FIRST NAME is a text field, select Text from the Data Type drop-down list box. Click the Size column and then type **25** in this column to make this field 25 characters long. Press Tab to move to the next row.

   The Field Definition dialog box should look like figure 2.15 when you are done. (Don't click OK yet, however, because you will modify some fields next.)

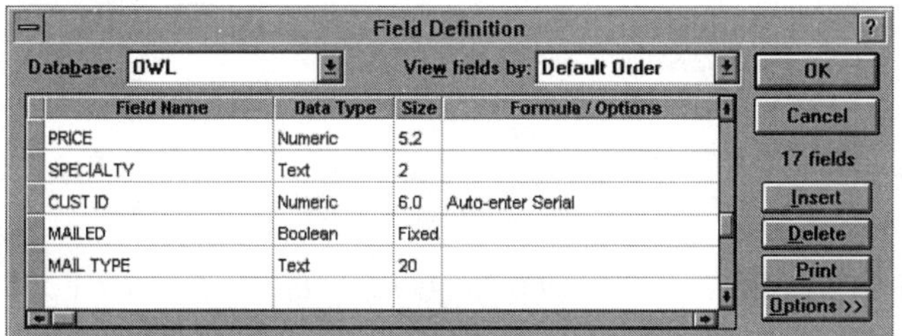

Fig. 2.15 Creating a new database for the Owl Publishing Company.

5. Select the CUST ID field. (If the CUST ID field isn't visible in the list box, use the scroll bars to bring it into view.) The information about the CUST ID field appears in the text boxes at the bottom of the Field Definition dialog box.

6. Choose **O**ptions. The Options section of the Creating New Database dialog box appears.

7. Choose the **S**erial Number Starting At option. Leave the default value of 1 for Serial Number Starting At and Incremented By.

8. Select the ZIP field.

9. Select the Validation tab.

10. Choose Formula i**s** True. The Formula dialog box appears.

11. Enter the following formula in the **F**ormula text box near the bottom of the dialog box (see fig. 2.16):

    Length(ZIP)=0 or Length(ZIP)=5 or Length(ZIP)=10

> **Note**
>
> This formula ensures that the length is 0 (so that you can leave the field blank if you don't know the zip code), 5 (standard zip code), or 10 (ZIP+4 with a dash).

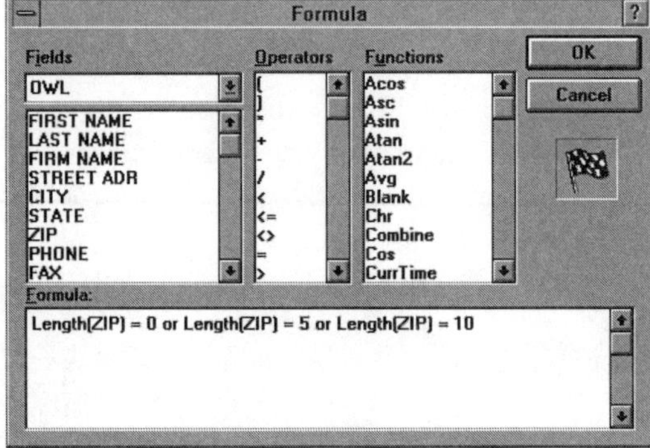

Fig. 2.16
Use the validation options to ensure that the zip code is correctly entered.

You can enter the formula by typing it or by choosing functions (Length), operators (Or), and field names (ZIP) from the appropriate lists in the Formula dialog box.

> **Note**
>
> If the OK button in the Formula dialog box is dimmed, your formula is either incorrect or incomplete. Check your formula carefully.

12. Click OK in the Formula dialog box and the Creating New Database dialog box. Approach creates the database and brings up the default form for data entry.

13. Open the **F**ile menu and choose **S**ave Approach File. Click OK in the Save View As dialog box to save the Approach file and the database.

Table 2.1 Fields in the Owl Publishing Database

Field Name	Data Type	Size
FIRST NAME	Text	25
LAST NAME	Text	35

Field Name	Data Type	Size
FIRM NAME	Text	60
STREET ADR	Text	60
CITY	Text	25
STATE	Text	2
ZIP	Text	10
PHONE	Text	12
FAX	Text	12
NEWSLETTER	Text	40
SUB START	Date	
SUB END	Date	
PRICE	Numeric	5.2
SPECIALTY	Text	2
CUST ID	Numeric	6.0
MAILED	Boolean	Fixed
MAIL TYPE	Text	20

From Here...

In this chapter you learned how to set up a database, including database design basics, selection of a file type, and construction of the database field. Approach's Default Value and Validation options were also discussed to show you how to customize the way a field works. You also learned how to use a worksheet to view your data in a simple format. Finally, you tried out your new skills by building a sample database.

Now that you have set up your database, it's time to enter data. For more information, refer to the following chapters in this book:

- Chapter 3, "Building Data Input Forms," explains the basics of building forms.

- Chapter 4, "Enhancing Data Input Forms," details how to add fields, graphics, illustrations, and text blocks to forms.
- Chapter 5, "Working with Your Data," teaches you how to enter information into the various types of database fields.

Chapter 3

Building Data Input Forms

In this chapter, you learn the basics of creating Approach forms. You learn that you can view individual records in your database by using forms. You also become familiar with Approach's layout tools, which help you position and align objects on a form, group objects together, set up a grid, and set the stacking order.

Besides forms, Approach enables you to build reports, mailing labels (see Chapter 7), and form letters (see Chapter 12). Together with forms, these constructs are often called *views* in Approach. Many of the techniques discussed in this chapter and in Chapter 4 can be used when building other types of views, especially reports.

In this chapter, you learn how to:

- Create and use a default form
- Rename and delete forms
- Change the properties of a form, including colors and lines
- Use Approach's objects and tools in designing your forms
- Set the print and preview attributes for forms
- Work with styles to simplify and standardize form design

Working with Forms

To enter, edit, or view the data in your Approach database, you use a *form*—an on-screen design that enables you to type the data you need. Forms can contain many objects, such as data fields, graphics, and buttons.

While you can use a worksheet to view multiple records at a time in a table, it's often inconvenient to edit data in a worksheet. Most databases contain more fields than the worksheet can fit on a screen. As a result, you must scroll left and right to view the fields in a record. A form, however, enables you to view a single record and fit all the fields in the record on the screen at one time.

Tip
You can use reports to view and edit multiple records at once. For more information, see Chapter 7.

The first time you create a database, Approach automatically creates a default form (Form 1) so that the data can be displayed. However, you can easily build your own forms in Approach's Design mode.

Approach has tools that enable you to add fields, graphics, and other objects to customize a form and make it more functional. You can change a form's size, color, font, and many other properties. You can also change the way a field is shown on a form to make entering data easier.

Because forms are the normal way to work with your data, they must be convenient to use. Approach lets you create multiple forms that show the data in the database in different ways. You can display different data from the database on different forms, and you can arrange fields to focus attention on certain aspects of the data.

The forms you design are stored in an Approach file (*.APR or *.APT). To load forms you already have designed, you must open the Approach file you want to use. If you make changes to forms, you must save those changes by saving the Approach file (open the **F**ile menu and choose **S**ave Approach File).

The examples in this chapter are based on the OWL.APR file created at the end of Chapter 2. To open the OWL.APR file, follow these steps:

1. Open the **F**ile menu and choose **O**pen.
2. Select OWL.APR from the list of files. You may need to adjust the directory and drive from which you are loading the file.
3. Click OK.

Using the Default Form

Approach automatically creates a default form under two circumstances: after you create a new database and save it by choosing OK in the Field Definition dialog box, and when you open a database directly by opening the **F**ile menu and choose **O**pen. You can use the second method if the database wasn't created with Approach (and therefore has no Approach file containing a form), or if you created a database with Approach but didn't save the Approach file when you exited Approach.

The format of the default form is less than ideal. First of all, the fields are laid out across the screen, as many as will fit. When Approach runs out of room on one line, it places fields on the next row, and so on (see fig. 3.1). Second, *all* of the fields in the database are included on the default screen. Most of the time you don't want all the fields to be visible on a particular screen! Finally, the labels for the fields on the form are the database field names. These labels may not be as descriptive as you'd like, and you're limited by the rules for naming fields in the database format.

Approach enables you to design the form you want easily, however, by starting from the default form. Because all the fields in the database are present, the default form is an excellent starting point for setting up a custom form.

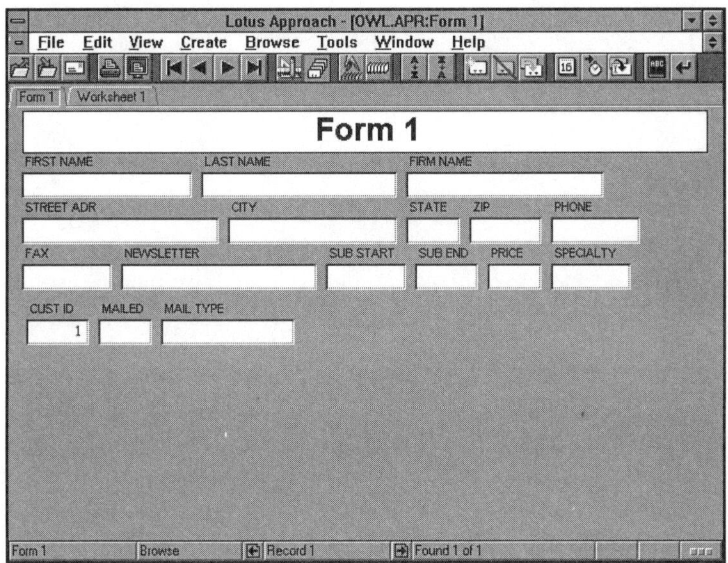

Fig. 3.1
Although the default form may be impractical for everyday use, use it as a starting point to set up a custom form.

Creating a New Form

You probably want to modify the default form simply because it's not a very effective form. You may also want to create a new form to achieve a custom field layout, add custom text instructions to the screen, dress up the form with pictures and graphics, and add buttons to perform common tasks. To create a new form, follow these steps:

1. With a view file open, switch to Design mode by clicking the Design SmartIcon, opening the **V**iew menu and choosing **D**esign, or selecting Design from the status bar.

2. Open the **C**reate menu and choose **F**orm or click the New Form SmartIcon. The Form Assistant dialog box appears (see fig. 3.2). The Sample Form box on the right side of the Form Assistant dialog box displays a preview of your form as you make your selections.

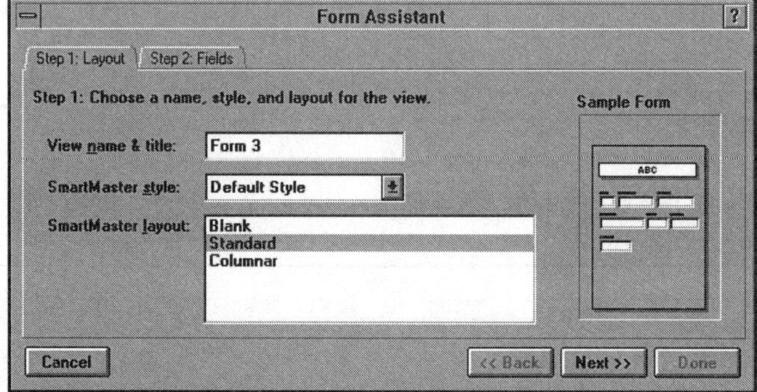

Fig. 3.2
Create new forms using the Form Assistant dialog box.

3. Type a name for the form into the View **N**ame & Title text box.

4. Choose a SmartMaster style from the SmartMaster **s**tyle drop-down list. A SmartMaster style gives a form a set of Info Box properties, such as a background color, text attributes, field borders, and field frames. Approach comes with a set of SmartMaster styles such as "3D Look1," "Chisel1," and "Executive."

5. Select a SmartMaster **L**ayout from the list. The Standard layout arranges the fields horizontally across the page. A Columnar layout arranges the fields vertically in columns. A Blank form provides an empty page for you to add your own fields using the various field tools. See Chapters 4 and 9 for more information on enhancing data input forms.

6. Click the Step 2: Fields tab or the Next button to move to the Fields section of the Form Assistant dialog box.

7. The Fields section contains two windows. The Database **F**ields list box lists all the fields for the current database. Click each field you want to add to the form, and then choose **A**dd after each selection to move each individual field to the Fields to **P**lace on View list box. To select multiple fields, press the Ctrl key as you click and then choose **A**dd. To select a range of fields, click the first field and then hold down the Shift key as you click the last field in the range.

8. Click Done. The new form appears as shown in figure 3.3. The fields are laid out vertically, just like on a default form.

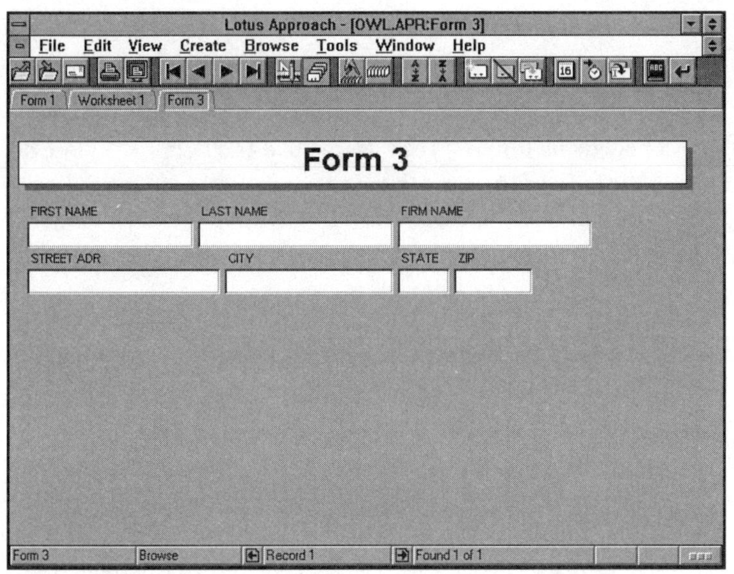

Fig. 3.3
The new form.

Note

If you change your mind about a field, select it in the Fields to **P**lace on View list box, and then choose **R**emove to remove the field from the list. You can also double-click the field in the Fields to **P**lace on View list box to remove it from the list.

Tip
You can also double-click single fields to add them to the Fields to Place on View list box.

Changing the Name of a Form

When you create a new form, Approach gives it a rather non descriptive default name, such as Form 1. After you create the form, you can change this name in the Info Box to describe more clearly what the form does—for example, Data Input or New Customer. When Approach creates a default form for a new database, however, you don't have an opportunity to set the name of the form; but you can rename the default form just like any other form.

To rename a form, follow these steps:

1. Switch to Design mode by opening the **V**iew menu and choosing **D**esign, clicking the Design SmartIcon, or selecting Design from the status bar.

2. If the form you want to rename isn't currently displayed on-screen, choose the form from the tabs across the top of the screen.

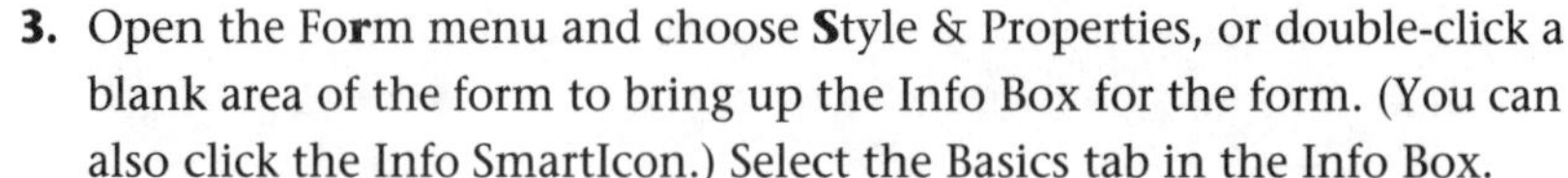

3. Open the Form menu and choose **S**tyle & Properties, or double-click a blank area of the form to bring up the Info Box for the form. (You can also click the Info SmartIcon.) Select the Basics tab in the Info Box.

4. Type a new name into the Form Name text box. Click the close box to close the Info Box. The form is renamed, and you can see the new name on the title bar. For the Owl Publishing example, rename the form to "Customer."

5. Save the view file by opening the **F**ile menu and choosing **S**ave Approach File, or clicking the File Save SmartIcon.

Tip
You can also rename a form in Design mode by double-clicking the form's tab. Edit the text of the tab to change the name.

Changing the Basic Properties of a Form

Besides changing the name of a form, you can set other properties from the Basics tab of the form's Info Box. You can choose the named style on which the form is based, whether the form is visible in Browse mode, and whether Approach displays the page margins. To open the form's Info Box, use steps 1–3 in the previous section.

To select a named style, choose the style from the Named styles drop-down list. For more information on creating named styles, see "Working with Named Styles" later in this chapter.

To hide the form in Browse mode, click the Hide view checkbox to place a check in the checkbox. To display a hidden form, click the Hide view checkbox to turn off the checkmark. To hide the page margins, click the Hide page margins checkbox to place a check in the checkbox. To display hidden page margins, click the Hide page margins checkbox again to remove the check.

Note

The Main Database drop-down lists let you change the database on which the form is based. The Main Database drop-down list is discussed in Chapter 9. The Attached menu bar lets you select a different menu bar for the form. Menu bars are discussed in Chapter 17.

Setting the Color and Line Properties of a Form

You may set the attributes of the background and lines that Approach displays on a form. To adjust these attributes, follow these steps:

1. Switch to Design mode by opening the **V**iew menu and choosing **D**esign, clicking the Design SmartIcon, or choosing Design from the status bar.

2. If the form you want to work with isn't currently displayed on-screen, choose the form from the tabs across the top of the screen.

3. Open the Form menu and choose **S**tyle & Properties, or double-click a blank area of the form to bring up the Info Box for the form. (You can also click the Info SmartIcon.) Select the Color tab in the Info Box.

4. To select a border width, click the Border width drop-down list. Select a line width from the available thicknesses.

5. To select a border color or form background fill color, select the Border color or Fill color drop-down list. Approach displays a palette of available colors. Click the color you want to use. The rectangle marked with a "T" makes the color transparent.

6. To select a frame style, click the Frame drop-down list. A variety of frame styles are available, including raised and recessed 3D-look frames. Select the one you want.

7. To select borders for the form's sides, use the checkboxes in the Borders section of the Info Box. Click the checkboxes to place checkmarks in the Left, Right, Top, and Bottom checkboxes.

Resizing the Form Page

Resizing the active area of the form on the page gives you more room to place fields, graphics, and other objects. To resize the active area of the form on the page, click the edge of the form. Approach draws a double line around the form. Move the mouse pointer over this double line. The mouse pointer becomes a two-headed arrow. Click and drag the double line to resize the form.

Duplicating a Form

You can copy a form so that you don't have to do all your work over again to create a similar form. To copy a form, follow these steps:

1. Switch to Design mode by opening the **V**iew menu and choosing **D**esign, clicking the Design SmartIcon, or choosing Design from the status bar.

2. If the form you want to duplicate isn't currently displayed on-screen, choose the form from the tabs across the top of the screen.

3. Open the **E**dit menu and choose **D**uplicate Form. Approach displays the duplicate of the form on-screen. You can change this duplicate without affecting the original—including changing its name.

Note

You should change the name of a form after you copy it. Approach does not allow two forms to have the same name.

Deleting a Form

You can delete a form once you no longer need it. To delete a form, follow these steps:

1. Switch to Design mode by opening the **V**iew menu and choosing **D**esign, clicking the Design SmartIcon, or choosing Design from the status bar.

2. If the form you want to delete isn't currently displayed on-screen, choose the form from the tabs across the top of the screen.

3. Open the **E**dit menu and choose D**e**lete Form. Approach displays the confirmation alert. Click **Y**es to delete the form.

Working with Objects

Approach enables you to place various objects on your forms, including fields, drop-down lists, graphics, and text. By placing objects on your form, you can customize the way the form looks and how it works. You also can resize and move objects. You have complete control over how and where objects appear on your form.

Selecting a Single Object

Before moving or resizing an object, you must select it. To select an object, switch to Design mode and click the item you want to modify. You can tell that the object is selected because four small black squares (called *sizing handles*) appear, one in each corner of the rectangle. The sizing handles define the limits of the object selected (see fig. 3.4).

Note

The form shown in figure 3.4 has been magnified (using the magnification setting on the status bar) to show the sizing handles better.

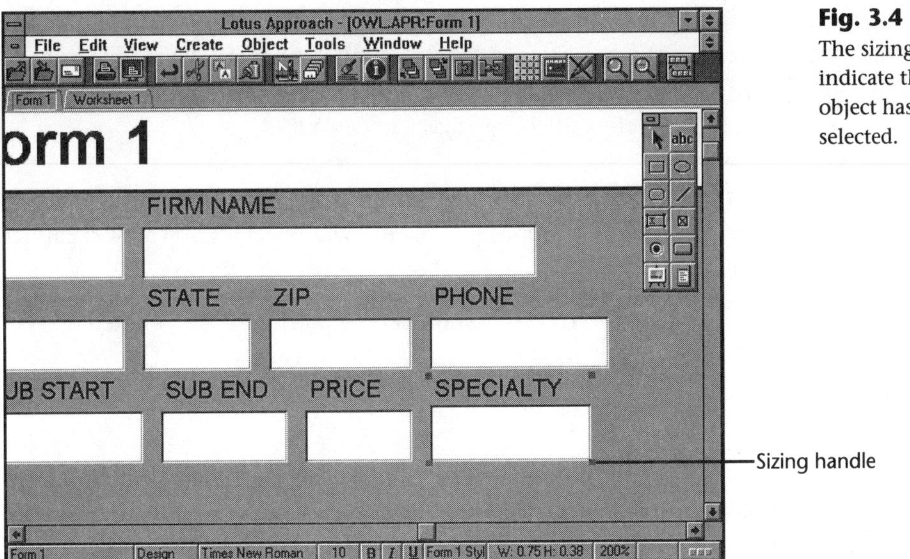

Fig. 3.4
The sizing handles indicate that an object has been selected.

Selecting Multiple Objects

You can select multiple objects in two ways. The first method is to move the mouse pointer to the upper-left corner of the area that includes the objects you want, and then hold down the left mouse button and drag to the lower-right corner of that area. All of the objects that are completely included in the dragged rectangle are selected (see fig. 3.5).

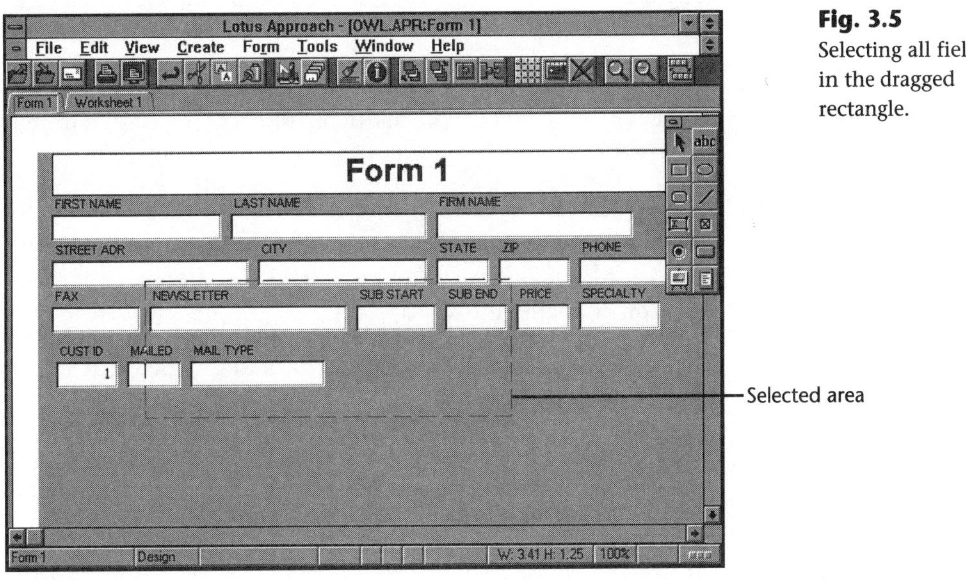

Fig. 3.5
Selecting all fields in the dragged rectangle.

The second way to select multiple objects is to click the first object you want to select, hold down the Shift key, and then click the other objects you want to select. If you accidentally click an object you don't want, hold down the Shift key and click the object again to deselect it.

Resizing Objects

As in most Windows applications, after you select an object, you can resize it. Follow these steps:

1. Click one of the four handles at the corners of the selected object.

2. Hold down the left mouse button and drag the corner until the object is the size you want.

Tip
You can tell when the mouse pointer is positioned over one of the sizing handles because the pointer changes into a small, two-headed arrow.

You can also adjust the size of an object using the object's Info Box. In the object's Info Box, click the Dimensions tab, which displays a rectangle with brackets around it. Set the width and height in the Dimensions panel.

When sizing a field on a form, try to make the field just long enough to hold the information that the database field will store. (This length depends on the font you plan to use for that field.) If you make the form field too short, you won't be able to see all the information you type into the field. On the other hand, if you make the form field too long, you waste screen space. Approach does not let you enter more characters on-screen than the length that was specified when the database field was created.

You can adjust the length of the field, if you find that it's too long or too short. Follow these steps:

1. Switch to Design mode by opening the **V**iew menu and choosing **D**esign, clicking the Design SmartIcon, or choosing Design from the status bar.

2. Double-click the text field to bring up the Info Box, and select the font tab (marked "az"). (You can also click the Info SmartIcon.) Set the font you want for the information in that field. (See Chapter 4 for more details on changing the font.)

3. Click the Browse SmartIcon to switch back to Browse mode.

4. Type the number of characters that the field should be able to hold. If the FIRST NAME field can hold 25 characters, for example, click the FIRST NAME field and type a text string of 25 characters (uppercase X works well as a place holder for this purpose).

5. Return to Design mode.

6. To adjust the length of the field, move the mouse pointer to one of the sizing handles; the pointer becomes a two-headed resizing arrow. Adjust the length in one of the following ways:

   If the field was longer than the text string you typed, resize the field to make it shorter.

   If the field wasn't long enough (the text string scrolled to the left as you typed the last few characters), resize the field to make it longer.

To make sure you can see the data you entered in Browse mode when you are in Design mode, open the **T**ools menu and choose **P**references to open the Preferences dialog box. Select the Display tab, and make sure the Data checkbox is set in the Show in Design section.

Memo type fields can have an unlimited length, and typing and editing text in a memo field is much easier if the field is more than one line deep. For memo fields, use the sizing handles to stretch the field into a box that's as wide as possible and at least three or four lines deep (see fig. 3.6). When you type in a memo field, the text scrolls up if you exceed the amount of space allotted for the field. Approach automatically wraps words in memo fields. Approach also lets you use multiline text fields in the same way.

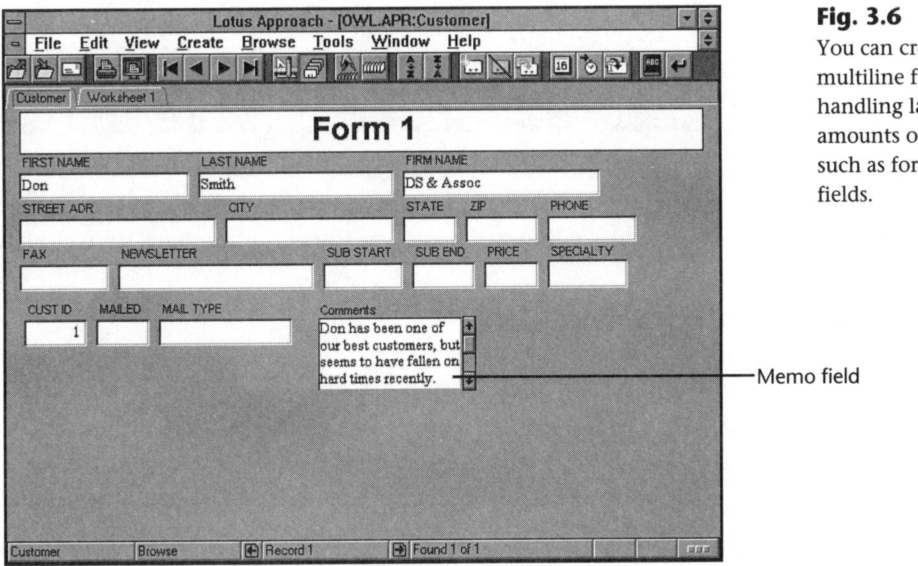

Fig. 3.6
You can create a multiline field for handling large amounts of text, such as for memo fields.

The Data Input form in the Owl Publishing example has the default field layout. To practice resizing objects on a form, try resizing the FIRST NAME and LAST NAME fields by following these steps:

1. Click the Design SmartIcon to switch to Design mode.

2. Click the FIRST NAME field near the top of the form, and drag the handle in the lower-right corner to make the field shorter.

3. Click the LAST NAME field and drag the sizing handle in the lower corner to make it shorter (see fig. 3.7).

Fig. 3.7
The FIRST NAME and LAST NAME fields have been shortened.

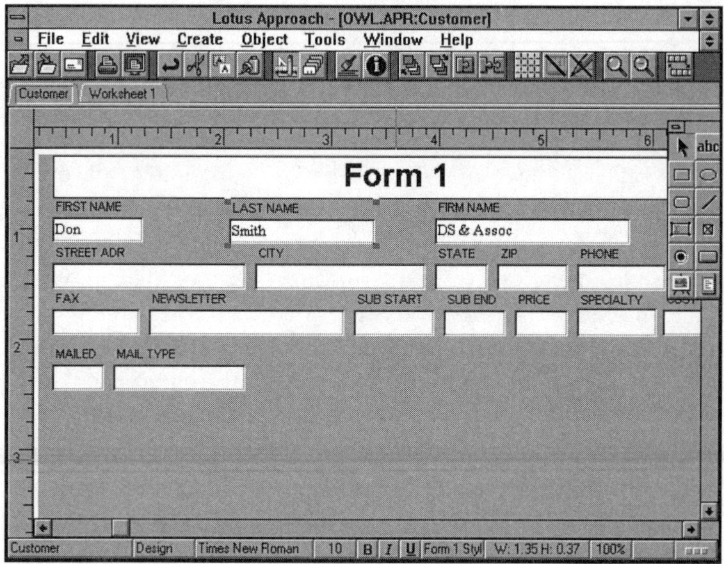

4. Open the **F**ile menu and choose **S**ave Approach File to save the file. (By saving the file, you are saving the new form design as well.)

Tip
To move a selected object(s) a little bit at a time, use the arrow keys on the keyboard. Each time you press an arrow key, the object(s) moves one screen pixel in the direction of the arrow.

Moving Objects

Approach lets you move objects so that you can rearrange them on the form. To move a single object, select the object, click the object again (anywhere except over a sizing handle), and then drag it to its new location. When the mouse pointer is positioned over a selected object, it turns into a shape that looks like a plus symbol with an arrowhead on each branch.

You can also relocate a single object using the object's Info Box. In the object's Info Box, click the Dimension tab and type in new Top and Left dimensions.

You can also move multiple objects as a group. Select all the objects you want to move (see the earlier section, "Selecting Multiple Objects"); click any selected object, hold down the left mouse button, and drag the whole group to its new location.

Suppose you want to rearrange some fields to make the layout of the Owl Publishing form more convenient. Moving the LAST NAME field to the right of the FIRST NAME field would help. To do this, follow these steps:

1. Click the LAST NAME field.
2. Move the mouse pointer anywhere inside the LAST NAME field. Hold down the left mouse button, and drag the LAST NAME field onto the same line as the FIRST NAME field, positioning the field just to the right of the FIRST NAME field (see fig. 3.8).

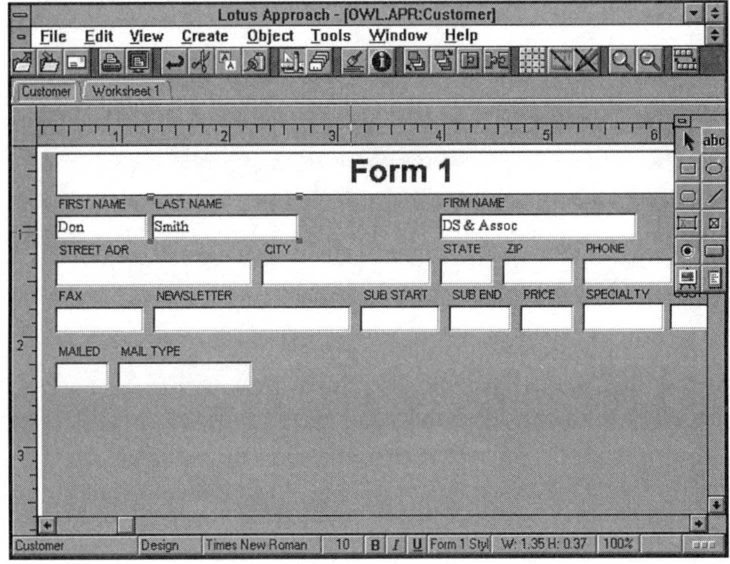

Fig. 3.8
After moving the LAST NAME field, there is more space on the form.

3. Open the **F**ile menu and choose **S**ave Approach File.

It's also a good idea to rearrange the fields on the Owl Publishing form so that they not only fit on one screen, but so they're also more friendly and usable. Figure 3.9 shows a good example of a modified form. To make these changes, click and drag the fields into the positions shown. To make the fields fit on the same line, you may also need to shrink some of them, notably the STATE field. When you are through rearranging and resizing the fields, open the **F**ile menu and choose **S**ave Approach File.

Fig. 3.9
The rearranged Owl Publishing form.

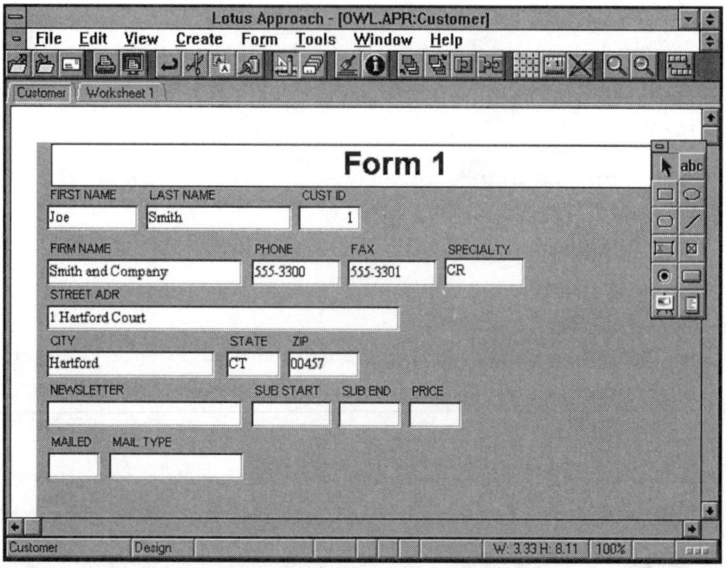

Cutting, Copying, and Pasting Objects

You can cut, copy, or paste objects on a form using options from the **E**dit menu. Cu**t** removes the selected objects from the form and places them on the Windows Clipboard. **C**opy copies the selected objects to the Clipboard; the original objects remain unchanged on the form. **P**aste takes the contents of the Clipboard (placed there by Cu**t** or **C**opy) and pastes them back on the form.

Tip
You can also use **C**opy and **P**aste to duplicate an object on the same form so that you can make minor changes to the object.

To use Cu**t** or **C**opy, first select the objects you want to cut or copy. To select multiple objects, hold down the Shift key and then click the objects you want, or drag a rectangle around the objects (see the earlier section, "Selecting Multiple Objects"). Open the **E**dit menu and choose either Cu**t** or **C**opy.

To paste the contents of the Clipboard back onto a form, click the form at the position you want to paste, and then open the **E**dit menu and choose **P**aste.

The combination of **C**opy and **P**aste is useful for copying objects from one form to another in Approach. Follow these steps:

1. Open the form that contains the object(s) you want to duplicate. To open the form, select the form from the form tabs.

2. Select the object(s) you want to copy.

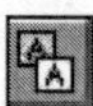

3. Open the **E**dit menu and choose **C**opy.

4. Switch to the form where you want to paste the object(s) by selecting the form's tab.

5. Click the form at the place where you want the object(s) pasted.

6. Open the **E**dit menu and choose **P**aste.

Deleting Objects from a Form

To delete objects from a form, select the objects and then open the **E**dit menu and choose Cu**t**, or press the Del key.

Using Approach's Layout Tools

Approach has several tools to help you design your form exactly the way you want. They help you position objects on-screen more accurately and adjust their appearance. These tools are rulers, status bar dimensions, an alignment tool, a snap-to grid, a magnification tool, a grouping tool, and an object-stacking-order tool.

Note

To use these tools, you must be in Design mode.

Using Rulers

Approach provides a set of rulers—one across the top of the screen and one down the left side—to help you align objects on the page. As you move the pointer, a set of lines moves in the rulers, showing where the pointer is in relation to the measurements on the ruler.

To turn on the rulers, open the **V**iew menu and choose Show **R**uler, or click the Show Rulers SmartIcon. A checkmark appears next to Show **R**uler in the menu. To turn off the rulers, click Show **R**uler again to remove the checkmark. Figure 3.10 shows how the rulers appear on-screen.

Rulers are very handy for working with text objects. When you select a text object, additional information about the text object appears in the ruler. This information includes margins, indents, and tabs, which are described below:

- The left and right edges of the text object are indicated as a pair of black, inward-facing arrowheads. You can't move these arrowheads; they are present in the ruler line for reference only. To adjust the size of the text box, click it and drag the sizing boxes.

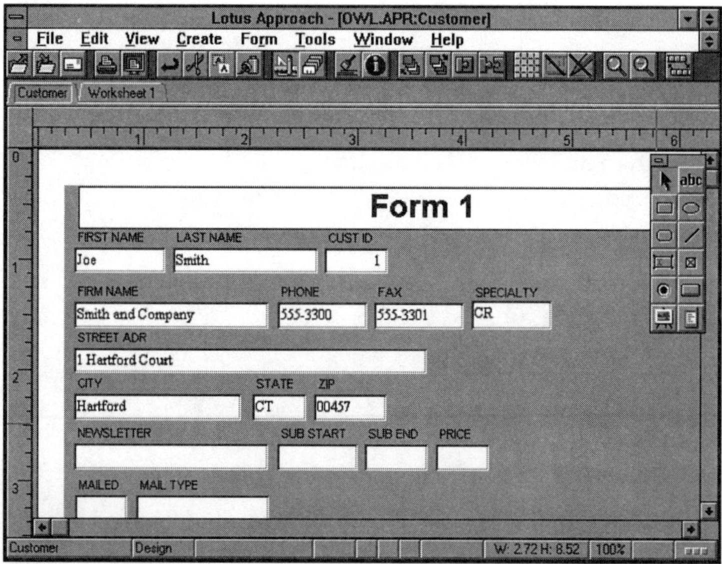

Fig. 3.10
The Design mode with rulers on.

- The right margin for text in the text object is indicated as a blue arrowhead. This arrowhead faces to the left and is located above the ruler line. Drag this arrowhead to set the right margin. However, you can't drag it to the right of the indicator for the right edge of the text box.

- You can place multiple tabs for the text in the text object. A tab is indicated as a small right-facing arrowhead with a line to its right. These tab indicators are located above the ruler line. To place a new tab, click above the ruler between the left and right edge of the text object. To move an existing tab, click the tab and drag it to its new location. To delete a tab, click the tab and drag it off the ruler.

- The left margin for text is indicated as a right-facing arrowhead with a line to its left. To adjust the overall left margin, click and drag the line and arrowhead to a new location. You can't drag the left margin past the left edge of the text object.

- The left margin arrowhead is split into top and bottom sections which you can drag independently. To set a first-line indent, drag the top portion of the arrowhead to the right of the bottom portion. To set a hanging indent, drag the bottom section of the arrowhead to the right of the top portion.

Activating the Status Bar Dimensions

To position objects precisely, you can show on the status bar the exact position (dimensions) of your mouse pointer to 1/100 of an inch or centimeter, depending on the measuring units you're using on the ruler. The mouse position is displayed only when no objects are selected. As you move the pointer, the numbers change to reflect the new pointer position. The first number shows the distance of the pointer from the left side of the form. The second number shows the distance of the pointer from the top edge of the form.

If you select an object, Approach can display either the x- and y-coordinates of the upper-left corner of the object or the height and width of the object (see fig. 3.11). To switch between displaying the left top x- and y-coordinates (the status bar displays L: and T:) and the width and height (the status bar displays W: and H:), click the dimension area of the status bar.

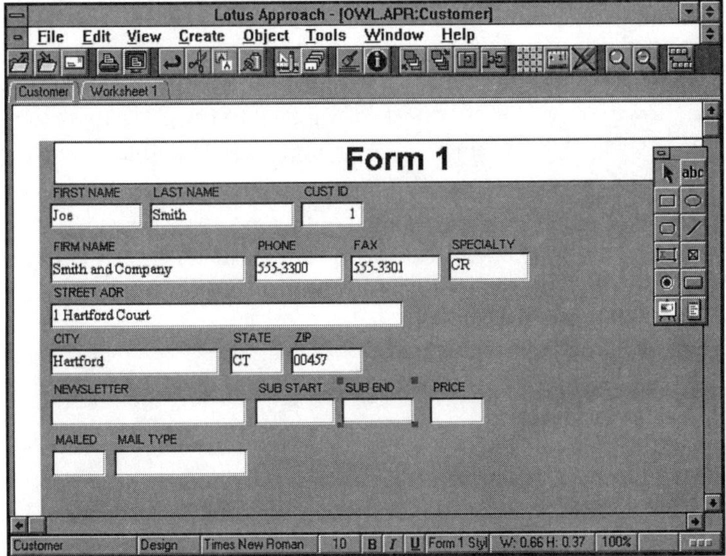

Fig. 3.11
An object's dimensions are shown on the status bar.

Using the Grid

Besides enabling you to align objects to each other, Approach has a grid to help you place objects. When the grid is turned on, an object's location is constrained to points on the grid. If you try to place an object so that it isn't on the grid, the object automatically moves to the nearest grid point. This feature helps you keep objects aligned on-screen.

If you try to resize an object with the grid turned on, Approach ensures that the adjusted edge is located on a grid point. If you try to size an object so that the adjusted edge isn't placed on the grid, that edge "snaps" to the closest grid point.

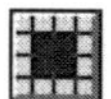 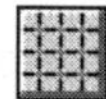

You have the options of snapping objects to the grid and viewing the grid. You can set these options independently. For example, you can snap objects to the grid, but not make the grid visible on the screen (an invisible grid); or you can view the grid (for alignment help) but not snap objects to the grid. To snap objects to the grid, open the **V**iew menu and choose Snap to **G**rid or click the Snap to Grid SmartIcon. A checkmark appears next to this menu item. To turn off the Snap to Grid, select this option again. To view the grid, open the **V**iew menu and choose Show Gr**i**d or click the Show Grid SmartIcon. A checkmark appears next to this menu item, and the grid becomes visible. When the grid is visible, Approach displays this icon with a line across it. To hide the grid, select this menu option again.

Aligning Objects to the Grid

As you learned earlier in this discussion, you can use the grid to align objects in your forms. If you have turned off the Snap to Grid and moved objects on the form, however, objects are no longer aligned to the grid. Approach therefore offers a feature that enables you to realign objects to the grid.

To align objects to the grid, follow these steps:

1. Switch to Design mode by opening the **V**iew menu and choosing **D**esign, clicking the Design SmartIcon, or choosing Design from the status bar.

2. Select the objects you want to align.

3. Open the **O**bject menu and choose **A**lign, or select the Align Objects SmartIcon. The Alignment dialog box appears.

4. Choose the To **G**rid button in the Align Objects box.

5. Select the other alignment options you want in the Horizontal Alignment or Vertical Alignment portions of the Align dialog box. (See the next section, "Aligning Objects to Each Other," for more information on alignment options.) The selected edge or center aligns to the nearest grid point. To align an object's top edge to the grid, for example, choose **T**op in the Vertical Alignment box.

> **Note**
>
> The objects in the Sample box don't move when you are aligning to the grid.

Aligning Objects to Each Other

Approach provides a powerful tool for aligning objects to each other that enables you to lay out a form quickly, and ensures that fields and other objects are lined up without having to tediously align them by hand. You can align objects horizontally or vertically:

- If you align the objects vertically, you can choose to align their top or bottom edges or their centers. You can also have Approach distribute the objects evenly in the vertical direction.
- If you align the objects horizontally, you can choose to align their left or right edges or their centers. You can also have Approach distribute the objects evenly in the horizontal direction.

To access the alignment tool, follow these steps:

1. Switch to Design mode by opening the **V**iew menu and choosing **D**esign, clicking the Design SmartIcon, or choosing Design from the status bar.

2. Select the objects you want to align.
3. Open the **O**bject menu and choose **A**lign or click the Align Objects SmartIcon. The Align dialog box appears (see fig. 3.12).

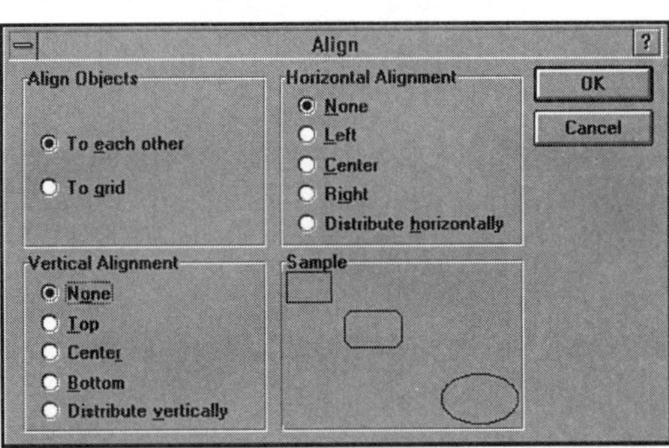

Fig. 3.12
Use the Align dialog box to specify how objects should align.

Tip
Remember, to select multiple objects, you click the first one, hold down the Shift key, and then click the others. Alternatively, you can drag a rectangle around the objects.

The Align dialog box is divided into four sections: Align Objects, Horizontal Alignment, Vertical Alignment, and Sample.

The Align Objects section contains two options. The To **E**ach Other button aligns the selected objects to each other. The To **G**rid button aligns the selected objects to the invisible grid. (See the earlier section, "Aligning Objects to the Grid," for details.)

To the right of the Align Objects options are the Horizontal Alignment options. To select the type of horizontal alignment you want, choose one of the following buttons:

- *None*. No horizontal alignment.
- *Left*. Approach aligns the left edges of all objects to line up with the left edge of the object farthest to the left.
- *Center*. Approach aligns all objects so that their horizontal (left-to-right) centers are lined up.
- *Right*. Approach aligns all objects so that their right edges line up with the right edge of the object that is farthest to the right.
- *Distribute horizontally*. Approach distributes all the objects evenly between the object that is farthest to the left and the object that is farthest to the right.

To select the type of vertical alignment you want, choose one of the following options in the Vertical Alignment section:

- *None*. No vertical alignment.
- *Top*. Approach aligns all objects so that their top edges line up with the top edge of the object that is highest on-screen.
- *Center*. Approach aligns all objects so that their vertical (top to bottom) centers are lined up.
- *Bottom*. Approach aligns all objects so that their bottom edges line up with the bottom edge of the object that is lowest on-screen.
- *Distribute vertically*. Approach distributes all objects evenly between the highest and lowest objects.

The Sample section, located in the lower-right corner of the dialog box, shows a sample of how the alignment options you have chosen will look. If you choose the Vertical Alignment Top option, for example, the sample objects move so that their top edges are lined up with the uppermost object in the Sample box.

On the Owl Publishing form, the CITY, STATE, and ZIP fields are on the same line, so they should be aligned to each other. To align these three fields, follow these steps:

1. Click the Design SmartIcon to switch to Design mode.

2. Click the CITY field.
3. Hold down the Shift key and then click the STATE and ZIP fields.
4. Open the **O**bject menu and choose **A**lign. The Alignment dialog box appears.

5. Choose **T**op in the Vertical Alignment box. Check the Sample box to see how the objects align (see fig. 3.13).

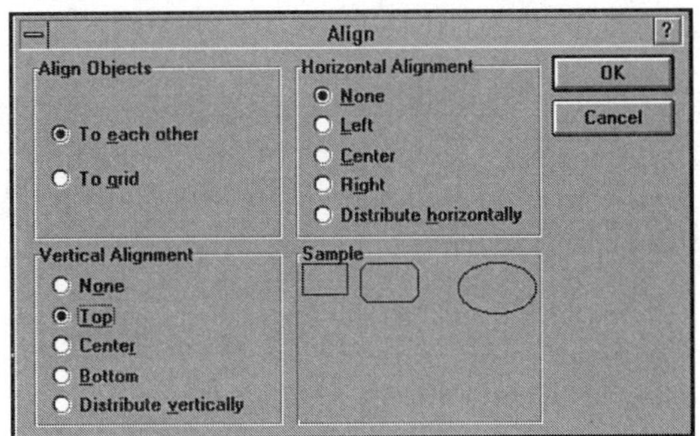

Fig. 3.13
Three fields are aligned by their top edges.

6. Click OK. The three fields align on the form so that all their tops are even.
7. Open the **F**ile menu and choose **S**ave Approach File to save the Approach file.

Using Magnification

Displaying the form in a larger size helps you place objects precisely. Displaying the form in a smaller size enables you to see more of the form on-screen at once.

To make the form larger, click the Zoom-In SmartIcon or open the **View** menu and choose **Zoom In**. Everything on the form appears larger, and you can't see as much of the form on-screen. If you want to view other parts of the form, use the scroll bars along the side of the screen.

To make the form smaller, click the Zoom-Out SmartIcon or open the **View** menu and choose **Zoom Out**. Everything on the form appears smaller, and you can see more of your form on-screen. Each time you choose the **Zoom Out** command the form halves in size, to a minimum of 25 percent of normal.

An alternate method for adjusting the amount of a form displayed on-screen is to use the magnification button in the status bar. When you click the magnification button, Approach lists the available magnifications in percentages. Select the magnification you want from this list. To return to the normal size, select 100% magnification from the status bar magnification list.

Note

If you have turned on the rulers, the measurements on them shrink or grow to reflect the new magnification of the form.

Grouping and Ungrouping Objects

Grouping objects on the form is helpful in several ways. By grouping objects, you can move, size, and set their properties as though they are a single object. This feature can save you a great deal of time.

For example, you can use the graphics tools in Design mode to construct a simple logo on the form. If you later decide to relocate this logo, however, you would have to make sure that all the portions of the logo were selected before you moved it; otherwise, you would leave pieces of the logo behind. If you needed to resize the logo, you would have to resize each graphic component individually.

After you group objects, however, you can click any part of the grouped object to display a single set of handles. You can then size or move this grouped object as you would any other object. Figures 3.14 and 3.15 help show the advantages of grouping objects.

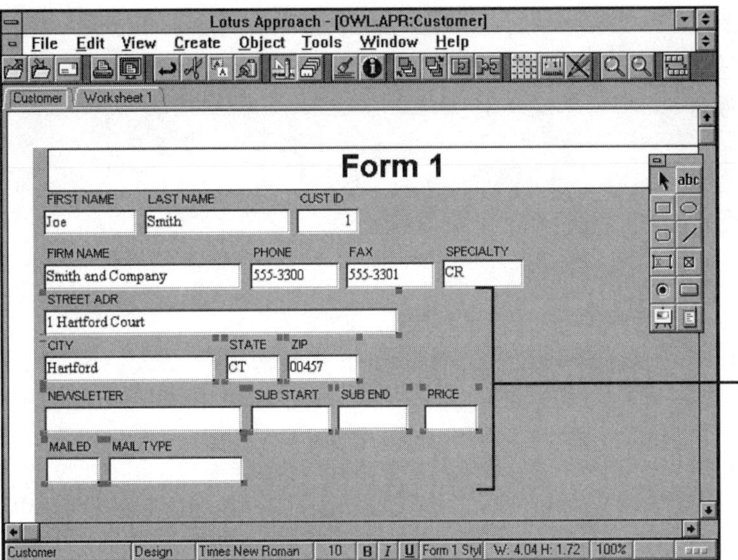

Fig. 3.14
Each object in this collection has individual sizing handles, making it difficult to size and move the objects together.

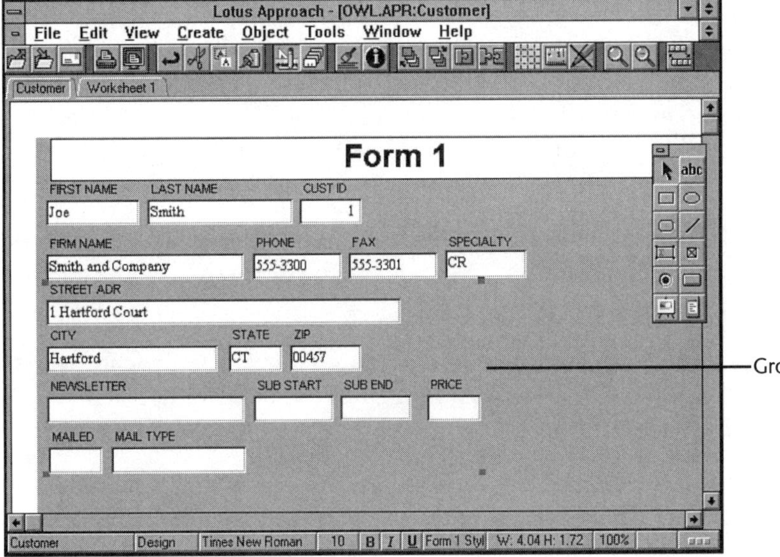

Fig. 3.15
These grouped objects have a single set of sizing handles, making it easy to size and move them as a single object.

Grouping Objects

To group objects, select the objects you want to include and then open the **O**bject menu and choose **G**roup, or click the Group Objects SmartIcon. Alternatively, you can click any selected object using the right mouse button, and then choose Group from the shortcut menu. A single set of four handles appears on the boundary of the group.

> **Note**
>
> After you group several objects into a grouped object, you can group the resulting group with other objects.

Ungrouping Objects

To ungroup the objects, select the group and choose **U**ngroup from the **O**bject menu or the shortcut menu. You can also select the Ungroup Objects SmartIcon. Approach separates the grouped object into its original objects or groups. If you combine a group with other objects, ungrouping leaves you with the original group and the objects. To separate the original group into its component objects, you must select that group and then open the **O**bjects menu and choose **U**nGroup again.

Stacking Objects

Another helpful layout feature is the capability to place objects on top of each other. Each object added to the screen is placed on its own layer, with more recently added objects being closer to the "top" layer. The most recently added object is on top, covering the other layers.

Tip
The stacking feature is useful when you're using graphics. For example, you can place a large box on-screen and then group several fields inside that box to indicate that they are related.

This stacking order affects how the objects appear on-screen and on the printout. If you have a form with fields on it and add a large box to the form, for example, the box covers up the fields because the box was added to the form after the fields.

Approach has four commands on the **O**bject A**r**range submenu: Send to **B**ack, Bring to **F**ront, **S**end Backward, and B**r**ing Forward. Use these commands to adjust the stacking order to get the effect you want.

To use any of these commands, you must be in Design mode. Click the object whose layer you want to modify, and use the commands or the optional SmartIcons as described below:

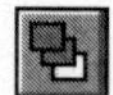

- To move an object behind all the others, open the **O**bject A**r**range submenu and choose Send to **B**ack, or click the Send to Back SmartIcon. This option places all other objects in front of the object. Figure 3.16 shows a red rectangle on the FIRST NAME and LAST NAME fields, and figure 3.17 shows the same rectangle after it is sent to the back.

- To move an object in front of all the others, open the **O**bject A**r**range submenu and choose Bring to **F**ront, or click the Bring to Front SmartIcon. This option places the object in front of everything else so that it is always visible.

- To move an object one layer forward, open the **O**bject A**r**range submenu and choose B**r**ing Forward, or click the Bring Forward SmartIcon.

- To move an object one layer back, open the **O**bject A**r**range submenu and choose **S**end Backward, or click the Send Backward SmartIcon.

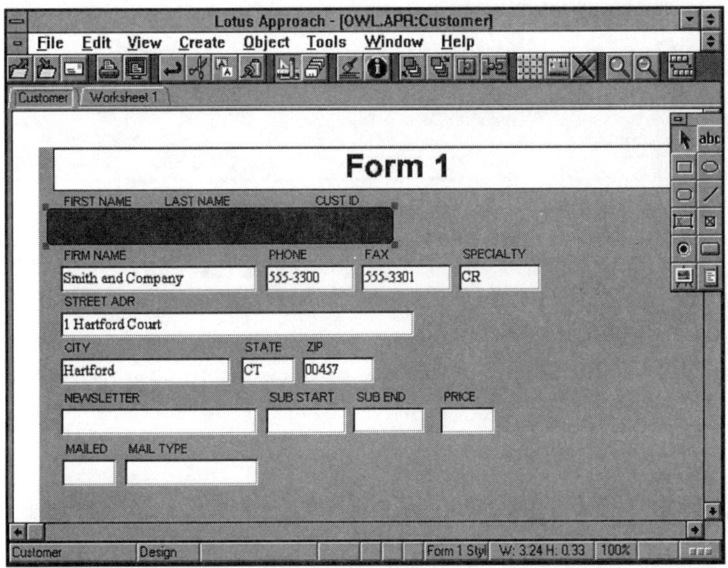

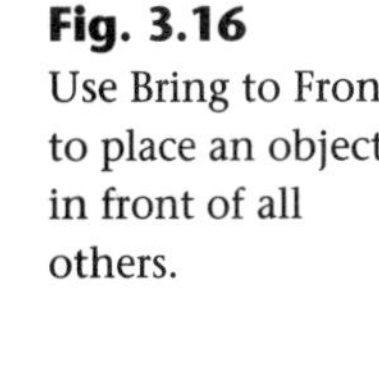

Fig. 3.16
Use Bring to Front to place an object in front of all others.

Note

You can use the B**r**ing Forward and **S**end Backward commands to adjust an object in relation to other objects. Adjusting an object by one layer, however, may not change how it looks in relation to another object, because the objects may not be next to each other in the stacking order. If so, execute the command several times until it has the desired effect.

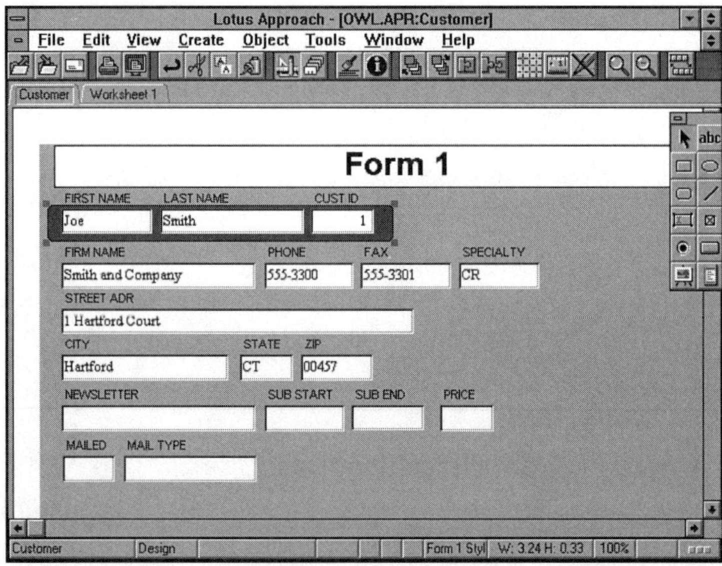

Fig. 3.17
Use Send to Back to move an object to the back.

Setting an Object's Print and Preview Attributes

You have the option to prevent an object from printing, show non-printing objects in Preview mode, and cause objects to relocate on the printout to close up the empty space on a form.

Preventing Objects from Printing

Normally, any object you place on a form is printed when you print the form and is displayed when you do a print preview. (See Chapter 7 for information on printing forms and reports.) But what if you don't want to print all of the objects? For example, you may not want to print complex graphics because they may slow down the print speed considerably. Similarly, because macro buttons don't contain any useful information, you have no reason to include them on a printout (these buttons default to non-printing).

To prevent an object from appearing on a printout or a print preview, follow these steps:

1. Switch to Design mode by opening the **V**iew menu and choosing **D**esign, clicking the Design SmartIcon, or choosing Design from the status bar.

2. Open the Info Box by selecting **S**tyle & Properties from the pop-up menu or by double-clicking the object. You can also open the Info Box

by selecting the object and clicking the Info Box SmartIcon, or by opening the **O**bject menu and choosing **S**tyle & Properties.

3. Click the Basics tab. Click the Non-printing checkbox to place a check in the checkbox. The checkbox shows a checkmark whenever you have selected an object that won't appear on a printout.

If you change your mind and decide to have the object appear on a printout, click the Non-printing checkbox to remove the checkmark.

Showing and Hiding Objects in Preview

If you decide to hide an object when you print the form you may also choose to hide the object in Preview mode. By hiding the object in Preview mode, the on-screen form will look like the printed form. Approach still displays the object in Browse mode, so you can add data to a data field. Of course, certain types of objects (such as buttons to activate macros) don't make sense to hide because you can't use them if you can't find them.

To show an object in Preview mode, follow these steps:

1. Switch to Design mode by opening the **V**iew menu and choosing **D**esign, clicking the Design SmartIcon, or choosing Design from the status bar.

2. Open the Info Box by selecting **S**tyle & Properties from the pop-up menu or by double-clicking the object. You can also open the Info Box by selecting the object and clicking the Info Box SmartIcon, or by opening the **O**bject menu and choosing **S**tyle & Properties.

3. Click the Basics tab. Click the Show in Preview checkbox to place a check in the checkbox. The checkbox shows a checkmark whenever you have selected an object that will appear in Preview mode. The Show in Preview checkbox is only available if you have also selected Non-printing.

If you change your mind and decide to have the object not appear in Preview mode, click the Show in Preview checkbox to remove the checkmark.

Using Slide Up and Slide Left

When you enter data into a field on a form, you can often leave blank spaces. Some empty space results if you don't enter data into all the fields on the form; empty space also appears when fields are much longer than the text they contain. Blank space doesn't represent a real problem, but ugly printouts can result. You can instruct Approach to move other fields and text or graphic objects on the form to close up the empty space when you print the form. Use Approach's Slide Up and Slide Left commands, coupled with the Reduce Boundaries command, to close up empty space. If you cause an object to slide up, it moves up to fill an empty line. If you cause an object to slide left, it moves to the left to fill in any space left in a field that is much longer than its contents (see fig. 3.18). In order for Slide Left to work, however, the objects' bottom borders must be aligned.

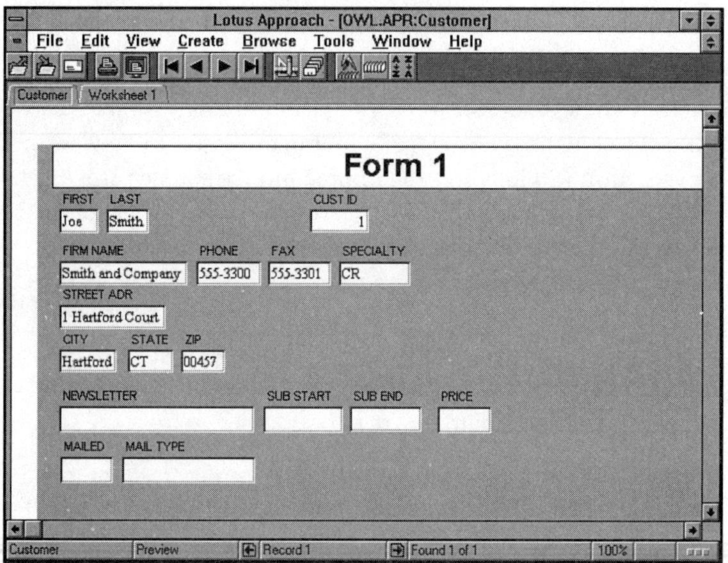

Fig. 3.18
When data does not fill a field completely, Slide Left closes up the empty space in Print Preview (and when you print).

To access the Slide Up and Slide Left commands, switch to Design mode, select the objects you want, and display the Info Box by choosing **S**tyle & Properties from the **O**bject or pop-up menu. Choose the Dimensions tab. To set an object to slide left, click the Left checkbox under the When printing, Slide heading. To set an object to slide up, click the Up checkbox in the When printing, Slide heading.

Under normal circumstances, fields take up a specific amount of room on the form. Thus, the Slide Left and Slide Up commands have no effect unless you allow Approach to adjust the size of any fields that contain blank space. To allow Approach to adjust the field size, select the Reduce checkbox on the Dimensions panel. The Reduce checkbox lets Approach shrink a field that contains empty space, potentially moving other objects left and up to fill in the empty space.

A related command is the Expand checkbox on the Dimensions panel. This checkbox enables Approach to increase the size of a screen field when the database field contains more information than can be displayed in the field on-screen. A good example of a use for the Expand checkbox is a memo field with more text than Approach can display in the allotted field space. If you check the Expand checkbox, Approach will insert enough space in the printout to fully print the contents of the memo field.

Note

You won't be able to see the changes on the form unless you are in Preview mode or Design mode with field data showing. To enter Preview mode, click the Preview SmartIcon or select Preview from the status bar. To show field data, open the **V**iew menu and choose S**h**ow Data, or click the Show Data SmartIcon. If the form is too small to read the text in Preview mode—and to see the effects of Slide Up or Slide Left—click the Zoom-In SmartIcon.

Working with Named Styles

Info Boxes are useful for setting the properties of objects on-screen. From an Info Box you can set the color, frame style, font, size, effects, field label attributes, and many other properties of an object. However, it can be tedious to set all the properties for each new object you create. If you set an attribute (for example, the font) to different values for different objects, the effect can look haphazard instead of well planned. For example, using too many colors or fonts on a form is distracting. Ideally, you should establish a scheme of object attributes and stick to it throughout an Approach application.

Approach can help you choose a scheme of object attributes with a named style. *Named styles* are named sets of object attributes that you can easily apply to any new or existing object on a form. When you apply a named style to an object, the object takes on all the attributes of the named style that are appropriate for that object. For example, if you apply a named style to a rectangle, the rectangle border width and color, as well as the fill pattern and color, take on the attributes of the named style. Even though the named style may have text attributes as well, these are not applied to the rectangle because a rectangle doesn't have any text.

Another advantage to named styles is that you can easily change the attributes of objects on a form. When you change the attributes of a named style, all the objects that use the named style automatically change to match the new style attributes. The exception is an object for which you have manually changed attributes using that object's Info Box. The new style attributes do not override any manual changes you may have made. For example, if you change the typeface of a named style from Arial to Times New Roman, all objects that use that style will change their typeface except those objects for which you previously changed the typeface manually.

Attaching a Named Style

To attach a named style to an object, you must be in Design mode. Open the Info Box by selecting **S**tyle & Properties from the pop-up menu or double-clicking the object. You can also open the Info Box by selecting the object and clicking the Info Box SmartIcon, or by opening the **O**bject menu and choosing **S**tyle & Properties. Select the Basics tab to open the Basics panel. Click the Named Style drop-down list to display a list of available styles. Select the style you want to use for the object.

Creating or Editing a Named Style

To create or edit a named style, open the **T**ools menu and choose select **N**amed Styles. The Named Styles dialog box opens (see fig. 3.19). A series of buttons down the right side of the Named Styles dialog box enables you to **E**dit an existing style, create a **N**ew style, or **C**opy an existing style. Copying an existing style is very handy when you want to change just a few attributes and create a new style from the result.

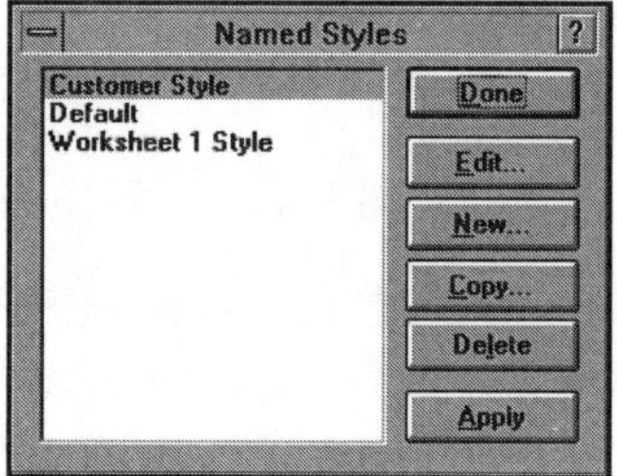

Fig. 3.19
Styles help you standardize your design and facilitate later changes.

Setting the Attributes of a Named Style

Once you select **E**dit, **N**ew, or **C**opy from the Named Styles dialog box, the Define Style dialog box opens (see fig. 3.20).

The top portion of the dialog box enables you to name and base your style on an existing style:

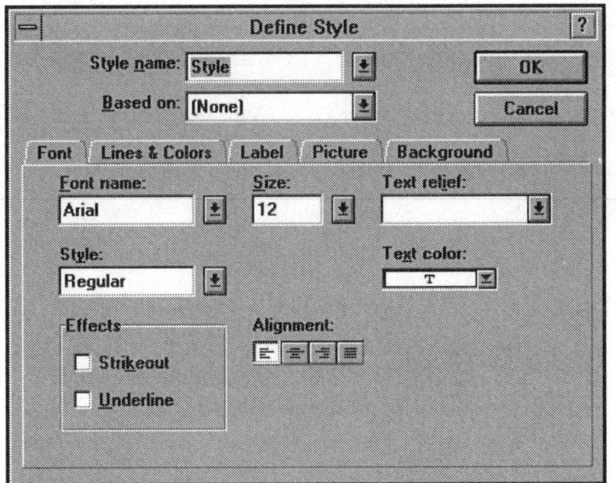

Fig. 3.20
A style sets all the properties of text, lines, pictures, fields, and labels.

- To name your style, type a new name into the Style **N**ame drop-down list. If you chose **E**dit from the Named Styles dialog box, Approach displays the name of the style you chose to edit in the Style **N**ame drop-down list. You can rename the style by typing a new name in the Style **N**ame drop-down list, or you can choose to edit another style by selecting the style from the list. If you choose **C**opy in the Named Styles dialog box, "Copy of" and the name of the copied style appears in the Style **N**ame drop-down list.
- You can base your style on another style. To select a style on which to base your style, select the style from the **B**ased On drop-down list.

The bottom portion of the Define Style dialog box looks much like an Info Box. There are five panels: Font, Lines & Colors, Label, Picture, and Background. To select a panel, click the tab for that panel. Set the properties you want on each panel as detailed below. When you're done setting the properties on all the panels, click OK to return to the Named Styles dialog box. You can set the following properties in the Define Style panels:

- *Font.* You can set the **F**ont name, St**y**le, Effects (Stri**k**eout and **U**nderline), **S**ize, Alignment, Text rel**i**ef, and Te**x**t color.
- *Lines & Colors.* You can set the Border **w**idth from a drop-down list, and Border **c**olor, **F**ill color, and S**h**adow color. You can choose a Fra**m**e and select on which sides you want the Border (**T**op, B**o**ttom, **L**eft, or **R**ight). You can also set a text Base**l**ine, make an object with this style Read-onl**y**, and have the Borders enclo**s**e a label.

- *Label.* In addition to setting all the attributes noted in Fonts, you can also set the Label **p**osition in relation to a field (Above, Left, Right, Below, or no label).
- *Picture.* The selections on this panel tell Approach how to handle a picture that is either too large or too small to fit in the space allocated for the picture on the form. If the picture is too large, you can have Approach **C**rop it or Shr**i**nk it to fit. You can also have Approach stretch a picture that is too small by checking **S**tretch If Too Small. Finally, you can allow the user to draw on a picture using the mouse pointer. For more information on fields that can hold pictures (PicturePlus fields), see Chapter 10.
- *Background.* You can set the Border **c**olor, **F**ill color, S**h**adow color, and Fra**m**e. You can also set the borders for the background by clicking the **T**op, B**o**ttom, **L**eft, or **R**ight checkboxes.

Deleting and Finishing with Named Styles

Use the De**l**ete button in the Named Styles dialog box to delete a named style. (You can't delete the styles that come with Approach, however.) If you delete a named style that is used by an object, the attributes of the object don't change, but you do lose the ability to change the object's attributes by changing the named style.

When you are finished creating and editing named styles, click the **D**one button to exit the Named Styles dialog box.

From Here...

In this chapter, you learned the basics of building a form. You created a new form, renamed an existing form, and added various objects to a form. After you placed an object on a form, you could move and resize it. You used Approach's layout tools (such as the rulers and the grid) to position the objects more easily on the form. The alignment, grouping, and stacking tools enabled you to define precisely how the objects were displayed in relation to each other. You also learned to use Slide Up and Slide Left to control how fields and other objects look on a printout, and learned how to create and use named styles.

To learn more about creating forms, refer to the following chapters in this book:

- Chapter 4, "Enhancing Data Input Forms," discusses how to add additional items to your forms.
- Chapter 7, "Creating Reports and Mailing Labels," details how to create reports that display multiple records on a page. Unlike other database applications, Approach enables you to enter data directly into reports.
- Chapter 14, "Using Worksheets and Crosstabs," shows you how to modify and work with the spreadsheet-like worksheet.

Chapter 4

Enhancing Data Input Forms

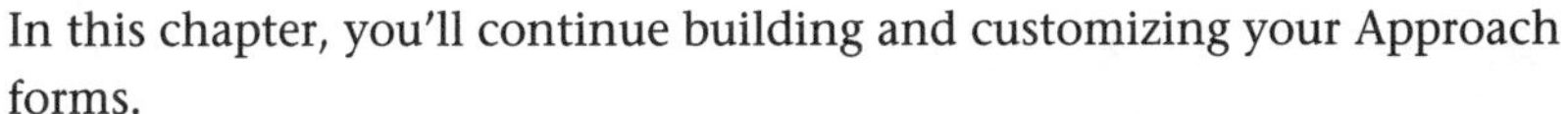

In this chapter, you'll continue building and customizing your Approach forms.

You customize your forms while in Design mode. To load forms you have already designed, you open the Approach file (APR) you want to use. If you make changes to your forms, you must save those changes by saving the Approach file (choose **S**ave Approach File from the **F**ile menu). Once you have laid out the structure of the database table (see Chapter 2, "Creating Database Tables"), you are ready to begin designing your data input forms.

In this chapter, you learn how to:

- Place fields on a form and customize how they look
- Change the data-entry format for a field, such as drop-down lists, checkboxes, and radio buttons
- Change field data-entry order
- Change the format for date, time, numeric, and text fields
- Use text boxes, lines, and graphics to enhance your forms
- Import illustrations to enhance your forms

Note

All the techniques illustrated in this chapter can be used with other types of views, such as reports and mailing labels.

Adding and Creating Fields

Because fields actually contain the data, they are the most important part of any form. A form without fancy text and pictures can be boring, but a form without data is useless.

You can add fields to a form at any time. You may want to add a field to a form after the form is created; for example, you may have neglected to specify the field when you first built the form. Alternatively, you can add a field to the database, and need to show that field on the form.

This section shows you how to place fields on a form as you design the form, and how to add fields to the database as you are designing a form. This section also provides an example of how to create a field in the database and add it to the Owl database form you created in Chapter 3.

Placing Fields on a Form

You can place a field on a form in two ways: by using the Add Field dialog box, or by using the menu or Draw Field tool from the Drawing toolbar. To place a field on the form using the Add Field dialog box, follow these steps:

1. Switch to Design mode by opening the **V**iew menu and choosing **D**esign, clicking the Design SmartIcon, or choosing Design from the status bar.

2. If the Add Field dialog box is not visible, open it by choosing **A**dd Field from the Fo**r**m menu (see fig. 4.1) or any object's pop-up menu. You can also select the Add Field tool from the Drawing toolbar.

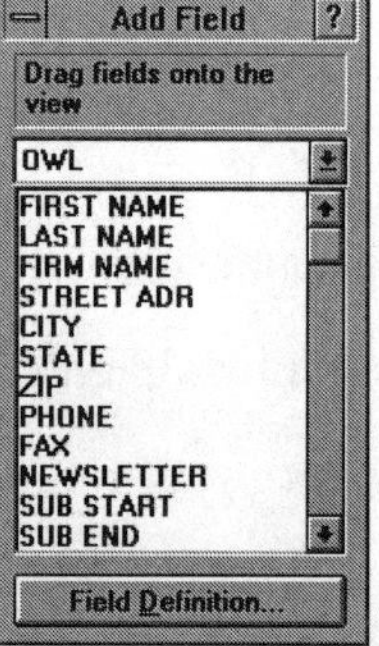

Fig. 4.1
Drag fields from the Add Field dialog box onto your form.

3. Click the field you want to add to the form and hold down the left mouse button. To add multiple fields to the form at one time, click the first field in the Add Field dialog box, hold down the Ctrl key, and then

click the remaining fields. To select all the fields between two fields, click a field, hold down the Shift key, and then click another field.

4. Drag the field out of the Add Field dialog box. The mouse pointer turns into a grabbing hand and the field name appears on a button attached to the mouse pointer.

5. Move the mouse pointer onto the form and release the mouse button where you want to add the field. Approach adds the field to the form.

Tip
To add a field to the database, click the Field **D**efinition button. For more information on adding database fields, see "Creating New Field Definitions for the Form" later in this chapter.

To place a field on the form using the menu or Draw Fields tool on the Drawing toolbar, follow these steps:

1. Switch to Design mode by opening the **V**iew menu and choosing **D**esign, clicking the Design SmartIcon, or choosing Design from the status bar.

2. Click the Draw Fields SmartIcon, click the Draw Fields tool in the Drawing toolbar, or open the **C**reate menu and choose Dr**a**wing **F**ield. The pointer turns into a crosshair.

3. Position the pointer where you want the field to start, hold down the left mouse button, and drag the pointer to the location where you want the field to end. You can also click the form to position the field in its default size.

4. Release the left mouse button. The Info Box for database fields appears. The left side of the Info Box displays a list of fields in the database.

5. From the list box, select the field you want to place on the form.

6. If you like, minimize the Info Box by double-clicking the Info Box title bar, or close the Info Box by double-clicking the close box.

Tip
To create a new field in the database, click the Field **D**efinition button. For more information on creating new database fields, see the next section, "Creating New Field Definitions for the Form."

Note

The field Info Box provides numerous other options for customizing the fields on the form. After you know how to use these options, you may want to set them up immediately after choosing the field. You always can change them later, however.

Creating New Field Definitions for the Form

If the field you want to place on your form doesn't yet exist in your database, you must add a new field definition to it before you can place the field on the form you are designing. You can add a new field to the database using either the field Info Box or the Add Field dialog box. To add a database field using the field Info Box, follow steps 1–4 in the preceding section to access the field Info Box, and then choose the Field **D**efinition button to open the Field Definition dialog box (see fig. 4.2). Add the new database field definition here, as discussed in Chapter 2.

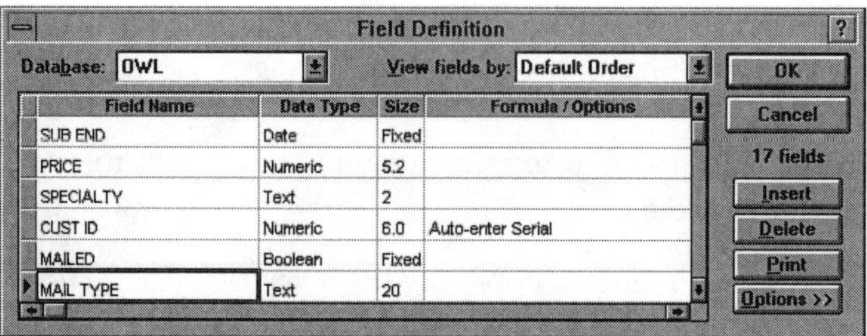

Fig. 4.2
You can add a new field to your database while designing a form.

After adding the new database field definition, click OK to return to the Info Box. The new field appears in the list of available fields, and you can place it on your form using the **C**reate menu or Draw Fields SmartIcon as discussed previously. Depending on your settings in Preferences, the Add Fields dialog box may also appear, displaying only the newly added fields.

> **Caution**
>
> You can modify any of the database fields while you are in the Field Definition dialog box—but remember that if you change the field type, you will usually delete all the data in that field. You can, however, convert field types to text type without losing your data.

To add a database field using the Add Field dialog box, open the Add Field dialog by choosing **A**dd Field from the Fo**r**m menu. Click the Field **D**efinition button to bring up the Field Definition dialog box. Enter your new field and click OK to add the field to the database and return to the Add Field dialog box. If the Show the **A**dd Field Dialog After Creating New Fields checkbox is checked in the General panel of the Preferences dialog box, the Add Field dialog displays only newly added fields when you return from the Field Definition dialog box. To display all the fields, click S**h**ow All Fields. Either way, you can add the new database field to the form by clicking and dragging the field onto the form.

Adding a Field to the Sample Database

When Owl Publishing sends out renewal notices, it wants to keep track of the number of notices it has sent out. Because the database doesn't contain a field for this purpose, you need to add one to the form.

To create the new field, follow these steps:

1. Click the Design button on the SmartIcon bar to switch to Design mode.

2. Click the Draw Fields SmartIcon. The pointer changes to a crosshair.

3. Move the pointer next to the MAIL TYPE field, and draw a small rectangle where the new field is to be placed (see fig. 4.3).

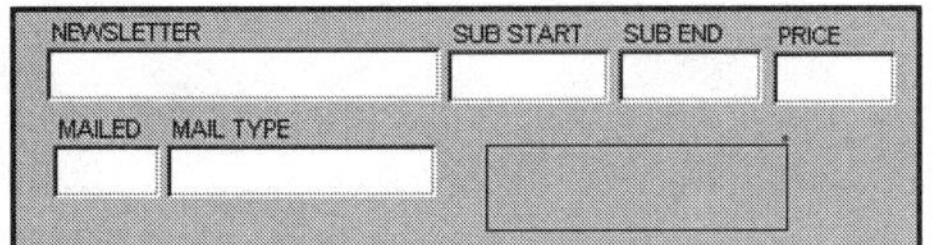

Fig. 4.3
Draw a rectangle where you want the new field to be placed.

4. Release the mouse button. The field Info Box appears.

5. Because the field doesn't yet exist, choose Field definition.

6. Scroll down to an empty line in the Field Definition dialog box. Type the new field information (see fig. 4.4). Type **RENEW NOTE** for the field name, choose Numeric as the data type, and type **2.0** for the size.

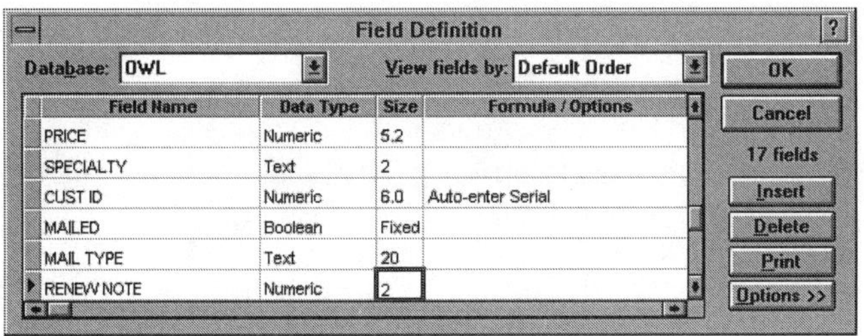

Fig. 4.4
Enter the specifications for the new field.

7. Click OK. The Field Info box appears again, with the new field selected (see fig. 4.5). Depending on your settings in Preferences, the Add Field dialog box can also appear. If it does, double-click the close box to hide it.

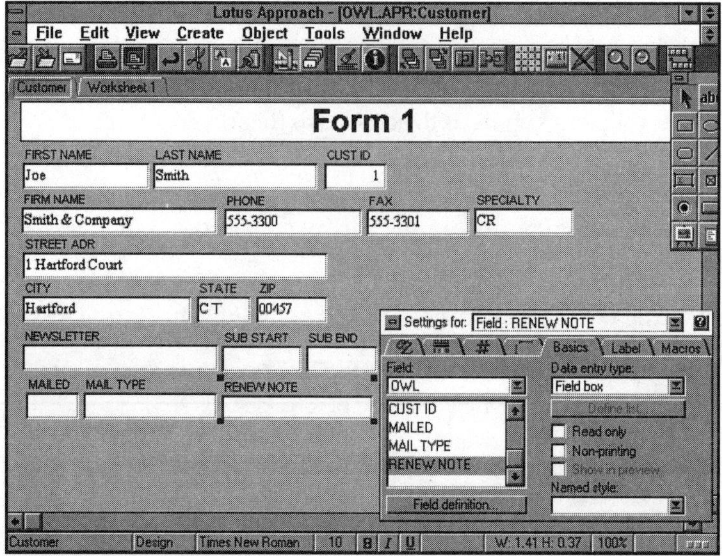

Fig. 4.5
The new field is added to the form.

8. Open the **F**ile menu and choose **S**ave Approach File to save the changes to the form. (Approach automatically saves the changes to the database itself in step 7.)

Changing the Data Entry Format of Fields

When you create a new form or place new fields on a form, the fields appear as a Field Box by default. The fields initially appear as text boxes into which you type information. Consider, for example, the data entry form that you created in Chapter 3 for Owl Publishing. First, make sure you are in Browse mode, and then click any field. You can type information into that field.

It makes sense that most fields appear in this default format. Fields for data such as names and addresses really don't work in any other format. For convenience, however, some fields can be represented other ways. Besides text boxes, your fields can use standard Windows devices such as drop-down lists, checkboxes, and radio buttons to enter and view data on a form.

For example, if a field will accept only one of a limited number of values, representing the field as a drop-down list containing those values is more convenient. You can use a drop-down list for a field that records the method of payment, such as Cash, Credit Card, and Check. Placing these three choices into a drop-down list simplifies data entry considerably, because you simply select a value from the list rather than remember and type the acceptable values.

Adding a Drop-Down List Field to a Form

Approach provides two drop-down list formats: Drop-Down List and Field Box & List. You can choose any value from a drop-down list field, but you can't type any other values. In a Field Box & List field, on the other hand, you can not only select a value from the drop-down list, but also enter a value that isn't already displayed in the list.

In the Owl Publishing example, the SPECIALTY field describes the legal specialties of Owl's potential customers. As Owl adds more and more newsletters, knowing what kind of law their potential customers specialize in will be important. Because the SPECIALTY field is limited to a small set of acceptable values, having it appear as a drop-down list on the form would be more convenient. That way, you can just click the desired value rather than type it each time.

To turn the SPECIALTY field into a drop-down list, follow these steps:

1. Switch to Design mode by opening the **V**iew menu and choosing **D**esign, clicking the Design SmartIcon, or choosing Design from the status bar.

2. Click the SPECIALTY field on the form. (Use the scroll bars to make this field visible on-screen.)

3. Open the Info Box by selecting **S**tyle & Properties from the pop-up menu or by double-clicking the object. You can also open the Info Box by selecting the object and clicking the Info Box SmartIcon or by opening the **O**bject menu and choosing **S**tyle & Properties. Click the Basics tab to display the Basics panel.

4. The Data Entry Type drop-down list contains the various types of field displays you can choose: Field Box, Drop-Down List, Field Box & List, Checkboxes, and Radio Buttons.

For this example, choose the Drop-Down List option. The Drop-Down List dialog box appears (see fig. 4.6).

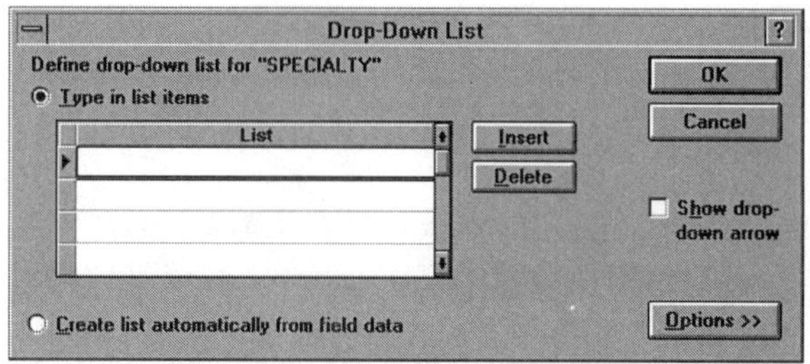

Fig. 4.6
Enter a list of acceptable values for your drop-down list.

> **Note**
>
> If you have never created a value list for this field, Approach automatically opens the Drop-Down List dialog box when you select Drop-Down List or Field Box & List from the Data Entry Type drop-down list in the Info Box. Otherwise, you must click the Define List button in the Info Box to open the Drop-Down List dialog box.

When you use the Drop-Down List or Field Box & List data entry formats, you must specify the values that are to appear in the list.

To add your own values to the value list, follow these steps:

1. In the Drop-Down List dialog box, select the **T**ype in List Items radio button.

2. Type one value on each line of the List box. After you type each value, click the next line with the mouse pointer. If you have more values than can fit in the List box, use the scroll bar to move down to an empty line. You can also click any line and edit the value on that line.

   For the Owl Publishing example, type each of the following values: **PF**, **PI**, **FM**, **EM**, and **CR**.

   > **Note**
   >
   > To remove a value from the list, select it in the List box and then press **D**elete. The value is removed from the list. To insert a new value into the list, click a line and then press **I**nsert. The selected value moves down, leaving a blank line for you to enter a new value.

3. Click the S**h**ow Drop-Down Arrow checkbox to display a drop-down list arrow on the form field. If you don't click this checkbox, the

drop-down list only shows the drop-down list arrow if you click the field or tab to it.

4. Click OK to close the Drop-Down List dialog box and place your drop-down list on the form.

5. Switch to Browse mode to view your new drop-down list on the form (see fig. 4.7). To switch to Browse mode, click the Browse SmartIcon.

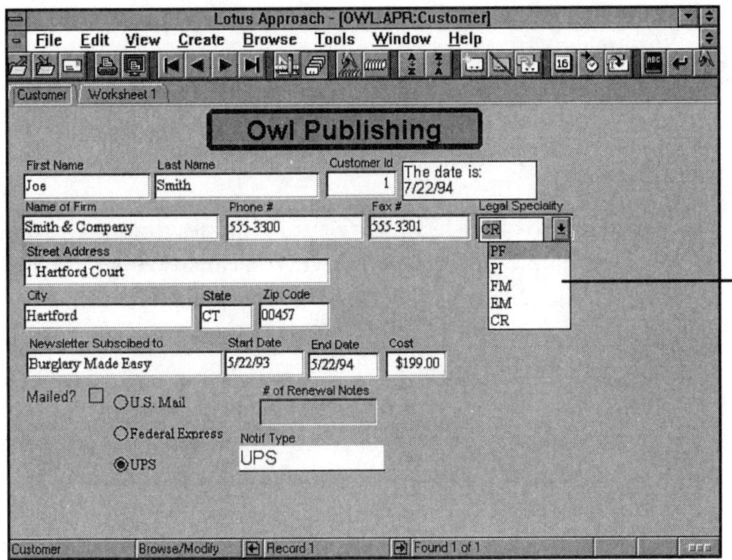

Fig. 4.7
The SPECIALTY field is formatted as a drop-down value list.

Tip
Typing a new value in a Text and Value List field doesn't add that value to the list that appears each time you enter the field. If the new value is one you plan to use often, you can add it to the list of values assigned to the drop-down list box.

Reordering Values

If you like, you can rearrange the values in the List box of the Drop-Down List dialog box. From the Drop-Down List dialog box, follow these steps:

1. Click the button at the left end of the value you want to move in the list. A right-facing arrowhead appears in the highlighted button.

2. Click the button again and hold down the left mouse button. The mouse pointer becomes an open hand.

3. Drag the value to the position you want it to have in the list. Approach indicates the proposed insertion point of the value in the list with a dark bar that appears between the two values where Approach will insert the moved value when you release the mouse button.

Using Values from the Field

If you have been entering values in a default format text field for some time, and decide to convert the field to a value list, remembering all the values that have been entered in the field can be difficult. In this case, Approach can create the value list from the values already entered in the field (rather than manually entering a list of acceptable values in the Value List dialog box).

To create a value list from fields already entered, follow these steps:

1. Switch to Design mode by opening the **V**iew menu and choosing **D**esign, clicking the Design SmartIcon, or choosing Design from the status bar.

2. Click the field whose Drop-Down List or Field Box & List values you want to modify.

3. Open the Info Box by selecting **S**tyle & Properties from the pop-up menu or by double-clicking the object. You can also open the Info Box by selecting the object and clicking the Info Box SmartIcon, or by opening the **O**bject menu and choosing **S**tyle & Properties. Click the Basics tab to display the Basics panel.

4. Select the Define List button. The Drop-Down List dialog box opens.

5. Select the **C**reate List Automatically from Field Data radio button. The List box displays all the current values in that field in all records in the database. Approach displays values only once—duplicate values aren't shown.

6. Click OK to return to the form.

> **Note**
>
> If you choose the **C**reate List Automatically from Field Data option with a Field Box & List field, you get a list containing values that already have been entered in the field, and you can add to the list by typing new values. This combination enables any user of the database to add new values to the list. Also, unnecessary values are removed from the drop-down list when all occurrences of those values are removed from the database field itself.

Returning to the Owl Publishing example, the SPECIALTY field actually would be more useful as a Field Box & List, with the values coming from the field. That way, any values you have forgotten to add to the list can be added simply by typing them. Also, as new specialties (hopefully from new customers) come up, they easily can be added to the list. To accomplish this change, follow these steps:

1. Switch to Design mode by clicking the Design SmartIcon.

2. Select the SPECIALTY field.

3. Open the Info Box by selecting **S**tyle & Properties from the pop-up menu or by double-clicking the object. You can also open the Info Box by selecting the object and clicking the Info Box SmartIcon, or by opening the **O**bject menu and choosing **S**tyle & Properties. Select the Basics panel by clicking the Basics tab.

4. Choose Define List in the Info Box. The Drop-Down List dialog box opens.

5. Select the **C**reate List Automatically from Field Data option.

Note

If you worked through the preceding set of steps, a list of the values used in this field will replace the custom list of values.

6. Click OK to close the Drop-Down List dialog box.

7. Switch to Browse mode (by clicking the Browse SmartIcon) to view the converted field format.

The SPECIALTY field on the form is now a drop-down field in which you can choose a value from the list or type a new value, as shown in figure 4.8. The list shows only the single value from the example record. No other values have been entered into the database field yet.

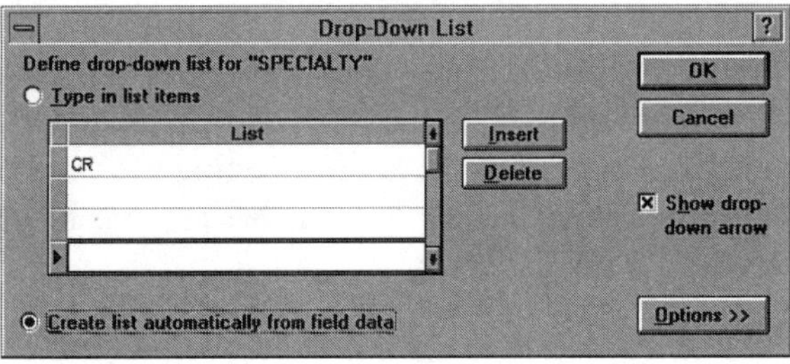

Fig. 4.8
The SPECIALTY field as a Field Box & List field, which allows users to type new values.

8. Open the **F**ile menu and choose **S**ave Approach File to save the changes to your form.

Note

You can also create a value list from entries made in a field in another database by using the selections available by clicking the **O**ptions button. To do so, however, the other database must be linked to the current database. See Chapter 8 for a general discussion of relational links; see Chapter 9 for information on using this particular option with relationally linked databases.

Restricting the Values in a Drop-Down List

When you create a list automatically from field data in the Drop-Down List dialog box, Approach normally makes all the previously entered values in the field available in the drop-down list. For example, if you have a Field Box & List that contains part numbers that your company orders from manufacturers, all the part numbers in the database are available in the drop-down list.

Approach enables you to set criteria to limit the values that appear in the drop-down list. For example, you can set criteria so that only the parts available from a certain manufacturer are available in the drop-down list when you enter a record for that manufacturer. This capability helps to limit mistakes, but works best with a fairly static list of values. For example, it would be quite cumbersome to continually have to enter a part number that is already in your list (but not available in the drop-down list) because you are now buying a part from another manufacturer.

To display a subset of values in the drop-down list for a field, follow these steps:

1. Switch to Design mode by opening the **V**iew menu and choosing **D**esign, clicking the Design SmartIcon, or choosing Design from the status bar.

2. Open the Info Box for the field whose values you want to filter by selecting **S**tyle & Properties from the pop-up menu or by double-clicking the object. You can also open the Info Box by selecting the object and clicking the Info Box SmartIcon, or by opening the **O**bject menu and choosing **S**tyle & Properties. Choose the Basics panel by clicking the Basics tab.

3. Select Define List. The Drop-Down List dialog box appears. Click the **O**ptions button to open the bottom portion of the dialog box.

4. Click the **F**ilter the List Based on Another Field option. The Define Filter dialog box opens (see fig. 4.9).

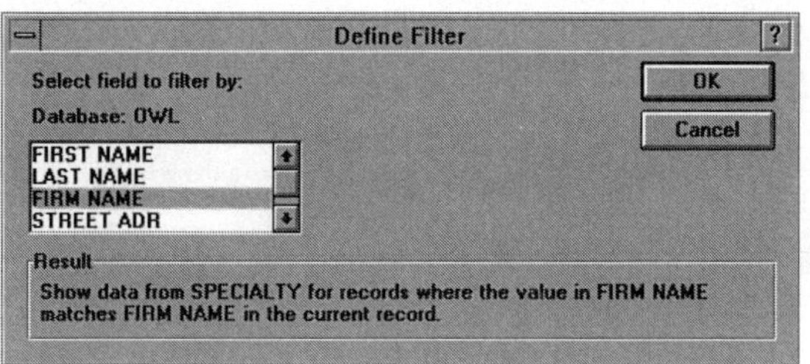

Fig. 4.9
The Define Filter dialog box limits the values listed in a drop-down list.

Note

The first time you establish a filter by clicking the **F**ilter the List Based on Another Field option, Approach automatically opens the Define Filter dialog box. To later modify an existing filter, you must click the D**e**fine Filter button.

5. Select the field to filter by from the list of database fields.

6. Click OK to return to the Drop-Down List dialog box. Values in the drop-down list are assembled only from database records in which the filter field you select matches the value of the filter field in the current record.

Caution

When you select the **F**ilter the List Based on Another Field option in the Drop-Down List dialog box, Approach creates the list automatically from the field data. Thus, any typed list items are lost if you choose this option.

Setting Up Checkboxes

In addition to the field box and drop-down list formats already discussed, Approach offers a format in which fields are displayed as checkboxes.

A checkbox is simply a small square. Clicking a blank checkbox places an X in it; clicking a checkbox already containing an X returns the box to its initial blank (off) condition. You can also tab to a checkbox and press the space bar to select or deselect the checkbox.

You can use checkboxes to format fields that accept only two values, such as Yes and No. If you have a field that indicates whether you have mailed a renewal flyer to a newsletter customer, for example, you can format that field as a checkbox. If the checkbox is blank, the flyer hasn't been mailed. When the flyer is mailed, the person doing the mailing clicks the checkbox to indicate that the flyer has gone out (see fig. 4.10).

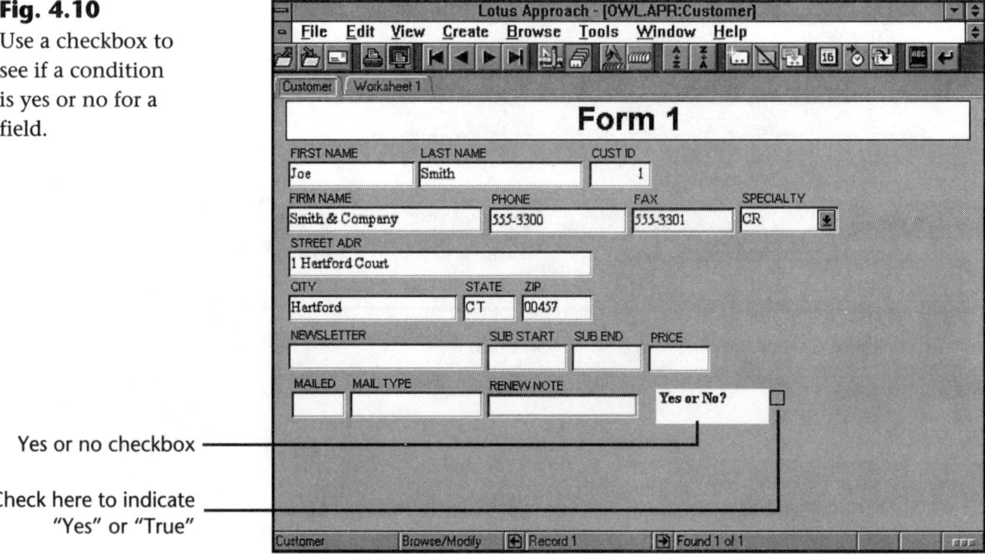

Fig. 4.10
Use a checkbox to see if a condition is yes or no for a field.

Creating a New Checkbox

To set up a checkbox, follow these steps:

1. Switch to Design mode by opening the **V**iew menu and choosing **D**esign, clicking the Design SmartIcon, or choosing Design from the status bar.

2. Click the Draw Checkboxes tool in the Drawing toolbar, or open the **C**reate menu and choose Dr**a**wing Checkbox. The mouse pointer becomes a crosshair.

3. Position the pointer at the desired location for the new checkbox on your form. Click and hold down the mouse button while dragging the pointer diagonally to set the size of the checkbox. When you release the mouse button, the Define Checkbox dialog box appears (see fig. 4.11).

4. Choose the field you want the checkbox to represent from the **S**elect the Checkbox Field list box in the bottom-left corner of the dialog box.

5. Enter the checked value, unchecked value, and checkbox label.

   The Checked Value text box contains the value stored in the database field if the checkbox is checked. The Unchecked Value text box contains the value stored if the checkbox is not checked. If the checkbox represents a database field of type Text, the checked value and unchecked value can contain any text up to the maximum length of the field. If the checkbox represents a database field of Boolean type (which is often the case), the values entered must be Yes/No. Any other values create an error condition.

The Checkbox Label is the text label that appears adjacent to the checkbox on the form. You can change the label using the Info Box for the checkbox.

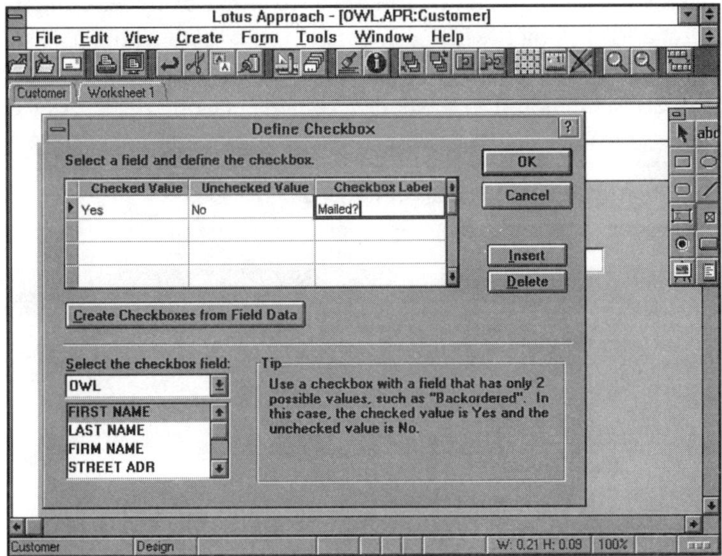

Fig. 4.11
Enter values to be represented by a check or no check.

6. To insert a new value into the list, click the line above where you want to insert a value, and then choose **I**nsert to insert a blank line. To delete an existing value, click the line you want to delete and choose **D**elete.

7. After setting up the checkbox, click OK to return to the form.

Note

You can create multiple checkboxes from a single field by filling in multiple lines in the Define Checkbox dialog box. Multiple checkboxes behave like radio buttons (see "Setting Up Radio Buttons" later in this chapter) in that only one checkbox can be selected at a time. If you click another checkbox, Approach unchecks the previous checkbox. With multiple checkboxes for one field, the checked value of the selected checkbox is stored in the database field.

Converting an Existing Form Field to a Checkbox

Approach makes it simple to convert an existing form field to a checkbox format. For example, you can convert the MAILED database field from a field box to a checkbox on the form by following these steps:

1. Switch to Design mode by opening the **V**iew menu and choosing **D**esign, clicking the Design SmartIcon, or choosing Design from the status bar.

2. Open the Info Box for the field you want to convert to checkboxes by selecting **S**tyle & Properties from the pop-up menu or by double-clicking the object. You can also open the Info Box by selecting the object and clicking the Info Box SmartIcon, or by opening the **O**bject menu and choosing **S**tyle & Properties. For this example, use the MAILED field. Switch to the Basics panel by clicking the Basics tab.

3. Select Checkboxes from the Data Entry Type drop-down list. The Define Checkbox dialog box opens. (It looks like the Define Checkbox dialog box shown in figure 4.11 except that it's missing the field selection list.)

> **Note**
>
> If you want to modify the attributes of a previously defined checkbox, click the Define Buttons button in the checkbox Info Box to reopen the Define Checkbox dialog box.

4. Enter the checked value, unchecked value, and checkbox label. For this example, enter **Yes** as the checked value, **No** as the unchecked value, and **Mailed?** as the checkbox label. Use the **I**nsert button to insert a new line and the **D**elete button to remove a line.

5. After setting up the checkbox, click OK to return to the form.

Reordering Checkboxes

If you like, you can rearrange the values in the Define Checkbox dialog box. Reordering the checkbox values causes Approach to rearrange the order of the checkboxes on the form. From the Define Checkbox dialog box, follow these steps:

1. Click the button at the left end of the value that you want to move in the list. A right-facing arrowhead appears in the highlighted button.

2. Click the button again and hold down the left mouse button. The mouse pointer becomes an open hand.

3. Drag the value to the position you want in the list. Approach indicates the proposed insertion point of the value in the list with a dark bar that appears between the two values where Approach will insert the moved value when you release the mouse button.

You can also rearrange groups of checkboxes on the form. When you first create a set of checkboxes, they are stacked vertically on the form. You can click and drag the group to relocate it, but you can't change the layout of the checkboxes (for example, you can't place the checkboxes alongside each other on the form).

To ungroup the checkboxes, click the set of checkboxes and then open the **O**bject menu and choose **U**ngroup, or click the Ungroup SmartIcon. Once you have ungrouped the checkboxes, you can move them around the form independently.

Note

When checkboxes are ungrouped, Approach no longer displays them in a single Define Checkbox dialog box. Instead, each checkbox has an Info Box from which you can modify the checked value, unchecked value, and checkbox label by clicking the Define Buttons button to open the Define Checkbox dialog box.

Once you have arranged the checkboxes the way you want them, you can regroup them so you can work with the checkboxes as a single unit again. To regroup the checkboxes, select the checkboxes and then open the **O**bject menu and choose **G**roup, or click the Group SmartIcon.

Creating Checkboxes from Database Values

You can create a set of checkboxes from data already entered into a database field. This is especially useful if you decide to convert a field to a checkbox format.

To create a set of checkboxes, click the **C**reate Checkboxes from Field Data button in the Define Checkbox dialog box. If the form field is of any type except a drop-down list or a Field Box & List, Approach populates the checked value lines of the Define Checkbox dialog box with the values in that database field. The checkbox label defaults to the checked value, but you can modify the label if you want.

For a drop-down list or a Field Box & List, Approach automatically creates the checkboxes with the same values as the drop-down list without using the

Define Checkbox dialog box. The label on each checkbox corresponds to the drop-down list value.

Setting Up Radio Buttons

Another useful format for displaying fields is as a group of radio buttons. A group of radio buttons is represented by a set of small circles. Clicking one of the circles selects that button (the circle is filled) and deselects all the other buttons in that set.

You can use a set of radio buttons to format a field in which you can enter only one of a small number of mutually exclusive values, such as High, Medium, or Low (see fig. 4.12). You can select only one button at a time; selecting another button deselects the initially selected button. This exclusivity applies because the group of radio buttons actually controls the value that Approach places in a single field—and a single field can contain only a single value.

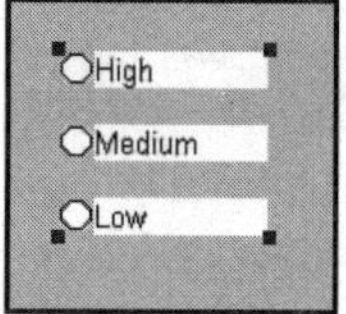

Fig. 4.12
Use radio buttons with fields that accept only one of a set of separate values.

Creating a New Radio Button Field

To set up a set of radio buttons, follow these steps:

1. Switch to Design mode by opening the **V**iew menu and choosing **D**esign, clicking the Design SmartIcon, or choosing Design from the status bar.

2. Click the Draw Radio Buttons tool in the Drawing toolbar, or open the **C**reate menu and choose Dr**a**wing Radio **B**utton. The mouse pointer changes into a crosshair.

3. Position the pointer at the desired location for the new set of radio buttons. Click and hold down the mouse button while dragging the pointer diagonally to set the size of the entire set of radio buttons. When you release the mouse button, the Define Radio Buttons dialog box appears (see fig. 4.13).

4. Choose the field you want the radio button to represent from the **S**elect Radio Button Field list box in the bottom-left corner of the dialog box.

5. Enter a clicked value and a button label.

The Clicked Value text box contains the value stored in the database field if you click the radio button and select it (the circle is filled in). If the radio button represents a database field of type Text, the clicked value can contain any text up to the maximum length of the field. If the radio button represents a database field of Boolean type (which is often the case), the values entered must be Yes or No. Any other values cause Approach to display all radio buttons as on whenever you click any radio button.

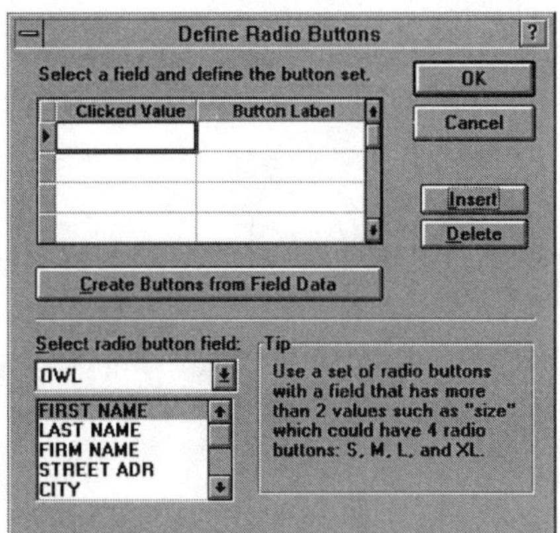

Fig. 4.13
The Define Radio Buttons dialog box.

The Button Label is the text label that appears adjacent to the checkbox on the form. You can change the label using the Info Box for the checkbox.

6. To insert a new value into the list, click the line above where you want to insert a value and then choose **I**nsert to insert a blank line. To delete an existing value, click the line you want to delete and choose **D**elete.

7. After setting up the radio button, click OK to return to the form.

Converting an Existing Field to a Set of Radio Buttons

Approach makes it simple to convert an existing form field to a radio button format. For example, Owl Publishing likes to track the way it sends individual renewal notices. The company sends renewal notices by one of three carriers: U.S. Mail, Federal Express, or UPS. You could use a drop-down list to represent these three choices, but for this example, radio buttons are used instead. To set up the buttons, follow these steps:

1. Switch to Design mode by opening the **V**iew menu and choosing **D**esign, clicking the Design SmartIcon, or choosing Design from the status bar.

2. Select the field you want to modify.

3. Open the Info Box for the field you want to convert to radio buttons by selecting **S**tyle & Properties from the pop-up menu or by double-clicking the object. You can also open the Info Box by selecting the object and clicking the Info Box SmartIcon, or by opening the **O**bject menu and choosing **S**tyle & Properties. Switch to the Basics panel by clicking the Basics tab.

   For this example, use the MAIL TYPE field.

4. From the Data Entry Type drop-down list, select Radio Buttons. The Define Radio Buttons dialog box opens. (It looks like the Define Radio Buttons dialog box shown in figure 4.13 except that it's missing the field selection list.)

> **Note**
>
> To modify the attributes of a previously defined radio button, click the Define Buttons button in the radio button Info Box to reopen the Define Radio Buttons dialog box.

5. Enter the clicked values and button labels. For this example, enter **U.S. Mail** for the first clicked value and button label; **Fed Express** for the second clicked value and **Federal Express** for the button label; and **UPS** for the third clicked value and button label. When you are finished, the Define Radio Buttons dialog box should look like figure 4.14.

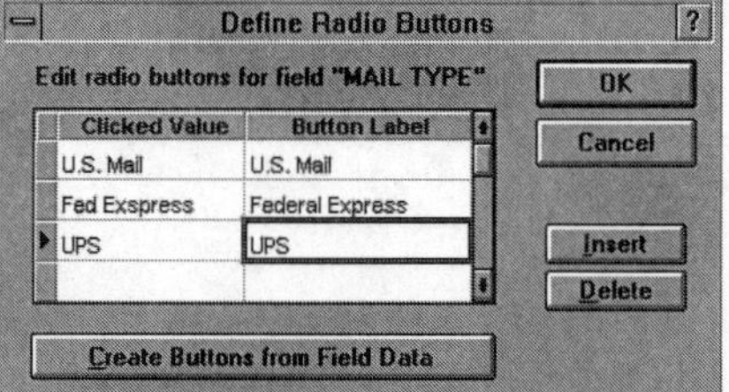

Fig. 4.14
The Define Radio Buttons dialog box for the MAIL TYPE field.

6. Click OK to return to the form with the new radio buttons in place (see fig. 4.15).

7. Open the **F**ile menu and choose **S**ave Approach File to save the changes to your form.

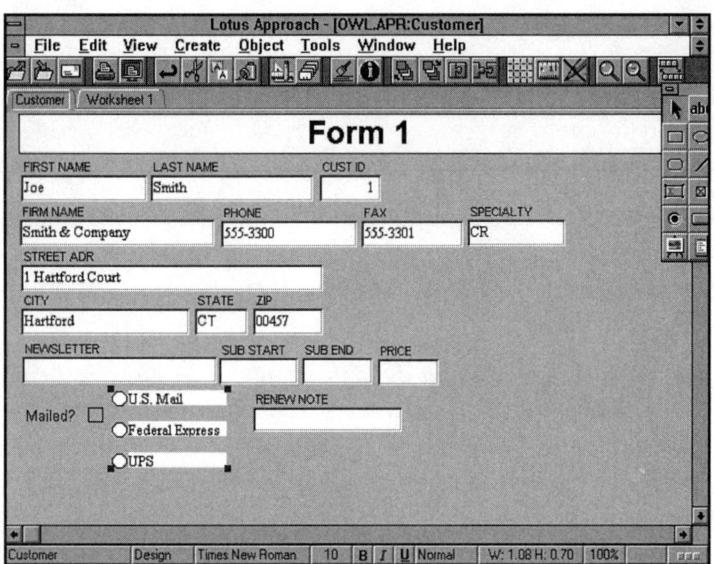

Fig. 4.15
The finished radio buttons represent ways of sending out renewal notices.

To see the effects of your work, select the Draw Fields icon from the Drawing toolbar. Click and drag a field on the form adjacent to the new radio buttons. Select MAIL TYPE as the database field from the list of fields in the Info Box. Return to Browse mode. Try clicking one of the radio buttons. Notice that the clicked value that you assigned in the Define Radio Buttons dialog box now appears in the MAIL TYPE field box on the form. The MAIL TYPE field displays the value that is actually stored in the database when you click one of the associated buttons.

Reordering Radio Buttons

If you like, you can rearrange the values in the Define Radio Buttons dialog box. Reordering the radio button values causes Approach to rearrange the order of the radio buttons on the form. From the Define Radio Buttons dialog box, follow these steps:

1. Click the button at the left end of the value you want to move in the list. A right-facing arrowhead appears in the highlighted button.

2. Click the button again and hold down the left mouse button. The mouse pointer becomes an open hand.

3. Drag the value to the position you want in the list. Approach indicates the proposed insertion point of the value in the list with a dark bar that appears between the two values where Approach will insert the moved value when you release the mouse button.

You can also rearrange groups of radio buttons on the form. When you first create a set of radio buttons, they are stacked vertically on the form. You can click and drag the group to relocate it, but you can't change the layout of the radio button (for example, you can't place the radio buttons alongside each other on the form).

You can ungroup the radio buttons by clicking them and then opening the **O**bject menu and choosing **U**ngroup, or by clicking the Ungroup SmartIcon. Once you have ungrouped the radio buttons, you can move them around the form independently.

When radio buttons are ungrouped, Approach no longer displays them in a single Define Radio Buttons dialog box. Instead, each radio button has an Info Box from which you can modify the Clicked Value and Button Label. To do this, click the Define Buttons button to open the Define Radio Buttons dialog box.

Note

You cannot use the Apply Format SmartIcon to apply another field's format to a grouped set of radio buttons. However, you can use the Apply Format SmartIcon to apply a format to individual radio buttons. See "Setting Field Properties" later in this chapter.

Once you have arranged the radio buttons the way you want them, you can regroup them so you can work with the buttons as a single unit. To regroup, select the radio buttons and then open the **O**bject menu and choose **G**roup, or click the Group SmartIcon.

Creating Radio Buttons from Database Values

You can create a set of radio buttons from data already entered into a database field. This is especially useful when converting a field to a radio button format.

To create a set of radio buttons from database values, click the **C**reate Buttons from Field Data button in the Define Radio Buttons dialog box. If the form field is of any type except a drop-down list or a Field Box & list, Approach populates the clicked value lines of the Define Radio Buttons dialog box with the values in that database field. The button label defaults to the clicked value, but you can modify the label if you want.

For a drop-down list or Field Box & List, Approach automatically creates the radio buttons with the same values as the drop-down list without using the

Define Radio Buttons dialog box. The label on each radio button corresponds to the drop-down list value.

Using Read-Only Fields on a Form

Formatting a field as "read only" on a form can often be helpful. If a field is in read-only format, the user can view the information in that field but can't change it. You can use this procedure, for example, when showing default text-formatted fields with their associated checkboxes and radio buttons. That way, the set of buttons is used to enter values into the field, and the text-formatted field displays those values without enabling the user to type a value that isn't represented by a button.

Owl Publishing wants its employees to use the U.S. Mail, Federal Express, and UPS buttons to enter MAIL TYPE values. The employees must not be able to enter a value in the MAIL TYPE field box that displays the database value. To change a field on a form to read only, follow these steps:

1. Switch to Design mode by opening the **V**iew menu and choosing **D**esign, clicking the Design SmartIcon, or choosing Design from the status bar.

2. Select the field you want to change—for this example, the MAIL TYPE field box.

3. Open the Info Box by selecting **S**tyle & Properties from the pop-up menu or by double-clicking the object. You can also open the Info Box by selecting the object and clicking the Info Box SmartIcon, or by opening the **O**bject menu and choosing **S**tyle & Properties. Select the Basics panel by clicking the Basics tab.

4. Select the Read Only checkbox. The field selected is now set to read-only on the current form.

5. Open the **F**ile menu and choose **S**ave Approach File to save the changes to the form.

Setting Field Properties

After you place your fields on the form, you can adjust the order in which the cursor moves through the fields. You can modify how the data in a form field appears by changing the color, font, background, shadow, frame, label attributes, and other properties.

Note

You can use the Apply Format SmartIcon to copy an object's format to another object. Click the object whose format you want to copy, select the Apply Format SmartIcon, and click the object(s) to which you want to copy the format.

You can also select **F**ast Format from an object's pop-up menu to copy that object's format to other objects. Click other objects to which you want to copy the format; then reselect **F**ast Format from any object's pop-up menu to turn off Fast Format.

Setting the Tab Order of Fields

When you are entering data in Browse mode, you can move from field to field on the form by pressing Tab. By default, Approach sets the tabbing order on a new form from top to bottom. After you create the form, Approach does not modify the tab order of the fields when you rearrange the fields on the form. If you later rearrange the fields on the form, you may find that the cursor jumps all over the screen as you press Tab. Also, any new fields you add to a form are placed at the end of the tabbing order, regardless of their location on-screen.

On the Owl Publishing Data Input form, the focus doesn't move through the fields in a logical order. Approach, however, enables you to change the tabbing order so that the cursor moves through the fields on the form in a more organized fashion. To change the tabbing order, follow these steps:

1. Switch to Design mode by opening the **V**iew menu and choosing **D**esign, clicking the Design SmartIcon, or choosing Design from the status bar.

2. Choose Show Data **E**ntry Order from the **V**iew menu. A checkmark appears next to the menu option.

   On the form, a small numbered box appears next to each field to indicate the field's tabbing order (see fig. 4.16).

3. To adjust the tabbing order, click a numbered square, backspace over the number, and then type a new number. Alternatively, you can double-click the right edge of a numbered square to erase the numbers in all the squares, and then click the squares in the desired tabbing order. New numbers appear in the squares as you click them.

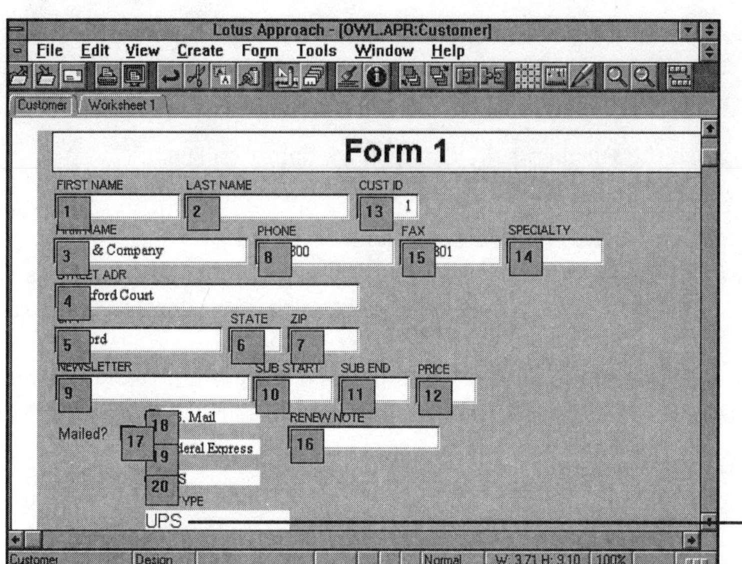

Fig. 4.16
The Owl Publishing form's tab order is indicated by numbered boxes.

For this example, double-click one of the tab order boxes to erase all the numbers, and then click the tab order boxes in the order shown in figure 4.17.

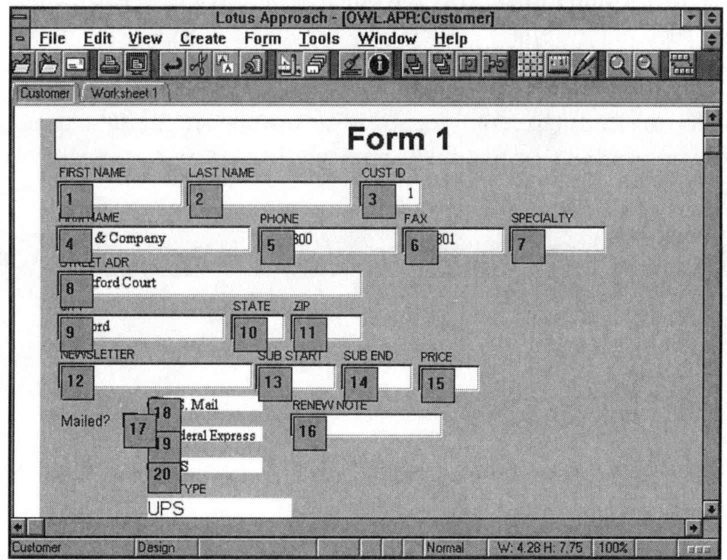

Fig. 4.17
The new tabbing order for the Owl Publishing Data Input form.

4. After adjusting the tab order, choose Show Data **E**ntry Order from the **V**iew menu to turn off the tab order boxes. The checkmark next to the menu option disappears.

5. Open the **F**ile menu and choose **S**ave Approach File.

Adjusting the Appearance of Fields

You can format the values typed into field boxes by changing font sizes and styles; text effects (for example, bold and italics); and other properties such as text alignment, the relief effect, and text color. You can emphasize a field containing the most important data in a record, for example, by formatting the value it contains to appear in a large point size with boldface.

To format the appearance of the value in a field, follow these steps:

1. Switch to Design mode by opening the **V**iew menu and choosing **D**esign, clicking the Design SmartIcon, or choosing Design from the status bar.

2. Select the field you want to modify, or select several fields to adjust multiple fields at once.

3. Open the Info Box by selecting **S**tyle & Properties from the pop-up menu or by double-clicking the object. You can also open the Info Box by selecting the object and clicking the Info Box SmartIcon, or by opening the **O**bject menu and choosing **S**tyle & Properties.

Tip

You can adjust the properties of multiple fields at one time by selecting the fields you want to modify and opening the Info Box. The Settings For text box at the top of the Info Box reads *Multiple Objects*.

4. Click the fonts tab (az) to move to the fonts panel. All the settings on this panel affect the text that Approach displays in the field (see fig. 4.18).

> **Note**
>
> The settings on the fonts panel do not affect the field label. For information on setting the attributes of the field label, see "Adjusting the Properties of Field Labels" later in this chapter.

5. Select the font you want to use from the Font **N**ame drop-down list in the upper-left corner of the dialog box.

6. Select a style or effect from the Style/Effect scrolling list. Styles include italic, bold, bold italic, underline, and strikethrough.

7. Select the desired font size from the available point sizes in the Size list.

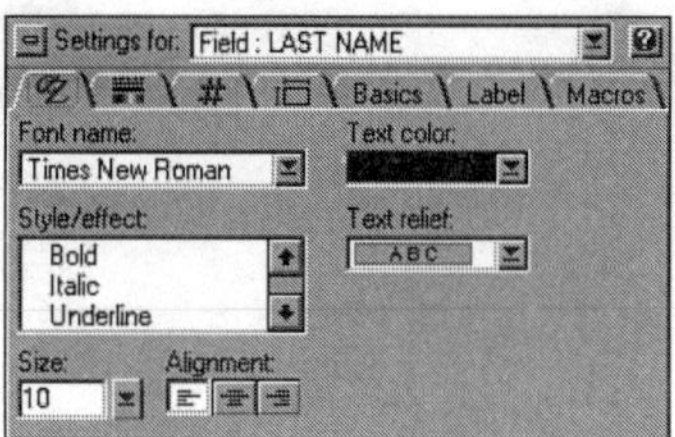

Fig. 4.18
The fonts panel lets you assign font type, size, and styles.

8. Choose one of the following alignment options to determine how the text will be aligned in the field:

Button	Description
	Aligns text against the left edge of the field (default)
	Centers text in the field
	Aligns text against the right edge of the field

Tip
Fonts are measured in points. There are 72 points in one vertical inch. If you want a letter that is 1/2-inch tall, for example, set the size to 36 points.

9. If desired, select a text color from the palette of colors that Approach makes available when you click the Text Color drop-down list. The block labeled with a T selects a transparent text color.

Note

The T in the color palette stands for Transparent, or no fill color. Without a fill color, anything below an object in the stacking order shows through. To select an object with no fill color, you must click the border.

10. Select an option from the Text Relief list box to change the look of your background and text.

Adjusting Other Properties of Field Data

In addition to adjusting font, size, style/effects, alignment, and color of field boxes, you can change the background fill and shadow color, border weight and color, and frame style. You can also add borders to highlight a field.

> **Note**
>
> For checkboxes and radio buttons, you can set only the fill color and shadow color.

To adjust these properties, follow these steps:

1. Switch to Design mode by opening the **V**iew menu and choosing **D**esign, clicking the Design SmartIcon, or choosing Design from the status bar.

2. Select the field you want to modify, or select several fields to adjust multiple fields at once.

3. Open the Info Box by selecting **S**tyle & Properties from the pop-up menu or by double-clicking the object. You can also open the Info Box by selecting the object and clicking the Info Box SmartIcon, or by opening the **O**bject menu and choosing **S**tyle & Properties. Click the Color tab to move to the Color panel (see fig. 4.19).

Fig. 4.19
Set colors and other graphical features from the Color panel.

4. Select the border width from the Border Width drop-down list. Available border widths range from hairline to 12 points (1/6 of an inch).

5. Select the border, fill, or shadow color from the Border Color, Fill Color, or Shadow Color drop-down lists. The box labeled T provides a transparent color.

6. Select a frame style from the Frame drop-down list. The frame style specifies the format in which Approach draws the border around the selected field.

7. Select the sides of the field on which you want Approach to draw borders by clicking the checkboxes in the Borders section. Besides drawing borders on the side of a field, you can add a text baseline by clicking the Baseline checkbox. A text baseline displays a line in the field box on which the text rests.

Tip
Some of the 3-D frame styles do not work well if the border is too narrow. If you want a 3-D frame style, select a border width of three points or greater.

8. You can either include the border within the boundaries of the field label, or display the label outside the field border. To include the label within the borders, check the Borders Enclose Label checkbox (see fig. 4.19).

Adjusting the Properties of Field Labels

You can adjust the properties of a field label using the field's Info Box. These properties include the font, style/effect, size, alignment, text, color, and position of the label text.

To adjust the label properties of a field, follow these steps:

1. Switch to Design mode by opening the **V**iew menu and choosing **D**esign, clicking the Design SmartIcon, or choosing Design from the status bar.

2. Select the field you want to modify.

3. Open the Info Box by selecting **S**tyle & Properties from the pop-up menu or by double-clicking the object. You can also open the Info Box by selecting the object and clicking the Info Box SmartIcon, or by opening the **O**bject menu and choosing **S**tyle & Properties. Click the Label tab to move to the Label panel (see fig. 4.20).

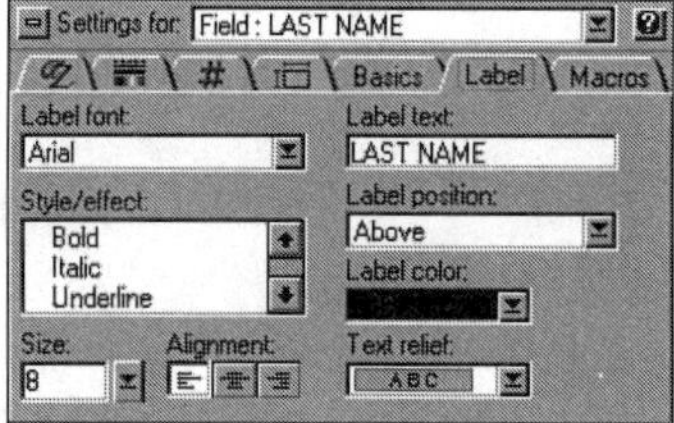

Fig. 4.20
Change the label properties from the Label panel.

4. Adjust the label's font, style/effect, size, alignment, color, and text relief as described earlier in "Adjusting the Appearance of Fields."

5. If desired, change the text of the label by typing your changes into the Label text box. The label text appears next to the field on the form.

> **Note**
>
> If you select multiple field boxes, you can't modify the label text. Also, if you select a grouped set of checkboxes or radio buttons, you must click the Define Buttons button in the Basics panel to open the dialog box (Define Checkboxes or Define Radio Buttons) that enables you to modify the checkbox or radio button labels.

6. Select the label position in relation to the field from the Label Position drop-down list. You can locate the label above or below the field, or to the left or right of the field. You can also select No Label from this list to turn off the label display.

So far, the fields on the sample Owl Publishing data input form have been labeled by default, using the name of the field in the database. You can customize these field labels so that they are more descriptive and look less computer-like. Follow the instructions provided earlier to format the labels to look like those in figure 4.21.

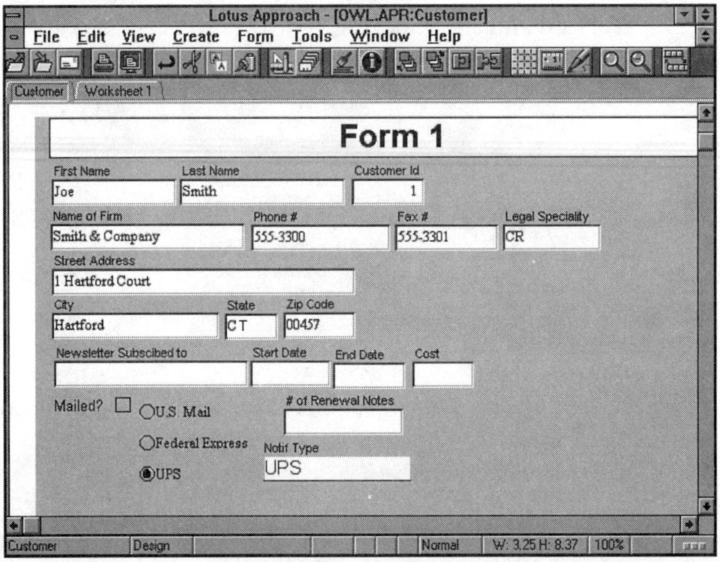

Fig. 4.21
The field labels on the Owl Publishing form.

Formatting the Display of Field Values

Approach can display the data you type into your field boxes in a wide variety of formats. These formats affect the appearance of date, time, numeric, and text values. You can change the display format of a field at any time. Changes affect the display format of new records and existing records on the form.

> **Note**
>
> The format changes discussed in this section affect only the appearance of the data. They normally don't modify how the data is stored in the database. However, if a text field is formatted as UPPER and Show Data Entry Format is on, Approach writes the data to the database in all uppercase (capital) letters.

To change the display format of field box values, follow these steps:

1. Switch to Design mode by opening the **V**iew menu and choosing **D**esign, clicking the Design SmartIcon, or choosing Design from the status bar.

2. Select the field box you want to format. When adjusting field box formatting, you can't select multiple field boxes.

3. Open the Info Box by selecting **S**tyle & Properties from the pop-up menu or by double-clicking the object. You can also open the Info Box by selecting the object and clicking the Info Box SmartIcon, or by opening the **O**bject menu and choosing **S**tyle & Properties. Switch to the Format panel by clicking the Format tab (#) as shown in figure 4.22.

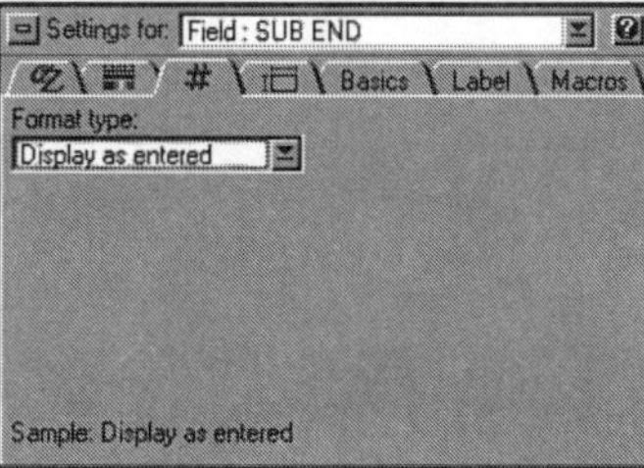

Fig. 4.22
You can change how the values of fields are displayed.

4. Choose one of the field formats from the Format Type drop-down list. Depending on the selection you make, Approach makes additional options (described below) available in the Info Box. The format types are:

   - Display as entered (default)
   - Date
   - Time
   - Numeric
   - Text

   These formatting options are discussed in the following sections of this chapter.

5. If you want Approach to display the data entry format in the field on the form as you enter data, check the Show Data Entry Format checkbox. If this checkbox is not checked, Approach does not display the selected format during data entry, but does reformat the field once you move to the next field.

> **Note**
>
> The Show Data Entry Format checkbox appears on every format except Display as Entered.

Using the Display as Entered Setting

The Display as Entered selection displays the value in the exact way that you enter it. Use this button to disable any other format you have selected.

Date Format Setting

Approach offers you a lot of flexibility in setting up date display formats. You can represent dates as 05 Feb 1994, 2/05/94, Saturday, February 5, 1994, 2nd Quarter, and so on. After choosing the date selection, you can determine the order in which parts of the date are displayed, the format of each part, and the character that separates them. You even can specify your own date format string.

Choosing the Date Order

To select the order of appearance of the day, month, and year in a date field, choose one of the selections in the Current format drop-down list: Day-Month-Year (common European format), Month-Day-Year (common American format), or Year-Month-Day.

Choosing the Format of Each Part of the Date

After you choose the order of the various parts of the date, the drop-down list boxes on the right side of the Info Box rearrange to reflect the chosen order (see fig. 4.23).

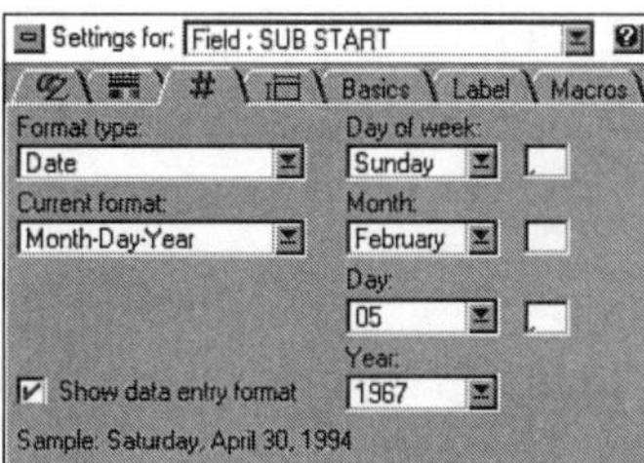

Fig. 4.23
You can select exactly how you want the date displayed.

These drop-down lists enable you to select the exact format of each part of the date:

- The Day of Week list enables you to use the full day name (Sunday) or an abbreviation (Sun). You can also leave the day of the week blank. You can select the character to separate the day of the week from the balance of the date. The default is a comma.

- The Day list lets you specify the number of digits used to represent the date. If you select the two-digit value, two digits are always used for the date (a leading zero appears if the date requires only one digit). The one-digit value uses only the digits required for the date (no leading zeroes). The day can be left blank. Enter the separator character to be used after the day (if any) in the box to the right of the Day drop-down list. Common characters are dashes (—) and slashes (/).

Tip
If you leave the day blank, make sure to erase the separator character as well.

- The Month list lets you use the full month name (February), an abbreviated month name (Feb), or the month number (such as 05). If you select the two-digit value, two digits are always used for the month number (a leading zero appears if the month requires only one digit). The one-digit value uses only the digits required for the month (no leading zeroes). The month can be left blank. Enter the separator character to be used after the month (if any) in the box to the right of the Month drop-down list. Common characters are dashes (—) and slashes (/).

- The Year list lets you specify whether you want the century displayed (1994) or just the year (94). The year can be left blank.

Using Alternative Date Formats

To use a date format other than those discussed in the preceding sections, choose Other Selection from the Current Format drop-down list. The Predefined Format Codes drop-down list appears, displaying still more ways to represent the date value typed into the field (see fig. 4.24). You can also type your own date format into the Format Code text box.

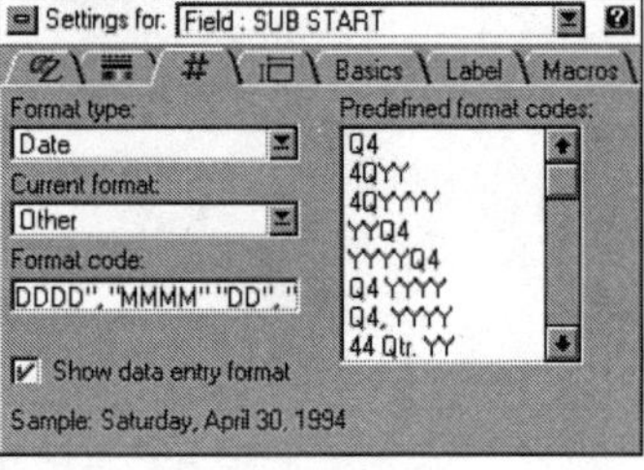

Fig. 4.24
Choose more date options from the Predefined Format Codes drop-down list.

Each alternative date format in the Predefined Format Codes list and the Format Code text box is divided into several parts. You can use the format 444QuarterYYYY to illustrate what those parts mean:

- The numeric part of the date format entry (444) serves two purposes: it breaks the year into periods (in this case quarters, indicated by the use of 4s) and indicates the place in the date format at which the period number (such as First) appears.

- The explanatory text part of the date format entry (Quarter) often indicates the type of period being used (such as Quarter); it can be used for any purpose you want, however.

- The year part of the date format entry (YYYY) indicates the year.

In Approach, the year can contain up to four periods. The value chosen for the numeric part of the date format entry indicates how many periods are to be used. Values from one to four are valid:

1: Annual (full year)

2: Semiannual (half a year)

3: Trimesters (thirds of a year)

4: Quarters (quarters of a year)

The chosen value can be repeated several times to change the appearance of the period number. A single-digit format entry (4) uses just the period number (1, 2, 3, or 4); a two-digit format entry (44) uses the corresponding abbreviation (1st, 2nd, 3rd, or 4th); and a three-digit format entry (444) uses the full word (First, Second, Third, or Fourth). If you use a three-period year (rather than traditional quarters), entering 3 yields period numbers 1, 2, or 3; entering 33 yields period abbreviations 1st, 2nd, or 3rd; and so on.

The explanatory text part of the date format string enables you to sandwich text between the period and the year. This text is normally used to indicate the name of the periods into which you have broken up the year (such as Quarters) or to provide an abbreviation of the period (such as Q for quarters).

Note

The explanatory text can be any word that doesn't contain the letter D, Y, or M. Approach reserves these three characters for another type of date string (see Table 4.1). If the text contains the letter d, y, or m, you must enclose the text in double quotes.

The final part of the date format string represents the year in one of two formats: YY and YYYY. Entering **YY** displays a two-digit year, ignoring the century (94). Entering **YYYY** displays the full year (1994).

If the date value is Dec. 27, 1994, for example, and you enter a custom date format of **444 Quarter YYYY**, the date displays as `Fourth Quarter 1994`.

Note

You can type the three parts of the alternative date format string in any order. The format string **YYQ444** is valid, for example, and displays Dec. 27, 1994 as `94QFourth`.

You can also type a date format string that uses d to represent date, m to represent month, and y to represent year (**dd/mm/yy**, for example). The number of characters you use for each part of the date (date, month, and year) determines the display characteristics for that part. Table 4.1 shows the valid entries and their meanings.

Table 4.1 Date Format Characters in Month/Date/Year Format Strings

Character	Description
d	Displays day using minimum necessary number of digits
dd	Displays day using two digits (adds a leading zero to single-digit dates)
m	Displays month number using minimum necessary number of digits
mm	Displays month number using two digits (adds a leading zero to single-digit months)
mmm	Displays month abbreviation (such as `Feb`)
mmmm	Displays full month name (such as `February`)
yy	Displays year using two digits (no century)
yyyy	Displays year using four digits (includes century)

You can embed other characters as separators in the date string (such as — or /). You also can type the **d**, **m**, and **y** character strings in any order (**mm/dd/yyyy** or **yy/mmmm/dd**, for example). Character strings containing m, y, or d must be enclosed in double quotes (for example, "The Year of Our Lord "YYYY"A.D.").

Time Format

The Time option enables you to format a field for 12- or 24-hour (military) time, select the current format, choose a character to separate the different parts of the time, and specify values for Approach to use to designate morning times and afternoon times.

To format the time for 12- or 24-hour time format, make the appropriate selection from the Time drop-down box. If you select 12-hour, Approach enables you to type the morning and afternoon time designators (AM and PM are the defaults) into the Time Suffix boxes. If you choose 24-hour, Approach enables you to type a single designator (default is blank) into the Time Suffix text box.

Note

You can leave the single time suffix blank, because time expressed on a 24-hour clock doesn't normally have a qualifier such as AM or PM.

A Current Format drop-down list lets you choose how exact you want the time display to be (see fig. 4.25). The options vary from displaying time accurate to the hundredth of a second (**2:03:45.23 PM**) to displaying the hour (**2 PM**).

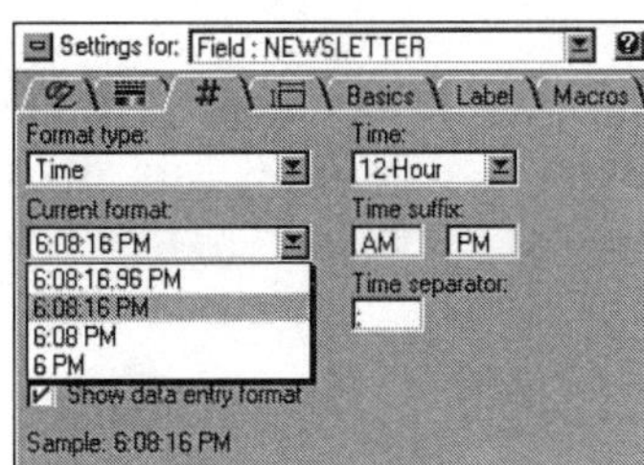

Fig. 4.25
Choose how much time to display using the Current Format drop-down list.

Type the character you want to use to separate the various portions of the time (for example, to separate the hours from the minutes) into the Time Separator text box.

Numeric Format

Choose the Numeric Selection from the Format Type drop-down list to format a numeric field. You can use the Current Format drop-down list to choose a common numeric format (see fig. 4.26). These formats include integer, scientific, currency, percent, phone number, social security number, and zip code. You also can type your own custom format in the Format code text box using the characters detailed in the following sections.

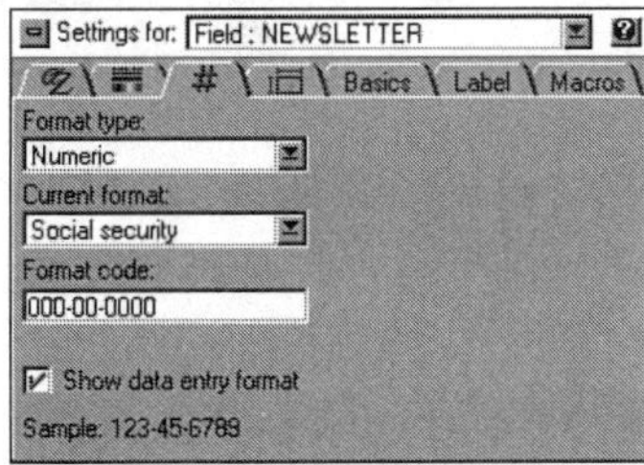

Fig. 4.26
Choose a numeric format from the drop-down list.

You can also embed separator characters in a numeric format. Two useful numeric formats in the drop-down list that use separator characters are the telephone number ((###)" "000-0000) and Social Security number (000-00-0000) formats.

The characters used to format numeric entries are zero (0), number or pound sign (#), decimal point (.), comma (,), semicolon (;), and percent sign (%). You can use quotation marks to embed special characters (such as spaces) in a format string.

Zero

Zeroes (0) specify the number of decimal places to the right of the decimal point and the minimum number of digits to the left of the decimal point. Any unused placeholders to the left or right of the decimal point are shown as zeroes (with a 000 format, for example, the entry **9** appears as `009`).

Number Sign

Number or pound signs (#) also specify the number of digits on either side of the decimal point. With number signs, however, any unused placeholders remain blank (with a ###.# format, for example, the entry **9** appears as `9`).

Decimal Point

The decimal point (.) specifies the location of the decimal point in a numeric string. With a format of #00.0#, for example, the numeric entry **9** is displayed as `09.0`.

Comma

The comma (,) specifies the presence of thousands separators (if zeroes or number signs enclose it). The number 9049, for example, when formatted as ##,##.#, is displayed as `9,049`.

Note

Notice that the actual location of the thousands separator in the string doesn't matter—Approach locates the thousands separator in the appropriate place.

Semicolon

The semicolon (;) separates a numeric format string into two separate parts. When a semicolon is used, the string to the left of the semicolon specifies the format for positive numbers and the string to the right of the semicolon specifies the format for negative numbers. The format ###.#;(###.#) displays negative numbers in the same general numeric format as positive numbers, but places them in parentheses. The number 9.2, for example, is displayed as `9.2`, but –9.2 is displayed as `(9.2)`.

Percent

The percent symbol (%) specifies that the number entered is to be multiplied by 100, and Approach displays a percent sign to the right of the resulting number. The numeric entry **.25**, formatted as ##.0%, appears as `25.0%`.

Comparison Operators

You can begin a format string with an integer and an equal sign (=), greater than sign (>), or less than sign (<). The format string applies only to data that has the number of digits specified by the integer and the sign. For example, the format string =7 000-0000 applies standard phone-number formatting to a string of exactly 7 numbers.

You can combine multiple format strings that begin with an integer and =, >, or <. You must separate the multiple format strings with the vertical OR sign (|). Suppose that a field has this format:

=7 000-0000|<7 "x"######|=10 (000)" "000-0000

If you enter a 7-digit phone number (for example, 5551212), Approach will display it as 555-1212. However, if you enter less than 7 digits (for example, 12345), Approach will display the number as x12345. Finally, if you enter a 10-digit number (for example, 5105551212), Approach displays it as (510) 555-1212.

Any Other Character

You can embed any character other than those mentioned in the preceding sections as a symbol or separator in a numeric format string. One common character used is the dollar sign ($). The string $##0.00, for example, displays the number **8.45** as `$8.45`. If you use the format string $##0.00;($##0.00), the entry **8.45** appears as `$8.45`, but the entry **–8.45** would appear as `($8.45)`. This special display occurs because the right portion of the format string, used for negative numbers, has the symbols (,), and $ embedded in it. However, symbols other than currency, dashes, and parentheses must be enclosed in double quotes.

In similar fashion, the format (###)" "000-0000 displays the entry **5105551212** as a phone number: `(510) 555-1212`. A blank is embedded in the string between the) and the first zero.

Another useful numeric format, 000-00-0000, displays the entry **566849482** as a Social Security number: 566-84-9482.

Table 4.2 shows some common numeric formats and how they would represent some numbers.

Table 4.2 Examples of Number Formats

Format	5345.89	–43	1.2
#,##0.###	5,345.89	–43	1.2
#,#00.00;(#,#00.00)	5345.89	(43.00)	01.20
$#,##0.00	$5,345.89	–$43.00	$1.20
$#,##0.00;($#,##.00)	$5,345.89	($43.00)	$1.20

Returning to the Owl Publishing example, you can format the Cost field as a dollar amount. To do so, follow these steps:

1. Switch to Design mode by opening the **V**iew menu and choosing **D**esign, clicking the Design SmartIcon, or choosing Design from the status bar.
2. Select the Cost field.

3. Open the Info Box by selecting **S**tyle & Properties from the pop-up menu or by double-clicking the object. You can also open the Info Box by selecting the object and clicking the Info Box SmartIcon, or by opening the **O**bject menu and choosing **S**tyle & Properties. Click the # tab to move to the data format panel.
4. Select Numeric from the Format Type drop-down list.
5. From the Current Format drop-down list, select the Currency with Decimals format.

6. Open the **F**ile menu and choose **S**ave Approach File.

The Cost field now displays numbers using the new format (see fig. 4.27).

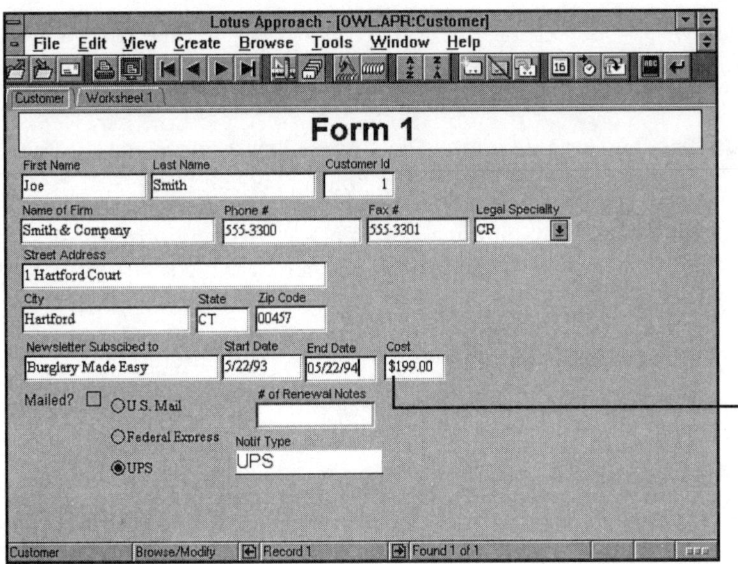

Dollar sign automatically prefaces the amount

Fig. 4.27
The Cost field displays a dollar sign before its value.

Text Format

You can set text formatting by selecting Text from the Format Type drop-down list. The Current Format drop-down list gives you three choices for text formatting: ALL CAPITALIZED, all lowercase, or First Capitalized. First Capitalized capitalizes the first character of every word (good for fields that contain proper names).

Working with Text Blocks

Approach enables you to add descriptive blocks of text to a form. You can use text blocks to give further details about the contents of a field; provide on-screen instructions; hold a page number, date, or time; or customize the form.

Inserting a Text Block

Text blocks often are used to place titles on a form. To create a title for the Owl Publishing form, follow these steps:

1. Switch to Design mode by opening the **V**iew menu and choosing **D**esign, clicking the Design SmartIcon, or choosing Design from the status bar.

2. Click the existing "Form 1" title and press the Delete key, or open the **E**dit menu and choose Cu**t**. Approach removes the default title text box.

3. Click the Text tool on the Drawing toolbar, or open the **C**reate menu and choose Dr**a**wing **T**ext. The pointer becomes an I-beam text cursor.

Tip
If there is not enough room available in the area where you want to insert the text block, select and move fields on the form to create an empty space.

4. Place the I-beam pointer at the upper-left corner of the position you have chosen for the text block and then drag the pointer diagonally to the bottom-right corner.

   For the Owl Publishing example, move the pointer to the empty area near the center top of the form. Click and drag an area about 2 1/2 inches long and about 1/2 inch high.

5. Release the mouse button. The text block appears with a blinking cursor (see fig. 4.28).

Fig. 4.28
A new text block, ready for you to enter its new contents.

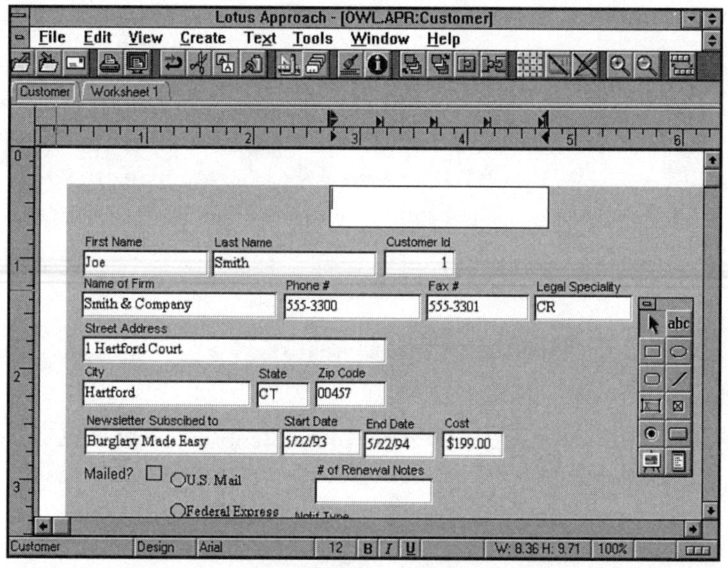

6. Type the text into the text block. For this example, type **Owl Publishing** (see fig. 4.29).

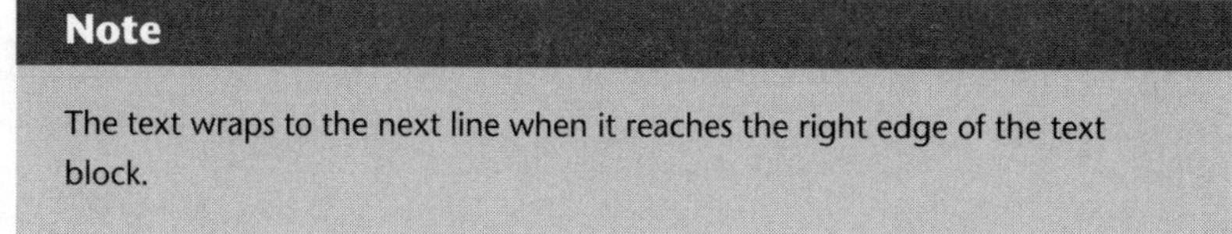

Note

The text wraps to the next line when it reaches the right edge of the text block.

7. Open the **F**ile menu and choose **S**ave Approach File to save the changes to the form.

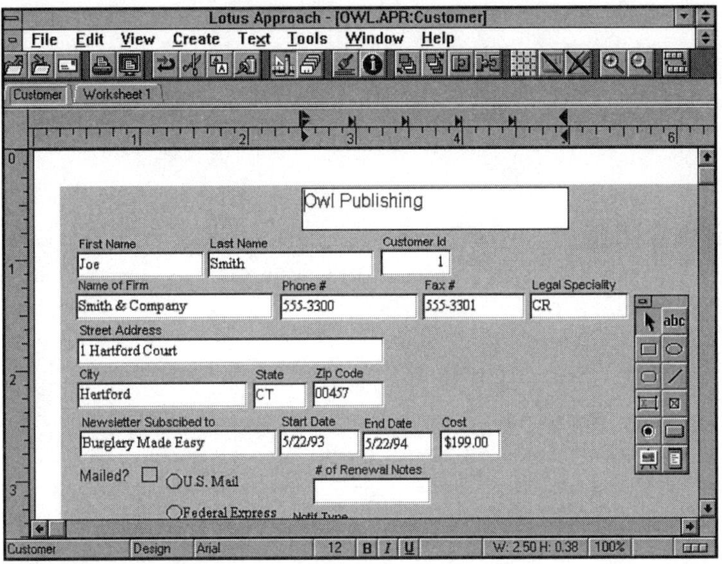

Fig. 4.29
The title block for the Owl Publishing form.

Editing a Text Block

You can edit the text in a text block. To switch to the text editing mode for the text block, select the Text tool from the Drawing toolbar and click the text block or single-click the text block twice with the mouse pointer. Once you are in text editing mode, you'll see the insertion point, a blinking cursor that indicates the place at which the next character you type will appear in the text. To move the insertion point in the text block, use the arrow keys or click at the desired insertion point.

To select text with the mouse, click and drag over the desired characters. To use the keyboard, place the cursor next to the text you want to select, hold down the Shift key, and use the arrow keys to move the cursor over the characters to be selected.

After selecting text, you can cut, copy, or paste:

- To cut the text (removing it from the text block) and place it on the Windows Clipboard, open the **E**dit menu and choose Cu**t** or click the Cut SmartIcon.

- To copy the text to the Windows Clipboard (leaving the original text in its place), open the **E**dit menu and choose **C**opy or click the Copy SmartIcon.

- To paste text that you have copied or cut, place the cursor at the desired insertion point and open the **E**dit menu and choose **P**aste, or click the Paste SmartIcon.

To delete selected text, press Backspace or Delete.

You can also reposition the text in the text block by clicking and dragging the margin indicators and tabs that appear above the ruler line whenever you select a text block.

Copying Text from Other Applications

You can also cut or copy text from another Windows application and paste it into the text block. Follow these steps:

1. Open the Windows application that contains the text you want to use.
2. Select the text in that application and place it on the Windows Clipboard. This task is normally accomplished by choosing the Cu**t** (Ctrl+X) or **C**opy (Ctrl+C) option on the other application's **E**dit menu.
3. Switch back to Approach.
4. Select the Text tool and click the text block at the location where you want to insert the new text.

5. Open the **E**dit menu and choose **P**aste or click the Paste SmartIcon to place the text into the text block.

Moving and Sizing Text Blocks

To resize a text block, click it to show the sizing handles. Drag any of the handles to adjust the size of the text block.

> **Note**
>
> If you've been typing into the text block, you must click somewhere else on the form first, and then click the text block to show the handles.

You can also resize a text block using the text block's Info Box. Click the Dimensions tab to switch to the Dimensions panel of the text block's Info Box. Type the new width and height for the text block into the Width and Height text boxes.

To move the text block, position the pointer inside the text block and then click and drag the block to its new location. To adjust the location of the text block from the Info Box's Dimensions panel, type the new location into the Top and Left text boxes.

Changing the Text Style of a Text Block

The title block entered earlier for the Owl Publishing form isn't quite right—it isn't centered, and the text is too small. It's easy to change the font, font style, size, alignment, or effects of the text in a text block by using the options in the Text Style dialog box. To modify the text block, follow these steps:

1. Switch to Design mode by opening the **V**iew menu and choosing **D**esign, clicking the Design SmartIcon, or choosing Design from the status bar.

> **Note**
>
> If you click a text block that is already selected (the sizing handles are visible), Approach places you in text editing mode, in which you can modify the text in the text block (see the following section, "Modifying Portions of Text in a Text Block"). To return to editing the properties of the text block, click somewhere else on the form and then click the text block again.

2. Open the Info Box by selecting **S**tyle & Properties from the pop-up menu or by double-clicking the text object. You can also open the Info Box by selecting the text object and clicking the Info Box SmartIcon, or by opening the **O**bject menu and choosing **S**tyle & Properties. Switch to the fonts panel by clicking the font tab (az) as shown in figure 4.30. This fonts panel is similar to the fonts panel for fields discussed earlier in this chapter.

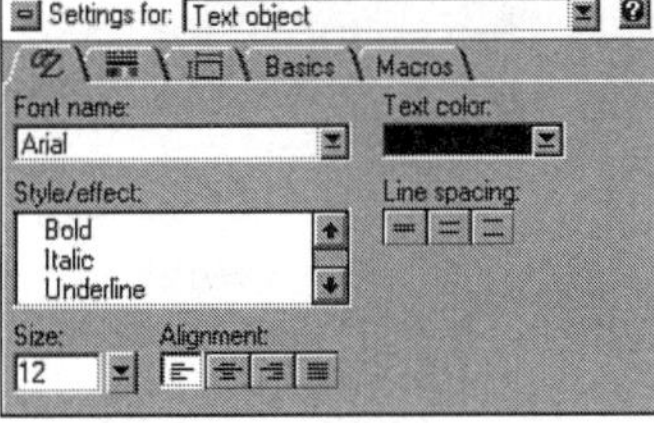

Fig. 4.30
You can easily change the font and style of a text block.

Tip
If necessary, resize the text block to see all the enlarged text.

3. Make the appropriate changes in the Info Box. You can change the font, style/effect, size, alignment, and text color. You can also choose the line spacing (single, double, or triple space) from the Line Spacing buttons. For the Owl Publishing example, select Bold in the Style/Effect

list box, 18 (or the nearest size your font offers) in the Size list box, and Center under the Alignment options.

4. Open the **F**ile menu and choose **S**ave Approach File to save the changes to the form.

Notice that the title block grabs your attention much more effectively now (see fig. 4.31).

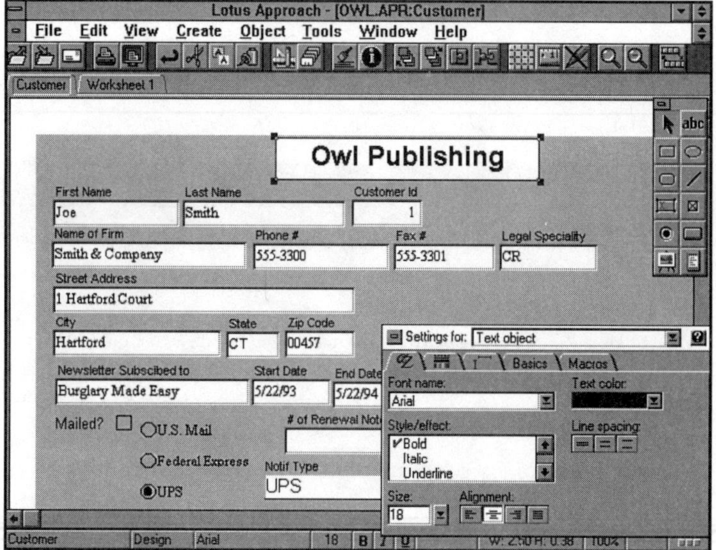

Fig. 4.31
The modified title block for the Owl Publishing form.

Modifying Portions of Text in a Text Block

You can modify selected portions of the text in a text block much as you would using your favorite word processor. To do so, follow these steps:

1. Switch to Design mode by opening the **V**iew menu and choosing **D**esign, clicking the Design SmartIcon, or choosing Design from the status bar.

2. To select a text block and enter text editing mode, click the Text tool in the Drawing toolbar or open the **C**reate menu and choose Dr**a**wing **T**ext, and then click the text block. You can also select the text block by single-clicking it twice with the arrow pointer.

3. To select a portion of the text, click and drag the mouse pointer across the characters you want to modify.

4. Open the Info Box by selecting **S**tyle & Properties from the **O**bject or pop-up menu or by clicking the Info Box SmartIcon. The Text Editing Info Box has a single panel for changing the text attributes. The panel is identical to the fonts panel for text blocks discussed in the last section.

5. Adjust the font, style/effect, size, alignment, color, and line spacing for the selected portion of the text in the text block.

Tip
To use the pop-up menu, position the mouse pointer over the selected text when you press the right mouse button.

Modifying the Other Properties of a Text Block

Careful selection of the colors and other properties you use in a text block can make the text block more effective. You can set the fill (background) and the pen (text) colors, border width and color, shadow color, and the frame style.

For example, you can fill the title block on the Owl Publishing data-entry form to make it more attractive. To modify the other nontext properties of a text block, follow these steps:

1. Switch to Design mode by opening the **V**iew menu and choosing **D**esign, clicking the Design SmartIcon, or choosing Design from the status bar.

2. Open the Info Box by selecting **S**tyle & Properties from the pop-up menu or by double-clicking the text block. You can also open the Info Box by selecting the text block and clicking the Info Box SmartIcon, or by opening the **O**bject menu and choosing **S**tyle & Properties. Select the Color tab to move to the Color panel (see fig. 4.32).

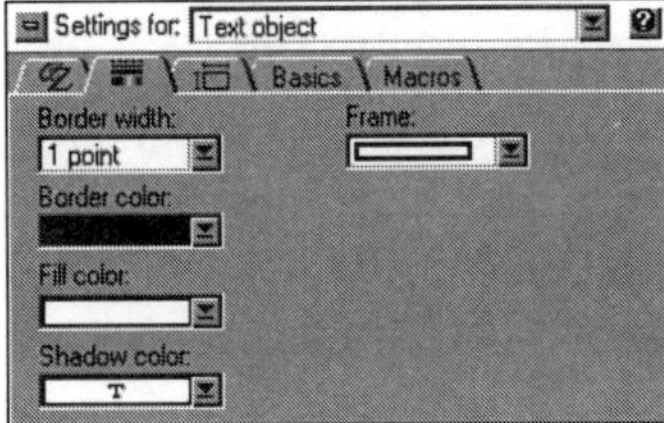

Fig. 4.32
Change colors and borders from the text block Color panel.

3. To set the border width, click the Border Width drop-down list and choose the weight of the border. You can choose a border width from hairline to 12 point (1/6 of an inch).

4. To set the border color, click the Border Color drop-down list and choose the color you want from among the available colors. Select T if you want a transparent (invisible) border.

> **Note**
>
> Text blocks always have borders—the only way to turn off the borders is to choose a transparent color for the borders.

5. To set the fill color, click the Fill Color drop-down list and choose the color you want from among the available colors. For the Owl Publishing form, choose a lighter color that offsets the dark text.

6. To set the shadow color, click the Shadow Color drop-down list and choose the color you want from among the available colors.

7. To select a frame style, click the Frame drop-down list and select the frame you want to use.

8. Open the **F**ile menu and choose **S**ave Approach File to save the changes to the text block.

Inserting a Field into a Text Block

You can insert one or more fields into a text block so that the text of the block changes as the values in the field(s) change. To insert a field into a text block, follow these steps:

1. Switch to Design mode by opening the **V**iew menu and choosing **D**esign, clicking the Design SmartIcon, or choosing Design from the status bar.

2. Click the Text tool in the Drawing toolbar or open the **C**reate menu and choose Dr**a**wing **T**ext. The mouse pointer turns into an I-beam cursor.

3. Select the desired text block or create a new text block.

4. Move the insertion point to the left edge of the position in the text where you want to place the field.

5. Choose I**n**sert **F**ield from the **T**ext menu, I**n**sert **F**ield from the pop-up menu, or click the Insert Field SmartIcon. The Add Field dialog box appears.

6. Select the field you want to place in the text block from the Add Field dialog box by double-clicking the field. The name of the file and field appears in the text, enclosed in insertion symbols (<< and >>).

7. Switch to Browse mode by opening the **V**iew menu and choosing **B**rowse, clicking the Browse SmartIcon, or choosing Browse from the

status bar. The value of the field for the current record appears in the text block (see fig. 4.33).

> **Note**
>
> Summary-calculated fields do not show their results on the form in Browse mode. These types of fields display their results only in Preview mode.

Tip
Inserting a field into a text block is a way to display field information without allowing the user to edit the field.

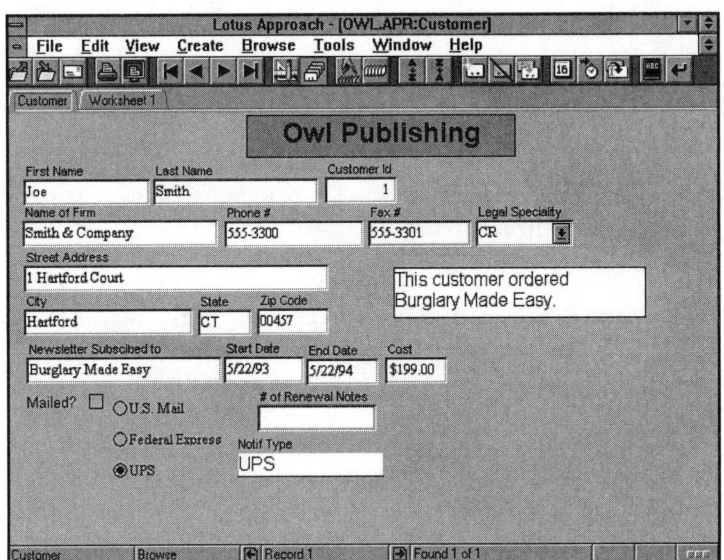

Fig. 4.33
The value of the inserted fields appears in the text block.

Inserting a Page Number, Date, or Time into a Text Block

You can easily create a new text block that contains the page number, date, or time. To do so, follow these steps:

1. Switch to Design mode by opening the **V**iew menu and choosing **D**esign, clicking the Design SmartIcon, or choosing Design from the status bar.

2. Open the **O**bject menu and choose I**n**sert. Select **D**ate, **T**ime, or **P**age # from the submenu. You can also click the SmartIcon for Insert Today's Date, Insert Current Time, or Insert Page Number.

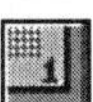

3. Approach creates a new text block containing the requested quantity. You can type additional text into the text block and format the text, border, and background.

You can also insert the page number, date, or time into an existing text block. Owl Publishing, for example, wants to show today's date on its form. Follow these steps:

1. Switch to Design mode by opening the **V**iew menu and choosing **D**esign, clicking the Design SmartIcon, or choosing Design from the status bar.

2. Click the Text tool in the Drawing toolbar or open the **C**reate menu and choose Dr**a**wing **T**ext. The mouse turns into an I-beam cursor.

3. Open the **V**iew menu and choose Show **R**uler to display the rulers to help you place the text block.

Tip
If you want, you can skip step 5 and place the page number or date in the form without any additional text.

4. Position the pointer at the desired location for the page number, time, or date, and then drag the pointer diagonally until the text block is the correct size. For this example, draw a text block about two inches long and 1/4 inch high in the upper-right corner of the form, near the title block.

5. Type any text you want into the text block. For this example, type **The date is:** in the new text block.

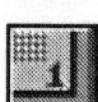

6. Choose I**n**sert from the Te**x**t or pop-up menu, and then choose the item you want to insert (**D**ate, **T**ime, or **P**age #) from the submenu. You can also click the SmartIcon for Insert Today's Date, Insert Current Time, or Insert Page Number.

   For this example, choose I**n**sert **D**ate from the Te**x**t menu. The date code appears in the text block in Design mode (see fig. 4.34). When you switch to Browse mode, the actual date, time, or page # is displayed on the form (see fig. 4.35).

7. Open the **F**ile menu and choose **S**ave Approach File to save your changes.

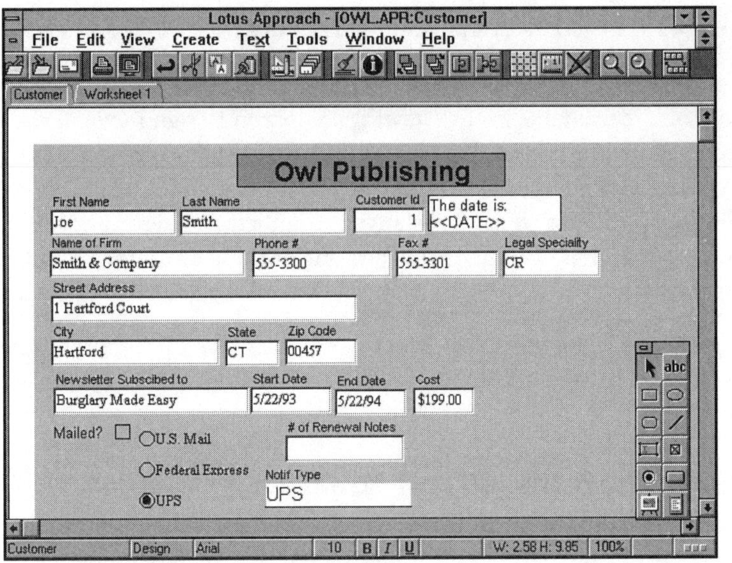

Fig. 4.34
The date is inserted into a text block in Design mode.

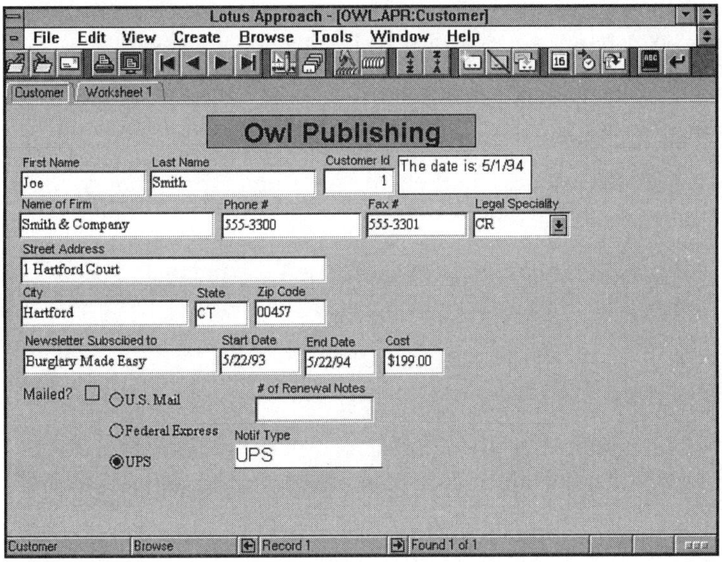

Fig. 4.35
The date is inserted into a text block in Browse mode.

Using Graphics to Enhance Forms

Approach's simple graphics tools enable you to place shapes on your forms. These tools are available in the Drawing toolbar in Design mode. If the Drawing Tools toolbar is not visible, open the **V**iew menu and choose Show Dra**w**ing Tools or click the Showing Drawing Tools SmartIcon. You can use these drawing tools to draw squares, rectangles, rounded rectangles and squares, ovals, circles, and lines. When you click one of these tools, the pointer turns into a crosshair.

After you draw a graphic object, you can edit its fill color, drop shadow, and the width and color of its boundary line. You can also move and resize the graphic object.

Drawing Rectangles and Squares

To draw a rectangle or a rounded rectangle, choose the Rectangle or Rounded Rectangle Drawing Tool icon. Position the pointer where the upper-left corner of the rectangle should appear. Click and drag to the point at which you want the bottom-right corner to appear, and then release the mouse button. The rectangle appears with visible sizing handles.

If you want to draw a square or rounded square, hold down the Shift key while dragging.

To add a rounded rectangle to the Owl Publishing form to box in the title, follow these steps:

1. Switch to Design mode by opening the **V**iew menu and choosing **D**esign, clicking the Design SmartIcon, or choosing Design from the status bar.

2. Click the Rounded Rectangle SmartIcon.
3. Place the pointer on the upper-left corner of the title box. The background fill color you added earlier makes this corner easy to find.
4. Hold down the left mouse button and drag the pointer to the bottom-right corner.
5. Release the mouse button; the rounded rectangle appears (see fig. 4.36).

6. Open the **F**ile menu and choose **S**ave Approach File to save the changes.

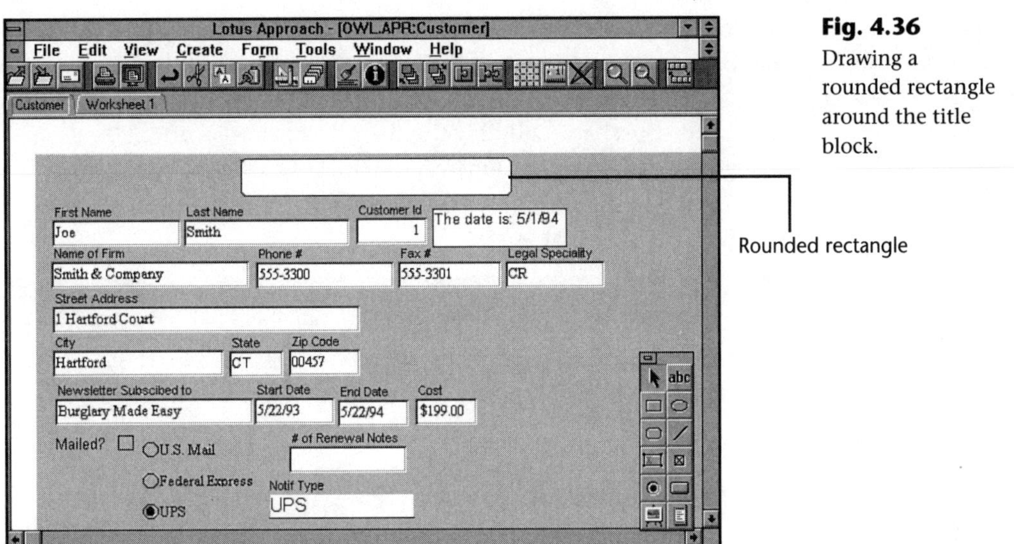

Fig. 4.36
Drawing a rounded rectangle around the title block.

Drawing Ovals and Circles

To draw an oval or a circle, choose the Oval Drawing Tool icon. Position the pointer where you want the center of the circle or oval to appear. Click and drag diagonally until the oval or circle is the size you want, and then release the mouse button. The oval appears with visible sizing handles around its boundary.

If you want to draw a circle, hold down the Shift key while dragging.

Drawing Lines

To draw a line, choose the Line Drawing Tool icon. Position the pointer where you want one end of the line to appear. Click and drag until the pointer reaches the other end of the line, and then release the mouse button. The line appears with visible sizing handles at either end.

Moving and Sizing Graphics Objects

After you draw a graphics object on your form, you can modify its size and shape. To modify a graphics object, switch to Design mode and then select the object. Click any of the sizing handles that appear and drag to stretch the shape in the direction you want. You can also change the location from the Dimensions panel of the Info Box. To adjust the position of the graphics object, type the new location of the upper-left corner of the object into the Top and Left text boxes.

Tip
If you hold the Shift key while dragging, the line is constrained to 45-degree angles.

Tip
You can group graphics objects (including lines) into a single object to make moving and sizing them easier. To do this, select the objects and choose **G**roup from the pop-up or **O**bject menu, or click the Group SmartIcon.

To move a shape, click the shape's border (for a line, click the line) and drag the shape to its new location. For any filled shape (for example, a rectangle, rounded rectangle, or oval with a fill color other than transparent), you can click inside the shape and drag the shape to its new location. You can also change the size from the Dimensions panel of the Info Box. To adjust the size of the graphics object, type the new width and height for the object into the Width and Height text boxes.

Note

The mouse pointer turns into an open hand when the pointer is correctly positioned to move a shape.

Setting the Properties of Graphic Objects

You can adjust the border, fill, and shadow color for filled objects (for example, rectangles, rounded rectangles, and ovals) to make them stand out on a form. You can also adjust the border width and frame style.

To change these properties for filled graphic objects, follow these steps:

1. Open the Info Box by selecting **S**tyle & Properties from the pop-up menu or by double-clicking the graphic object. You can also open the Info Box by selecting the graphic object and clicking the Info Box SmartIcon, or by opening the **O**bject menu and choosing **S**tyle & Properties. Switch to the Color panel by clicking the Color tab.

2. Select the border, fill, or shadow color from the Border Color, Fill Color, or Shadow Color drop-down list. The T box provides a transparent (invisible) color.

3. Select the border width you want from the Border Width drop-down list. The available widths are hairline to 12 point (1/6 of an inch).

4. Select a frame style for the border from the Frame drop-down list.

To change the properties of a line, follow these steps:

1. Open the Info Box by selecting **S**tyle & Properties from the pop-up menu or by double-clicking the line. You can also open the Info Box by selecting the line and clicking the Info Box SmartIcon, or by opening the **O**bject menu and choosing **S**tyle & Properties. Switch to the Color panel by clicking the Color tab.

2. Choose the line or shadow color from the Line Color or Shadow Color drop-down list. The T box provides a transparent (invisible) color.

3. Select a line width from the Line Width drop-down list. The available widths are hairline to 12 points (1/6 of an inch). To make the rounded rectangle around the Owl Publishing title block more distinct, select a three-point line width.

4. Choose a line style from the Line Style drop-down list.

5. Choose **S**ave Approach File from the **F**ile menu to save your work.

Working with Overlapping Objects

Because the rounded rectangle was the last object drawn in the Owl Publishing example, it completely covers the title block. It appears in a higher layer of the form than the title block and hides everything below it. To fix this problem, open the **O**bject menu and choose A**r**range Send to **B**ack to move the title block on top of the rounded rectangle layer. Another solution is to choose a transparent fill color for the rounded rectangle so that the title block beneath it shows through.

If you haven't made the frame quite large enough, choosing A**r**range Send to **B**ack can cover part or all of the rectangle with the title block. If you run into this problem, drag the sizing handles of the rectangle to make the frame slightly larger.

If you use the Send to **B**ack command, choose A**r**range Bring to Front from the **O**bject menu to restore the rectangle to its original layer.

To choose a transparent color fill, select the rounded rectangle. Open the Info Box by selecting **S**tyle & Properties from the pop-up menu or by double-clicking the rectangle. You can also open the Info Box by selecting the rectangle and clicking the Info Box SmartIcon, or by opening the **O**bject menu and choosing **S**tyle & Properties. Change to the Color panel and click the Fill Color drop-down list. From the palette of available colors, select the box marked T in the upper-left corner of the palette. Approach provides a transparent color. The title text now shows through, framed by the rounded rectangle border. Increase the border width to three points and set the border color to a deep blue (see fig. 4.37).

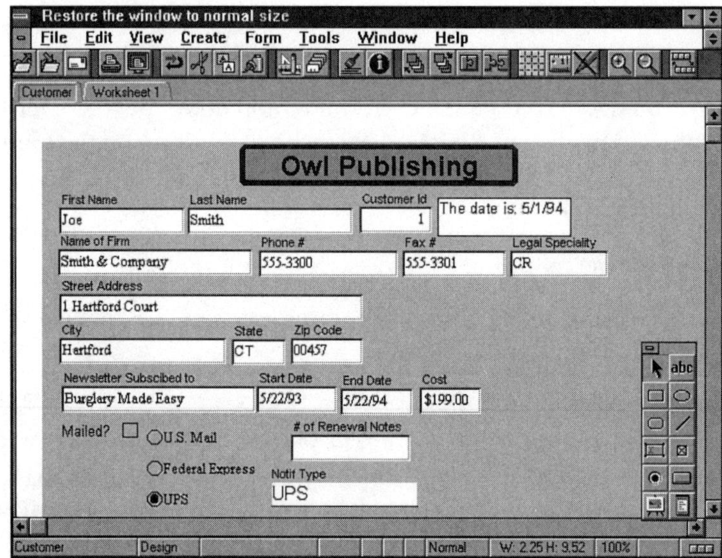

Fig. 4.37
The title bar with its border frame.

Adding Illustrations to Forms

Approach also enables you to place illustration files on your form, using several popular formats. To do so, you can use the standard Windows copy and paste operations, or you can paste an illustration directly from a file onto your form. The second option enables you to create and save an illustration using a drawing package and then import it into Approach. The following sections discuss both methods for placing illustrations on a form.

Using Cut and Paste to Add Illustrations to Forms

To place an illustration on a form using the standard Windows Clipboard cut, copy, and paste operations, follow these steps:

1. Open the application that contains the illustration that you want to add to your form (or that you will use to create the picture).

2. Load or create the graphic and then select it.

3. Open the **E**dit menu and choose Cu**t** or **C**opy to place the illustration on the Windows Clipboard.

4. Switch back to Approach.

5. Switch to Design mode by opening the **V**iew menu and choosing **D**esign, clicking the Design SmartIcon, or choosing Design from the status bar.

6. Click the form at the location where you want to place the illustration.

7. Choose **P**aste from the **E**dit menu to place the illustration on the form.

8. Use the sizing handles to stretch or shrink the illustration if necessary. You can also click in the picture and drag it to a new location. Use the Dimensions panel of the Info Box to set the location and size.

Pasting an Illustration onto a Form

To make the Owl Publishing form more attractive, you can put a logo in the upper-right corner. The graphic used in this example is a PCX file, but you can perform the same actions with any of the file types supported by Approach, including BMP, WMF, TIF, GIF, TGA, and EPS files.

Choose a graphics file in any of the formats listed in the following steps. If you don't have a graphics file handy, create and save one using Windows Paintbrush.

To paste the illustration directly from a file, follow these steps:

1. Switch to Design mode by opening the **V**iew menu and choosing **D**esign, clicking the Design SmartIcon, or choosing Design from the status bar.

2. Click the location where you want the illustration to appear. For the Owl Publishing example, click near the upper-right corner of the form.

3. Open the **E**dit menu and choose Paste from **F**ile. The Paste from File dialog box appears (see fig. 4.38).

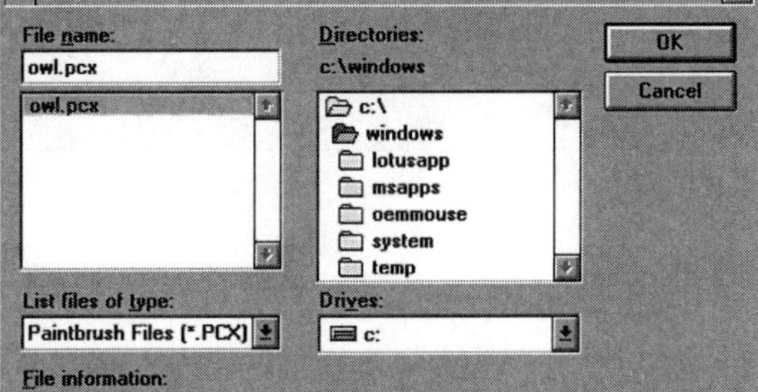

Fig. 4.38
The Paste from File dialog box.

4. Use the **D**irectories list box and the Dri**v**es drop-down list to select the directory and drive where your graphics file is stored.

5. From the List Files of **T**ype drop-down list, select the file type of the picture you want to import.

6. Select the desired file from the list box below the File **N**ame text box.

7. Click OK. The illustration appears on your form.

8. Use the sizing handles to stretch or shrink the illustration if necessary. You can also click the picture and drag it to a new location. Use the Dimensions panel of the Illustration's Info Box to type in new values for the location and size.

9. Open the **F**ile menu and choose **S**ave Approach File to save the changes.

Figure 4.39 shows what the finished form looks like with the owl logo added.

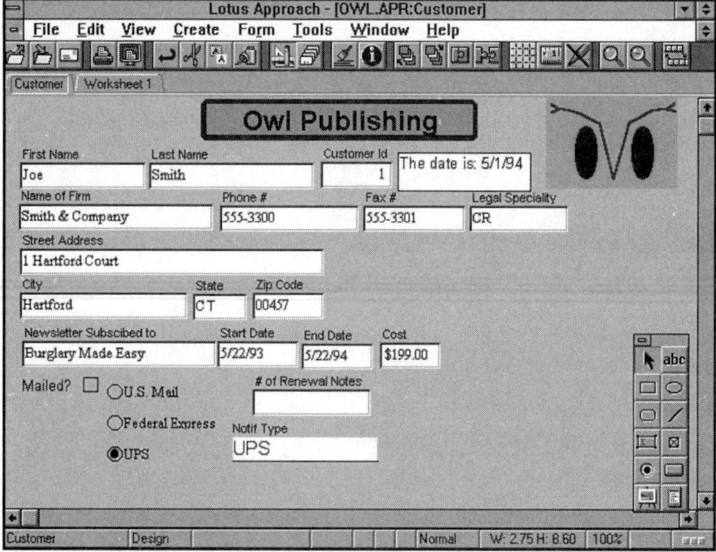

Fig. 4.39
An illustration is pasted onto a form from a file.

From Here...

In this chapter, you learned to enhance your data entry forms. You can now place text fields, radio buttons, checkboxes, text blocks, and graphics on the form. You can adjust the color, border, shadow, and text attributes of these objects. You can also choose the display format for database fields on a form. You can edit the text in text blocks, adjust the properties of labels, and add illustrations from other applications to a form.

The concepts learned in Chapter 4 are applicable to many other Design mode objects. For more information, refer to the following chapters in this book:

- Chapter 7, "Creating Reports and Mailing Labels," teaches you how to use many of the techniques you learned in this chapter to build other types of views.
- Chapter 9, "Designing Advanced Forms," shows you how to build more complex forms.
- Chapter 12, "Creating Advanced Reports," expands on Chapter 7 to show you how to build advanced reports.

Chapter 5

Working with Your Data

As you work with your database, you'll spend the bulk of your time entering, finding, and sorting records. In this chapter, you learn how to create records and enter data into fields in Approach forms. This chapter focuses on the various types of fields that Approach allows, and tells you how to enter data into each. You also learn how to move through your records and sort them in the order you want. After defining your database and laying out forms, you are ready to choose a form and to start entering data.

Note

You must use Browse mode to work with the data in your database.

In this chapter, you learn how to:

- Access an Approach form for entering data
- Create, duplicate, and delete records
- Enter data into the various types of fields, such as data and time fields
- Navigate through records using the status bar, SmartIcon toolbar, and keyboard commands
- Sort records using various criteria
- Spell check your data entry using Approach's built-in checker

Accessing Forms

Tip
If the View tabs aren't visible across the top of the screen, open the **V**iew menu and select Show View **T**abs.

Because Approach can create multiple forms, you need a way to switch between them. To switch from one form to another, click the view tab to choose the form you want from the view tab line. If you can't see the view tab because so many other view tabs are in the way, use the left and right arrows on the tab line to scroll the view tab line. You can also choose another form by selecting the form name from the button at the left end of the status bar. Clicking this button pops up a list of available forms (as well as reports, form letters, and mailing labels). Select the form you want from this list (see fig. 5.1).

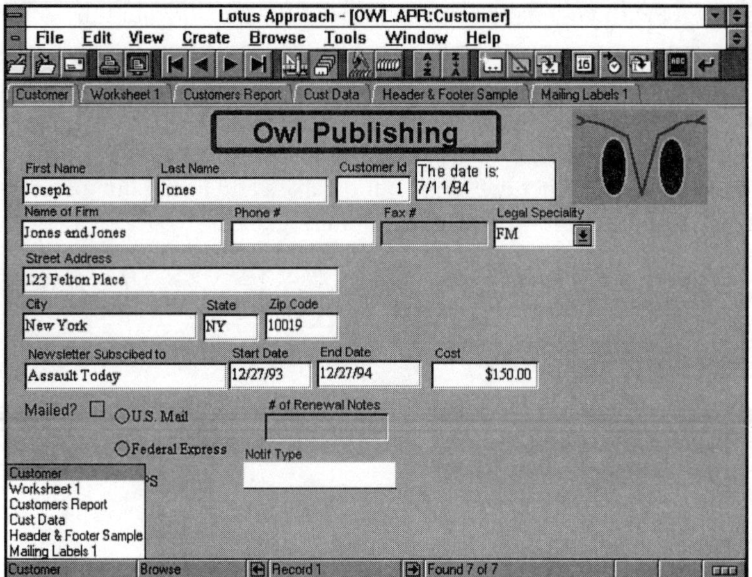

Fig. 5.1
Select a form by clicking Approach's status bar.

Manipulating Records

Approach provides three ways to work with database records on a form: you can create a new record, duplicate an existing record, and delete an existing record.

Creating a New Record

After accessing the desired form, you can create a new record. To do so, click the New Record SmartIcon, press Ctrl+N, or open the **B**rowse menu and choose N**e**w Record. Each time you create a new record, Approach presents you with a blank form in which to enter your data.

Duplicating a Record

Sometimes creating a new record is easier if you copy and modify an existing record. To do so, move to the record you want to copy by using the Record Forward or Record Backward SmartIcons (see "Navigating Through Your Records" later in this chapter for complete instructions), and then open the **B**rowse menu and choose **D**uplicate Record. You can also click the Duplicate Current Record SmartIcon.

After you copy the record, make the necessary changes to the duplicate. Be sure to change any fields that were designated as **U**nique in the Validation section of the Field Definition Options dialog box. You can't duplicate the values contained in those fields (see Chapter 2 for details concerning this restriction).

Deleting a Record

To delete a record, move to the record you want to delete and click the Delete Record SmartIcon, or open the **B**rowse menu and choose De**l**ete Record. Approach asks whether you really want to delete the record. Choose **N**o if you want to keep the record.

Tip

You can also delete multiple records in Approach, but first you must use the Find function to generate a found set that includes all the records you want to delete.

If your database uses a dBASE III+ or dBASE IV file type, deleting a record doesn't actually remove that record from the database file. The record is marked in a special way so that it no longer appears on-screen, but it remains in the database file and continues to take up space. To remove such records from the database file and recover the lost space, follow these steps:

1. Open the **T**ools menu and choose **P**references to open the Preferences dialog box.

2. Click the Database tab to open the Database panel.

3. Click the **C**ompress button in the dBASE and FoxPro Compression section of the Database panel.

Moving Through Fields

On a form, the field available for data entry has the focus. You can tell when a field box has the focus because the blinking text cursor appears in the field box. To move the focus to another field, use one of the following methods:

- Move the mouse pointer to the field you want and click it.

- Press Tab to move to the next field in the tabbing order (see Chapter 4 for more information about setting the tabbing order). Press Shift+Tab to move to the previous field in the tabbing order.

- If the Use **E**nter Key To Move Or Tab Between Fields In Browse checkbox is checked in the General panel of the Preferences dialog box, you can move between fields using the Enter key.

If the selected field is a text-format field, the cursor becomes a blinking insertion point, and you can begin typing your data.

Note

To duplicate a value from the last newly created record, click the field and choose the Duplicate Data from Previous Record SmartIcon, or open the **B**rowse menu and choose **I**nsert **P**revious Value.

Entering Data into a Form

The process of entering data into a form is relatively straightforward. The data-entry technique used to enter data, however, depends on the format of the field (text, checkbox, button, and so on).

Field Box

To enter information in a text field box, simply type it. The length of the text to be entered can't exceed the length of the database field as specified in the Field Definition or Creating New Database dialog boxes. If you exceed this length, Approach warns you when you try to type more characters than the field can hold (see fig. 5.2). Most fields on the Owl Publishing form (such as LAST NAME and FIRST NAME) are text fields.

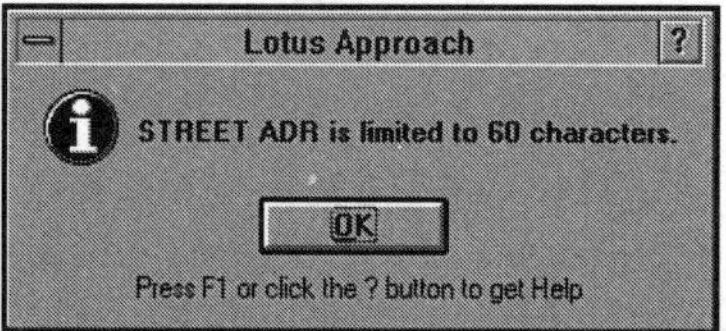

Fig. 5.2
Approach warns you when you type longer values than allowed.

Tip
Refer to Chapter 3 for some tips on sizing form fields to match the length of the fields in the database.

If the Show Data Entry Format box is checked in the Format panel of a text field box Info Box, Approach displays the text you type in the specified format. If this checkbox is not checked, the text takes on the specified format when you move to another field.

The blinking insertion point indicates where the next character you type will appear. To move the insertion point, use the arrow keys or click the desired position.

You can select text using either of the following techniques:

- Click and drag over the text you want to select.
- Use the arrow keys to position the blinking insertion point immediately to the right or left of the text you want to select, hold down the Shift key, and then use the arrow keys to select the text. You can also double-click on a word to select just that word.

After you select text, you can delete it by pressing Delete or Backspace. You can also replace it by typing new text; whatever you type replaces the selected text.

You can cut or copy selected text to the Windows Clipboard by choosing Cu**t** or **C**opy from the **E**dit menu. To place the contents of the Clipboard into the text at the insertion point, choose **P**aste from the **E**dit menu.

Numeric Fields

You can enter only numbers in numeric fields. (In the Owl Publishing database, numeric fields include COST and # OF RENEWAL NOTES.) If you try to enter text into a numeric field, Approach warns you when you try to leave the field. If you mix numbers and letters, Approach warns you that the value entered is not a number (see fig. 5.3) and it refuses to accept the value.

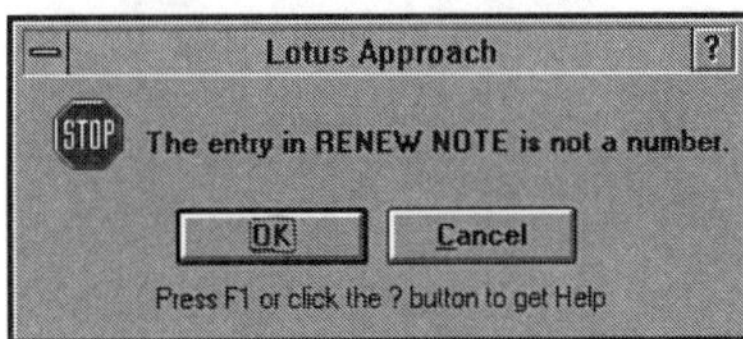

Fig. 5.3
Approach warns you when you type a non-numeric value into a numeric field.

> **Note**
>
> If you need to mix numbers and letters, you must use a text field. The exception to this rule is that you can create a numeric format string that includes non-numeric characters (for example, telephone numbers).

The length of the number that you enter in a numeric field can't exceed the database field length as specified in the Field Definition dialog box. If you exceed the length of the field, Approach warns you that your entry is too long when you try to type more characters than the field can hold.

If the Show Data Entry Format checkbox is checked in the Format panel of a numeric field Info Box, Approach displays the formatting characters and underlines to specify the maximum number of characters you can type (see fig. 5.4). If the checkbox is not checked, Approach reformats the numbers you type into the correct format when you move to the next field.

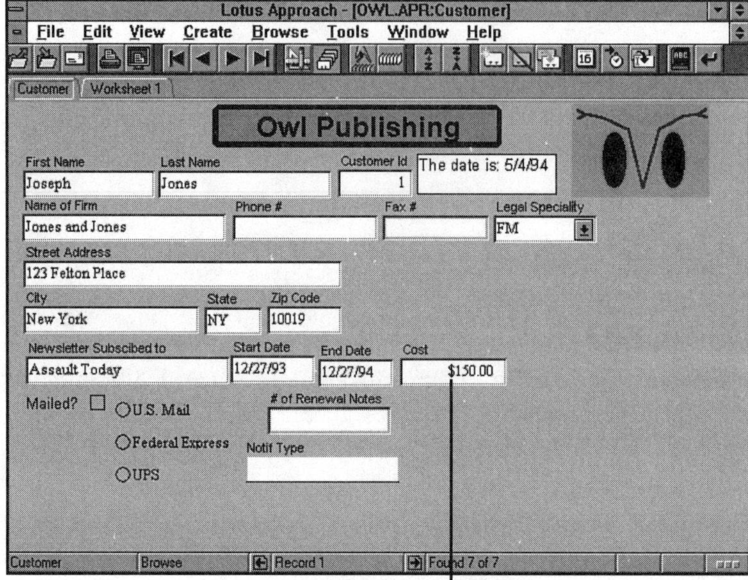

Underline shows maximum length

Fig. 5.4
A numeric field can display a line to indicate how many digits you can enter.

Date Fields

You must enter dates in the format set for short dates in the Windows International Control Panel. If you select the standard U.S. short date format (mm/dd/yy), for example, you can enter up to 10 characters in the date field, including the slashes. Approach displays the slashes for you—you don't need to type them. When you select a date field, the date is displayed as numbers separated by slashes (for example, 12/27/94). When you leave the field, the date is reformatted according to the display format options you have set for this field. In the Owl Publishing database, SUB START and SUB END are examples of date fields.

Time Fields

Time fields can contain up to 12 digits, depending on the format you have set in the Windows Control Panel. You can type hour, minute, and second values into the field, separating them with colons (HH:MM:SS). If you enter tenths or hundredths of a second, separate them from the whole second value with a decimal point (HH:MM:SS.00). You don't have to enter such a detailed time value, however; you can enter just the hour (HH) if you like, or the hour and minute (HH:MM).

You can also type **am** or **pm** after the time. If you enter the time in 24-hour format in a time field that uses the 12-hour format, Approach reformats the field in a 12-hour format and adds the AM or PM for you when you leave the field; you can enter a time such as **13:10** or **1:10pm**, for example. You can also specify a more exact time, such as **1:10:34pm**.

If the Show Data Entry Format checkbox is checked in the Format panel of a time field Info Box, Approach displays the formatting characters and underlines to specify the maximum number of characters you can type. If this checkbox is not checked, Approach reformats the numbers you type into the correct format when you move to the next field.

Memo Fields

To enter information into a memo field, type and edit it just like a text field. Memo fields have no length constraints. As you type, Approach scrolls the text automatically to make more room. You can move up and down through the text using the arrow keys. If you type more text than the memo field can display on the form, Approach provides a scroll bar to the right of the memo field when you move to the next field so that you can scroll through the text.

Boolean Fields

When entering data in Boolean fields, you are limited to a small set of clearly defined values. To indicate true or yes, enter **Y**, **Yes**, or **1**. To indicate false or no, enter **N**, **No**, or **0**. All other entries are interpreted as Yes or 1. Approach reformats the contents of Boolean fields to Yes or No, depending on your entry. The MAILED? field in the Owl Publishing database is an example of a Boolean field. However, a checkbox, not the actual Y/N, True/False values, indicates the value for this field on the form.

Drop-Down Lists

A drop-down list provides a list of values from which to choose. You can enter data into the field only by choosing values from this list. An arrow always appears next to the field if the S**h**ow Drop-Down Arrow checkbox is checked in the Drop-Down List dialog box (accessed from the Define List button in the Basics panel of the Info Box). If this checkbox is not checked, the arrow only appears when you select the field.

To choose a value, click the arrow adjacent to the field to drop down the list of values. A list of up to eight value choices appears (see fig. 5.5). If the list contains more values, a scroll bar also appears.

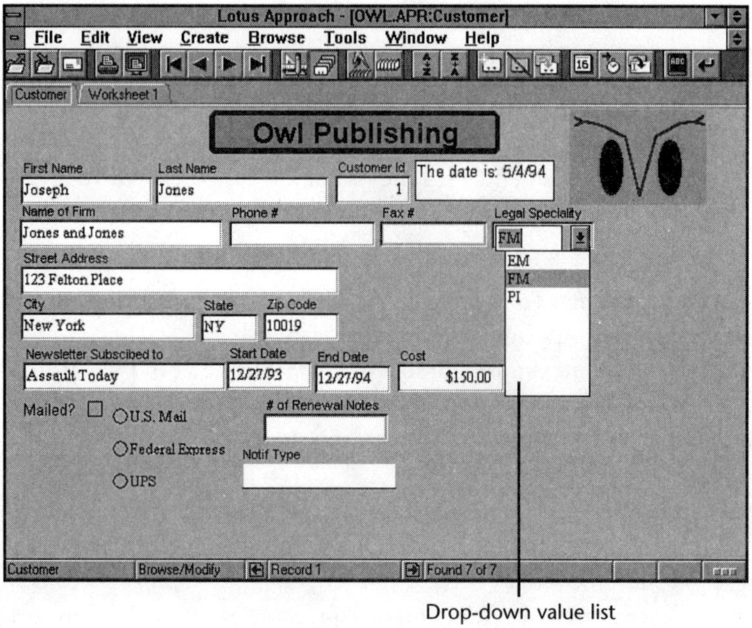

Fig. 5.5
The selection bar shows the value to be selected when you press Enter or Tab.

Drop-down value list

Drop-down lists can include any type of textual or numeric information. They are useful for selecting from a list of states, employees, zip codes, and so forth.

Use one of the following methods to choose a value from the list:

- Click the value with the mouse pointer.
- Move the selection bar to the value using the arrow keys and then press Enter (which makes the selection and enters the new or updated record) or Tab (which makes the selection and moves to the next field).
- In a long list of values, jump to the first value that begins with a certain letter by pressing that letter. This procedure is helpful if you have entered the values in the list in alphabetical order.

Field Box & List

A Field box & list enables you to choose a value from a drop-down list or to type a new value into the field. An arrow appears next to the field at all times if the Show Drop-Down Arrow checkbox is checked in the Drop-Down List dialog box (accessed from the Define List button in the Basics panel of the Info Box). If the checkbox was not checked, the arrow only appears when you select the field.

To choose a value, click the arrow adjacent to the field to drop down the list of values. A list of up to eight value choices appears. If the list contains more values, a scroll bar also appears. You can also type a new value into the Field box & list. The SPECIALTY field in the Owl Publishing database is an example of a Field box & list.

Note

Within a Field box & list field using typed-in values, you cannot move to a value in the list by typing the first letter of the value. Your keystroke is interpreted as the first character of a typed-in value.

Checkboxes

Checkboxes are useful when a field can have only one of two possible values (such as On/Off, Yes/No, or Satisfied/Unsatisfied). Checkboxes have on and off values, which are set using the Define Checkbox dialog box (discussed in Chapter 4). Clicking a checkbox turns it on (an X appears in the box) and stores the on value in that field of the database. Clicking it again turns it off (the X disappears) and stores the off value instead.

In the Owl Publishing database, the MAILED? field is an example of a checkbox.

Radio Buttons

To choose from a set of radio buttons, click the button that corresponds to the value you want to enter. Clicking another button in the set selects that button and deselects the first one. In a set of three radio buttons denoting shipment methods in the Owl Publishing database, for example, you can choose only one of three options: U.S. Mail, Federal Express, or UPS.

Entering Sample Records

Owl Publishing has its first customer! You need to enter that customer's record into the database that you created in Chapter 2.

Note

Before trying the next example, delete any sample records you may have added. Also be sure that the CUSTOMER ID field (a serial-number field whose value Approach sets automatically) starts with 1 for the records you enter. Otherwise, the records added in the following example will have a different customer ID number.

To reset the customer ID serial number, follow these steps:

1. Open the **C**reate menu and choose Field **D**efinition to open the Field Definition dialog box.

2. Click the CUST ID field in the Field Definition dialog box.

3. Click the **O**ptions button. The bottom portion (Default Value and Validation) of the Field Definition dialog box appears.

4. Make sure that a 1 is in the **S**erial number starting at the text box. If any other number appears, change it to 1. Then click the **S**erial number starting at the button.

5. Click OK to return to the form.

6. Click the Delete Record SmartIcon to delete any sample records you may have built.

7. Open the **F**ile menu and choose **S**ave Approach File.

To enter the first record of the Owl Publishing database, follow these steps:

1. Open the **V**iew menu and choose **B**rowse to switch to Browse mode.

2. Click the New Record SmartIcon.

3. Click the FIRST NAME field in the form; then type **Joseph**.

4. Press Tab to move to the LAST NAME field; then type **Jones**.

5. Type **Jones and Jones** for the FIRM NAME field.

6. Type **123 Felton Place** for the STREET ADDRESS field.

7. For the CITY, STATE, and ZIP CODE fields, type **New York**, **NY**, and **10019**.

8. For the LEGAL SPECIALTY field, type **FM**.

> **Note**
>
> You don't need to enter a mail type value (from the radio buttons) or # of Renewal Notes value for every record, because renewal notes aren't sent to companies with subscriptions that aren't about to expire.

9. For the NEWSLETTER SUBSCRIBED TO field, type **Assault Today** as the newsletter name.

10. Enter a START DATE of **12/27/93** and an END DATE of **12/27/94**.
11. Enter a COST of **150.00**.
12. Press Enter.

Now you can practice entering some additional records into the database. (This way, you will also have some records to experiment with later.) Table 5.1 shows values for some of the fields in the database. You won't place a value in every field, but you can enter values in the other fields, if you like.

Tip
You can also press Tab from the last field on a record to enter the record and move to the first field on a new record.

Note

Remember to click the New Record SmartIcon before entering each new record. If you don't want to add another new record, press Esc to cancel the record—the previous record will still be saved.

Table 5.1 Records for the Owl Publishing Database

First Name:	**John**	Newsletter Title:	**Assault Today**
Last Name:	**Roberts**	Sub Start:	**12/15/93**
Firm Name:	**Diddle & Diddle**	Sub End:	**12/15/94**
Street Address:	**217 Romie Lane**	Price:	**$150**
City:	**New York**	Renew Notes:	**1**
State:	**NY**	Mail Type:	UPS
Zip:	**10019**	Specialty:	PI
First Name:	**Marcy**	Newsletter Title:	**Burglary Made Simple**
Last Name:	**Pettis**	Sub Start:	**1/12/93**
Firm Name:	**Pettis and Co.**	Sub End:	**1/12/94**
Street Address:	**98 Snider Road**	Price:	**$175**
City:	**New York**	Renew Notes:	**0**
State:	**NY**	Mail Type:	
Zip:	**10023**	Specialty:	FM

(continues)

Table 5.1 Continued			
First Name:	**David**	Newsletter Title:	**Assault Today**
Last Name:	**Green**	Sub Start:	**11/14/93**
Firm Name:	**Black and Blue, Inc.**	Sub End:	**11/14/94**
Street Address:	**1902 Christina Ave.**	Price:	**$150**
City:	**Buffalo**	Renew Notes:	
State:	**NY**	Mail Type:	
Zip:	**10342**	Specialty:	EM
First Name:	**George**	Newsletter Title:	**Burglary Made Simple**
Last Name:	**Kinder**	Sub Start:	**05/12/93**
Firm Name:	**Kinder & Garten**	Sub End:	**05/12/94**
Street Address:	**444 Yearling Ave.**	Price:	**$175**
City:	**Smallville**	Renew Notes:	**2**
State:	**NY**	Mail Type:	U.S. Mail
Zip:		Specialty:	EM
First Name:	**Martin**	Newsletter Title:	**Employment Today**
Last Name:	**Braun**	Sub Start:	**11/12/92**
Firm Name:	**Brainz & Braun**	Sub End:	**11/12/93**
Street Address:	**12239 Park Ave.**	Price:	**$195**
City:	**New York**	Renew Notes:	**2**
State:	**NY**	Mail Type:	U.S. Mail
Zip:	**10019**	Specialty:	EM
First Name:	**Harriet**	Newsletter Title:	**Employment Today**
Last Name:	**Dee**	Sub Start:	**12/12/93**
Firm Name:	**Fiddle, Dee & Dee**	Sub End:	**12/12/94**
Street Address:	**909 High Street**	Price:	**$195**

City:	**Buffalo**	Renew Notes:	
State:	**NY**	Mail Type:	
Zip:	**10342**	Specialty:	EM

Navigating Through Your Records

After you have a few records in your database, you must be able to page through them. You can use the SmartIcons, the status bar, or the keyboard to do so. The following sections discuss these different methods.

Using the SmartIcon Bar to Navigate Records

You can use the group of arrow keys that appear on the SmartIcon bar to move through the database:

- To move to the next record in the database, click the Next Record SmartIcon.

- To move to the preceding record in the database, click the Previous Record SmartIcon.

- To move to the first record in the database, click the First Record SmartIcon.

- To move to the last record in the database, click the Last Record SmartIcon.

Using the Status Bar to Navigate Records

The status bar also contains three controls that you can use to move through the database (see fig. 5.6):

- To move to the next record in the database, click the Next Record button.
- To move to the preceding record in the database, click the Previous Record button.
- To move to any record in the database, click the Record Number button. The Go To Record dialog box appears. Enter the appropriate record number and then click OK.

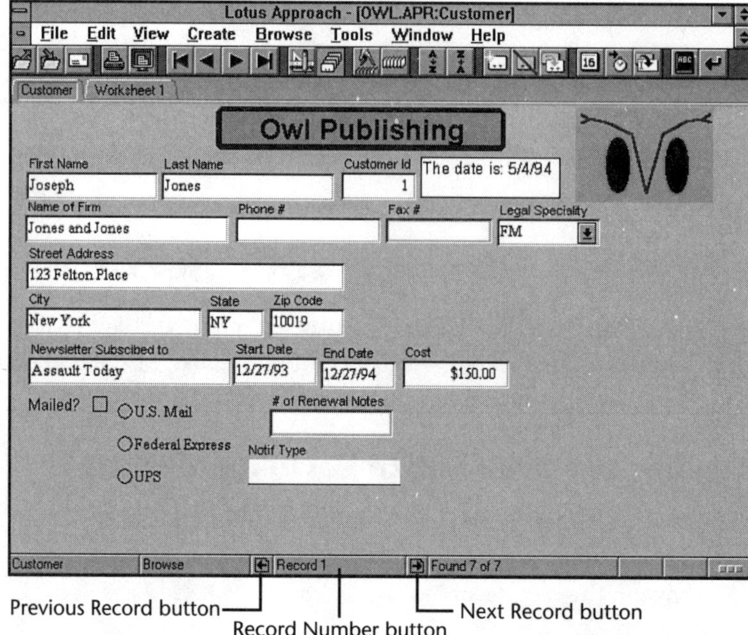

Fig. 5.6
Navigation controls on the status bar.

Using the Keyboard to Navigate Records

You can also use the keyboard to navigate through your records:

- To move to the next record in the database, press PgDn.
- To move to the preceding record in the database, press PgUp.
- To move to the first record in the database, press Ctrl+Home.
- To move to the last record in the database, press Ctrl+End.

Sorting Records

By default, Approach displays records in the order in which they were entered. This order may not always be the one you want. Rearranging the records in a certain order makes finding groups of similar records easier.

Tip
Descending order is especially helpful for date fields because the most recent date appears at the top of the list.

You can sort, or rearrange, the records temporarily based on the values contained in one or more fields. You can also establish a default sort order for records. The default sort order is the order in which the records are displayed when no other (temporary) sort orders are in effect. For any sort, the field values can be sorted in ascending or descending order. In ascending order, the records are sorted from lowest value to highest value. Text values are sorted A-Z; numeric values are sorted low to high; dates and times are sorted earliest to latest. In descending order the opposite is true—the records are sorted from highest to lowest value.

After you sort your records, the new order affects how the records are viewed, updated, and printed. For example, if you sort the subscription database by newsletter names, all subscriptions for a particular newsletter appear together. If you sort by date instead, all subscriptions appear in chronological order.

Note

Except for the default sort order, all sort orders are temporary. If you perform a query (as discussed in Chapter 6), click the Show All SmartIcon, or close the view, the records revert to their default sort order. However, you can establish a macro that recreates the sort order with the click of a button (see Chapter 13 for more information about macros).

Sorting On One Field

The simplest type of sort is the single-field sort. As the name implies, you choose a single field in the database in which to sort the records. For example, in the sample database, you can sort the database by firm name to get an idea of which firms are subscribing to which newsletters. To sort on one field, follow these steps:

1. Switch to Browse mode by opening the **V**iew menu and choosing **B**rowse, clicking the Browse SmartIcon, or choosing Browse from the status bar.

2. Open the **B**rowse menu and choose Sor**t** De**f**ine, or click the Open Sort Dialog SmartIcon. The Sort dialog box appears.

3. In the Database **F**ields list box at the left side of the dialog box, select the field you want to use for your primary sort field (the field by which the database is sorted). For Owl Publishing, select FIRM NAME from the field list.

   Your Sort dialog box should look like the one shown in figure 5.7.

4. Click the **A**dd button or double-click the field to move the field to the Fields To **S**ort On list box.

5. Choose Asc**e**nding or **D**escending to determine whether the database is sorted in ascending or descending order on that field. Use Asc**e**nding for this example.

6. Click OK to sort the records.

Tip
Rather than performing steps 3 and 4, you can double-click the field to move it to the **S**ort list box.

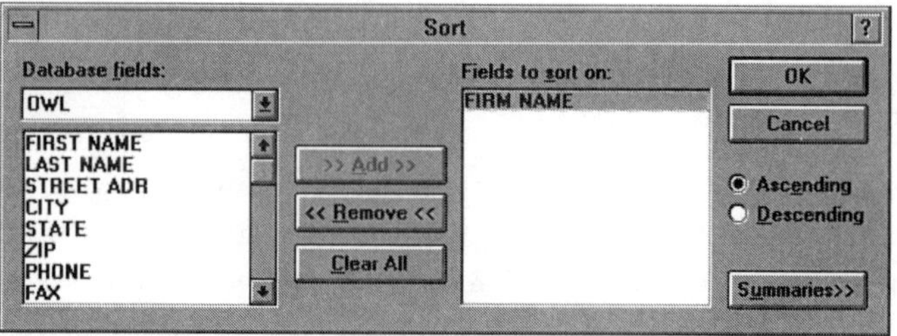

Fig. 5.7
Setting up to sort records by FIRM NAME.

When you return to the form, try paging through the records. Now they appear in alphabetical order by FIRM NAME rather than in the order in which they were entered. Figure 5.8 shows the Worksheet view of the records in the database (see Chapter 14 for information on how to create worksheets). The records appear in their sorted order.

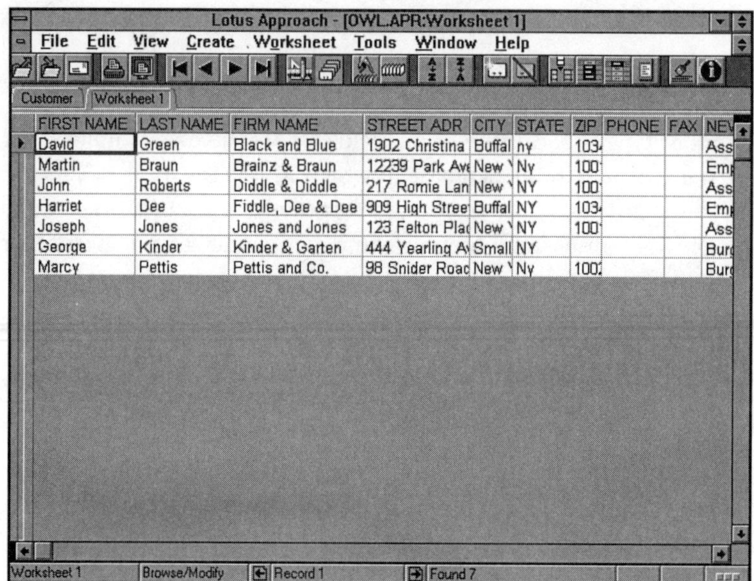

Fig. 5.8
The records appear in order in the Worksheet view.

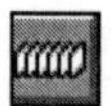

If you want to return to the default order (the order in which the records were entered), click the Show All SmartIcon or open the **B**rowse menu and choose Show **A**ll.

There is another way to easily sort the records on a single field in ascending order. Simply click the field you want to sort and then open the **B**rowse menu and choose Sor**t** **A**scending, or click the Sort Ascending SmartIcon.

To sort the records in descending order, click the field and open the **B**rowse menu and choose Sor**t** **D**escending, or click the Sort Descending SmartIcon.

Sorting Records on Multiple Fields

You can sort your database on more than one field by adding more fields to the **S**ort list box before clicking OK in the Sort dialog box. To do so, select additional fields in the order you want them sorted, clicking the **A**dd button for each selected field to move it to the **S**ort list. To establish the sort order for each additional field, choose Asc**e**nding or **D**escending.

These newly added fields, called secondary sort fields, affect the sort order of the database within the order established by the primary sort field. In other words, the records are sorted first by the primary field; and then, for all records with the same primary sort field value, the records are sorted by the first secondary field. If any records have the same values for the primary and secondary fields, they are sorted by the next secondary field, if any, and so on.

If the primary field in the Fields To **S**ort On list is NEWSLETTER (the Newsletter subscribed to, in Asc**e**nding order), for example, and the secondary field is SUB START (the Start Date, in **D**escending order), the newsletter subscriptions are sorted in alphabetical order by the name of the newsletter. The first block of records includes all the entries for *Assault Today*, followed by a block of records for *Burglary Made Simple*, and so on. All the entries for *Assault Today* would be sorted by their subscription date, with the most recent subscriptions appearing first. All the entries for *Burglary Made Simple* would also be sorted by subscription date.

Figure 5.9 shows a list of some records that may appear in the new sort order.

If you decide that you don't want one of the fields in the Fields To **S**ort On list, select it and choose **R**emove or double-click the field. If you make a mistake and decide to start over, choose **C**lear All to erase all fields in the Fields To **S**ort On list box (thus making them available again in the Database **F**ields list).

After you set up the sort order the way you want it, click OK to sort the records. Although Approach is very fast, the program may pause while it sorts the records.

Setting the Default Sort Order

Approach enables you to set the default sort order for a database. This default order is the order in which the records appear when no other sort order is in effect. To disable other sort orders and return to the default sort order, you can change views, open the **B**rowse menu and choose Show **A**ll, or click the Find All Records SmartIcon.

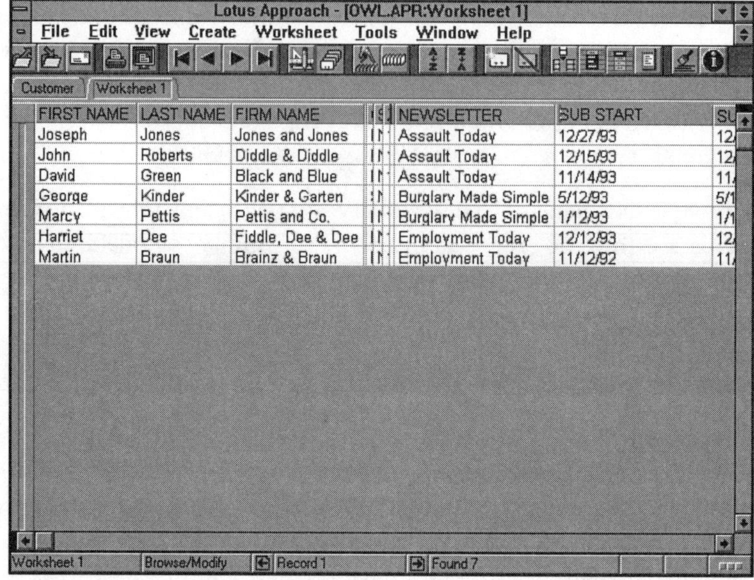

Fig. 5.9
Records sorted by newsletter name and subscription date.

To set the default sort order, open the **T**ools menu and choose **P**references to open the Preferences dialog box. Click the Order tab to move to the Order panel (see fig. 5.10). Select the database for which you want to maintain the default sort order from the **M**aintain Default Sort For drop-down list. Set the default order using the Database **F**ields list and Fields To **S**ort On list. When you are finished setting up the sort order, click OK or the **S**ave Default button.

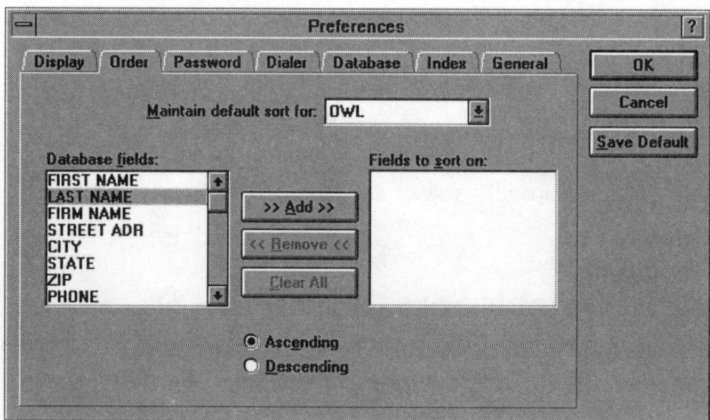

Fig. 5.10
You can set the default database sort order using the Preferences dialog box.

Using the Spell Checker

Approach can check the spelling of text in your Approach files and databases. The text that Approach checks for you depends on which mode you are in:

- In Browse mode, Approach checks the spelling of data in all fields, including memo fields, checkboxes, radio buttons, and PicturePlus fields.
- In Design mode, Approach checks the spelling of text in field labels and text objects, including text in the body of form letters. Approach also checks headers and footers on reports.

> **Note**
>
> The spell checker is not available in Preview or Find modes.

Approach's spell checker compares the appropriate entries with the contents of a main dictionary and user dictionary. The main dictionary comes with Approach and can't be edited. The user dictionary is for words that are not in the main dictionary. These words often include proper names and technical terms. You can add and delete words from the user dictionary at any time.

Running the Spell Checker

You must be in Browse or Design mode to run the spell checker. Follow these steps:

1. Select any text you want to spell check. If you don't select any text before running the spell checker, Approach checks all text.

   In Browse mode, you can select all or part of the text in a field. In Design mode, you can select text in a text object or an entire text object. If you select a text object, Approach checks all the text in the text object.

2. Open the **T**ools menu and choose **S**pell Check or click the Spell Check SmartIcon. The Spell Check dialog box opens (see fig. 5.11). Select the options you want for the spell check:

   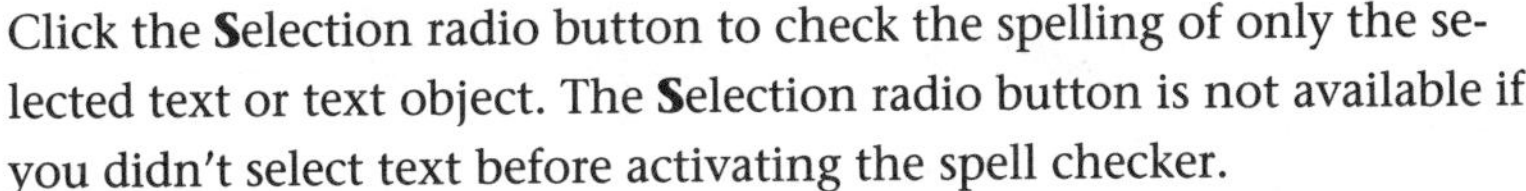

   Click the **S**election radio button to check the spelling of only the selected text or text object. The **S**election radio button is not available if you didn't select text before activating the spell checker.

   Current Record (Browse mode) spell checks all the text in fields in the current record. **C**urrent View (Design mode) spell checks all the text in the current view (form, report, form letter, or mailing label).

Found Set (Browse mode only) spell checks all records in the found set. A found set is a special set of records that meet criteria you specify (see Chapter 6 for more information on Finds). After you specify the Find criteria, Approach displays all records that match this criteria.

Selection **A**cross Found Set (Browse mode only) spell checks the selected text in all records in the found set. This option is not available if you did not select text prior to running the spell checker.

Click the **M**emo Fields Only checkbox if you only want to check the text in memo fields. This is handy because you often type the bulk of the text you want spell checked into memo fields. Other fields also often contain proper names and technical terms that are not in your dictionary.

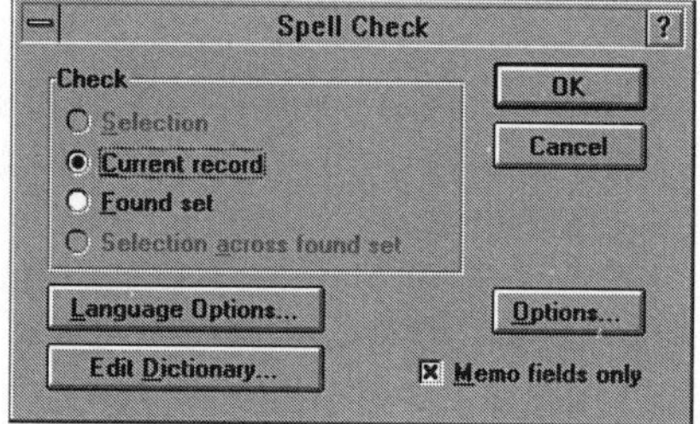

Fig. 5.11
The Spell Check dialog box.

3. Click OK. Approach begins the spell check. If Approach finds a word that is not in its dictionary, another Spell Check dialog box opens (see fig. 5.12). Approach displays the unknown word on a line at the top of the dialog box. If Approach does not find any unknown words, an alert box pops up to inform you that the spell check is complete.

Spell Check
Unknown word: U.S
Replace with: U.S
Alternatives:
US
Replace All
Replace
Skip All
Skip
Add To Dictionary
Close

Fig. 5.12
Approach displays a word that may be misspelled.

4. For unknown words, Approach suggests possible replacements in the **Al**ternatives list. To pick an alternative, click the word so that it appears in the Replace **W**ith text box. You can also type in a replacement word or edit one of the alternatives in the Replace **W**ith text box.

To replace the word, click R**e**place or **R**eplace All. R**e**place replaces this occurrence of the unknown word. If the word appears again later, Approach will question it again. **R**eplace All replaces all occurrences of the word in the text you are checking.

To skip a word, click S**k**ip or **S**kip All. S**k**ip skips this occurrence of the word. If the unknown word appears again later, Approach will question it again. **S**kip All skips all occurrences of the word in the text you are checking.

To accept a word and add it to the dictionary, click **A**dd to Dictionary. Approach will not question the word in future spell checks in any Approach file.

5. Once you have decided what to do with a questioned word, click OK in the Spell Check dialog box. Approach moves to the next unknown word. When Approach has completed checking the spelling, it displays an alert box to let you know that the spell check is complete.

Setting the Spell Checker Options

You can specify different spell checker options, such as whether you want Approach to find repeated words. These options take effect when you click OK and become the new default for the spell checker. The following are some options you can select:

- *Check for* ***R****epeated Words*. This option finds words that appear twice in a row, such as "the the."
- *Check Words with* ***N****umbers*. This option checks words that contain numbers, such as "Junior2." The number must be included in the word in the dictionary or Approach will flag the word as unknown.
- *Check Words with* ***I****nitial Caps*. This option checks the spelling of words that begin with a capital letter, such as Berlin. Approach checks all words at the beginning of a sentence whether this option is checked or not.
- *Include* ***U****ser Dictionary Alternatives*. This option includes words from the user dictionary when Approach displays possible replacement words.

Editing the User Dictionary

The user dictionary contains any words that you have added to the main dictionary. The contents of the user dictionary are often proper nouns or technical terms that are not found in a general-purpose dictionary. If you click **A**dd to Dictionary when Approach displays an unknown word, the new word is added to the user dictionary. You can edit the user dictionary to add or delete words from it. To edit the user dictionary, follow these steps:

1. Open the **T**ools menu and choose **S**pell Check or click the Spell Check SmartIcon. The Spell Check dialog box opens.

2. Click Edit **D**ictionary. The Edit Dictionary dialog box opens (see fig. 5.13).

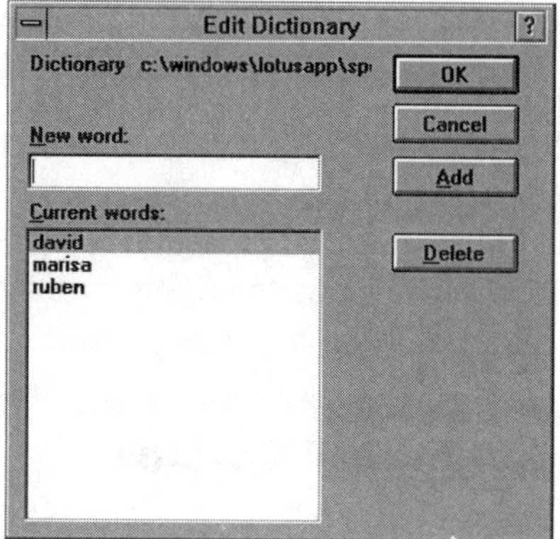

Fig. 5.13
Use the user dictionary to add, edit, and delete words.

3. To add a new word to the dictionary, type the word in the **N**ew Word text box. Click the **A**dd button to add the word to the list of current words contained in the dictionary.

4. To delete a word, click the word in the **C**urrent Words list box and then click **D**elete.

5. Click OK to save the changes, or Cancel to return to the previous version of the user dictionary.

Tip
Once you click the **C**urrent Words list box, you can move the selection bar to pick a word using the arrow keys.

From Here...

In this chapter, you learned how to enter data into the carefully crafted forms that you build in Approach. You also learned how to create and delete records, move through fields on a form, enter data into fields and value lists, and use checkboxes and radio buttons. You also explored the constraints for entering data into date, number, time, and Boolean fields.

After you had a database full of records, you moved from one record to another and sorted the records to look at them in a desired order. Finally, you learned how to spell check your work.

Once you have data in your database, there is quite a lot you can do. For related information, see the following chapters in this book:

- Chapter 6, "Finding Records," teaches you how to locate specific data in your database.
- Chapter 14, "Using Worksheets and Crosstabs," discusses how to look at your data in a spreadsheet-like format and create special cross-reference reports called "crosstabs."
- Chapter 15, "Creating Charts," shows you how to create a pictorial representation of your data.

Chapter 6

Finding Records

Computer-based databases excel at finding records that match the criteria (search conditions) you define. In fact, this capability to locate information quickly is probably what persuades people to switch to a computer for storing their records.

Suppose your address book has a section that indicates all the people who sent you Christmas cards last year. If you want to create a list of those people, you would need to search through your address book by hand. With Approach, you can tell the computer to find that information for you, and even to create a set of mailing labels to send cards to those people this year.

Approach has a powerful set of functions for locating information and making it available to you by an operation called *performing a find*. Performing a find enables you to locate records in your database that contain information in which you are interested. For example, you can find all the records for customers that live in California. Approach can handle some very sophisticated finds, such as finding everyone whose Legal Specialty is "EM" or "PI."

The *found set* consists of those records that meet the find criteria. After performing a find and obtaining the found set, you can perform operations on just the found records until you decide to return to the entire database.

The more advanced querying functions, such as conditional finds (IF) and "sounds-like" finds, are discussed in Chapter 11.

In this chapter, you learn how to:

- Set up and run a search
- Perform searches for specific types of data, such as text, dates, and times
- Find a range of values or duplicate values

- Find blank or non-blank values
- Modify or cancel a search
- Use multiple criteria for a search
- Hide or delete a found set of records

Setting Up and Running a Find

To perform a find, Approach uses the data input forms you created earlier in Chapters 3 and 4. The first step in setting up a find is to decide which form you want to use. The form you choose must contain the field(s) for which you want to specify criteria.

After you decide which form to use, switch to Browse mode by opening the **V**iew menu and choosing **B**rowse, clicking the Browse SmartIcon, or by choosing Browse from the status bar. Select the form you want to use by clicking the form tabs (see fig. 6.1). You can also use the status bar to select the form.

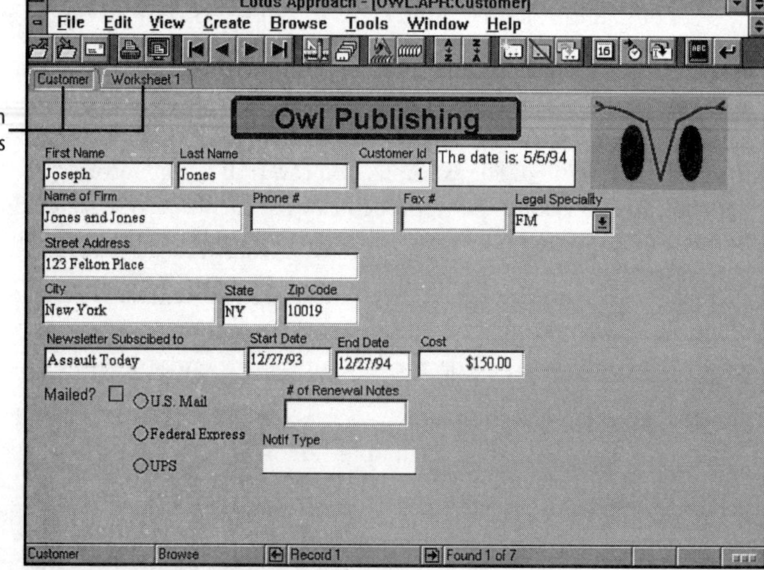

Form tabs

Fig. 6.1
Before searching, select your form using the form tabs.

To build the find, open the **B**rowse menu and choose **F**ind, click the Find SmartIcon, or select Find from the status bar. The form clears and none of your data is visible. Approach displays the Find SmartIcon bar.

Enter the Find Criteria on the form. You can enter find criteria for multiple fields before executing the find. To enter the find criteria, follow these steps:

1. Click each field (or move to the field using the tab key on the keyboard) in which you want to enter find criteria.

2. Type the find criteria, including any find operators. You can type in a find operator (such as a question mark) or click the equivalent SmartIcon to place that operator in the criteria. The find operators are discussed in Table 6.1, and the following sections explain how to specify find criteria.

3. When you are done entering the find criteria on all fields you want to include in the find, press Enter, click OK in the Find bar, or click the Enter SmartIcon.

Figure 6.2 illustrates a query for which you want to find all records where the newsletter title is *Assault Today*. The text string `Assault Today` is the search criteria, and the field being searched is the NEWSLETTER SUBSCRIBED TO field.

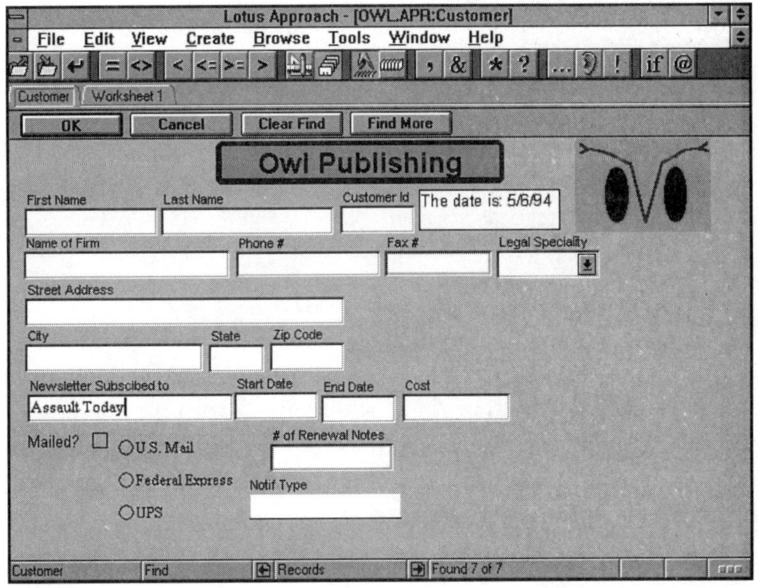

Fig. 6.2
Type your search criteria in the appropriate field.

The find executes and creates the found set. The status bar at the bottom of the screen indicates how many total records in the database are in the found set (see fig. 6.3).

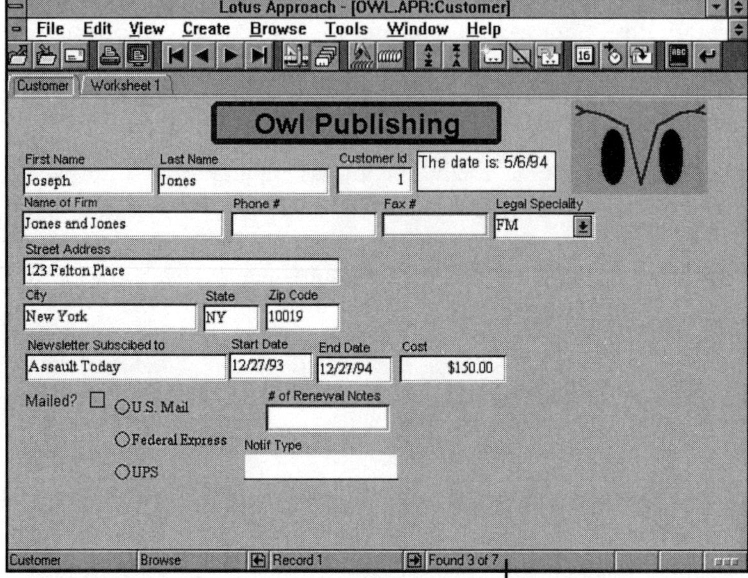

Fig. 6.3
The status bar shows how many records meet your criteria.

While the found set is active, use the arrow buttons on the SmartIcon bar, the page icons on the status bar, or the keyboard record navigation keys (PgUp, PgDn, Ctrl+Home, and Ctrl+End) to move through only the found set.

To return to the full set of records in your database, click the Show All SmartIcon or open the **B**rowse menu and choose Show **A**ll. The status bar now indicates that all records are available.

Specifying the Find Criteria

When you enter the find criteria into a field, you can use text and special find operators that modify how Approach interprets the text you have entered. These operators are symbols such as !, =, &, ?, and *, and are described in Table 6.1. Used with standard text, find operators enable you to specify further searching operations for Approach.

While Approach is in Find mode, find operators appear on the SmartIcon bar. Table 6.1 also shows these SmartIcons.

If you need to enter find criteria that contains one of these operators, you must enclose the text in the criteria in single quotation marks. For example, if you are looking for the phrase Guilty? in the NAME OF FIRM field, you would type **'Jones and Jones?'** (enclosed in single quotes) in the NAME OF FIRM field.

Table 6.1 The Approach Find Operators

Operator	Description	SmartIcon
=	Finds exact matches (by itself, finds blank records)	=
<	Less than	<
>	Greater than	>
< =	Less than or equal to	<=
> =	Greater than or equal to	>=
...	Within the range	...
, (comma)	Separates multiple criteria in a single field (OR)	,
*	Wild card for any number of characters	*
?	Wild card for one character	?
@	Field compared to result of following formula. Must be used with a comparison operator	@
!	Case sensitive	!
~	Sounds like	
&	Combines criteria in a single field (AND)	&
< >	Field doesn't match; by itself, finds non-blank records	<>
IF	Conditional finds	if

The next few sections discuss how to create and execute some of the finds in Approach. See Chapter 11 for information on performing more advanced finds.

Finding a Text String

To find all records that match a string of characters, type the text string into the appropriate field. Approach then finds all records in which the contents of that field start with the typed characters. For example, if you type **A** into the NAME OF FIRM field, Approach finds all records in which the firm name begins with the letter A.

Suppose that Owl Publishing wants to find the customer records for all subscribers to *Assault Today*. Follow these steps:

1. Switch to Browse mode by opening the **V**iew menu and choosing **B**rowse, clicking the Browse SmartIcon, or choosing Browse from the status bar.
2. Choose the form you want from the form tabs or the status bar. For this example, select the Customer form from the tabs.

3. Open the **B**rowse menu and choose **F**ind, click the Find SmartIcon, or select Find from the status bar.
4. In the NEWSLETTER SUBSCRIBED TO field, type **Assault**.
5. Press Enter.

Approach finds all records in which the newsletter title begins with the word `Assault`. This search is sufficient for finding all subscribers to *Assault Today* because no other newsletter title begins with that word. If Owl Publishing adds a new newsletter entitled *Assault Monthly*, however, you need to revise the find criteria to **Assault T** to find only *Assault Today* subscribers.

Running Case-Sensitive Finds

Approach isn't normally case sensitive when searching dBASE- or FoxPro-formatted databases. In other words, if you type a string of characters into a field, the records are found whether the string appears in uppercase (capital letters) or lowercase. Typing **dee** into the NAME OF FIRM field, for example, finds all firm names that begin with `dee`—whether they are spelled `Dee`, `dEe`, or `DEE`. To find only those records that match the exact case of what you type, use an exclamation mark (!) in front of the text string. For example, to find only `dee` (and not `Dee`), type **!dee**.

> **Note**
>
> Paradox finds are normally case sensitive. However, you can disable the default using the Database panel of the Preferences dialog box. Click the Case Insensitive radio button to turn off Paradox case sensitivity except when you use the case-sensitive operator (exclamation mark, or !).

Finding an Exact Match

When you type a text string into a field to perform a find, Approach searches to find all records that begin with the text string. However, you can tell Approach to find only those records in which the value in the field exactly matches the text string you entered. To do so, use an equal sign (=) in front of the text string. For example, if you type **=Dee** in the NAME OF FIRM field, you get a list of all records in which the firm name is just `Dee`—but not `Dee and Dee` or any other variation (see fig. 6.4).

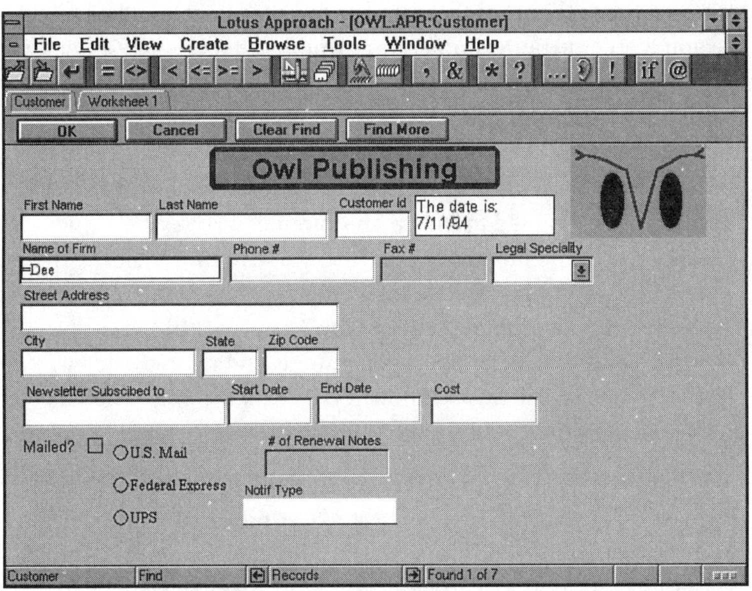

Fig. 6.4
Use an equal sign (=) to find an exact match.

> **Note**
>
> This match isn't case sensitive—you can still get variations such as DEE and dEE. Because you can't combine find operators such as ! and = in a single find criteria, you can't create an exact match and case-sensitive find with a single find criteria.

Using Multiple Search Operators to Find Records

You can use an ampersand (&) to combine find criteria for a single field. Suppose that you want an exact match of a text string. You can't combine the exact match symbol (=) with the match case symbol (!) unless you use the & symbol. This symbol connects both halves of the criteria. Therefore, to match the text string `Dee` exactly, you would enter **!Dee&=Dee** as the criteria in the field.

> **Note**
>
> DO NOT leave any spaces around the & symbol unless the string you are searching for includes a trailing space or a leading space.

Using Wild-Card Characters

With wild-card characters, you can search for text strings when certain characters vary or when you know only a portion of the text string. Suppose that you want to find all the firms where the firm name contains the name `Dee`. Because you aren't guaranteed that this name is the first word in the firm name, using the text search described in the preceding section may not find all occurrences. Therefore, you can use wild cards.

Approach has two wild-card characters:

- The asterisk (*) is used to match any number of characters (including no characters). In the preceding example, you can find the firm(s) you are looking for by typing ***Dee*** as the criteria in the NAME OF FIRM field. This criteria shows any records in which the text string `Dee` appears anywhere in the firm name. If you enter a find criteria, such as **Burg***, in the NEWSLETTER SUBSCRIBED TO field, a list of newsletters whose name begins with `Burg` appears.

- The question mark (?) is used to match a single character. You can enter as many question marks as you want. To find a text string that is exactly four characters long and begins with B, for example, type **B???** as the criteria. To find a text string with any two characters, followed by the text `day` and two more characters, type **??day??** as the criteria.

You can combine the * and ? in a single search criteria. For example, to find a string that begins with any single character, followed by the text string `day`, and followed by anything else, you enter **?day*** (see fig. 6.5).

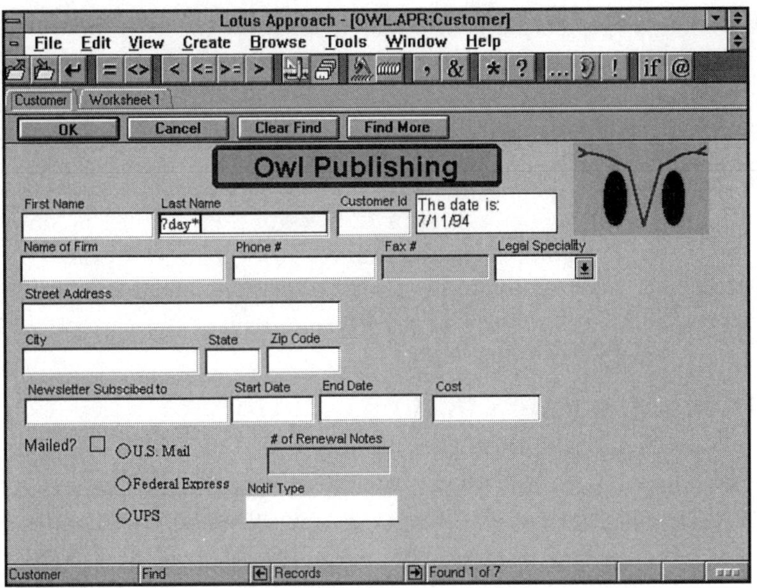

Fig. 6.5
You can combine wild-card characters for powerful searches.

Finding Numbers, Dates, and Times

Numbers, dates, and times work differently from text values. Finds on values typed into numeric, date, and time fields are always exact matches—you never need to use the = operator to specify an exact match with these types of fields.

> **Note**
>
> Make sure that the field into which you type your criteria is truly a numeric, date, or time field. Often, text fields are used to store numeric, date, or time values. The rules for finding values in text fields apply to these fields. Using the text field search rules can actually be advantageous in certain circumstances. Zip codes, for example, are assigned according to a system—codes starting with 9 are in west coast states. If you want to send mail to customers in these states, you can use a simple criteria in the ZIP CODE field: **9**. If the ZIP CODE field is numeric, you need more complex criteria.

The criteria for finding numbers, dates, and times is as follows:

- To find a number in a numeric or calculated field, type the number into the field and press Enter. (See Chapter 10 for more information on calculated fields.)

- To find a date in a date or calculated field, type the date into the field and press Enter. Type the date as numbers separated by a non-numeric character such as the slash character (for example, **12/31/94**). Entering the date in this format finds the date in any format.

- To find a time in a time or calculated field, use the hh:mm:ss syntax, using 24-hour (military) time or 12-hour time. Press Enter. Be sure to fill in zeroes for missing digits (for example, use **03** for 3 am) and separate the portions of the time with colons. Entering the time in 24-hour or 12-hour format finds the time in either format.

Entering Values in Checkbox, Button, and Value-List Fields

During a find, you can type the needed criteria into text, numeric, date, and time field boxes. However, checkbox, radio button, and drop-down list fields don't allow you to type in values, even during a find. To enter the criteria for these field types, you must enter the value just as you would when filling in those values on a form, as follows:

- For checkboxes, click the checkbox to indicate that you want to search for all instances in which the checkbox is marked. To search for all instances in which the checkbox is not selected, click the checkbox twice—once to turn on the checkbox (an X appears), and again to turn it off (the checkbox is empty). Otherwise, the checkbox is not used as part of the selection criteria.

- For radio button sets, click the button that represents the value for which you want to search (see fig. 6.6).

- For drop-down lists and Field box & list fields, either click the list to make it drop down and select the value you want, or type the value you want to search for. To search for a particular specialty on the Owl Publishing form, you can click the LEGAL SPECIALTY field and select the Specialty code you want. You can also type in the code.

Note

Because you can't type values into checkboxes or buttons, you can't use any of the special query operators (wild cards, ranges, OR, AND, and so on). If you need to use these operators to search checkboxes or buttons, you must create another form in which these fields are formatted as default (text) field boxes rather than as checkboxes or buttons. You can also use an IF find, as discussed in Chapter 11.

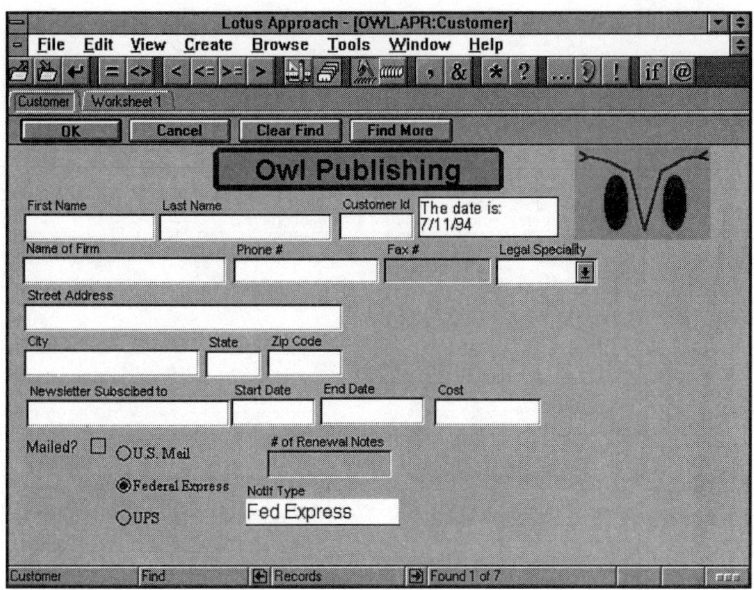

Fig. 6.6
Clicking a radio-button value simplifies searching.

Finding a Range of Values

Approach can find records in which fields are greater than a given value, less than a given value, or between two values (range). You can use text, numeric, and date and time fields in a range find. Range finds are discussed in the following sections.

Finding a Greater Than Value

To find values in a field that are larger than a comparison value, use the > (greater than) symbol, followed by the comparison value. To include records in which the fields also contain the comparison value in the found set, use the >= (greater than or equal to) symbol instead.

For example, to find all text values that don't begin with A (that is, text values that begin with B, C, D, and so on), type **>Az** or **>=B**. To find a date later than 01/01/94, type **>01/01/94**. To find a number greater than or equal to 0, type **>=0**.

Finding a Less Than Value

To find values in a field that are smaller than a comparison value, use the < (less than) symbol, followed by the comparison value (see fig. 6.7). To include fields that also contain the comparison value in the found set, use the <= (less than or equal to) symbol instead.

For example, to find all text values that are "less than Bob" (those that start with an earlier combination of letters in the alphabet, such as "Albert" or "Bab") type **<Bob**. To find all dates earlier than 1994, use **<01/01/94** or **<=12/31/93**. To find all negative numbers, use **<0**.

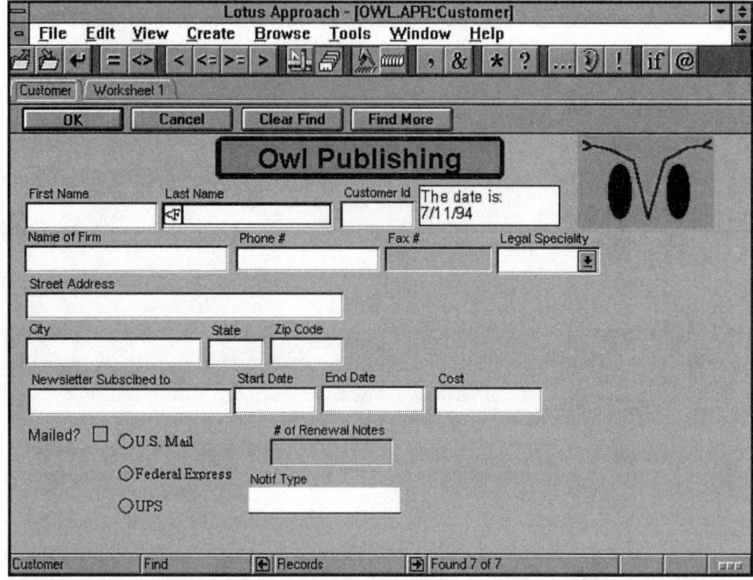

Fig. 6.7
Use the < symbol to find all records where a value is less than your search criteria.

Finding a Value Between Two Values

To find fields with values that fall between two specified values, use an ellipsis (indicated by three dots, or ...) between the two values that define the range. To find all dates in 1994, for example, type **01/01/94...12/31/94**. The values that define the range are included in the range of the found set. In this example, fields with a value of 01/01/94 or 12/31/94 are included in the found set.

> **Note**
>
> You must specify the range with the lower value on the left and the higher value on the right (12/31/94 is later than 01/01/94, and is a higher value). Approach cannot find records if you fail to specify your ranges in this manner.

To find a range of numbers in a numeric field, type the limits of the range. For example, to find all values between 1 and 10, inclusive, type **1...10**. If your range includes negative numbers, remember that negative numbers get smaller as the number value gets larger (–100 is smaller than –10).

Finding ranges of text works the same way. To find all text strings that begin with letters in the first half of the alphabet, type **A...M**.

> **Note**
>
> Only certain operators can be combined in a single criterion. You can combine multiple wild-card operators (such as ***day?** or **??d*a***). You can also combine single criterion with the & symbol. However, you can't combine any other operators in a single criterion. Thus, you can't use wild cards with the range find. Also, because you can't combine the ! operator with the range find, the find is not case sensitive.

Let's return to the Owl Publishing example for a moment. Suppose that Owl Publishing wants to find all subscription-end dates in 1994. Switch to Find mode by opening the **B**rowse menu and choosing **F**ind, clicking the Find SmartIcon, or by selecting **F**ind from the status bar. Type **01/01/94... 01/01/95** into the END DATE field (see fig. 6.8) and press Enter.

After you finish inspecting the records that meet this criteria, click the Show All SmartIcon to return to the entire database.

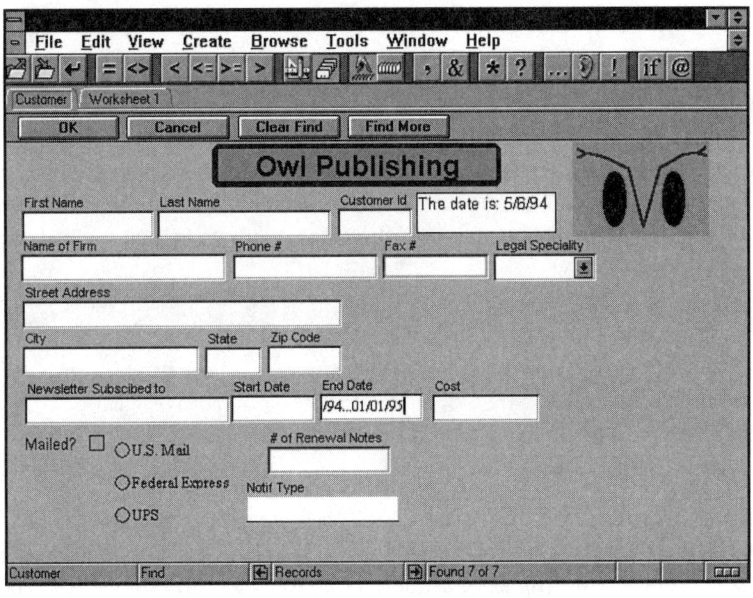

Fig. 6.8
Use the ellipsis to find records within a date range.

Using the & Symbol

You can use the & symbol with the comparison operators (<, >, > =, and < =) to define a range search. Although using the & symbol involves more typing than using the ellipsis, you can be more specific about the limits on the range. With the ellipsis, you must include the ends of the range in the found set. With the & symbol and comparison operators, however, you can specify the ends of the range without including those ends in the found set. That is, you can find all values between `Ab` and `Mo`, excluding those values (or including only one of them).

You can set up a & find in three steps:

1. Use the < or < = operator, as described earlier, to define the high end of the range.
2. Use the > or > = operator, as described earlier, to define the low end of the range.
3. Join the two criteria with &.

For example:

- To find all text strings in a field between `Ab` and `Mo` but excluding those values, type **>Ab&<Mo** in the field.
- To include the low end of the range (`Ab`) and everything up to `Mo` but excluding `Mo`, type **>=Ab&<Mo**.
- To include the high end of the range (`Mo`) and everything down to `Ab` but excluding `Ab`, type **>Ab&<=Mo**.
- To include both ends in the range and everything in between, type **>=Ab&<=Mo**. This syntax has the same result as using an ellipsis.

Note

Remember, you can't use wild-card, case-sensitive, or exact-match operators in this type of range find because these operators cannot be combined with any other operators.

Finding Duplicate Records

In the process of entering large amounts of data, you can enter some records with duplicate data. Approach provides a way to find all the records with duplicate data in any combination of fields. You can select any fields on a form, including drop-down lists, radio buttons, and checkboxes, although these types of fields will usually have values that duplicate other records.

To find duplicate records, follow these steps:

1. Switch to Browse mode by opening the **V**iew menu and choosing **B**rowse, clicking the Browse SmartIcon, or choosing Browse from the status bar.

2. Open the **B**rowse menu and choose Find Spe**c**ial. The Find Special dialog box appears (see fig. 6.9).

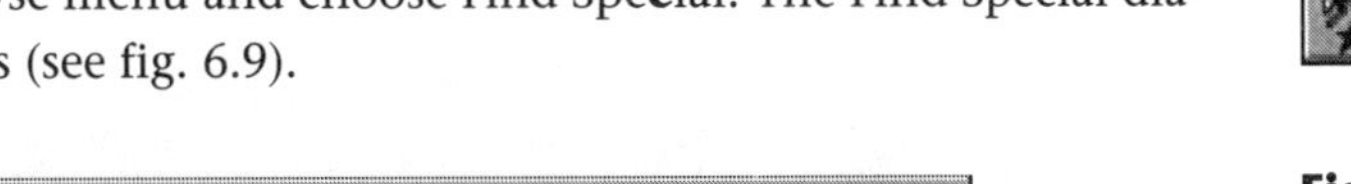

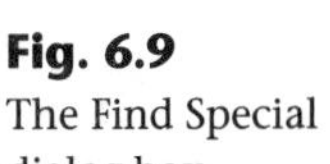

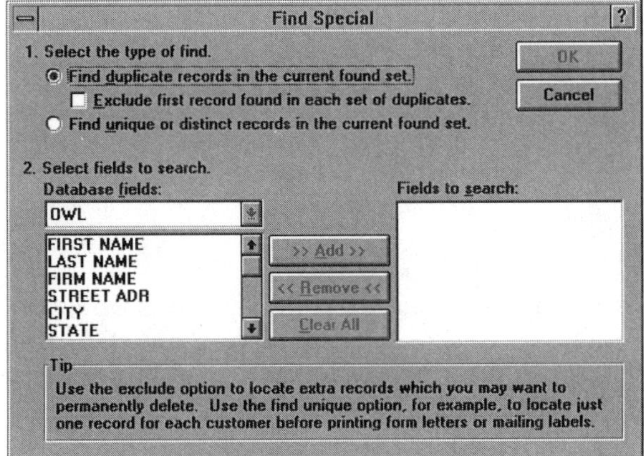

Fig. 6.9
The Find Special dialog box.

3. From the Database **F**ields list box on the left side of the dialog box, click the first field that you want to check for duplicates.

4. Click **A**dd to move the field to the Fields to **S**earch list box. (To remove a field from the Fields to **S**earch list box, select that field and then click **R**emove.) You can also double-click a field to add or remove it.

5. Repeat steps 3 and 4 as needed to move all the fields that you want to check for duplicates to the Fields to **S**earch list box. Only records that contain duplicates in all the specified fields are included in the found set.

Note

You must select the fields one at a time from the Fields to **S**earch list box and move them by clicking the **A**dd button. The Find Duplicates dialog box doesn't enable you to select multiple fields at one time.

6. At the top of the Find Special dialog box are a pair of radio buttons and a checkbox. Choose the appropriate button:

Option	Description
Find **D**uplicate Records in the Current Found Set	Includes all duplicate records in the found set. This option is handy if you suspect that the duplicates are really errors and you want to edit the values in the fields. If you check the **E**xclude First Record Found in Each Set of Duplicates checkbox, Approach excludes the first duplicate record from the found set. This is handy if the duplicates are errors that you want to delete but you want to leave one record in the database. (See "Deleting the Found Set" later in this chapter.)
Find **U**nique or Distinct Records in the Current Found Set	This option is handy if your database has many duplicates and you want to extract the unique records, perhaps to create a new database with just those records.

Finding Blank Values in Fields

Finding blank fields is important. These fields often represent data omissions. You may not have had the information that went into these fields, or the field is newly added and you need to fill in the information. To find a blank value in a field, type an equal sign (=) into the field on the query form. The found set includes all records in which that field is blank.

Owl Publishing suspects that not all their customers' addresses contain zip codes. To find the blank records for the company using the Data Input form, follow these steps:

1. Switch to Find mode by opening the **B**rowse menu and choosing **F**ind, clicking the Find SmartIcon, or by selecting Find from the status bar.

2. Select the ZIP CODE field.

3. Type = and then press Enter. Any records that have blank zip codes are found.

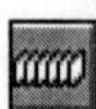

4. After you finish inspecting the found record(s), click the Show All SmartIcon to return to the entire database.

Finding Non-Blank Values in Fields

Finding fields that are not blank is important. Suppose you want to send out a large volume of mail. You don't want to generate mailing labels for customers for whom you don't have a complete address. By checking for non-blank fields, you can generate a found set of customers with values in all the address fields.

To find a non-blank value in a field, switch to Find mode and type < > in the field in which you want to search for non-blanks on the query form. Press Enter to execute the search. The found set includes all records in which that field is not blank.

Using Multiple Criteria in a Single Field

You can find records in which the value in a field matches any of several different criteria. This type of find is called an *OR find* because the record will be part of the found set if the first condition is met OR the second condition is met OR the third condition is met, and so on. The record will be part of the found set if the field meets any of the criteria you type into the field. To build such a find, type the multiple criteria you want into the field, and separate each part with a comma. Do not insert a space after the comma.

If you want a list of all customers whose last name begins with `A` or `J`, for example, type **A,J** into the LAST NAME field.

You can also use this technique in conjunction with the = operator for full-string matches. To find the records of the last names `Abercrombie` or `Johnson`, for example, type **=Abercrombie,=Johnson**. There is no limit to the number of items you can add to this list.

OR searches can contain virtually any operators or combination of operators that are valid in each individual criterion:

- You can use wild cards in OR searches. For example, you can type ***Shell,A??n** to find any value in a field that ends in the word `Shell` or contains a 4-character value beginning with `A` and ending with `n`.
- You can use comparison operators such as > and <. For example, you can find all dates before 1994 or after 1994 (but excluding any dates in 1994) by typing

  <01/01/94,>12/31/94

- You can combine multiple criteria by using the & operator. For example, to find an exact match (including case) on `Dee` or any text strings beginning with `C`, type

  !Dee&=Dee,C

- You can combine all these operators into a complex find. For example, to find an exact match on `Dee`, all text beginning with `C`, or all text starting with `E` through `Z`, type **!Dee&=Dee,C,>=E** (for the last criterion, you can substitute **E...Z** for **>=E**).

Owl Publishing wants to find all the records with the names Roberts or Pettis in the LAST NAME field. To find specific records, follow these steps:

1. Switch to Find mode by opening the **B**rowse menu and choosing **F**ind, clicking the Find SmartIcon, or by selecting Find from the status bar.
2. Type **Roberts,Pettis** in the LAST NAME field (see fig. 6.10). Press Enter.

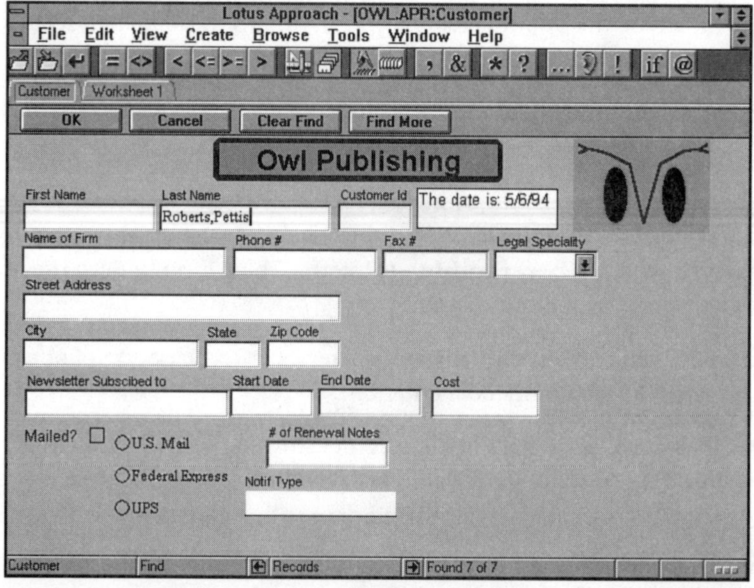

Fig. 6.10 Doing an OR search finds records that contain two different last names.

3. Only two records are now available, those for John Roberts and Marcy Pettis. Inspect them by using the arrow buttons in the SmartIcon bar.

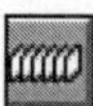

4. Click the Show All SmartIcon to return to the entire database.

Using Multiple Criteria in Different Fields

Approach can search for records in which find conditions have been specified in several different fields. Two different types of multiple field finds are available—an AND find and an OR find.

Setting Up a Multiple-Field AND Find

In a multiple-field AND find, a record is included in the found set only if the first criterion is satisfied AND the second criterion is satisfied AND the third criterion is satisfied, and so on. The record is included only if the fields in the record match all the criteria specified in the find.

You can use any of the operators and techniques discussed earlier on any of the fields, including an OR condition (multiple criteria in a field separated by commas). For example, to find all customers whose last names begin with A or C and who subscribe to the *Burglary Made Simple* newsletter, type **A,C** in the LAST NAME field and **Burglary Made Simple** in the NEWSLETTER SUBSCRIBED TO field (see fig. 6.11). Only those firms that meet both sets of criteria are included.

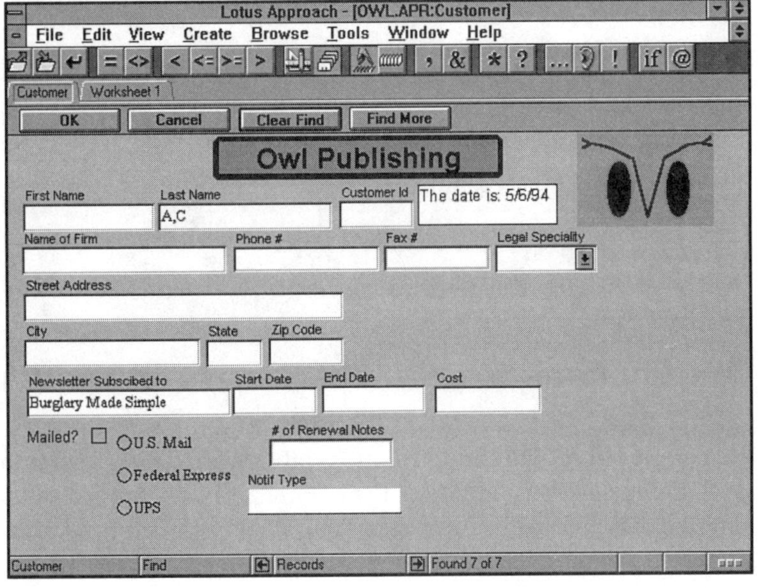

Fig. 6.11
Entering criteria in multiple fields.

In this example, assume that Owl Publishing wants to mail some announcements about a new newsletter. The company only wants to send the newsletter to people who have full addresses in the database. At a minimum, the address must include the FIRST NAME, LAST NAME, STREET ADDRESS, CITY,

STATE, and ZIP CODE. If any of these fields are blank, a mailing label is not made for that subscriber.

To set up a multiple-field AND find to gather all the records in which these fields aren't blank, follow these steps:

1. Switch to Find mode by opening the **B**rowse menu and choosing **F**ind, clicking the Find SmartIcon, or selecting Find from the status bar.
2. Type the criteria into the appropriate fields. For this example, type **< >** into the FIRST NAME, LAST NAME, STREET ADDRESS, CITY, STATE, and ZIP CODE fields (see fig. 6.12).
3. Press Enter.

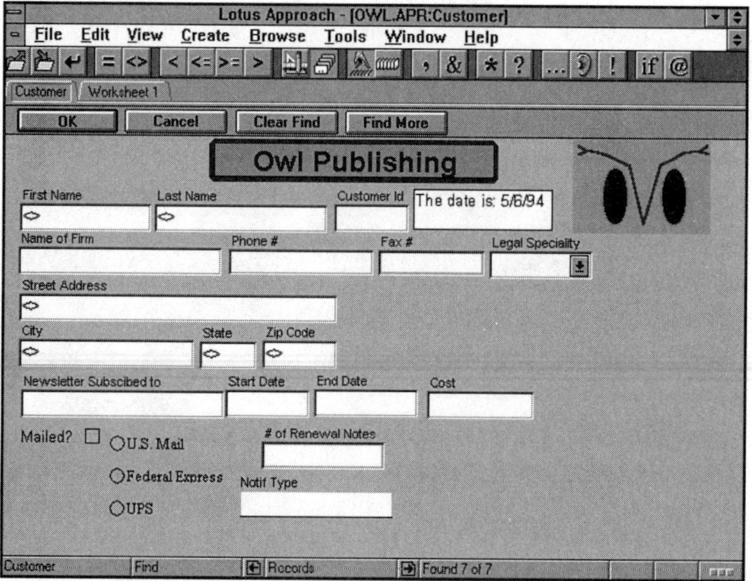

Fig. 6.12
Using < > in fields prevents a mailing label from being printed for incomplete addresses.

Approach begins its search, and the records with valid addresses appear in the found set. If you have been following the examples so far in this book, one record in the database is missing from the found set because it has a blank zip code.

Setting up a Multiple-Field OR Search

In a multiple-field OR find, Approach uses more than one find form so that you can specify each set of find criteria. You can use any technique detailed so far (including single-field OR conditions and multiple-field AND conditions) to fill out a find form.

Each find form is called a *request*. A record is included in the found set if the fields in the record match any requests specified in the find. The record is included if the first request is satisfied OR the second request is satisfied OR the third request is satisfied, and so on.

Suppose Owl Publishing wants to find out which of its customers have subscriptions to *Burglary Made Simple* or to *Assault Today* that end in 1994. To set up a multiple-field OR find using this criteria, follow these steps:

1. Switch to Find mode by opening the **B**rowse menu and choosing **F**ind, clicking the Find SmartIcon, or by selecting Find from the status bar. The form clears and you are ready to set up a find.

2. Type the criteria for the first request into the first find form. For the Owl Publishing example, type **Burglary Made Simple** into the NEWSLETTER SUBSCRIBED TO field and **01/01/94...12/31/94** into the END DATE field (see fig. 6.13). Notice that the text you type can be longer than the space provided on the form.

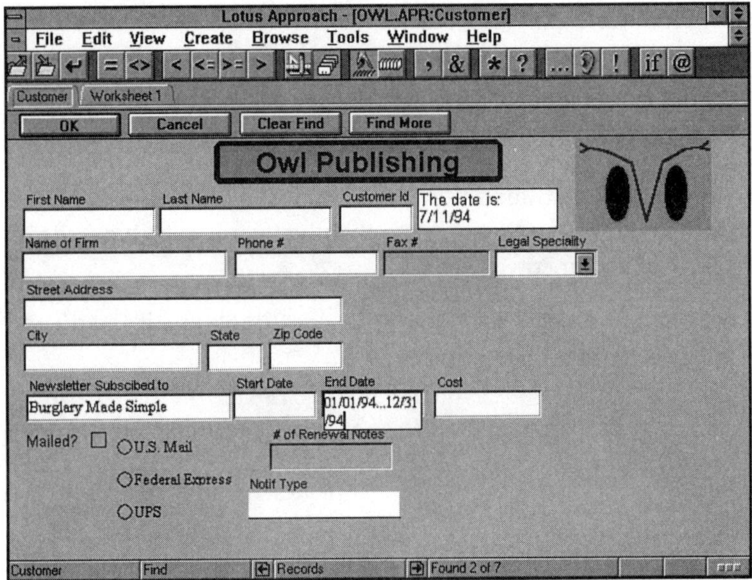

Fig. 6.13
Enter the first search criteria for OR searches.

3. Click the Find SmartIcon again, click the Find More button, or open the **B**rowse menu and choose **F**ind More. A new blank find form opens.

4. Type the criteria for the second request into the second find form. For this example, type **Assault Today** into the NEWSLETTER SUBSCRIBED TO field and **01/01/94...12/31/94** into the END DATE field (see fig. 6.14).

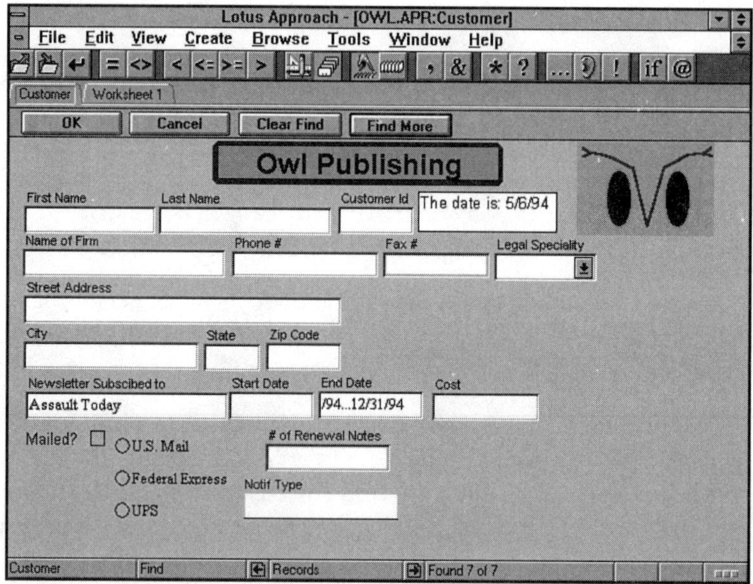

Fig. 6.14
Enter more unique find criteria for your OR search.

> **Tip**
> Move through multiple find requests and use the SmartIcons for Next Find, Previous Find, First Find, and Last Find criteria. You can also use the page buttons on the status bar.

Repeat steps 3 and 4 to specify as many OR requests as you want. Records that meet any of the requests are included in the subsequent found set.

5. Press Enter after you finish specifying all requests.

6. Use the arrow buttons on the SmartIcon bar to move through the records in the found set to verify that the found set includes the records that match your criteria.

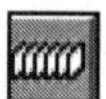

7. After you finish viewing the records, click the Show All SmartIcon.

When you fill out each find request in a multiple-field OR query, you can either type a value into a single field, or you can type values into multiple fields before moving to the next request. If you type multiple values into a single form before moving on to the next request, the find is evaluated in the following manner:

- For each request, records are included if they meet all the conditions on the find form—that is, an AND search is done on the database for that request.

- Approach builds the found set by joining the sets of records that satisfy each of the AND finds on the individual requests.

Modifying Your Last Find

Setting up a find can take considerable time. Sometimes you may notice that the find you have constructed doesn't quite give you the found set that you want. You can modify your last find by opening the **B**rowse menu and choosing Find A**g**ain. After your last find appears on-screen, you can edit any of its criteria and try again. You can also create a macro that reruns any find you build (see Chapter 13 for more information on automating your work).

Canceling a Find

If you want to clear the find criteria from a form, click the Clear Find button in the find button bar just below the form tabs.

If you decide that you don't want to execute a find that you have started to build, press the Esc key at any time to cancel the query. The previous found set is still active.

Another way to cancel a find is to click the Show All SmartIcon, or open the **B**rowse menu and choose Show **A**ll. If you cancel a find this way, the entire database becomes available.

Working with the Found Set

You can perform two especially useful operations on a found set—you can delete the entire found set, or you can fill a field with a value.

Deleting the Found Set

Opening the **B**rowse menu and choosing Delete F**o**und Set deletes all found records from the database. Deleting the found set is useful if you can write a find that gathers all the records you no longer need. If you no longer plan to send mail to firms with a specialty of EM, for example, you can write a find for all firms with that specialty and discard those records.

To delete the found set, follow these steps:

1. Perform the find that gathers the records you no longer want.
2. Open the **B**rowse menu and choose Delete F**o**und Set. Approach requests verification (see fig. 6.15).
3. When you click OK, the records are discarded.

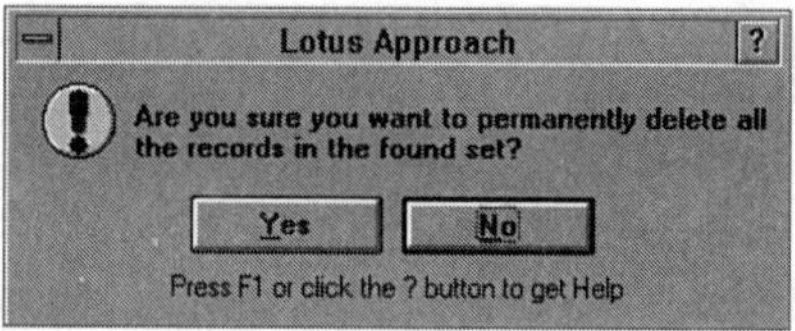

Fig. 6.15
You can delete a set of records that meet your find criteria.

Filling Fields in a Found Set

Approach can fill any field in a found set (or in the whole database) with a value. Opening the **B**rowse menu and choosing F**i**ll Field is useful if you just added a new blank field to a database, and the majority of the records have the same value in that field. You can fill the field with this value, and then go through and change only the few values that are different.

This operation is also handy if you create a find that gathers records that have the same value in a field. You can then put the appropriate value into that field. For example, you can write a find that gathers all firms located in Houston and Dallas. You then can fill the STATE field with TX, because both cities are in Texas.

To perform a F**i**ll Field operation, follow these steps:

1. Switch to Browse mode by opening the **V**iew menu and choosing **B**rowse, clicking the Browse SmartIcon, or by choosing Browse from the status bar.

2. If you are changing only the records in a found set, create and run a find that specifies the found set. Otherwise, fill field will use the entire database.

3. Click the field for which you want to enter a value. This field doesn't have to be empty, but the value you insert replaces any value in that field in the found set (or the entire database, if no current found set is active).

4. Open the **B**rowse menu and choose F**i**ll Field. The Fill Field dialog box appears (see fig. 6.16).

5. In the box provided, type the value that you want placed in the field. Approach doesn't allow you to type a longer value than fits into the field.

6. Click OK to insert the value into every record.

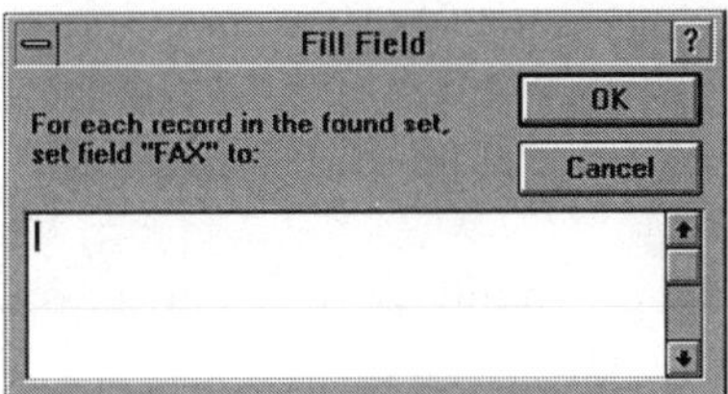

Fig. 6.16
During a find, you can update a field using the Fill Field dialog box.

Hiding Records

With Approach, you can hide any records you don't want to work with. Hiding records makes them temporarily unavailable—it doesn't erase them.

Hiding records can be useful if you don't want to work with just a few records in the found set. Often, you create a simple find that retrieves not only all the records you want, but also a small number you don't want. Perhaps you could create a much more complex find that retrieves only the records you want, but hiding the few records you don't need is often simpler.

Note

Hidden records are still included in any finds you perform. This is because executing a find undoes the **H**ide Records function, making all records available to be found in the find. In other words, all records are available in any find.

To hide records, follow these steps:

1. Switch to Browse mode by opening the **V**iew menu and choosing **B**rowse, clicking the Browse SmartIcon, or choosing Browse from the status bar.

2. Move to the record you want to hide by using the Next Record or Previous Record SmartIcons, the record navigation keys on the keyboard, or the status bar.

3. Open the **B**rowse menu and choose **H**ide Record. The record is no longer available. You can also press Ctrl+H.

Repeat steps 2 and 3 to hide all the records you don't want to work with. To make hidden records available again, click the Show All SmartIcon.

From Here...

This chapter discussed how to find records that meet the find criteria that you type into fields on a find form. Special operators are used to find the records you want. After this "found set" is obtained, you can perform operations on just those found records.

For more information on using Approach's find function, refer to the following chapters in this book:

- Chapter 7, "Creating Reports and Mailing Labels," shows you how to create reports and mailing labels, which can be very useful in displaying and using the results of a find.
- Chapter 9, "Designing Advanced Forms," shows you how to display the results of a find in a sophisticated form that includes multiple joined databases.
- Chapter 11, "Performing Advanced Finds," shows you how to perform even more powerful finds.

Chapter 7

Creating Reports and Mailing Labels

As powerful as Approach's forms are, they can't perform certain functions. For one thing, a form can't present the information from more than one record at a time. A form also can't summarize information across multiple records in the database. Approach's powerful report builder, however, gets around the limitations of forms.

Approach also enables you to build mailing labels quickly and easily. You can set up custom mailing labels or use standard sizes from Avery. If you use standard sizes, Approach does all the work of setting sizes and margins for you.

If you are comfortable with designing forms, you should have no trouble getting used to designing reports and mailing labels—they work almost exactly the way forms work.

In this chapter, you learn how to:

- Create blank, columnar, and standard reports
- Change the report name and basic specifications
- Set the number of columns in a report
- Delete or duplicate a report
- Add a header or footer to a report
- Customize a report with text, lines, boundaries, and more
- Add a title page to a report
- Create a mailing label

- Delete or duplicate a mailing label
- Preview and print a report or mailing label

Understanding the Differences between a Form and a Report

Reports present information in the database in ways that circumvent the limitations of forms. Consider the following capabilities of reports:

- Reports can show multiple records on a page. When you print a form, each page holds only a single record. In contrast, when you print a report, each page can hold the information for many records. You can adjust the size of the "body" box that holds each record to provide more or less room between records on a report.
- Reports can summarize information in different ways, without you having to reenter the data. In the Owl Publishing database, for example, a report can summarize all firms that subscribe to a certain newsletter. If you kept a record of the salespeople who contacted specific firms to sell them newsletter subscriptions, you could also get a report of all sales, grouped by salesperson.
- Reports have formatting options that aren't available on forms. These include title pages, headers, and footers.

Reports are also similar to forms in many ways. Consider the following traits:

- You can use reports as well as forms to input information. If you change a field in a report, those changes are stored in the database, just as if you were changing that record on a form.

> **Note**
>
> Reports often don't include all the fields necessary to enter a record completely. If you type data in such a report, the records will be incomplete because information in some fields will be missing.

- You can customize fields on a report by using most of the options available on a form, such as specifying the data-entry format and display format.
- You can perform finds and sorts on a report.

Creating a Report

To create a report, follow these steps:

1. Open the **C**reate menu and choose **R**eport or click the New Report SmartIcon. The Report Assistant dialog box appears (see fig. 7.1).

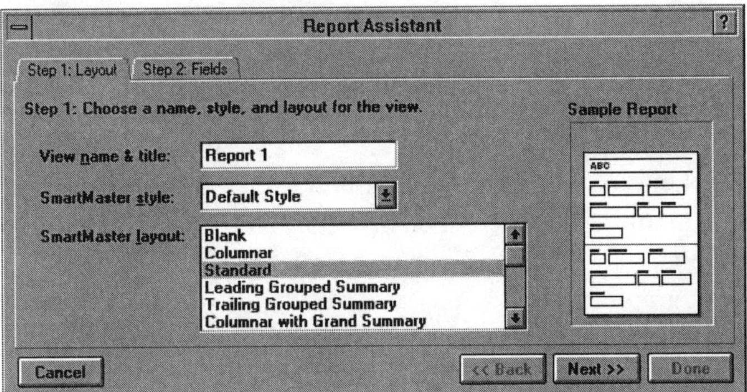

Fig. 7.1
The Report Assistant dialog box.

2. Type the name of the report in the View **N**ame and Title text box.

3. Select a SmartMaster style from the SmartMaster **S**tyle drop-down list. The SmartMaster styles give the report a consistent look, such as shadowed, executive, chiseled, and so on.

4. Select the SmartMaster layout you want from the SmartMaster **L**ayout drop-down list, as discussed in the following section, "Choosing the Type of Report."

5. For all reports except Blank and Summary-only reports, select the fields to include on the report, as discussed in "Choosing Fields for the Report."

6. Click OK. Approach creates the report according to your specifications.

Choosing the Type of Report

Select the SmartMaster layout from the SmartMaster **L**ayout drop-down box in the Report Assistant dialog box. The SmartMaster layouts determine the layout of the report. The SmartMaster layouts are Blank, Columnar, Standard, Leading Grouped Summary, Trailing Grouped Summary, Columnar with Grand Summary, and Summary-only reports. The summary reports summarize data across multiple records and place the summary results in various locations on the report. Summary reports are discussed in Chapter 12. Blank, standard, and columnar reports are discussed in the following sections.

Note

If you have two or more joined tables in your database, another type of Report SmartMaster is available—Repeating Panel. See Chapter 12 for more information on Repeating Panel reports.

Creating a Blank Report

To create a blank report, select Blank from the SmartMaster **L**ayout drop-down list. A blank report opens a blank report template, with no fields or formatting present. You can use the techniques discussed later in this chapter to add fields, graphics, illustrations, text, headers, footers, and a title page to a blank report.

Creating a Standard Report

To create a standard report, select Standard from the SmartMaster **L**ayout drop-down list. When you create this type of report, any fields you place on the report initially appear on lines across the report. (See "Choosing Fields for the Report" later in this chapter.) When there is no more room on a line, Approach moves down one line and continues placing fields on the report. This configuration is similar to the default forms that Approach creates (see fig. 7.2).

Creating a Columnar Report

To create a columnar report, select Columnar from the SmartMaster **L**ayout drop-down list. In a columnar report, each record appears as a row in the report, and each field appears as a column. The name of the field appears as a column heading at the top of the column (see fig. 7.3).

Note

The name of the column is not a field label, as in a Form or a Standard report, but a text item that can be moved independently of the column and that has its own Info Box.

If you include in a columnar report more columns than can fit across the page, Approach uses multiple pages (see fig. 7.4). You can see the page break as you scroll the display to the left and right. Approach does not attempt to keep all fields on one page—if the field is located at the right edge of a page, the column header and field text may be split across the pages. The best solution is to restrict columnar reports to one page wide by selecting fewer fields or choosing a smaller font.

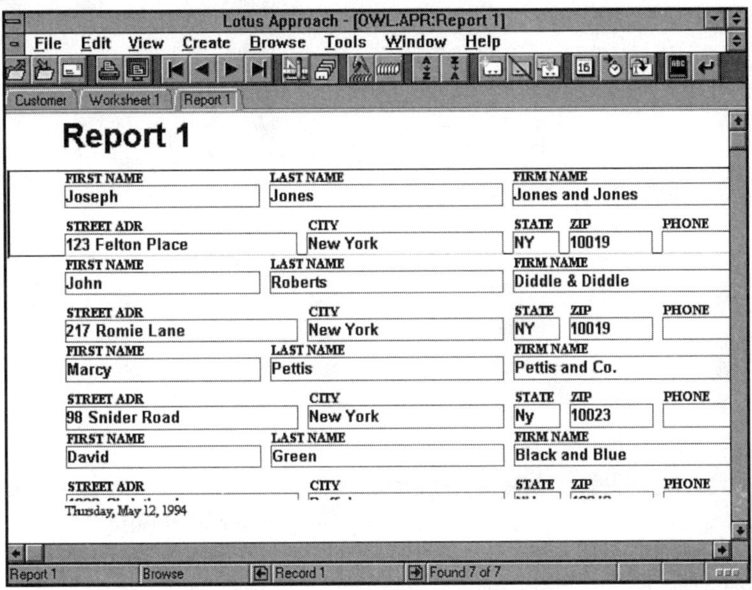

Fig. 7.2
A standard report, like the default form, contains fields across the page.

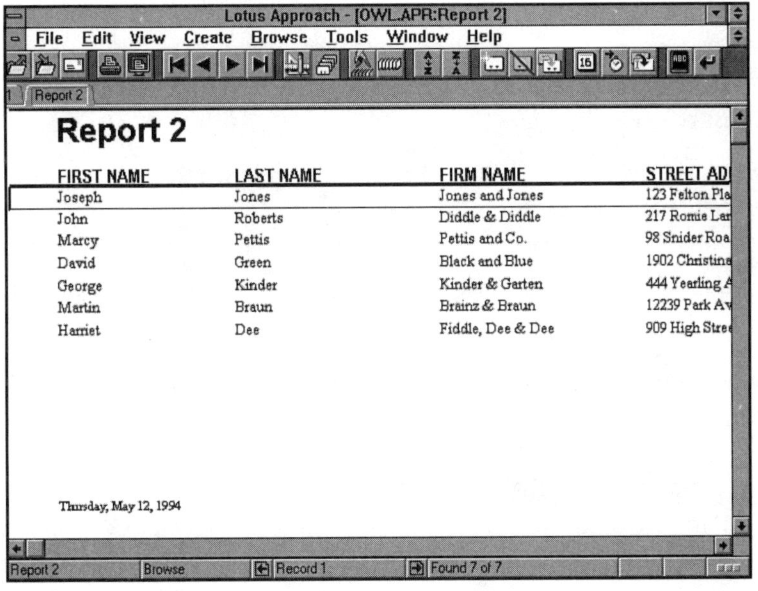

Fig. 7.3
A columnar report lists one record per row and a field in each column.

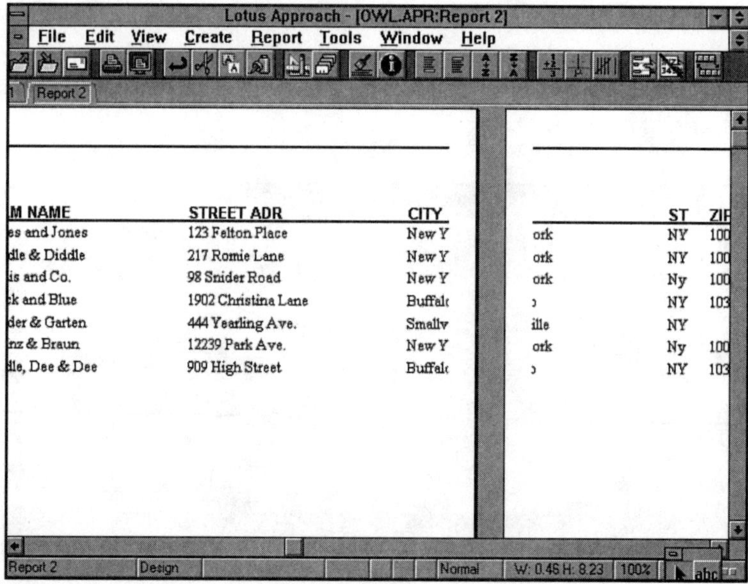

Fig. 7.4
A columnar report may sometimes break across pages.

Choosing Fields for the Report

For all reports except Blank and Summary-only, you can choose the fields that Approach puts on the report. From the layout panel, click the Step 2: Fields tab or the Next button to move to the Fields panel. The Database **F**ields list on the left side of the Fields panel displays all the fields in the database. To add a field to the report, select the field from the Database **F**ields list box and click **A**dd. Approach moves the field to the Fields to **P**lace on View list box. You also can double-click the field to move it to the Fields to **P**lace on View list box.

To select multiple fields, click the first field, hold down the Ctrl key, and click any other fields you want to select.

If you want to remove a field from the list of report fields, select the field in the Fields to **P**lace on View list box and click **R**emove. You also can double-click a field to remove it from the Fields to **P**lace on View list box.

You can return to the Layout panel by clicking the Layout tab or the Back button.

Creating a Sample Report

Owl Publishing wants to create a columnar report listing all its customers. This report will include only customer names and newsletter titles so that each record can fit on one row. Follow these steps to create such a report:

1. Switch to Design mode by opening the **V**iew menu and choosing **D**esign, clicking the Design SmartIcon, or by choosing Design from the status bar.

2. Open the **C**reate menu and choose **R**eport or click the Create a New Report SmartIcon. The Report Assistant dialog box appears (refer to fig. 7.1).
3. Type **Customers Report** in the View **N**ame & Title text box.
4. Choose Executive from the SmartMaster **S**tyle drop-down list.
5. Choose Columnar from the SmartMaster **L**ayout list.
6. Click the Step 2: Fields tab to move to the Fields panel.
7. In the Database **F**ields list, select FIRST NAME. Hold down the Ctrl key, and then click LAST NAME, FIRM NAME, and NEWSLETTER.
8. Click **A**dd. The fields appear in the Fields to **P**lace on View list box (see fig. 7.5).

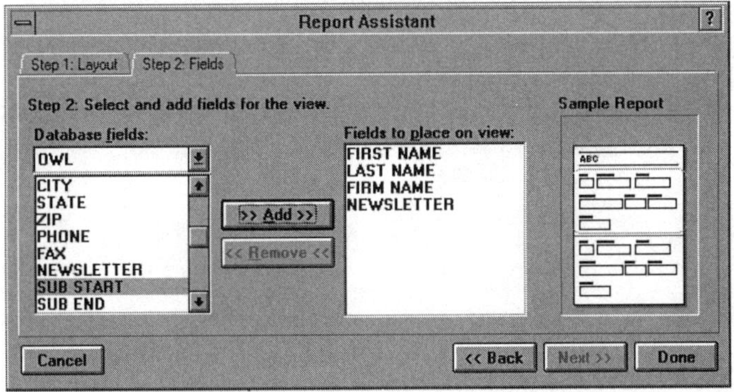

Fig. 7.5
Select the field names you want to add to your columnar report.

9. Click Done. The new report appears as shown in figure 7.6. If the report shows data instead of the field names, select S**h**ow Data from the **V**iew menu (turning off the checkmark) to show the field names instead of the data.
10. Switch to Browse mode to view the report (see fig. 7.7).
11. Open the **F**ile menu and choose **S**ave Approach File to save the file.

Owl Publishing also wants to create a standard report that includes all the information from the form. Follow these steps to create such a report:

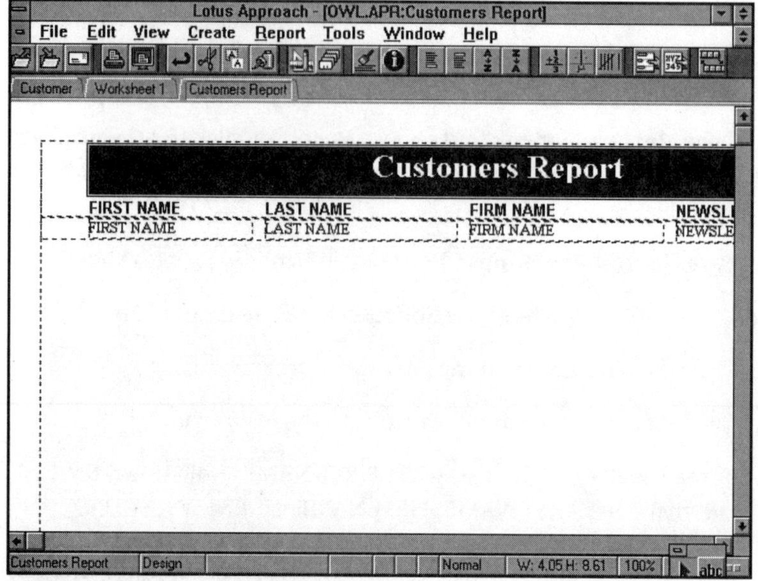

Fig. 7.6
The columnar report for Owl Publishing's customers (in Design mode).

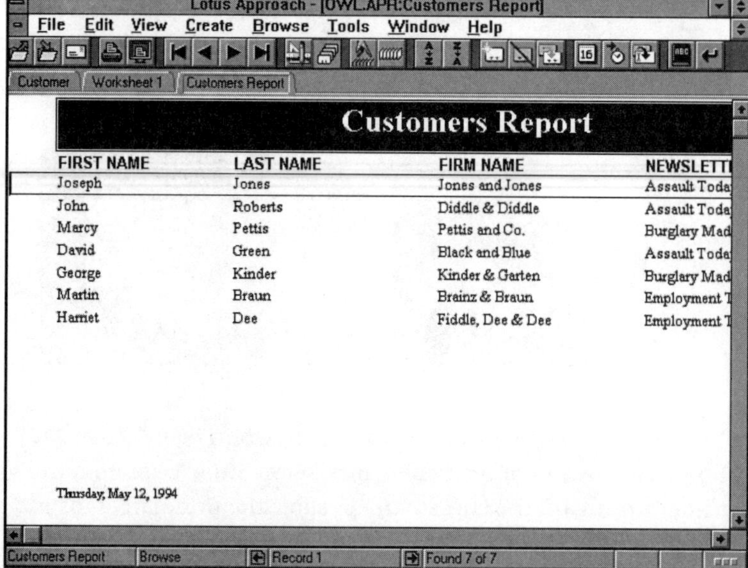

Fig. 7.7
The columnar report in Browse mode.

1. Switch to Design mode by opening the **V**iew menu and choosing **D**esign, clicking the Design SmartIcon, or choosing Design from the status bar.

2. Open the **C**reate menu and choose **R**eport or click the Create a New Report SmartIcon. The Report Assistant dialog box appears.

3. Type **All Data** as the name of the report.
4. Choose Shadowed from the SmartMaster **S**tyle drop-down list.
5. Choose Standard from the SmartMaster **L**ayout list.
6. Click the Next button to move to the Fields panel.
7. Select FIRST NAME in the Database **F**ields list and click **A**dd to move the field to the Fields to **P**lace on View list. Continuing clicking **A**dd until all the fields from the database are available in the Fields to **P**lace on View list. The selection bar moves down the list of fields in the Database **F**ields list automatically as you click **A**dd.

Tip
Approach is smart enough to remember what Smart-Master style and layout you last used.

Caution

Don't get too enthusiastic when clicking the **A**dd button! If you continue to click **A**dd after you have added all the fields in the database to the Fields to **P**lace on View list, Approach returns to the top of the list and begins adding the fields to the Fields to **P**lace on View list a second time.

8. Click Done. The new report appears (see fig. 7.8). If the report displays field data instead of the field names, choose S**h**ow Data from the **V**iew menu to turn off the field data.
9. Switch to Browse mode to view the report (see fig. 7.9).
10. Open the **F**ile menu and choose **S**ave Approach File to save the report.

Changing the Report Name and Basic Specifications

You can adjust many of a report's properties from the report's Info Box. You can change the name of a report, adjust the number of columns, and have the option of keeping each record together on a page. You make all these changes from the Basics panel of the Info Box shown in figure 7.10.

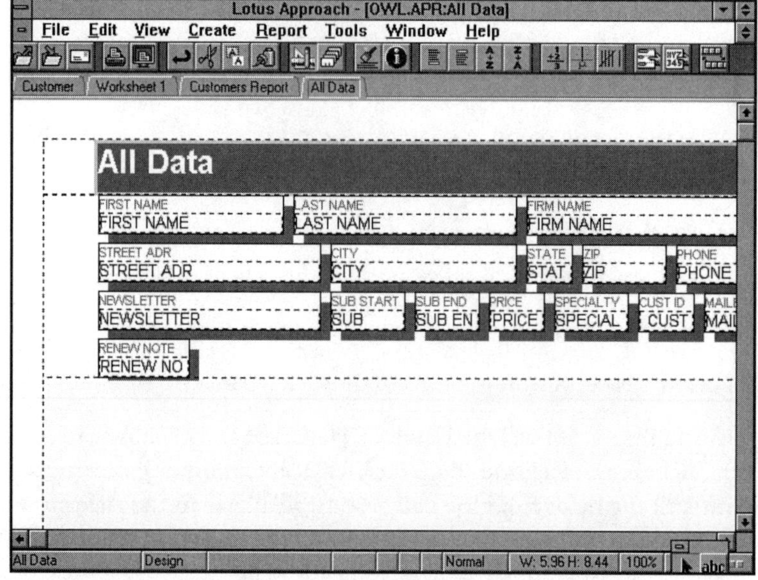

Fig. 7.8
A standard report for Owl Publishing's customers (in Design mode).

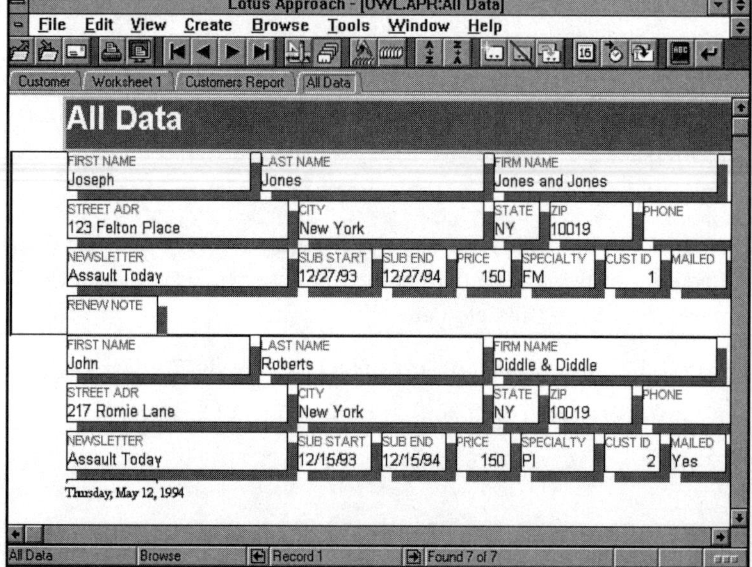

Fig. 7.9
The standard report in Browse mode.

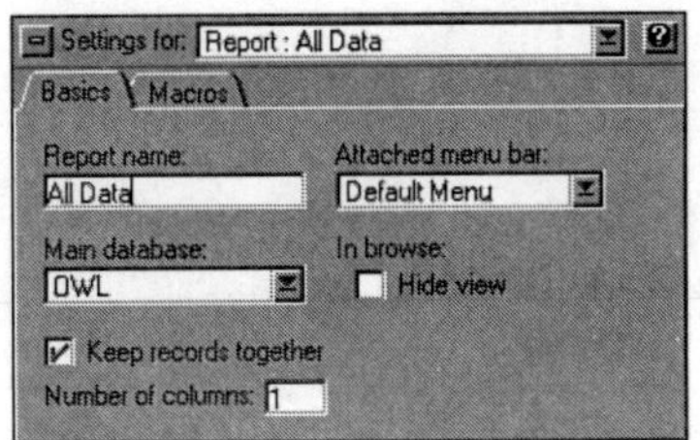

Fig. 7.10
The Report Info Box.

To adjust the properties of the report, follow these steps:

1. Switch to Design mode by opening the **V**iew menu and choosing **D**esign, clicking the Design SmartIcon, or choosing Design from the status bar.

2. If the report you want to modify isn't the one currently on-screen, click the tab for the report you want. You can also switch to the appropriate report by using the status bar.

3. Make sure nothing on the report is selected (click a blank area of the report to deselect anything, if necessary).

4. Choose **S**tyle & Properties from the **R**eport or pop-up menu. The report Info Box appears. Click the Basics tab to move to the Basics panel.

5. To change the name of the report, type the new name in the Report **N**ame text box.

6. To hide the report in Browse mode, click the Hide View checkbox. Approach will not display the report in the view tabs or the list of views in the status bar.

7. To change the number of columns, type the number of columns you want in the Number of Columns text box. See the following section, "Setting the Number of Columns," for more information.

8. To keep each record together, check the Keep Records Together checkbox. When this checkbox is checked, Approach does not split a record across different pages. If all the information about one record won't fit on the remainder of a page, Approach moves the record to the top of the next page.

Suppose the report name for the Owl database standard report isn't descriptive enough. To change its name, follow these steps:

1. Switch to Design mode by opening the **V**iew menu and choosing **D**esign, clicking the Design SmartIcon, or choosing Design from the status bar.

2. Select the All Data report by clicking the All Data tab or selecting the report from the status bar.

3. Open the Info Box by choosing **S**tyle & Properties from the **R**eport or pop-up menu. You can also open the Info Box by clicking the Info Box SmartIcon.

4. Type **Cust Data** in the Report Name text box.

5. Open the **F**ile menu and choose **S**ave Approach File.

Setting the Number of Columns

The Number of Columns text box in the Report Info box enables you to set the number of columns you want printed in the report. By using more columns, you can place more information (sets of fields) on the page. If you specify more than one column, Approach prints your records from top to bottom in the first column, then moves to the second column, and so on.

Note

Using multiple columns is different from a columnar report. In a columnar report, Approach uses a single column for each field. Thus, a five-field report has five columns. When you create a multiple column report, Approach repeats all the fields used in each column. Thus, a columnar report with three fields, for which you specified two columns, would actually contain six columns—the three field columns in the first report column, and the three field columns in the second report column. Approach's usage of columns in these two contexts is very confusing.

Using Multiple Columns in a Standard Report

If you are creating a standard report that has short fields and labels, for example, you can see more records on each page if you use two or more columns (see fig. 7.11).

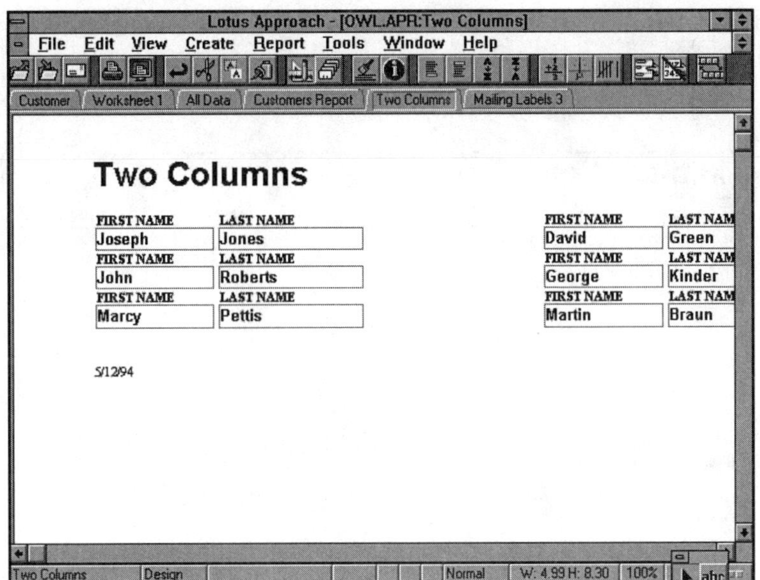

Fig. 7.11
Using multiple columns for your report can save paper.

Using Multiple Columns in a Columnar Report

In a columnar report, multiple columns are advantageous if your report includes only a few fields across the page. Each column contains all the selected fields for the report. Thus, if you choose two fields and two columns for the report, four columns of data will appear on the report—the two fields selected, in each of the two columns. With multiple columns, you can fit more records on the page (see fig. 7.12).

Viewing a Multi-Column Report

There are several ways to view a multi-column report. To see the actual data in the report, use Preview or Design mode with field data showing (click the Show Data Instead of Field Names SmartIcon, or choose S**h**ow Data from the **V**iew menu, to display data instead of field names). You *cannot* use Browse mode because all data is hidden in this mode. Approach displays the column borders if you are in Design mode with field names displayed instead of data. A vertical dashed line shows the edge of each column (see fig. 7.13).

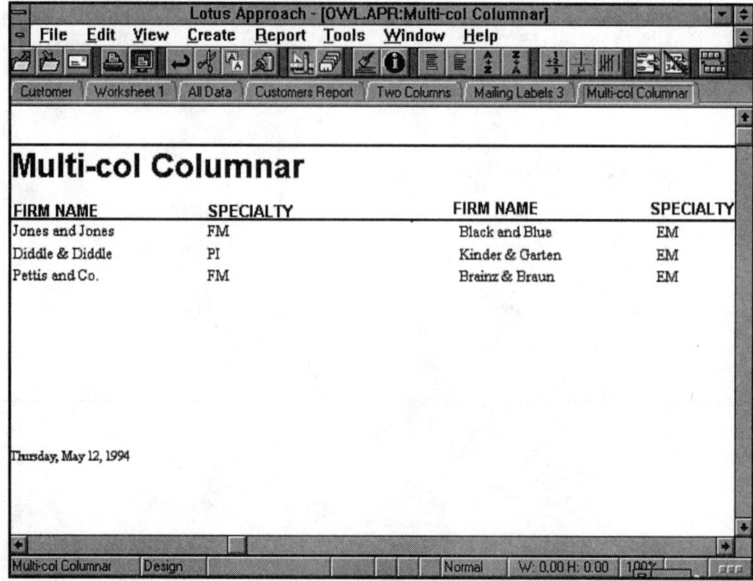

Fig. 7.12 Use multiple columns in a columnar report to fit more records on the page.

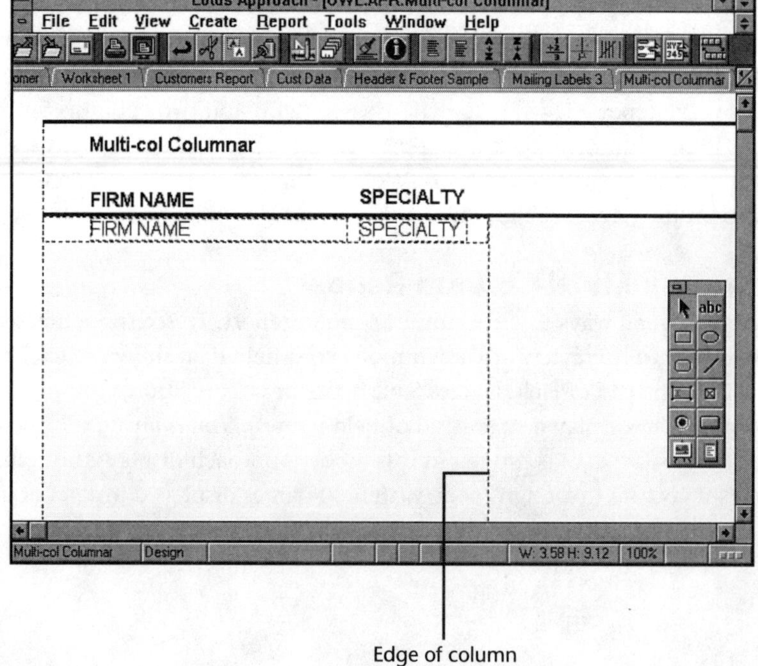

Fig. 7.13 Viewing a two-column columnar report in Design mode.

Deleting a Report

If you don't need a report anymore, you can delete it. To delete a report, follow these steps:

1. Switch to Design mode by opening the **V**iew menu and choosing **D**esign, clicking the Design SmartIcon, or choosing Design from the status bar.

2. If the report you want to delete is not on-screen, choose the report from the view tabs or from the status bar.

3. Open the **E**dit menu and choose D**e**lete Report. Confirm that you want to delete the report when Approach asks you.

Duplicating a Report

Approach enables you to duplicate an existing report to give you a head start in creating a report that is similar to one you already have. Making a duplicate is especially useful when you need to create complex mailing labels. To copy a report, follow these steps:

1. Switch to Design mode by opening the **V**iew menu and choosing **D**esign, clicking the Design SmartIcon, or choosing Design from the status bar.

2. If the report you want to duplicate is not on-screen, choose the report from the view tabs or from the status bar.

3. Open the **E**dit menu and choose **D**uplicate Report. The duplicate of your report appears on-screen. You can make changes (for example, change fonts, add and remove fields, or rearrange fields) to the duplicate without affecting the original.

Approach gives the duplicate report the same name as the original with the words "Copy of" in front of the name. If you duplicate the Cust Data report, for example, Approach names the duplicate "Copy of Cust Data." Use the Basics panel of the report Info Box to change the name of the report, or double-click on the report's tab and edit the name.

Customizing a Report

Approach enables you to customize reports in many different ways. You can add, remove, move, and size fields; specify the text attributes of fields and labels; change the text of a label; and add graphics. In fact, you can change reports in virtually all the ways you can modify forms.

Reports also have new elements that are not present on forms. For example, you can add a header or footer to a report page and a title page for the report. Another new element is the body panel. On a form, each record occupies the entire form, but a report page can display multiple records. The rectangular portion on a report page that holds a single record is called a *body panel*. As we will discuss, you may set various properties for body panels, such as color and border style.

Almost all the changes work the same way on reports as they do on forms. Therefore, whenever a function is the same for a form as for a report, only a summary of the function is covered in this chapter. For a more comprehensive discussion of each function, see Chapter 4.

You must make all changes to a report in Design mode.

Adjusting the Attributes of a Body Panel

Tip
To display small report panel labels that identify the parts of a report, open the **V**iew menu and choose Show Panel **L**abels, or click the Show Panel Labels SmartIcon.

A body panel is the rectangular area on a report that surrounds the fields that make up a single record. In Design mode, body panels appear differently, depending on whether you are displaying field names or field data:

- If you are displaying field names, Approach shows you a single body panel with all the fields you included in the report from a single record (see fig. 7.14). If you select the body panel by clicking an area of the body panel in which there are no fields present, Approach draws a heavy line around the body panel. All records in the report follow the format of this single record.

- If you are displaying field data, Approach displays all the records in the database, with the body panel boundary around the selected record (see fig. 7.15). The layouts of all the records are identical. Changes you make to any record's body panel are reflected in all records. Displaying field data helps you see how a record will look in Browse mode as you adjust the record layout. However, it can be confusing to see all the data as you are attempting to modify the layout, and Approach does run slower when the data is displayed.

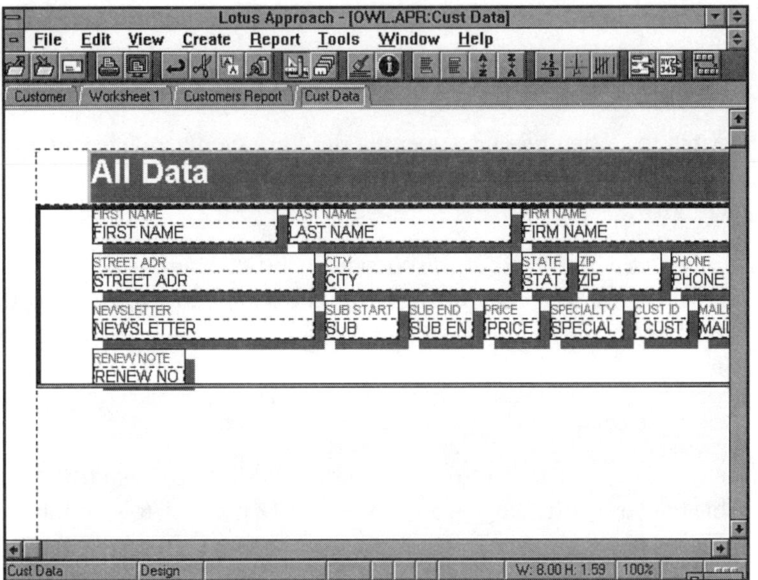

Fig. 7.14
Approach displays the field names when displaying a single body panel in Design mode.

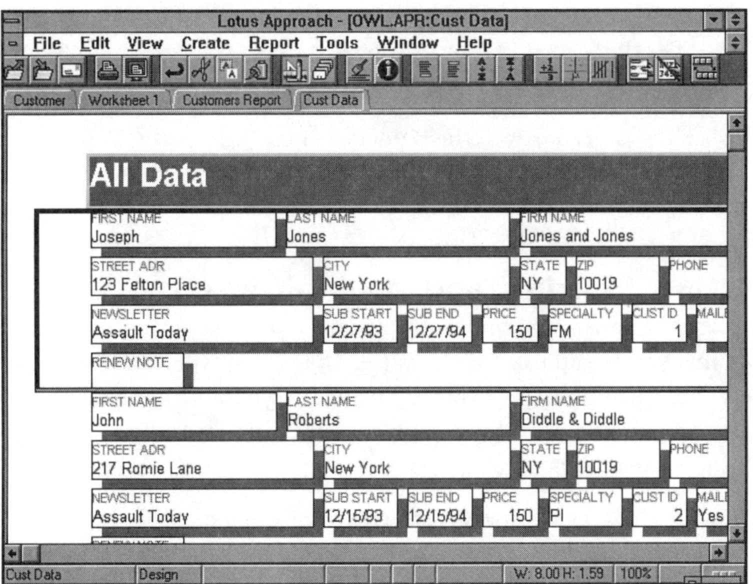

Fig. 7.15
When field data is shown in Design mode, Approach displays multiple records in body panels.

Note

To avoid confusion, it's probably best to make adjustments to a report with only the field names showing.

You can adjust the border and fill color of a body panel, as well as the border width, frame style, and the sides of the body panel on which Approach displays a border. To adjust these properties, follow these steps:

1. Switch to Design mode by opening the **V**iew menu and choosing **D**esign, clicking the Design SmartIcon, or choosing Design from the status bar.

2. Bring up the Info Box for the body panel by clicking the body panel and choosing **S**tyle & Properties from the pop-up menu, selecting the Info Box SmartIcon, or selecting **S**tyle and Properties from the **R**eport menu.
3. Select the colors panel by clicking the Colors tab.
4. Select the border width from the Border Width drop-down list. Available border widths range from hairline to 12 point (1/6 of an inch).
5. Select the border and fill color from the Border Color and Fill Color drop-down lists. Select the box labeled T for transparent, or no color.
6. Select a Frame style from the Frame drop-down list. The Frame style specifies the format in which Approach draws the border around the body panel.
7. Click the checkboxes in the Borders section (Left, Right, Top, and Bottom) to select on which sides of the body panel you want Approach to display a border.

Selecting, Resizing, and Moving Objects

You can select, resize, and move objects on a report using the same techniques that you would use on a form (see Chapter 3). You can select multiple objects with the mouse, resize objects by clicking and dragging sizing handles, and move objects by clicking and dragging them. You can also cut, copy, and paste objects on a report.

To make the Cust Data report for the Owl Publishing database easier to read (and to practice modifying reports), try rearranging some fields. First, make sure that only field names are displayed on the report (choose S**h**ow Data from the **V**iew menu if data is displayed on the report). Then follow these steps:

1. Switch to Design mode.
2. Select the FIRST NAME field.

3. Drag one of the right sizing handles to the left to make the field smaller.

4. Select the LAST NAME field.

5. Drag the LAST NAME field closer to the FIRST NAME field to close the gap.

6. Rearrange the rest of the report as shown in figure 7.16. Note that most of the field labels have been turned off to save room. To turn off the field label, select No label from the Label Position drop-down list on the Label panel of the Info Box.

7. Change the title of the report in the text box from All Data to Customer Data. To change the title, click the text twice with the mouse, highlight the existing title, and type in the new title. The finished report should look like figure 7.16.

8. Open the **F**ile menu and choose **S**ave Approach File to save the file.

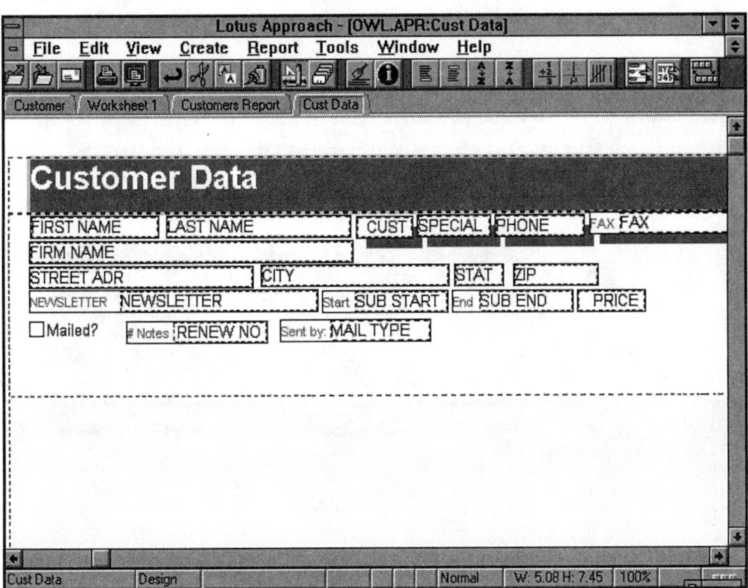

Fig. 7.16
The new layout of the Cust Data report.

Adjusting the Boundary of a Record

If you rearrange the fields in a standard report so that the fields require less space, you end up with a great deal of blank space at the bottom of the body panel. To have Approach move the next record up to fill this space, you must adjust the boundary of the body panel in Design mode. If you don't adjust

Tip
To make sure you click on the bottom of the body panel (and not the bottom of a field in the body panel), hold down Ctrl while you click the bottom border.

the boundary of the body panel, Approach shows and prints the report with blank space at the end of each record because the space allotted for each record hasn't been changed (see fig. 7.17).

To resize the body panel, move the mouse pointer over the bottom border of the body panel. The mouse pointer becomes a two-headed arrow. Hold down the left mouse button and drag the bottom border to change (shrink or increase) the size of the body panel.

To make better use of the space on the Cust Data report, Owl Publishing wants to adjust the record boundary to get rid of all the blank space between the records. Follow these steps:

1. Switch to the Cust Data report by using the view tabs or the status bar.

2. View the report from Browse mode. Notice how much white space is between the records.

3. Switch to Design mode by opening the **V**iew menu and choosing **D**esign, clicking the Design SmartIcon, or choosing Design from the status bar.

4. To make the record boundary visible, use the left mouse button to click anywhere in the record EXCEPT in a field. You can also press and hold down the Ctrl key and click anywhere in the record with the left mouse button.

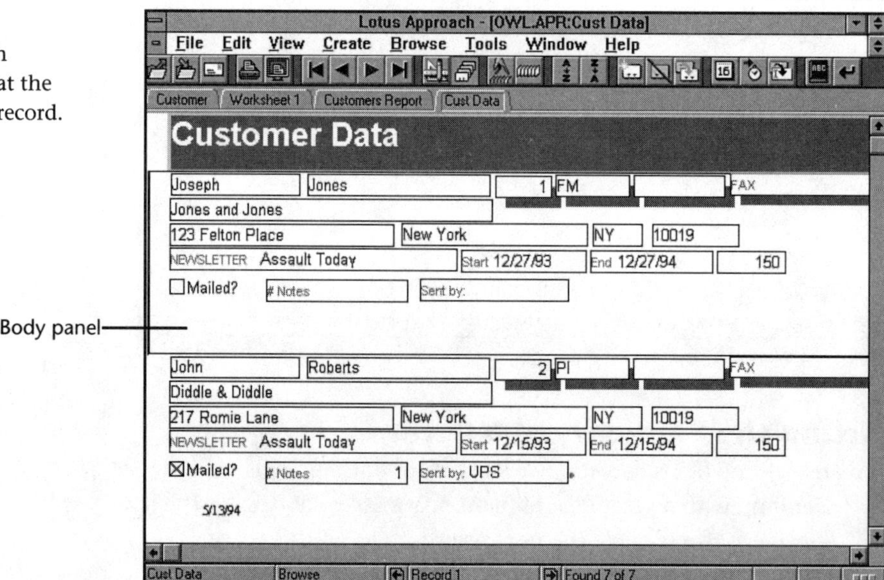

Fig. 7.17
A report with blank space at the end of each record.

A black line appears around the panel, except at the bottom, where the line is gray. You must click and drag the gray bottom line to adjust the size of the body panel (see fig. 7.18).

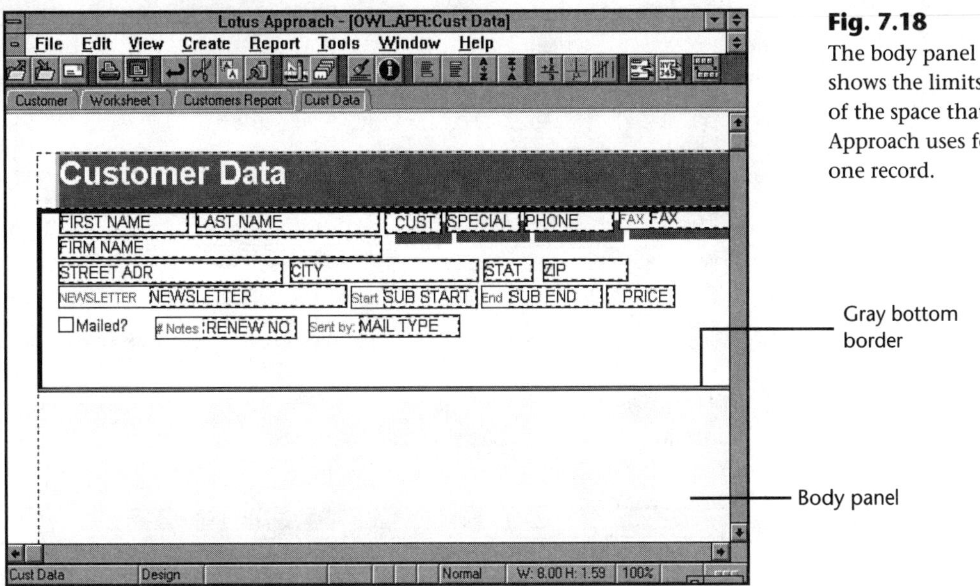

Fig. 7.18 The body panel shows the limits of the space that Approach uses for one record.

5. To adjust the body panel, drag the gray bottom border until it is just below the bottom line of fields.
6. Switch back to Browse mode. Notice that the wasted white space is gone.
7. Open the **F**ile menu and choose **S**ave Approach File to save the file.

Figure 7.19 shows the resulting report, without excessive blank space between the records.

You may have a similar problem with columnar reports. If you shrink the font of the header line (which holds the labels for the columns) or the record body panel, the space taken up by these lines becomes partially empty. Click anywhere except in a field in the header line or the body panel to see the boundary. Or, hold down the Ctrl key and click anywhere in the header or body panel. Drag the gray bottom border to close up the space on either line (see fig. 7.20).

Tip
Drag the body panel that holds the records to make it larger and give more room to each record.

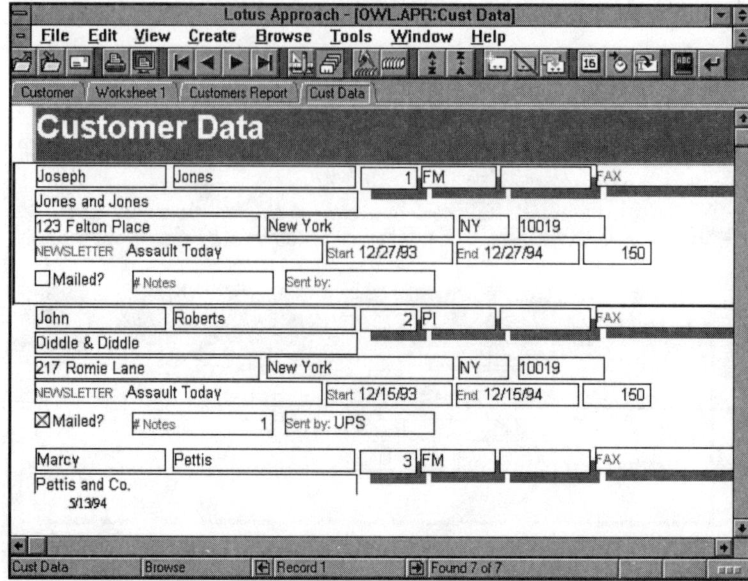

Fig. 7.19
Drag the gray border to remove wasted space at the end of each record.

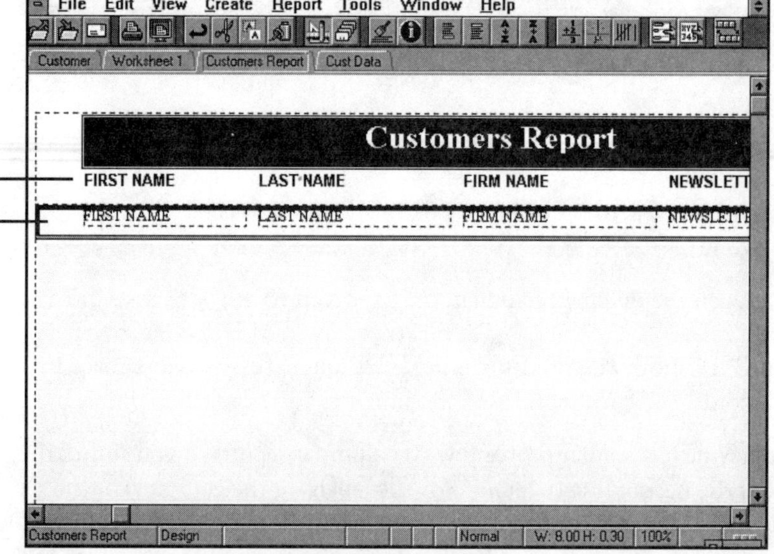

Fig. 7.20
Closing up the space on the header line or the body panel in a columnar report.

Working with Report Columns

Approach makes it easy for you to work with whole columns (a column and its header) on a columnar report. While you are working with whole columns, you can move or resize a column and its header at the same time. Otherwise, the columns and headers behave like separate objects that you can move and resize independently.

To work with whole columns, you turn on columns and show data rather than field names.

> **Note**
>
> You must show data before Approach will allow you to turn on columns.

To show data, open the **V**iew menu and choose S**h**ow Data or click the Show Data SmartIcon. To turn on columns, Open the **R**eport menu and choose Turn On **C**olumns or click the Columns SmartIcon.

When you first create a columnar report, Approach displays the columns in the order you specified in the Report Assistant dialog box. Approach automatically sets the column and header width to the field width. However, you can reposition, resize, or delete a column and its header.

- To resize a column, click the column data. Approach highlights the column (see fig. 7.21). Move the mouse pointer over the right edge of the column. The mouse pointer becomes a two-headed arrow. Hold down the left mouse button and drag the right edge of the column to make it larger or smaller. You can resize only the right edge of a column.

- To move a column, click the column data. Approach highlights the column. Move the mouse pointer over the column. The mouse pointer becomes an open hand. Hold down the left mouse button and drag the column to its new position. Approach automatically repositions other columns to move them out of the way and close up the gap left by the relocated column.

- To delete a column, click the column data. Approach highlights the column. Press the Delete key or choose Cu**t** from the **E**dit menu. Approach deletes the column and moves other columns to the left to close up the hole.

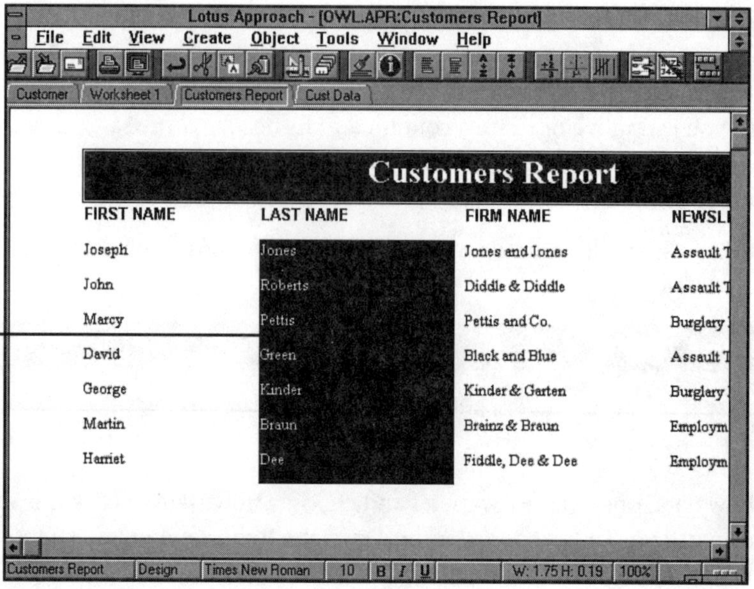

Fig. 7.21
A columnar report with a column selected.

Selected column

Using Slide Up and Slide Left

Reports and mailing labels often contain blank areas (see "Creating Mailing Labels" later in this chapter for more on mailing labels). These blanks occur for two main reasons: if some of the fields on the label aren't used, or if a field contains text that doesn't completely fill the field. For example, you can specify two address lines in your database to handle long addresses, but some records may leave the second line blank because it isn't needed. Or, you may have left room for a long city field, but the city name for a particular record is short.

As with forms, Approach provides two special commands to close the gaps that result from these conditions—Slide Left and Slide Up. These checkbox options are available from the Dimensions panel of a field or graphic object's Info Box.

When the Reduce checkbox in a field's Info Box is checked, Slide Left closes any gap that appears when text doesn't completely fill a field. If the CITY and STATE fields are on the same line in the mailing label, for example, using Slide Left moves the STATE field to the end of the CITY field, leaving just one space between them. In order for Slide Left to work, however, the objects must be aligned along their bottom borders and not touching.

If the Reduce checkbox in a field's Info Box is checked, Slide Up closes any gap that appears when a line isn't used. If the second address line on a label isn't used, for example, all the lines below it are moved up. Another good place to use Slide Up is for memo fields in which the entire field is not filled with text. Approach moves up information below the partially empty memo field to fill in the unused space.

To cause a field or graphic object to slide left or up, follow these steps:

1. Switch to Design mode by opening the **V**iew menu and choosing **D**esign, clicking the Design SmartIcon, or choosing Design from the status bar.

Tip
Slide Up and Slide Left don't work if fields overlap, if the bottoms are not aligned, or if field boundaries touch.

2. Click the field or graphic object.

3. Open the Info Box for the field or object, and switch to the Dimensions panel of the Info Box.

4. Click the Left or Up checkboxes in the When Printing, Slide section of the Dimensions panel.

Note

You won't be able to see the changes on the report unless you are in Preview mode or Design mode with field data showing. To enter Preview mode, click the Preview SmartIcon or select Preview from the status bar. To show field data in Design mode, open the **V**iew menu and choose S**h**ow Data, or click the Show Data SmartIcon. If the form is too small to read the text in Preview mode—and thus to see the effects of Slide Up or Slide Left—click the Zoom-In SmartIcon.

Under normal circumstances, fields take up a specific amount of room on the form. Thus, the Slide Left and Slide Up commands have no effect unless you allow Approach to adjust the size of any fields that contain blank space. To allow Approach to adjust the field size, select the Reduce checkbox on the Dimensions panel. The Reduce checkbox enables Approach to shrink a field that contains empty space, and potentially move other objects left and up (if you have enabled Slide Left or Slide Up for those fields) to fill the empty space.

A related command is the Expand checkbox on the Dimensions panel. This checkbox enables Approach to increase the size of a screen field and the body panel on the printout when the database field contains more information than can be displayed in the field on the screen. You must ensure that there are no other fields to the right or beneath the field you allow to expand, because Approach will print over those fields. A good example of a use for the

Expand checkbox is a memo field with more text than Approach can display in the allotted field space. If you check the Expand checkbox, Approach will insert enough space in the printout to fully print the contents of the memo field.

Using the Layout Tools

Approach has a number of tools to help you get the layout of a report just right. These layout tools work the same way they do when you're laying out a form.

These layout tools include using the rulers, showing the screen coordinates of the mouse pointer or the selected object, and using the grid to align objects. You can also align objects to each other, magnify objects so you can place them more precisely, shrink objects so you can see more of them on-screen, and group objects. Another handy layout tool is adjusting the way objects are layered on top of each other. Last, you can prevent selected objects from printing or displaying in Browse mode. All of these Approach features are discussed in detail in Chapter 3.

Adding Fields to a Report

From Design mode, you can add fields to a report using either the Draw Fields tool in the Drawing toolbar or the Add Fields dialog box. To add a field using the Draw Fields tool, follow these steps:

1. Click the Draw Fields tool. The pointer turns into a cross-hair pointer.

2. Drag a rectangle to define the location and size of the field. The Field Info Box appears.

3. From the Field list box, select the field you want to add. If the field you want doesn't exist yet, choose the Field Definition button to open the Field **D**efinition dialog box. Add the field you want and then choose OK to return to the Field Info Box. The new field will be selected in the field list.

To add a field from the Add Field dialog box, click the field you want to add and drag the field into a body panel on the report. If you need to create a new field, click the Field **D**efinition button to open the Field Definition dialog box. Add the field you want, and click OK to return to the Add Field dialog box. You can now click and drag the new field onto the report.

> **Note**
>
> You can also create a new field by copying an existing field (open the **E**dit menu and choose **C**opy) and then pasting that field back onto the report (open the **E**dit menu and choose **P**aste). Then, double-click the copied field to bring up the Info Box. Select the field you want from the field list, or create a new field by clicking the Field **D**efinition button. Creating a field on the report in this way duplicates the attributes of the field you used to copy/paste.

Modifying the Report Field Display

You can change how a field is displayed on a report in all the same ways you can change the field display on a form. You can display fields as a drop-down list, field box and list, checkbox, and radio button. You can also set the values for a drop-down list (or field box and list), and set the on/off values for a checkbox, and the on value for a radio button.

To keep the user from entering something in a field, you can make it read-only. You can also adjust the order in which the user moves through the field by changing the tab order. Adjusting the tab order is useful because you can input data into a report, just like a form.

You can change the font, size, effects, and color of the text entered into a field and the text of the field's label. You can also set the field background and shadow color, frame style, position of the field borders, and line width of the border.

You can move and resize fields either by clicking and dragging or by using the Dimensions panel of the Info Box.

Finally, you can change the display format of the field so that the entered data is displayed in the text, numeric, time, or date format you prefer.

Customizing Your Report

Blocks of text, graphics objects, and illustrations from graphics files add color and impact to a report. Adding these items to a report is done in exactly the same way that you add them to a form.

The text tool, graphics tools, and copy/paste commands all work in exactly the same way as they do on a form. On a text block, you can change the text font, size, effects, and color, as well as the text block fill and shadow color. You can also place a database field, the page number, time, or a date into a text block on a report. Finally, for graphics objects, you can change the line color and weight, frame style, as well as the fill and shadow color. You can move and resize text blocks and graphics objects by clicking and dragging or by using the Dimensions panel of the object's Info Box.

On a report, you have the option of placing text blocks, graphics objects, and pictures from graphic files in headers and footers. By placing these items in a header or footer, you can ensure that they appear on every page of the report.

Working with Headers and Footers

Headers and footers are unique to reports. You can use headers and footers to display certain information on each page. You can add text, graphic objects, OLE objects, database fields, and almost any other object that Approach supports to a header or footer. If you want the page number and date to appear on each page, for example, you can place these features in a text block in the header or footer.

If you set up a header, it appears at the top of every page. If you set up a footer, it appears at the bottom of every page. Figure 7.22 shows a sample report with a header and footer.

Note

When specified, a header or footer appears on every page of the report, including the first page. To suppress the header or footer on the first page of the report (or to use a different header or footer on that page), create a title page (see "Working with Title Pages" later in this chapter). A title page enables you to make the first page different from the balance of the report.

Adding a Header or Footer

To add a header or footer to a report, follow these steps:

1. Switch to Design mode.

2. If the report you want isn't on-screen, select it from the view tabs. You can also select the report from the status bar.

3. Open the **R**eport menu and choose Add **H**eader to add a header, or Add F**o**oter to add a footer. When a header or footer is present in the report, these menu options show checkmarks in the menu.

Header and Footer Sample

FIRST NAME Joseph LAST NAME Jones
FIRM NAME Jones and Jones PHONE
STREET ADR 123 Felton Place CITY New York
STATE NY ZIP 10019

FIRST NAME John LAST NAME Roberts
FIRM NAME Diddle & Diddle PHONE
STREET ADR 217 Ramie Lane CITY New York
STATE NY ZIP 10019

FIRST NAME Mercy LAST NAME Pottir
FIRM NAME Pottir and Co. PHONE
STREET ADR 98 Snider Road CITY New York
STATE Ny ZIP 10023

FIRST NAME John LAST NAME Roberts
FIRM NAME Diddle & Diddle PHONE
STREET ADR 217 Ramie Lane CITY New York
STATE NY ZIP 10019

FIRST NAME Mercy LAST NAME Pottir
FIRM NAME Pottir and Co. PHONE
STREET ADR 98 Snider Road CITY New York
STATE Ny ZIP 10023

FIRST NAME David LAST NAME Green
FIRM NAME Black and Blue PHONE
STREET ADR 1902 Christina Lane CITY Buffalo
STATE NY ZIP 10342

Page 1

Fig. 7.22
A report with a header and a footer displays information that is the same on every page.

After you insert a header or footer in your report, it appears on the page with a black box around it when selected in Design mode (see fig. 7.23). You must scroll down to the bottom of the page to see the footer. It is helpful to turn on the report panel labels by clicking the Show Panels Labels SmartIcon.

> **Note**
>
> When you create a report with Report Assistant (except for a blank report), Approach places a header and footer in the report automatically. The default header contains a text block with the name of the report; the default footer contains a text block with the date and page number.

Deleting a Header or Footer

To delete a header or footer from a report, follow these steps:

1. Switch to Design mode.
2. If the report you want isn't on-screen, select it from the view tabs. You can also select the report from the status bar.

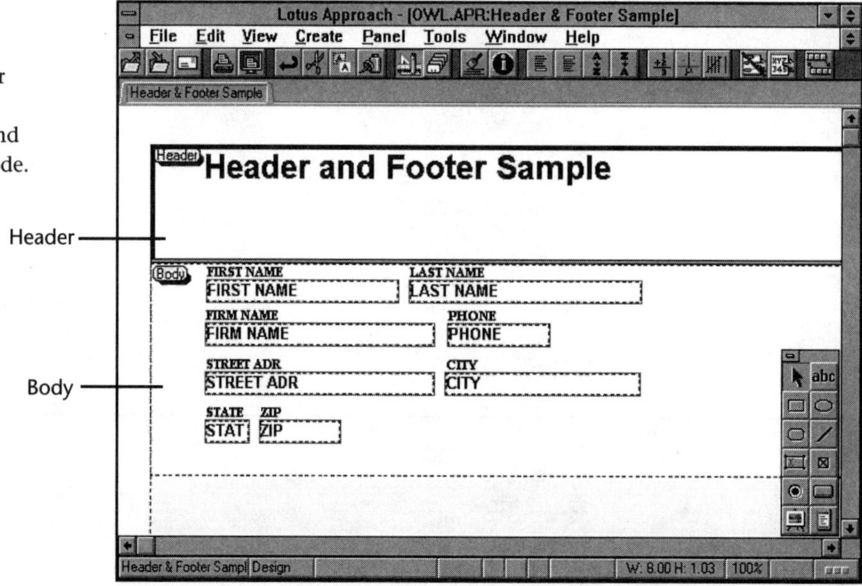

Fig. 7.23 The selected header or footer has a black boundary around it in Design mode.

3. To delete the header from the selected report, open the **R**eport menu and choose Add **H**eader. This turns off the checkmark and the header disappears. To delete the footer, choose Add F**o**oter from the **R**eport menu. This turns off the checkmark and the footer disappears.

Resizing a Header or Footer

When you initially create a header or footer in Approach, it is approximately one text line high (about 1/4 inch). You may need to make the header or footer larger to accommodate more lines of text, graphics, or graphics files. To resize headers and footers, follow these steps:

1. Switch to Design mode.
2. If the report you want isn't on-screen, select the report from the view tabs or the status bar.
3. Scroll the report page until the header or footer area is visible (depending on which one you want to resize).
4. To select the header or footer area, click anywhere in the header or footer area EXCEPT where an object is positioned. You can also press and hold down the Ctrl key and click anywhere in the header or footer.

   When a header or footer is selected, a black border appears around three sides of the header or footer. One edge of the header or footer is gray.

The gray edge is the bottom border of the header or the top border of the footer. The gray border is placed on the bottom edge of the header because you can resize the header only by stretching its bottom border down the page. The gray border is placed on the top edge of the footer because you can resize the footer only by stretching its top border up the page. (The gray border works just like the gray borders discussed earlier in this chapter for resizing a report body panel.)

5. Move the mouse pointer over the gray border. The pointer becomes a double-headed arrow. Drag the gray border until the header or footer is the size you want, and then release the left mouse button.

Adding Objects to Headers and Footers

Once you add a header or footer to a report, you can customize the header or footer to suit your purposes. Although a header or footer you add is empty initially, you can add text blocks, graphics drawn with the graphics tools, and illustrations (graphics files). You can also add all of these objects to the default header or footer that Approach places on a report.

> **Note**
>
> If you add a database field (or a text block containing a database field) to the header or footer, that field will contain the value from the first record on the page. In Browse mode, the field appears in the header or footer exactly the same way it appears in Design mode, with the label and database field name. However, the field displays its value in Preview mode.

You add objects to a header or footer in Design mode the same way you place them elsewhere on a report. To add a text block to a header, for example, click the Text tool in the Drawing toolbar, and then click and drag with the mouse pointer to define the limits of the text block in the header.

After you add a text block, you can modify it in the following ways:

- Resize it by dragging the sizing handles or using the Info Box Dimensions panel.
- Move it by dragging the text block to a new location or using the Info Box Dimensions panel.
- Customize it by selecting the text block, opening the Info Box, and using the font panel or color panel.

- Insert a page number, time, or date into it (select the text block and choose I**n**sert **D**ate, **T**ime, or **P**age # from the **O**bject or pop-up menu).

Let's return to the Owl Publishing example for a moment. Suppose that the company has decided to customize their Cust Data report by adding header and footer information to it. First, switch to Design mode and remove the default header or footer by opening the **R**eport menu and choosing Add **H**eader or Add F**o**oter. To add a new header, follow these steps:

1. Select Cust Data from the view tabs or the status bar.

2. Turn on the rulers by opening the **V**iew menu and choosing **S**how Ruler.

3. Open the **R**eport menu and choose Add **H**eader. The header appears on the report.

4. Click the Text tool in the Drawing toolbar.

5. Move the mouse pointer into the header, and click and drag a text block about 1 1/2 inches long and 1/4 inch high. Locate the text block on the left side of the header.

6. Type **Date:** in the text block.

7. Open the Te**x**t menu and choose I**n**sert **D**ate to insert the current date into the text block (see fig. 7.24).

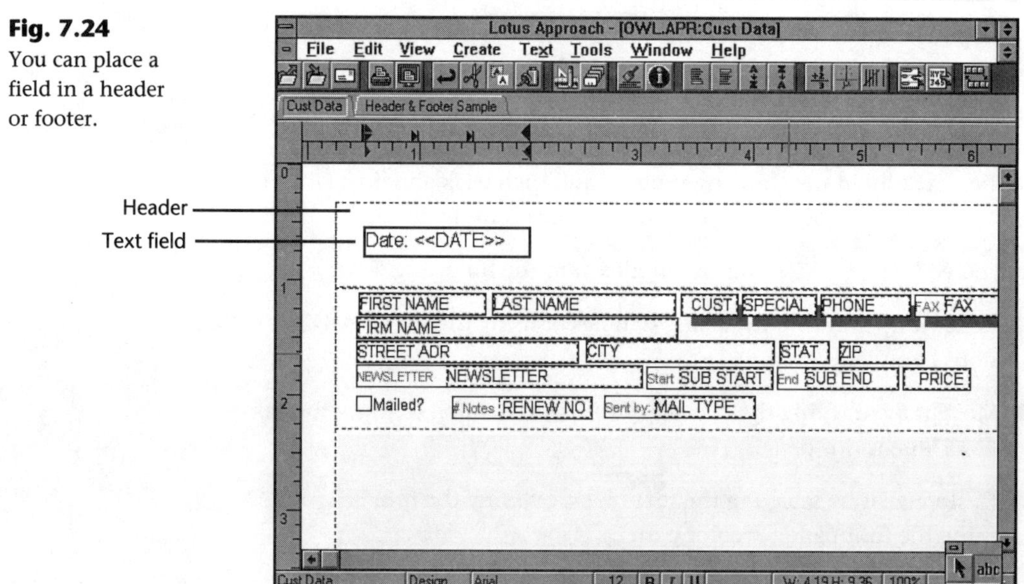

Fig. 7.24
You can place a field in a header or footer.

To add a footer, follow these steps:

1. Open the **R**eport menu and choose Add F**o**oter. The footer appears on the report.

2. Click the Text tool in the Drawing toolbar.

3. In the footer, drag a text block about 1 1/2 inches long and 1/4 inch high. Locate the text block in the center of the footer.

4. Type **Page No:** in the text block.

5. Open the Te**x**t menu and choose I**n**sert **P**age # to insert the page number into the text block.

6. Click anywhere in the footer except in the text block to make the border visible. You can also hold down the Ctrl key and click anywhere in the footer.

7. Drag the gray border up about 1/2 inch. This step increases the size of the footer (see fig. 7.25).

8. Open the **F**ile menu and choose **S**ave Approach File.

9. Switch back to Browse mode.

10. Click the Print Preview SmartIcon to view the report (see fig. 7.26).

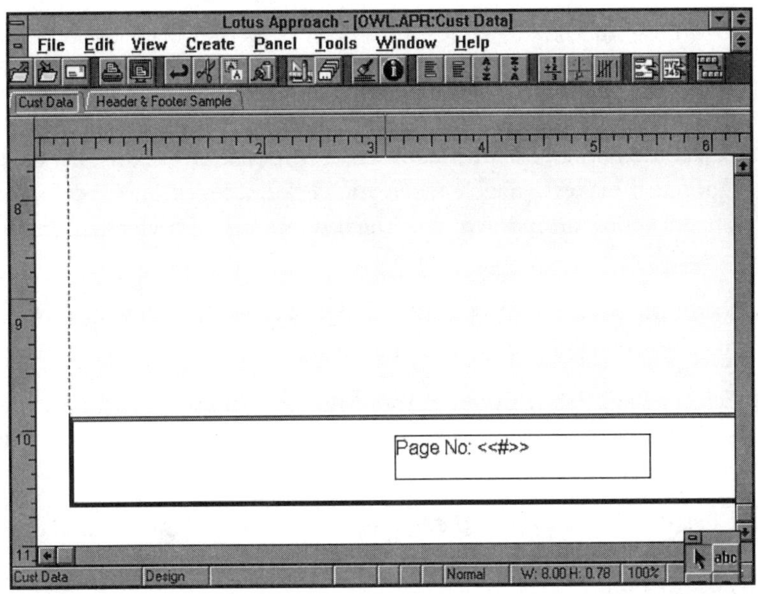

Fig. 7.25
You can make the footer bigger, if necessary.

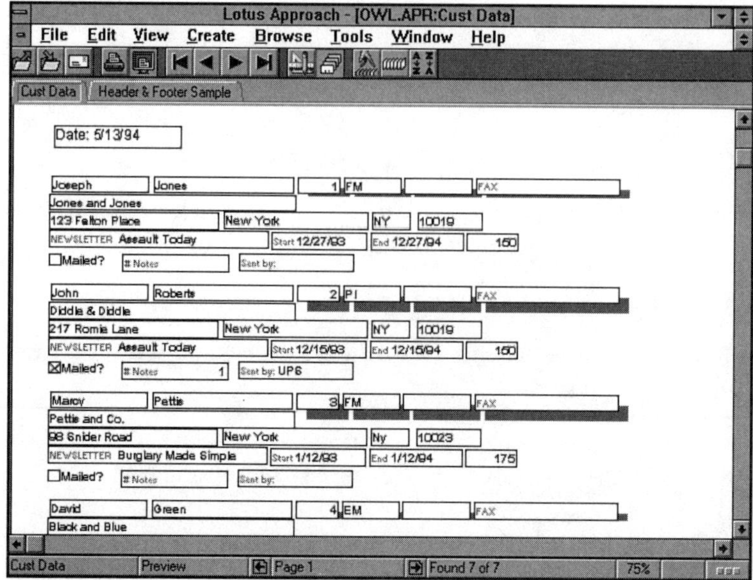

Fig. 7.26
The print preview of the Cust Data report.

Setting the Properties of a Header or Footer

You can set the properties of a header or footer from the Info Box by following these steps:

1. Switch to Design mode.

2. Open the Info Box by choosing **S**tyle & Properties from the **P**anel menu or the pop-up menu. Switch to the colors panel by clicking the Colors tab.

3. Select the border, fill, or shadow color from the drop-down list that Approach makes available when you click Border color, Fill color, or Shadow color drop-down lists. The box labeled T provides a transparent color.

4. Select the border width from the Border Width drop-down list. Available border widths range from hairline to 12 point (1/6 of an inch).

5. Select a Frame style from the Frame drop-down list. The Frame style specifies the format in which Approach draws the border around the selected field.

6. Click the checkboxes in the Borders section (Left, Right, Top, and Bottom) to select on which sides of the body panel you want Approach to display a border.

Working with Title Pages

A report can have a title page that is different from the main pages of a report. Title pages are useful for displaying information that you want shown just once in the report, such as your name. A title page initially looks just like the report page. If the report page has a header or footer, the title page also contains one, but the header and footer on the title page are initially blank. You can customize anything on the title page (including the header and footer) independently of the report page.

Adding a Title Page

To add a title page to a report, follow these steps:

1. Switch to Design mode.
2. If the report you want isn't on-screen, choose it from the view tabs or the status bar.
3. Open the **R**eport menu and choose Add Title **P**age. A checkmark appears next to this command on the **R**eport menu.
4. To display the title page instead of the report layout page, choose Show Title **P**age on the **R**eport menu. A checkmark appears next to this command and Approach displays the title page.

> **Note**
>
> Once you choose Show Title **P**age on the **R**eport menu, you are working with the title page. To switch back to working with the main page of the report, choose Show Title **P**age again to turn off the checkmark. Any changes you make to the title page are limited to the title page—they do not affect the main report page.

Deleting a Title Page

To delete a title page you no longer need, open the **R**eport menu and choose Add Title **P**age. If you change your mind, you can add the title page back again, but any customizing you did will be lost.

Modifying a Title Page

When you initially add a title page, it looks exactly like the main page of the report except that any header or footer is blank. The title page has the same field layout in the record, and all the properties of the fields, graphic objects, and body panels are preserved on the title page. You can make the following types of changes to customize a title page:

- Add a header or footer to the title page. These items can be different from the header or footer on the other pages of the report. You also can have a header or footer on the title page without the rest of the report having one.

- Resize an existing header or footer. If the title page already has a header or footer (because the report page contains them), modifying the header and footer on the title page doesn't affect the header and footer on the main page. Although the title page has a header or footer if the report page has one, the header or footer on the title page is blank—any objects added previously to the report header or footer DO NOT appear on the title page header or footer.

- Add objects to the title page, such as graphics, illustrations (graphics files), and text blocks. You can also add page numbers, times, and dates to the text blocks.

Note

As with headers and footers on the report page, you can place a database field or a text block containing a database field in a title page header or footer. However, this database field will always contain the value of that field in the first record on that page. Also, the field value will not be visible, except in Preview or Design mode with field data showing.

The body panel, which contains the field layout for each record, is visible on the title page (see fig. 7.27). If you don't make any further changes to the title page, it will include records when you print it.

The body panel that contains the record layout on the title page is the same one shown on the report page. If you make any changes to this layout (remove, resize, or move fields), all records in the report are affected. If you resize the body panel in the title page, the records in the rest of the report are also modified.

Setting the Number of Records on the Title Page

When you size the header and footer on the title page, all space remaining between the bottom of the header and the top of the footer is used to print records.

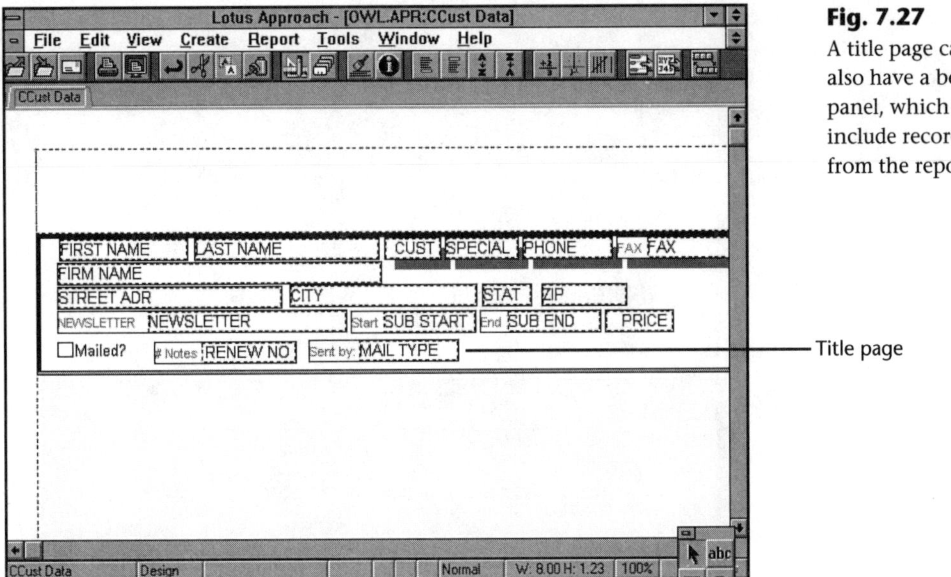

Fig. 7.27
A title page can also have a body panel, which can include records from the report.

The number of records that show on the title page depends on how much room is between the header and the footer. If you don't want any records to print on the title page, size the header and footer so that the bottom of the header and the top of the footer meet. The record layout still shows on the page in Design mode (see fig. 7.28), but no records print on the title page.

To check this layout, switch to Preview mode (see fig. 7.29) or display field data in Design mode (choose S**h**ow Data from the **V**iew menu). Title pages cannot be viewed in Browse mode.

In the Owl Publishing example, suppose the company wants to add a title page—without records—to its main report. Follow these steps to add the title page:

1. Switch to Design mode.

2. Select the Cust Data report from the view tabs or the status bar. You should see the report page showing the record layout.

3. Open the **R**eport menu and choose Add Title **P**age, and then choose Show Title Pa**g**e. The title page is now visible.

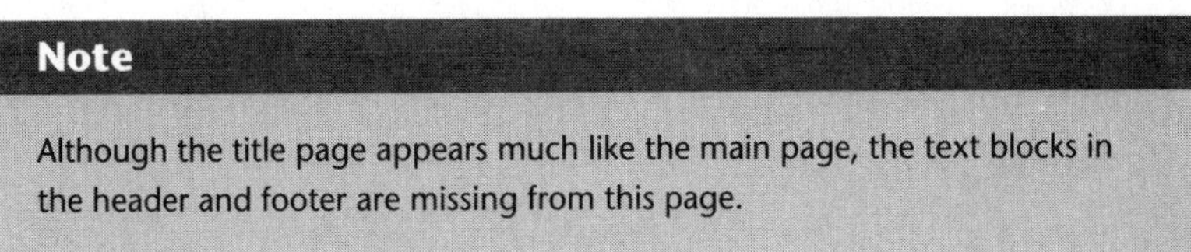

Note

Although the title page appears much like the main page, the text blocks in the header and footer are missing from this page.

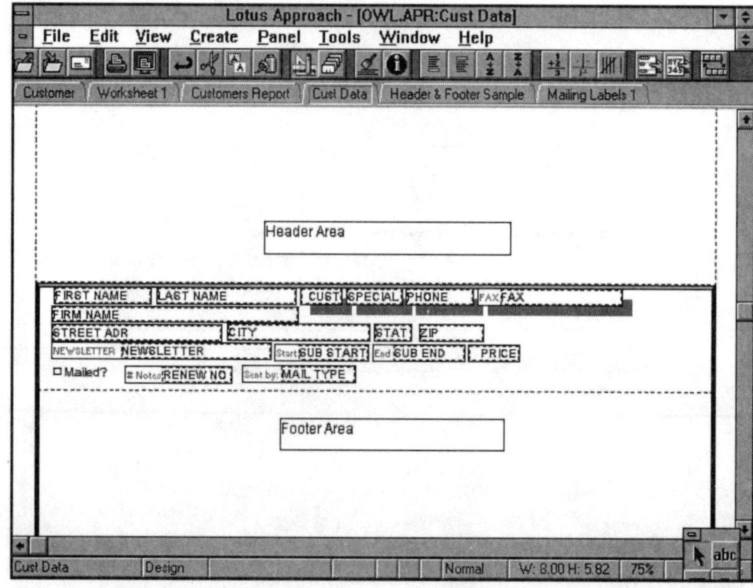

Fig. 7.28
A title page in Design mode that includes a header, footer, and body panel.

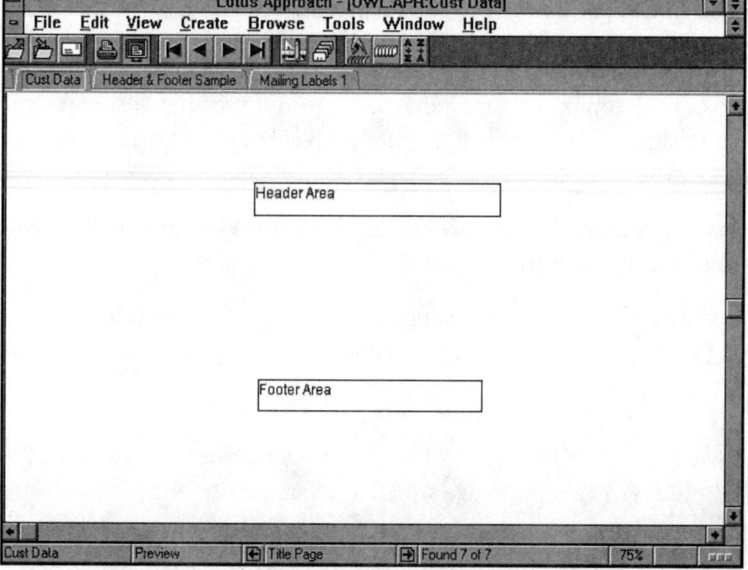

Fig. 7.29
The same title page in Preview mode, with no records showing.

Now, resize the header and footer so that no records print on the title page. Follow these steps:

1. Click in the header to show the black border with the gray bottom border.

2. Drag the gray bottom border down the page so that the header spans the upper-half of the page. Notice that as you make the header bigger, the record layout moves down the page to get out of the area taken by the header.

3. Scroll down the page until you can see the footer. Click the footer to show the black border and the gray top border.

4. Drag the gray top border up the page so that the top border of the footer meets the bottom border of the header. The footer overlays the record layout.

Next, add a text block to the title page header. Follow these steps:

1. If the rulers aren't visible on-screen, open the **V**iew menu and choose Show **R**uler.

2. Click the Text tool in the Drawing toolbar.

3. Move the pointer into the header near the top of the screen, and drag a text block about 3 inches down from the top of the form. The text block should be about 3 inches long and 1/2 inch high.

4. Type **Owl Publishing Customer Report** in the text block.

5. Click the Pointer tool in the Drawing toolbar.

6. Drag the text block in the header so that it is centered on the page.

7. Double-click the text block to open the Text Info Box; or click the text block, open the **O**bject menu and choose **S**tyle & Properties; or click the Info SmartIcon.

8. Switch to the font panel by clicking the Font tab. Select Bold from the Style/Effect list and choose a larger point size (14 point works well) from the Size drop-down list.

9. Switch to Preview mode (click the Preview SmartIcon) to see the title page (see fig. 7.30).

10. Open the **F**ile menu and choose **S**ave Approach File.

Note

The only item that appears on the title page is the text block you placed there. Because you left no room for records on the page, none appear (see fig. 7.30).

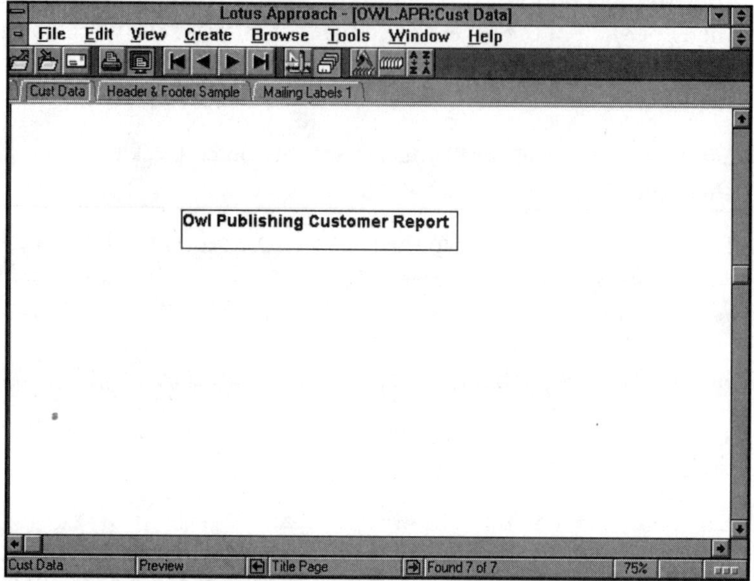

Fig. 7.30
The finished title page for the Cust Data report.

Creating Mailing Labels

One of the most useful features of a database is its capability to generate mailing labels as well as other kinds of labels. If the database contains names and addresses, you can use these labels to mail information. If the database contains a list of the titles in your videotape collection, you can generate labels to place on the videotapes. A wide variety of labels are commercially available, and Approach can format information to fit on most of the popular sizes.

A mailing label is a special type of report, one in which Approach provides extra help in setting the dimensions to match the common sizes of labels available. Because mailing labels are just reports, you can modify mailing labels in most of the same ways you can modify a report. You can even enter data on a label. However, the information for fully specifying a record is rarely present in the limited space available on a label.

You can customize a mailing label in most of the same ways you can customize a form (see Chapter 4 for details on these features). On a mailing label, you can do the following:

- Add, delete, and customize fields
- Customize the text format of a field
- Customize the display format of a field
- Customize the data-entry format of a field
- Add and customize field labels
- Draw graphics, using the graphics tools
- Paste or import illustrations (graphics files)
- Use all the layout tools (rulers, dimensions, grid, alignment, grouping, and so on) to place fields
- Add text blocks and customize them

To practice using mailing labels, follow these steps to create labels for Owl Publishing:

1. Open the database from which you want to generate mailing labels and switch to Design mode.

2. Open the **C**reate menu and choose **M**ailing Labels. The Mailing Label Assistant dialog box appears (see fig. 7.31).

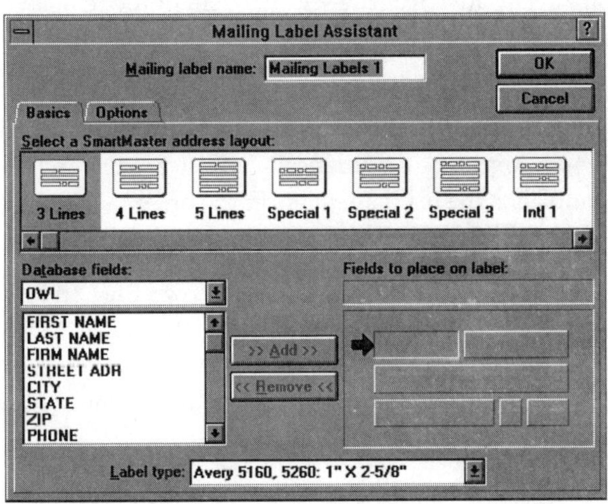

Fig. 7.31 Create mailing labels through the Mailing Label Assistant dialog box.

3. Select a SmartMaster Address Layout from the scrolling list across the top of the Mailing Label Assistant dialog box. The SmartMaster Address Layout sets the template of the address label, including the number of lines of text and the general placement of the field place holders. Approach displays the Fields to Place on La**b**el template in the bottom-right corner of the Mailing Label Assistant dialog box. For the Owl Publishing example, choose 3 Lines from the SmartMaster Address Layout.

Note

You aren't limited by the layout you choose in the Mailing Label Assistant dialog box. You can change the field layout on the mailing label by relocating and sizing fields, and adjusting the font size of the fields.

4. Approach displays one of the template place holders in blue—this is the selected place holder. When you add a database field to the template (as detailed below), Approach adds the database field to the selected place holder. To select where the next database field will be added to the template, click one of the place holders in the template.

5. The database fields are listed in the Da**t**abase Fields list box on the left side of the Mailing Label Assistant dialog box. Select the fields you want on the mailing labels, using these selection methods:

   - To select one field, click it and choose the **A**dd button, or double-click the field. Approach adds the database field to the template and automatically advances the selected field in the template to the next field.

   - To select more than one field at a time, click the first field, hold down the Ctrl key, and click any other fields you want and then click **A**dd. Approach automatically advances the selected template field and adds the database fields in the order in which they are listed in the Da**t**abase Fields list.

   - For the Owl Publishing example, hold down the Ctrl key and click the following fields: FIRST NAME, LAST NAME, STREET ADR, CITY, STATE, and ZIP. Choose **A**dd. The selected fields move to the Fields to Place on La**b**el template on the right side of the Mailing Label Assistant dialog box (see fig. 7.32).

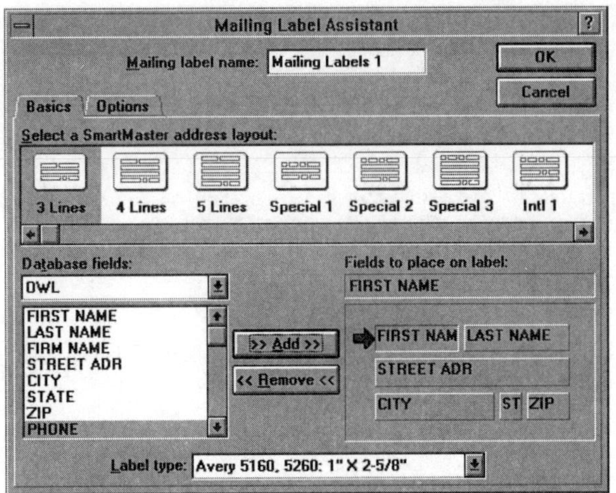

Fig. 7.32
Select the fields you want on Owl Publishing's mailing labels.

6. To specify a standard label, select the type of label you want from the **L**abel Type drop-down list. For this example, select Avery 5161. This label is sheet-fed, with three labels across and 10 labels down (30 to a sheet). If you are using a tractor-feed printer, choose 5261 instead.

   To specify a custom label, choose the Options tab. For more information on specifying a custom label, see "Specifying the Label Characteristics" later in this chapter.

7. Type the name of the mailing label report in the **M**ailing Label Name text box. For this example, leave it as the default name, Mailing Labels 1.

8. Choose OK. Approach creates the mailing label and places it on-screen so that you can make any changes you want (see fig. 7.33).

Tip
To remove a field from the Fields to Place on La**b**el template, click the field and choose **R**emove. You can also double-click the field to remove it.

Note

Approach may place fields outside the boundaries of the label because of the limited space on the label. You need to rearrange the fields so that they are all within the label (see "Arranging the Fields on a Label" later in this chapter). You may also need to specify a smaller font size to fit all the information you want on the label. The rounded rectangle provides a guide to where the label edges are located. This rectangle does not print.

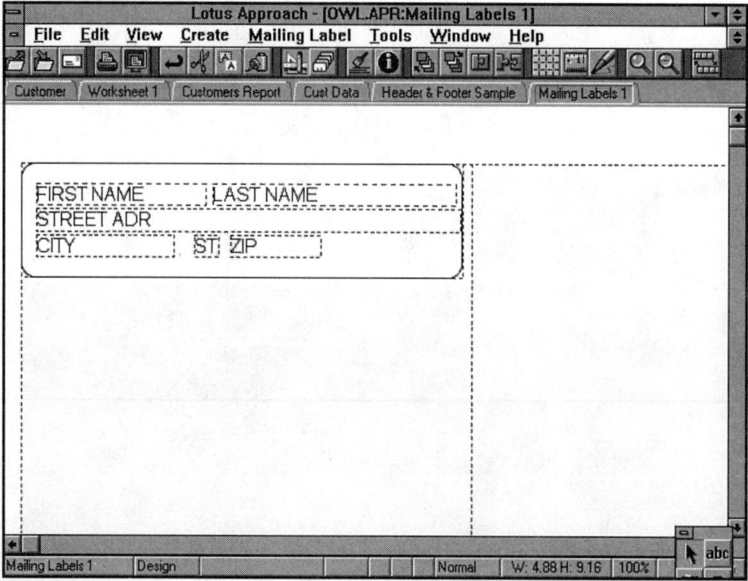

Fig. 7.33
A default mailing label, ready to be customized.

Deleting a Set of Mailing Labels

If you decide you don't need a set of mailing labels anymore, you can delete them by following these steps:

1. Switch to Design mode by opening the **V**iew menu and choosing **D**esign, clicking the Design SmartIcon, or choosing Design from the status bar.

2. If the set of mailing labels you want to delete are not on-screen, choose the set of mailing labels from the view tabs or from the status bar.

3. Open the **E**dit menu and choose D**e**lete Mailing Labels. Confirm that you want to delete the set of mailing labels when Approach asks you.

Duplicating a Set of Mailing Labels

To give you a head start in creating a set of mailing labels that are similar to a set you already have, Approach enables you to duplicate an existing set of mailing labels. Making a duplicate is especially useful when you need to create complex mailing labels. To copy a set of mailing labels, follow these steps:

1. Switch to Design mode by opening the **V**iew menu and choosing **D**esign, clicking the Design SmartIcon, or choosing Design from the status bar.

2. If the set of mailing labels you want to duplicate is not on-screen, choose the set of mailing labels from the view tabs or from the status bar.

3. Open the **E**dit menu and choose **D**uplicate Mailing Labels. The duplicate of your mailing labels appears on-screen. You can make changes (for example, change fonts, add and remove fields, or rearrange fields) to the duplicate without affecting the original.

Approach gives the duplicate set of mailing labels the same name as the original with the words "Copy of" in front of the name. Use the Basics panel of the report Info Box to change the name of the report.

Specifying the Label Characteristics

The Mailing Label Assistant dialog box provides two options for specifying the size and shape of the mailing labels: the **L**abel Type drop-down list and the Options tab.

The **L**abel Type drop-down list provides choices that include the common sizes of Avery labels. Because Avery is the most common brand of computer labels made, you have a good chance of finding your labels on this list. The list includes a wide variety of mailing labels, audio and video tape labels, floppy disk labels (5 1/4-inch and 3 1/2-inch), shipping labels, name badges, Rolodex cards, postcards, file folder labels, and more. If you aren't using Avery labels, you may be able to use the Avery definition if your labels have the same dimensions as a supported Avery label.

The Options tab opens the second panel of the Mailing Label Assistant dialog box so that you can specify custom dimensions for your labels (see fig. 7.34).

Note

You can change the custom options of a mailing label in Design mode. To do so, click the Edit Label Options button in the Mailing Label Info Box. This button opens the Mailing Label Options dialog box. This dialog box is identical to the Mailing Label Assistant Options panel.

Type the name of your custom label definition in the Custom **L**abel field box and list. Click the **A**dd button to add the custom label name to the list. You can also select a custom label name from the list, change the label specifications (as detailed below), and click the **C**hange button.

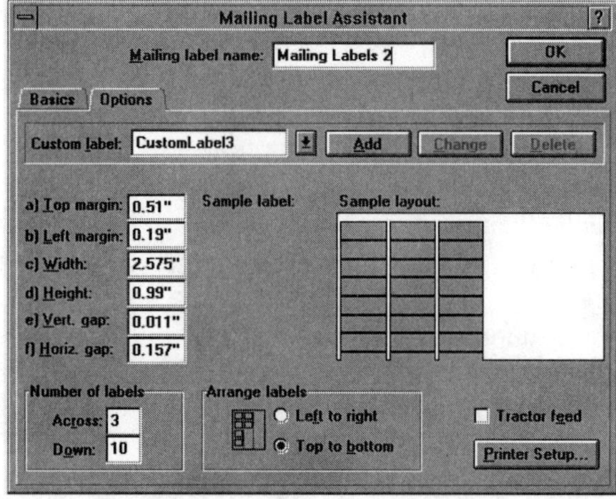

Fig. 7.34
Customize label dimensions through the Mailing Label Assistant dialog box.

To delete a custom label definition, select the label from the Custom **L**abel list and click the **D**elete button.

Enter the dimensions of your custom labels in the center section of the Options panel. As you enter the dimensions, the Sample Layout changes to give you an idea of how Approach will print the labels on the page. The label dimensions are:

- **T**op Margin: The distance between the top line of labels and the top edge of the page.
- **L**eft Margin: The distance between the left edge of the labels and the left edge of the page.
- **W**idth of each label.
- **H**eight of each label.
- **V**ert. gap: The vertical gap between labels on the page.
- **H**oriz. gap: The horizontal gap between labels on the page.

In the Arrange Labels section, choose the printing option you want. **L**eft to Right tells Approach to print the labels in order of rows across the page. **T**op to Bottom tells Approach to print the labels in order by columns.

Set the balance of the label specifications across the bottom of the Options panel:

- In the Number of Labels section, type the number of labels Ac**r**oss the page and the number of labels D**o**wn the page. The Sample Layout adjusts to display your label layout.

- If you are using tractor-fed labels, choose the Tractor F**e**ed checkbox. If you are using sheet-fed labels (such as those used by laser or inkjet printers), make sure the Tractor F**e**ed checkbox is not checked.

- Type the size of the respective margins in the T**o**p Margin, L**e**ft Margin, R**i**ght Margin, and **B**ottom Margin text boxes.

Note

You do not need to enter top margin measurements for tractor-fed labels.

When you choose the **P**rinter Setup button in the bottom-right corner of the Options panel, the Print Setup dialog box appears. In this dialog box, you can configure your printer with all its normal options.

Arranging the Fields on a Label

After you specify the label size and select the fields, you can size and arrange the fields on the label. You may also need to change the font and size of the fields so that all the information fits on the mailing label. You perform these operations on mailing labels the same way you perform them on forms or reports. The following paragraphs summarize these actions:

- To size a field, select it, and then drag its sizing handles until the field is the size you want. You can also use the dimensions panel in the field's Info Box.

- To move a field, select it, place the pointer inside the field, and drag the field to its new location. You can also use the dimensions panel in the field's Info Box.

- To change the font, size/effect, alignment, text color, and relief, select the field and choose the options you want from the font panel in the field's Info Box.

- To close up empty spaces when printing, check the Left and Up checkboxes on the dimensions panel of the field's Info Box (see the earlier section, "Using Slide Up and Slide Left").

- Use the colors panel in the field's Info Box to set the border width, frame style, border color, fill color, shadow color, and the border location (left, right, top, and bottom).
- Use the Label panel in the field's Info Box to set the label font, style/effect, size, alignment, label text, position, color, and text relief. Normally, mailing labels don't use labels because of the limited space. To suppress a field's label, set the Label position to No label.

Setting the Mailing Label Properties

Aside from the fields, a mailing label design in Approach consists of three other parts: a rounded rectangle graphic, a body panel, and the mailing label background.

Approach uses the rounded rectangle to delineate the borders of each label. You can select the rounded rectangle by clicking anywhere in a mailing label except where there is a field. By default, the rounded rectangle is non-printing, but you can set it to print with the mailing labels by unchecking the Non-printing checkbox on the Basics panel of the rectangle's Info Box. As with any other graphic object, you can adjust the border width, border color, fill color, shadow color, and frame from the colors panel of the Info Box. Of course, unless you are going to print the rounded rectangle, there is little point in adjusting its properties.

The body panel sets the boundaries of each label. The panel itself is not normally visible because it is covered by the rounded rectangle discussed above. However, you can select the body panel by clicking anywhere in the mailing label while holding down the Ctrl key. You can adjust the border width, border color, border location, fill color, shadow color, and frame from the colors panel of the Info Box. You can make the body panel visible by setting the fill color of the rounded rectangle to T (transparent).

Click between the labels in a mailing label layout to gain access to the Mailing Labels background. From the Basics panel of the Mailing Label's Info Box, you can change the mailing label's name by typing a new name into the Mailing Label Name field box. You can also use the colors panel to set the border width and location, frame style, border color, and fill color. However, the properties of the colors panel are always identical for the mailing labels and body panel.

Printing Records

You can have Approach print your currently selected form or report. If you have sorted the records, they print in the current sort order. If you have performed a find operation, only the records in the found set print.

Before printing, take the following steps to ensure that you print only what you need:

1. Switch to the form or report that you want to print. Approach prints the form or report that you now are using.
2. Choose the set of records that you want to print. Approach prints the current found set of records (or all records, if there is no found set).
3. Sort the records in the order in which you want them printed. Approach prints the records in the sort order you now are using.

Previewing the Printout

Before printing, you may want to see what the output will look like, in case you want to make some last-minute changes. The Print Preview feature shows how the report will look when printed.

If you have formatted certain objects as non-printing, or if you are using options such as Slide Up or Slide Left, what appears on the printout will be different from what appears on-screen. With Approach's Print Preview feature, you can check the report before wasting paper.

To preview a page, first make sure you are in Browse mode. Click the Preview SmartIcon, choose Preview from the status bar, or open the **F**ile menu and choose Pre**v**iew. The previewed page shows on your screen at 75 percent of normal size. To see the previewed page in a larger size, click the left mouse button or select an alternate magnification from the status line.

To exit Preview mode, click the Preview SmartIcon again, select a different mode from the status line, or choose Pre**v**iew again from the **F**ile menu.

Printing the Report

To print the form or report, open the **F**ile menu and choose **P**rint. The Print dialog box appears (see fig. 7.35). The specifications for your printer are listed at the top of the dialog box. To change these specifications, click the **S**etup button.

From the Print dialog box, you can print to your printer or to a file.

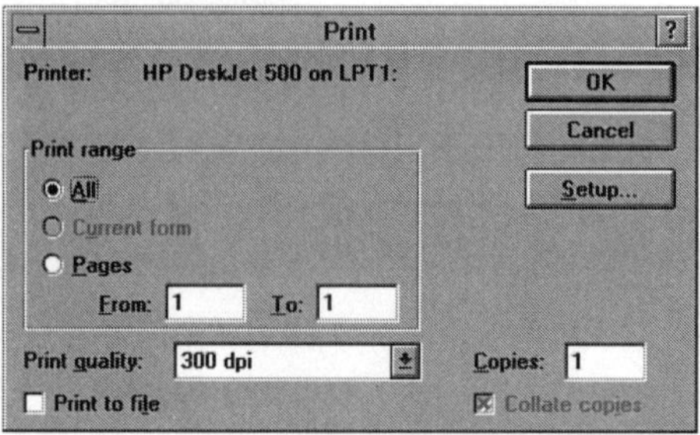

Fig. 7.35
Set your print options through the Print dialog box.

Printing to the Printer

Before printing to your printer, you may want to set some options in the Print dialog box. Use the option buttons in the Print Range section to set the pages you want to print:

- The **A**ll button prints all the records in the current set.
- C**u**rrent Form prints only the form page you have on-screen. This option is valid only for form letters and forms.
- The **P**ages option enables you to specify exactly the range of pages you want printed. Choose **P**ages, and enter the number of the first page you want printed in the **F**rom text box. Enter the last page you want printed in the **T**o text box. To print from a page to the end, enter a number only in the **F**rom text box. To print from the beginning to a page, enter a number only in the **T**o text box.

The Print dialog box also provides two other options:

- In the **C**opies text box, you specify the number of copies you need.
- In the Collate Cop**i**es checkbox, you specify how you want multiple copies printed. If you leave this box blank, Approach prints multiple copies of the first page, followed by multiple copies of the next page, and so on. If you select Collate Cop**i**es so that the checkbox contains an X, Approach prints all pages of the entire first copy, all pages of the second copy, and so on.

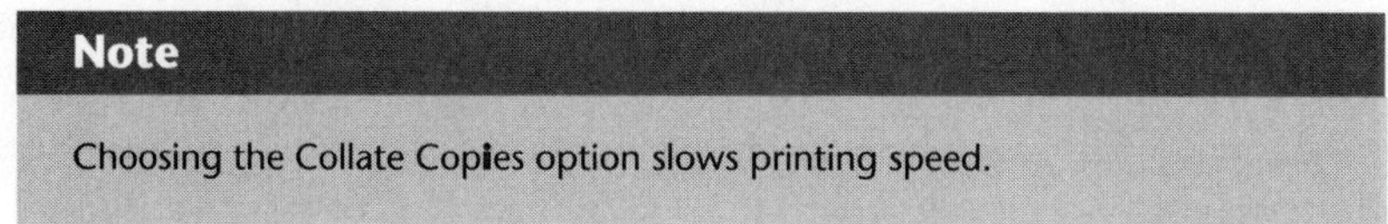
Note

Choosing the Collate Cop**i**es option slows printing speed.

After you finish setting your options, click OK to print your information.

Printing to a File

Printing to a file saves a printed version of your document to a file. You can then print it later or transmit the report by modem. The saved file contains all the information necessary to send that file to the configured printer. If you have an HP LaserJet as your selected printer, for example, the file is saved with all the PCL commands embedded. A file saved in this format (or in PostScript format, if you have a PostScript printer configured) is not readable on-screen.

Tip
To save a printed disk file in a format that you can read on-screen, reset your printer configuration to Windows' Generic/Text Only printer driver.

To print to a file, follow these steps:

1. Choose Print to Fi**l**e in the Print dialog box so that an X appears in the checkbox.

2. Click OK in the Print dialog box, and the Print to File dialog box appears (see fig. 7.36).

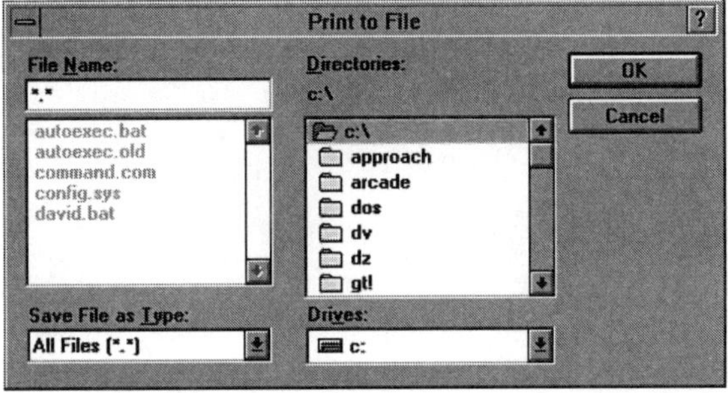

Fig. 7.36
The Print to File dialog box.

3. In the File **N**ame text box, type the name of the file you want to print.

4. Use the **D**irectories list and the Dri**v**es drop-down list to specify where you want Approach to save the file.

5. Click OK in the Print to File dialog box to save the printed file.

From Here...

As you've seen, reports are similar to forms in many ways, but have some important differences as well. You learned how to build a report, add fields to the report, and customize the format of those fields. You also saw how to "dress up" reports with graphics and text. Headers, footers, and title pages—not available for forms—enable you to customize a report by adding items that appear on every page and to create a special first page. Mailing labels are a special kind of report; they enable you to create labels using the data in your database and to place that data on commercial labels.

You can do much more with reports. For more information, refer to the following chapters in this book:

- Chapter 10, "Using Advanced Field Types," tells you how to create more complex field types which can be very useful on a report.
- Chapter 12, "Creating Advanced Reports," continues the lessons learned in this chapter, discussing how to create reports that include summary information.
- Chapter 15, "Creating Charts," shows you how to make colorful graphs and charts to include in reports.

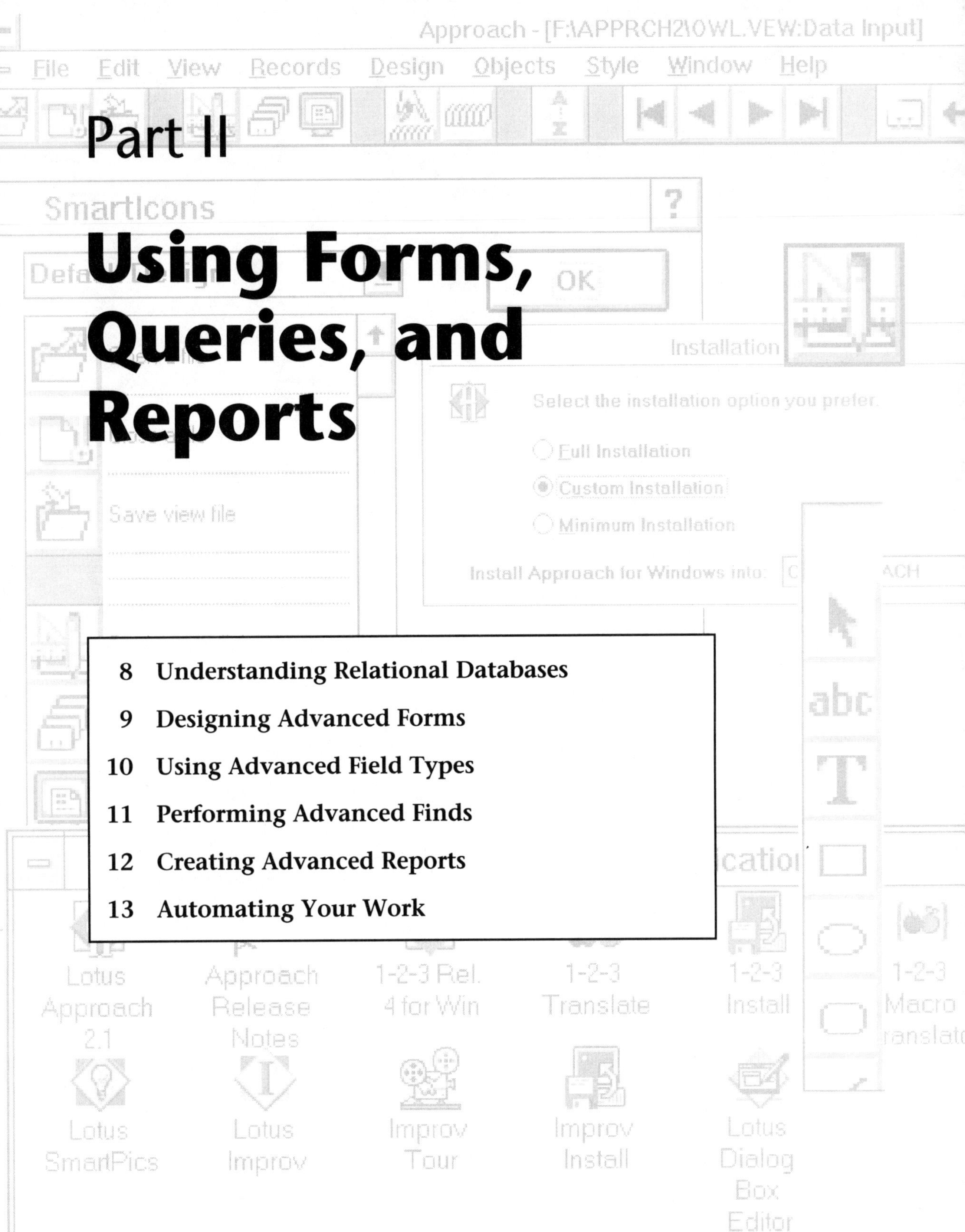

Part II

Using Forms, Queries, and Reports

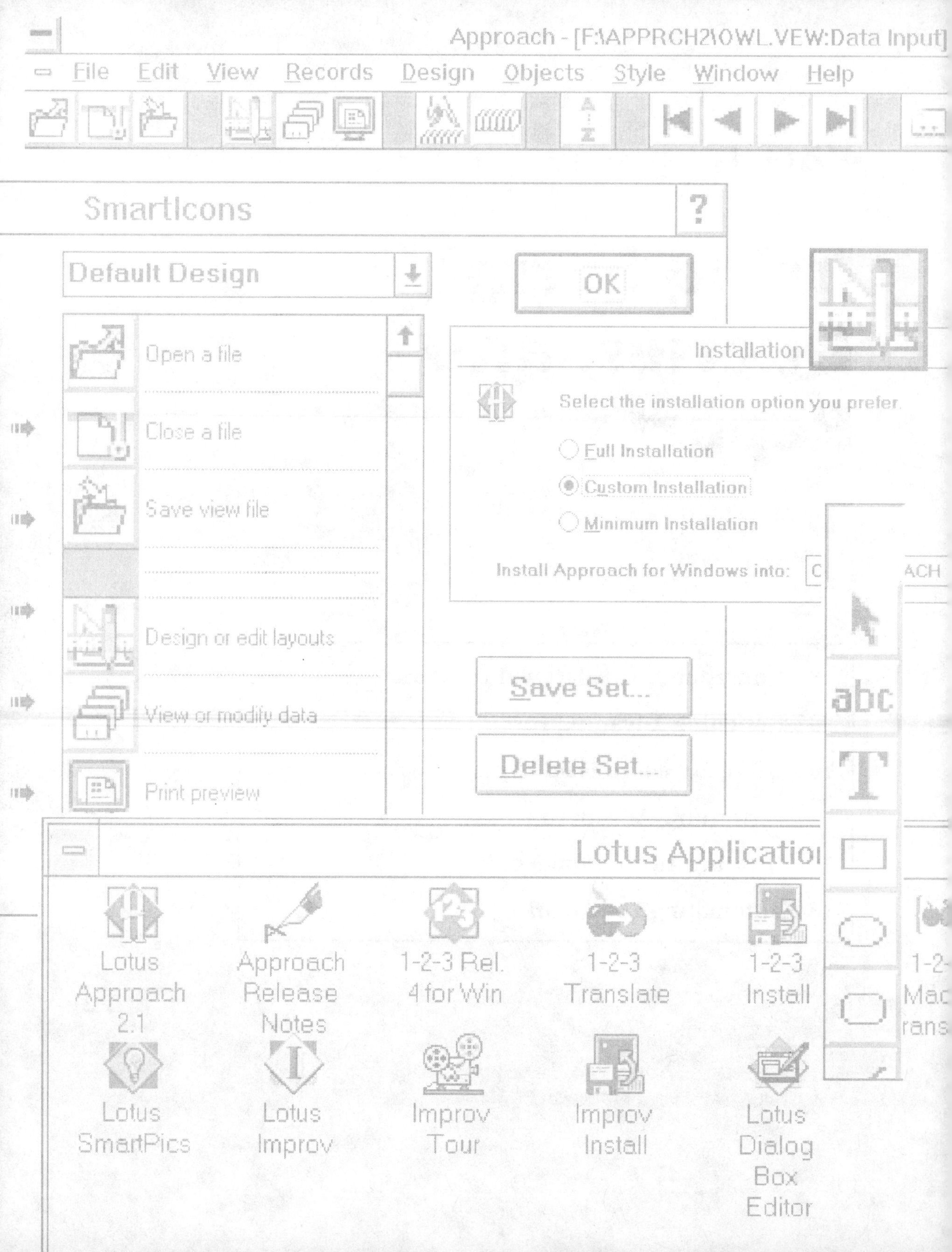

Approach - [F:\APPRCH2\OWL.VEW:Data Input]
File Edit View Records Design Objects Style Window Help
SmartIcons
Default Design
OK
Open a file
Close a file
Save view file
Design or edit layouts
View or modify data
Print preview
Save Set...
Delete Set...
Installation
Select the installation option you prefer.
Full Installation
Custom Installation
Minimum Installation
Install Approach for Windows into:
abc
T
Lotus Applicatio
Lotus Approach 2.1
Approach Release Notes
1-2-3 Rel. 4 for Win
1-2-3 Translate
1-2-3 Install
Lotus SmartPics
Lotus Improv
Improv Tour
Improv Install
Lotus Dialog Box Editor

Chapter 8

Understanding Relational Databases

8

Up to this point, this book has discussed keeping all data in a single table. A database that stores everything in a single table is called a *flat file*. This chapter introduces a powerful new kind of database called a *relational database*. You will learn the advantages of a relational database over a flat-file database, as well as how to set up relational databases. You will also completely rebuild the Owl database near the end of this chapter to make it relational.

In this chapter, you learn how to:

- Distinguish flat-file from relational databases and the advantages of each
- Set up a relational link, including many-to-many, many-to-one, and one-to-one relationships
- Set up relational options
- Join aliased databases
- Set data-entry options for relational databases

Understanding the Disadvantages of Flat Files

The advantage of a flat-file database is that designing one is very straightforward. Keeping all your data in a single table, however, has some significant disadvantages. These disadvantages include wasting disk space, typing unnecessary data, and having to change data in multiple places.

Consider the Owl Publishing database. It includes customer information, such as names, addresses, and phone numbers. It also includes the name of the newsletter to which the customer subscribes, the price, and the subscription dates.

What would happen, however, if one customer wants to subscribe to more than one newsletter? Handling such a situation with the current design would be very difficult. You could create another record for that subscriber, complete with all the information about that person (such as address, phone number, and so forth). The new record would also contain the information about the additional newsletter. Thus, if a person wants to subscribe to three newsletters, that subscriber would have three separate records with three sets of customer information in the database (see fig. 8.1).

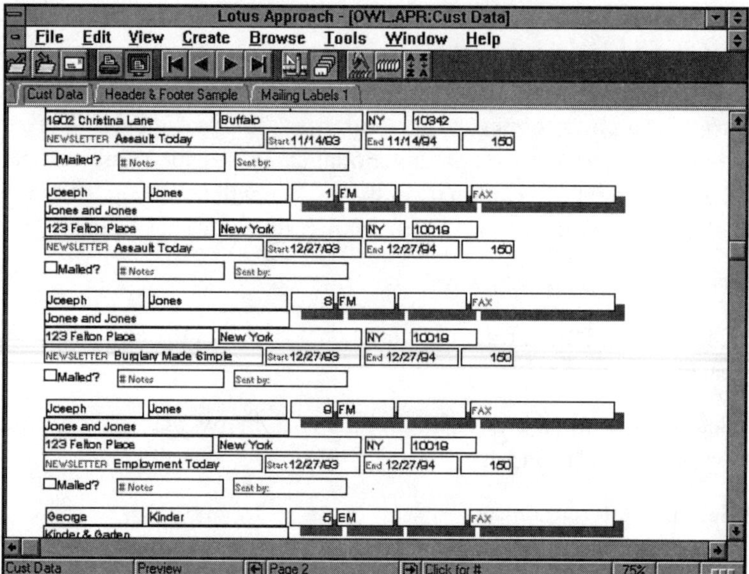

Fig. 8.1
A flat-file database requires redundant information for repeat customers.

Using multiple records in this situation presents the following problems:

- Information that is largely a duplicate of information stored in another record takes up quite a bit of disk space.
- Typing in all those extra records takes a good deal of time. Imagine if Owl Publishing were a large publishing house, with hundreds of newsletters. Would you want to retype all those addresses into the database?

- What if one of your larger customers changed addresses? Someone would have to go through the multiple records and change the address in each record.

You may have thought of a potential solution already—creating multiple sets of fields in the database (and on the form) for holding newsletter information. You can create, for example, the fields NEWSLETTER1, NEWSLETTER2, NEWSLETTER3, and so on to hold the title information. However, this "solution" presents some problems of its own:

- How many sets of fields do you make? If you create only a few sets, the day will come when you run out of fields. At that point, you will have to create more sets of fields, revising the database and the form to hold them. If you create a large number of sets, you are wasting space in the database and on the form—and you can still run out of fields.

- How do you find information in a query? Suppose that you want to find all subscribers of a particular newsletter. The name of that newsletter may appear in the NEWSLETTER1 field on one record, in the NEWSLETTER3 field in another record, and so on. Approach enables you to find all records in which the contents of one field match your criteria OR the contents of another field match your criteria. These queries become unwieldy, however, when you need to check the contents of a large number of fields.

These problems are difficult, and this example has considered only the case in which one set of data (the newsletter data) occurs multiple times. If another set of data also occurs multiple times (such as a firm with multiple entries in the SPECIALTY field), the problem quickly becomes unmanageable with a flat-file database.

Finding the Relational Database Solution

The solution to this dilemma is to use multiple tables (databases)—that is, not to store all your information in a single table. For the preceding example, you could store the information about the customers (name, address, phone) in one table, and the newsletter subscription information (newsletter name, price, subscription dates) in another table. Because the two tables must have a relationship that identifies which newsletter subscription information belongs to each customer, this type of database is called a "relational" database. Approach enables you to construct and use relational databases.

Setting Up a Relational Link

To create a relationship between two databases, you must join them. A *join* identifies one or more fields in each database that relates records in the two databases. It's usually best to use a unique ID value in each database, but you can use a combination of fields that uniquely identify a record in one of the databases. Because the join establishes the relationship between two databases, a join is also called a *relational link* between two databases. When you specify a record in one database, the value in the join field(s) of that database is used to find the matching record(s) in the other database. Join field(s) are the only place in which information from one database also is stored in another database.

In the Owl Publishing example, the customer database would contain customer information such as name, address, phone, and so forth. One of the fields would be Customer ID (CUST ID), which would contain a unique number that identifies a customer.

The Subscription database would contain information on subscriptions (newsletter title, subscription start date, subscription end date, and so forth). Clearly, you would need a field in the Subscription database to identify which customer the subscription belongs to. You would need the Customer ID (CUST ID) field in the Subscription database as well. The CUST ID field would be the field that relates the two databases—the relational link.

Note

The relational fields don't have to have the same name in the two databases, but using the same name is helpful since it makes identifying the related fields easier.

When you identify a customer record in the customer database, Approach automatically has the value in the CUST ID field. With this information, Approach can obtain the records with the matching value in the CUST ID field of the subscription database.

Understanding the Advantages of a Relational Database

The advantages of a relational structure are significant:

- You enter data only once. The subscription information database doesn't contain the customer address information. Such information appears only in the Customer database. Even customers that subscribe to multiple newsletters have only a single record in the customer database. Thus, the customer's address is typed only once.

- Data is stored only once. The customer database contains the address information in a single record. If the customer moves, you need to change just a single record for that customer in the customer database to update all your address information for that customer.

- You can enter an unlimited number of related records in the Subscription database. If a customer subscribes to another newsletter, all you need to do is enter the new subscription information in the subscription database with the CUST ID for that customer.

Deciding When to Use a Relational Database

If you haven't used a relational database before, deciding when you should switch from a flat-file design to a relational design may be unclear. The answer is actually quite simple: any time you need to store more than one occurrence of a piece of information, you need to think about using a relational design. In the Owl Publishing example, you found that you needed to store multiple occurrences of subscription information. Thus, you needed to build a new database to hold that information. If Owl Publishing decides that the company needs to keep track of multiple specialties (SPECIALTY), that information also would be a good candidate for a separate—yet related—database.

Deciding What a Related Database Should Contain

The related database should contain all the information that is directly connected to the subject of that database. The Owl subscription database, for example, would contain the newsletter title, subscription start date, subscription end date, and price, because each quantity can occur only once for a given subscription. A subscription can have only one subscription start date. If the subscription start date changes (the customer re-subscribes), you enter a new record in the subscription database for this new subscription.

Using Information from Related Databases

After you build relationships between databases, you can place the information from related databases on the same form. The form is based on a "main" database, as discussed in Chapter 9. This form also can contain fields from related databases (called *detail databases*). When you change the data on a form for a field that comes from a detail database, the information in the detail database is updated automatically.

Understanding the Types of Database Relationships

Databases may be related to one another in three ways: many-to-one, one-to-one, and one-to-many.

Many-to-One Relationships

In a many-to-one relationship, a record in the primary database has no more than one matching record in another database, but a record in the other database matches more than one record in the primary database (see fig. 8.2).

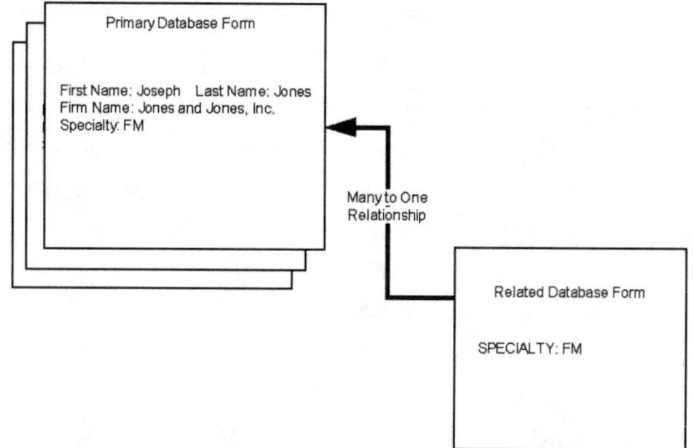

Fig. 8.2 A many-to-one relationship, where several subscribers may have a value of FM in the SPECIALTY field.

Many-to-one relationships are very useful for performing lookups. When you enter the value for the relational field on your form, a lookup can retrieve other information about that value from the related database. You then can place this related data on your form (see Chapter 9 for information on how to set up a form this way). You don't have to type the data retrieved from the related database, nor do you need to store it in your primary database.

Suppose that you have a database that contains a field for the two-character SPECIALTY code. Each record in the Specialty database can also contain other data, such as a text field explaining what the code means. After your Customer database and your Specialty database are related (by the SPECIALTY field in each database), the information in the Specialty database would be available on the Customer form. Entering the SPECIALTY code (or choosing it from a list) on the Customer form establishes the matching record in the Specialty database. You then can place the text explanation from this record onto the Customer form—without having to type it (see fig. 8.3).

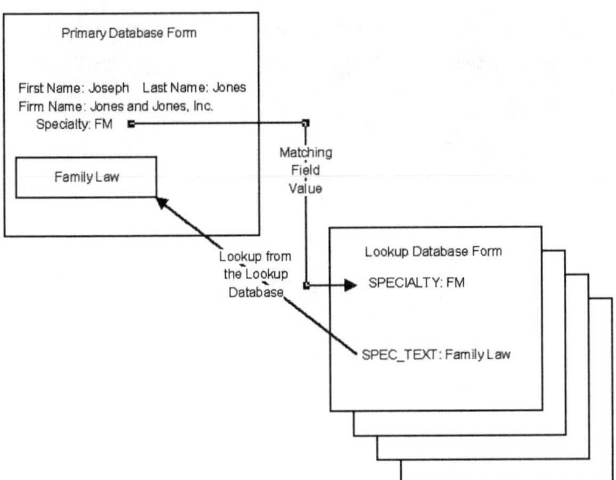

Fig. 8.3
Establishing a link between the Customer and Specialty databases.

For a lookup to work properly, the linking field must come from the primary database for the form or report. In the example above, the SPECIALTY field displayed on the form must come from the Customer database (although the SPECIALTY field is present in both databases).

One-to-One Relationships

In a one-to-one relationship, a record in the primary database has no more than one matching record in another database. At first, you could include the field for that information in your primary database. However, there are some good reasons for occasionally using one-to-one relationships.

One good reason for setting up a one-to-one relationship is for security and confidentiality. You may have, for example, employee information that includes mailing address and salary. Clerical staff may enter the addresses, but the salary information is confidential. You could set up the address information in a database with its own form, and then set up another database that contains the salary information. The two databases can be joined by Employee ID.

Chapter 9 shows how you can look up the employee address from the address database and place this information on the Salary form when working with the Salary database (see figs. 8.4 and 8.5).

It is rare that you need to use one-to-one relationships in Approach. You could achieve the same results as in the example above by including the confidential data in the main database, but providing multiple Approach files. The Approach file used by the clerical staff would display only nonconfidential fields, while another (password-protected) Approach file contains forms and reports that display all the data, including the confidential salary information.

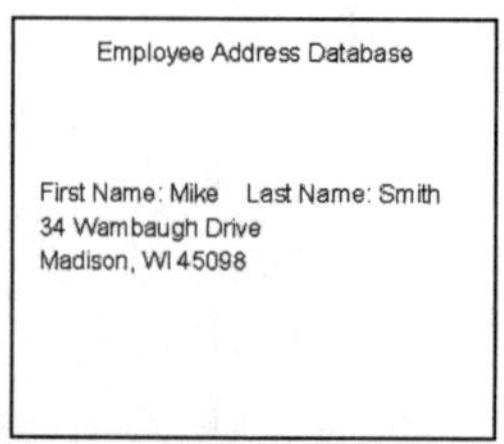

Fig. 8.4
Entering an address in the Employee Address view file.

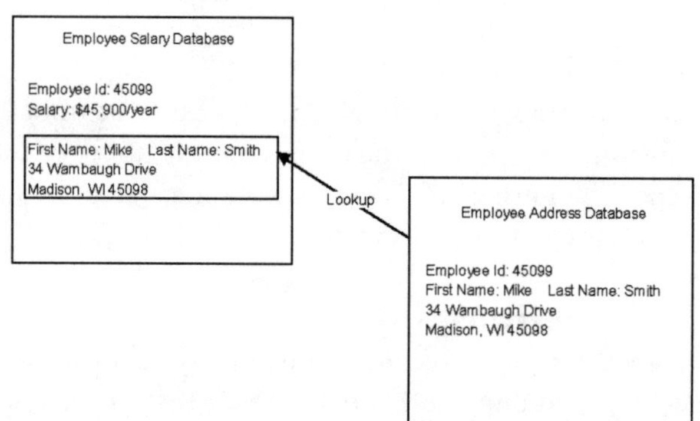

Fig. 8.5
Looking up and placing the address on the form in the Salary view file.

One-to-Many Relationships

In a one-to-many relationship, a single record in the primary database can have many matching records in another (detail) database (see fig. 8.6).

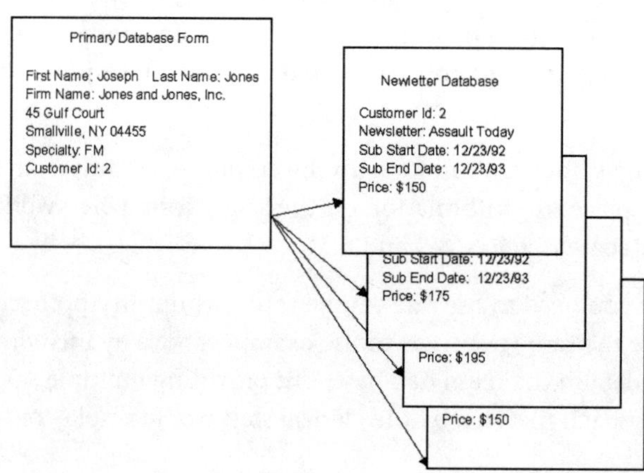

Fig. 8.6
A one-to-many relationship, where a customer can have a subscription to many different newsletters.

The newsletter example illustrates this relationship well. Each customer record in the Customer database can have many matching subscription records in the Subscription database. Approach enables you to see these many records on a form in a repeating panel. A *repeating panel* is a small table that displays records from a related database on a form.

The field(s) that relates the two databases in a one-to-many relationship should identify each record uniquely in the primary database. Thus, using a unique Customer ID works well. In contrast, if the values in the related fields aren't unique, strange things can happen. Suppose that you run a search for a customer whose last name is Brown. If you use LAST NAME as the related field, Approach finds the same set of matching records in the secondary database for everyone named Brown, which is clearly not correct.

Note

Although a single record in the primary database can have multiple related records in the secondary database, each record in the secondary database must match no more than one record in the primary database. For Owl Publishing, each customer record can have multiple subscription records, but each subscription record must be related to only a single customer record, because the related field is the unique CUST ID field.

Circumstances do exist, however, in which each record in the secondary database matches more than one record in the primary database. Suppose that you have a list of customers and a list of sales representatives. If each customer has multiple sales reps, and each sales rep calls on multiple customers, you have a many-to-many relationship. Relational databases can't handle many-to-many relationships directly, although you can work around this limitation (as discussed in Chapter 16).

Joining Databases

Setting up the relational link between two or more databases is called joining them. To join two or more databases, you must do the following:

- Identify two or more databases to be joined.
- Identify the field(s) in each database to be the basis of the relationship.

After you define a join, it's stored as part of the Approach file. Any databases you open in the Join dialog box and join to other databases also are stored as part of the Approach file. Opening the Approach file opens all the joined databases and establishes any relational links you have defined.

Note

All databases you open in the Join dialog box must be joined to each other—that is, you must be able to navigate from any one database to any other database in the Join dialog box by traversing the join links. If you haven't set up the Join dialog box this way, the OK button will be dimmed.

Approach enables you to join up to 50 databases together. You have considerable flexibility in how you join the databases. You could join multiple databases to one main database, for example, or you could join database A to database B, join database B to database C, and so on.

Note

Approach doesn't allow you to join two databases that are joined to the same database. If, for example, database A is joined to database B, and database B is joined to database C, you can't join database A to database C because A and C are joined to B. However, you may use database Aliases to circumvent this limitation. See "Joining Aliased Databases" later in this chapter.

To join two databases, follow these steps:

1. Open the **F**ile menu and choose **O**pen. From the Open dialog box, select the Approach file you want to open. Any databases used by the selected Approach file open automatically when you open the Approach file.

   Note

   The Approach file you open is the one that stores the relational information you define.

Tip
You can click any field in a database in the Join dialog box. Approach displays the field name, type, and length in the dialog box.

2. Open the **C**reate menu and choose **J**oin. The Join dialog box appears (see fig. 8.7). Any database associated with the Approach file opened in step 1 becomes visible in the working area of this dialog box, and a list of fields appears under the heading for each database.

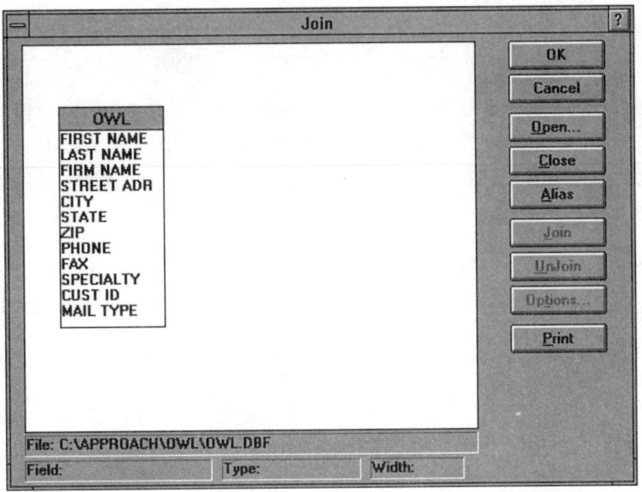

Fig. 8.7
Join databases through the Join dialog box.

3. Choose **O**pen to open a database you want to join to any databases already available in the Join dialog box. The Open dialog box opens (see fig. 8.8).

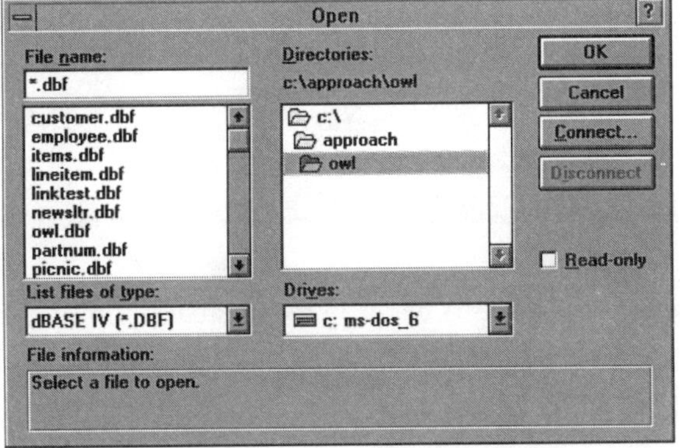

Fig. 8.8
Select a database to which you want to relate.

4. From the list box on the left side of the dialog box, select the database you want to add to the Join dialog box. The name of the database appears in the File **N**ame box.

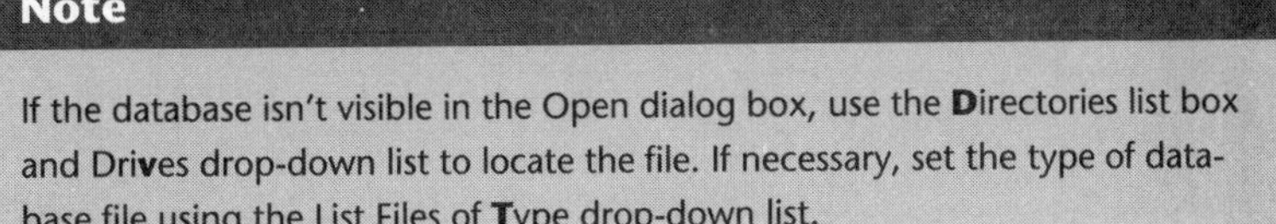
Note

If the database isn't visible in the Open dialog box, use the **D**irectories list box and Dri**v**es drop-down list to locate the file. If necessary, set the type of database file using the List Files of **T**ype drop-down list.

Tip
Approach lets you join databases of different types. For example, you can join a dBASE III+ database to a Paradox database.

5. Click OK. The database you selected in the Open dialog box now appears in the Join dialog box, with its list of fields (see fig. 8.9).

6. Select a database (such as the OWL database in fig. 8.9), and choose the field that will link this database to the newly opened database. The linking field may be a field already used to link to another database. Approach highlights the field name.

7. Select a field in the newly opened database (the NEWSLTR database in fig. 8.9) that you will use to link to the first database. Approach highlights the field name.

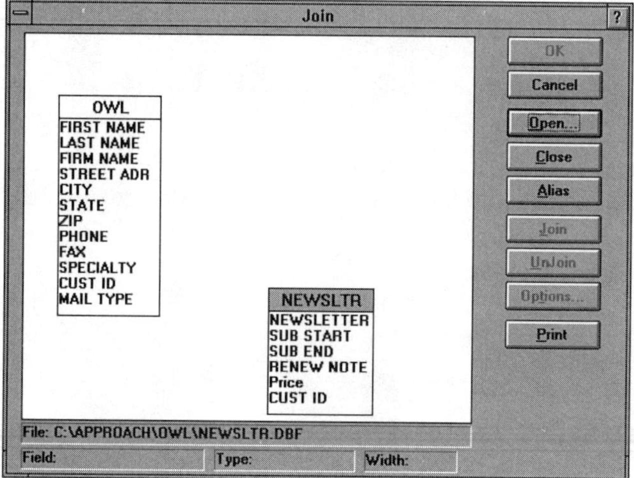

Fig. 8.9
Both databases are displayed in the Join dialog box.

8. Click **J**oin. A line appears between the databases, linking the fields selected in steps 7 and 8 (see fig. 8.10).

9. If you are going to join two databases in more than a single field, repeat steps 7–9 to establish the additional joins.

Note

You can also establish a join between two databases by clicking a join field in the first database and dragging to the join field in the second database. When you release the left mouse button, Approach creates the join line. You can also use the click and drag method to create multiple-field joins between databases.

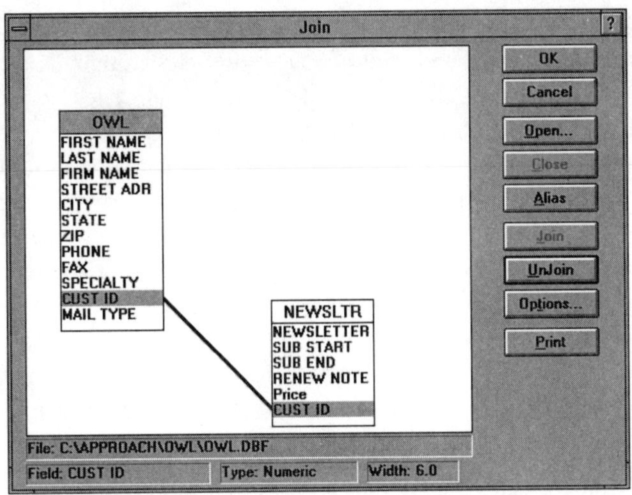

Fig. 8.10
The line between the two databases indicates they are joined.

To rearrange the database boxes in the Join dialog box, drag them to new locations (see fig. 8.11). Approach redraws the join lines automatically. Rearranging the databases makes them easier to see and use. Approach saves the new configuration in the Approach file.

You can print the Join diagram by selecting **P**rint. Click OK in the Print dialog box to create a printed version of your joins.

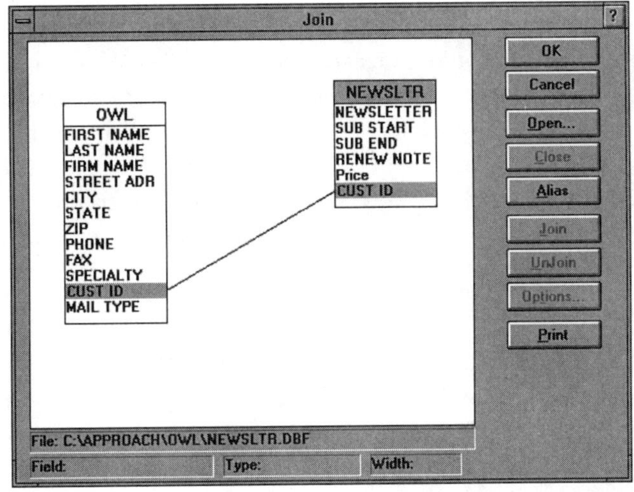

Fig. 8.11
You can rearrange the database boxes to make room for other joins.

Joining Aliased Databases

One of the more difficult problems you face when designing relational databases is the need to occasionally join a database to itself. The classic example of this is the employee/manager relationship. At first glance, you might set this up with two databases. The Employees database contains a list of employees; the Managers database contains a list of managers. Each employee has one manager, but a manager may have many employees—a one-to-many relationship between a manager and his or her employees. Unfortunately for this scenario, managers are also employees, and also reside in the Employees database. To handle this situation, you must join the Employees database to itself. In addition to other information, each record in the Employees database must contain two IDs: the employee's ID (Empl ID) and the employee manager's ID (Mgr ID). The values that go in the Mgr ID field must be valid Empl IDs.

To join a database to itself, you must create a "copy" of the database in the Join dialog box. The copy is not an actual copy of the database, but only another instance of the same database called an *alias*. Once you create an alias, you can set up a join between the alias and any database just as you would with any two databases. In the example discussed above, you would create an alias of the Employee table. This alias serves as the Managers table. You join the original Employee table and its alias using the relational link fields of Mgr ID (Employee table) and Empl ID (alias of Employee table). Since aliases are treated the same as any other joined databases, you can even create a form that displays a manager and all of the manager's employees (see fig. 8.12).

To create an alias of a database in the Join dialog box, click the database you want and select **A**lias. Approach creates the alias and displays it in the Join dialog box (see fig. 8.13). You may create multiple aliases of a database. Approach appends a 1 to the original database name. The alias has the same name as the original database with a 2 (or 3, 4, and so on) appended to it: for example EMPLOYEE:1 and EMPLOYEE:2. These numbers do not actually affect the database name; Approach just uses the numbers to distinguish between the database and its aliases.

Approach does not permit circular joins; however, you can avoid this limitation by using aliases. For example, if you join database A to B, and B to C, you normally could not join A to C. However, you CAN join A to an alias of C to achieve the same result.

Setting the Relational Options

After you join two databases, you can set some relational options that define certain features of the join. Many database relationships are structured so that adding a record in the first database automatically adds a record to the second database. If the Departments database is joined to the Employees database, for example, adding a new record to the Departments database also adds a new record to the Employees database, since a department must have at least one employee.

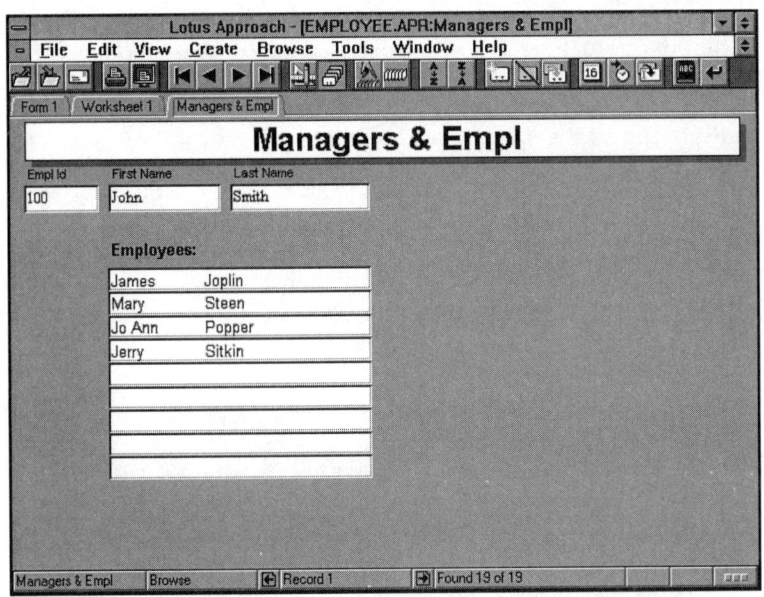

Fig. 8.12
Using an Employee database alias, you can display a manager and of all that manager's employees.

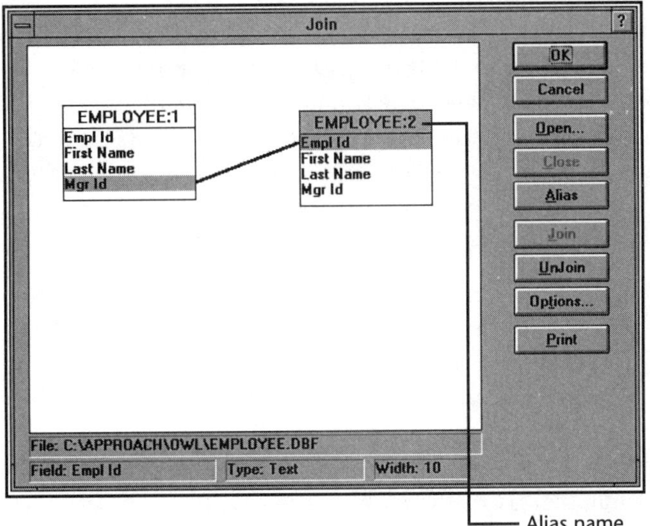

Fig. 8.13
For each alias, Approach appends a number (1, 2, 3, and so on) to the original database and its aliases.

Sometimes deleting a record in the second database makes sense when the matching record has been deleted from the first database. If a record is deleted from the Departments database, for example, you may want to delete all the employees in that department, but not if you will be transferring them to another department. With the relational options, you can make these types of decisions.

To set the options for the relationship between two databases, follow these steps:

1. Open the **C**reate menu and choose **J**oin. The Join dialog box opens, displaying all the open databases and the relationships between them.

2. Click the line connecting the two databases for which you want to define the relational options.

3. Click the Op**t**ions button. The Relational Options dialog box appears (see fig. 8.14). You can also double-click the join line to open the Relational Options dialog box.

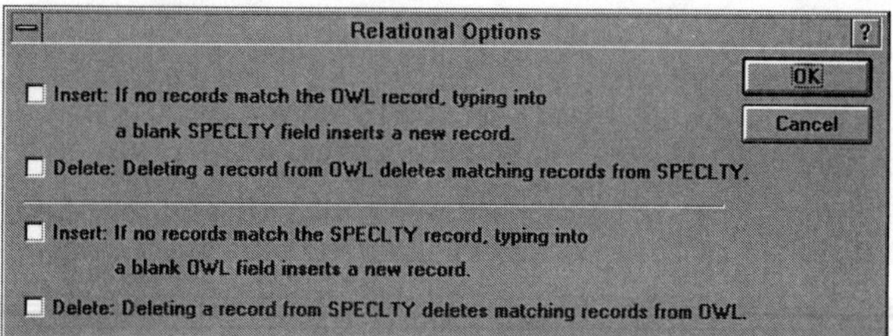

Fig. 8.14
Set relational options in the Relational Options dialog box.

4. Select one or more of the four check box options that define the options you want to set. The two options above the line determine what occurs in the second database when you add or delete a record to the first database. The two options below the line determine what happens in the first database when you add or delete a record in the second database. These options are described as follows:

   - *Insert.* For a form based on the first database that also has fields from the second database on it, choose the Insert option above the line so that a record is added automatically to the second database when you add a record to the first database. Typing information into the fields on the form that come from the second database enters the typed information into the new record in the second database. For example, say the first form is based on the Owl Customer database, and it contains fields from the Newsletter (second) database. Use this option so that entering information in the newsletter database fields on the form automatically creates a record for the newsletter in the second database. If you didn't use this option, you would have to go to a form based on the Newsletter database to create a new record for the newsletter (including the Customer ID). At that point, you would then be able to see the information in that record on the first form.

For a form based on the second database that has fields from the first database on it, choose the Insert option below the line so that a record automatically is added to the first database when you add a record to the second database. Typing information into the fields on the form that come from the first database enters the typed information into the new record in the first database.

- *Delete.* When a form is based on the first database, choose the Delete option above the line so that all joined records in the second database are deleted automatically when you delete a record from the first database. For example, say the first form is based on the Owl Customer database, and it contains fields from the Newsletter (second) database. If you use this option, when you delete the Customer from the first database, all of that customer's Newsletter records are deleted from the Newsletter (second) database. If you didn't use this option, you would still have "orphaned" records in the Newsletter database (that is, there would be records in the Newsletter database that belonged to customers you had deleted).

  When a form is based on the second database, choose the Delete option below the line so that all joined records in the first database are deleted automatically when you delete a record from the second database.

Caution

Be very careful about using the Delete option for databases joined in a one-to-many relationship. You normally don't want to delete a record from the "one" database when you delete a record from the "many" database. If the Departments database is linked to the Employees database, for example, you usually don't want to delete the Department record when you delete one of the Employees in that department. Similarly, you wouldn't want to delete a subscriber when that subscriber cancels one of several subscriptions.

5. Click OK twice to close the Relational Options and Join dialog boxes.

Unjoining Databases

After you join two databases, you can *unjoin* them. Approach doesn't let you modify a join, however. If the wrong field joins two databases, you must unjoin the databases and rebuild the join. You can also unjoin two databases if you find that you no longer need the relationship between them.

Unjoining a database and closing it from the Join dialog box deletes all forms, reports, form letters, repeating panels, and mailing labels for which the database that you unjoined was the main database. (See Chapter 9 for information on assigning "main" databases for a form and on repeating panels.) The highlighted database box is closed when you click the **C**lose button in the Join dialog box. Forms, reports, form letters, and mailing labels for which this database is the main database will be lost if you close it.

To unjoin a database, follow these steps:

1. Open the **C**reate menu and choose **J**oin. The Join dialog box appears.
2. Select the relationship line that you want to delete.
3. Choose **U**njoin. The relationship line disappears (see fig. 8.15).
4. Click the database(s) that has been unjoined and then click **C**lose.
5. Click OK in the Join dialog box.

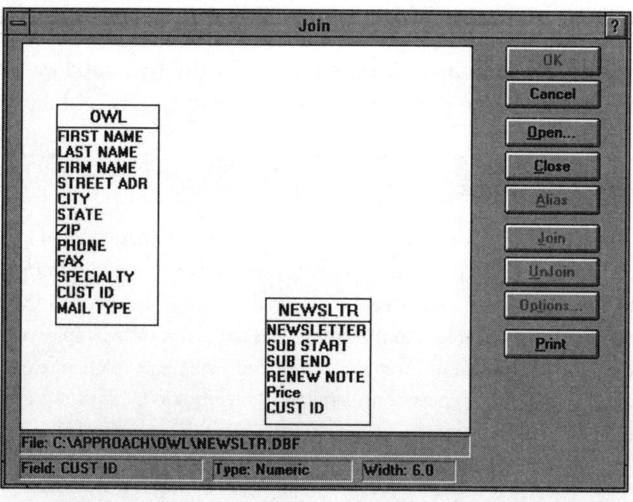

Fig. 8.15
Unjoining the selected OWL database from the NEWSLTR database.

Setting Data-Entry Options for Related Databases

As you learned in Chapter 2, the Options button in the Field Definition dialog box enables you to enter data validation criteria for a field. If the criteria aren't met, Approach doesn't accept the value typed into the field.

When you set up relational joins that link one or more databases, additional options become available in the Validation panel of the Field Definition dialog box. To set these options, follow these steps:

1. Open the Create menu and choose Field Definition. The Field Definition dialog box appears.

2. Click the Options button to open the lower section of the dialog box. Select the Validation tab to switch to the Validation panel (see fig. 8.16).

3. When you are working with joined databases, more than one database is available for you to use. Select the database you want to work with from the Database drop-down list.

4. Select the field for which you want to modify the data-entry options in the Validation panel.

In Field and Formula is True are the validations that offer additional options when relational links have been defined. These validations are discussed in the following sections.

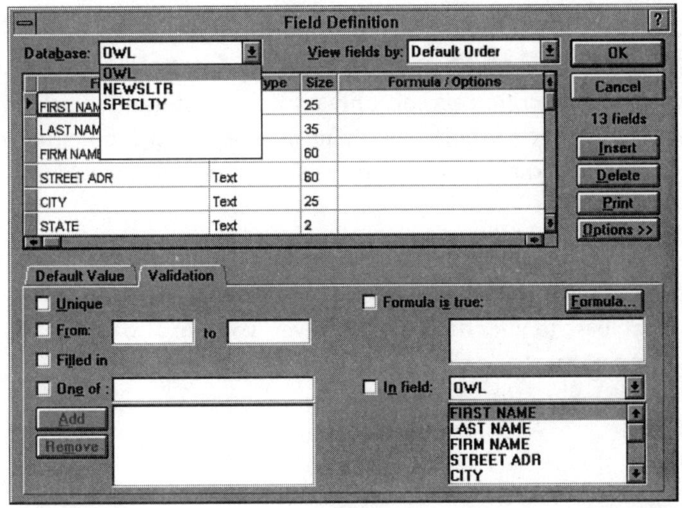

Fig. 8.16
The Field Definition dialog box, with additional databases shown.

Using the In Field Option to Set Up a Validation List

The **In** Field option ensures that the value entered into a field is a value already entered into another field (called a validation field) in the same or in a different database. In Chapter 2, you learned how to select a validation field from the database in which your field is located. After you join a related database to your database, however, you can select the validation field from a related database.

Setting up the **In** Field option to validate against a field in another database is very useful. You can change the list of valid entries simply by adding or deleting a value in another database—perhaps a protected database to prevent the average user from changing its values. One interesting use for the **In** Field option in our Employee/Manager example would be to ensure that the value entered into the Mgr ID field is a value that is already in the Empl ID field.

To set up the **In** Field option to validate against a field in a related database, follow these steps:

1. Follow steps 1–4 in the preceding section to access the Field Definition dialog box displaying the Validation panel.
2. Select the **In** Field checkbox.
3. Drop down the list box next to the **In** Field option for a list of all related databases. From this list, select the database you want to use.
4. Select the validation field from the field list just below the database drop-down list box.
5. Click OK to close the Field Definition dialog boxes.

Using Related Databases Fields in Formula is True

The Formula **is** True option accepts only a value typed into the field if the typed value causes the formula to evaluate as true. If you choose the **F**ormula button, the Formula dialog box opens to assist in building a valid formula (see fig. 8.17).

In Chapter 2, you learned how to include in the formula a field from the same database in which the validated field is located. After you join a relational database to your database, however, you can also select fields from related databases.

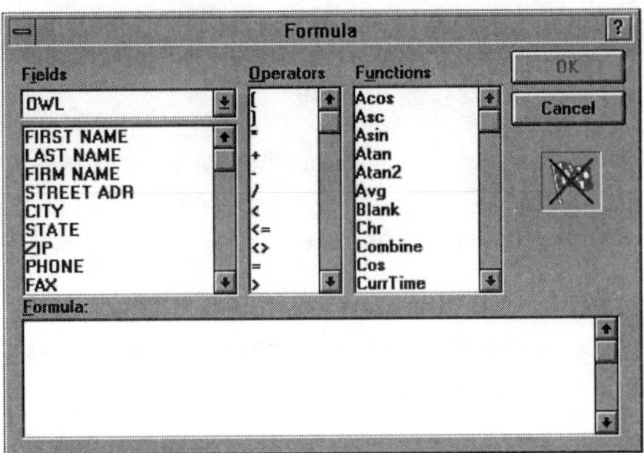

Fig. 8.17
You can use fields from joined databases in the Formula dialog box.

To include a field from a related database in the formula, follow these steps:

1. Follow steps 1–4 in "Setting Data-Entry Options for Related Databases" earlier in this chapter to open the Field Definition dialog box with the Validation panel displayed.
2. Select the Formula **is** True checkbox.
3. Click the **F**ormula button. The Formula dialog box appears.
4. From the drop-down list box just below F**i**elds, select the database you want to use from the list of all related databases.
5. From the list box below the F**i**elds option, select the field you want to include in the formula. The field appears in the **F**ormula text box at the bottom of the dialog box.
6. Continue building the formula. (You can change databases at any time by repeating step 4.) Refer to Chapter 2 for information on how to use the Formula dialog box.
7. When the formula is complete, click OK to close the Formula dialog box.

Note

If the OK button is dimmed, a problem exists with the syntax of the formula. Correct the syntax and click OK.

8. Click OK to exit the Field Definition dialog box.

Setting Up and Joining the Owl Publishing Databases

The Owl Publishing database that you used in Part I of this book served your purposes well, but it suffers from all the disadvantages of flat-file databases. Now, converting the Owl Publishing database application to a relational design is important so that you can do the following:

- Efficiently record the necessary information when Owl's customers subscribe to multiple newsletters.
- Perform data lookups so that you don't have to retype a great deal of information.

Building the Newsletter and Specialty Databases

The first step in revising the Owl Publication application is to build two new databases to hold newsletter and specialty information. Follow these steps to build the Newsletter database:

1. Switch to Design mode.
2. Open the **F**ile menu and choose **N**ew. The New dialog box appears.
3. Type **Newsltr** in the File **N**ame box and then click OK. The Creating New Database dialog box appears (see fig. 8.18).
4. By using the Field Name, Data Type, and Size columns, define the following fields for the Newsltr database:

Field Name	Data Type	Size
NEWSLETTER	Text	40
SUB START	Date	
SUB END	Date	
RENEW NOTE	Numeric	2
PRICE	Numeric	5.2
CUST ID	Numeric	6

After you finish entering this information, the Creating New Database dialog box should look like figure 8.19.

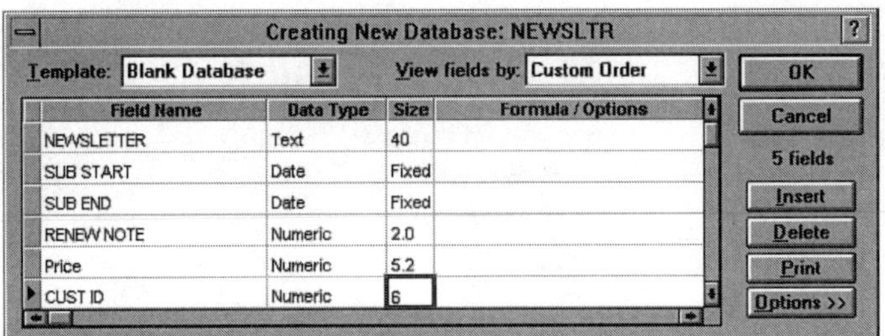

Fig. 8.18
The field definitions for the Newsltr database.

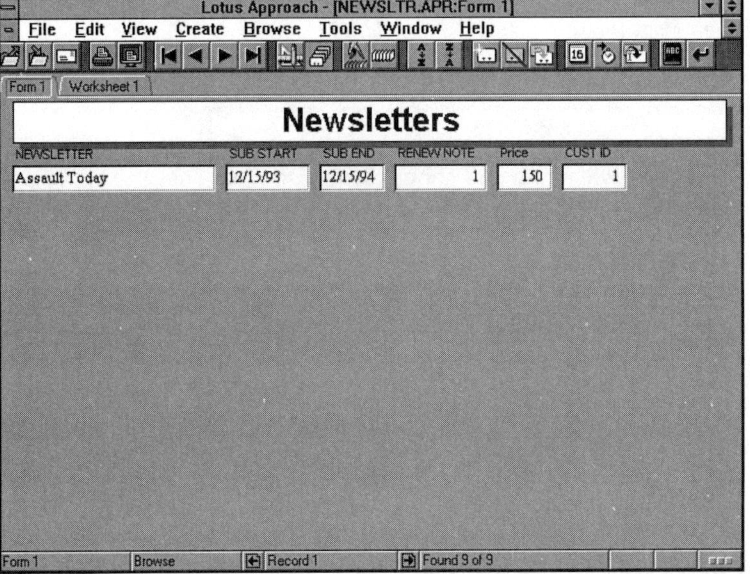

Fig. 8.19
The default form for the Newsltr database.

5. Click OK to close the Creating New Database dialog box, create the database, and open the default form (see fig. 8.19). Change the text block in the title to "**Newsletters**."

6. To enter the following records for the database, first click the New Record SmartIcon. Then type the information for one record and press Enter to save the record. Repeat this step for each record.

NEWSLETTER	SUB START	SUB END	RENEW NOTE	PRICE	ID CUST
Assault Today	12/15/93	12/15/94	1	150	1
Burglary Made Simple	1/12/93	1/12/94	0	175	2

(continues)

NEWSLETTER	SUB START	SUB END	RENEW NOTE	PRICE	ID CUST
Assault Today	11/14/93	11/14/94	0	150	3
Burglary Made Simple	5/12/93	5/12/94	0	175	4
Employment Today	11/12/92	11/12/93	2	195	5
Employment Today	12/12/93	12/12/94	0	195	6
Personal Injury for Profit	6/1/93	6/1/94	0	215	3
Burglary Made Simple	7/2/93	7/2/94	0	175	1
Personal Injury for Profit	8/4/93	8/4/94	0	215	4

7. Open the **F**ile menu and choose **S**ave Approach File. The Save Approach File dialog box appears.
8. Click OK.
9. Choose **C**lose from the **F**ile menu.

The next step in revising the Owl Publishing application is to build a database to hold the information for legal specialties. Repeat the steps for building the Newsletter database, except use the data in Tables 8.1 and 8.2 for defining the fields and entering the records. Call the file "SPECLTY."

Table 8.1 Field Definitions for the Specialty Database

Name	Type	Length
SPECIALTY	TEXT	2
SPEC TEXT	TEXT	20

Table 8.2 Record Data for the Specialty Database

SPECIALTY	SPEC TEXT
PI	Personal Injury
FM	Employment Law
RP	Real Property
CR	Criminal Law

Removing Information from the OWL Database

Because the information about newsletter subscriptions is now stored in the NEWSLTR database, you no longer need the fields in the OWL database. You also no longer need the fields that display this information on the Customer form. You need to remove the fields from the OWL database and the Customer form. (In Chapter 9, you will rebuild the Data Input form to add information from the SPECLTY and NEWSLTR databases.)

> **Note**
>
> Just removing the fields from the form doesn't remove them from the database. Also, you aren't removing the Specialty field data from the form or the database because the SPECLTY database is used only to validate the Specialty values and provide a description of the specialty code.

To clean up the OWL database and Customer form, follow these steps:

1. Open the **F**ile menu and choose **O**pen. The Open dialog box appears.
2. Select OWL from the list of Approach files. If the file isn't visible, use the **D**irectory list box and Dri**v**es drop-down list to move to the drive and directory in which the OWL.APR file is stored.
3. Click OK.
4. Switch to Design mode.

5. If the Customer form isn't on-screen, select it from the view tabs or the status bar.
6. While holding down the Shift key, click the following fields on the form: Newsletter Subscribed to, Start Date, End Date, # of Renew Notes, and Cost.
7. Open the **E**dit menu and choose Cu**t** to remove these fields from the form (see fig. 8.20).

8. Open the **C**reate menu and choose **F**ield Definition. The Field Definition dialog box appears.
9. Select each of the following fields and choose Delete after each selection to remove it from the database: NEWSLETTER, SUB START, SUB END, RENEW NOTE, and PRICE. Confirm that you want to remove the field each time Approach prompts you for confirmation.

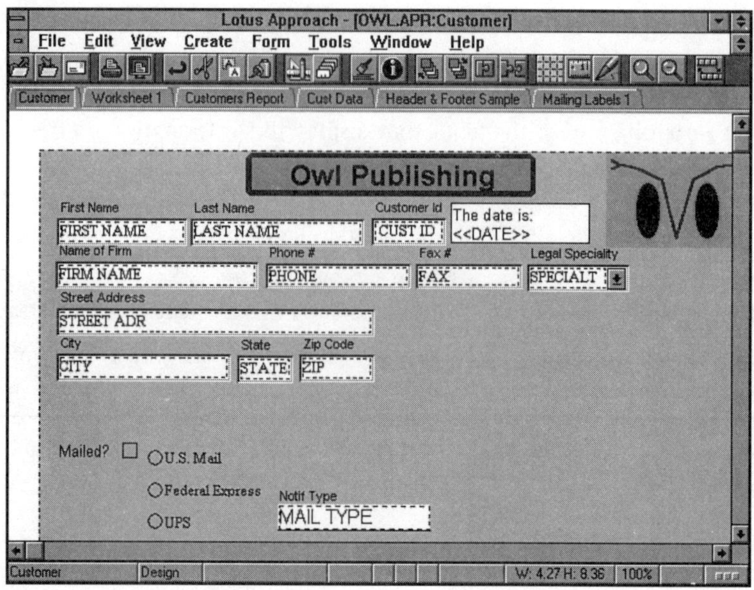

Fig. 8.20
The Owl Publishing form without the newsletter fields.

10. Click OK.

11. Open the **F**ile menu and choose **S**ave Approach File.

Joining the Three Databases

The next step is setting up the relationships between the databases in the OWL Publishing application. To join the databases, follow these steps:

1. Make sure that the OWL Approach file is open and its form on-screen.
2. Open the **C**reate menu and choose **J**oin. The Join dialog box appears, showing the OWL database (see fig. 8.21).
3. Choose **O**pen in the Join dialog box. The Open dialog box appears.
4. Select the NEWSLTR database from the list of available databases.
5. Click OK in the Open dialog box. The Join dialog box appears with the OWL and NEWSLTR databases listed.
6. Select the CUST ID field in the OWL database box.
7. Select the CUST ID field in the NEWSLTR database box.
8. Click the **J**oin button. A line appears between the two databases, indicating that they are joined (see fig. 8.22).

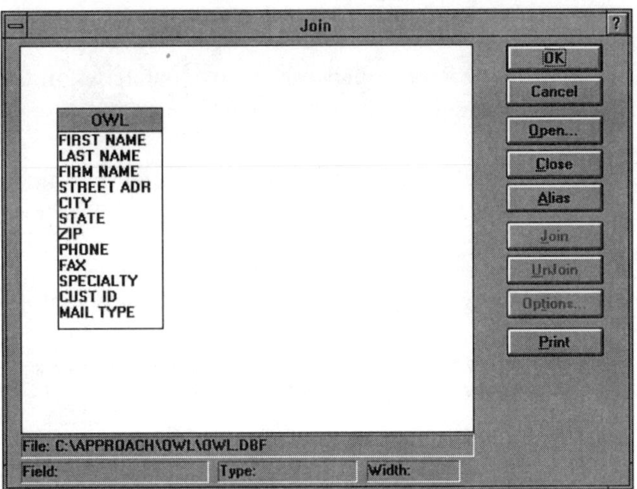

Fig. 8.21
The Join dialog box and the OWL database are ready to be joined.

The join links the records in the OWL database (customers) with the newsletters to which they subscribe in the NEWSLTR database. The linking field is the CUST ID field in both databases.

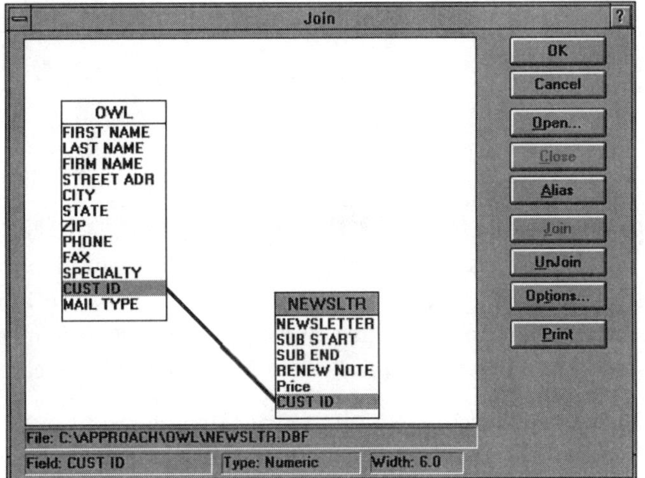

Fig. 8.22
The joined OWL and NEWSLTR databases.

9. Choose **O**pen in the Join dialog box. The Open dialog box appears.
10. Select the SPECLTY database from the list of available databases.
11. Click OK. The Join dialog box reappears, with the three databases listed.
12. Select the SPECIALTY field in the OWL database.

13. Select the SPECIALTY field in the SPECLTY database.

14. Choose **J**oin. A line appears between the two databases, indicating that they are joined (see fig. 8.23).

The join serves as the basis for a lookup: when you enter the value of the two-digit SPECIALTY code in the OWL database form, the SPECLTY form provides the long description of that code.

You still have a few things left to do, so don't close the Join dialog box yet.

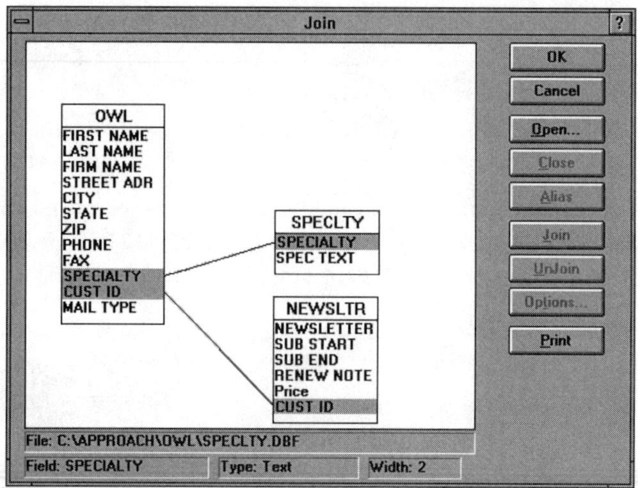

Fig. 8.23
The joined OWL and SPECLTY databases.

Setting the Relational Options for the Owl Databases

The final step in changing the flat file Owl Publishing application into a relational design is to set the relational options. To join the relationship between the OWL database and the NEWSLTR database, you want the following relationships to be true (these are typical values for a one-to-many relationship):

- If you add a new record to OWL, add a matching record to NEWSLTR. This enables you to easily fill in information about the newsletter subscription for that customer.

- If you delete a record from OWL, delete all matching records from NEWSLTR. If you no longer have information about the customer, you don't need information about the newsletter subscriptions.

- If you add a new record to NEWSLTR for which no matching record exists in OWL, add a new record to OWL. Otherwise, there would be no customer for the Newsletter to be attached to.

- If you delete a record from NEWSLTR, don't remove the matching record from OWL, because the record in OWL may match other records in NEWSLTR.

To set up these options, you should be in the Join dialog box. Then follow these steps:

1. Click the line joining OWL to NEWSLTR to select it.
2. Click the Op**t**ions button. The Relational Options dialog box appears.
3. Check the Insert and Delete checkboxes above the line and the Insert checkbox below the line (see fig. 8.24).

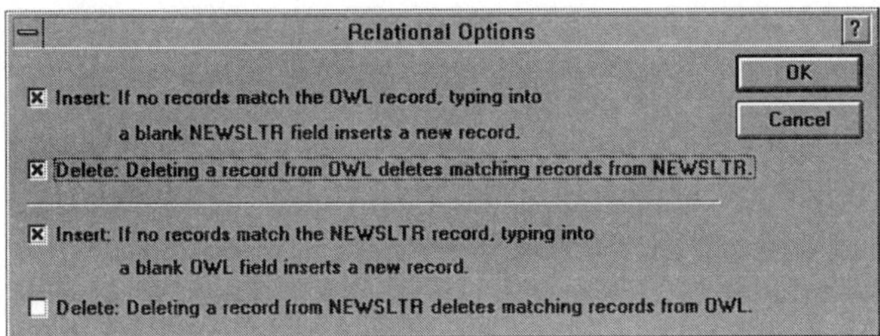

Fig. 8.24
Relational options are set between the OWL and NEWSLTR databases.

4. Click OK in the Relational Options dialog box to return to the Join dialog box.

The relationships between the OWL and SPECLTY databases are quite a bit different from the OWL to NEWSLTR database relationship, because the SPECLTY database is used as a lookup (many-to-one relationship). The following relationships therefore must be true:

- If you add a new record to OWL, don't add a new record to SPECLTY. A new customer doesn't necessarily need a new value of SPECLTY, because the values in SPECLTY are used for multiple customers.
- If you delete a record from OWL, don't delete the matching record in SPECLTY. A value in SPECLTY may be used by multiple customers, so don't delete the value in SPECLTY just because you deleted one of the customers that uses that value.
- If you add a record to SPECLTY, don't add a new record to OWL. This new value of SPECLTY may not be used by any customer currently.
- If you delete a record from SPECLTY, don't delete the matching records from OWL. Even if you choose not to track a particular value of

SPECLTY, that doesn't necessarily mean that you don't care about customers with that value of SPECLTY—those customers still have newsletter subscriptions.

To set up these options, you should be in the Join dialog box. Then follow these steps:

1. Click the line joining OWL to SPECLTY.
2. Click the Op**t**ions button. The Relational Options dialog box appears.
3. Select any checked boxes to uncheck them.
4. Click OK twice to exit the dialog boxes and to return to the Data Input form.

5. To save the Approach file, open the **F**ile menu and choose **S**ave Approach File.

The next time you open this file, all three databases will be available. They also are linked as you have set them up in this example.

From Here...

Once you begin to use Approach as a relational database, you begin to tap into its real power.

This chapter introduced how you can use Approach as a relational database. You learned how to set up relational links, including the options that specify how those links operate and the relationships that can exist between databases. This chapter also discussed using linked databases to provide a valid value list and to construct validation formulas. Finally, you rebuilt the Owl database to turn it into a relational application.

To learn more about using Approach as a relational database, refer to the following chapters in this book:

- Chapter 9, "Designing Advanced Forms," teaches you how to build forms that support one-to-many relationships using "repeating panels."
- Chapter 12, "Creating Advanced Reports," teaches you how to create relational reports, as well as use options to summarize data across multiple linked databases.
- Chapter 16, "Exploring Advanced Database Relationships," teaches you how to design a many-to-many relational database.

Chapter 9

Designing Advanced Forms

Approach can build sophisticated forms that go beyond the capabilities of those discussed in Chapters 3 and 4. If you link databases relationally, you can build powerful forms based on multiple databases. For example, you can place fields from related databases on a form. You can use repeating panels to display multiple joined records on a form, and use related databases to provide the values in drop-down lists. You can also add objects from other Windows applications to a form.

In this chapter, you learn how to:

- Add fields from related databases to a form
- Create and modify repeating panels
- Work with records in repeating panels
- Duplicate or delete records in a repeating panel
- Add a drop-down list based on another field's values
- Add a description to a drop-down list
- Embed objects in an Approach form or report

Adding Fields from a Related Database

If databases are relationally linked, you can place fields from the linked databases on a single form. It doesn't matter when you place fields from a linked database—you can add them when you create the form, or later when you use the Draw Field tool in the Drawing toolbar or the Add Field dialog box.

After these fields appear on a form, you can edit them. Approach automatically updates the field in the linked database to reflect the new value you have entered.

The related information comes from a another database. For example, you can display a customer's billing information on an invoice. The customer information is stored in a customer database, and the specific invoice information is stored in an invoice database. For each record in the invoice database, Approach finds the matching customer fields for that invoice based on the customer's identification number (which must also be present in the invoice database).

Adding Relational Fields When You Create a Form

To add fields from multiple databases to a form when you create a form, follow these steps:

1. Open the **C**reate menu and choose **F**orm or click the Create New Form SmartIcon. The Form Assistant dialog box appears (see fig. 9.1).

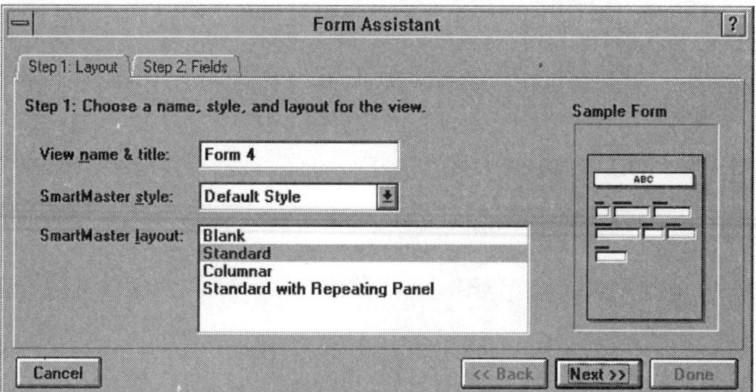

Fig. 9.1
The Form Assistant dialog box.

2. Type the name of the form into the View **N**ame & Title text box, select a form style from the SmartMaster **S**tyle drop-down list, and choose a form layout from the SmartMaster **L**ayout list. For any layout except Blank, click the Step 2: Fields panel or click the Next button to move to the Fields panel.

Note

When working with multiple joined databases, a new SmartMaster layout appears in the SmartMaster Layout list: Standard with Repeating Panel. We will discuss working with this option in "Working with Repeating Panels" later in this chapter.

3. From the Database Fields drop-down list, select the name of the database from which you want to add field(s) to the form (see fig. 9.2). The Database Fields list box displays the fields for that database.

Note

When building a form based on related databases, the first database you add fields from is considered the "main" database for that form. The importance of the "main" database for a form is discussed in "Understanding the Main Database for a Form" later in this chapter.

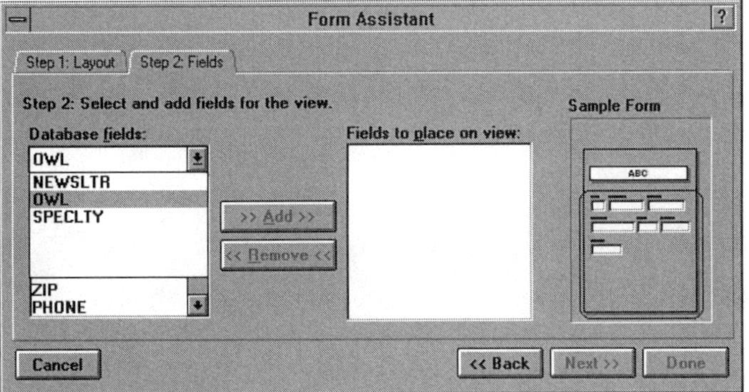

Fig. 9.2
The Database drop-down list contains the names of all related databases in the view.

4. Select the fields you want to add to the form from the Database Fields list box.

5. Choose Add or double-click to move those fields to the Fields to Place on View list box.

6. If you want to add fields from another database to the form, repeat steps 3–5 to select another database and place the database fields on the form.

Tip
You can also return to a database you've already used to add more fields.

7. Choose Done. Approach displays the Define Main Database dialog box. You can select the main database for the form from the Main Database drop-down list. As discussed above, the default main database is the first database you used to place fields on the form.

8. Click OK in the Define Main Database dialog box to create a form containing all the fields selected in the Create Form dialog box. The fields are laid out in their default format (see fig. 9.3). Because the Approach file has joined databases, the fields are listed in the form DATABASE.FIELD NAME.

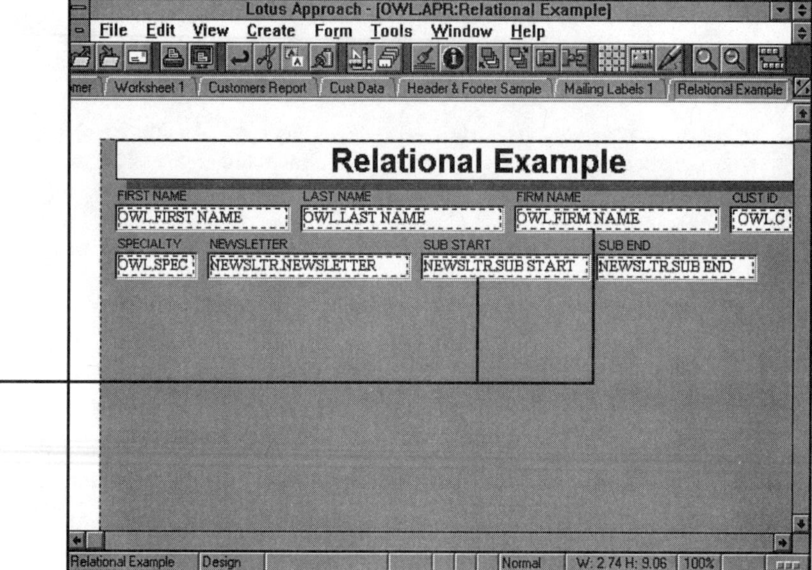

Fig. 9.3
The form with fields from multiple databases. The field name is prefixed with the name of the database that contains the field.

Adding Relational Fields to an Existing Form

To add a field from a linked database to an existing form, select the form to which you want to add the fields from the view tabs or from the status bar. You may create a field on the form either by using the Add Field windows or by using the Draw Field tool from the Drawing toolbar.

To add a field using the Add Field window, follow these steps:

1. If the Add Field window is not showing, open it by opening the **F**orm menu and choosing **A**dd Field. The Add Field window appears.

2. Select the database from which you want to add a field from the drop-down list near the top of the Add Field window. All related databases are available in this drop-down list.

3. Approach displays the fields from the selected database in the field list. Select the field you want to add to the form and drag it onto the form.

4. If you wish, you can customize the field using all the tools in the Info Box, including field font, size, style/effect, and color; label font, size, style/effect, and color; border width, location, and color; shadow color; size; data entry type; and field display format.

To add a field using the Draw Field tool from the Drawing toolbar, follow these steps:

1. Select the Drawing Field tool. The field Info Box automatically appears. Drag a rectangle on the form to define where you want the field.

2. Near the upper-left corner of the Info Box is a drop-down list of available related databases (just below the text "Field:"). Select the database from which you want to add a field. The field list displays all the fields in the selected database.

3. Select the field you want to add to the form.

Note

If you create a field on the form using the Draw Field tool, you must adjust the text of the label using the Label panel of the field's Info Box. Approach sets the initial label text to the name of the first field in the form's main database.

4. If you wish, you can customize the field using all the tools in the Info Box, including field font, size, style/effect, and color; label font, size, style/effect, and color; border width, location, and color; shadow color; size; data entry type; and field display format.

Note

If you need to create a new field for the database before you can add it to the form, you can select the Field **D**efinition button in the Info Box or in the Add Field window. You can also open the **C**reate menu and choose Field **D**efinition.

Owl Publishing wants to display the description joined to the two-digit specialty code stored in the SPECIALTY field. These descriptions already are stored (with the SPECIALTY field code) in the SPECLTY database. Because of the relational link between these two databases, all you need to do is add the description field (SPEC TEXT) from the SPECLTY database to the Customer form. The descriptive contents of that field then will appear automatically whenever you add a value for SPECIALTY to a record.

To add the new field from the related database, follow these steps:

1. Switch to Design mode by opening the **V**iew menu and choosing **D**esign, clicking the Design SmartIcon, or choosing Design from the status bar.
2. If the Customer form is not on-screen, select it from the view tabs or from the status bar.
3. If the Add Field window is not on-screen, display it by opening the Fo**r**m menu and choosing **A**dd Field. Select the SPECLTY database from the drop-down list in the Add Field window.

4. To see the rulers, open the **V**iew menu and choose **S**how Ruler.
5. Click the SPEC TEXT field in the Add Field dialog box and drag the field onto the form just below the LEGAL SPECIALTY Field box and list. Drop the field on the form.
6. Open the Info Box for SPEC TEXT, and click the Label panel. Select No Label from the Label position drop-down list.
7. Click the sizing handles and shrink the SPEC TEXT field to one line. Drag it up just under the LEGAL SPECIALTY field. (see fig. 9.4).

Switch to Browse mode. The description now appears on the form. If you modify the description on the form, it changes in the data SPECLTY database where the data is actually stored.

Understanding the Main Database for a Form

A form always has a single database that is considered the "main" database. By default, the main database is the first database from which you add fields to a form when you create the form using the Form Assistant.

It's important to understand which database is the main database for a form. If you unjoin and close the database, all forms, reports, or repeating panels for which the unjoined database is the main database will be deleted. In addition, the Insert and Delete options in the Relational Options dialog box operate only if the form used to add or delete a record in a database is based on that database (that is, that database is the main database for the form). The form must also contain fields from the joined databases.

Fig. 9.4
Creating a new field to hold the specialty description.

In a report, you see each record from the main database once as a line item in the body of the report. You could write a report to list all of Owl Publishing's customers and group them by Newsletter using summary panels (see Chapter 12 for more information on grouping records). For a report that uses joined data, the report must be based on the database from which you want to display each record once.

In the Owl database example, you want to see all customers and their newsletter subscriptions. In this case, the main database must be the Newsletter database so that each newsletter is displayed only once. The report displays all the customers for each newsletter. If you base the report on the Owl database, you'll see each customer only once in the report, despite the fact that the customer might subscribe to multiple newsletters (and should thus appear multiple times—once for each newsletter he or she subscribes to). Another way to say this is when a report is based on two databases that have a one-to-many relationship, the main database must be the "many" database.

The main database for a form is the database whose name appears in the Main Database drop-down list in the Form Info Box. After you create a form, you can change the main database by selecting a new database from the list of related databases that Approach displays in the Main Database drop-down list.

Working with Repeating Panels

Because you need only a single field on the form to show the related value, placing a field on a form works well for lookups (many-to-one) and one-to-one relationships. In a one-to-many relationship, however, a single field cannot show all the matching records in the joined database. To display the results of a one-to-many relationship on a form, Approach provides a repeating panel (see fig. 9.5).

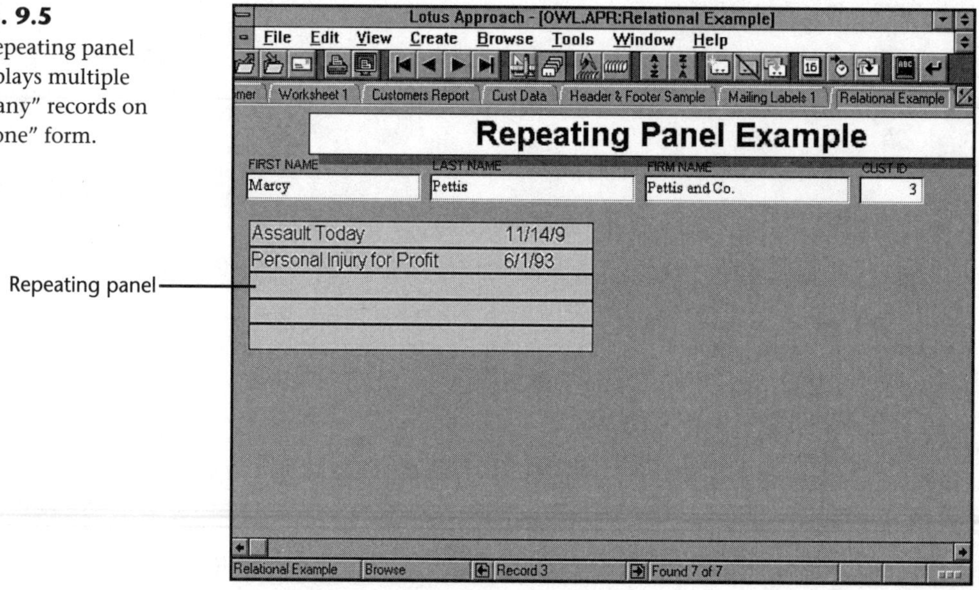

Fig. 9.5
A repeating panel displays multiple "many" records on a "one" form.

A repeating panel looks like a columnar-style report: each column is a field, and each row is a record. When designing a repeating panel, you specify the fields (columns) that will appear, as well as how many lines the repeating panel will display. One matching record from the related database is displayed on each line. If there are more lines in the repeating panel than there are matching records, some lines remain blank. If there are more matching records than lines in the panel on which to display them, the repeating panel provides a scroll bar that enables you to scroll through the extra records.

Understanding the Parts of a Repeating Panel

When viewed in Design mode, a repeating panel is made up of three parts: the field bar, the data fields, and the body (see fig. 9.6).

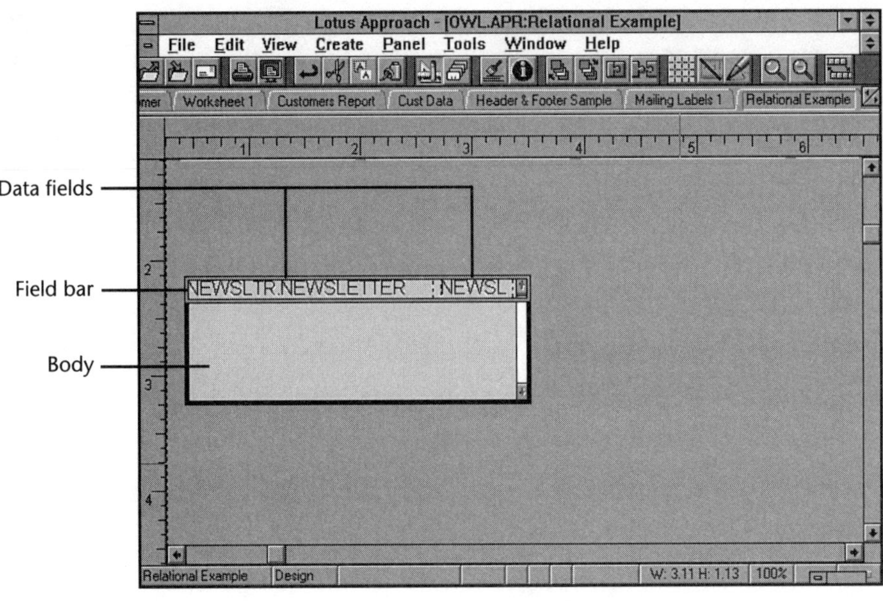

Fig. 9.6
The three different parts of a repeating panel.

The parts of the repeating panel are described as follows:

- The *field bar*—the first line at the top of the repeating panel—contains the data fields. It also sets the overall width of the repeating panel and the height of each record in the panel.
- The *data fields* are the fields from the related database. These fields are selected when you build the repeating panel, as described in the following section. The fields must reside within the field bar. You can add additional fields to the field bar (as discussed in "Modifying a Repeating Panel" later in this chapter).
- The *body* of the repeating panel is the portion of the panel that isn't taken up by the field bar. The body indicates the size of the panel on the form. In Browse mode, the entire body of the repeating panel is filled with rows of records; each row is the size of the field bar.

Tip
You can adjust the width and height of the field bar (see "Modifying a Repeating Panel" later in this chapter).

Creating a Repeating Panel

Before creating a repeating panel, make sure that you have built your database links as described in Chapter 8.

A repeating panel displays the many parts of a one-to-many relationship on a form. The database that represents the "one" side of the relationship must be the main database for the form to which the repeating panel is being added.

If you have assigned the main database incorrectly for a form, Approach won't allow you to create a repeating panel based on the database you require. However, as noted earlier, you can change the main database for a form.

A repeating panel must be based on a detail or "many" database.

You can create a repeating panel when you initially create the form, or add a repeating panel to an existing form.

Adding a Repeating Panel During Form Creation

To include a repeating panel on a form when you create the form, follow these steps:

1. Open the **C**reate menu and choose **F**orm. The Form Assistant dialog box opens. Type the form name into the View **N**ame & Title text box. Select a form style from the SmartMaster **S**tyle drop-down list.

2. Select Standard with Repeating Panel from the SmartMaster **L**ayout list.

3. Click Next or the Step 2: Fields tab to move to the Field panel. Select the fields you want from the form's main database in the Database **F**ields list and add them to the Fields to **P**lace on View list. Do not select fields from the database you will use to create the repeating panel. You can select a field and click Add or double-click the field to add it to the Fields to **P**lace on View list.

4. Click Next or the Step 3: Panel tab to move to the Repeating Panel page.

5. Select a database from the Database **F**ields drop-down list. You must select a detail ("many") database.

6. Select the fields you want in the repeating panel in the Database **F**ields list and add them to the Fields to Place in **P**anel list.

> **Note**
>
> Don't place the field that provides the relational connection into the repeating panel. When you create a new record in the repeating panel, Approach automatically fills in the value of the connecting field in the related database. This process ensures that the new record in the repeating panel is associated with the current record in the main portion of the form. Thus, you don't need to waste space in the repeating panel for the connecting field. Also, leaving off the field prevents you from accidentally changing the join data, causing the detail record to become unjoined from the main record and joined to a different main record.

7. Click Done to create the form with a repeating panel.

Adding a Repeating Panel to an Existing Form

To add a repeating panel to an existing form, follow these steps:

1. If the form to which you want to add the repeating panel is not currently on-screen, select it from the view tabs or the status bar.

2. Open the **C**reate menu and choose Repeating **P**anel. The Add Repeating Panel dialog box appears (see fig. 9.7).

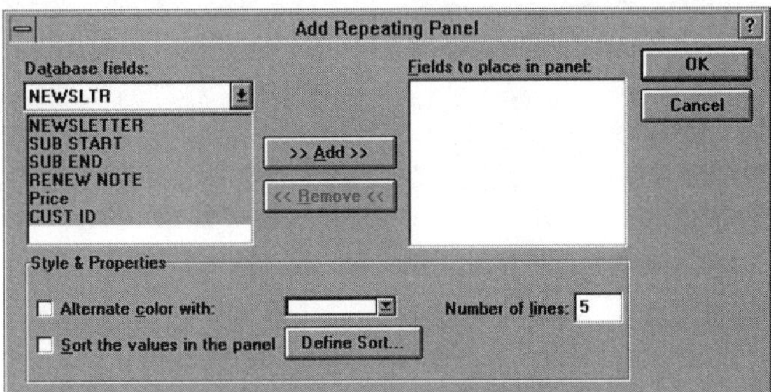

Fig. 9.7
Select fields to include in your repeating panel.

3. Select a database from the Database **F**ields drop-down list.

> **Note**
>
> The main database for the form does not appear in the list of available databases for the repeating panel. If the database you want for the repeating panel doesn't appear in the list, confirm that the form is based on the proper main database.

4. Select the fields you want in the repeating panel in the Database **F**ields list and add them to the Fields to Place in **P**anel list. Add the fields by double-clicking them or by selecting a field and clicking **A**dd.

5. In the Number of **L**ines text box, type the number of lines you want to appear in the repeating panel.

6. To make each record stand out, you can alternate the fill color of every other line in the repeating panel. Choose the Alternate **C**olor checkbox. Then click the box to the right of the option and select the color you want to use from the color palette that appears.

Tip
If you don't want a field in the panel, select the field in the **F**ields to Place in Panel list and then choose **R**emove; or double-click the field in the **F**ields to Place in Panel list.

7. If you want to sort the values in the repeating panel, click the **S**ort the Values in the Panel checkbox. To define the sort order, click the Define Sort button. The Sort dialog box opens. Select the fields to sort on in the Database **F**ields list and add them to the Fields to **S**ort On list. To add a field to the sort list, either double-click the field or click the field and then click the **A**dd button. Select the Asc**e**nding or **D**escending radio button at the right side of the Sort dialog box.

8. Click OK to create the repeating panel.

Note

A repeating panel can contain only the fields for which it has room. The width of the page limits the width of the repeating panel. If you specify more fields than can fit in a full-page width repeating panel, some fields won't appear in the repeating panel. These fields can be added later.

Owl Publishing wants to display the one-to-many relationship between the OWL database and the NEWSLTR database. The company will do this by placing on the Customer form a repeating panel that shows all the newsletters to which a customer in the OWL database subscribes.

To add a repeating panel to the Customer form, follow these steps:

1. If the Customer form is not on-screen, select it from the view tabs or the status bar.

2. Open the **C**reate menu and choose Repeating **P**anel. The Add Repeating Panel to Form dialog box appears.

3. Make sure that the NEWSLTR database is displayed in the Database **F**ields drop-down list box. If it isn't, select NEWSLTR from the drop-down list.

4. In the Da**t**abase Fields list box, select the NEWSLETTER field. Then hold down Ctrl and click the SUB START, SUB END, and RENEW NOTE fields.

5. Click **A**dd to move the fields to the **F**ields to Place in Panel list box.

6. Click OK. The repeating panel appears on the Customer form (see fig. 9.8).

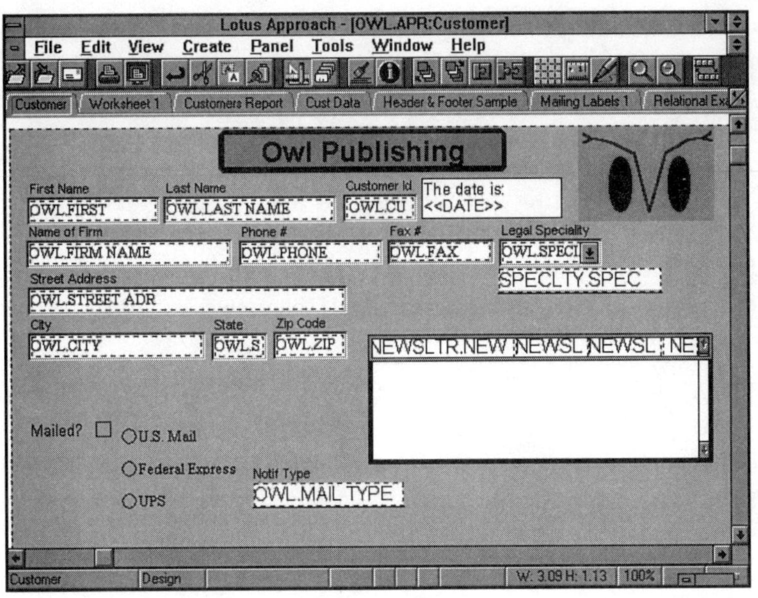

Fig. 9.8
The repeating panel for recording newsletter subscription information.

Modifying a Repeating Panel

After you build a repeating panel on a form, you can customize the panel in many different ways:

- You can move the panel on the form.
- You can change the size of the panel.
- You can add or delete fields.
- You can change field sizes.
- You can specify borders, frame style, and data-entry formats for the fields.
- You can specify the fill, shadow, and border color of the panel.
- You can specify the fill and pen color of the fields in the panel.
- You can customize the font, size, style, effects, and alignment of the text in the fields.

You must perform all customizing of the panel in Design mode. The customizing options are discussed in the following sections.

Moving a Repeating Panel

To move a repeating panel, click the body portion of the panel. A black border appears around the panel. Drag the repeating panel to its new location.

Changing the Size of a Repeating Panel

You can resize a repeating panel at any time. If you want to add fields to a repeating panel, for example, you need to widen the panel. If you remove fields from the repeating panel, you may want to shrink the panel to remove the empty gaps in the panel. Also, the fields themselves can be resized, which may require resizing the panel.

To change the size of a repeating panel, you must change the size of the field bar. As you widen or shrink the field bar, the entire repeating panel changes width to match. You can also change the height of the field bar. The field bar represents the height of each record in the repeating panel. If you make the field bar taller, the entire repeating panel grows in height based on the specified number of records (see figs. 9.9 and 9.10).

The first step in resizing the field bar is to select the repeating panel. Approach displays the field bar with a gray border around it. Move the mouse cursor over any edge of the field bar. The cursor turns into a two-headed arrow. Drag to change the size of the field bar (as well as the entire panel). Dragging a side border increases or decreases the width of the panel. Dragging the top or bottom increases or decreases the height of the panel.

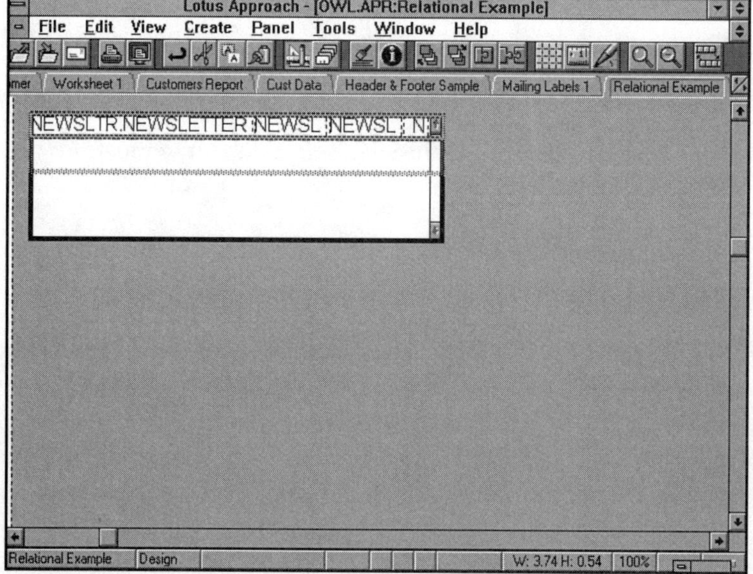

Fig. 9.9
The repeating panel must be large enough to contain the number of records specified.

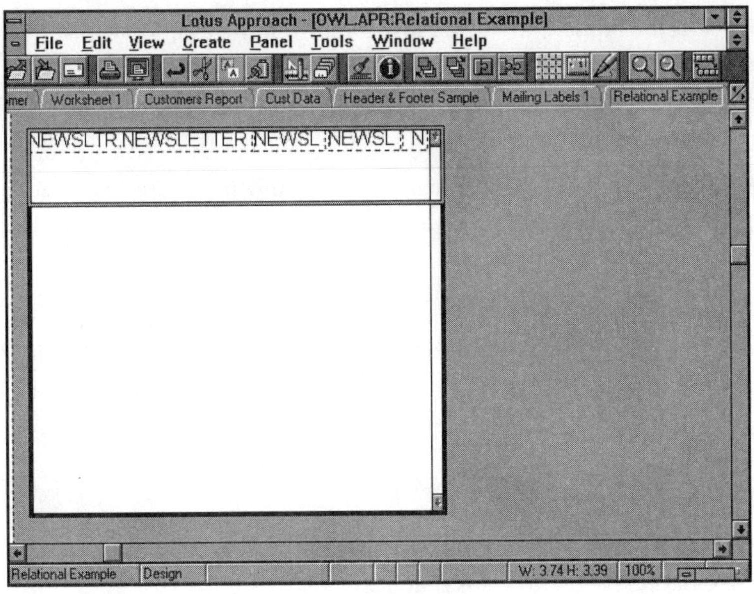

Fig. 9.10
Changing the size of the field bar causes the repeating panel to change size.

Changing the Options on a Repeating Panel

You can change repeating panel options from the Basics panel of the Info Box:

- Change the main database by making a selection from the Main Database drop-down list. However, the repeating panel MUST be based on the database for which you want to show all the records in the panel—it would be very rare to change the main database.

- Change the number of lines displayed in the repeating panel by typing the new number into the Number of Lines text box.

- Sort the values in the repeating panel by selecting the Sort Panel Values checkbox. Click the Define Sort button to display the Sort dialog box and define the sort order.

Changing the Other Properties of a Repeating Panel

You can change the fill, shadow, and border colors of a repeating panel. You may also select a border width and location, frame style, and alternate line fill colors. You set these options from the Colors panel of the Info Box:

- Select the border width for each row in the repeating panel from the Border Width drop-down list. Available border widths range from hairline to 12 point (1/6 inch).

- Select the border, fill, or shadow color from the drop-down list that Approach displays when you click the Border Color, Fill Color, or Shadow Color drop-down lists. The box labeled T provides a transparent color.
- Select a Frame style from the Frame drop-down list. The Frame style specifies the format in which Approach draws the border around each line in the repeating panel.
- Click the checkboxes in the Borders section (for example, Left, Right, Top, and Bottom) to select which sides of each line you want Approach to display borders.
- If you want an alternate fill color on every other line, click the Alternate Fill Color checkbox.

Working with Fields in Repeating Panels

The field bar contains the fields that are displayed in the repeating panel. These fields work just like fields on the rest of the form. You can add, delete, move, resize, and change the characteristics of a field in a repeating panel.

> **Note**
>
> Because of the limited space in a repeating panel, you normally don't want to use field labels. Approach defaults to no labels for fields placed in a repeating panel when you create it. For any fields you add later, however, you may have to turn off the field labels by selecting No Label from the Label Position drop-down list.

Tip
To test if fields are contained in a repeating panel, move the panel. If the fields move with it, they are contained in the panel.

To delete a field in the field bar, select the field and then click Delete, or open the **E**dit menu and choose Cu**t**.

To resize a field, select the field and then drag any of its sizing handles until the field is the size you want. You can also resize a field using the Dimensions panel in the Info Box.

To move a field, click inside it and then drag the field to its new location. You can modify the order of fields in the field bar by rearranging the fields in this manner. You can also change the location using the Dimensions panel of the Info Box.

Note

After resizing or moving a field, make sure that the field is still fully contained within the boundaries of the field bar. If the field is not fully contained, it does not appear in each of the multiple records in the repeating panel (see figs. 9.11 and 9.12).

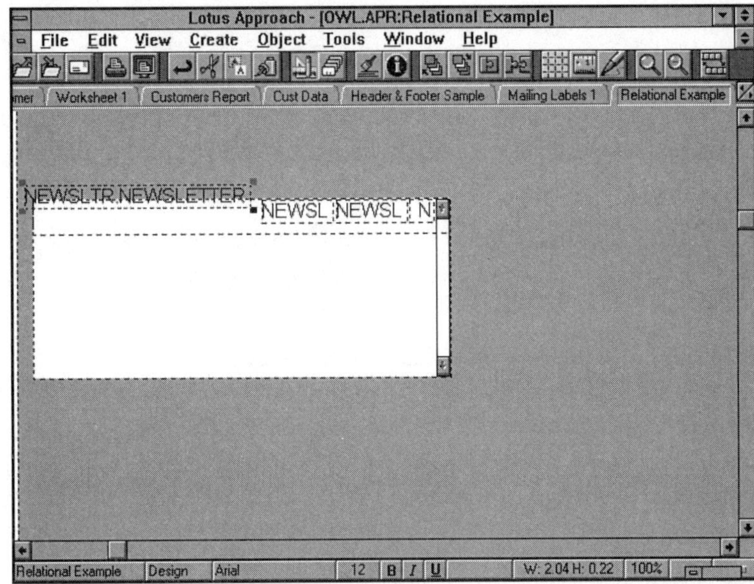

Fig. 9.11
A field that is not fully inside the field bar.

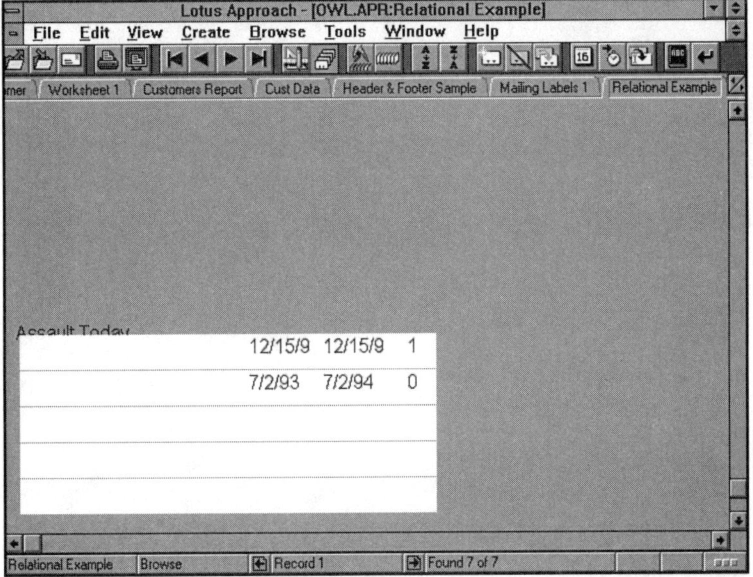

Fig. 9.12
The effect of a field that is not fully contained.

Adding a Field to a Repeating Panel

To add a field to a repeating panel, make sure that the field bar is large enough to hold the new field. If the field bar is not large enough, enlarge it as described earlier. You can drag a field from the Add Field dialog box into the field bar. You can also use the Draw Field tool in the Drawing toolbar. To use the Draw Field tool, follow these steps:

1. Click the Draw Field tool.
2. Click and drag the new field rectangle inside the field bar.
3. From the field Info Box, select the database and field you want to use. Make sure to turn off the label by selecting No Label from the Label Position drop-down list.
4. If you wish, you may further customize the text, colors, and border characteristics of the field using the Info Box (see next section).

Tip
You can copy an existing field and paste it in the panel, and then change the database and field from the Info Box. The copied field retains the formatting characteristics of the original field.

Adding Column Headings to a Repeating Panel

To identify the fields in a repeating panel, you can add column headings by placing text blocks above each column (see fig. 9.13). Use the Text SmartIcon to drag the text blocks above each column. Adding these headings should be the last step in the design of the repeating panel; add them after you define all the fields in the field bar and set the location and size of the fields.

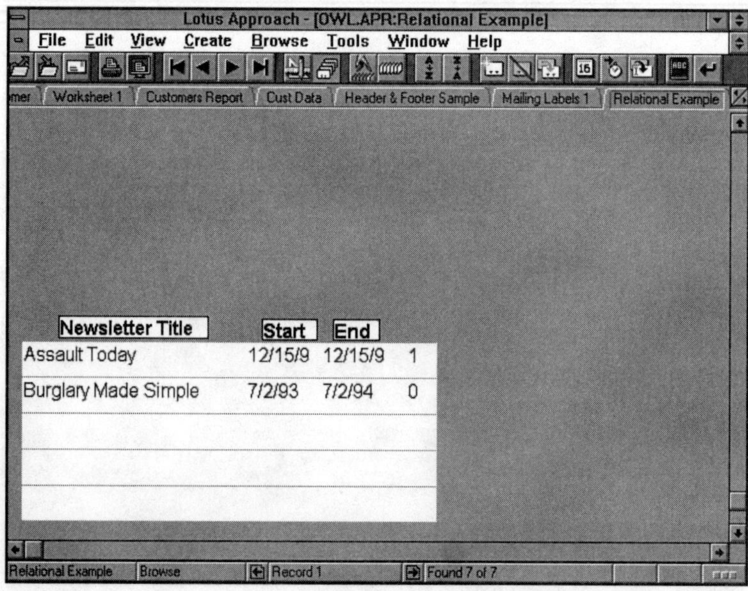

Fig. 9.13
Add column headings to a repeating panel.

Customizing the Owl Publishing Form

In the Owl Publishing example, the repeating panel you added earlier to the Customer form needs to be customized to make it more useful. You need to perform the following tasks:

- Center the panel along the bottom of the form.
- Make every other line a different color.
- Add a new field to the repeating panel.
- Add column headings to the repeating panel.
- Change the field text color.

To perform these tasks, follow these steps:

1. Switch to Design mode by opening the **V**iew menu and choosing **D**esign, clicking the Design SmartIcon, or choosing Design from the status bar.

2. If the Customer form is not on-screen, select it from the view tabs or the status line.
3. Rearrange the fields in the lower-left corner of the form. Move the Mailed? checkbox, the Notif Type text field, and the notification type radio buttons up under the LEGAL SPECIALTY field.
4. Click the body of the repeating panel and drag it to the center in the lower portion of the Data Input form. Leave enough room above the repeating panel for column headings that you will add later.
5. Click the body of the repeating panel. The field bar's gray borders become visible. Drag the right border of the field bar to make the repeating panel wider.
6. If the Add Field dialog box is not visible, select **P**anel **A**dd Field. Select the NEWSLTR database from the list of databases in the Add Field dialog box.
7. Select the PRICE field from the field list and drag it into the field bar of the repeating panel.
8. To customize the field, select the Labels panel in the Info Box and choose No Label in the Label Position drop-down list. If necessary, resize the field to fit into the field bar.

   Select the Colors panel in the Info Box and choose a Fill Color or select T (transparent). Also check to make sure no borders are checked.

When you're finished, the repeating panel should look like figure 9.14.

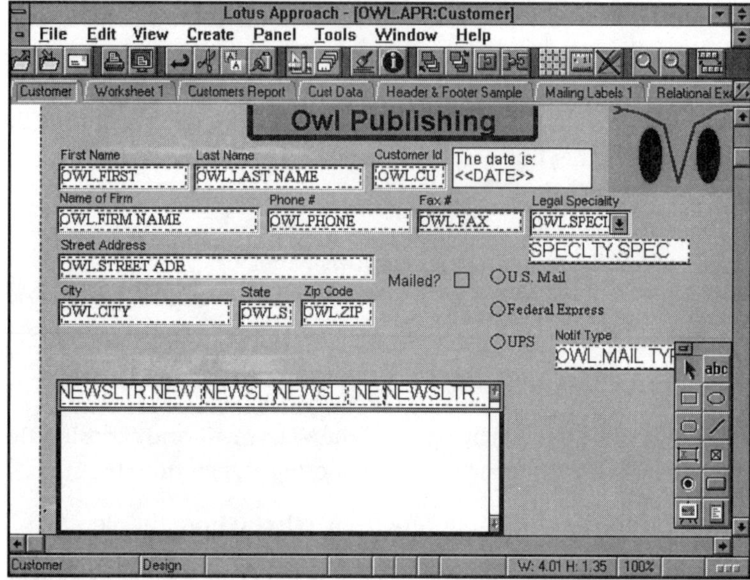

Fig. 9.14
Adding a repeating panel to the Owl Publishing database.

9. Select the repeating panel by clicking the body of the repeating panel. Click the Alternate Fill Color checkbox to alternate the colors on each line of the checkbox.

10. Select the Draw Text tool from the Drawing toolbar. Drag a rectangle over the NEWSLETTER column. Type **Newsletter** into the text block.

Repeat this step for the other columns, using **Start Date**, **End Date**, **# of notes**, and **Price** for the headings (see fig. 9.15).

Working with Records in a Repeating Panel

After you define the repeating panel on the form, you can add, delete, duplicate, and edit records in the panel, as discussed in the following sections. The setting of the relational options (in the Relational Options dialog box), however, affects the technique for adding a record. For a reminder on how to change the Relational Options settings, see the next section. All record operations are done in Browse mode.

Adding a Record to a Repeating Panel

When you add a record to a repeating panel, Approach automatically enters the information you type into the related database.

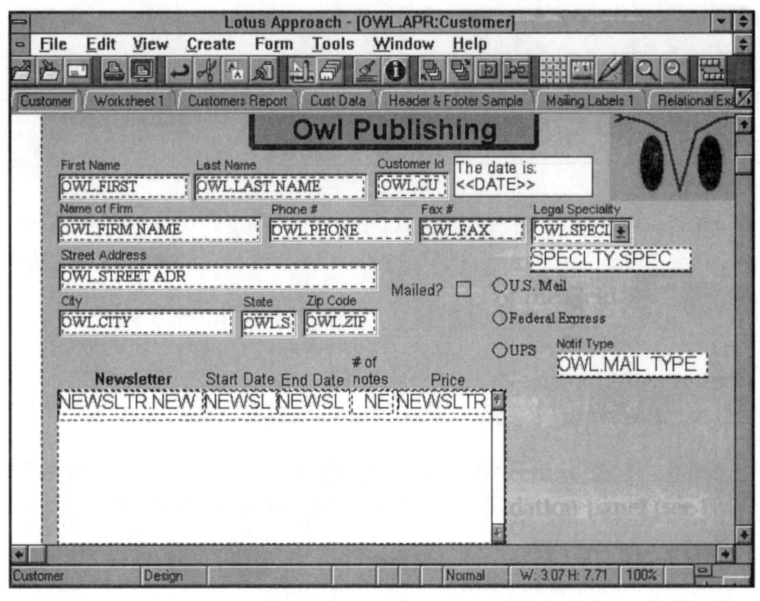

Fig. 9.15
Using column headings to identify each field.

Also, you don't need to enter the value of the field in the related database that provides the relational connection. Approach automatically enters the value in the join field of the related database that matches the value in the join field in the main database so that the record in the repeating panel is properly associated with the record in the main database.

The procedure for adding a new record to a repeating panel depends on the settings in the Relational Options dialog box (see fig. 9.16).

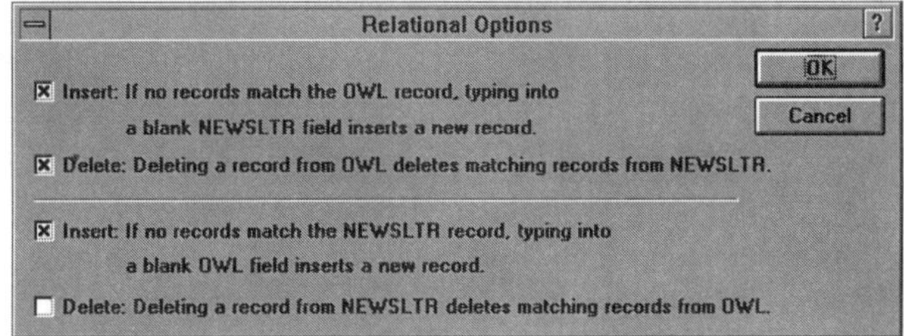

Fig. 9.16
The Relational Options dialog box controls how records are added.

If the first checkbox (Insert) in the Relational Options dialog box is checked, click the first blank line of the repeating panel, type values into the fields, and press Enter.

If all the lines in the repeating panel are full, scroll the lines up to display a blank line. Enter the new record in the blank line.

Note

The scroll bar appears next to the repeating panel automatically when you have filled all the lines in the repeating panel.

If the first checkbox in the Relational Options dialog box is not checked, follow these steps:

1. Click any existing record in the repeating panel. If the repeating panel has no existing records, you must use the first Insert option. To use this option, you must change the relational options. The steps are covered in the following section, "Adjusting Relational Options."

2. Create a new record by opening the **B**rowse menu and choosing N**e**w Record or clicking the New Record SmartIcon. A blank line appears in the repeating panel.
3. Type the new information into the blank line.
4. Press Enter.

Adjusting Relational Options

If you need to change the relational options in the Relational Options dialog box so that you can add records to a repeating panel, follow these steps:

1. Open the **C**reate menu and choose **J**oin. The Join dialog box appears.
2. Choose the line linking the two databases on the form (one is the main database; the other is the repeating panel database).
3. Choose Op**t**ions or double-click the join line. The Relational Options dialog box appears.
4. Click the Insert checkbox above the line.
5. Click OK twice to close the Relational Options and Join dialog boxes.

Duplicating a Record in a Repeating Panel

To duplicate records in a repeating panel, click any field in the record that you want to duplicate. Then open the **B**rowse menu and choose **D**uplicate Record.

Deleting a Record from a Repeating Panel

To delete a record from a repeating panel, click the record you want to delete and then open the **B**rowse menu and choose De**l**ete Record. Approach asks for confirmation. Click OK to delete the record.

Editing a Record in a Repeating Panel

To edit the fields displayed in a repeating panel, use the same methods as you would for editing fields on the main form:

- *Field Box.* Type values into field boxes. Values can't exceed the length of the field in the database. To select the text in a text field, use the mouse pointer to click and drag the text. You can also select text by using Shift and the arrow keys. Once selected, you can delete, cut, or copy the text.
- *Date or Time Fields.* Type valid dates or times into these fields.
- *Drop-Down Lists.* Click the drop-down list to display the value. Either click the value you want to use, or select the value with the arrow keys.
- *Field Box & List.* Select the field box & list to display the values, and then select the value you want to use. If the value you need is not in the list, type it in.
- *Memo Fields.* Type the values you want into a memo field. To select the text in a memo field, use the mouse pointer to click and drag the text. You can also select text by using Shift and the arrow keys. Once selected, you can delete, cut, or copy the text. A memo field can be multiple lines, even in a repeating panel.
- *Checkboxes.* Click the checkbox to place an X in the box. Click the box again to remove the X (leaving the box blank).
- *Radio Buttons.* Click the button to select it. A selected button is filled in.

Transferring to Another Form from a Repeating Panel

Repeating panel displays records that are stored in a related database. Repeating panels often do not display all the fields in the related database. To edit those fields, you must switch to another form. Approach enables you to select a record in the repeating panel and switch to another form. If the form is based on the related database, all the information from the selected record may be displayed on the form. You can then use the form to edit the record. To switch to another form from a record in a repeating panel, follow the steps on the next page.

1. Select the record in the repeating panel that you want to work with.
2. Select the form you want to switch to from the view tabs or the status bar.

Owl Publishing wants to switch from a record in the repeating panel on the Data Input form to a form displaying the specific newsletter record. To do this, follow these steps:

1. Open the **C**reate menu and choose **F**orm. The Form Assistant dialog box appears.
2. Type **Newsletter Input** in the View **N**ame & Title text box.
3. Choose Default Style from the SmartMaster **S**tyle drop-down list. Select Standard from the SmartMaster **L**ayout list. Click the Next button to move to the Field panel.
4. Select the NEWSLTR database from the drop-down list just below the Database **F**ields text.
5. Select the NEWSLETTER field in the Database **F**ields list box. Hold down Ctrl and click the SUB START, SUB END, RENEW NOTES, PRICE, and CUST ID fields.
6. Choose **A**dd to move the fields to the Fields to **P**lace on View list.
7. Choose Done to create the default form.

8. Switch to Browse mode by opening the **V**iew menu and choosing **B**rowse, clicking the Browse SmartIcon, or choosing Browse from the status bar.
9. Select the Customer form from the view tabs or the status bar.
10. Click any record in the repeating panel to make it the current record.
11. Select the Newsletter Input form from the view tabs or the status bar. Approach transfers to the Newsletter Input form.

The record you selected on the Customer form is now the current record in the Newsletter Input form.

Summing a Repeating Panel

Repeating panels hold multiple records. Those records often contain numeric values. For example, on a main form containing invoice information, a repeating panel can hold the individual line items that make up the invoice. One of the fields on a line might be the cost of the item. If the lines are summed, the result is the total cost of the items attached to the invoice.

Approach makes it possible to sum a field in a repeating panel and to place the result on the form. To accomplish this, you must add a field to the form to hold the result. This field contains a calculation that sums a field in the repeating panel (see Chapter 10 for more information on calculated fields).

To set up a sum for a field in a repeating panel, follow these steps:

1. Switch to Design mode by opening the **V**iew menu and choosing **D**esign, clicking the Design SmartIcon, or choosing Design from the status bar.
2. Click the Draw Field tool from the Drawing toolbar.
3. Drag the area outside of the repeating panel where you want the summed field to be located. Approach creates a field on the form.
4. Click Field Definition in the Info Box. The Field Definition dialog box appears (see fig. 9.17).

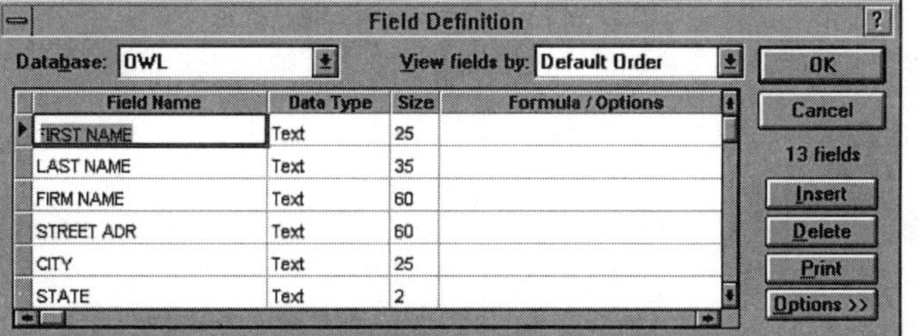

Fig. 9.17
Add calculated fields through the Field Definition dialog box.

> **Note**
>
> Because calculated fields are saved with the Approach file and not within a database, you don't have to select the database at this step as you do when you are adding a new database field.

5. Find a blank line in the Field Definition dialog box. In the Field Name text box, type the name of the new field that will hold the result of the calculation (for example, **HOLD SUM**).

6. Select Calculated in the Data Type drop-down list. The Options section at the bottom of the Field Definition dialog box opens to display the Define Formula panel (see fig. 9.18).

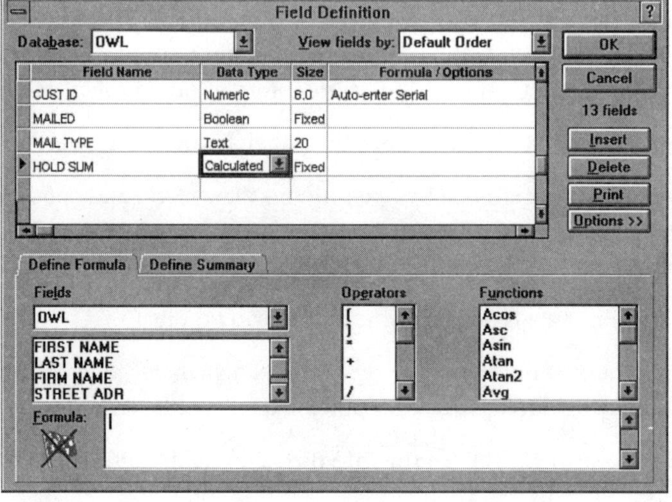

Fig. 9.18
The Formula panel in the Field Definition dialog box.

Tip
To reach the SSUM function, use the scroll bars to scroll through the F**u**nctions list.

7. Select the SSUM function from the F**u**nctions list box so that it appears in the **F**ormula list box near the bottom of the dialog box.

8. Make sure that the database displayed in the list box just below the Fie**l**ds text is the database that provides the information in the repeating panel (that is, the NEWSLTR database). If it's not, select the correct database from the drop-down list. The list box just below the database name displays the fields for that database.

9. Select the field on which you want to sum from the left-hand list box. (For this example, use the PRICE field.) The field appears between the parentheses after the SSUM function in the **F**ormula list box.

10. Click the Define Summary tab to move to the Define Summary panel. From the **S**ummarize On drop-down list box, select the item that summarizes all the records in the appropriate database.

Note

Remember that this database must be the one that provides the information in the repeating panel. If the repeating panel is based on the NEWSLTR database, for example, the selection should read `Summarize on all records in NEWSLTR`.

11. Click OK to return to the form with the new calculated field. Adjust the text of the label using the Label panel in the Info Box. For this example, call the field "Price Sum."

Tip
If the OK button isn't active, the formula you've added is not correct. Double-check the formula you added.

The new field appears on your form. As you page through the records in the main form, this field sums only the related records in the repeating panel (see fig. 9.19). The calculated field does not have the file name in front of it because the calculated field is not attached to a database—it exists only in the Approach file.

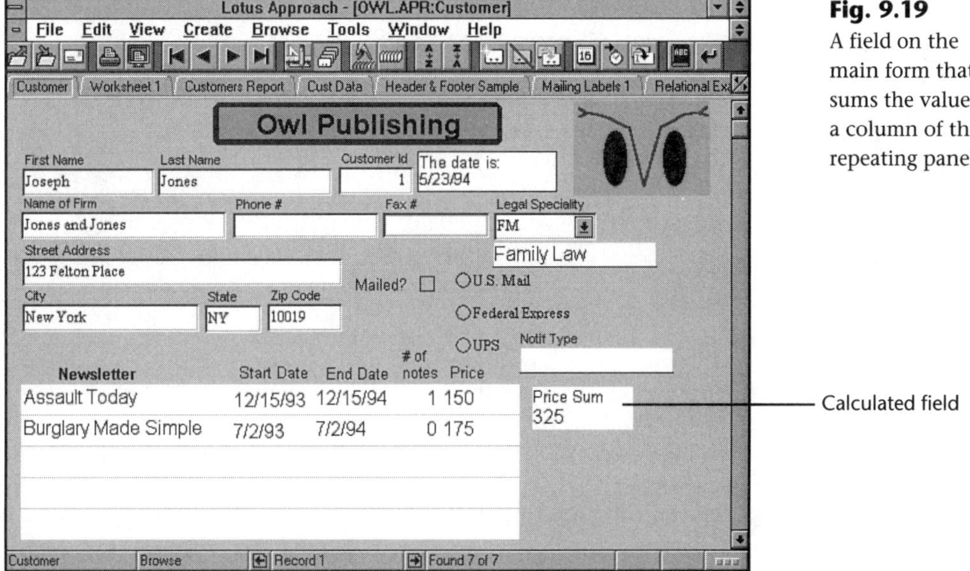

Fig. 9.19
A field on the main form that sums the values in a column of the repeating panel.

Note

Summing a repeating panel is the only type of summary calculation where the value appears in Browse mode. Summary calculations based on other groupings only display a value in Preview mode.

Adding a Drop-Down List Based on Another Field's Values

When the display entry format of a field is set to Drop-Down List or Field Box & List, a drop-down list of values appears when you click the field. You can then select a value from the list. For the Field Box & List, you can also type a value.

Setting the data-entry format of a field to Drop-Down List or Field Box & List is appropriate if the list of possible values is relatively small. To select these data-entry format options, choose these options from Data Entry Type drop-down list in the Basics panel of the field Info Box.

To specify the values in the list, click the Define List button. The Drop-Down List dialog box appears (see fig. 9.20).

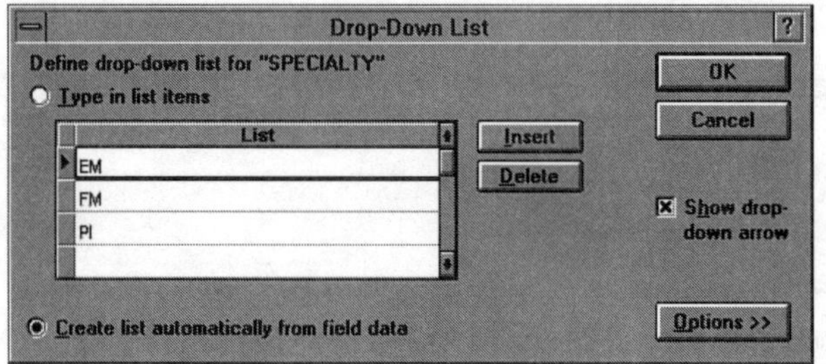

Fig. 9.20
The Drop-Down List dialog box enables you to specify the values for a drop-down list.

The values in the list can come from two different places:

- If you select the **T**ype in List Items radio button, you can type the values into the Drop-Down List dialog box.
- If you select the **C**reate List Automatically from Field Data radio button, Approach draws the values from the values already entered into a field. The default field that Approach draws the values from is the Drop-Down List field itself. However, you can draw the values from another field, either in the same or a related database.

Because the **C**reate List Automatically from Field Data option enables you to add valid values from another related database—perhaps one that is protected from normal users—it is the most powerful of the options.

To draw a drop-down list from another database, join the database to your main database by opening the **C**reate menu and choosing **J**oin. After you create the join, follow these steps:

1. Switch to Design mode by opening the **V**iew menu and choosing **D**esign, clicking the Design SmartIcon, or choosing Design from the status bar.

2. Select the field that will be formatted as a drop-down list or Field Box & List.

3. Open the Info Box by selecting **S**tyle & Properties from the pop-up menu or by double-clicking the object. You can also open the Info Box by selecting the object and clicking the Info Box SmartIcon, or by opening the **O**bject menu and choosing **S**tyle & Properties.

4. If the data entry format is not a Drop-Down List or Field Box & List, choose the appropriate format in the Data Entry Type drop-down list in the Basics panel of the Info Box.

5. Choose Define List. The Drop-Down List dialog box appears.

6. Select the **C**reate List Automatically from Field Data radio button.

7. Choose **O**ptions to open a new section in the Drop-Down List dialog box (see fig. 9.21).

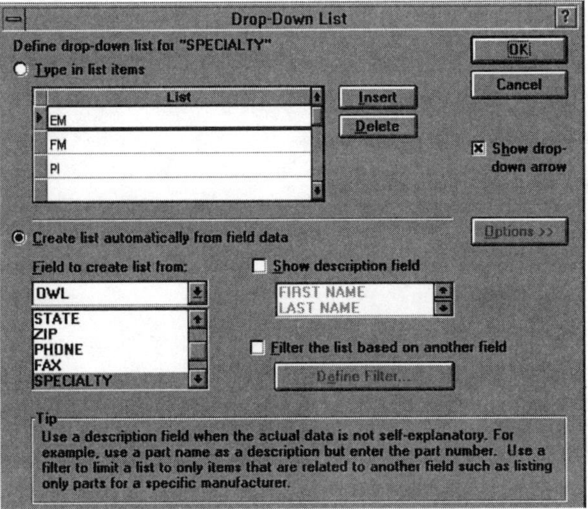

Fig. 9.21
The Drop-Down List dialog box provides some powerful options.

8. Select the database that contains the values you want to use for your drop-down list field from the **F**ield to Create List From drop-down box.

9. Select the field that contains the values you want to use for your drop-down list from the **F**ield to Create List From drop-down box. The List list box at the top-left displays the current values in the field you selected.

10. Click OK to close the Drop-Down List dialog box and to return to the main form.

The drop-down list in the main field is now drawn from the specified field in the linked database. If you change the contents of the field supplying the drop-down list, the drop-down list that appears when you click the main field also changes.

Here's a simple illustration of using a field in another database to supply the values for a drop-down list. A database called ITEMS contains two fields: ITEM NUM (item number) and ITEM DESC (item description). The ITEMS database is joined to another database called PICNIC. It has two fields as well: ITEM NUM and QUANTITY (see fig. 9.22).

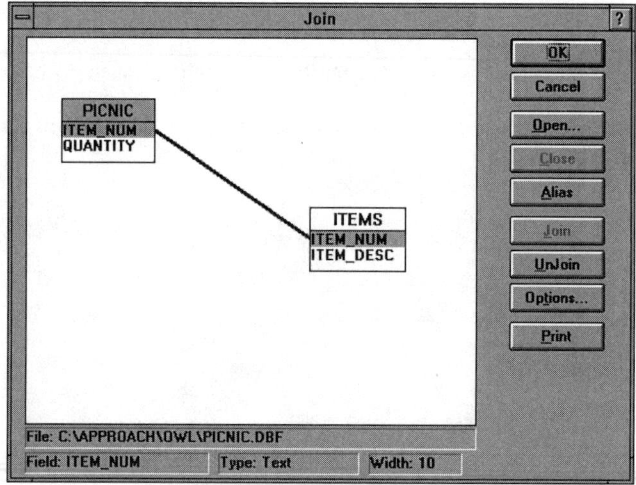

Fig. 9.22
The ITEMS database is joined to the PICNIC database by the ITEM NUM field in each database.

By using the preceding steps, you set the data-entry format of the ITEM NUM field in the PICNIC database to a drop-down list in the field Info Box. The drop-down list for the ITEM NUM field in PICNIC comes from the ITEM NUM field in ITEMS (see fig. 9.23).

When you click the ITEM NUM field on the PICNIC form, a drop-down list of values appears (see fig. 9.24). This list comes from the field ITEM NUM in the ITEMS database.

Adding a Description to a Drop-Down List

Often, the information entered into fields in a database is in the form of alphanumeric codes—instead of long descriptive text, you simply enter a code that means the same thing. For example, the code K could be used for the text string Ketchup. This practice dates back to the days when the only way information could be entered in a database was to type it. Codes were often used in place of text for the following reasons:

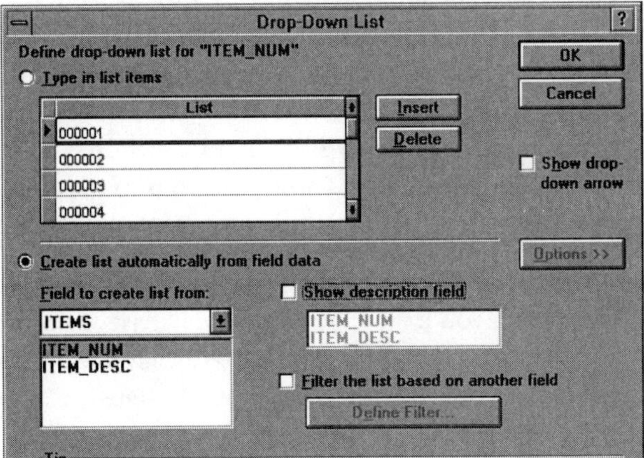

Fig. 9.23
The Drop-Down List dialog box shows that ITEM NUM in ITEMS is supplying the drop-down list for ITEM NUM in PICNIC.

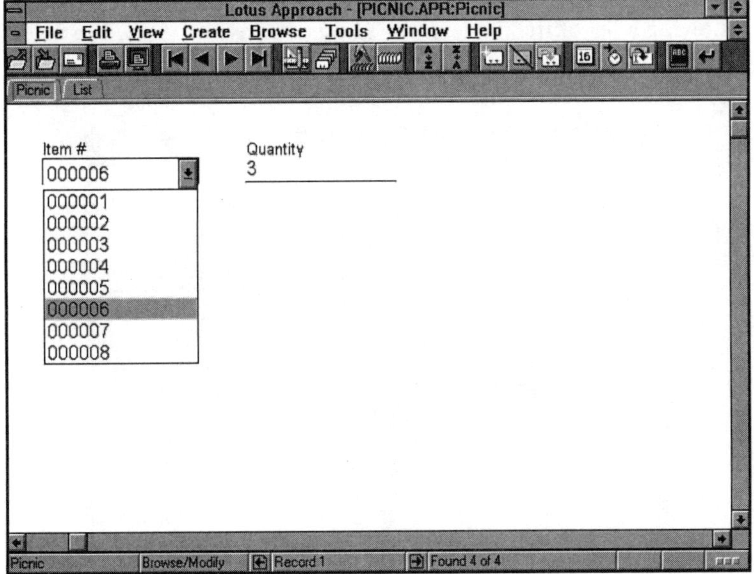

Fig. 9.24
The list of drop-down values comes from the ITEM NUM field in the ITEMS database.

- Typing long descriptive phrases took much longer than typing codes.
- Ensuring that the text was typed accurately was difficult. If errors were inadvertently created, a text search might miss that record.
- Codes took up less room than text on-screen and on disk.

Deciphering a particular code can be difficult! When you click the ITEM NUM field on the PICNIC form, for example, a list of codes such as `00006` appears. But what happens if you don't remember that `00006` means Ketchup?

Approach provides a mechanism to help you identify the codes. Instead of using codes, Approach displays descriptions in the drop-down list. When you select a description, Approach inserts the corresponding code into the field. In the previous illustration, the drop-down list would contain descriptions such as Ketchup or Hot Dogs. When you click the Ketchup description, however, the code for Ketchup (`00006`) would be entered into the field.

To use descriptions instead of codes, follow steps 1–9 in the "Adding a Drop-Down List Based on Another Field's Values" section earlier in this chapter, to get to the point at which you have specified the database and the field that contains the drop-down list you want to use. To display the descriptions in the drop-down list instead of the codes, follow these steps:

1. From the Drop-Down List dialog box, click the **O**ptions button to access the expanded Drop-Down List dialog box. Select the **S**how Description Field checkbox. The list box below this option then becomes available, showing a list of the fields in the same database in which the field that is providing the drop-down list is stored (see fig. 9.25).

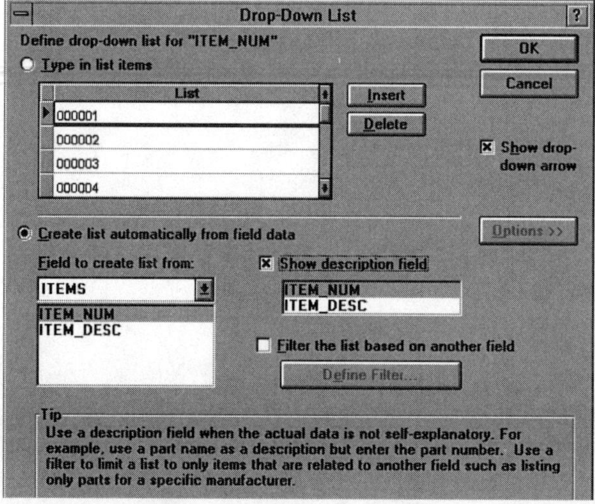

Fig. 9.25
Click the Show Description Field checkbox to see a list of available fields.

2. Select the field that contains the description you want to use. The List list box displays the descriptions (see fig. 9.26).

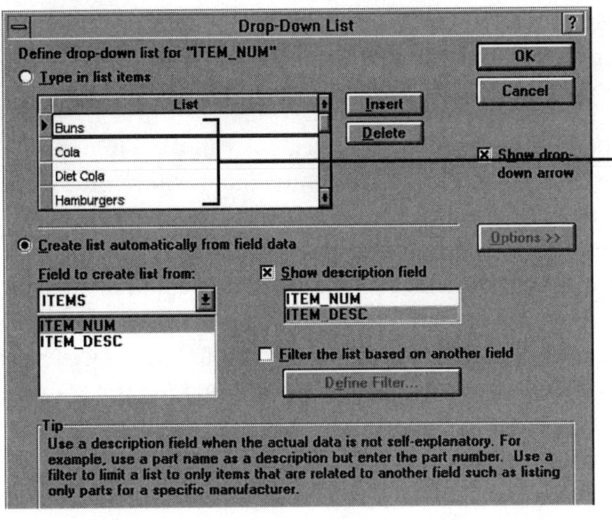

Fig. 9.26
The codes in the List box are replaced by descriptions.

3. Click OK to close the Drop-Down List dialog box and to return to the main form.

You are now using two fields from the linked database: the code (ITEM NUM) field and the description (ITEM DESC) field. The description field supplies the descriptions for the drop-down list that appears when you click the drop-down list field. The code field (in the same record) supplies the actual value that is entered in the drop-down list field on the main form when you make a selection from the drop-down list.

Restricting List Values from a Related Database Field

In Chapter 4 you learned how to filter the values available in a record for a drop-down list based on a field. Briefly, you can specify a field that Approach uses to filter records (the "filter field"). The values in the drop-down list come only from records in which the value of the filter field matches the value in the filter field of the current record. For example, a drop-down list might contain the values in the PART field. You can filter the values available in the current record to just those PART fields for which the value in the MANUFACTURER field (the filter field) matches the value in the MANUFACTURER field of the current record.

In Chapter 4, you used a single database for matching—the field containing the values and the filter field were in the same database. One difficulty with this approach is that you must build up a set of values in the single database before setting up the filter. If you don't create records before setting up the filter, you may end up with drop-down lists that contain no values.

Once you have joined several databases, you can use a joined database to contain the drop-down list and match the filter field in the current database against the filter field in the joined database. The advantage to doing this is that you can create records in the joined database before starting to enter data into the current database. For example, you could build another database (Parts) that contains Parts and their Manufacturers, and use Manufacturer as the filter field. When you create an order in your Orders database (which is linked to your Parts database) you could use the Manufacturer with whom you are placing the order to filter the available Parts. To define a filter based on a related database, follow steps 1–9 in the "Adding a Drop-Down List Based on Another Field's Values" section earlier in this chapter to draw the values in a drop-down list or field box & list from a related database. Then follow these steps:

1. Click the **F**ilter the List Based On Another Field checkbox. The Define Filter dialog box opens (see fig. 9.27).

> **Note**
>
> The first time you click the **F**ilter the List Based On Another Field checkbox, the Define Filter dialog box opens automatically. To open the Define Filter dialog box after the initial opening, click the Define Filter button.

2. Select the database that contains the filter field from the **U**sing the Current Value In drop-down list. All related databases are available in this list. The selected database must be the one that also holds the field containing the list of values.

3. Select the filter field from the list of fields in the database. Approach will assemble the values in the drop-down list only from database records in the related database in which the filter field you selected matches the value in the filter field in the current database.

Embedding Objects

In Chapters 4 and 7 you learned how to paste objects created in other applications into a form or report. You can use these objects to create custom effects in the form or report. Approach also enables you to embed an object directly in a form or report.

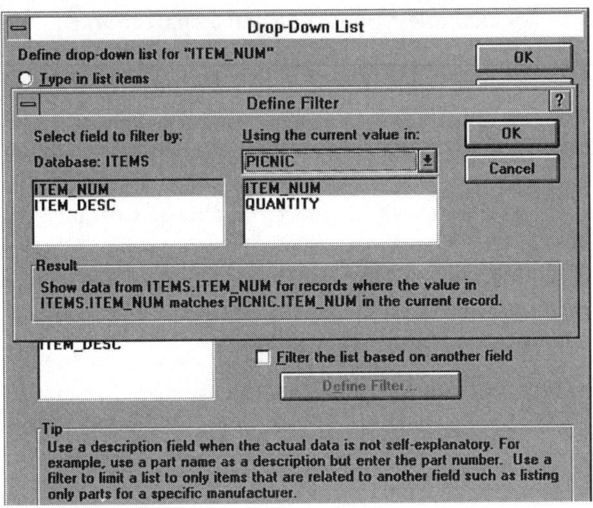

Fig. 9.27
Use a filter to limit the size of your drop-down list.

Embedding is a special technique that not only has all the capabilities of Paste, but that also makes it much easier to edit the object. With embedding, Approach "remembers" which application created the object you have placed on the form.

Note

The application that created the object is called the *server application*, because it provides the information to Approach. Approach is called a *client application*, because it informs server applications when information is needed, and then receives that information. Although we will only discuss using Approach as a client application here, Approach can also be a server application. For more information on using Approach as a server application, see Chapter 20.

When you need to edit an object that a server application has provided, you can ask Approach to open the server application that created the object (see "Editing an Embedded Object" later in this chapter). You can then use the server application to perform the editing. When the editing is complete, you can exit the server application and return to Approach. The object is then automatically updated on the form or report. This process of embedding an object and using the original application to edit it is part of Object Linking and Embedding (OLE).

Editing the object in the server application enables you to use that application's tools to perform the changes. The tools in the server application are usually much better at modifying the objects you need than the tools built into Approach. For example, you can embed a chart from a 1-2-3 for Windows spreadsheet. If you need to change the chart, it is much easier to do this in 1-2-3 for Windows than in Approach. You can also create more complex graphics in a program such as Microsoft Draw or Freelance Graphics than you can by using Approach's drawing tools.

The Approach view file stores the object you choose to embed on a form or report. You can move the view file to another computer and the embedded object moves with it. However, if the other computer doesn't have the server application installed, the object can't be modified.

Embedding an Existing Object

You can embed an existing object several ways. If you don't need to modify the object before embedding it, you can choose the Create from **F**ile option from the **O**bject dialog box under the **C**reate menu. If you do need to modify the object before embedding it, you can cut and paste the object from the active server application to Approach. You can also use the Create **N**ew option from the **O**bject dialog box under the **C**reate menu to start the server application and then load the object so it can be copied into Approach.

To embed an object that you don't need to modify, follow these steps:

1. Choose the form or report into which you want to embed the object.

2. Switch to Design mode by opening the **V**iew menu and choosing **D**esign, clicking the Design SmartIcon, or choosing Design from the status bar.

3. Click the area where you want to insert the embedded object.

4. Open the **C**reate menu and choose **O**bject. The Insert Object dialog box appears.

5. Click the Create from **F**ile radio button. Approach displays a Fil**e** text box (see fig. 9.28). Type in the name of the file you want to embed, or click the **B**rowse button to open the Browse dialog box and choose a file from a list of files.

6. Click OK to return to the form or report. Approach displays the embedded object on the form. You can edit the object (see "Editing an Embedded Object" later in this chapter).

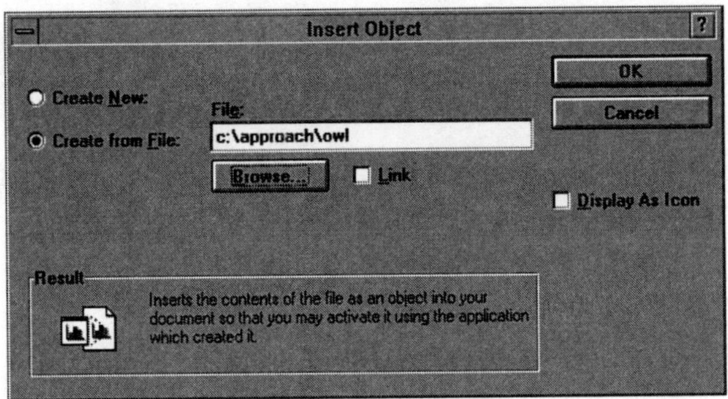

Fig. 9.28
The Insert Object dialog box.

To embed an existing object through the server application, follow these steps:

1. Start the server application, and load the file that contains the object you want to embed.
2. Select the object in the server application.
3. Open the **E**dit menu and choose **C**opy. The selected object is copied to the Windows clipboard.
4. Switch to Approach.
5. Choose the form or report into which you want to embed the object from the view tabs or the status bar.
6. Switch to Design mode by opening the **V**iew menu and choosing **D**esign, clicking the Design SmartIcon, or choosing Design from the status bar.

7. Click the form or report in the area where you want the object embedded.
8. Open the **E**dit menu and choose **P**aste. The object is embedded in the form or report.

As an alternative method of embedding an object that you need to modify, you can open the **C**reate menu and choose **O**bject. Follow these steps:

1. Choose the form or report into which you want to embed the object.
2. Switch to Design mode by opening the **V**iew menu and choosing **D**esign, clicking the Design SmartIcon, or choosing Design from the status bar.

3. Click the area where you want to insert the embedded object.

4. Open the **C**reate menu and choose **O**bject. The Insert Object dialog box appears.

5. If it's not already selected, click the Create **N**ew radio button (see fig. 9.29). Select the type of object you want to create in the Object **T**ype list box.

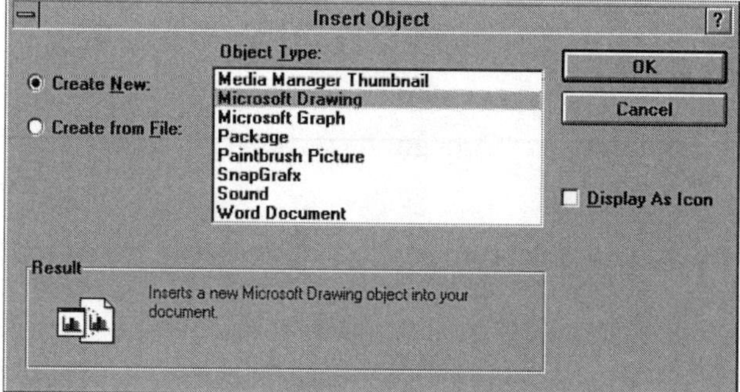

Fig. 9.29
The Insert Object dialog box.

Note

Depending on which OLE server applications you have installed on your computer, your list of object types (as displayed in the Insert Object dialog box) may be different than the list in the illustration.

6. Click OK in the Insert Object dialog box. Approach opens the server application. The title of the server application's window is the name of the Approach file you are working with, prefixed with the name of the server application (see fig. 9.30).

7. Load the file to be embedded. Use the server application's tools to edit the file before embedding it.

Note

Some server applications (notably Microsoft's Sound Recorder and Paintbrush) can't embed an object after loading a file using the File Load command. These applications often have other ways of "loading" a file for embedding. For example, to load a file into Sound Recorder, open the **E**dit menu and choose **I**nsert File; to insert a file into Paintbrush, open the **E**dit menu and choose Paste **F**rom.

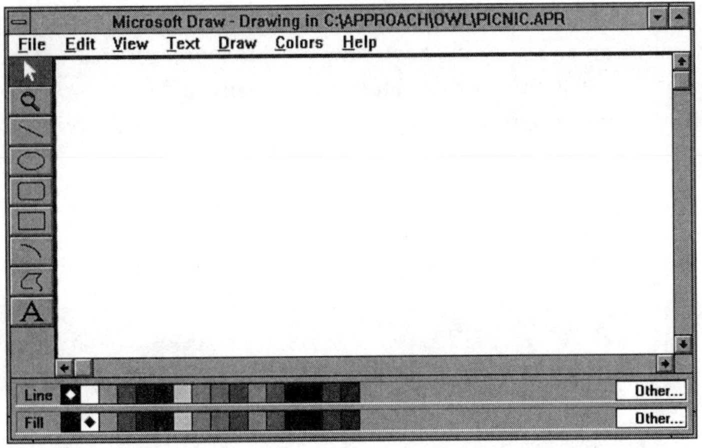

Fig. 9.30
The server application window identifies the Approach file and the server application.

8. Open the **F**ile menu and choose **U**pdate in the server application.

> **Note**
>
> Some server applications do not provide an Update menu item on the File menu. If this is the case, open the **F**ile menu and choose **C**lose. When the server application asks whether you want to update the Approach file, choose Yes.

9. Open **F**ile menu and choose **C**lose in the server application to return to Approach. The embedded object appears in the form or report.

Embedding a New Object

The previous steps show you how to embed an object that's already been created. To embed a new object, follow these steps:

1. In Approach, choose the form or report into which you want to embed the object.

2. Switch to Design mode.

3. Click the area where you want to insert the embedded object.

4. Open the **C**reate menu and choose **O**bject. The Insert Object dialog box appears.

5. Click the type of object you want to create in the Object Type list box.

6. Click OK in the Insert Object dialog box. Approach opens the server application and provides a window in which you can create the object you want. The title of the window is the name of the Approach view file you are working on, prefixed with the name of the server application.

7. Create the object you want to embed.

8. Open the **F**ile menu and choose **U**pdate in the server application.

> **Note**
>
> Some server applications do not provide an Update menu item on the File menu. If this is the case, Open the **F**ile menu and choose **C**lose. When the server application asks whether you want to update the Approach file, choose Yes.

9. Choose **C**lose in the **F**ile menu in the server application to return to Approach. The embedded object appears in the form or report.

Viewing an Embedded Object

Some embedded objects (for example, Paintbrush pictures) can be viewed in Approach. Other objects, however, display only the icon of the server application that created them (see fig. 9.31). Typically, these are objects that can't be readily displayed in a graphics environment. For example, how would you display the "picture" of a Sound Recorder sound?

To view the objects that display only the server icon, double-click the icon. In Design mode, you can alternatively select the appropriate menu item (which varies depending on the type of object) in the **O**bject menu. If you embed a sound object in an Approach form or report, for example, you can listen to it by either double-clicking the icon or (in Design mode) by choosing Sound **O**bject **P**lay from the **O**bject menu.

Working with Embedded Object Icons

As mentioned in the previous section, some embedded objects can be viewed directly on an Approach form or report. These objects tend to be graphic files, such as a Paintbrush picture or a single frame from a video animation. However, if space is tight on your report or form, you may not want to always display an embedded object. Instead, you can display the embedded object as an icon on the form. You can also change the icon from the default icon of the server application (for example, the microphone icon for Microsoft Sound) to another icon, and change the icon for embedded objects that always display as icons.

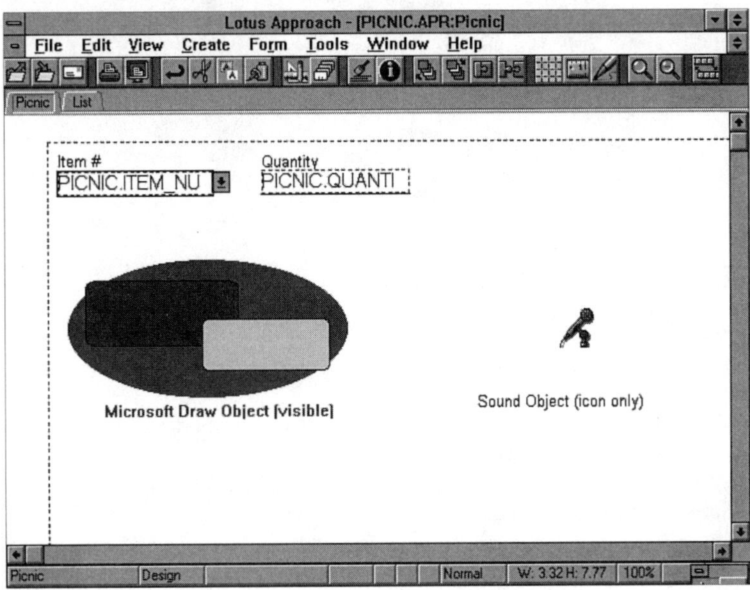

Fig. 9.31
Some embedded objects are visible in the form or report, while other objects display only the icon of the application that created them.

To show an embedded object as an icon on the form or report, select the **D**isplay As Icon checkbox in the Insert Object dialog box. The default icon of the server application appears just below this checkbox. Approach also displays a Change **I**con button. To change the icon that Approach displays for an embedded object, follow these steps:

1. From the Insert Object dialog box, click the Change **I**con button. If the button is not visible, click the **D**isplay as Icon checkbox.

2. The Change Icon dialog box opens (see fig. 9.32).

3. Select the option for the icon you want. You can choose the **C**urrent icon, the **D**efault icon (the icon of the server application), or select an icon **F**rom File. If you select an icon from a file, you type the name of the file in the **F**rom File text box, or click the **B**rowse button to select a file from disk. Any icons contained in the typed or selected file are displayed in the area below the file name. Click the icon you want to use.

4. Type the label for the icon into the **L**abel text box and click OK to return to the Insert Object dialog box. Click OK to place the embedded object on the form.

Tip
Many files contain icons that you can borrow. A good source of icons is MOREICONS.DLL (in your Windows directory) or any file ending in ".ICO."

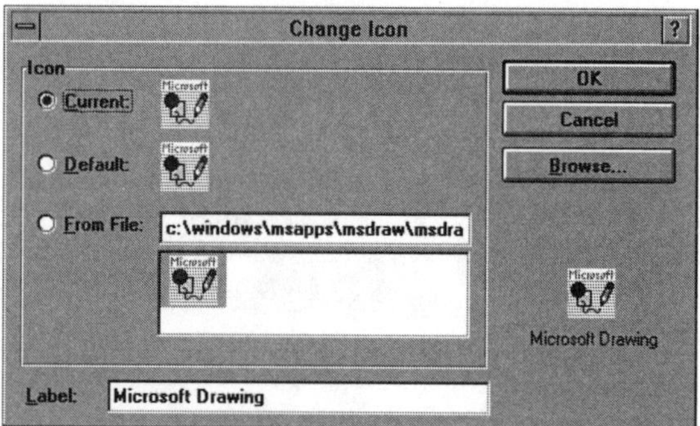

Fig. 9.32
An embedded object appears as a simple icon.

Editing an Embedded Object

To edit the contents of an embedded object, follow these steps:

1. Switch to Design mode.
2. Choose the form or report that contains the embedded object by using the view tabs or the status line.
3. Select the embedded object.
4. Select the command for editing the object from the **O**bject menu or the shortcut menu. The server application that created the object opens on-screen and displays the object.
5. Use the server application to make the changes you want.
6. Open the **F**ile menu and choose **U**pdate in the server application.

> **Note**
>
> Some server applications do not provide an Update menu item on the File menu. If this is the case, open the **F**ile menu and choose **C**lose. When the server application asks whether you want to update the Approach file, choose Yes.

7. Choose E**x**it from the **F**ile menu in the server application. You return to Approach with the object updated on-screen (see figs. 9.33, 9.34, and 9.35).

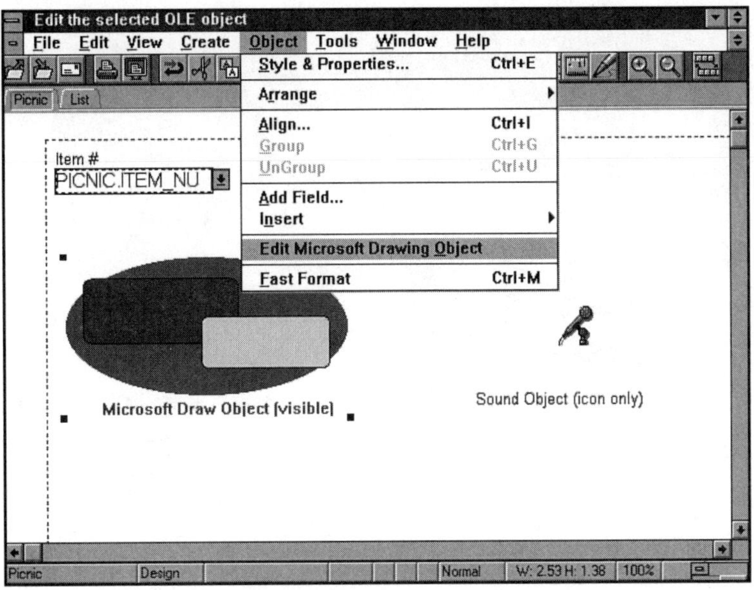

Fig. 9.33
To edit an embedded object, select it and choose the edit command from the Object or shortcut menu.

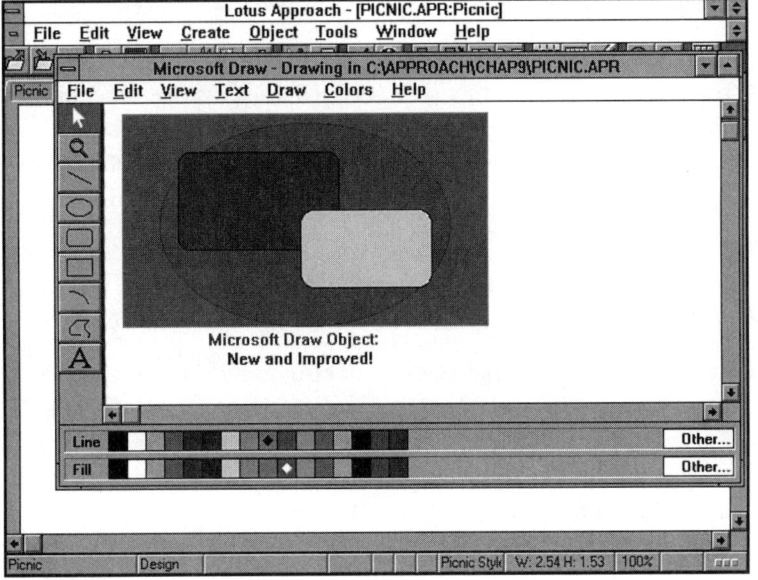

Fig. 9.34
The server application opens and you can make changes to the object.

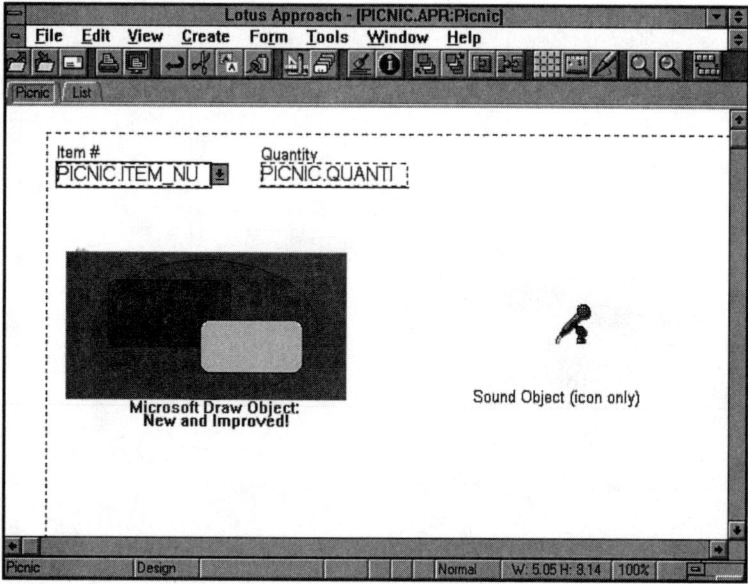

Fig. 9.35
When you return to Approach, the embedded object is automatically updated.

When selecting a menu item to edit an embedded object, keep in mind the following:

- The menu item for editing an embedded object varies depending on the type of object. For objects that display their contents on-screen, the menu item displays the word `Edit` and the name of the object (for example, `Edit Microsoft Drawing Object`), as shown in figure 9.36.

- For objects that display only the server application icon, choose the name of the object (for example, Sound **O**bject) from the **O**bjects menu or the shortcut menu. From the submenu, choose **E**dit (see fig. 9.37).

- For most embedded objects, you can also double-click the object to open the server application. However, you can't use this technique if you are using any type of embedded sound or animation. Double-clicking a sound or animation application icon plays the sound or animation; it doesn't open the application.

- The embedded objects can't be activated or edited if the Approach file is moved to a system without the server application, or if the server application is removed from the system.

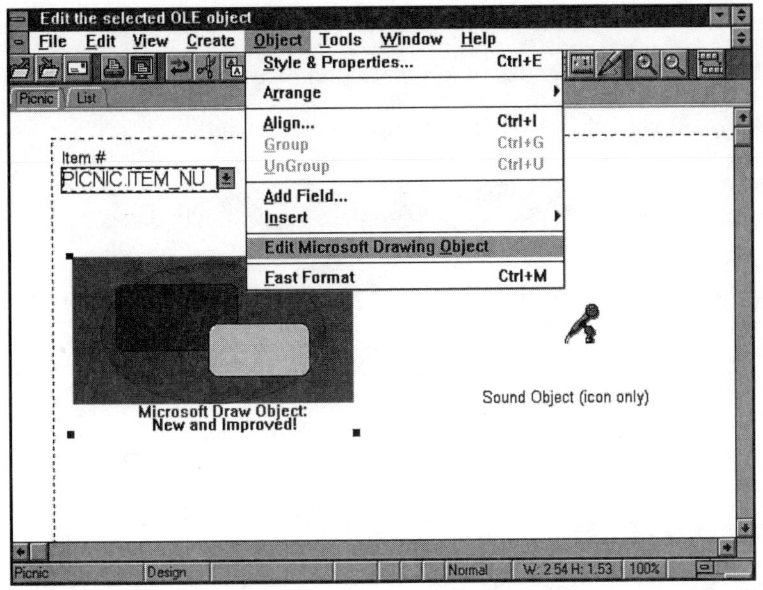

Fig. 9.36
Choose the item from the Edit menu for objects that display their contents on-screen.

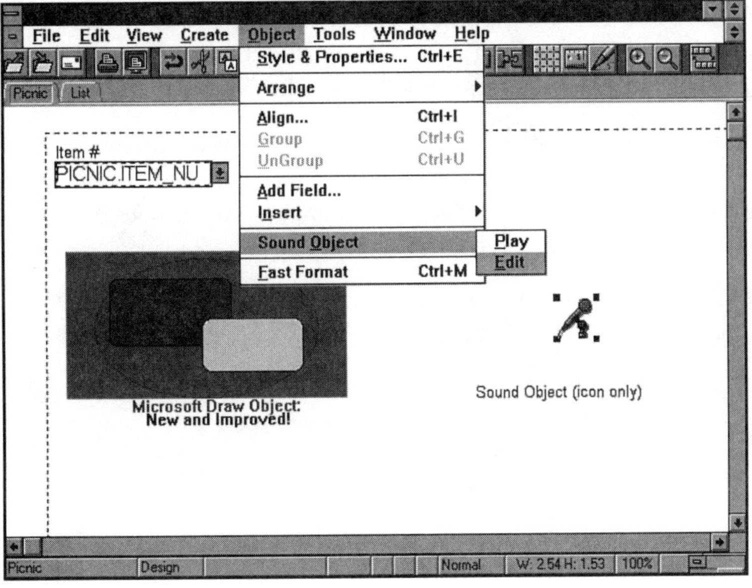

Fig. 9.37
Choose the item from the Edit menu for objects that display the server icon on-screen.

Approach enables you to edit embedded objects in Design mode:

- To move an embedded object, click and drag it to a new location.
- To resize an object, click and drag the sizing handles.

Note

Approach automatically scales the embedded object to fit into the space allowed for it on-screen. That is, if you enlarge the boundaries of the object, Approach increases the size of the object to fill the new boundaries. If you make the boundaries for the object smaller, Approach shrinks the object to a smaller size so that it continues to fit in the allotted space.

From Here...

In this chapter, you learned how to create advanced forms that enable you to use relational databases. You also learned advanced techniques for defining forms, such as using repeating panels for showing the parts of a one-to-many relationship. You discovered that embedded objects can be used on a form to display objects that can't be created directly within Approach.

Now that you have mastered these skills, you'll also want to learn about advanced reports, how to use Approach as an OLE server, and how to combine its power with other Lotus products. For more information on these topics, refer to the following chapters in this book:

- Chapter 12, "Creating Advanced Reports," tells you how to extend what you've learned to writing reports.
- Chapter 20, "Using Approach with the Lotus SmartSuite," tells you how to combine Approach's power with other products in the SmartSuite. It also covers how to use Approach as an OLE server.

Chapter 10

Using Advanced Field Types

Besides the field types discussed in Chapter 2 (Boolean, date, memo, numeric, text, and time), Approach enables you to use more powerful fields. These advanced fields make it possible to perform calculations, store values temporarily, and place graphic and OLE (linked and embedded) objects in database fields.

In this chapter, you learn how to:

- Define a calculated field
- Add a calculated field to an existing report or form
- Change the appearance of a calculated field
- Create a formula for a calculated field
- Use functions in a calculated field
- Create variable fields
- Add a variable field to an existing report or form
- Change the appearance of a variable field
- Create PicturePlus fields
- Add a PicturePlus field to an existing report or form
- Change the appearance of a PicturePlus field
- Add or remove an image or object to or from a PicturePlus field

Using Calculated Fields

Simply put, a *calculated field* is a field that contains a formula. When you define the formula for the calculated field, Approach performs the calculation and displays the result in the field. You can define calculated fields when you first create a database, or you can add them later.

Unlike other types of fields, calculated fields don't "belong" to any one database in an Approach file. Instead, they reside in the Approach file itself. Calculated fields appear in the available field list for all databases in a view.

> **Note**
>
> Because calculated fields are part of the Approach file, the calculated field defined in one Approach file will not be available if you open the database(s) in another Approach file.

Parts of a Calculated Field

Calculated fields are constructed from four kinds of building blocks:

- References to field values
- References to constant values
- Operators (arithmetic, comparison, and Boolean)
- Functions

These items are detailed in the following sections.

References to Field Values

You can use the contents of fields in a formula for the calculated field. The fields you use can come from the same database as the calculated field or from any relationally linked database.

> **Note**
>
> If the field name contains spaces, enclose the field name in double quotation marks (" "). You can also select the field name from the list of fields and Approach adds the database name or quotations as needed.

References to Constant Values

Constants are values you enter into a formula that don't change from record to record. You must follow certain rules when typing constants into a formula:

- Enclose text string constants in single quotation marks (for example, **'Approach'**).
- Type date constants in the order mm/dd/yy, separated by slashes, and enclosed in single quotation marks (for example, **'03/12/56'**).
- Type time constants in the order of hours, minutes, seconds, and hundredths of seconds. Separate hours, minutes, and seconds with a colon (:). Separate seconds from hundredths of seconds with a decimal point. Enclose time constants in single quotation marks (for example, **'12:25:00.45'**).
- Type Boolean constants as **'Yes'** or **'No'** and enclose them in single quotation marks. You can also use **1** for Yes and **0** for No.
- Don't type numeric constants in scientific notation.

Arithmetic Operators

You can use arithmetic operators to build arithmetic equations in the formula for the calculated field. The arithmetic operators include multiplication (*), division (/), addition (+), subtraction (–), percentage (%), and negation operator (NOT). You can also use parentheses to group arithmetic operations.

Arithmetic operations are evaluated in a specific order:

- Multiplication and division operations are evaluated first.
- Addition and subtraction operations are evaluated second.
- The percentage operation is third, followed by the negation operation.
- If any operations are on the same evaluation level (such as multiplication and division), they are evaluated from left to right in the formula.

You can modify the evaluation order of arithmetic operators by using parentheses. Approach always evaluates the contents of parentheses before evaluating other parts of the formula. Within a set of parentheses, the evaluation order is as described in the preceding list.

> **Note**
>
> In Approach, your formula can have multiple sets of parentheses. If Approach finds a problem with your formula, the OK button on the Formula dialog box will be inactive and there will be a red "X" through the checkered flag. Check to see that you have the same number of left and right parentheses. If the formula is unbalanced (the number of parentheses don't match), it's not considered a valid formula.

Comparison Operators

You can use comparison operators to compare two values or fields. The comparison operators include equals (=), greater than (>), less than (<), not equal to (<>), greater than or equal to (>=), and less than or equal to (<=).

Boolean Operators

You can use Boolean operators to connect parts, or clauses, of the formula. The Boolean operators are AND and OR.

The clause containing the AND operator evaluates as true only if both parts connected by the AND are true. For example, 5>6 AND 'A'<'B' is false; although 'A' is less than 'B', 5 isn't greater than 6. However, 5<6 AND 'A'<'B' is true because both parts of the equation are true.

The clause containing the OR operator evaluates as true if either part connected by the OR is true. For example, 5>6 OR 'A'<'B' is true because 'A' is less than 'B'. However, 5>6 OR 'A'>'B' is false because both sides are false.

You connect multiple clauses with combinations of ANDs and ORs. Clauses normally are evaluated from left to right (AND and OR have the same evaluation level). You can use parentheses to modify this order, however. The result of each clause (true or false) is then used to evaluate the next clause.

Look at the formula 5>6 AND 'A'<'B' OR 10<12, for example. This equation evaluates to be true. The first clause is 5>6 AND 'A'<'B'. Because 5 isn't greater than 6, this whole clause evaluates as false. The result (FALSE) is then used with OR 10<12. Because 10 is less than 12, this clause becomes FALSE OR TRUE, which evaluates as true.

Functions

Approach supports 84 functions that can perform various operations on text and numeric values. The value on which a function operates (called an *argument*) can be a field or constant value. If a function uses multiple arguments, you must separate the arguments using commas (or the list separator in the

Windows International Control Panel). The Middle function, for example, returns a text string of a specified size from a specified position in another text string. It has the form Middle (Text, Position, Size). AND or OR can connect multiple functions in the same clause.

Creating a Calculated Field

As with all other types of fields, to create calculated fields you need to use the Field Definition dialog box. You can create a calculated field when you first define the database or add the field later.

Defining a Calculated Field for a New Database

When creating a new database, follow the steps detailed in the "Designing a Database" section in Chapter 2 to define the fields you need. Briefly, these steps are:

1. Define the information you need to track. List all the database fields you think you might need.
2. Refine the list you built in step 1 to make sure you have everything you need. Ensure that you are not keeping extraneous information, and that you will be storing fields in a format that will enable you to get your work done.

Then continue as follows:

1. Open the **F**ile menu and choose **N**ew. The New dialog box appears.
2. Type the database name in the File **N**ame text box and select the file type from the List Files of **T**ype drop-down list.
3. Click OK. The Creating New Database dialog box appears (see fig. 10.1).

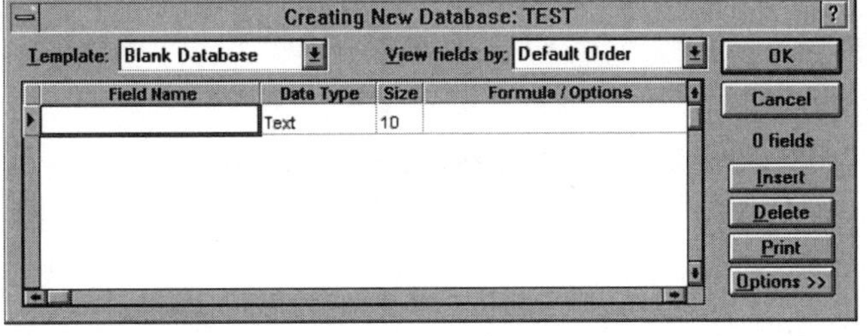

Fig. 10.1
You can add calculated fields from the Creating New Database dialog box.

4. Type the field name of the calculated field into one of the lines in the Field Name column.

5. From the Data Type drop-down list, select Calculated. The Creating New Database dialog box expands to display the Options section at the bottom. Use the expanded section to define the calculated field's formula (see fig. 10.2).

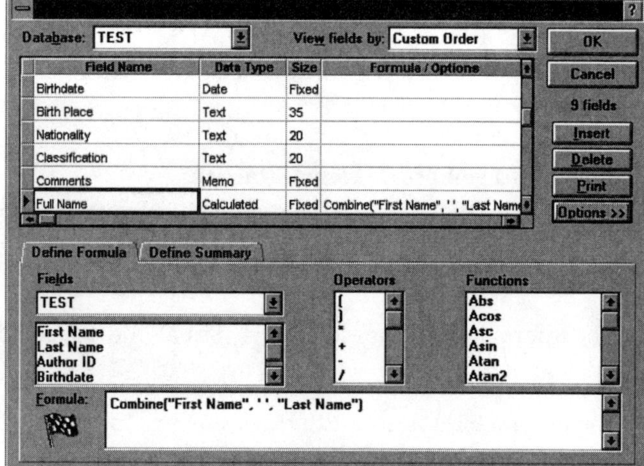

Fig. 10.2
The Options section allows you to build a calculated formula.

6. To define the formula you need, use the Fields, Operators, and Functions list boxes in the expanded Creating New Database dialog box.

7. When the formula is complete, click OK to close the Creating New Database dialog box.

Note

If you need to return to the Formula dialog box to revise the formula, select the calculated field in the list of fields in the Creating New Database dialog box, and then click the **O**ptions button.

Adding a Calculated Field to an Existing Database

To define a calculated field in an existing database, follow these steps:

1. Switch to Design mode.

2. Open the **C**reate menu and choose Field **D**efinition. The Field Definition dialog box appears.

3. Type the field name on an empty line in the Field Name column. From the Data Type drop-down list, choose Calculated. The Field Definition dialog box expands to show the Options section. Use the expanded section to define the calculated field's formula.

4. To define the formula you need, use the Fields, Operators, and Functions list boxes in the expanded Field Definition dialog box.

5. When the formula is complete, click OK to close the Field Definition dialog box.

Adding an Existing Calculated Field to a Form or Report

After you define a calculated field, you can add it to an existing form or report just like any other field. Follow these steps:

1. Switch to Design mode.

2. Either click and drag the calculated field onto the form from the Add Field dialog box, or:

3. Click the Draw Field tool from the Drawing toolbar, drag a rectangle to define the position and size of the calculated field, and select the calculated field form the field list in the Basics panel of the field Info Box.

Note

Calculated fields are displayed in italic text at the end of the field list in the Info Box. If an Approach file has any variable fields, they are listed before calculated fields, in italics.

Changing the Appearance of a Calculated Field

You can change the appearance of a calculated field on a form or report just as you can any other field by resizing, moving, changing the fill and pen colors, setting borders, and adjusting the attributes of the text for the contents of the field and the label.

To make changes to the field, switch to Design mode, and then perform any of the following procedures:

- To move the field, drag it to its new location or adjust the location from the Dimensions panel of the Info Box.

- To resize the field, drag one of the sizing handles until the field is the size you want. You can also adjust the width and height from the Dimensions panel of the Info Box.
- Select the border, fill, or shadow color from the drop-down list that Approach makes available in the Colors panel of the Info box when you click the Border Color, Fill Color, or Shadow Color drop-down lists. The box labeled T provides a transparent color.
- Select the border width from the Border Width drop-down list in the Colors panel of the Info Box. Available border widths range from hairline to 12 point (1/6 of an inch).
- To change the font, size, style/effect, color, alignment, or text relief, make the appropriate selections from the Font panel of the Info Box.
- To change the label font, size, style/effect, color, alignment, position, text, or text relief, make the appropriate selections from the Label panel of the Info Box.
- Click the checkboxes in the Borders section (for example, Left, Right, Top, and Bottom) of the Colors panel in the Info Box to select which sides of the field you want Approach to display borders.
- Select a frame style from the Frame drop-down list in the Colors panel of the Info Box. The frame style specifies the format in which Approach draws the border around the selected field.

Creating a Formula

To build a formula for a calculated field, use the **O**ptions section of the Creating New Database dialog box (for a new database) or the Field Definition dialog box (when working with a calculated field in an existing database). For a calculated field, the **O**ptions portion of these dialog boxes displays the Define Formula panels (see fig. 10.3). The Define Formula panels are divided into five main sections: the Fie**l**ds list box, the Operators list box, the Functions list box, the **F**ormula text box, and the Define Summary panel. The following sections describe how to use these sections.

Tip
Rather than selecting a field name from this list, you can type the field name into the **F**ormula text box.

The Fields List Box

The Fie**l**ds list box in the Define Formula panels contains a list of all the fields in the database whose name appears in a drop-down list box just above the Fie**l**ds list box. When you select a field in the Fie**l**ds list box, it appears in the **F**ormula text box near the bottom of the dialog box.

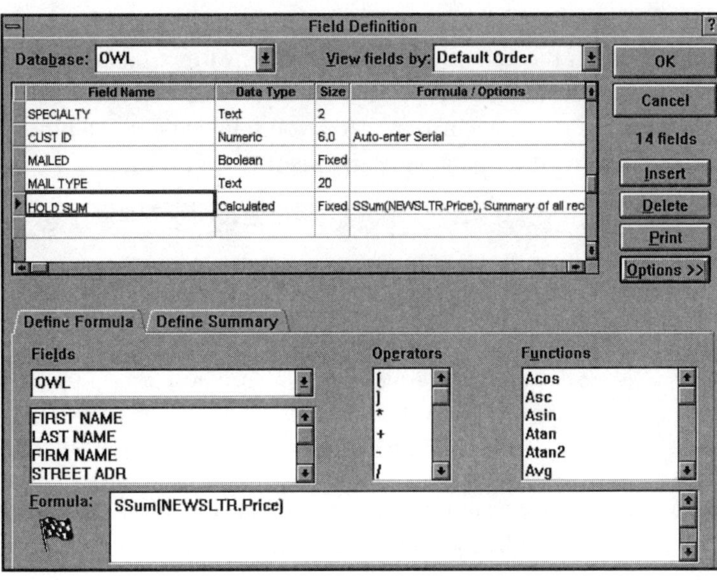

Fig. 10.3
The Define Formula panels make it simple to create and edit a formula.

You can include fields in the formula from any other database that is contained in the current Approach file. You can switch to another database and view the fields by selecting it from the drop-down list box just above the Fields list box. After selecting the database name, the Fields list box displays the fields in that database.

Note

If a calculated field displays <circular> in Browse mode rather than a value, this means the field has a reference back to itself called a circular reference. Check the formula for the field, or the fields it uses as references, to find and correct the problem.

The Operators List Box

The **O**perators list box displays all the operators available for building a formula. These include arithmetic operators, comparison operators, Boolean operators, and parentheses for grouping expressions. To select an operator, you can select it from this list or type the operator into the **F**ormula text box.

The Functions List Box

From the F**u**nctions list box, you can select any of the 84 powerful functions that Approach contains to build a formula. These functions include conversion, date, logical, time, trigonometric, string, financial, summary, mathematical, and statistical functions. To enter a function into a formula, select the function from the list box or type the function into the **F**ormula text box.

Many functions operate on one or more values, or arguments. These values are entered between the parentheses that follow the function name. They can be field values or constant values. To enter a field value, select the field or type it. If you want to use a constant value, you must type it. If a function uses multiple arguments, separate the arguments with commas.

> **Note**
>
> Approach gets various settings from the Windows International control panel that affect formulas. These settings include the default list separator (a comma in the United States), the default data format (MM/DD/YY in the United States), and the default time format (HH:MM:SS.00 in the United States). If these settings have been changed, enter the formula using the current settings in this control panel.

The Middle function, for example, returns a text string of a specified size from a specified position in another text string. It has the following format:

```
Middle(Text, Position, Size)
```

You can use functions as arguments in a function. To indicate whether the LAST_NAME field is blank, for example, you can combine the If function with the Isblank function:

```
If (Isblank(LAST_NAME),'Blank','Not Blank')
```

In this example, the Isblank function and its argument are used as the first argument in the If function.

The Formula Box

The **F**ormula text box displays the formula as you build it. At any time, you can edit the formula in this box.

> **Note**
>
> The OK button in the Define Formula panels is dimmed and unavailable unless the formula displayed in the formula area has a valid syntax. If the OK button is dimmed, check the syntax of the formula. Likewise, the flag appears with a red X across it if the formula is invalid.

Now you can practice using the **F**ormula text box to create a formula. For example, Owl Publishing's newsletters are always sold in one-year subscriptions—by knowing the start date of a subscription, you can calculate the end date. Calculating the end date saves time because then you don't have to enter the end date on each new subscription. To create a field that calculates the end date of a subscription, follow these steps:

1. Switch to Design mode. Open the Info Box if it is not open on the form.

2. Select the Customer form from the view tabs or the status line.
3. Select the SUB END field in the repeating panel. (See Chapter 9 for information on setting up repeating panels on a form.)
4. Click the Field Definition button in the Info Box. When defining a new calculated field, leave the old field (SUB END) in the database in case you make a mistake.
5. Scroll down the Field Definition dialog box until you reach an empty line. Click the empty line and type **SUB END CC** in the Field Name column.
6. Set the Data Type to Calculated. The Define Formula panel opens at the bottom of the Field Definition dialog box.
7. Enter the following formula in the **F**ormula text box:

```
NEWSLTR."SUBSTART"+365.25+If(MOD(YEAR(NEWSLTR."SUBSTART")+1,4)=0,1,0)
```

   This formula calculates the date one year after SUB START and corrects for the extra day in leap years (see fig. 10.4).

Tip
Remember, the fields, operators, and functions can be typed in or selected from the lists within the formula section of the Field Definition dialog box.

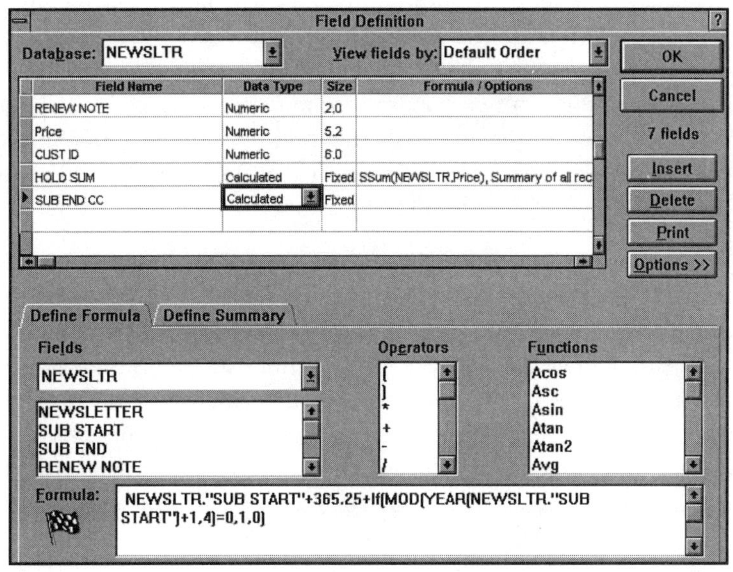

Fig. 10.4
The SUB END CC calculated field calculates the ending date for a one-year subscription.

8. Click OK to close the Field Definition dialog box. Approach returns to the Customer form. The SUB END field in the repeating panel has now been replaced with the new SUB END CC calculated field (see fig.10.5).

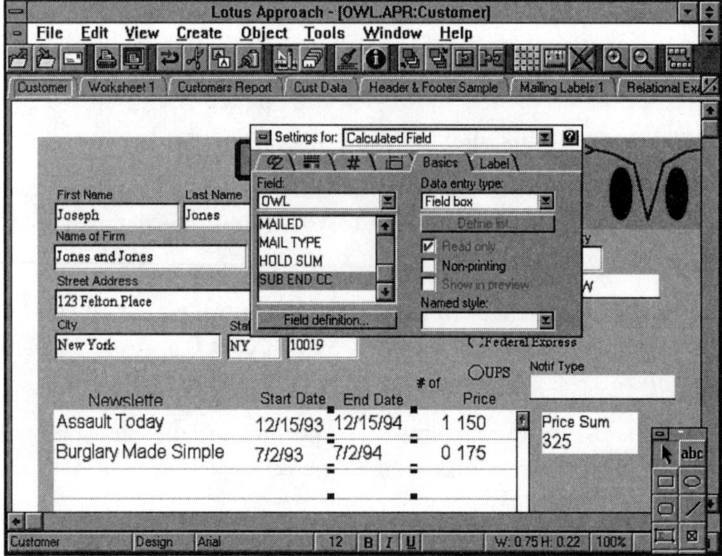

Fig. 10.5
The calculated subscription ending date is displayed in the repeating panel.

The Define Summary Panel

For certain functions (called *summary functions*), a calculated field can calculate and display a value that is summarized for the database in which the calculated field appears, for the summary panel in which the field is placed, or for all databases to which the field's database is relationally linked. You can select the summary option you want from the **S**ummarize On drop-down list box in the Define Summary panel. The three options are Summarize On All Records In (current database), Summary Panels Where This Field is Placed, or Summarize On All Records in All Databases:

- *Summarize On All Records In (current database).* This option summarizes across all the current records in any one database, and appears once for each database in a view file. Thus, in your example, this option appears three times: once for the OWL database (for example, Summarize on all records in OWL), once for the NEWSLTR database, and once for the SPECLTY database. Use this option when the formula contains only fields located in a single database. Only the records that are currently in use are summarized. Thus, if you are currently working with a found set after performing a find, only the records in the found set are included in the summary calculation.

- *Summary Panels Where This Field is Placed.* In Chapter 12 you'll learn to create summary panels on a report. A summary panel groups and summarizes records on the report by the value in a certain field. For example, you can create a summary panel to group and summarize information by SPECIALTY. The Summary Panels Where this Field is Placed option tells Approach to summarize on the same field that is used in the summary panel. This is a useful option—you can create a single summary field, for example, SUBTOTAL—and reuse it in different summary panels, even on different reports.

- *Summarize On All Records in All Databases.* This option summarizes across all the databases in the Approach file. Use this option if the formula contains fields from more than one database. It is especially useful for summarizing across records in a database that are related to the main database in a one-to-many relationship.

Note

The **S**ummarize On drop-down list in the Define Summary panel is not available if the formula does not include a summary function.

Using Functions in Calculated Fields

Although calculated fields are often used to calculate and display mathematical results, Approach's functions give you considerably more power than just handling numbers. Approach enables you to do the following:

- Use text functions to find characters within a string, combine fields, and split off portions of fields

- Use conversion functions to convert one type of data to another (for example, number to text)

- Use date functions to extract information about a supplied date (for example, the week of the year a particular date falls into)

- Use logical functions to decide what calculations to perform based on the value of a field

If an argument is a constant (that is, not a reference to a field value), you must follow certain rules when typing the argument into the function:

- *Text string.* Enclose text strings in single quotation marks (**'ABCDEFG'**).

- *Date.* Type the date as numbers, separated by slashes, and enclosed in single quotation marks (**'10/20/93'**).

- *Time.* Type the time as numbers and enclose in single quotation marks. Separate the hours, minutes, and seconds with a colon (:), and separate the seconds from the hundredths of seconds with a decimal point. Use the AM or PM qualifier (**'10:20:34.02 AM'**). Any time value entered without a qualifier is taken as 24-hour time.
- *Numbers.* Don't enter numbers in scientific notation. Numeric data can come from a numeric field, or a text field containing numeric data.

The following sections discuss some of Approach's more powerful functions, with examples illustrating their use. The entire list of Approach functions can be found in Appendix A of the Approach manual.

Working with Text Functions

You can manipulate the contents of text fields using the functions Left, Right, Length, Middle, Position, Combine, and Trim, as described in the following sections.

> **Note**
>
> In a text string, spaces are considered characters. It's important to take spaces into account when using functions that rely on factors like position.

Left. Left requires two arguments—a text string and a number: `(n): Left(text,n)`. The function returns the first `n` characters of the text string, counting from the left. If the text argument is the name of a text-type field, the value in that field is used in the function.

For example, if the NAME field contains the value `ABCDEFG`, `Left(NAME,3)` returns `ABC`.

Right. Right requires two arguments—a text string and a number: `Right(text,n)`. The function returns the first `n` characters of the text string, counting from the right (that is, it returns the last `n` characters in the string). If the text argument is the name of a text-type field, the value in that field is used in the function.

For example, if the NAME field contains the value `ABCDEFG`, `Right(NAME,3)` returns `EFG`.

Length. Length requires a text string for its single argument: `Length(text)`. It returns the length of the text string. If the text argument is the name of a text-type field, the value in that field is used in the function.

For example, if the NAME field contains the value `ABCDEFG`, `Length(NAME)` returns `7`.

Middle. Middle requires three arguments—a text string and two numbers: `Middle(text, start, size)`. It extracts a string of characters from the text string. The string of characters starts at the position given by start. If the text argument is the name of a text-type field, the value in that field is used in the function. If the number arguments are names of numeric fields, the values in those fields are used in the function.

For example, if the NAME field contains the value `ABCDEFG` and the START field contains `3`, `Middle(NAME, START, 3)` returns `CDE`.

Position. Position requires three arguments—two text strings and a number: `Position(text, search, start)`. Position searches through the text string for the string of characters given by search. The search begins at the position given by start. If the search string of characters is found in text, Position returns the character position at which the search string is found. If the search string isn't found, Position returns zero. If the text and search arguments are the names of text-type fields, the values in those fields are used in the function. If the start argument is the name of a numeric field or a text field containing a number, the value in that field is used in the function.

For example, if the NAME field contains the value `ABC EFG`, `Position(NAME,' ',1)` returns `4` because the first blank space in the contents of the NAME field is at position 4. Alternately, if the formula used for this value is `Position(NAME,' ',5)`, the value returned is `0` because the space is before the starting position given in the function.

Combine. Combine requires a list of text-type arguments: `Combine(argument list)`. It links all the arguments in the list to form one text string. If the argument list includes field names, the function uses the values in the fields. Spaces and other text items are added in single quotation marks and separated by a comma.

For example, if the FIRST NAME field contains `John` and the LAST NAME field contains `Doe`, `Combine(FIRST NAME,' ',LAST NAME)` results in `John Doe`.

Trim. Trim requires a single text-type argument: `Trim(text)`. It returns the supplied text with all leading and trailing spaces removed. If the argument is a text-type field name, the value in the field is used in the function.

For example, `Trim('London ')` returns `London` (with no trailing spaces). Spaces within the text string are ignored. For example, `Trim('Walnut Creek ')` returns `Walnut Creek` (with no trailing spaces). The space within the string remains unaltered.

Combining Text-String Functions

Approach enables you to combine string functions to perform many complex string operations. You can extract single words from a field that contain multiple-word strings, for example. Thus, if the FULLNAME field contains a person's full name (first name and last name), setting up calculated fields that extract the first or last name from the full name is possible:

- Define the LASTNAME field using the following formula:

  Right(FULLNAME,Length(FULLNAME)–
  Position(FULLNAME,' ',1))

  The Position(FULLNAME,' ',1) portion of the formula finds the first blank in the full name (the blank between the first and last name). Subtracting this number from Length(FULLNAME) gives the length of the last name in the field. The Right function uses this result to extract the last name from the full name string.

- Define the FIRSTNAME field using the following formula:

  Left(FULLNAME, Position(FULLNAME,' ',1))

This formula takes any text from the FULLNAME field from the beginning of the field until the first space.

You can use the Combine function to combine the contents of fields for use in reports or mailing labels. You can combine, for example, the FIRST NAME and LAST NAME fields into a single calculated field:

Combine("FIRST NAME",' ',"LAST NAME")

You also can combine the CITY, STATE, and ZIP fields into a single field. The Trim function removes any trailing spaces:

Combine(Trim(CITY),', ',Trim(STATE),' ',Trim(ZIP))

Building a calculated field in this manner ensures that no large spaces are left between the city, state, and zip code on a mailing label. You could also use the When Printing Slide Left checkbox on the Dimensions panel of the Info Box to close up spaces between fields in a form, report, or mailing label (see fig. 10.6).

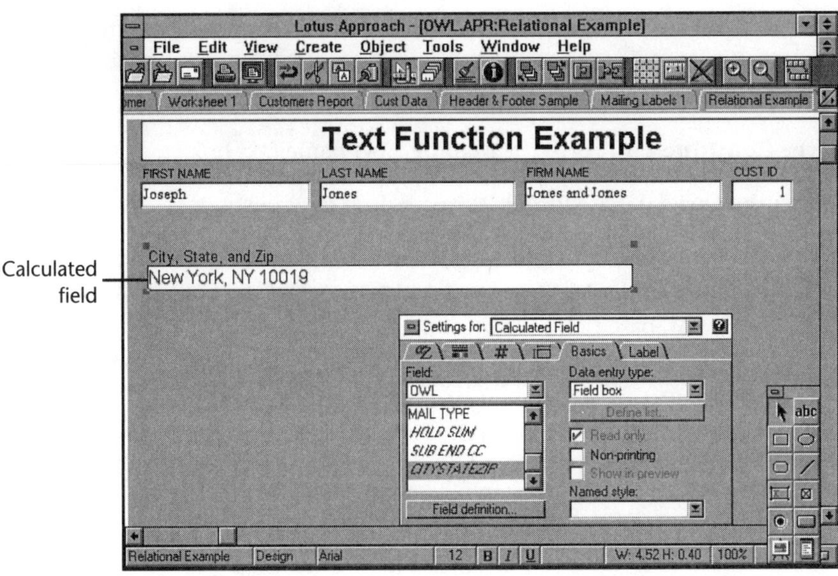

Fig. 10.6
Using calculated fields and string functions to create custom string formats.

> **Note**
>
> The preceding example assumes that ZIP is a text field. If ZIP is a numeric field, use the conversion function NumToText to convert the ZIP value into a text value (see the next section, "Working with Conversion Functions"). The Combine function then would look like the following:
>
> **Combine(Trim(CITY),',',Trim (STATE),' ',NumToText(ZIP,'00000')).**

Owl Publishing wants to create some mailing labels using the Combine function so that the City/State line can include a comma. Follow these steps:

1. Use the techniques detailed in the preceding "Creating a Formula" section to create a calculated field called CITYSTATEZIP. The formula for this field is:

   Combine(Trim(CITY),', ',Trim(STATE),' ',Trim(ZIP))

2. Use the techniques detailed above to create a calculated field called FULLNAME. The formula for this field is:

   Combine("FIRST NAME",' ',"LAST NAME")

3. Open the **C**reate menu and choose **M**ailing Label. The Mailing Label Assistant dialog box appears. Choose the 3 Lines SmartMaster address layout.

4. Type **Combine Labels** in the **M**ailing label name text box.

5. Select the Owl database in the **D**atabase drop-down list box.

6. Click the long center label field in the Field to Place on La**b**el diagram on the left side of the Mailing Label Assistant. Select the STREET ADR field in the Da**t**abase fields list box and click **A**dd.

7. Select Avery 5161 labels from the **L**abel Type drop-down list.

8. Click the upper-left label field in the Field to Place on La**b**el diagram. Select FULLNAME from the Da**t**abase Fields list and click **A**dd.

9. Click the bottom-left label field in the Field to Place on La**b**el diagram. Select CITYSTATEZIP from the Da**t**abase fields list and click **A**dd.

10. Click OK to complete the mailing labels. Figure 10.7 shows the labels in Design mode when **Sh**ow Data is chosen from the **V**iew menu. Notice that the labels are formatted exactly as you want.

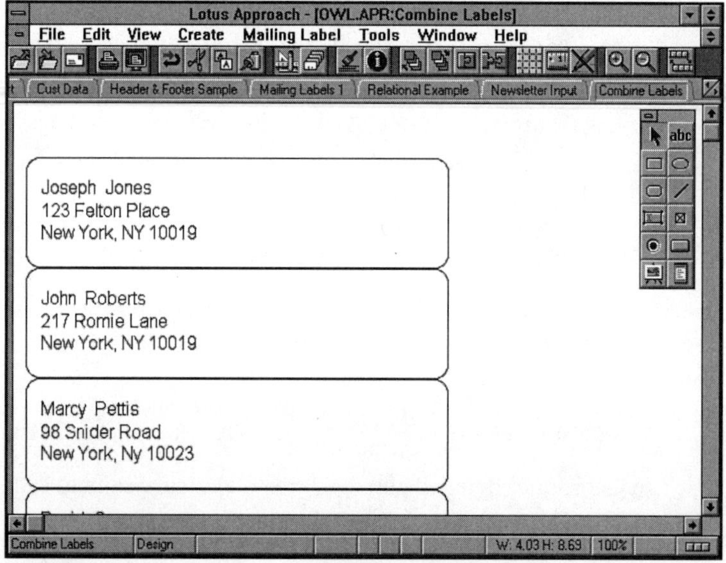

Fig. 10.7
The mailing labels with calculated fields.

Working with Conversion Functions

To use functions that require a specific type of value, changing one type of value (such as numeric) into another type of value (such as text) is often necessary. You see this in the preceding section, in which a number had to be converted to a string.

Approach supports the DateToText, NumToText, TextToBool, TextToDate, and TextToTime conversion functions. These functions are discussed in the following sections.

DateToText. DateToText requires two arguments—a date and a text string: `DateToText(date,'text')`. This function converts a date into a formatted text string. The date to convert is given by the date argument. If this argument is a field name, the value in the field is used in the formula. The text argument, enclosed in single quotation marks, supplies the format string for the date that determines how the converted date is displayed (see Chapter 4 for information on date formats).

For example, `DateToText('3/22/94','MMMM DD, YYYY')` returns `March 22, 1994`.

NumToText. NumToText requires two arguments—a number and a text string: `NumToText(number,'text')`. This function converts a number into a text string. The number to convert is given by the number argument. If this argument is a numeric field or a text field containing a number, the value in the field is used in the formula. The text argument, enclosed in single quotation marks, supplies the format string for the number that determines how the converted number is displayed (see Chapter 4 for information on numeric formats).

For example, if the NUMBER field contains 8.45, `NumToText(NUMBER,'$00.00')` returns `$08.45`.

TextToBool. TextToBool requires a single text-type argument: `TextToBool(text)`. This function returns `No` if the first character in the text argument is NO, no, N, n, or 0. If the first character in the text argument is any other character, this function returns `Yes`. If the text argument is the name of a text-type field, the value of the field is used in the function.

For example, `TextToBool('Fred')` returns `Yes`.

TextToDate. TextToDate requires a single text-type argument: `TextToDate(text)`. This function returns the date equivalent of the text argument so that text can be used in date-oriented functions (such as WeekOfYear). Enter the text string in the format mm/dd/yy (any other format returns an error message). If the text argument is the name of a text-type field, the value of the field is used in the function.

For example, `WeekOfYear(TextToDate('01/03/93'))` returns `1` (this date is in the first week of the year).

TextToTime. TextToTime requires a single text-type argument: `TextToTime(text)`. This function returns the time equivalent of the text argument so that text can be used in time-oriented functions. Enter the time string in one of the following formats:

- hh
- hh:mm
- hh:mm:ss
- HH:MM:SS.00

You can add AM or PM at the end of any of these text strings. If the text argument is the name of a text-type field, the value of the field is used in the function.

For example, `TextToTime('10:30 PM')` returns `10:30 PM` as a time value.

Working with Date Functions

Approach provides a wide range of functions for working with dates. By using these functions, you can extract information about a date or perform calculations using dates. Date functions include Date, Day, DayName, DayOfWeek, DayOfYear, Month, MonthName, Today, WeekOfYear, and Year.

All these functions require a single date-type argument. You can enter the argument as a constant or a date-type field name. If you enter the argument as a constant, you must use the format mm/dd/yy and enclose it in single quotation marks.

Date. Date returns a date value corresponding to the numbers given as arguments: Date(day, month, year).

`Date(3,22,94)` would return the date value `3/22/94`.

Day. Day returns the day of the month from a date.

For example, if the SUB END field contains 12/27/92, `Day(SUB END)` returns `27`.

DayName. DayName returns a text string containing the name of the day, given the date. This function also can accept a number from 1 to 7 as the argument (`1` is Sunday, `2` is Monday, and so on).

For example, if the SUB END field contains 01/27/93, `DayName(SUB END)` returns `Wednesday`.

DayOfWeek. DayOfWeek returns a number equal to the number of the day of the week (`1` is Sunday, `2` is Monday, and so on).

For example, `DayOfWeek('01/27/93')` returns `4` (Wednesday).

DayOfYear. DayOfYear returns a number equal to the number of days since January 1 of the year in the supplied date.

For example, if the SUB END field contains 2/13/93, `DayOfYear(SUB END)` returns `44`.

Month. Month returns a number representing the month of the supplied date.

For example, `Month('3/12/92')` returns `3`.

MonthName. MonthName returns a text string containing the name of the month in the supplied date.

If, for example, the SUB END field contains 3/12/93, `MonthName(SUB END)` returns `March`.

WeekOfYear. WeekOfYear returns a number representing the number of weeks since January 1 of the year in the supplied date.

For example, `WeekOfYear('1/28/93')` returns `5`.

Year. Year returns a number representing the year in the supplied date. The year returned is the full four-digit year (includes century).

For example, if the SUB END field contains 1/27/93, `Year(SUB END)` returns `1993`.

Working with Logical Functions

Logical functions determine if a condition given is true or false. They can be used with constants or, more likely, with field data. Logical functions also provide the opportunity for different values in a calculated field, based on how the contents are evaluated versus the condition given.

Blank. Blank tests to see if a field is blank. If it is, it returns a given value. If it is not, it returns the field information. It needs two arguments, the field and the value: Blank(field, value).

For example, `Blank("M INITIAL", 'NMI')` would return the text string `NMI` (no middle initial) if the Middle Initial field is blank.

IsBlank. IsBlank tests to see if a field is blank, and returns a Yes if it is blank or a No if it is not. It needs just one argument, the field name: `IsBlank(field)`.

For example, `IsBlank(PAID)` would equal `Yes` if the PAID field is empty.

IsBlank can also be combined with Not to evaluate when a field is not blank. `Not IsBlank(PAID)` would equal `No` if the PAID field is empty.

If. One of the most powerful functions Approach offers is the If function. With this function, you can test for a condition and perform calculations based on whether the condition is true or false.

The If function requires three arguments: a condition and two values: If(condition, truevalue, falsevalue).

The condition is a logical statement that must evaluate as true or false. Some examples follow:

- Comparing the values in two fields: FIELD1>FIELD2. If the contents of FIELD1 for the given record are greater than the contents of FIELD2, the result of this condition is true. Otherwise, the result of this condition is false.

- Checking to see whether a field is blank. The IsBlank function determines whether or not a field is blank. The single argument is a field name: IsBlank(FIELD). IsBlank(FIELD) returns true if FIELD is blank, otherwise it returns false.

- Comparing a date field to the current date. The Today function returns the date on the system clock. It has no arguments, but you must still use the parentheses: Today( ). For example, you can compare the contents of the SUB END field to the current date with `SUB END>Today()`. This condition returns true if date in the SUB END field is later than the current date. If the date in the SUB END field is earlier than the current date, however, the condition returns false.

- Comparing two text strings. The Exact function compares two text strings. It uses two text-type arguments, which can be text fields: Exact(text1, text2). Exact returns true if the two text strings are exactly the same (including spacing and case). Otherwise it returns false.
- Checking to see whether multiple conditions are true using the AND and OR operators. FIELD1>20 AND FIELD2<100; DATEFIELD<Today() OR DATEFIELD>(Today()+30).

Truevalue is any value, including a constant, a calculation, or a field reference. The If formula returns truevalue if the condition evaluates as true.

Falsevalue is also any value, including a constant, a calculation, or a field reference. The If formula returns falsevalue if the condition evaluates as false.

Suppose that an employee database has a field (BIRTHDATE) that contains the birthday of the employee. A calculated field can be used to compute the current age of the employee. The entire If statement looks like the following:

If(IsBlank(BIRTHDATE),'No Date of Birth', Trunc
(((Today()-BIRTHDATE)/365.25),0))

The formula is built as follows:

1. Check to see whether the BIRTHDATE field is blank. To do so, use the IsBlank function. IsBlank returns true if the BIRTHDATE field is empty. If a value is in the BIRTHDATE field, IsBlank returns false.
2. If the BIRTHDATE field is blank, return the text string `'No Date of Birth'`.
3. If the BIRTHDATE field isn't blank, use the following age formula to calculate the age:

   Trunc(((Today()-BIRTHDATE)/365.25),0)

The clause `(Today()-BIRTHDATE)/365.25` returns a decimal number for the number of years that the employee has been alive (for example, 38.458). Because ages are counted in whole numbers, however, you need to remove the decimal portion of the age. The Trunc function is used for this purpose. It requires two arguments: the number that is being truncated, and a whole number indicating how many decimal places the final result should have. The rest of the decimal places are discarded. In this example, you want no (0) decimal places.

Tip

You can leave off the number of decimal places for Trunc; this function will then return the number truncated to zero decimal places.

Nested If Functions. You can place an If function, using additional If statements, inside the truevalue or falsevalue arguments. This is called a "nested" If, because it is nesting inside another If. By nesting If statements, you can test for multiple conditions. Consider a simple one-level nest:

```
If(condition1,truevalue1,If(condition2,truevalue2,falsevalue))
```

If condition1 in the outside If statement is true, truevalue is returned. If condition1 is false, however, the nested If is executed as the false value. If condition2 is true, truevalue2 is returned. If condition2 is false, falsevalue is returned. Realize that falsevalue could still be another If statement, and so on.

Consider an employee database that records the date that an employee joined the company in a field called SERVEDATE. The number of years that an employee has been with the company could be calculated and displayed in a field called SERVE:

```
Trunc(((Today()-SERVEDATE)/365.25),0)
```

This company has a set of rules that determines the stock options for which an employee is eligible based on the years of service: Basic, Supplemental, Plus, and Full. You can use a nested If statement in a calculated field to calculate and display the stock option for which an employee was eligible:

```
If(SERVE<=5,'Basic',If(SERVE<=10,'Supplemental',If(SERVE<=15,'PLUS','FULL')))
```

In this example,

- If the employee has five or less years of service, the condition in the first If is true, and the text string `Basic` is placed in the calculated field.
- If the employee has more than five years of service, the condition is false, and the second If is executed.
- If the employee has between 6 and 10 years of service, the condition of the second If statement is true, and the text string `Supplemental` returns.
- If the employee has more than 10 years of service, the condition in the second If is false, and the third If executes.
- If the employee has between 11 and 15 years of service, the condition in the third If is true, and the text string `Plus` returns.
- If this last condition is false (the employee has more than 15 years of service) the text string `Full` returns because it's the false result for the last If statement.

Working with Summary Functions

Summary functions perform calculations across a range of records and display the value in the calculated field. Non-summary functions work within a single record.

As an example of a non-summary function, a sales commission might take the SALES TOTAL for each record and calculate that value times a percentage to give a commission amount. Commission has one value per record in the database. A summary function calculates a value for a field over an entire group of records, such as the sum of all SALES TOTAL fields for the year of 1993.

You use the summary functions with the **S**ummarize On drop-down list in the Define Summary panel of the Define Field dialog box.

The summary functions are as follows:

- SAverage (Summary Average)
- SCount (Summary Count)
- SMax (Summary Maximum)
- SMin (Summary Minimum)
- SNPV (Summary Net Present Value)
- SStd (Summary Standard Deviation)
- SSum (Summary Sum)
- SVar (Summary Variance)

These functions are discussed in the following sections.

SAverage (Summary Average). The summary average function has a single argument that must be a numeric field or a text field containing numeric data: SAverage(field). It calculates the average value for non-blank occurrences of the specified field for the current range of records.

For example, if the NUMBER field contained 2, 3, 4.3, and 6 in four records, the SAverage(NUMBER) is 3.825 for that four-record group.

SCount (Summary Count). The summary count function has a single argument that must be a field: SCount(field). It calculates the number of non-blank occurrences for any value in the specified field for the current range of records. Blank values aren't counted.

For example, if the NUMBER field contained 2, 3, 4.3, and 6 in four records, the SCount(NUMBER) is 4 for that four-record group.

Tip

You can use date or time fields to obtain the latest date or time.

SMax (Summary Maximum). The summary maximum function has a single argument that can be any type of field: SMax(field). It returns the largest value in the field for the current range of records.

For example, if the NUMBER field contained 2, 3, 4.3, and 6 in four records, the SMax(NUMBER) is 6 for that four-record group.

SMin (Summary Minimum). The summary minimum function has a single argument that can be any type of field: SMin(Field). It returns the smallest value in the field for the current range of records.

For example, if the NUMBER field contained 2, 3, 4.3, and 6 in four records, the SMin(NUMBER) is 2 for that four-record group.

SNPV (Summary Net Present Value). The summary net present value function needs two arguments. The first is a field; the second is a constant: SNPV(Field,.05). The SNPV returns the net present value of an investment based on a series of yearly cash flows (contained in the field) and a discount rate (the constant value). The discount rate is usually stated in percent (for example, 8 percent) but is entered into the formula as a decimal number (for example, .08). The periodic cash flows can be positive (income) or negative (investment). The value in the field in the first record in the database represents the investment made in the first year. The value in the field in subsequent records represents the investment or income for subsequent years (for example, the second record is for year 2, the third record is for year 3, and so on).

For example, the PAYMENT field can have positive values of 6, 4.3, 2, and 3 in four records, one for each year. The interest rate is 8%. SNPV(PAYMENT,.08) is 13.035.

SStd (Summary Standard Deviation). The summary standard deviation function has a single argument that must be a numeric field or a text field containing a number: SStd(Field). It returns the standard deviation of the values in the specified field for the current range of records. The standard deviation is a measure of how widely dispersed the values are from the average value.

For example, if the NUMBER field contained 2, 3, 4.3, and 6 in four records, the SStd(NUMBER) is 1.497 for that four-record group.

SSum (Summary Sum). The summary sum function has a single argument that must be a numeric field or a text field containing a number: SSum(Field). It returns the sum of all the values in the specified field for the current range of records.

For example, if the NUMBER field contains 2, 3, 4.3, and 6 in four records, the SSum(NUMBER) is 15.3 for that four-record group.

SVar (Summary Variance). The summary variance function has a single argument that must be a numeric field or a text field containing a number: SVar(Field). It returns the variance of the values in the specified field for the current range of records.

For example, if the NUMBER field contains 2, 3, 4.3, and 6 in four records, the SVar(NUMBER) is 2.242 for that four-record group.

Using Variables

A variable is a temporary holding place for data. It is useful for holding intermediate data and for passing results from one record to another. Variables are also very useful in macros (see Chapter 13 for some examples of using variables).

When you store data in a variable field, this value is a single value that is available to every record in the database. The variable field, because it has only one value, will appear to be the same for every record in the database. Like a calculated field, the variable field is part of an Approach file, and is not stored in the database file.

Variable fields have a field type that determines the type of data they can store (such as Text, Date, Boolean, and so on). You can format variable fields like any other field—they can be formatted, displayed on a form or report, and used in calculations.

Creating Variable Fields

As with all other types of fields, to create variable fields you must use either the Creating New Database or the Define Field dialog box. You can create a variable field when you first define the database, or you can add it later.

Defining a Variable Field for a New Database

When creating a new database, follow the steps detailed in the "Designing a Database" section in Chapter 2 to define the fields you need. Then proceed as follows:

1. Open the **F**ile menu and choose **N**ew.
2. In the New dialog box, type the database file name and select the file type.
3. Click OK. The Creating New Database dialog box appears.
4. To define a variable field in the Creating New Database dialog box, type the name of the variable field into the Field Name column.

5. Select Variable from the drop-down list in the Data Type column. You can also type a **V** to select a variable Data Type.

6. Click **O**ptions. The Creating New Database dialog box expands to display the Variable Options panel (see fig. 10.8).

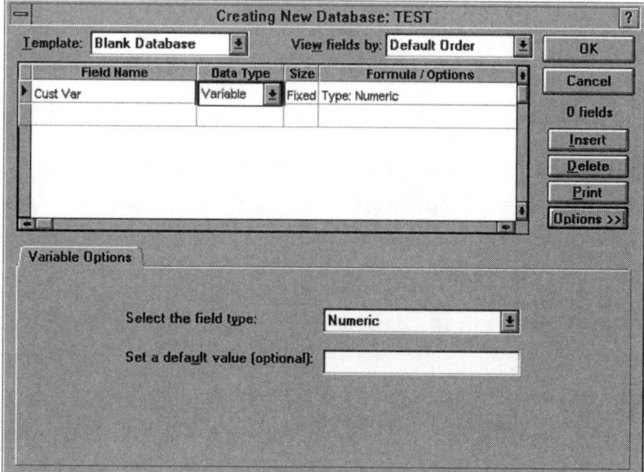

Fig. 10.8
A variable field, like a calculated field, is another Data Type.

7. From the Select the Field **T**ype drop-down list, select the field type. You can assign a field type of Boolean, Date, Numeric, Text, or Time.

8. If you wish, you can set a default value for the variable field. To do so, click the Set a Defa**u**lt Value (Optional) text box. Type the default value for the variable field.

9. Continue designating fields for the database. When you are done, click OK in the Field Definition dialog box to create the database.

Note

If you need to return to the Variable Options dialog box, select the variable field in the list of fields in the Field Definition dialog box, and then click **O**ptions. Variable fields are displayed in field lists in italics. They are shown after "real" database fields and before calculated fields.

Adding a Variable Field to an Existing Database

To define a variable field in an existing database:

1. Open the **C**reate menu and choose Field **D**efinition. The Field Definition dialog box appears.
2. To define a variable field in the Field Definition dialog box, type the name of the variable field into the Field Name column.
3. Select Variable from the drop-down list in the Data Type column. You can also type a **V** to select a variable Data Type.
4. Click **O**ptions. The Field Definition dialog box expands to display the Variable Options panel.
5. From the Select the Field **T**ype drop-down list, select the field type. You can assign a field type of Boolean, Date, Numeric, Text, or Time.
6. If you want, you can set a default value for the variable field. To do so, click the Set a Defa**u**lt Value (optional) text box. Type the default value for the variable field.

Adding an Existing Variable Field to a Form or Report

After you define a variable field, you can add it to an existing form or report just like any other field:

1. Switch to Design mode.

2. Either click and drag the variable field onto the form from the Add Field dialog box, or:
3. Click the Draw Field tool from the Drawing toolbar, drag a rectangle to define the position and size of the variable field, and select the variable field form the field list in the Basics panel of the field Info Box.

Changing the Appearance of a Variable Field

You can change the appearance of a variable field on a form or report just like you can any other field by resizing, moving, changing the fill and pen colors, setting borders, and adjusting the attributes of the text for the contents of the field and the label.

To make changes to the field, switch to Design mode, and then perform any of the following procedures:

- To move the field, drag it to its new location or adjust the location from the Dimensions panel of the Info Box.
- To resize the field, drag one of the sizing handles until the field is the size you want. You can also adjust the width and height from the Dimensions panel of the Info Box.
- Select the border, fill, or shadow color from the drop-down list that Approach makes available in the Colors panel of the Info box when you click the Border Color, Fill Color, or Shadow Color drop-down lists. The box labeled T provides a transparent color.
- Select the border width from the Border width drop-down list in the Colors panel of the Info Box. Available border widths range from hairline to 12 point (1/6 of an inch).
- To change the font, size, style/effect, color, alignment, or text relief, make the appropriate selections from the Font panel of the Info Box.
- To change the label font, size, style/effect, color, alignment, position, text, and text relief, make the appropriate selections from the Label panel of the Info Box.
- Click the checkboxes in the Borders section (for example, Left, Right, Top, and Bottom) of the Colors panel in the Info Box to select which sides of the field you want Approach to display borders.
- Select a frame style from the Frame drop-down list in the colors panel of the Info Box. The frame style specifies the format in which Approach draws the border around the selected field.

Using PicturePlus Fields

A PicturePlus field can contain graphics and special objects called OLE objects. OLE objects are objects created in other Windows applications that connect back to this application to be edited or updated. They include objects such as sound, charts, and written documents. PicturePlus fields enable you to include a wide variety of objects and information in your database. Approach provides quite a few ways in which you can add information to PicturePlus fields.

Unlike Calculated and Variable fields, PicturePlus fields are part of the database. However, the contents can only be accessible through Approach, and not other applications that can read the same database format.

Creating PicturePlus Fields

As with all other types of fields, PicturePlus fields are created using the Field Style dialog box. You can create a PicturePlus field when you first define the database, or you can add it later.

Defining a PicturePlus Field for a New Database

When creating a new database, follow the steps detailed in the "Designing a Database" section in Chapter 2 to define the fields you need. Then proceed as follows:

1. Open the **F**ile menu and choose **N**ew.
2. In the New dialog box, type the database file name and select the file type.
3. Click OK. The Creating New Database dialog box appears.
4. Type the name of the PicturePlus field into the Field Name column.
5. Select PicturePlus from the Data Type drop-down list. You can also type a **P**.
6. Click **O**ptions. The Creating New Database dialog box expands to display the PicturePlus Options panel (see fig. 10.9).

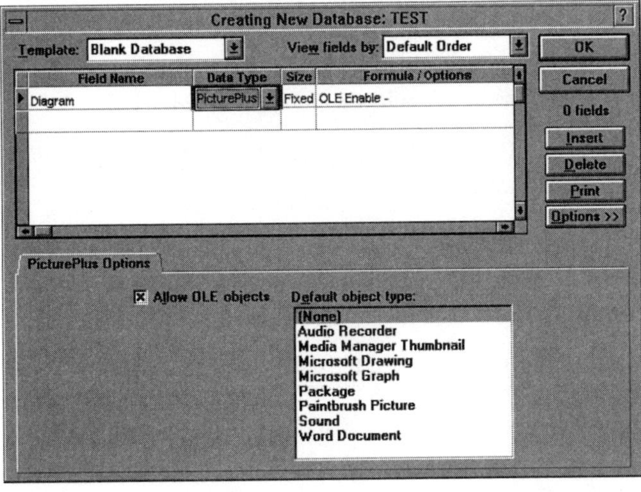

Fig. 10.9
The PicturePlus field can use OLE objects from other Windows applications.

7. If desired, choose **Al**low OLE Objects to set this option. When the checkbox is selected (default), Approach enables you to place OLE objects in the PicturePlus field. When the checkbox isn't selected, Approach enables you to place only graphics files in the PicturePlus field—it doesn't let you place OLE objects.

8. If the A**l**low OLE objects checkbox is selected, choose the default OLE application from the D**e**fault Object Type list or leave the setting at the default None. This application opens when you double-click the PicturePlus field to place an object in the field (see "Adding an Object Using Embedding" later in the chapter).

9. Continue designating fields for the database. When you are done, click OK in the Creating New Database dialog box to create the database.

> **Note**
>
> If you need to return to the PicturePlus Options dialog box, select the PicturePlus field in the list of fields in the Field Definition dialog box, and then click **O**ptions.

Adding a PicturePlus Field to an Existing Database

To define a PicturePlus field in an existing database:

1. Open the **C**reate menu and choose Field **D**efinition. The Define Field dialog box opens.

2. To define a PicturePlus field in the Field Definition dialog box, type the name of the PicturePlus field into the Field Name column.

3. Select PicturePlus from the drop-down list in the Data Type column. You can also type a **P** to select a PicturePlus Data Type.

4. Click **O**ptions. The Define Field dialog box expands to display the PicturePlus Options panel.

5. If desired, choose **A**llow OLE objects to set this option. If the option is on, select a default OLE application from the Default Object type list or leave this setting at the default None.

6. Click OK in the Field Definition dialog box.

Adding an Existing PicturePlus Field to a Form or Report

After you define a PicturePlus field, you can add it to any existing form or report:

1. Switch to Design mode.

2. Either click and drag the PicturePlus field onto the form from the Add Field dialog box, or:

   Click the Draw PicturePlus Field tool from the Drawing toolbar, drag a rectangle to define the position and size of the PicturePlus field, and select the PicturePlus field from the field list in the Basics panel of the field Info Box. Unlike other types of fields placed on a form or report using the Draw Fields tool, Approach only displays PicturePlus fields in the field list.

3. Drag a rectangle to define the position and size of the PicturePlus field.

4. Select the PicturePlus field from the field list in the Basics panel of the field Info Box. Unlike other types of fields placed on a form or report using the Draw Fields tool, Approach only displays PicturePlus fields in the field list.

Changing the Appearance of a PicturePlus Field

You can change the appearance of a PicturePlus field on a form or report just like you can any other field by resizing, moving, changing the fill and pen colors, setting borders, and adjusting the attributes of the text for the contents of the field and the label.

To make changes to the field, switch to Design mode, and then perform any of the following procedures:

- To move the field, drag it to its new location or adjust the location from the Dimensions panel of the Info Box.

- To resize the field, drag one of the sizing handles until the field is the size you want. You can also adjust the width and height from the Dimensions panel of the Info Box.

- Select the border, fill, or shadow color from the drop-down list that Approach makes available in the Colors panel of the Info box when you click the Border Color, Fill Color, or Shadow Color drop-down lists. The box labeled T provides a transparent color.

- Select the border width from the Border Width drop-down list in the Colors panel of the Info Box. Available border widths range from hairline to 12 point (1/6 of an inch).

- To change the font, size, style/effect, color, alignment, or text relief, make the appropriate selections from the Font panel of the Info Box.

- To change the label font, size, style/effect, color, alignment, position, text, and text relief, make the appropriate selections from the Label panel of the Info Box.

- Click the checkboxes in the Borders section (for example, Left, Right, Top, and Bottom) of the Colors panel in the Info Box to select which sides of the field you want Approach to display borders.

- Select a frame style from the Frame drop-down list in the Colors panel of the Info Box. The frame style specifies the format in which Approach draws the border around the selected field.

Changing the PicturePlus Options

You can set how Approach displays an image in a PicturePlus field when the image and the field are not the same size. To set the PicturePlus options, you must be in Design mode, with the Options panel of the PicturePlus field's Info Box displayed (see fig. 10.10).

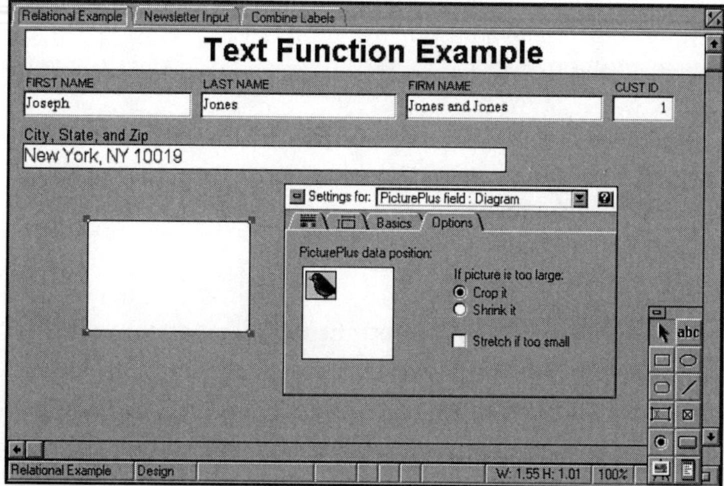

Fig. 10.10
You can set how the image appears in a PicturePlus field.

You can specify the following options for the PicturePlus field:

- Choose Crop It if you want Approach to crop an object that is too large to fit into the field. A cropped object displays only as much of the image as will fit into the PicturePlus field frame.
- Choose Shrink It if you want Approach to shrink an object that is too large to fit into the field. The object is reduced in size, proportionally, until it fits into the PicturePlus field. This can cause some distortion in the image.
- Choose Stretch If Too Small if you want Approach to enlarge an object proportionally to fit in the PicturePlus field. If this checkbox is left blank, space shows around the edges of an object that is too small.
- Choose the PicturePlus data position option to specify where the object appears within the PicturePlus field if the object doesn't fill the whole field. Nine positions are possible from a grid of three rows and three columns. Click a place in the box to indicate which of the positions you want, or you can click and drag the sample image.

Adding Images and Objects to a PicturePlus Field

After you place a PicturePlus field on a form or report, you can insert graphic images or OLE objects into the PicturePlus field. Because a PicturePlus field has a different value in every record, PicturePlus fields provide a mechanism for including images or OLE objects in each record.

You can insert a graphic image or OLE object into a PicturePlus field in two ways: by embedding the object and by linking the object. Embedding and linking are similar in that they enable you to easily edit the image or OLE object. They differ, however, in that they store the image file or OLE object file in different places. The techniques for embedding and linking OLE objects are discussed in the following sections.

Defining Object Embedding

Embedding is a special technique used for inserting information into a PicturePlus field. It not only works very much like Paste (in fact, you can use Paste from the Edit menu), but also makes editing the object much easier. With embedding, Approach "remembers" which application created the object you have placed on the form.

Embedded objects in a PicturePlus field can be edited or updated, just like embedded objects in an Approach file (described in Chapter 9 in the section "Embedding Objects").

Defining Object Linking

A linked object in a PicturePlus field is similar in many ways to an embedded object:

- You create the linked file in a Server application outside of Approach (Approach is the "Client" application).
- You instruct Approach to open the server application to easily edit the linked file (see "Editing a PicturePlus Field Containing a Linked Object" later in this chapter). You can then use the server application to perform the edits. When the edits are complete, you can close the server application and return to Approach, automatically updating the linked object in the PicturePlus field.

Unlike an embedded object, linked objects are not stored in the Approach database file. Instead, they are stored as normal files on disk. Because they are stored as normal files, you can edit them using the same server application that created them—even when Approach isn't running. If you link an Excel chart to a PicturePlus field on an Approach form, for example, you can open Excel and edit the chart.

If you do modify a linked file, the next time you open the Approach file to which it is linked, Approach can update the link, displaying the latest version of the file in the PicturePlus field. You can initiate this update automatically or manually, depending on the Link options you set in Approach.

Linked files require more effort to set up and maintain than embedded files. Because you store a linked file separately from the Approach database file, however, you can link any given file to more than one Approach database file. You also can link the file to other Windows application files that support object linking. For example, you can link the same Excel chart to multiple Approach database files, and to a Word for Windows document.

Linking a single file to multiple Approach databases (and other Windows application files) uses less disk space than embedding, in which the file must be stored in each application file to which it is linked. Also, if you update the single linked file, all Approach database files (and any other application files) to which the file is linked can be updated to reflect the changes.

> **Note**
>
> For embedding and linking to work, the application providing the object must be a "server" application. That is, it must be specifically designed to take advantage of object linking and embedding. This is called being *OLE Aware*. Many, but not all, Windows applications can act as server applications. Although copying and pasting an image into an Approach PicturePlus field from a non-server application is still possible, the image isn't connected to the originating application. To modify such an image, you must open the originating application, load and modify the image, copy it in the originating application, and paste it into Approach.

Adding an Object Using Embedding

Approach offers five different ways to embed an object in a PicturePlus field:

- Open the **E**dit menu and choose Paste
- Open the **E**dit menu and choose Paste Special
- Paste from a file
- Drag and drop a file
- Open the **C**reate menu and choose **O**bject

These methods of embedding objects in a PicturePlus field are described in the following sections.

Using Paste to Embed an Object. You can use Paste to embed an object in a PicturePlus field. This option enables you to paste the entire object or only a portion of the object into the PicturePlus field. To use Paste to embed an object, follow these steps:

1. Open the application from which you want to paste an object.
2. Load the file containing the object or create the object using the application.
3. Select the object (or portion of the object) you want to place into Approach.
4. From the application, open the **E**dit menu and choose **C**opy.
5. Open Approach or switch to Approach if it is open already.
6. Switch to Browse mode.

7. Select the form or report you want from the view tabs or the status bar.

8. Click the PicturePlus field to select it.

9. Open the **E**dit menu and choose **P**aste. The selected object appears in the PicturePlus field (see fig. 10.11).

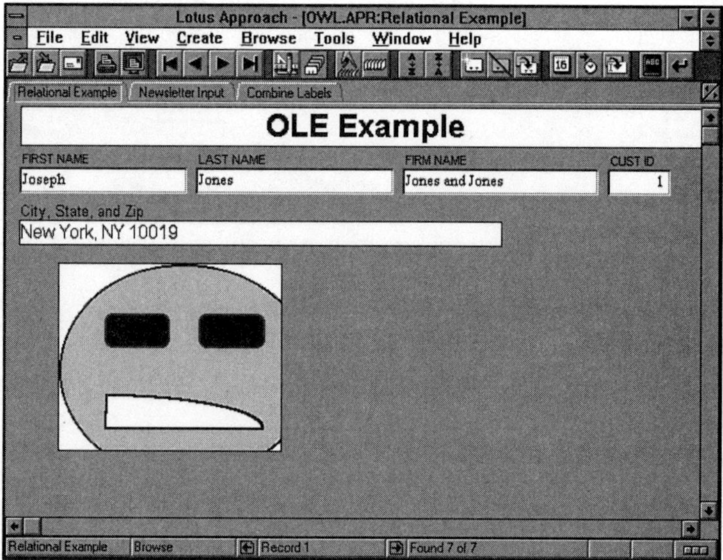

Fig. 10.11
After using Paste, the embedded object appears in the PicturePlus field.

If the application providing the object isn't OLE Aware, the Paste still works (for images only), but the image isn't connected to the originating application. To modify an image pasted into Approach from a non-OLE Aware application, follow these steps:

1. Open the application that created the image.

2. Load the image (or copy it from Approach and paste it into the application).

3. Modify the image using the application's tools.

4. Copy it from the application and paste it back into the Approach PicturePlus field.

Using Paste Special to Embed an Object. You can choose Paste **S**pecial from the **E**dit menu to embed an object in a PicturePlus field. This option enables you to paste the entire object or only a portion of the object into the PicturePlus field. To use Paste Special to embed an object, follow these steps:

1. Open the application from which you want to paste an object.
2. Load the file containing the object or create the object using the application.
3. Select the object (or portion of the object) you want to place into Approach.
4. From the application, open the **E**dit menu and choose **C**opy.
5. Open Approach or switch to Approach if it is open already.
6. Switch to Browse mode.

7. Select the form or report using the view tabs or the status bar.
8. Click the PicturePlus field to select it.
9. Open the **E**dit menu and choose Paste **S**pecial. The Paste Special dialog box appears (see fig. 10.12).

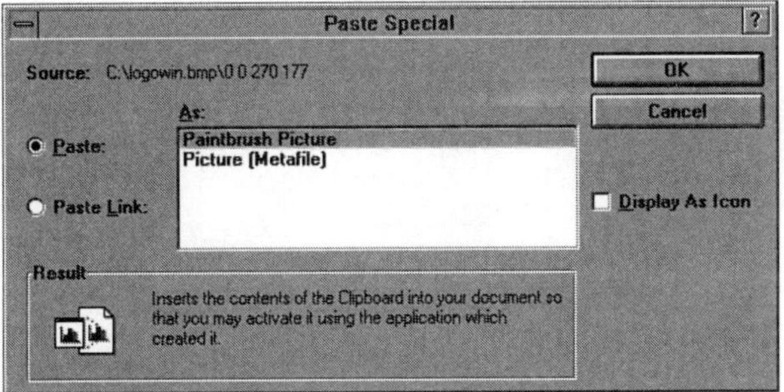

Fig. 10.12
Special paste options from the Paste Special dialog box.

10. The Paste Special dialog box displays a list of types of objects. Select the object type for the object you want to embed in the PicturePlus field.

> **Note**
>
> To maintain the connection between the object and the application that created it, you must select an object type in the Paste Special dialog box that includes the name of the server application (for example, "Paintbrush Picture Object"). For an image, if you select an option that doesn't include the application name (for example, "Bitmap"), the image is pasted into the PicturePlus field, but no connection to the application that created the object exists.

11. Click OK in the Paste Special dialog box to place the object in the PicturePlus field.

Using Paste from File to Embed an Object. You can choose Paste from **F**ile in the **E**dit menu to embed an object in a PicturePlus field. This option, however, allows embedding of an entire object only (that is, you can't embed only a portion of an image). Because Approach can recognize these image file formats, you don't need a server application to be able to use these files in a PicturePlus field.

To embed an object using Paste from File, follow these steps:

1. Switch to Browse mode.
2. Select the form or report containing the PicturePlus field from the view tabs or the status line.
3. Click the PicturePlus field.
4. Open the **E**dit menu and choose Paste from **F**ile. The Paste from File dialog box appears (see fig. 10.13).

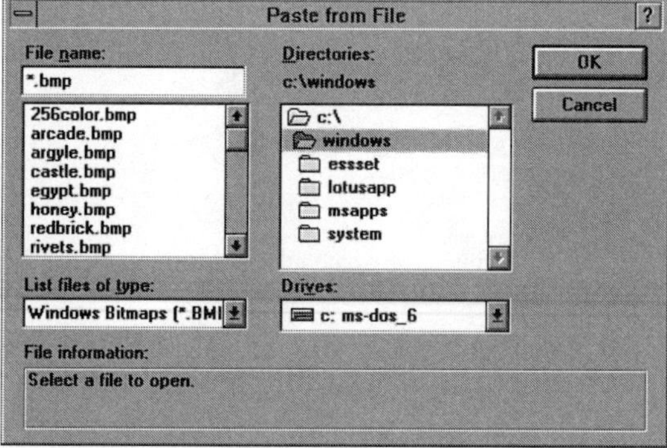

Fig. 10.13
The Paste from File dialog box.

5. From the List Files of **T**ype drop-down list, select the type of file you want.

Note

Approach recognizes a number of image file types, including BMP, PCX, EPS, GIF, TIF, TGA and WMF. If you select another type of file (such as a WAV sound file) which Approach doesn't recognize, Approach gives you a `Sharing Violation` error, and the Paste will be unsuccessful. You can embed some of the unsuccessful types of files, however, using Insert Object (see "Using Insert Object to Embed an Object" later in this chapter).

6. Adjust the location from which you want to select the file by using the **D**irectories box and the Dri**v**es drop-down list in the center of the Paste from File dialog box.

7. Select the file you want to embed from the box below the File **N**ame box. The file selected appears in the File **N**ame text box.

8. Click OK to embed the object in the PicturePlus field.

Using Drag and Drop to Embed an Object. You can use Drag and Drop to embed an object in a PicturePlus field. Drag and Drop refers to using File Manager to locate a file in a directory, then dragging the file name onto the Approach form and dropping it into the PicturePlus field. This option allows embedding of an entire object only. Again, you don't need a server application installed for compatible formats.

To embed an object using Drag and Drop, follow these steps:

1. Switch to Browse mode.

2. Select the form or report containing the PicturePlus field from the view tabs or the status line.

3. Resize the Approach window so that it takes up as little room on-screen as possible, with the PicturePlus field still visible. This can be done by moving the mouse pointer to the edge of the window where it becomes a double-headed arrow. Hold down the mouse button and drag the edge of the window to adjust its size.

4. Click the PicturePlus field to select it.

5. Open File Manager and size the File Manager window so that it is visible alongside the shrunken Approach window.

6. Move to the drive and directory in File Manager that contains the file you want to embed.

7. Select the file name in the File Manager window.

8. Hold down the mouse button and drag the file name to the PicturePlus field (see fig. 10.14). Release the mouse button.

9. The file appears in the PicturePlus window.

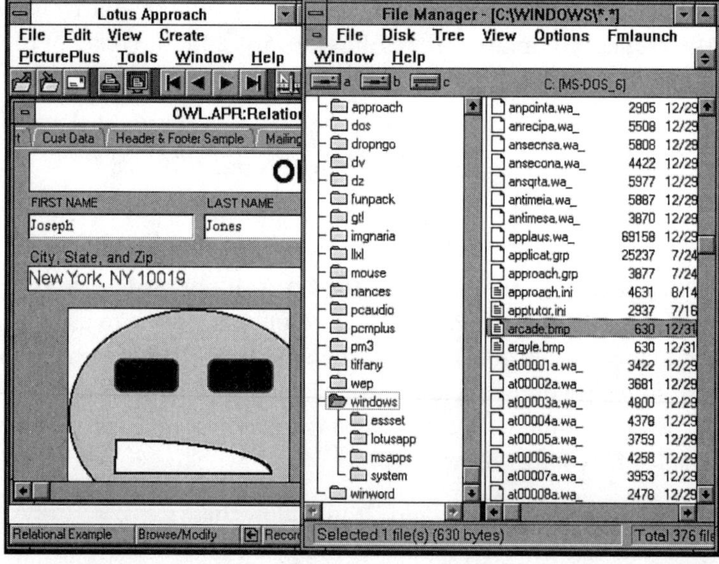

Fig. 10.14
Drag the file from File Manager and drop it in the PicturePlus field in Approach.

> **Note**
>
> Approach recognizes a number of file types, including BMP, PCX, EPS, GIF, TIF, TGA and WMF. If you select another type of file (such as a WAV sound file) which Approach doesn't recognize, Approach gives you a `Sharing Violation` error, and the Drag and Drop will be unsuccessful. You can embed some of the unsuccessful types of files, however, by using Insert Object (see "Using Insert Object to Embed an Object" below).

Using Insert Object to Embed an Object. You can open the **C**reate menu and choose **O**bject to embed an object in a PicturePlus field. This option has some advantages over Drag and Drop and Paste from File. Because you must tell Approach what type of object you are embedding, you won't get `Sharing Violation` errors if Approach can't recognize the type of object. However, like Drag and Drop and Paste from File, you can insert only an entire object.

This method, like the others, starts by selecting the PicturePlus field the image will be inserted into. After that point, the steps are identical to those used in Chapter 9 in the "Embedding Objects" section.

Editing a PicturePlus Field Containing an Embedded Object

To edit the contents of a PicturePlus Field, follow these steps:

1. Switch to Browse mode.

2. Select the form or report that contains the PicturePlus field using the view tabs or the status bar.

3. Click the PicturePlus field to select it.

4. Select the **P**icturePlus Edit menu selection for the object you want to edit. To edit a Microsoft Drawing object, for example, choose Edit Microsoft Drawing **O**bject from the **P**icturePlus menu. The server application that created the object opens and displays the object.

> **Note**
>
> For most types of embedded objects, you also can double-click the PicturePlus field to open the server application. You can't use this technique, however, if you are using any type of embedded sounds or animation. Double-clicking a sound or animation application icon plays the sound or animation; it doesn't open the server application.

5. Use the server application to make the changes you want.

6. Choose Update from the **F**ile menu in the server application.

> **Note**
>
> Some server applications don't provide an Update menu item in the File menu. If this is the case, select Close from the **F**ile menu. When the server application asks whether you want to update the Approach file, select the Yes button.

7. Choose Exit from the **F**ile menu in the source (server) application. You are returned to Approach with the object updated on-screen.

Adding an Object Using Linking

Linking provides a link back to a file created within a server application. To link a PicturePlus field to an object file, you must meet the following conditions:

- You must create and save the object file before you can link it to a PicturePlus field. If you have not created the object file, open the server application and create a new object file. Be sure to save the new object file, however, before you try to link it to a PicturePlus field in Approach.
- Make sure that Approach and the server application are running at the time you create the link. After you create the link, you can close the server application.

To place a linked object into a PicturePlus field, follow these steps:

1. Open the server application. Load the file that contains the object you want to link to a PicturePlus field. If the object file doesn't exist, create one using the server application and save the file.
2. In the server application, select the object (or portion of the object) you want to link to the PicturePlus field in Approach.
3. From the server application, open the **E**dit menu and select **C**opy.

> **Note**
>
> Don't choose Cut—the link won't be created if you choose Cut. Also, leave the server application running because you have not yet created the link.

4. Switch to Approach.
5. Select the form or report containing the PicturePlus field from the view tabs or the status bar.

6. Switch to Browse mode.
7. Click the PicturePlus field.
8. Open the **E**dit menu and choose Paste **S**pecial. The Paste Special dialog box appears (see fig. 10.15).
9. Choose Paste **L**ink and click OK. The Paste Special dialog box disappears, and the linked object is placed into the PicturePlus field.

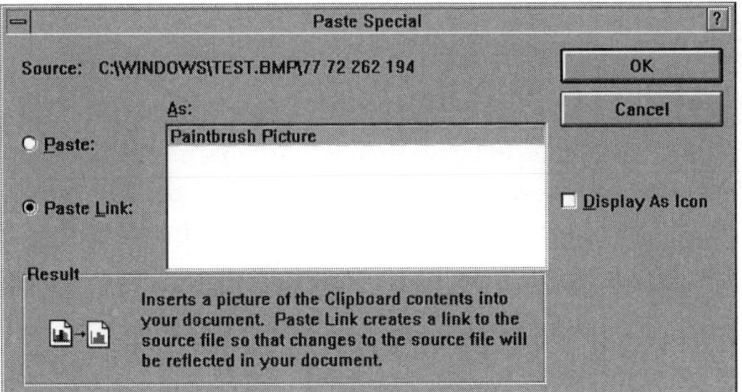

Fig. 10.15
The Paste Special dialog box. Paste Link is now available.

Working with Established Links

After you establish a link between a server application and an Approach PicturePlus field, you can:

- Set the update status of the link
- Delete the link
- Repair a broken link

The Links dialog box (see fig. 10.16) provides the tools to perform these tasks.

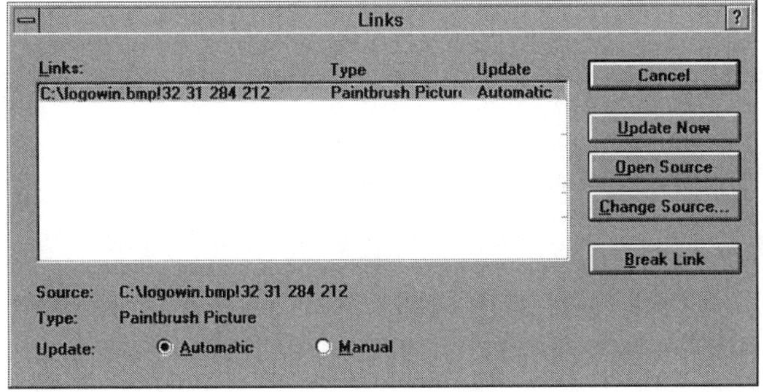

Fig. 10.16
The Links dialog box.

> **Note**
>
> The changes to links detailed in the following sections must be made in Browse mode. Although Approach allows access to the Links dialog box in Design mode, the Links dialog box is empty—no links are displayed. Therefore, to see links between server applications and PicturePlus fields, you must be in Browse mode and in the correct record.

Selecting the Link Status. A link can have one of two possible statuses: Automatic or Manual. These statuses determine how the link behaves when a change is made to the object file to which the PicturePlus field is linked.

If a link is automatic, it is updated when the Approach file is opened. Thus, if at any time you used the server application to change the file to which the PicturePlus field is linked, the Approach file displays the latest version.

If the server application is open at the same time as Approach, a PicturePlus field with an automatic link displays the changes in the field as you make them in the server application. This occurs even if you don't save the file in the server application after you make changes. If you make changes in the server application and don't save the file, however, an automatic link becomes "out of synch" with the stored file until the next time you open the Approach file. That is, the contents of the PicturePlus field don't reflect the contents of the linked file on disk. This occurs because the PicturePlus field reflects the changes being made in the server application—but those changes were not saved.

To bring the link back into synch with the stored file without closing and reopening the View file, choose **U**pdate Now in the Links dialog box (see "Updating a Link" later in this chapter).

If a link is set to manual update, it isn't updated when the Approach file is opened. It also doesn't reflect changes that are made in the server application. To update the link and display the current version of the linked object, choose **U**pdate Now in the Links dialog box (see "Updating a Link" later in this chapter).

Setting the Link Status. To set the status of a link:

1. Select the form or report containing the PicturePlus field for which you built the link.

2. Switch to Browse mode.
3. Click the PicturePlus field containing the linked object.
4. Open the **E**dit menu and choose L**i**nks. The Links dialog box appears with the link for the object in the selected PicturePlus field.
5. Choose **A**utomatic (default) or **M**anual.
6. Click OK.

Updating a Link. You should manually update a link for two reasons:

- To display the latest version of the object file in the PicturePlus field.
- To correct automatic links that get "out of synch" with the object file. This occurs if you make changes with the server application while Approach is open and don't save the changes in the object file.

To update a link so that the PicturePlus field displays the latest version of the object file:

1. Select the form or report that contains the PicturePlus field for which you built a link using the tabs.
2. Switch to Browse mode.

3. Click the PicturePlus field that contains the linked object.
4. Choose L**i**nks from the **E**dit menu. The Links dialog box appears with the link for the object in the selected PicturePlus field.
5. Click the link and choose **U**pdate Now.
6. Click Close to return to the Approach form or report. The PicturePlus field displays the latest version of the object file.

Deleting a Link. Approach enables you to break the link between an object and the server application. You can break a link in two ways. The first method is to use the Links dialog box. The second method is to use Clear in the Edit menu.

To use the Links dialog box, follow these steps:

1. Select the form or report containing the PicturePlus field for which you built the link.
2. Switch to Browse mode.

3. Click the PicturePlus field that contains the linked object.
4. Open the **E**dit menu and choose L**i**nks. The Links dialog box appears. Click the link for the selected PicturePlus field.
5. Choose **C**ancel Link. The link disappears from the Links box.
6. Click OK.

If you break the link between an object file and a PicturePlus field using the Links dialog box, the object remains in your PicturePlus field as it last appeared. Any future changes you make to the file, however, are not reflected in the contents of the PicturePlus field. You also can no longer edit the object, as described in "Editing a PicturePlus Field Containing a Linked Object" later in the chapter.

Note

If the object displays only the icon of the server application that created it, the graphic of the icon continues to be displayed in the PicturePlus field.

To use Clear in the Edit menu, follow these steps:

1. Select the form or report containing the PicturePlus field for which you built the link.

2. Switch to Browse mode.

3. Click the PicturePlus field on the form or report.

4. Open the **E**dit menu and choose Cl**e**ar. The object disappears from the PicturePlus field and the link is deleted.

Changing the Source of a Link. Changing the source of a PicturePlus field lets you specify a new application and file as the source for the PicturePlus field without going through the effort of opening the server application, loading or creating an object file, and using Paste **S**pecial from the **E**dit menu. Further, if you change the name of a linked object file or move it to a new location (for example, to a new directory or drive), Approach can't update the object because it won't be able to find the file. If a link is broken in this manner, you can reconnect it by telling Approach the new location or name for the file (for example, the new link source).

Note

When a link is broken, Approach does not give you any warning when you open the Approach file or the form on which the PicturePlus field is located. However, if you attempt to edit the linked object, Approach gives you an `OLE Server Busy` error message.

To specify a new source, follow these steps:

1. Open the Approach file that contains the link whose source you want to modify.

2. Select the form or report containing the PicturePlus field with the link whose source you want to modify.

3. Switch to Browse mode.

4. Click the PicturePlus field to select it.

5. Open the **E**dit menu and choose L**i**nks. The Links dialog box appears. Highlight the object for which you want to modify the link source.

6. Choose **C**hange Source. The Change Source dialog box appears (see fig. 10.17).

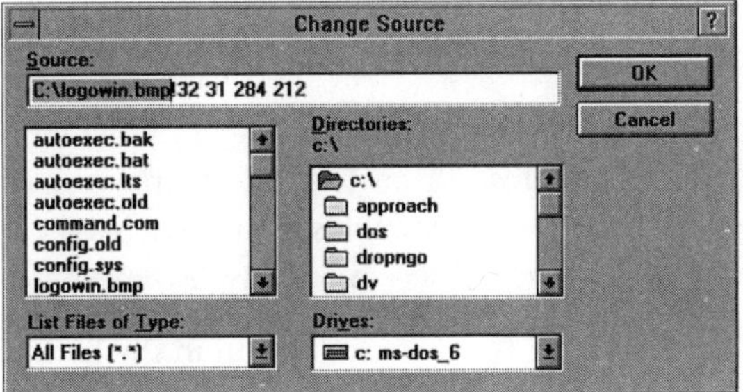

Fig. 10.17
The Change Source dialog box.

7. Select the file name from the list of files on the left side of the dialog box. Use the **D**irectories box and the Dri**v**es list in the center of the Change Link dialog box to locate the object file you need. If necessary, use the List Files of **T**ype list to display the correct type of file.

8. Click OK in the Change Source dialog box to return to the Links dialog box.

> **Note**
>
> If you choose an invalid source (for example, a file that has no application associated with it), Approach warns you and gives you the opportunity to choose another source. If you insist on an invalid source, Approach establishes the link, but you can't open the source and edit the linked file. Approach continues to display the graphic from the last valid source.

9. Click the **U**pdate Now button if you want to update the PicturePlus field to show the latest version of the file for the reestablished link.

10. Click OK.

Editing a PicturePlus Field Containing a Linked Object

To edit a linked object, use the server application that created the object. You can do this from Approach or from the server application in Windows by opening the application and editing the file just like any other file created with that application.

To edit a linked object from Approach, follow these steps:

1. Switch to Browse mode.

2. Select the form or report containing the PicturePlus field for which you built the link.

3. Click the PicturePlus field to select it.

4. Choose the **P**icturePlus menu item for the object you want to edit. For example, to edit a Microsoft Drawing Object, choose Edit Microsoft Drawing **O**bject from the **P**icturePlus menu. The server application that created the object opens on-screen and displays the object.

   You can also select the **O**pen Source button in the Links dialog box.

> **Note**
>
> For most types of embedded objects, you also can double-click the PicturePlus field to open the server application. You can't use this technique, however, if you are using any type of embedded sounds or animation. Double-clicking a sound or animation application icon plays the sound or animation; it doesn't open the server application.

5. Use the server application to make the changes you want.

6. Choose Save from the **F**ile menu in the server application.

7. Choose E**x**it from the **F**ile menu in the server application. You are returned to Approach.

Note

If the link is an automatic link, the change is displayed in the PicturePlus field immediately. If the link is manual, you must use the Links dialog box to update the PicturePlus field (see "Updating a Link" earlier in this chapter).

Viewing an Embedded or Linked Object in a PicturePlus Field

Some embedded or linked objects display their contents in the PicturePlus field in Approach (see fig. 10.18). Typically images (such as Paintbrush and Draw) are visible in the PicturePlus field on the form or report.

Other objects, however, display only the icon of the server application that created them (see fig. 10.18). These include objects such as sound files, for which no way really exists to "display" the contents.

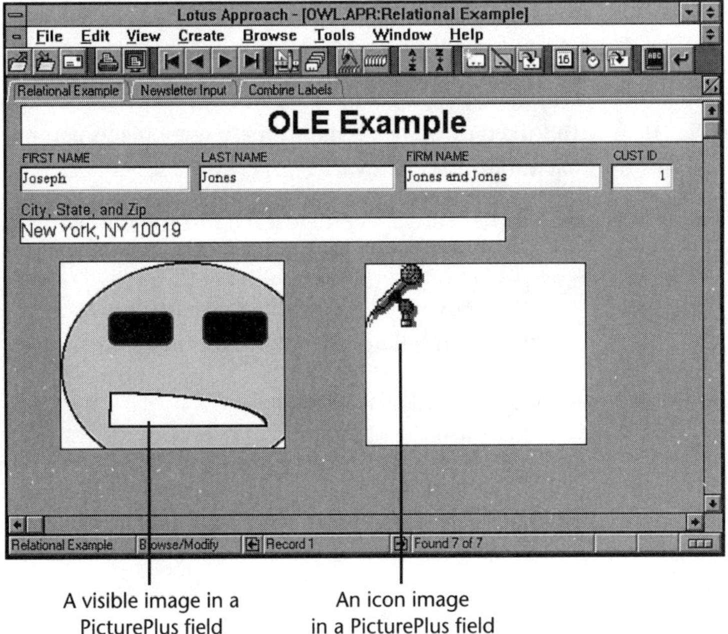

Fig. 10.18
Some embedded or linked images are normally visible in the PicturePlus field, while others display only the icon of the server.

To view objects that display the icon of the server application, double-click the PicturePlus field. You can also click the PicturePlus field and select the appropriate menu item (which varies depending on the type of object) in the **P**icturePlus menu. For example, if you embed a sound object in a PicturePlus field, you can listen to it by double-clicking the icon in the PicturePlus field, or by selecting the PicturePlus field and choosing Sound **O**bject **P**lay from the **P**icturePlus menu.

Clearing an Object from a PicturePlus Field

To remove an object from a PicturePlus field, switch to Browse mode. Click the PicturePlus field, open the **E**dit menu, and choose Cl**e**ar.

From Here...

Calculated and variable fields allow Approach to provide more information specific to your database. With the great variety of functions available, many tasks that might be difficult if you had to define your own formula become quite easy by using an Approach function.

For another method of including a greater range of information, use the PicturePlus field with linked or embedded objects. These objects can be stored within Approach, but used in a variety of creative ways.

For more information on these advanced fields, refer to the following chapter in this book:

- Chapter 12, "Creating Advanced Reports," shows you how to use calculated fields and variables to add powerful functions to reports.

Chapter 11

Performing Advanced Finds

Chapter 6, "Finding Records," discussed Approach's ability to find records that meet certain criteria. Most of the time, the methods discussed in Chapter 6 are sufficient to locate the records you need. However, Approach enables you to search for records using more complex and powerful find criteria.

In this chapter, you learn how to:

- Search for records with fields whose contents "sound like" the criteria you typed
- Specify find criteria in a calculated field
- Search for records with fields whose contents match the results of an IF statement, even if you can't type find criteria into those fields (for example, radio buttons)
- Search for records with fields that contain the value in another field
- Search for records with fields that match the results of a formula
- Search for the contents of a field in a related database

Performing a "Sounds Like" Search

When searching for a text string, you may not always know exactly how to spell the text for which you are looking. In the Owl Publishing database, for example, you want to find the record for a customer with a first name of John or Jon. Approach enables you to perform a "sounds like" search.

This type of find selects records in which the text string sounds like what you typed in. A find in a STATE field for "Illinoise" would locate any records where the field searched contains the correctly spelled Illinois, and also any records with phonetically similar misspellings ("Illinoise"), such as the one used for the find criterion.

To perform a "sounds like" search, follow these steps:

1. Switch to Browse mode.
2. Select the form or report you want to work with from the tabs or the status bar. For the Owl Publishing example, select the Customer form.

3. Click the Find SmartIcon, open the **B**rowse menu and choose **F**ind, or select the Find mode from the status bar.
4. Select the desired field. For this example, select the FIRST NAME field.

5. Type ~ (tilde) in the search field or click the Sounds Like SmartIcon, and then enter the text that sounds like your search field. For this example, type **~Jon** (see fig. 11.1).

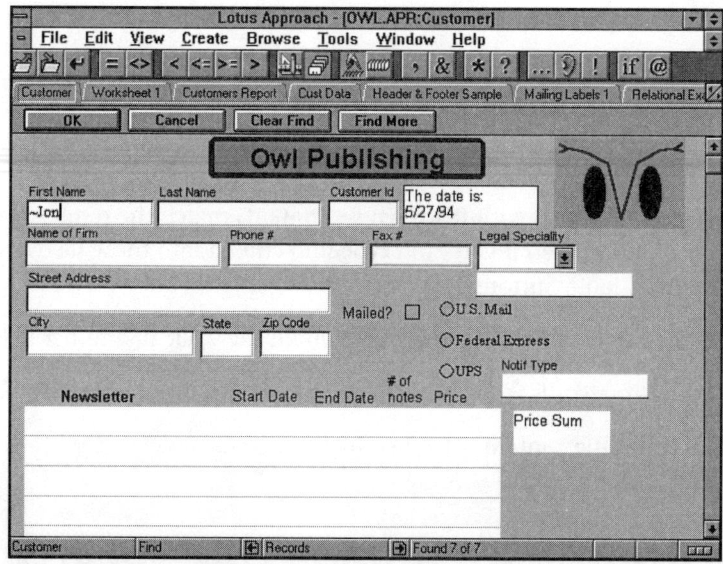

Fig. 11.1
Performing a "sounds-like" search on the FIRST NAME field.

Tip
You can also type search criteria into other fields to perform an AND find.

6. Click the Enter SmartIcon or press Enter. The record for John Roberts appears.

Searching on a Calculated Field

Calculated fields return the result of a calculation that you define when you create the field. Although you can't type a value into a calculated field in Browse mode, you can type find criteria into a calculated field.

By running a find on a calculated field, you can find values you may not be able to locate with Approach's standard find functions. For example, to find all records in which the combination of the first and last names exceeds a certain length would be very difficult using Approach's standard find functions. With a calculated field, however, you can create a formula using the `Length` and `Combine` functions to calculate the length of the combination of the two strings. This calculation could be handy for locating records for which you must use a larger mailing label. Use the following formula when defining the calculated field:

```
Length(Combine(FIRST NAME,LAST NAME))
```

With this calculated field, the search is simple to perform. For the find criterion, specify a number greater than the length you desire. If you want to find all combinations of the first- and last-name strings greater than 40 characters, for example, type **>40** in the calculated field.

Entering Criteria in Calculated Fields

Criteria entered in calculated fields are subject to the same rules as criteria entered in other types of fields. Thus, criteria entered in calculated fields can:

- Reference constants and field values
- Use comparison operators (<, >, <>, >=, <=)
- Include a range of values 

- Be case sensitive 

- Include wild cards 

- Search for an exact match (=) 

- Join multiple criteria
- Separate multiple criteria. Approach finds all records in which the value in the calculated field matches any of the criteria (an OR query). 

Entering Find Criteria in a Calculated Field

To enter find criteria in a calculated field, follow these steps:

1. Choose Browse mode.
2. Select the form or report you want to work with using the view tabs or the status bar.

3. Click the Find SmartIcon, open the **B**rowse menu and choose **F**ind, or select the Find mode from the status bar.
4. Type the criterion in the calculated field. You can also type search criteria into other fields to perform an AND find, or add additional find requests for an OR find.

5. Click the Enter SmartIcon or press Enter.

Using a Formula in a Find

You can type a formula into any field during a find. Approach compares the contents of the field with the result of the formula. If the comparison is true, the record is included in the found set.

> **Note**
>
> A formula used in a find must be preceded by a comparison operator (=, <, >, > =, < =, or < >) and the @ symbol.

Using Items in the Formula Find

You can reference the following items in a formula find:

- Field names
- Functions
- Arithmetic operators
- Constants

Field Names

The formula can reference other fields in the Approach file. Approach uses the value contained in the referenced field when it evaluates the formula.

For example, if a variable field called REGIONVAR contained the value North, doing a find in the database field REGION for =@REGIONVAR would return a found set of all records where the REGION field matched the current value in the variable field, North. You might use this capability to allow the user to enter his search criteria on a special form you use just for finds. This special "find form" might contain just the variable field for the user to enter what he wants to search for. You could then execute a macro that uses the contents of the field in a find.

Functions

You can include many of Approach's functions in formulas. Certain functions aren't appropriate, however, because they don't return a value. An example is the Fill function, which fills one string, or group of text characters, with the contents of another string.

A common find performed with a function is =@TODAY() in a field that contains date values. This finds any records where the field used in the find contains today's date.

Arithmetic Operators

You can perform arithmetic operations as part of the formula. However, you can't use the multiplication operator (*), because Approach interprets it as the wild-card find symbol rather than as the multiplication operator. Because the formula already contains a comparison operator, the one needed at the beginning of the find, you can't include any other find operators in the formula—a find criterion can contain only one find operator.

An example of this could be a product inventory system. To find records where the field containing the stock level, STOCK, is at least five units over the minimum stocking level, stored in a second field called STOCK MIN, you could do a find on STOCK for >@STOCK MIN+5. All records in the found set would be at a stock level at least five units above the minimum level.

Note

To search for a value in a field whose contents must match the result of a formula that includes a multiplication, you can compare the contents of the field to the contents of a calculated field that contains the formula (see "Searching for the Value in Another Field" later in this chapter).

Constants

You can include constants as part of the formula. When entering a formula, follow these rules:

- Enclose text string constants in single quotation marks (for example, **'Approach'**).
- Type date constants in the order month-day-year, separated by slashes (for example, **03/12/56**).
- Type time constants in the order of hours, minutes, seconds, and hundredths of seconds. Separate hours, minutes, and seconds with a colon (:). Separate seconds and hundredths of seconds with a decimal point (for example, **12:25:00.45**).
- Type Boolean constants as **'Yes'** or **'No'** (enclosed in single quotation marks), or use the numbers **1** or **0**.
- Don't type numeric constants in scientific notation.

Creating a Formula for a Search

To create a formula search, follow these steps:

1. Choose Browse mode.
2. Select the form or report you want to work with using the view tabs or the status bar.

3. Click the Find SmartIcon, open the **B**rowse menu and choose **F**ind, or select Find mode from the status bar.
4. Select the field for which you want to specify the find criteria.
5. Type the comparison operator, followed by the @ symbol (for example, type <@ for a less-than comparison). Type the rest of the formula you want to use.

6. Click the Enter SmartIcon or press Enter.

You can use the following example formulas in finds:

- To determine whether a field contains the current date, use

```
=@Today()
```

- To determine whether a field contains a date that is more than 30 days old, use

```
<@Today()-30
```

- To determine whether a field contains the name of the month given contained in the SUB START field, use

```
=@Monthname("SUB START")
```

- To determine whether a field other than LAST NAME contains the first letter in the LAST NAME field, use

```
=@Left("LAST NAME",1)
```

- If the FULL NAME field contains the first and last name separated by a space, use the following formula to determine whether a field contains the last name portion of the FULL NAME field:

```
=@Right(FULL NAME, Length(FULL NAME) - Position(FULL NAME,
' ',    1))
```

- To determine whether a field is greater than or equal to the sum of a number and the contents of the numeric field NUMBER, use

```
>=@(75+NUMBER)
```

- If the contents of the TEXTDATE field is a text string in a date format, use the following formula to determine whether a date field contains a date less than the "date" in TEXTDATE:

```
<@TextToDate(TEXTDATE)
```


Searching for the Value in Another Field

You can enter criteria in a find field that compares the contents of the field with the contents of another field. The fields can be of any type except PicturePlus.

To construct the find, type a comparison operator and the name of the compared-to field into the find field. You can use any of the following comparison operators:

- Equal (=)

- Greater than (>)

- Less than (<)

- Greater than or equal (>=)

- Less than or equal (<=)

- Not equal (< >)

The found set returns all records in which the criterion evaluates to be true.

By using a calculated field as the compared-to field, Approach enables you to compare the contents of the find field with the result of a formula. Follow these steps:

1. Add a calculated field containing the formula to the database (see Chapter 10).

2. Place the calculated field on the form. Now you're ready to specify the comparison between the find field and the calculated field.

3. Switch to Browse mode. To save this new calculated field, save the form by opening the **F**ile menu and choosing **S**ave Approach File.

4. Select the form or report you want to work with using the view tabs or the status bar.

5. Switch to Find mode by opening the **B**rowse menu and choosing **F**ind, clicking the Find SmartIcon, or selecting Find from the status bar.

Tip
Without the @ symbol, Approach would find the field name rather than the field's contents for an exact match on a text string.

6. Select the field for which you want to specify the find criteria.

7. Type the comparison operator, followed by the @ symbol (for example, type **=@** for an equals comparison).

8. Type the name of the field whose contents you want to compare to the find field (see fig. 11.2). If you are comparing the contents of the search field to a calculated field, type in the name of the calculated field.

9. Click the Enter SmartIcon or press Enter.

Note

You can also compare the contents of the find field to a formula by entering the formula into the field during the find (see "Creating a Formula for a Search" earlier in this chapter). Formulas entered directly into a field during a find, however, can't include the multiplication operator (*).

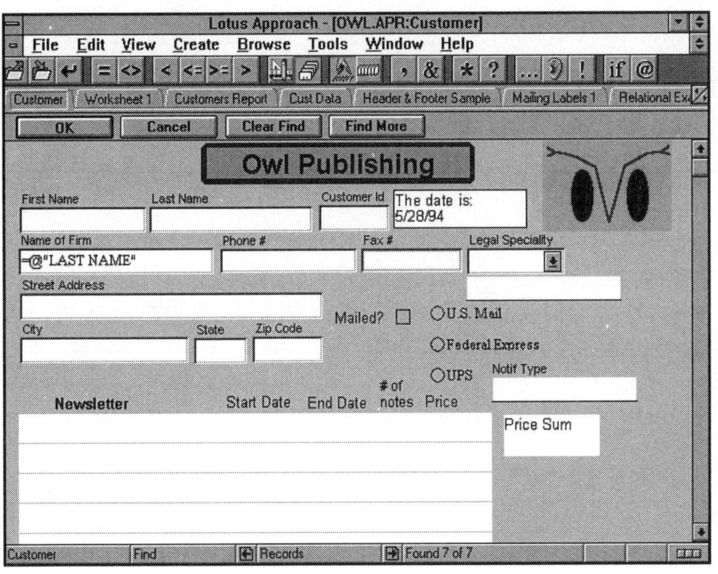

Fig. 11.2
Use =@ to find records in which one field contains the value in another field.

Using the IF Function in a Search

You can use the IF function in a find to retrieve all records in which the expression in the IF statement evaluates as true. To do so, type the IF function into any field on the form that accepts typed text during a find.

> **Note**
>
> You don't need to include in the expression the field into which you type the IF function. If you type **IF("LAST NAME">='P')** into the FIRST NAME field, for example, all records in which the last name starts with any letter from P to Z are returned in the found set.

Using IF in a find enables you to build complex criteria and perform finds you can't perform using Approach's other find functions.

Using Items in an IF Expression

The expression in an IF statement can contain any of the following items, as explained in the next few sections:

- Field names
- Functions

- Arithmetic operators
- Constants
- Comparison operators
- Boolean operators

Field Names

Approach uses the value contained in the field when it evaluates the expression. For example, IF `("LAST NAME"='Smith')` would return a found set where the LAST NAME field contained `Smith`. The double quotes (" ") around the LAST NAME field name are necessary because there is a space in the field name.

Functions

Approach has 84 functions that perform various operations on text and numeric values. The value on which a function operates (called a *parameter*) can be a field value or a constant value. If a function uses multiple parameters, use commas to separate the parameters. Connect multiple functions in the same clause with AND and OR.

Arithmetic Operators

The expression may contain the division (/), addition (+), and subtraction (–) arithmetic operators. An IF expression can't use the multiplication operator (*), however, because Approach interprets the asterisk as the wild-card find operator. Approach evaluates the arithmetic operations in the expression in a specific order:

- The division (/) operation is evaluated first.
- Addition (+) and subtraction (–) operations are evaluated second.
- If any operations are on the same evaluation level (such as addition and subtraction), they are evaluated from left to right in the formula.

You can modify the evaluation order of arithmetic operators by enclosing the operation that you want performed first in parentheses. Approach always evaluates the contents of parentheses before evaluating other parts of the formula. Within a set of parentheses, the evaluation order is as described in the above bulleted list.

To demonstrate this, consider the following two finds, again using STOCK and STOCK MIN. The find IF(STOCK MIN=(STOCK + 5)/2) would find all records where the minimum stocking level equals the half of the quantity the current stocking level plus five units. The find IF(STOCK MIN=STOCK+5/2) would find all records where the minimum stocking level equals the current stocking plus two and one-half units.

Constants

You can use constants as part of the formula. Follow these rules:

- Enclose text string constants in single quotation marks (for example, **'Approach'**).
- Type date constants in the order month-day-year, separated by slashes (for example, **03/12/56**).
- Type time constants in the order of hours, minutes, seconds, and hundredths of seconds. Separate hours, minutes, and seconds with a colon (:). Separate seconds and hundredths of seconds with a decimal point (for example, **12:25:00.45**).
- Type Boolean constants as **'Yes'** or **'No'**, with single quotation marks enclosing them, or the numbers **1** or **0**.
- Don't type numeric constants in scientific notation.

Comparison Operators

Use comparison operators to compare two values or fields. The comparison operators are =, >, <, <>, >=, and <=.

Perhaps you're doing a company mailing and need to search for records within a range of zip codes, described by the first three digits of the zip code. This find can be done with an IF find and the Left function. The find `IF(LEFT(Zip,3)='940')`, for example, would return a found set of all records where the first three digits of the value stored in the ZIP field matched the find criteria, 940.

Boolean Operators

You can connect clauses in the IF statement with the AND and OR Boolean operators, as follows:

- In an AND clause, the clause evaluates as true when both sides of the AND are true (for example, 5<6 AND 'B'>'A').

- In an OR clause, the clause evaluates as true when either side (or both sides) of the OR are true (for example, 5>6 OR 'B'>'A').

Creating a Find Using the IF Function

To create a find using the IF function, follow these steps:

1. Switch to Find mode by opening the **B**rowse menu and choosing **F**ind, clicking the Find SmartIcon, or selecting Find from the status bar.
2. Select the form or report you want to work with using the view tabs or the status bar.
3. Select the field into which you want to type the IF expression.
4. Type the IF expression into the field (see fig. 11.3). You can also type search criteria into other fields to perform an AND find, or add additional find requests for an OR find.

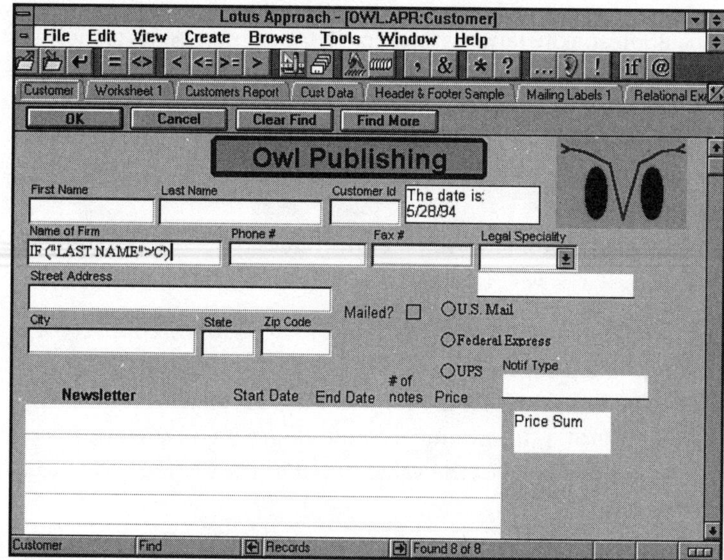

Fig. 11.3
Using an IF expression.

5. Press Enter or click the Enter SmartIcon.

Using the IF Function to Perform More Complicated Finds

The IF function often can duplicate other find techniques. You can type a comparison formula such as **IF("LAST NAME">'P')** into a field. Of course, you can perform the same operation by simply typing **>P** into the LAST

NAME field. Using the IF function enables you to perform finds that can't be done with the normal find functions, however, as the following sections explain.

Using IF for Finds on Drop-Down Lists, Checkboxes, and Radio Buttons

One limit of Approach's "normal" find functions is that you can't type criteria into fields that don't accept typed text (that is, checkboxes and radio button fields). Standard finds that involve these types of fields are limited to a single value unless you resort to multiple find (Find Mores). You can select a single value in a drop-down list field, for example, to find all records in which the field contains the value. Because a drop-down List field can't accept typed text, however, you can't specify multiple values (for example, all records in which the SPECIALTY field contains EM or CR).

You can type an IF function into any field on a form that accepts typed text. Thus, the IF function enables you to specify a find criteria for these types of fields that do include multiple values.

Let's return to our fictitious company for a moment. Owl Publishing wants to find all the records in which UPS or Federal Express is used to send out renewal notices. Because these are buttons, you can't simply type the two values into the MAIL TYPE field. Instead, you can use an IF search, as follows:

1. Switch to Find mode by opening the **B**rowse menu and choosing **F**ind, clicking the Find SmartIcon, or selecting Find from the status bar.

2. Select the Customer form from the view tabs or the status bar.

3. Select the STREET ADDRESS field.

4. Type **IF("MAIL TYPE"='UPS' OR "MAIL TYPE"='Fed Express')** (see fig. 11.4).

5. Press Enter. All records with UPS or Federal Express are returned in the found set.

Using IF to Compare the Values in Two Fields

Use the IF function to compare the contents of two fields, as shown below:

```
IF(Sales92<Sales91)
```

This formula returns all records in which the value in field `Sales92` is less than the value in the field `Sales91`.

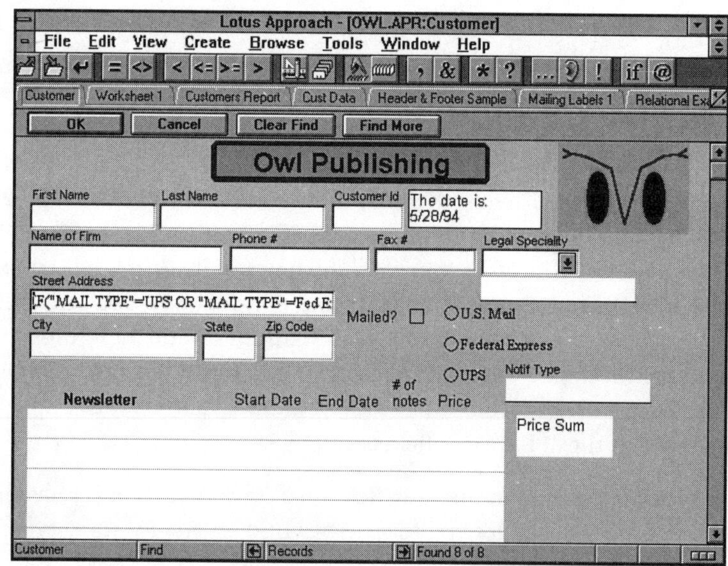

Fig. 11.4
Finding multiple values of a radio button field.

Using IF to Evaluate a Formula

You can use the IF function to evaluate a complex formula. For example, to evaluate whether the result in the SUB END date is within 90 days of the current date, use

```
IF ("SUB END"-Today()<=90)
```

The formula may contain many functions and multiple clauses connected by AND and OR operators. If, for example, you want to see all records in which more than 90 days have passed since the date in `INVOICEDATE`, and a customer owes you money (`BALANCEDUE` is greater than zero), use

```
IF (((INVOICEDATE-TODAY())>90) AND (BALANCEDUE>0))
```

Using IF on a Field Not Displayed on the Current Form

You can use the IF function to find records where fields contain a matching criterion, even if that field isn't displayed on the current form. In mailing labels, for instance, you may not display the SPECIALTY field. You can find all records in which the SPECIALTY field includes the value CR from this field, however, by using the following formula in the STREET ADDRESS (or any other text-type) field:

```
IF(SPECIALTY='CR')
```

Finding on a Field in a Related Database

Forms and reports can include fields from related databases. These fields appear in the main body of the form/report or in a repeating panel (only on a form).

You can find on a field in a related database as easily as you can find on a field from the main database. As with fields from the main database, to perform a find, type your criteria into the fields from the related database. All the same find limits and capabilities apply to this type of find (see "Entering Criteria in Calculated Fields" earlier in this chapter). Multiple-field AND finds can include related fields.

Exactly what the find returns depends on whether you type the find criteria into a related field in the main body of the form or report or into a repeating panel:

- If the related field is located in the main body of the form or report, the found set includes all records that match the criteria of the search. If a repeating panel is also in use, all related records in the repeating panel are returned as well.

- If the related field is located in a repeating panel and if the contents of the find field in any record in the repeating panel matches the criteria, the found set contains the main record and the matching record from the repeating panel (see figs. 11.5 and 11.6).

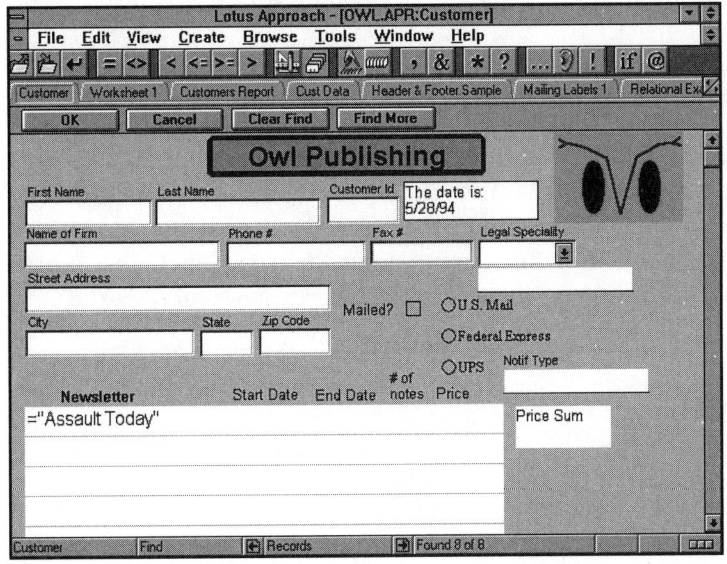

Fig. 11.5
The Find criteria in a repeating panel.

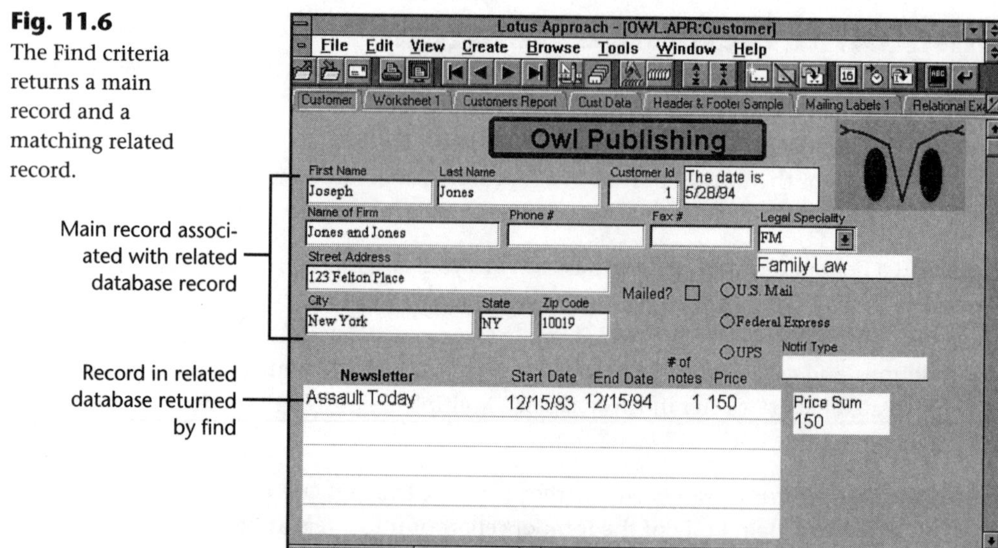

Fig. 11.6
The Find criteria returns a main record and a matching related record.

Finds in an Approach File with Related Files

When you use an Approach file that has related files, the find creates a found set within the database that the current form or report is based on. If you switch to a different form or report based on the same file, you'll still have the found set. If you switch to a form or report that's based on a different database, however, the data returns to an "unfound" state—that is, all records in the database on which the form or report is based are available.

From Here...

As you have seen, Approach enables you to search for records using complex and powerful find criteria. The techniques covered in this chapter include finds with formulas, finds using the IF function, and doing a find with multiple criteria for a field that cannot use standard text input. And, as before, these criteria can be combined further to create powerful AND and OR finds.

Once you know how to create complex finds, it is important to present the found information in reports, as well as show the results in crosstabs and graphs. For more information, refer to the following chapters in this book:

- Chapter 12, "Creating Advanced Reports," shows you how to create reports that include summary panels, use calculated fields, and build form letters.
- Chapter 13, "Automating Your Work," shows you how to create Macros that use finds. With a macro, you can use predefined find criteria with the click of the mouse.
- Chapter 14, "Using Worksheets and Crosstabs," shows you how to display the results of a find in a worksheet or a crosstab report.
- Chapter 15, "Creating Charts," shows you how to display the results of a find in a variety of chart styles.

12

Chapter 12

Creating Advanced Reports

In Chapter 7, you learned how to print detailed records in standard or column format. In this chapter, you'll discover how you can use additional reporting features and calculations to organize and analyze your data.

Along with reports, another type of view that's often printed are form letters. The Approach Form Letter Assistant allows you to quickly and easily create letters that include fields from your database.

In this chapter, you learn how to:

- Create Summary reports
- Create a Repeating Panel report
- Use PowerClick reporting to modify reports
- Add summary calculations to a report
- Modify the attributes of a report panel or object
- Create, edit, and print form letters

Understanding Summary Reports

The reports created in Chapter 7 were composed of different parts, or *panels*. The section that contains the fields that are displayed for each record is called the *body panel*. Additionally, the report can have a header, footer, or both.

Another panel that's available for use in reporting is called a *summary panel*. The summary panel is used to create various groupings of the data in the report.

> **Note**
>
> A summary panel is different from a body panel in that a summary panel is displayed only in Preview or Design mode. If the report includes both body and summary panels, only the body panel is displayed in Browse mode.

Summary panels, like body panels, can display field data. Generally they are not used to display all data in a record. Instead, a summary panel often contains information specific to the current group. In the Owl Publishing database, for example, you might group the newsletter subscribers by state, using the summary panel to separate each state grouping. Since the current group's state would be the same for each record in the group, it can be displayed in the summary panel rather than for each record in the body panel.

Summary panels are also used to display summary calculations. A *summary calculation* is a special calculation type that gives a value over a group of records or all records in a database. For example, in the Owl Publishing database you know which customers receive which newsletters, and the newsletters' subscription prices. You can create a summary calculation based on these customers' records that displays the total amount from all newsletter subscriptions.

If your report has a summary group based on a field value, such as a grouping by state, you can display the same summary calculated field you used for the grand total in the group panel. In this case, though, the value displayed in each state grouping would be the total amount for all newsletters in that state. Of course, the report can have both a grouping by state and a grand total (see fig. 12.1).

You can set a summary panel to be displayed before the records it is grouping, as a leading panel, or after, as a trailing panel. To display information both before and after the group, you can define two panels for the same group, one leading and one trailing. You can also define a panel to appear to the left or right of a detail record, rather than above or following, but this is less common. A report can have up to eight different summary panels.

You can set a summary panel to add a page break. For instance, there might be a new page after every trailing summary grouping by state. The page break occurs before a leading summary panel, or after a trailing summary.

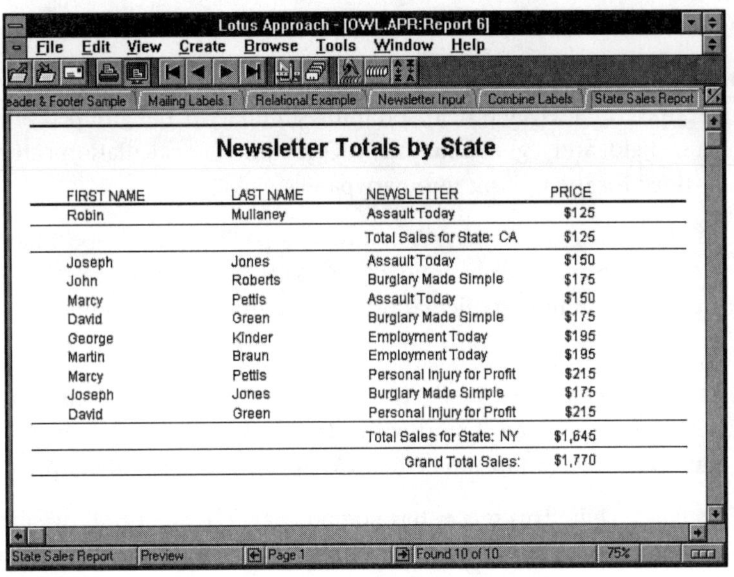

Newsletter Totals by State

FIRST NAME	LAST NAME	NEWSLETTER	PRICE
Robin	Mullaney	Assault Today	$125
		Total Sales for State: CA	$125
Joseph	Jones	Assault Today	$150
John	Roberts	Burglary Made Simple	$175
Marcy	Pettis	Assault Today	$150
David	Green	Burglary Made Simple	$175
George	Kinder	Employment Today	$195
Martin	Braun	Employment Today	$195
Marcy	Pettis	Personal Injury for Profit	$215
Joseph	Jones	Burglary Made Simple	$175
David	Green	Personal Injury for Profit	$215
		Total Sales for State: NY	$1,645
		Grand Total Sales:	$1,770

Fig. 12.1
This report shows newsletter customers grouped by state with a grand total.

Three types of summary groupings are available:

- *All records.* This grouping creates a grand summary for whatever file is used for the report. For example, an all-records grouping might be used to show a sales total for a file based on the year's sales records.
- *Records grouped by a field.* This grouping, one of the most common uses of a summary panel, enables you to group detail records by distinct values in a field. For example, you might group sales records by region in order to display regional totals, or you might group customers by zip code for a bulk mailing.
- *Every certain number of records.* This grouping displays a summary panel after a certain number of records. The number of records is set by the user.

Creating Advanced Reports with the Report Assistant

The Report Assistant lists several different predefined report types. In Chapter 7, the Report Assistant was used to create blank, standard, and columnar reports. The remaining report types use summary panels. They can have, but don't necessarily include, a body panel. These reports can be used as is after they are created or they can be customized as needed.

These additional report types are:

- *Leading Grouped Summary.* This report has a leading summary panel grouped on a selected field, a trailing summary panel grouped on the same field, and a grand summary. One summary calculation can be defined for the trailing summary panels.
- *Trailing Grouped Summary.* A trailing grouped summary report has a trailing summary panel grouped on a selected field, and a grand summary. One summary calculation can be defined for the summary panels.
- *Columnar with Grand Summary.* The columnar with grand summary reports is a columnar report with a trailing grand summary panel. One summary calculation can be defined for the grand summary panel.
- *Summary Only.* This report has no body panel. It has a trailing summary panel grouped on a selected field and a grand summary. One summary calculation can be defined for the summary panels.
- *Repeating Panel Report.* This report is an easy way to print all records that appear in a repeating panel, without running into the display limit of a repeating panel on a form. This report has a leading and trailing summary panel based on a field, and a trailing grand summary panel. One calculated field can be defined for the trailing summary panels.

Tip
The Repeating Panel report, like the repeating panel for a form, is only available when you have files that are relationally joined in your Approach file.

Creating reports with the Report Assistant uses several common steps. A few differences still exist within the various types of reports.

The Leading Grouped Summary, Trailing Grouped Summary, and Columnar with Grand Summary reports are similar in that they each contain both body and summary panels. See the following section, "Creating a Leading Grouped Summary Report," for instructions on creating this type of report.

The Summary Only report has, as the name implies, only summary panels. A smaller number of fields are usually displayed in this type of report, since it doesn't include detail records. See "Creating a Summary Only Report" for instructions on creating this report.

Finally, the Repeating Panel report lets you print data that's normally displayed on a form with a repeating panel, without the display restrictions of a repeating panel. This report is described in the section, "Creating a Repeating Panel Report."

Creating a Leading Grouped Summary Report

Imagine you want a list of Owl Publishing's customers, grouped by subscribers of each newsletter. If a customer subscribes to more than one newsletter, that customer will be listed more than once. Also included in this report is the start date and stop date for each customer's subscription, and, in a summary calculation, the oldest start date for each newsletter.

To create the Leading Grouped Summary report, follow these steps:

1. Open the **C**reate menu and choose **R**eport. The Report Assistant appears (see fig. 12.2).

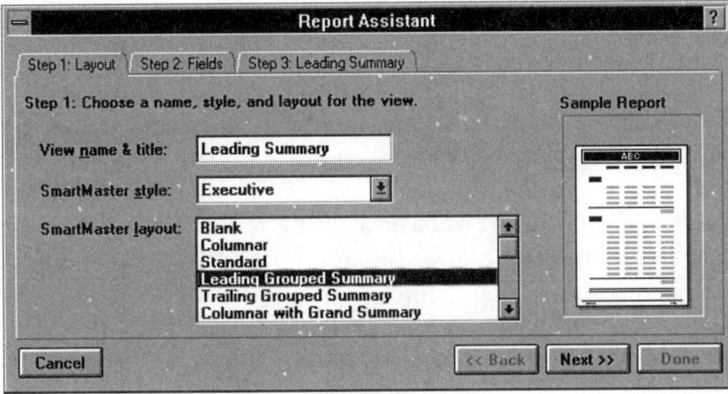

Fig. 12.2
The Report Assistant shows a sample picture of the report you want to create.

> **Note**
>
> The number of panel tabs in the Report Assistant varies by the selected report type. The default type—blank—has only one tab. Standard and columnar have two, and the remaining types have three. If you notice you don't get the proper tab to define a section that you need, return to the first tab and reselect the report type. The dialog will change, giving you the selections you require.

2. Type the report name, **Leading Summary**, into the View **N**ame & Title text box.

3. Choose the Executive SmartMaster **S**tyle from the drop-down list.

4. Select Leading Grouped Summary from the SmartMaster **L**ayout.

5. Click the Next button to proceed to the second panel, Fields (see fig. 12.3).

II

Forms, Queries, & Reports

Fig. 12.3
The sample picture shows where the selected fields will be placed.

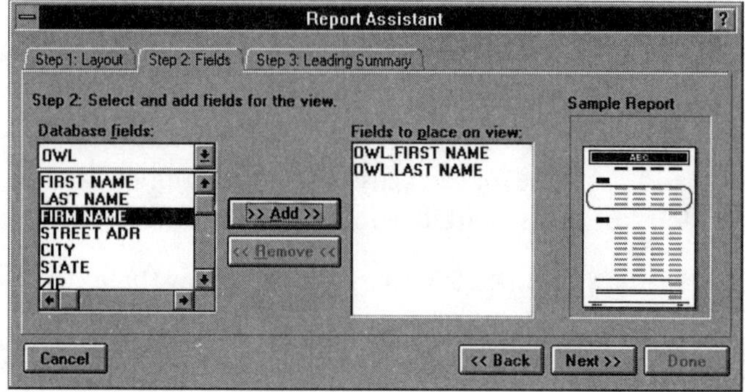

6. If the Database **F**ields option doesn't show the database from which you want to add fields, select the database from the drop-down list immediately below Database **F**ields.

   For the report, choose the Owl database.

7. Choose the fields you want to add to the report from the Database **F**ields list box. To choose multiple fields, click the first field, hold down the Ctrl key, and click any additional fields.

   From Owl, select the FIRST NAME and LAST NAME fields.

8. Choose **A**dd to add the fields to the Fields to **P**lace On View list box.

9. To add fields from a relationally linked database, return to step 6 and choose a new database.

   For this example, choose Newsltr. Add the fields SUB START and SUB END, the starting and ending date for each customer's subscription.

10. Click the Next button to continue to the third panel, Leading Summary (see fig. 12.4).

Tip
To remove a field from the Report Fields list box, choose the field and select **R**emove.

Fig. 12.4
The grouping field and calculation are defined in the Leading Summary panel.

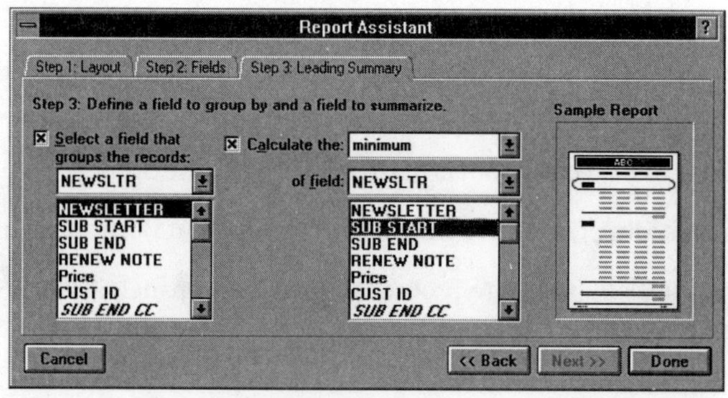

11. Select the grouping field in the **S**elect a Field That Groups the Records drop-down list. This field can be from any relationally linked database.

    When the grouping field is selected, the checkbox to the left is checked. If this box remains unchecked, a leading summary won't be created. A grand summary would still be created, however.

    Select the NEWSLETTER field from the Newsltr database as the field by which the records will be grouped.

12. Define a summary calculation. Choose the type of calculation from the Calculate The drop-down list. Each one of the selections creates an Approach calculated field using a summary function. The following selections, each showing its related summary function, are available:

    - *Average—SAverage.* The average of a value from all records in the current grouping; for example, average yearly income.
    - *Count—SCount.* The number of fields with non-blank values in a group; for example, the number of newsletter subscribers per state.
    - *Sum—SSum.* The sum of all values of a field in the group; for example, the sales for a product in a region.
    - *Minimum—SMin.* The minimum of a group; for example, a store with the least amount of returned products.
    - *Maximum—SMax.* The maximum of a group; for example, the number of sales per representative.
    - *Standard Deviation—SStd.* The standard deviation (how far values are from the mean) of a field's values over the current grouping. Used for statistical reporting.
    - *Variance—SVar.* The variance of a field's values over the current grouping. Used for statistical reporting.

    Select the database field the calculation will use from the field list. If necessary, select the required database from the Of **F**ield drop-down list. If the checkbox for the calculation section is unchecked, no calculated field is created.

    This report will show the oldest start date for each newsletter grouping. To show the oldest start date, select the minimum of field SUB START, the subscription start date.

Caution

Either a grouping field or summary calculation, or both, needs to be defined to create the Leading Summary report. If neither of the checkboxes on the Leading Summary panel are checked, the Done button will remain dimmed and won't allow you to exit.

13. Click Back if you need to make any changes or adjustments in the Report Assistant. Choose Done when you are finished designing the report.

14. If fields from more than one relationally linked file are included in the Fields panel, the Define Main Database dialog box appears, asking for the main database for the body panel of the report (see fig. 12.5). Choose the database from which you want the detail records.

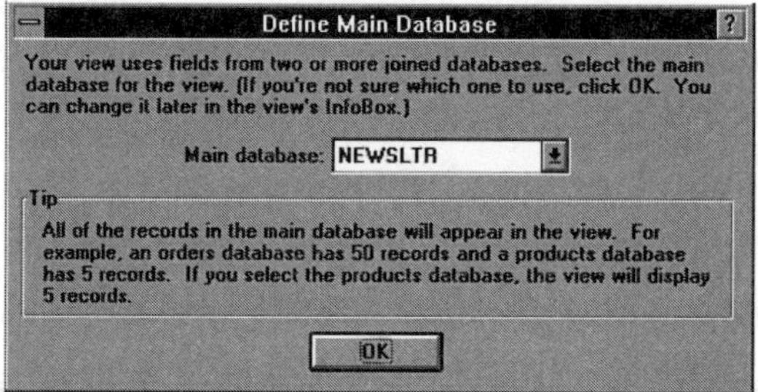

Fig. 12.5
When using fields from multiple databases, you must choose the main database for your report.

In this example, you want to display a detail record for each customer who receives a certain newsletter. Although we're displaying customer names, we're listing them by the start and stop date of each newsletter. Because the Newsltr database contains the individual newsletter subscription information, it is the main database for this report.

Tip
If you're not sure which database should be the main database for a report, pick the one you think is correct. It can be adjusted later through the Info Box.

Note

Although it's showing customer information, the report displays one record for each newsletter subscription. These subscription records are in the Newsltr database; thus, the main database is the Newsltr database. The database for which you want the report to display all the records is the main database for the report.

You can see the completed report either in Design mode, with Show Data on, or in Preview mode (see fig. 12.6). In Browse mode, only the header, footer, and body panel are displayed.

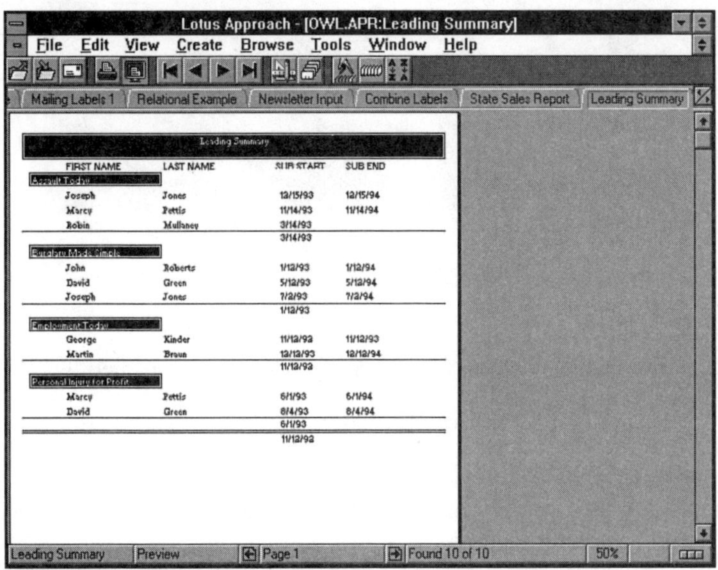

Fig. 12.6
The completed leading summary report of newsletter subscribers.

Each newsletter is a new group in the leading summary panel. The next set of lists are the detail records for each grouping. The trailing summary panel lists the oldest start date for each subscription. In the grand summary panel, the minimum date calculation occurs again, but this time it lists the minimum for all records, since that is what the panel summarizes, rather than a subgroup.

Creating a Summary Only Report

The Summary Only report, as the name implies, contains no detail records. Instead, it contains only summary panels, and usually summary calculations. It is another way to produce the newsletter report by the minimum subscription date. Rather than listing each subscriber, though, the report lists each newsletter, its oldest subscription date, and the oldest overall date in a grand summary.

To create a Summary Only report, follow these steps:

1. Open the **C**reate menu and choose **R**eport. The Report Assistant appears on the Layout panel (see fig. 12.7).

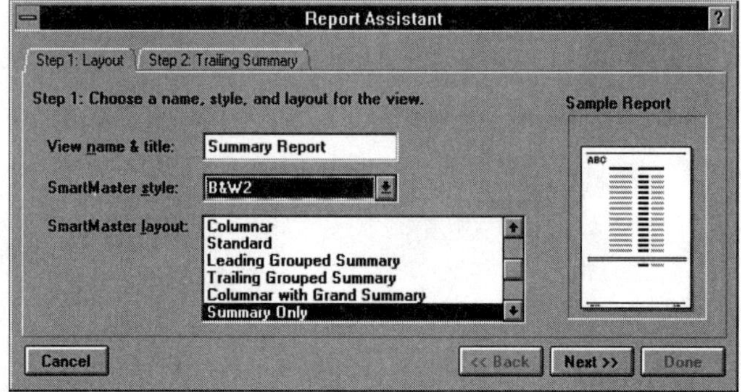

Fig. 12.7
The Layout panel of the Report Assistant with settings for a Summary Only report.

2. Type the report name, **Summary Report**, into the View **N**ame & Title text box.
3. Choose the B&W2 SmartMaster **S**tyle from the drop-down list.
4. Select Summary Only from the SmartMaster **L**ayout drop-down list.
5. Click the Next button to proceed to the Trailing Summary panel (see fig. 12.8). Notice that this time there is no Fields panel, since there is no body panel in the report.

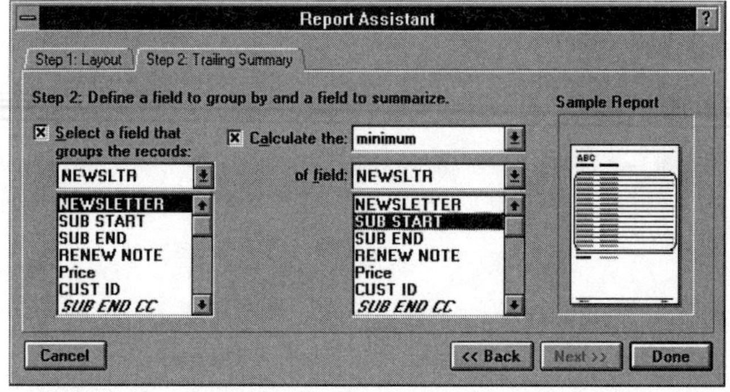

Fig. 12.8
The Trailing Summary panel for the Summary Only report allows you to define your summary data.

6. Select the grouping field in the **S**elect a Field That Groups the Records drop-down list. This field can be from any relationally linked database.

   When the grouping field is selected, the checkbox to the left is checked. If this box remains unchecked, a leading summary won't be created, although a grand summary would still be created.

Select NEWSLETTER from the database Newsltr as the field by which the records will be grouped.

7. Define a summary calculation, if you want one. Choose the type of calculation from the Calculate The drop-down list. Each one of the selections creates an Approach calculated field using a summary function. The following selections are available, each showing its related summary function:

   - Average—SAverage
   - Count—SCount
   - Sum—SSum
   - Minimum—SMin
   - Maximum—SMax
   - Standard Deviation—SStd
   - Variance—SVar

   Select the database field the calculation will use from the field list. If necessary, select the required database from the Of Field drop-down list. If the checkbox for the calculation section is unchecked, no calculated field is created.

   This report shows the oldest start date for each newsletter grouping. To show the oldest start date, select the minimum of field SUB START.

8. Click Back if you need to make any changes or adjustments in the Report Assistant. Choose Done when you're finished defining your report.

Tip
Consider what kind of printer you'll be using when you design a report. You don't need any colors, for example, if you will be printing to a black-and-white printer.

You can view the completed report either in Design mode, with Show Data on, or in Preview mode (see fig. 12.9). Because there's no body panel, Approach won't allow you to enter Browse mode when this report is the current view.

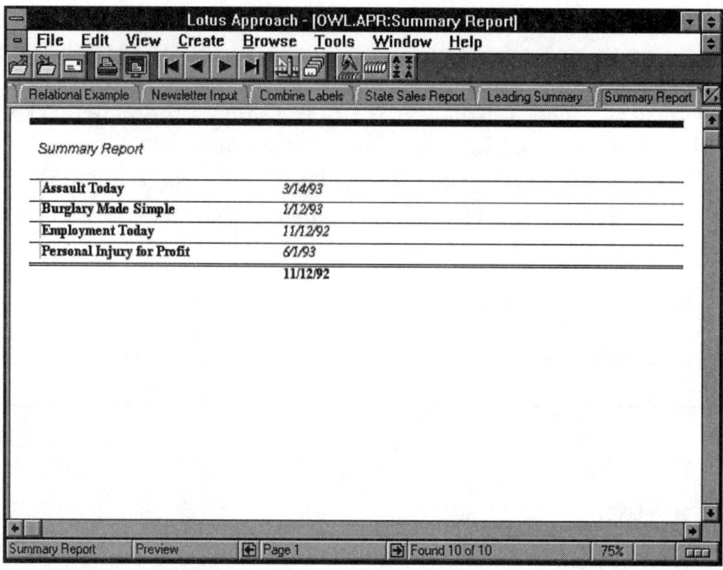

Fig. 12.9 The completed Summary Only report of the oldest newsletter subscriptions.

If you compare the report that was created with the one in figure 12.6, you see that they do contain the same summary data. The listings for the newsletters and the minimum start dates are the same. The Summary Only report can be useful for getting a quick overview. If more information is required, a similar report with detail information can then be constructed.

Creating a Repeating Panel Report

Repeating panels are a way to show how many records from one database file are joined to a main record in another database file. An example of this is the main Owl Publishing customer information screen, shown in figure 12.10. For this form, the main database is Owl. The detail database, with one or more possible records, is Newsltr.

Repeating panels are helpful in that they can display or be used to enter relational information. One problem, though, is that the repeating panel is set to display a certain number of records. Although the number of detail records can be quite large, only a certain number of records are displayed by a repeating panel. You can view those records that aren't within the number shown by the repeating panel by scrolling through the panel.

Tip
Remember, a Repeating Panel report is only an option if you have joined databases.

The Repeating Panel report enables you to print all needed detail records, without any limits. The report is grouped by the same unique value that is used for the form, which in this case is the Customer ID. It also lists information from the detail database, Newsltr. Of course, this report might just as easily be used for any number of other one-to-many tasks, such as invoices or purchase orders.

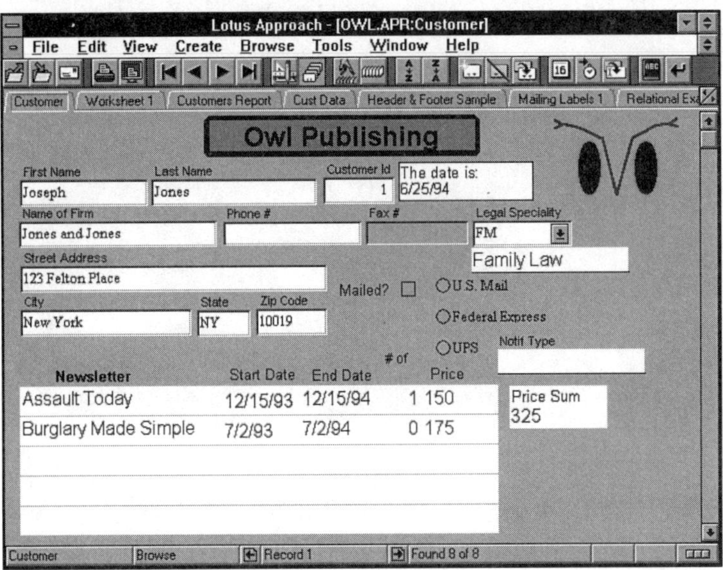

Fig. 12.10
The Owl Publishing customer form includes a repeating panel that lists all newsletters for each customer.

To define a Repeating Panel report, follow these steps:

1. Open the **C**reate menu and choose **R**eport. The Report Assistant appears on the Layout panel (see fig. 12.11).

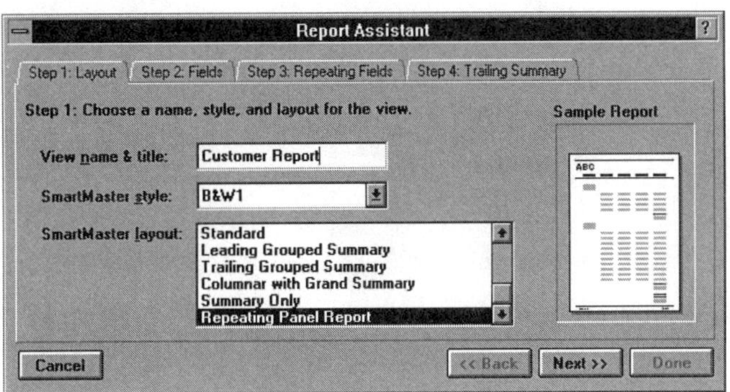

Fig. 12.11
A Repeating Panel report contains four steps.

2. Type the report name, **Customer Report**, into the View **N**ame & Title text box.

3. Choose the B&W1 SmartMaster **S**tyle from the drop-down list.

4. Select Repeating Panel Report from the SmartMaster **L**ayout drop-down list.

5. Click the Next button to proceed to the second panel, Fields (see fig. 12.12).

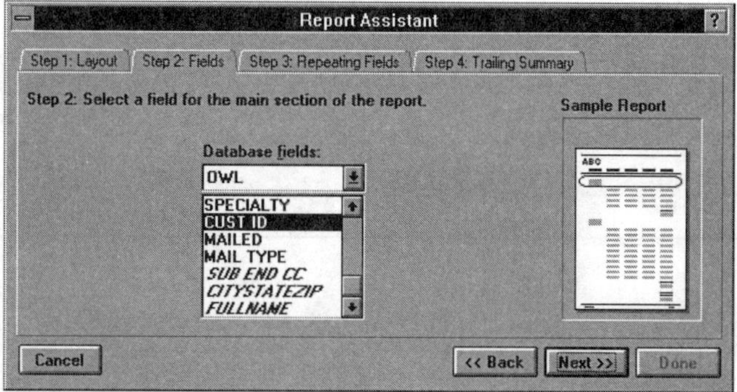

Fig. 12.12
Selecting a main field for the Repeating Panel report.

6. If the Database **F**ields option doesn't show the database from which you want to select the main field, select the database from the drop-down list.

   For the report, choose the Owl database, since it's the main database for the form with the repeating panel.

7. Choose the fields you want for the main section of the report in the Database **F**ields drop-down list. Only one field can be selected. More fields can be added to the report in Design mode, if necessary.

   From Owl, select the customer ID field, CUST ID.

8. Click the Next button to continue to the third panel, Repeating Fields (see fig. 12.13).

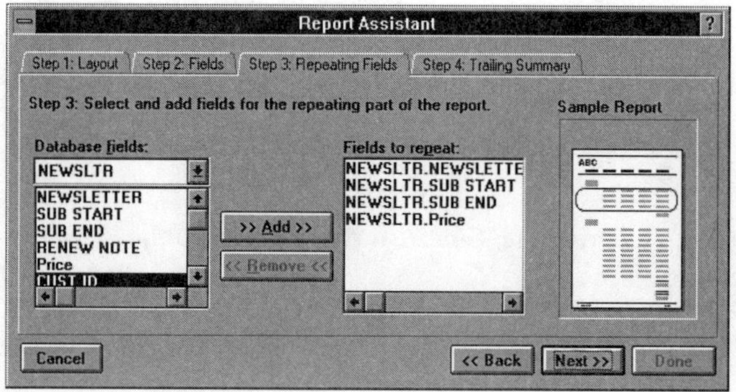

Fig. 12.13
The fields for the detail records are selected on the Repeating Fields panel.

9. If the Database **F**ields option doesn't show the database from which you want to add fields, select the database from the drop-down list.

   For the report, choose the Newsltr database.

10. Choose the fields you want to add to the report from the Database **F**ields drop-down list. To choose multiple fields, click the first field, hold down the Ctrl key, and click any additional fields.

    From Newsltr, select the NEWSLETTER, SUB START, SUB END, and PRICE fields.

11. Choose **A**dd to add these fields to the Fields to Re**p**eat list box.

12. To add fields from a relationally linked database, return to step 9 and choose a new database.

    In this example, all of the repeating fields have already been selected.

13. Click the Next button to continue to the Trailing Summary panel (see fig. 12.14).

Tip
To remove a field from the Fields to Re**p**eat list box, select the field and click **R**emove.

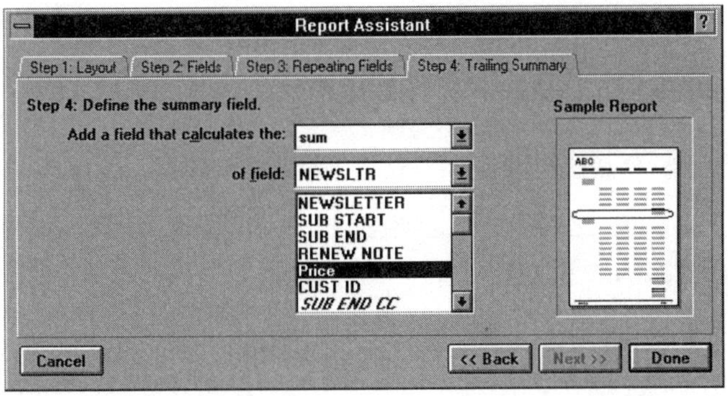

Fig. 12.14
Select the type of calculation for the Trailing Summary panel.

14. Define a summary calculation. Choose the type of calculation from the Add a Field That C**a**lculates The drop-down box. Each one of the selections will create an Approach calculated field using a summary function. The following selections are available, each showing its related summary function:

    - Average—SAverage
    - Count—SCount
    - Sum—SSum
    - Minimum—SMin

- Maximum—SMax
- Standard Deviation—SStd
- Variance—SVar

Select the database field the calculation will use from the Of **F**ield drop-down list. A calculation must be defined for this report.

15. Click Back if you need to make any changes or adjustments in the Report Assistant. Otherwise, click Done when you are finished defining your report.

16. If fields from more than one relationally linked file are included in the Fields panel, the Define Main Database dialog box appears, asking for the main database for the repeating fields section of the report. Choose the database upon which the repeating panel is based.

You can see the completed report either in Design mode, with Show Data on, or in Preview mode (see fig. 12.15). In Browse mode, only the header, footer, and repeating records are displayed.

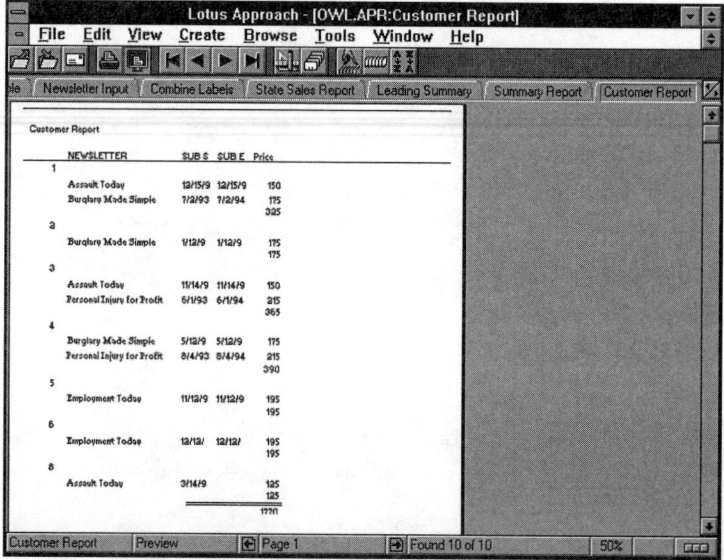

Fig. 12.15
The Repeating Panel report lists newsletters grouped by customer ID.

Each listing of a customer ID is a new grouping of the leading summary panel; after that is the repeating records for each grouping. The trailing summary panel lists the sum of the prices for each customer's newsletter subscriptions. In the grand summary panel, the total of all newsletter subscriptions is displayed.

The Repeating Panel report didn't add the customer's name or any other customer information. That can easily be added later in Design mode.

Modifying Reports

So far, the focus has been on creating reports through the Report Assistant. Although it will often produce the report you need, sometimes additional modification or customization is necessary to get the exact report you want.

Approach offers several features such as show data, columnar editing, and PowerClick reporting that make it easy to modify a report. To use these features, it's important to understand what they are and when they are available.

A simple columnar report is used to demonstrate these features. The report shown in figure 12.16 lists each Owl Publishing customer and his or her legal specialty. This report is based on the Owl database.

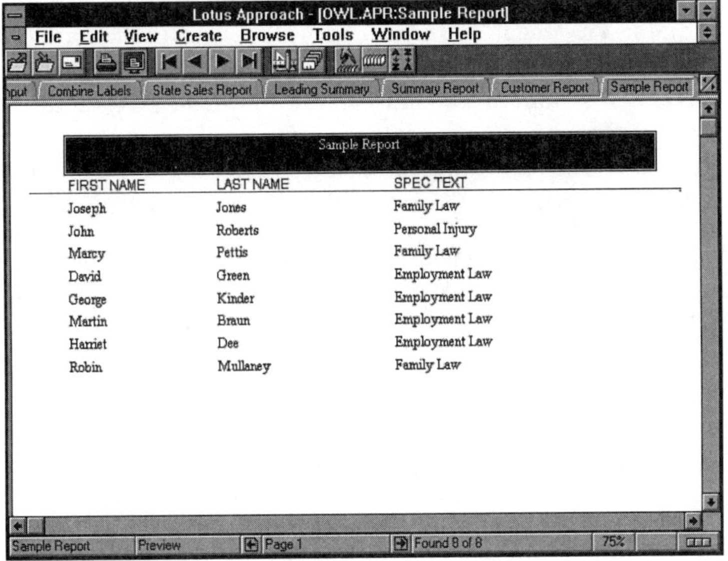

Fig. 12.16
A simple columnar report.

Using Show Data

Show Data mode is a way to show actual data, rather than just report bands and objects in Design mode (see fig. 12.17).

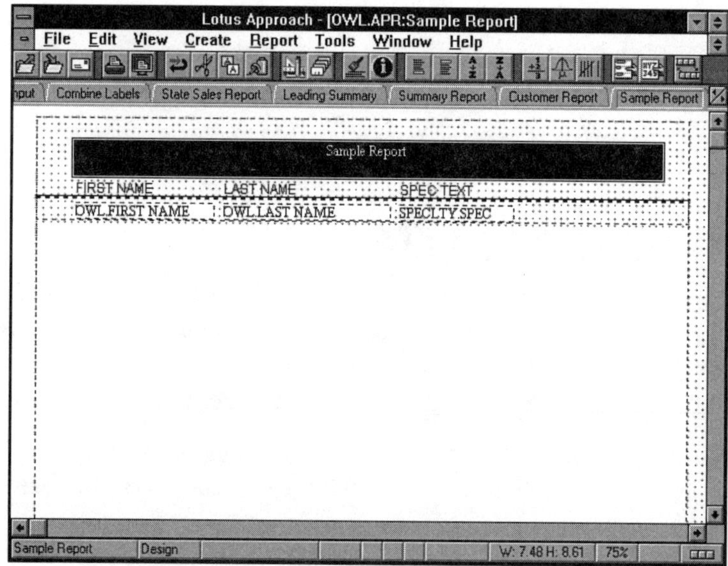

Fig. 12.17 The simple columnar report in Design mode with Show Data off.

To turn on Show Data, follow these steps:

1. Switch to Design mode, if you're not already there.

2. Open the **V**iew menu and choose S**h**ow Data or click the corresponding SmartIcon. When Show Data is on, the menu item will have a checkmark in front of it and the SmartIcon will have a slash through it.

The Show Data menu item and SmartIcons work as a toggle. To turn them off again, select the icon or menu item again.

When Show Data is on, the report looks much like it did in Preview mode in figure 12.16, except that the panels and objects can be selected and manipulated in Design mode.

Working in Columnar Mode

When a report is in Design mode with Show Data on, the fields in the report can act as a single column. This allows you to select, resize, and move data, and get instant feedback on what the final result will look like.

To work in Columnar mode, follow these steps:

1. Switch to Design mode, if you're not already there.

2. Open the **R**eport menu and choose Turn On **C**olumns or click the corresponding SmartIcon. When Column editing is on, the menu item will

have a checkmark in front of it, and the SmartIcon will have a slash through it.

Click a column to select it. The entire column is selected (see fig. 12.18). Once a column is selected you can:

- *Resize it.* Click the right edge of the column, and you get the resize cursor. Click and drag it to the left or right to make the column narrower or wider.
- *Move it.* Click in the column and drag the column to the left or right to reposition it.
- *Delete it.* Click in the column to select it, and then open the **E**dit menu and choose Cu**t**.

- *Copy it.* Click in the column to select it, and then open the **E**dit menu and choose **C**opy.

II

Forms, Queries, & Reports

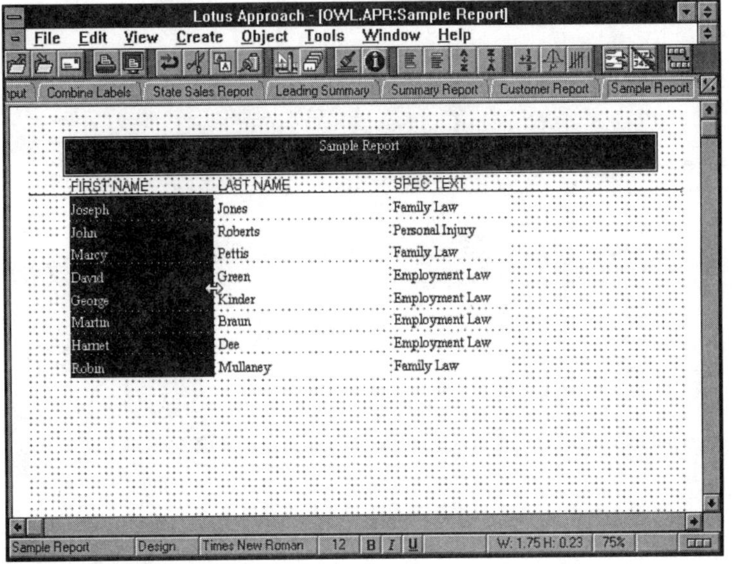

Fig. 12.18
Resizing the First Name field column with Show Data on.

When a column is modified, the other columns move as needed. If a column is moved over an existing column, the existing column and any columns to the right of it will move to the right. This prevents one column from being placed over another.

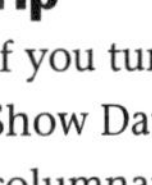

Tip
If you turn off Show Data, columnar editing is also turned off.

Adding a Field to the Report

The easiest way to add a field to a report is by dragging it from the Add Field dialog box.

To add a field, follow these steps:

1. Switch to Design mode.
2. Open the Add Field dialog box by clicking the SmartIcon, or open the **R**eport menu and choose **A**dd Field. When the Add Field dialog box is open, the menu item will have a checkmark in front of it and the SmartIcon will have a slash through it.
3. In the Add Field dialog box, select the database for which you want the field listing. In this case, the report might list the newsletter to which each customer subscribes. Select the Newsltr database.
4. Choose the field you want to add and drag it into the body of the report. Choose the NEWSLETTER field (see fig. 12.19). Click the mouse to drag it off Add Field and then release the mouse when it's positioned over the report.

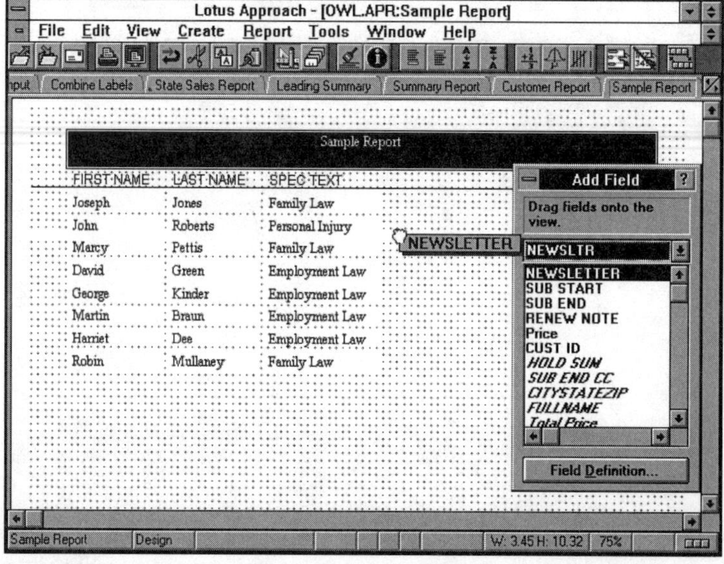

Fig. 12.19
You can drag and drop fields onto the report design.

Tip
Close the Add Field dialog box by double-clicking the control menu in the top-left corner.

You can also add the PRICE field from the Newsltr database to the report using the same method.

Using PowerClick Reporting

You can use PowerClick reporting to quickly add summary panels or summary calculations to a report. A trailing grand summary with an SSum calculated field can be added to a report in Design mode just by clicking the mouse.

To use PowerClick reporting to add a trailing grand summary, follow these steps:

1. Switch to Design mode.
2. Click the Trailing Summary SmartIcon. Since no fields are selected, this becomes a trailing grand summary. (If there had been a field selected, this would be a trailed summary grouped by that field value.)
3. Click a field to select it.
4. Click the Sum SmartIcon to sum the contents of the field.

Figure 12.20 shows the sample report with a PowerClick summary added to the PRICE field.

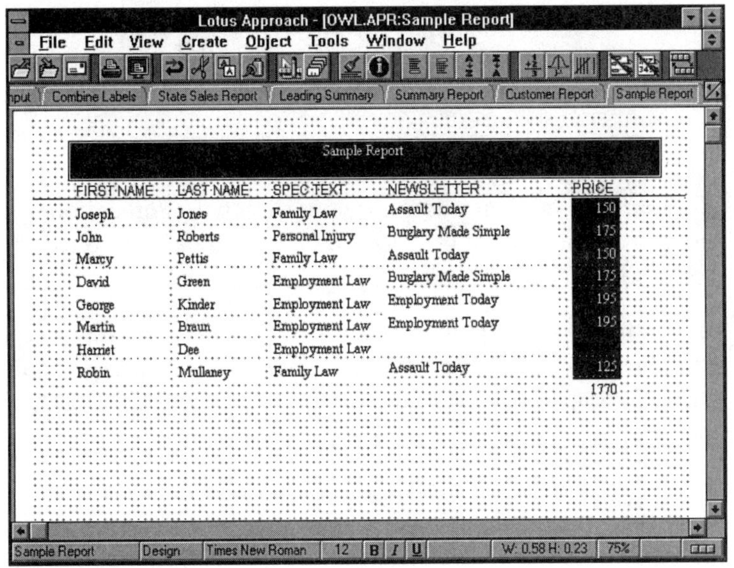

Fig. 12.20
Using PowerClick, the PRICE field has gained a trailing grand summary and a summary calculation.

With PowerClick reporting, you can add summary panels:

- The Leading Summary SmartIcon adds a leading grand summary panel if no fields are selected. If a field is selected, the summary panel groups over unique values in that field.

- The Trailing Summary SmartIcon adds a trailing grand summary panel if no fields are selected. If a field is selected the summary panel groups over unique values in that field.

PowerClick reporting can also be used to add summary calculations. These calculations are described in the "Using Summary Functions in a Calculated Field" section, later in this chapter.

Adding a Summary Panel

So far, you've seen how to add summary panels by using the Report Assistant and PowerClick reporting. You can also use the Summary dialog box to add a summary panel to a report (see fig. 12.21).

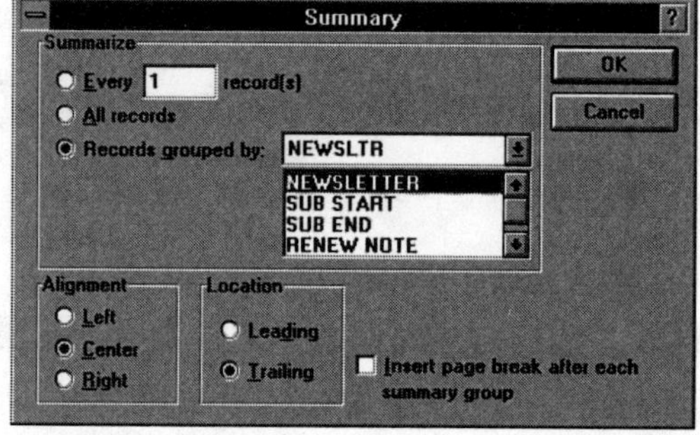

Fig. 12.21 The Summary dialog box shows the options available when adding a summary panel.

The Summary dialog box has these features:

- The Summarize section lists the various summarization options. A database can be summarized on **E**very specified number of records, **A**ll records, or Records **g**rouped by a specific field.
- The alignment—**L**eft, **C**enter, or **R**ight—refers to the panels' placement with respect to a body panel. Center is used by the Report Assistant and PowerClicking. Left places a summary panel to the left of a body panel; Right places a summary panel to the right.
- The location, Lea**d**ing or **T**railing, tells the panel to display either before or after the records it is grouping.

Tip
If you want leading and trailing panels on the same group, you need to define two panels.

Summary panels must be added in Design mode. To add a summary panel, open the **C**reate menu and choose **S**ummary. The Summary dialog box appears. Adjust the summary options and click OK. The new summary is now added to the report.

Modifying Summary Options

The modification options for a summary panel are the same as the options when adding a new panel. You can adjust the summarize options, the alignment, or the location.

To modify a panel, follow these steps:

1. Switch to Design mode.
2. Double-click a summary panel to display an Info Box, or click the Info Box SmartIcon.
3. Click the Basics panel in the Info Box to display the Summarize options (see fig. 12.22).

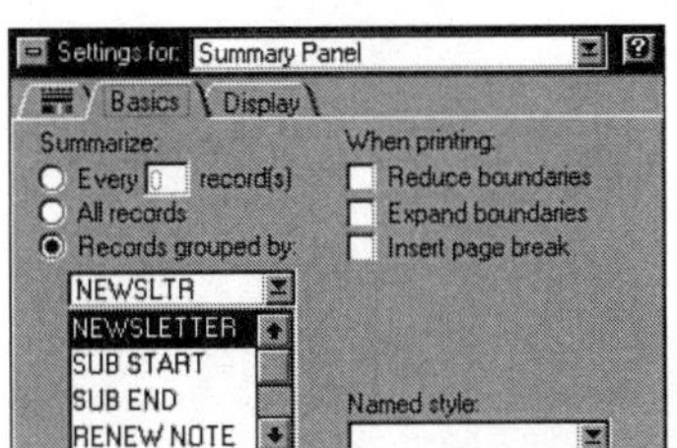

Fig. 12.22
The Info Box for a Summary panel.

4. Click the Display panel in the Info Box to set alignment and location options (see fig. 12.23).

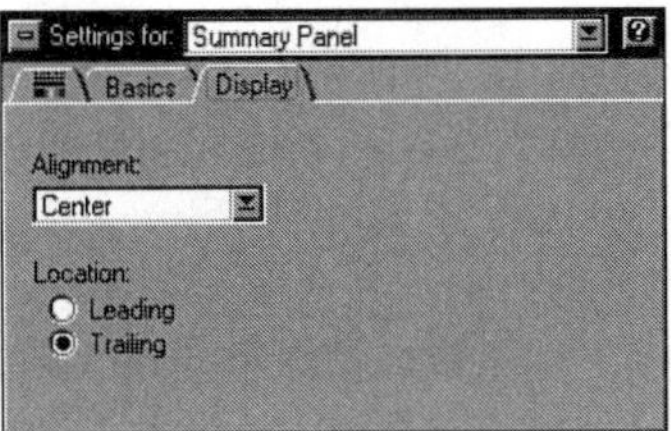

Fig. 12.23
Use the Display panel to adjust display options for a Summary panel in the Info Box.

If you're working in Show Data when you do the modifications, you'll see any changes immediately. If Show Data is off, you'll see alignment and location changes immediately but not the actual data. New grouping options won't be apparent until you go to Preview mode or turn on Show Data.

Showing Panel Labels

Panel labels, located on the left side of the report panel, let you know what the options are for that panel. For example, figure 12.24 shows the panel labels for the header, a trailing summary grouped by newsletter, and two occurrences of the body panel.

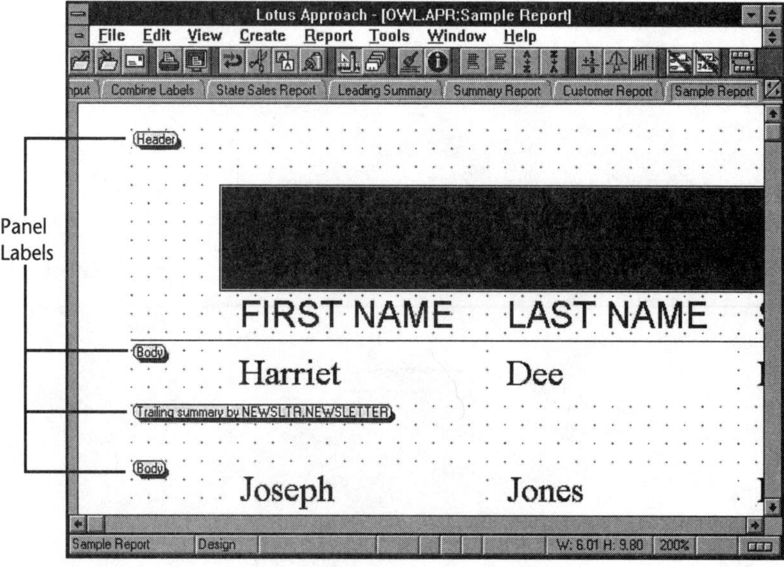

Fig. 12.24 Panel labels help clarify the various parts of your report's design.

Panel labels are controlled by both a menu item and a SmartIcon. To toggle the panel labels on or off, open the **V**iew menu and choose Show Panel **L**abels, or click the Panel Labels SmartIcon. When panel labels are on, the menu item has a checkmark in front of it, and there is a slash through the SmartIcon.

Using Summary Functions in a Calculated Field

The Report Assistant and PowerClick reporting are two methods that have been used to define and add summary calculations. Each assistant option and PowerClick SmartIcon can define a calculation using one of Approach's summary functions.

Tip
If Show Data is turned off, each panel is displayed only once. If Show Data is turned on, a panel label is displayed multiple times.

> **Caution**
>
> Calculated fields using summary functions or any calculated fields based on a summary calculated field will only display a value in Preview or Design mode with Show Data on. If your summary calculation is blank, check which mode you are in.

Defining Approach Summary Functions

Approach has eight different summary functions. The following functions can be defined or modified either by the Report Assistant, PowerClick reporting, or through the Field Definition dialog box. These functions are:

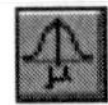

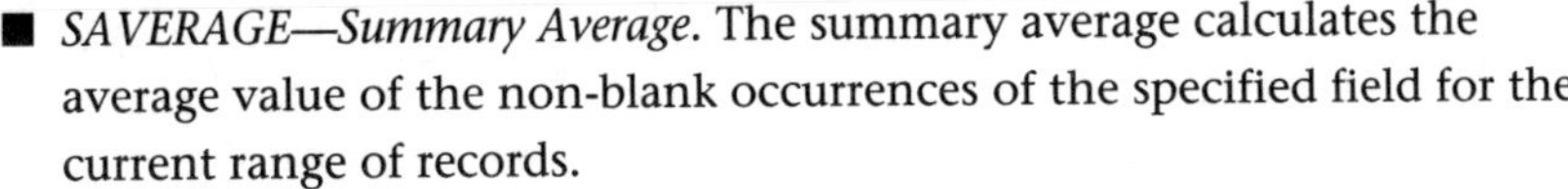

- *SAVERAGE—Summary Average.* The summary average calculates the average value of the non-blank occurrences of the specified field for the current range of records.

- *SCOUNT—Summary Count.* The summary count calculates the number of occurrences of all non-blank values in the specified field for the current range of records. Blank values are not counted.

- *SMAX—Summary Maximum.* The summary maximum function returns the largest value in a field for the current group of records. It can use numeric, date, or time values.

- *SMIN—Summary Minimum.* The summary minimum function returns the smallest value in the field for the current range of records. It can use numeric, date, or time values.

- *SNPV—Summary Net Present Value.* The summary net present value function needs two parameters. The first is a field, the second is a constant: SNPV(Field, .05). The SNPV returns the net present value of an investment based on a series of yearly cash flows (contained in the field) and a discount rate (the constant value). The discount rate is usually stated as a percentage (8 percent) but is entered into the formula as a decimal number (.08). The periodic cash flows can be positive (income) or negative (investment). The value in the field in the first record in the database represents the investment made in the first year. The value in the field in subsequent records represents the investment or income for subsequent years (the second record is for year 2, the third record is for year 3, and so on).

- *SSTD—Summary Standard Deviation.* The summary standard deviation function has a single parameter that must be numeric. It returns the standard deviation of the values in the specified field for the current range of records. The standard deviation is a measure of how widely dispersed the values are from the average value.

- *SSUM—Summary Sum.* The summary sum function has a single parameter that must be a field containing a numeric value. It returns the sum of all the values in the specified field for the current range of records.

- *SVAR—Summary Variance.* The summary variance function has a single parameter that must be a field containing a numeric value. It returns the variance of the values in the specified field for the current range of records.

Setting Summary Options

When a summary calculation is added to a summary panel through the Report Assistant or through PowerClicking, it is defined to evaluate where placed. This means that the summary will evaluate the function over the current summary grouping.

For example, if a summary calculation is calculating the number of customers and is placed into a summary panel that's grouping by state, the calculated field will give the total number of customers for each state that displays in the report. If the calculation is also placed into a trailing grand summary, the field displayed in that panel will show the total number of customers in the database.

You can also define a summary field to evaluate over a defined report panel. This is done using the Define Summary panel in the Field Definition dialog box's options (see fig. 12.25). The panel you use needs to be from the same report that the field will be used in, or the field won't evaluate and will remain blank.

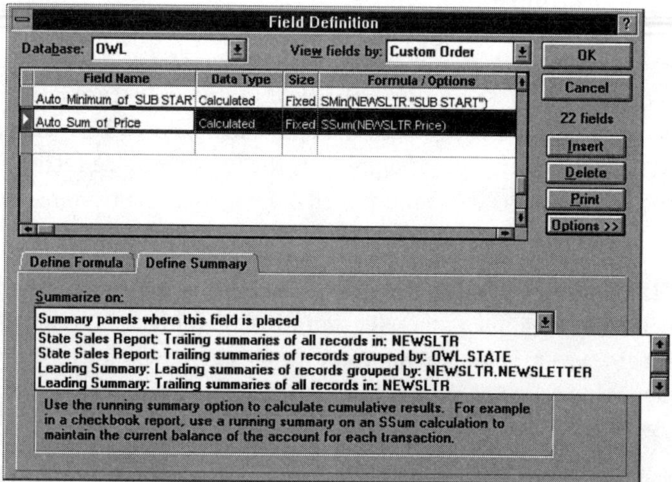

Fig. 12.25
A summary calculation can be defined as where it is placed or attached to a specific summary panel.

To set or modify a summary calculation's options:

1. Open the **C**reate menu and choose Field **D**efinition.

2. Click the field name to select it. The fields defined automatically will have names like AUTO SUM OF PRICE or AUTO COUNT OF CUSTOMER.

3. Click the Options button.

4. Click the Define Summary tab to bring that option panel to the front.

5. Select the new setting from the **S**ummarize On list. This list includes defaults where the field is placed, summarized over each individual database, and summarized over all databases. It also has a selection for each summary panel defined in a report.

A summary that's defined over a certain range can be used within summary panels that have a different grouping than the one for which the calculation is defined. For example, you might define a summary calculation as the SSum as sales for a company, summarized over a report's trailing grand summary. Then, within a regional summary, you can display the total of sales for that region with a Where Placed SSum of Sales. The same panel can also have the total sales company-wide as a comparison figure. If the company sales weren't defined as over the grand summary grouping, it would display the same value as the regional summary, since the two are summarizing the same field. By defining the company's sales over a specific group, it can be used anywhere within the report.

Defining a Running Summary

You can use a summary calculation based on a certain panel because the calculation can be used as a running summary. A running total or running count, for example, shows an updated value for each detail record in a report. Let's look at two examples of how a running total and a running count might be used.

A running total can be used to show cumulative sales figures in a region. The regional sales report contains the sales of the current sales representative in each record. A running total showing the sales of the current representative summed with each representative from the region listed in the previous records can also appear in each record.

A running count can be used to number each record in a report. The calculation with the summary count function appears in each record. As long as the field for which the running count is defined contains only non-blank values, each record has a new number.

The calculated field used for the running summary must be summarized over a set report panel. The running summary can't be defined as where placed in the Field Definition dialog box's summary options. If the summary panel is a grand summary, the running summary will evaluate its formula over every detail record in the report. If the summary panel is a grouping on a field, the running summary will evaluate for each record within a group and begin again for a new grouping.

For example, let's say Owl Publishing wants to add a count of all customers to a report:

1. The running summary must be added in Design mode.

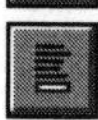

2. If there's no trailing grand summary in the current report, click the Trailing Summary SmartIcon to add one. If a field is selected when the icon is clicked, use the Info Box to change the grouped summary to a grand summary.

3. Select a field that will be present in every record, such as CUSTOMER ID or LAST NAME field.

4. Open the Info Box and select the newly added SCOUNT field to see what it's been named.
5. Open the **C**reate menu and choose Field **D**efinition.
6. Select the field that was added to be a running summary.
7. Click the Options button.
8. Select the Define Summary tab in the Field Definition dialog box.
9. In the **S**ummarize On list, choose the trailing grand summary for the current report. Also, click the Make Calculation a **R**unning Summary checkbox (see fig. 12.26).
10. Click OK to close the Field Definition dialog box.
11. Place the RUNNING COUNT field into the body panel in the report.

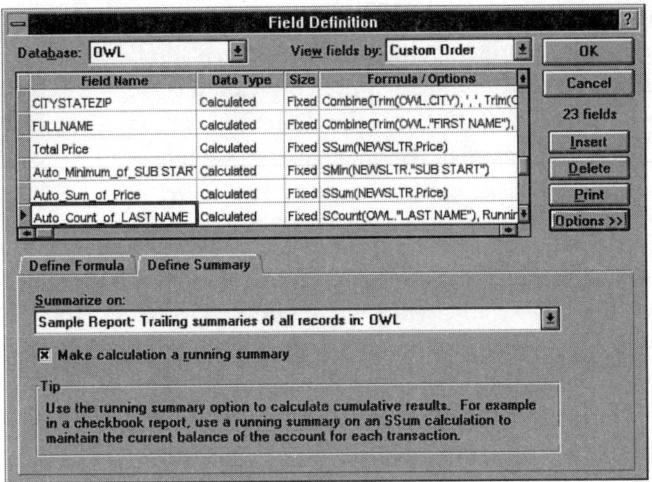

Fig. 12.26
An SCount calculation can number the records in a customer report.

12. View the results in Design or Preview mode (see fig. 12.27). As a summary calculation, the running total won't display in Browse mode.

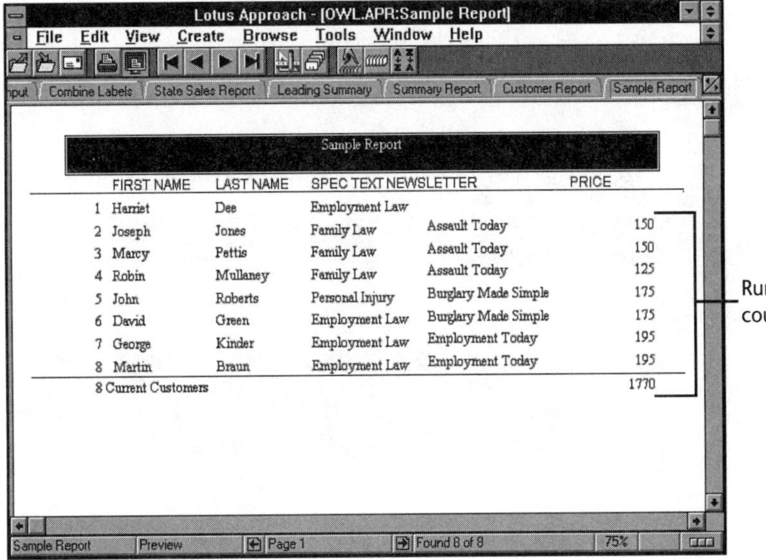

Fig. 12.27
The result is a running customer count on a report.

Reordering Summary Panels

Summary panels need to follow a certain order to display the groupings properly. In a leading summary, the largest group should be the top panel. In a trailing summary, the largest group should be the bottom panel.

For example, if your report has a leading group by region, and within that group has a subgrouping by state, the region panel should be above the state panel. A leading grand summary, if present, should be above both panels. If the order is not set properly, the report groupings will be incorrect. Instead of having state as a subgroup of region, region might appear as a subgroup of state—the opposite of the grouping you've tried to define.

To change the order of summary panels, click the panel and drag it up or down. You can change the order easily when Show Data is turned off. Also, this change is relative to the set location, leading, or trailing. If the actual location needs to be changed from leading to trailing, for example, it is done through the Info Box.

Modifying Panel and Object Attributes

Report panels and objects are like objects in a form or other view. They have attributes that can be set through the Info Box. For example, you can select a panel and add a border around it or fill it with a color using the lines and colors tab.

You can resize a panel border by clicking it and dragging the resize cursor up or down. A border with a light gray color can be resized; borders with a darker gray can't be. Also, you'll only get the resize cursor on a border that can be resized (see fig. 12.28).

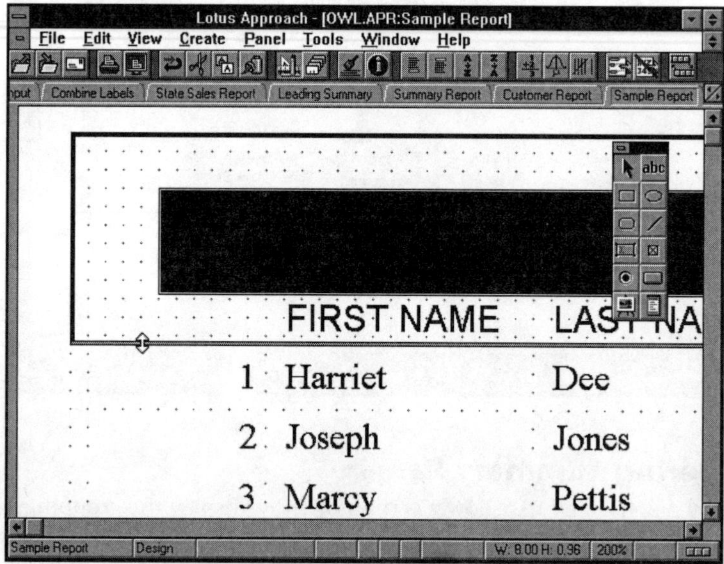

Fig. 12.28
Resizing a report header.

Similarly, you can modify or resize fields within a report panel. Make sure the field is fully contained within the panel, though, or it will not display as expected. If necessary, a panel can always be resized to accommodate a larger field.

You can add features such as graphic objects, circles, and squares to any panel, just like you would add them to a form. You can also add pictures to a report panel using the Clipboard or the Paste From File dialog box.

Tip
The more objects you add to a report, the longer the report will take to print.

Removing a Summary Panel

A summary panel can be removed by clicking the panel to select it and clicking the Delete key on the keyboard. Objects within the panel are also deleted from the view, but not necessarily from the Approach file. For example, you can add a summary panel with a grouping by state, and include an SCount calculation. If you select that panel and delete it, the panel and the calculation field object are removed from the view. The defined calculation remains in the Approach file and can be deleted using the Field Definition dialog box if it's not needed.

Caution

Deleting a summary panel can't be undone. When you choose to delete a panel, make sure it is the correct one. If you accidentally delete a panel that would be difficult to re-create, you can close the Approach file without saving and reopen it to return to your most recently saved version. This recovery option works best when you save your file often.

Using Form Letters

A *form letter* is a document that combines text with the fields in a database. The text is the same in every letter, but the values in the fields change because each form letter is generated using the fields in a different record. The letters are *personalized* by including unique information in the letter. A form letter to customers whose subscriptions are about to expire, for example, can include the subscriber's name, address, and the name of the expiring newsletter.

Approach can help you generate form letters using the fields in your database. An Approach form letter consists of blocks of text and database fields. You can create and edit text, add and rearrange fields, and change the style of text and fields. You can also change the format of fields. Before you print the form letters, you can perform a find to limit the form letters to just the found set of records.

Note

Unlike other Approach views, you can't modify the contents of fields inserted into text blocks on a form letter. However, you can insert fields into a form letter outside of a text block that can be modified.

Creating a Form Letter

To create a form letter, follow these steps:

1. Open the **C**reate menu and choose Form **L**etter, or click the Create Form Letter SmartIcon. The Form Letter Assistant opens to the Layout tab (see fig. 12.29).

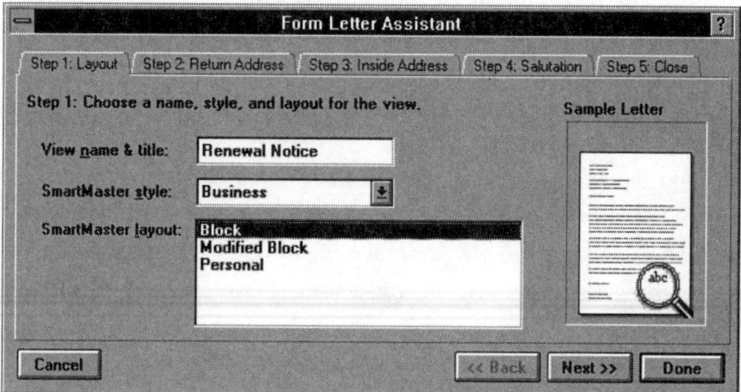

Fig. 12.29
The Form Letter Assistant offers several letter and layout styles.

2. Type the name of the form letter into the View **N**ame & Title text box.
3. Select the font style from SmartMaster **S**tyle list.
4. Select the letter style from the SmartMaster **L**ayout list.
5. Click the Next button to continue to the second tab, Return Address (see fig. 12.30).
6. Enter the return address or select **N**one. After you've defined a form letter, the return address section remains for the next time you use the Form Letter Assistant and can be modified as needed.

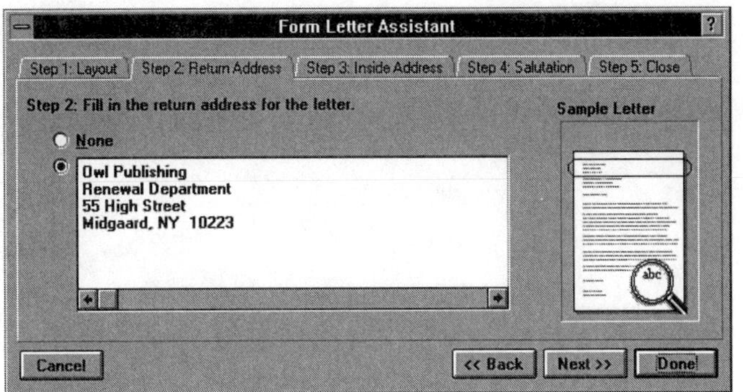

Fig. 12.30
The return address setting is saved for future form letters.

7. Click the Next button for the third tab, Inside Address (see fig. 12.31).

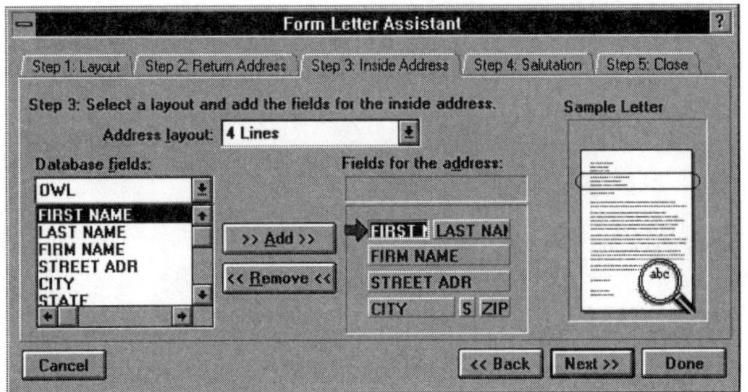

Fig. 12.31
Select database fields to use for the return address.

8. Adjust the number of lines for the address in the Address **L**ayout section. The Fields For the A**d**dress section shows where it expects fields to be placed.

9. Select a field and click **A**dd to move the fields from the Database **F**ields list box to the Fields For the A**d**dress box. A red arrow moves next to the place holder that will be used for the field. If you keep clicking **A**dd, the fields from the list box will be added in the order entered.

10. Repeat step 9 to add fields to the form letter from other databases.

11. Click the Next button to move to the Salutation panel (see fig. 12.32).

12. Choose the one or two fields to display in the salutation. Select **N**one to skip a field. You can also customize the greeting and the punctuation, or select **N**one to leave this section blank.

    Once you've created a form letter, the text entered for the salutation will remain until you change it.

Tip
If you need to remove a field from the Fields For the A**d**dress box, select the field and choose **R**emove.

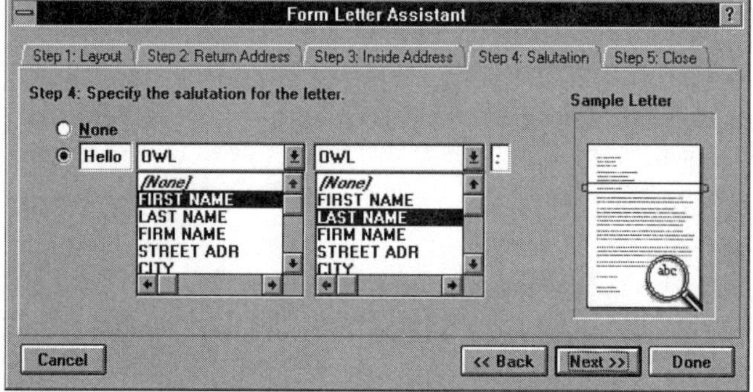

Fig. 12.32
Customize your greeting in the Salutation panel.

13. Click the Next button to continue to the last panel, Close (see fig. 12.33).

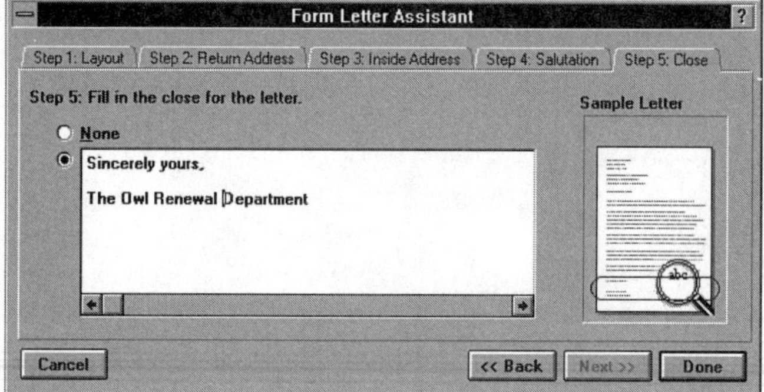

Fig. 12.33
Personalize the close of your letter.

14. In the Close panel, you can type a personalized close, or choose **N**one to leave it blank. The close that you use is available for future form letters until you modify it.

15. Click Done to create the form letter.

The new form letter appears. The fields you identified in the Create Form Letter dialog box appear on the form letter in insertion brackets (<< >>), as shown in figure 12.34.

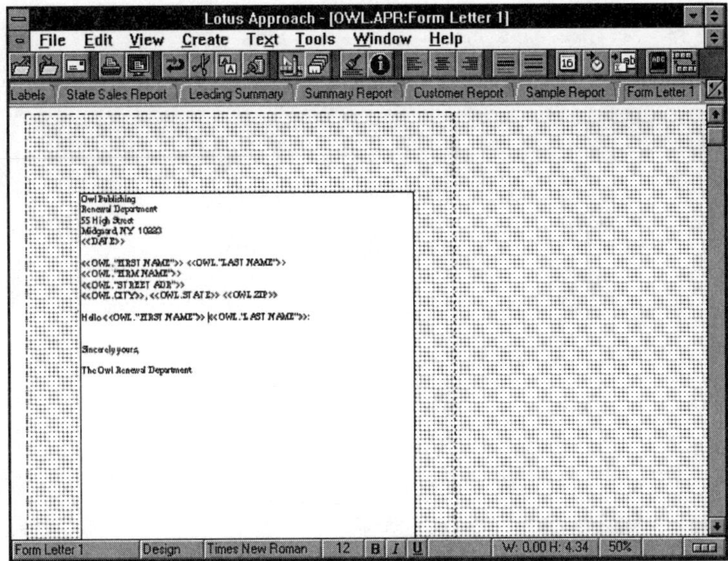

Fig. 12.34
A newly created form letter in Design mode.

Creating Text in a Text Block

The newly created form letter consists of a single text block containing the fields that you identified in the Create Form Letter dialog box. The text block fills the entire form letter page. You can add and change text in this text block.

For example, you can add body text to the letter that was created for Owl Publishing:

1. The Text tool is selected immediately after creating the form letter. If it's not still active, select it from the Drawing Tools palette. Open the **C**reate menu and choose Dr**a**wing, and then select **T**ext.

2. Click the form letter below the greeting.

3. Type in the text, for example:

   "We're sorry to inform you that your Owl Publishing newsletter subscription is almost expired. Please take a moment to renew your subscription."

4. View the letter in Browse or Preview mode to see how it will look when printed (see fig. 12.35).

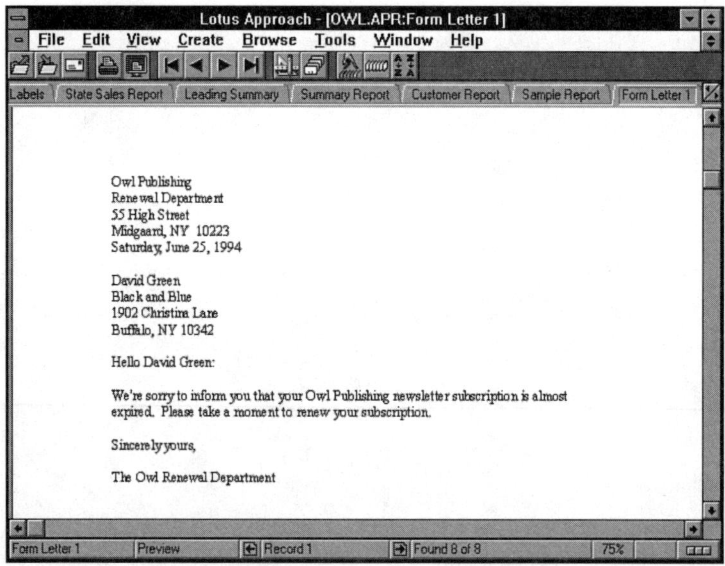

Fig. 12.35
Your personalized form letter, ready for printing.

Editing a Form Letter

The form letter is no different than any other Approach text block. The text attributes can be set with the Info Box, either by selecting the entire block for a global change, or by selecting text within the block to change a particular section of the text.

To insert new fields into the text block, follow these steps:

1. Choose the Text SmartIcon. Click in the form letter's text block where you want to add the new field.

2. Open the Te**x**t menu and choose I**n**sert, and then choose **F**ield.

3. Choose the field from the Insert Field dialog box. If necessary, change the database from the drop-down list. In this example, you might add the SUB END field to show the customer exactly when the subscription ends.

The field is inserted as a text object, like the other fields in the form letter, so it can't be used like a standard field object.

You can cut and paste text into the text block from elsewhere in the block or from another application, and add formatting such as italics or bold to individual words or letters in the text block. In addition, you can use logos or other graphics to modify form letters. Since these objects are not text, they are placed on the form letter outside of the main text block.

Note

A form letter can be only a single page long. Consider this when deciding what field information you want to insert into your form letter.

Printing the Form Letters

After you finish setting up your form letter, you will want to print it. Approach prints one copy of the form letter for each current record. If you perform a find before printing the form letters, only the records in the found set are used to print the form letters.

To print the form letters, follow these steps:

1. Switch to **B**rowse mode.

2. Choose Select the Form Letter from the list of forms and reports in the status bar or by its view tab.
3. If you wish, use a Field On Another View to perform a find to locate the records for which you want to print the form letter.
4. Open the **F**ile menu and choose **P**rint or select the Print SmartIcon.

5. Click OK to print the form letters.

From Here...

In this chapter, you learned how reports can give you greater control of both data and display attributes than any other type of Approach view. You learned how to create and modify reports using Report Assistants and PowerClicking, and by adjusting panel and calculated field options.

You also learned that a form letter—while not nearly as complex in its construction as a report—is a specialized way to merge text and field information. You can use form letters to cover your basic mailing needs in Approach, rather than moving your data to a Word Processor application.

For a quick way to work with or analyze the data in a database, consider using a worksheet or crosstab, or even a chart. To find out more, refer to the following chapters in this book:

- Chapter 14, "Using Worksheets and Crosstabs," describes how to use worksheets and crosstabs to display and analyze data.

- Chapter 15, "Creating Charts," shows you how Approach data can be charted from either the Chart Assistant or directly from a crosstab. Charts can be placed into report panels for a visual analysis of a field in the database.

Chapter 13

Automating Your Work

The macro features of Approach help simplify your database work by automating routine activities. A *macro* is a series of operations that are saved by Approach under a macro name that you assign. When you want to perform those operations, you simply run that macro.

Note

Approach macros are quite different from those you may have used before. Many other programs use the term *macro* to refer to a series of keystrokes that you record and play back whenever you want. By contrast, you create an Approach macro by selecting actions in a special dialog box—not by recording keystrokes.

In this chapter, you learn how to:

- Create and use macros
- Assign commands to a macro
- Run a macro
- Edit or delete an existing macro
- Assign a macro to a button or object
- Attach macros to fields and views

Almost any series of operations you can perform yourself in Approach can be assisted or completely automated by a macro—or by a set of macros that you chain together. This means that you can use macros for a wide variety of operations. For example, you can use macros to create a menu-driven application that rivals the sort of product you would expect from a professional programmer.

After you create a macro, either you or anyone else can perform the operations embodied in the macro—no matter how complex—simply by running it. You can run a macro in any of the following ways:

- Make a menu selection
- Use a function key
- Click a special command button—or a graphics or text object—that you add to a form or report design
- Start up or exit Approach
- Enter or exit a particular view
- Tab into or out of a particular field
- Change the value of a particular field

Creating a Macro

To help introduce the concept of working with macros, you will create a simple macro whose only purpose is to switch from the current view to another one. For example, if your Approach file contains 25 different views, you could use a macro to switch to the view named "Worksheet 1."

Note

When you create a new macro, Approach stores it as part of the current Approach file.

To create a new macro, follow these steps:

1. Open the Approach file in which you want to create the macro.
2. Switch to Browse, Define, or Preview mode. (You can't define a macro in Find mode.)
3. Open the **T**ools menu and choose **M**acros. You'll see a dialog box similar to the one shown in figure 13.1.

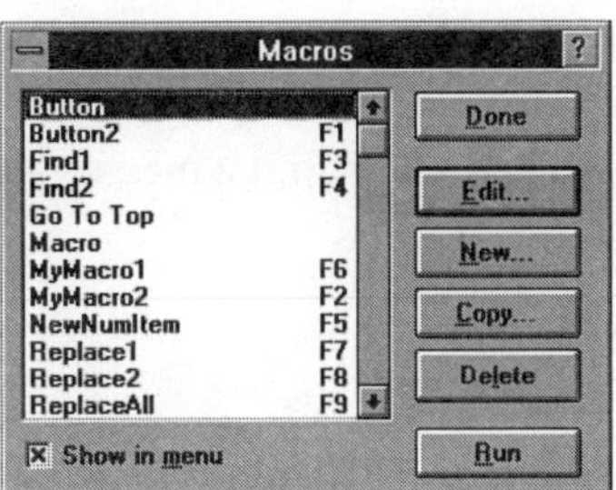

Fig. 13.1
Use the Macros dialog box to begin defining a new macro.

4. Click the **N**ew button, and the dialog box shown in figure 13.2 appears. You'll use this box to define the entire macro.

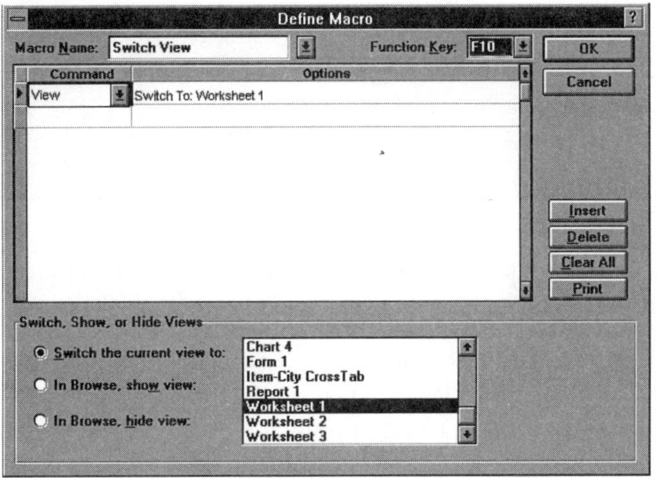

Fig. 13.2
Start defining your macro from the Define Macro dialog box.

5. In the top-left edit box labeled Macro **N**ame, enter a unique name for the new macro. This can be any set of up to 24 characters, including spaces and special characters.

6. To assign a function key to this macro, select it in the drop-down list box labeled Function **K**ey. Now you can begin to create the command for this new macro.

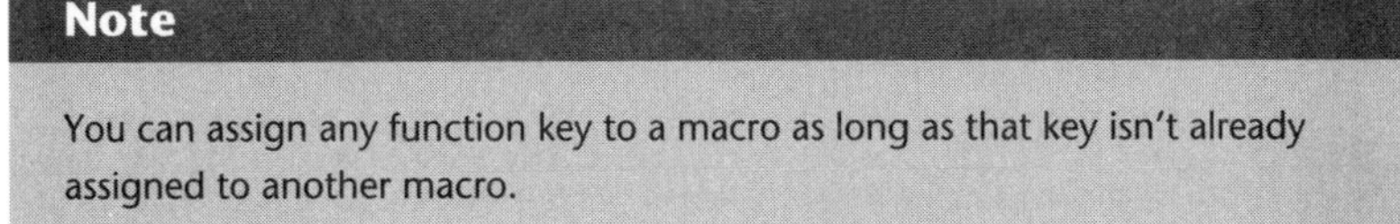
Note

You can assign any function key to a macro as long as that key isn't already assigned to another macro.

Tip
In the Define Macro dialog box, you can pull down the Macro Name list box to see what other macros have already been defined.

7. Click the down-arrow in the column labeled Command. The list that appears extends across most of the dialog box and shows all the possible commands you can use within a macro (see fig. 13.3).

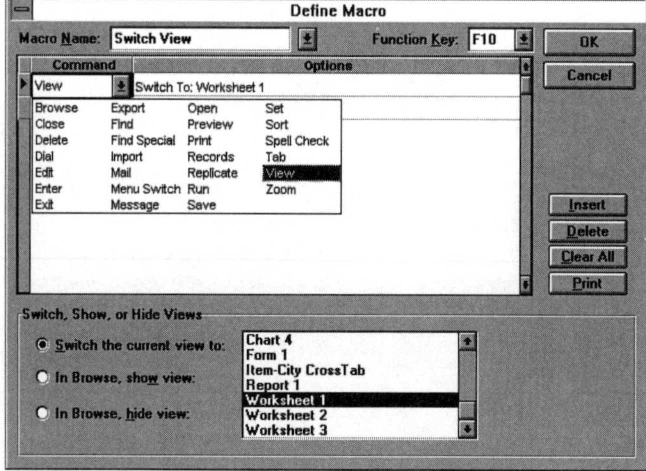

Fig. 13.3
Select a command to insert into the macro.

8. Click the command View (this command was already selected by default, but the practice will do you good).

9. In the lower part of the dialog box, click the radio button labeled **S**witch the Current View To, then choose the view labeled "Worksheet 1." If this view doesn't exist in your current file, choose one of your favorites from the list. Note that the option you choose appears in the upper part of the dialog box in the right-hand column labeled Options.

10. To save the new macro, click OK and then click **D**one.

Your new macro consists of the single command you selected, which we can refer to as "View, Switch to: Form 1." Each time you run the macro, this single command will be executed.

Now let's practice running this macro. Remember, the idea is that each time you run it, the macro will switch to the view you selected in step 9 above.

Here's how to run your macro:

1. To begin, switch to a view other than the one you selected in the macro above.

2. Make sure that you're in either Preview or Browse mode. (You can't run a macro when Approach is in either Design or Find mode.)

3. Open the **T**ools menu and choose **R**un Macro.

4. When the list of current macros appears, choose the one you just created. The macro will run, switching to the new view.

Note

Each macro is saved as part of an Approach file, which you must save after creating a new macro. If you can't find a previously recorded macro, you probably didn't save the corresponding Approach file after creating the macro, or you're in the wrong Approach file.

Working with Macros

The preceding example describes the basic steps for creating a new macro. However, this simple macro consists of only a single operation—switching to a particular view. This is fine as a simple practice example, but in reality you can create macros consisting of many different operations.

This section describes how to create macros that consist of many different commands. It will also describe how to edit and save the macros you create.

Creating a New Macro

To begin creating a new macro, display the Define Macro dialog box by opening the **T**ools menu, choosing **M**acros, and then choosing **N**ew. Enter a unique name for the macro in the upper-left edit box. You can optionally select a function key for the macro in the upper-right list box. This function key will then be reserved so that whenever you press it, the macro will run.

Entering Commands

You build a macro by selecting the commands for it. When you choose a new command, it becomes part of the list on the upper-left part of the Define Macro dialog box in the column labeled Command. The order in which the commands appear on-screen (top to bottom) is the order in which they will execute each time you run the macro. For example, the macro shown in figure 13.4 consists of the following three commands:

Records, First

View, Switch To: Worksheet 1

Zoom, In

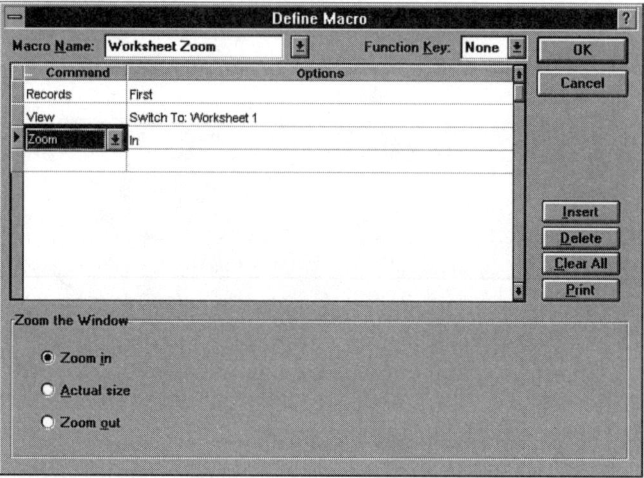

Fig. 13.4 This macro consists of three commands.

You can insert each new command anywhere in the current list of commands—at the bottom, in the middle, or at the top. You can order the commands any way you want, provided they make sense. For example, you could create a macro consisting of the following two commands, but they don't make any sense because you can't move past the last record in a database file:

Records, Last Record. This command moves Approach to the last record in the current database file.

Records, Next Record. This command moves Approach to the next record in the database file.

To enter a new command, follow these steps:

1. In the column labeled Command, select where you want to insert the new command:

   To enter a command at the bottom of the current command list, click the first blank line below the last command. For example, in figure 13.4 you would click immediately below the command Zoom, In.

   To enter a new command before an existing one, click on that existing command, click the **I**nsert button, and then click the new blank space that's highlighted.

2. Click the pull-down arrow that appears, and you'll see the entire list of available commands. A description of each of the available commands is listed later in this chapter.

3. Click the command you want to insert.

4. If there are any options associated with this command, they will appear at the bottom of the dialog box. Select the one you want for the command. For instance, in figure 13.4 the Zoom **I**n option is selected.

Repositioning and Deleting Commands

As you build a new macro, you may find errors as you recheck your work. To correct them, you can do the following:

- Edit an existing command, either by selecting new options for it or by replacing it with another command
- Delete a command
- Rearrange the order in which the commands appear

These are important features because they allow you to correct errors before they become big problems.

To edit an existing command, follow these steps:

1. Click anywhere on the line displaying that command.

2. Change the options at the bottom of the dialog box.

3. To replace the command with another one, click it in the Command column, pull down the list of commands, select the new command, and then select its options.

To move a command from one location in the command list to another, follow these steps:

1. Click the row marker at the far-left end of the command you want to move, so that the entire line is highlighted (see fig. 13.5).

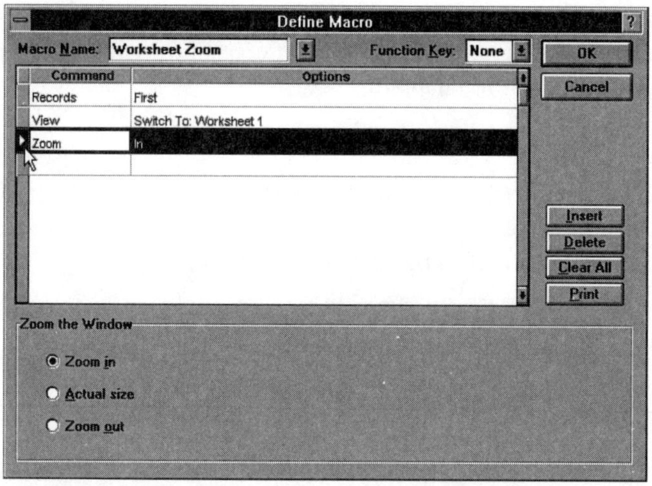

Fig. 13.5
To move a command, first click its row marker.

2. Holding down the mouse button, drag the row marker up or down to where you want to reposition it. Notice the heavy guideline that appears (see fig. 13.6). This line indicates the upper boundary of the new position for the command.

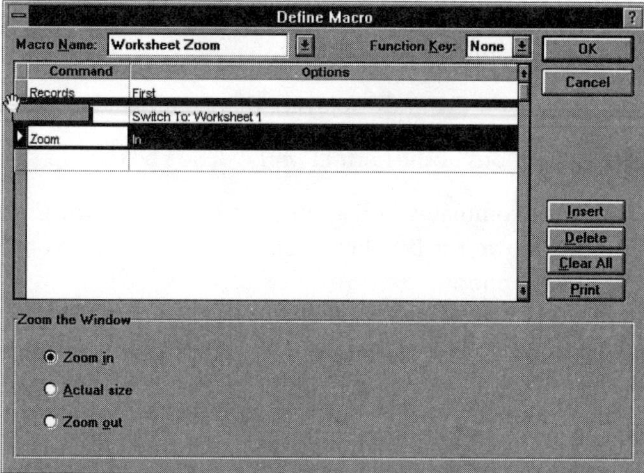

Fig. 13.6
Reposition a command by dragging it.

3. When the command is where you want it, release the mouse button.

If you need to delete a command, follow these steps:

1. Click the row marker for the command you want to delete, so that the entire line becomes highlighted, or click anywhere in that row. You can

delete a macro step by clicking anywhere in the line and then clicking the Delete button.

2. Click the Delete button.

Note

If you accidentally delete a command, you can recover—provided you don't mind losing all of your unsaved current work—by choosing the Cancel button. Approach then gives you the opportunity to undo all of your current changes to the macro.

Editing and Deleting an Existing Macro

You can edit an existing macro by repositioning, modifying, and deleting existing commands, and by adding new ones. These operations are identical to those described in the preceding sections.

To edit a macro, you first select it from the list of current macros, then make your changes:

1. Open the **T**ools menu and choose **M**acros.
2. When the list of macros appears, double-click the name of the macro you want to edit. Alternatively, you can click the macro name and then click the **E**dit button. The Define Macro dialog box appears.
3. Make whatever changes to the macro you want, using the techniques described in the preceding sections.
4. To save your changes, click the OK button.

You can easily delete a macro that is no longer needed by following these steps:

1. Open the **T**ools menu and choose **M**acros.
2. Click the name of the macro.
3. Click the Delete button.
4. When Approach asks you to confirm the deletion, choose **Y**es (unless you suddenly change your mind, in which case you should choose **N**o).

Saving Your Macros

Each macro you edit or create is part of the Approach file that's currently open. When you save the Approach file, the macros you have edited or created are also saved.

From another point of view, if you create a new macro and then later exit the Approach file without saving it, your macro will be lost.

Note

Each macro is restricted to the file in which you created it. Consequently, if you create a macro for file A, you can't use it directly with file B. Instead, you'll have to open file B and then recreate the macro from scratch.

The Available Macro Commands

When building new macros, you can choose from 27 different major types of macro commands. We refer to these as "major" commands because many of them have several options from which to choose. A few commands offer you virtually unlimited choices. Consequently, you have at your disposal a gigantic variety of different commands, offering endless possibilities for automating your work.

This section lists the 27 major types of commands, along with a brief description of each one. They are listed in the order in which they appear in the Define Macro dialog box, except for the most commonly used commands, which are listed first.

Set

This command sets the value of the field you specify to a particular value which you also specify. Using this command together with Approach's built-in IF function allows you to selectively set field values under specific conditions.

Run

This powerful command runs a macro you specify. You can include If/Else conditions, so that the macro you choose runs only if certain conditions exist. You can also use the Run command to run the current macro again—starting from the top. This feature provides the mechanism for creating looping macros. This command can also run another macro, and then return to the original macro and continue running the original macro.

View

View switches to the view you choose in the current Approach file. This could be a form, a worksheet, or any other type of view.

Records

This versatile command has several options. You can use it to go to a particular record in the current Approach file, such as the first record, last, next, and so on. Alternatively, you can set up this command to create a new record, hide a record, or duplicate an existing record.

Find

Find performs a preset find operation using the find options you specify when creating the macro. Alternatively, you can set up this command to pause the macro when it runs, displaying the Find screen for user input. Other command options include Find Again, Show All Records, Refresh the Found Set, and Run a Macro if No Records are Found.

Browse

Browse switches from the current view mode to Browse mode. This command is of limited value because you can use a macro to switch to Browse only from Preview mode.

Note

Remember that you can't run a macro from either Find or Design mode.

Close

This command closes the current Approach file. If you've made any changes since the last time you saved the file, Approach asks you if you want to save them now.

Delete

This powerful—but extremely dangerous—command gives you the option of deleting either the current record, the current found set, or a particular file. To make the command even more potentially lethal, you can turn off Approach's standard dialog box that warns you of an impending deletion.

Caution

Be very careful when using the Delete command. If you use the Delete command incorrectly, you can wipe out part or all of an Approach database.

Dial

This command dials the telephone number contained in the field you specify, and for the record that is current when the macro runs. Approach uses whatever dial-up settings are currently in effect.

> **Note**
>
> For information on customizing the autodialer feature of Approach, see Chapter 17.

Edit

Using the Edit command, you can perform any of the following:

- Remove the current selection (for example, whatever you have currently highlighted on the screen) and copy it to the Windows Clipboard. This is equivalent to opening the **E**dit menu and choosing Cu**t**.
- Copy the current selection to the Clipboard (equivalent to opening the **E**dit menu and choosing **C**opy).
- Paste the Clipboard contents to the current position of the text cursor (equivalent to opening the **E**dit menu and choosing **P**aste).
- Select the entire database file. This option is equivalent to opening the **E**dit menu and choosing Select **A**ll, and it is effective only when a worksheet is displayed in Browse mode.
- Display the Paste Special dialog box. If this option is in effect, the macro—when it runs—pauses when the Paste Special dialog box is displayed, so that you can make your selection there.

Enter

Enter is equivalent to either pressing the Enter key or clicking the Enter icon. Its main use is to accept the record currently being entered or edited.

Exit

This command exits from Approach, unlike the Close command which just closes the currently opened Approach file. If you have made any changes since the last save, Approach asks you if you wish to save them.

Export

Export automatically performs an export operation, using the set of options you select when creating the macro. Alternatively, you can set up this command to pause the macro when it runs, displaying the Export Data dialog box for user input.

Find Special

This command performs a Find Special operation, using the options you select when creating the macro. Alternatively, you can set up Find Special to pause the macro when it runs, displaying the Find Special dialog box for user input. You can also set the command to run a particular macro in the event that the Find Special operation doesn't locate any records.

Import

Import performs an import operation, using the options you select when creating the macro. Alternatively, you can set the command to pause the macro when it runs, displaying the Import Data dialog box for user input.

Mail

Mail displays the Send Mail dialog box, pausing the macro for user input. Alternatively, you can set this command to send mail automatically, using the Send Mail options you select when creating the macro.

Menu Switch

This command switches to another menu, which you specify when creating the macro.

Message

Message displays a dialog box with the message you set up as part of the command.

Open

This command option opens a file, which you select when creating the macro. Alternatively, you can use this command to pause the macro when it runs, displaying the File Open dialog box for user input.

Preview

This command switches to Preview mode.

Print

Print performs a print operation when the macro runs, using the print options you select when creating the macro. Alternatively, you can set the command to pause the macro when it runs, displaying the Print dialog box for user input.

Replicate

This command option replicates a Notes database, using the options you establish when creating the macro. Alternatively, you can use the command to pause the macro when it runs, displaying the Replicate dialog box for user input.

Save

This command saves the current Approach file. Or, you can set the command to pause the macro when it runs, displaying the Save As dialog box for user input.

Sort

Sort performs a sort operation, using the options you select when creating the macro. Or, you can use this command to pause the macro when it runs, displaying the Sort dialog box for user input.

Spell

Spell opens the Spell Check dialog box, pausing the macro for user input.

Tab

This command tabs the cursor to a specific tab number. When creating the macro, you must specify the tab number to go to.

Zoom

Zoom either zooms in, zooms out, or switches the magnification to the actual size.

Running Macros

After you have created a macro, you can set it up to run in several different ways:

- Press the function key—if any—that you have assigned to the macro.
- Open the **T**ools menu and choose **R**un Macro, then select the macro from the list that is displayed.
- Click the macro name from the Macros dialog box and then click the **R**un button.
- Click a button or other object to which you assigned a macro.

Note

If your macro fails to run, make sure you're not in either Design or Find mode, because no macros will ever run there. If your macro runs incorrectly, you'll have to try tracking down the problem—perhaps on a step-by-step basis. Try deleting every command in the macro except the first one, then run it. If it does what you expect, add another command and run the macro again until you find the troublesome command(s).

You can also have a macro run automatically under any of the following circumstances:

- Opening or closing a particular Approach file
- Tabbing into or out of a specific field
- Changing the value in a specific field
- Switching into or out of a particular view

Open and Close Macros

You can create a macro that runs automatically each time you open a particular Approach file. To accomplish this, open the file you want, create the macro, and assign it the name "Open." Similarly, if you assign the name "Close" to a macro, it will automatically run each time you close its associated file.

Because each macro is saved as part of the Approach file that's open when you create it, you can create a separate pair of Open and Close macros for each of your Approach files.

Attaching Macros to Fields

You can assign up to three macros to a particular field:

- A macro that runs whenever you tab into the field. For example, for certain fields you might want to display a note indicating that the fields need to be updated periodically.
- A macro that runs whenever you tab out of the field. For example, you may want to perform special calculations on a field to verify its value.
- A macro that runs whenever you change the value of the field. For example, you could display a message telling the user to verify the new value of the field.

Tip

You can assign a macro to a field only in Design mode. Also, this technique won't work for either Worksheet or Crosstab views.

To assign one or more of these types of macros with a field, follow these steps:

1. Switch to a Form view, and then switch to Design mode.
2. Double-click the field you want to use, so that its Info Box appears.
3. Click the Macros tab so that the Info Box resembles figure 13.7.

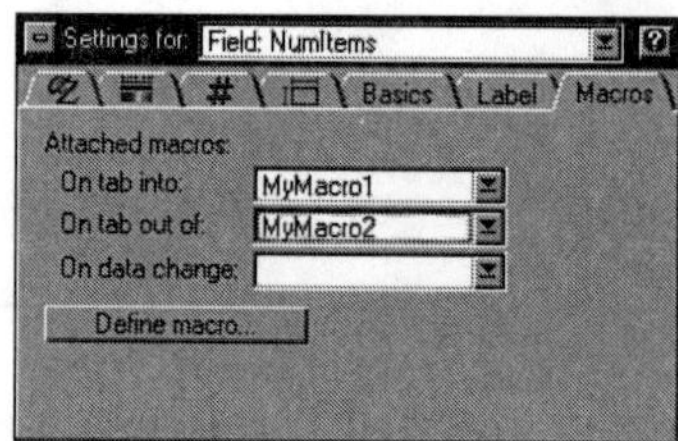

Fig. 13.7
Use this Info Box to attach macros to a field.

4. If you haven't yet created one or more of the macros, choose the button labeled Define Macro, then build the macro or macros. When you're finished, exit from the Macros dialog box.
5. Assign the macros you want by using the appropriate drop-down boxes.

If you want to detach a macro from a field, follow the above steps, but choose the blank item in the corresponding drop-down list box.

Attaching Macros to Views

You can attach a macro to a particular view so that it runs whenever you switch to that view. You can also attach another macro that runs whenever you switch out of the view. To set up one or both of these macros, follow these steps:

1. Switch to the view you want, then switch to either Browse or Design mode.

2. Display the Info Box for this view (the easiest way is to click the Info Box icon).
3. Click the tab labeled Macro so that the Info Box resembles figure 13.8.

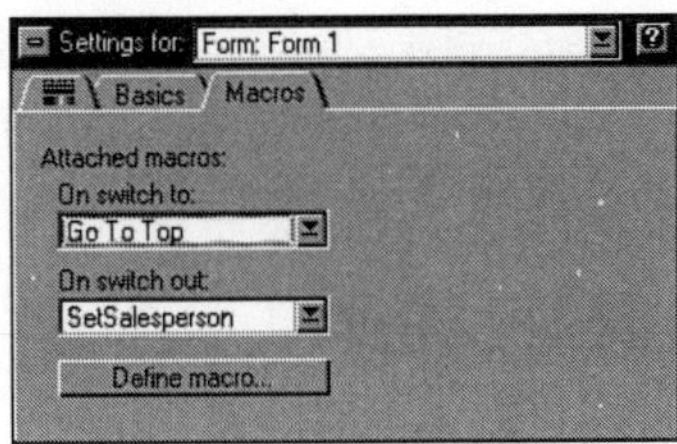

Fig. 13.8
Use this Info Box to attach macros to a view.

4. If you haven't yet created one or both of the macros, choose the button labeled Define Macro, then build the macros. When you're finished, exit from the Macros dialog box.

5. Assign the macros you want by using the appropriate drop-down boxes.

If you want to detach a macro from a view, follow the preceding steps, but choose the blank item in the corresponding drop-down list box.

Running Macros with Buttons and Objects

You can attach a macro to either a text or graphic object you create within Approach. You can then run the macro simply by clicking the object.

You can also create a standard macro button and attach it to a macro; clicking the button runs the macro. You can create the macro first and then create the button and attach the macro, or you can create the button and the macro at the same time.

Text and Graphics Objects

You can attach a macro to any text or graphic object you have already created on a form. This is a handy feature because it allows you to create highly customized objects to use as buttons for running macros. For instance, you could create a macro that prints the current view, then attach it to a graphic object in the shape of a printer, as shown in figure 13.9. When you click this object, Approach prints the view.

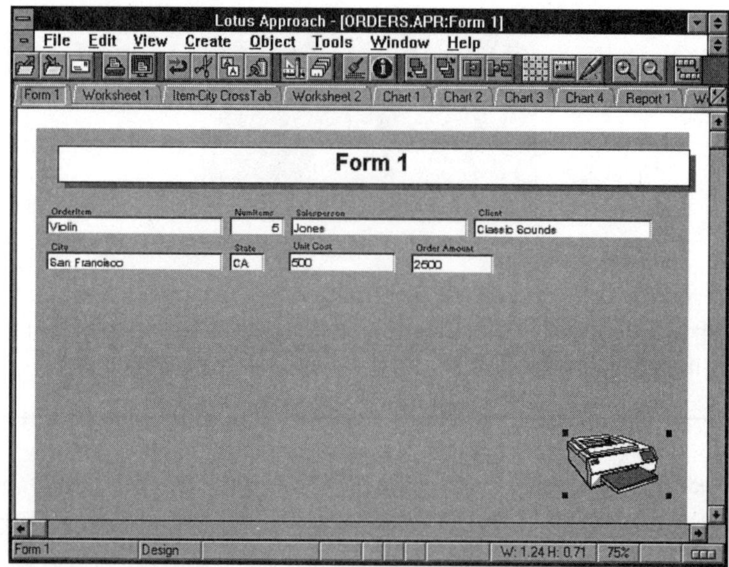

Fig. 13.9 You can create highly customized graphic objects as macro buttons.

To attach a macro to a text or graphic object you have already created, follow these steps:

1. Switch to the view containing the text or graphic object.

2. Switch to Design mode.
3. Click the object you want to use.

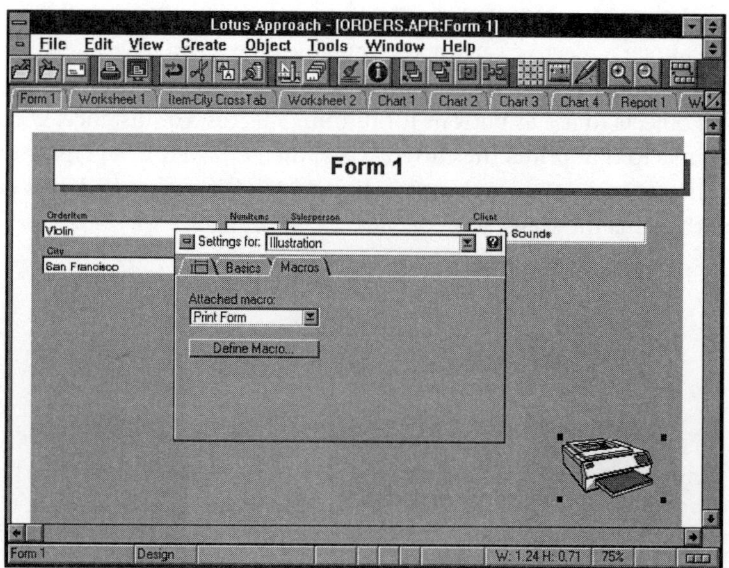

Fig. 13.10 Use the Info Box to attach a macro to a text or graphic object.

4. Display the Info Box for the object, then click the tab labeled Macros so that the Info Box resembles figure 13.10 on the preceding page.

5. If you haven't yet created the macro, choose the button labeled Define Macro, then build the macro.

6. Using the displayed drop-down list box, select the macro you want to attach.

Macro Buttons

You can create a standard macro button on any of your forms or reports, and then attach a macro to the button. When you click the button, the macro will run. A macro button looks exactly like a real button, and you can add descriptive text to the button so that a user will have no doubt as to the button's purpose.

Here's how to create a macro button and assign it to a particular macro:

1. Display the form or report you want to use.

2. Make sure that you're in Design mode.

3. Display the Tools palette. Either click the Show Drawing Tools icon or open the **View** menu and choose Show Dra**w**ing Tools.

4. Click the Button icon on the Tools palette, then click where you want the button to appear on the form or report. If necessary, drag the button to exactly where you want it.

5. Double-click the new button to display its Info Box. Then click the tab labeled Basics, so that the Info Box resembles figure 13.11.

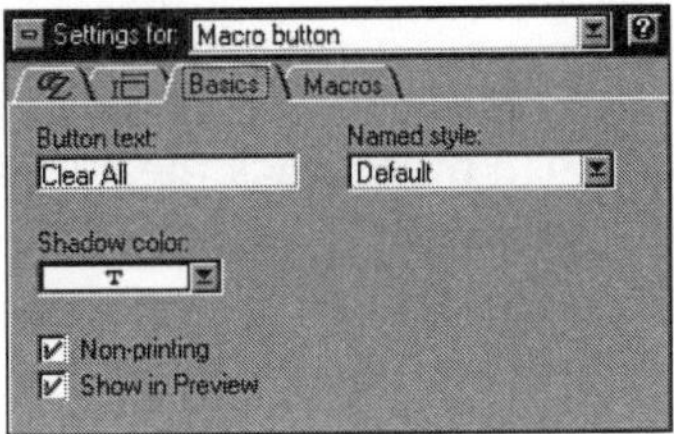

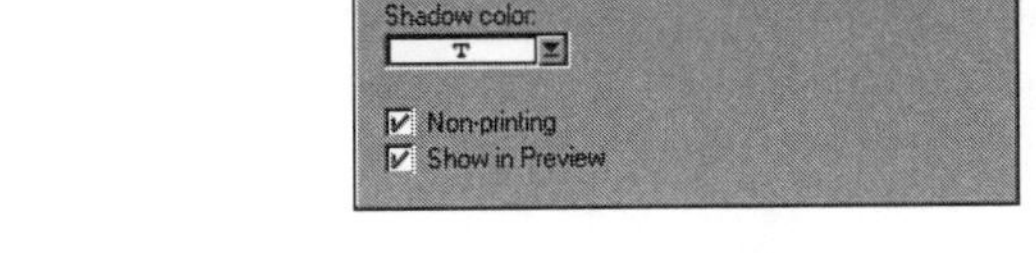

Fig. 13.11
Enter the text for a macro button.

6. Enter the text that you want to appear on the button.

7. If necessary, you can resize the button by grabbing and dragging a corner handle, so that the button conveniently displays all the text.

8. If you want the button to appear in Preview mode, choose the Show in Preview option.

9. Click the tab labeled Macros, so that the Info Box appears as shown in figure 13.12.

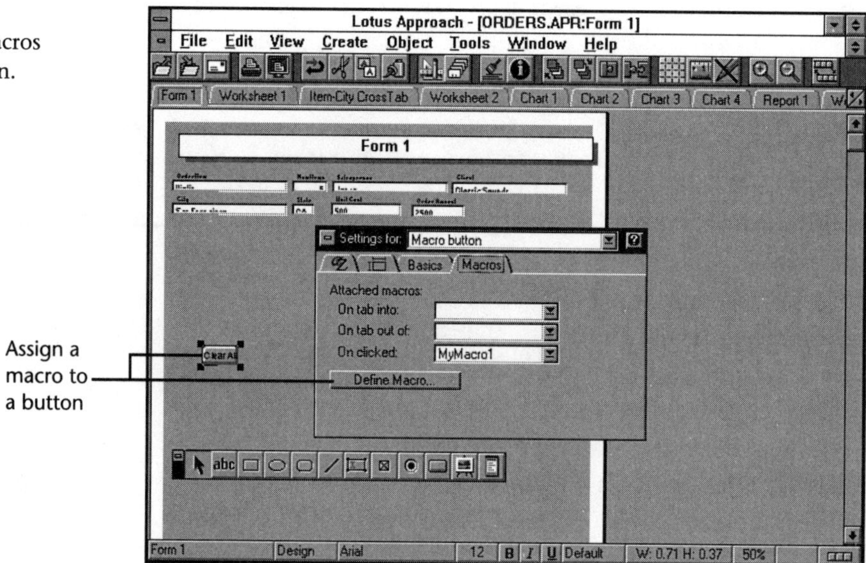

Fig. 13.12
Select the macros for the button.

10. If you haven't yet created the macro for this button, choose the button labeled Define Macro, then create the macro. When you're done, exit from the Macros dialog box.

11. In the drop-down list box labeled On Clicked, choose the macro you want to assign to the macro button.

You can easily delete a macro button you no longer want to appear in a view. Select the view, switch to Design mode, click the button, and then press the Delete key; or open the **E**dit menu and choose Cu**t**. Note that the macro that was attached to the button is not deleted; it remains part of the associated file so that you can use it again.

Macro Examples

The best way to learn how to create macros is to study as many different examples as possible. This section presents several types of macros that you can use most effectively by reproducing and running them on your own computer.

To duplicate each of the examples in this section, you would begin the same way—by opening the **T**ools menu and selecting **M**acros. When the Macros dialog box appears, click the **N**ew button so that the Define Macro dialog box appears.

Sorting Records

Frequently you may want to work with a group of records that are sorted into a particular order. For instance, you might want to perform a weekly operation that requires sorting a file of Orders records by state, and then for each state by city.

To create a macro to perform this particular type of sort operation, fill in the Define Macro dialog box as shown in figure 13.13.

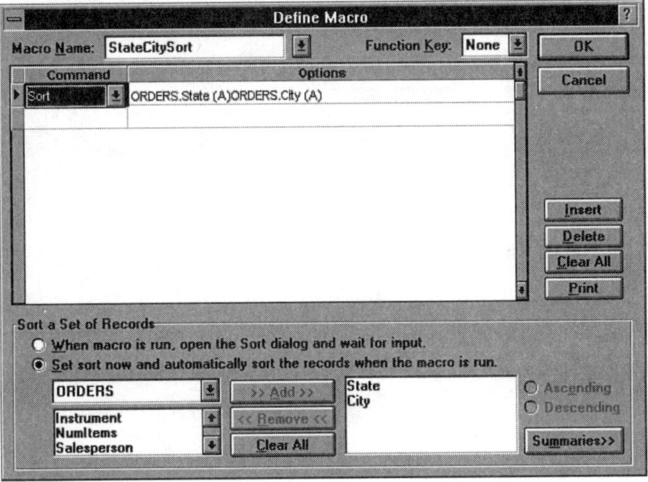

Fig. 13.13
Use this macro to perform an automatic sort.

As a review, let's go through the steps for accomplishing this:

1. In the text box labeled Macro Name, enter a new name for this macro.
2. Pull down the list of commands and then click Sort.
3. In the lower part of the dialog box, choose the **S**et Sort Now and Automatically Sort the Records When the Macro is Run option, and then copy the STATE and CITY field names from the left-hand list box to the right-hand one.
4. When you're done, click OK.

Replacing Field Values

There are many ways you can use macros to automatically replace the contents of one or more records. As a simple example, figure 13.14 shows a macro that replaces the NUMITEMS field of the current record with zero.

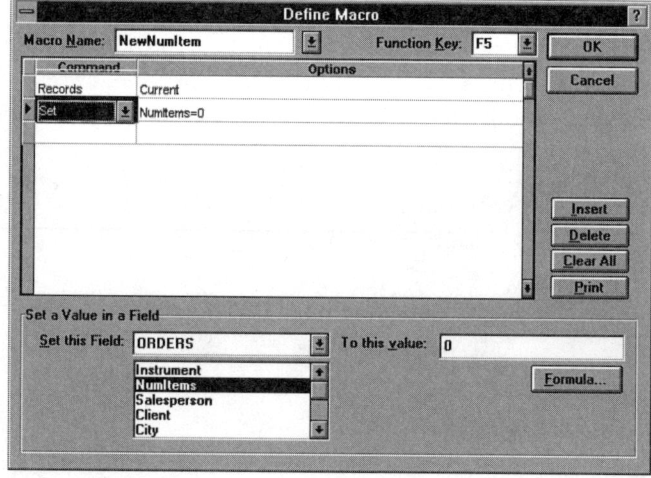

Fig. 13.14
Use this macro to replace a field value in the current record.

Tip
When using a macro to modify a record, use the Records command to select that record.

This macro consists of two commands:

Records, Current. When you set up this command, you choose the Current Record option at the bottom of the dialog box. The complete command tells Approach to set up the current record (whichever one you have currently selected when the macro runs) for modification.

Set, NumItems=0. As part of this command, you choose the NumItems field and the value 0. When the macro runs, this command sets the NUMITEMS field to a value of zero.

Note

For each of the remaining macro examples in this section, we'll present a figure similar to 13.14, listing the commands that make up the macro. For each command, the entry in the Options column indicates the corresponding options you would select at the bottom of the Define Macro dialog box.

A Looping Example: Replacing a Field Value for All Records

One of the most powerful features of the macro language is its ability to perform loops, whereby a macro is repeated over and over again—each for a different record.

To illustrate how a looping macro works, let's expand on the previous example by creating a macro that sets the NUMITEMS field to zero *for every record in the database file*. This macro is shown in figure 13.15.

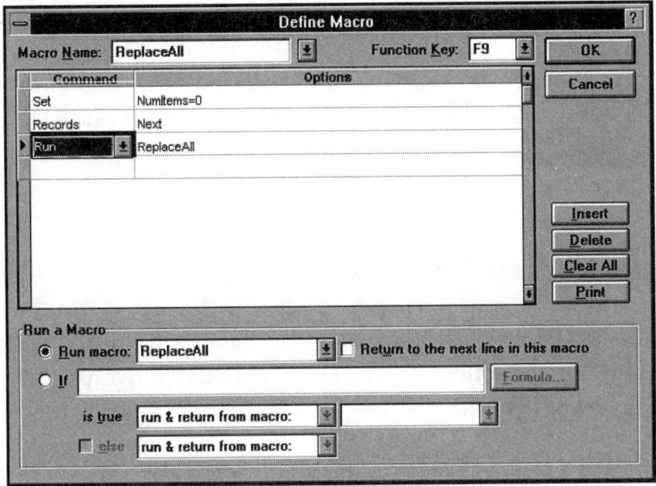

Fig. 13.15
You can use macros to replace a field value in all records.

Let's go through the different commands that make up this macro:

Set, NumItems=0. This command replaces the value of the NUMITEMS field to zero *in the current record.*

Records, Next. This command moves to the next record in the current database file.

Run, Replace All. Use this command to cause the macro to loop. To accomplish this, you select the Run Macro option, as shown in figure 13.15. Using this option, you select the name of the macro you want to run—in this case, the name of the current macro. In other words, when the Run command in this macro executes, the macro runs itself again! Therefore, the three commands that make up the macro repeat themselves—including the Run, ReplaceAll command, which then repeats the macro again, and so on.

Here are some important points to note about this macro:

- Each time the macro repeats itself, the NUMITEMS field of a different record is modified because of the command Records, Next, which moves to the next record in the database file.
- The macro automatically stops running when there are no more records in the current database file. This is a handy feature that simplifies your programming a great deal.
- The macro doesn't automatically begin at the first record in the database file. Instead, it starts with whatever record you happen to have selected when you run the macro. To make the macro modify every record in the file, you must manually click the first record in the file before running the macro. (An improvement on this macro would be to have it begin by automatically jumping to the first record in the file. You'll see how to accomplish this in the next example.)

Another Looping Example

The problem with the previous macro example is that before you run it you must remember to click the first record in the database file; otherwise, not every record will be modified. We can eliminate this shortcoming by creating a *second* macro that does the following:

- Jumps to the first record in the current database file.
- Runs the macro "ReplaceAll" (the one in the previous example).

Figure 13.16 shows the two commands in this macro. The Records, First command causes Approach to jump to the first record in the current database file. Then the Run, ReplaceAll command tells Approach to run the macro named ReplaceAll. As described in the previous example, this macro then replaces values in the NUMITEMS field, starting with the current record (which is the first one in this case).

Note that in this new two-macro set, you would run the macro Go To Top, which would do its setup and would then run the macro ReplaceAll.

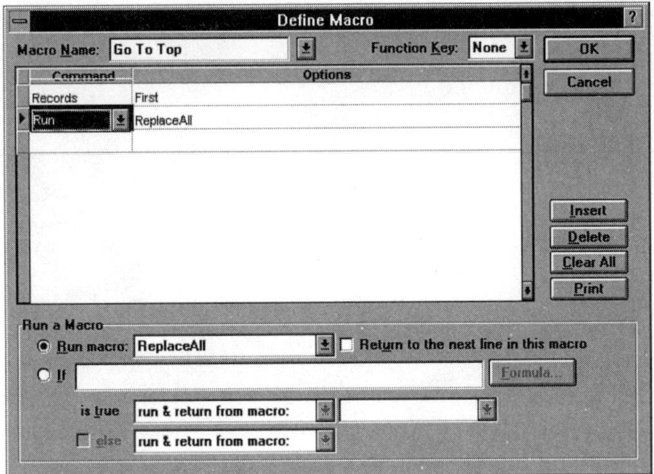

Fig. 13.16
Use this macro to go to the first record and begin a looping macro.

Finding a Group of Records

As you work with Approach database files, you'll often need to locate particular groups of records. For example, you might want to view only those records for a particular city or for a particular salesperson.

Approach offers two different types of macro techniques for finding groups of records. With the first, you preselect the search conditions you want to use so that whenever you run the macro, it locates the records satisfying just those search conditions.

With the second method, you set up a macro so that each time it runs, it pauses with the Find dialog box displayed, so that you can enter whatever search conditions you wish. After you do, Approach will first find and display the records satisfying your search conditions and then resume running the macro.

Presetting a Group of Find Conditions

Figure 13.17 shows a macro in which you preset a group of find conditions.

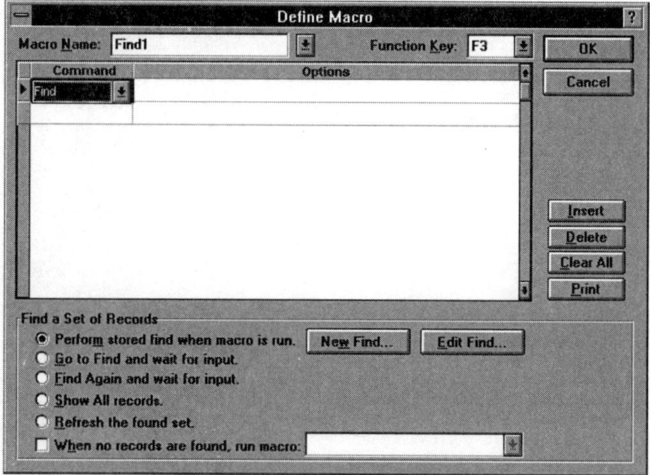

Fig. 13.17
You can use this macro to preset a group of find conditions.

To create this macro, follow these steps:

1. Open the **T**ools menu and choose **M**acros. Next, click the **N**ew button to display the Define Macro dialog box.

2. Enter a name for the new macro.

3. Pull down the list of commands, then choose the Find command.

4. Choose the Perform **S**tored Find When Macro is Run option, then click the Ne**w** Find button.

5. When the Find screen appears, as shown in figure 13.18, fill in the find conditions you want.

6. Press the Enter key to return to the Define Macro dialog box.

7. Click OK to save the new macro.

The single-command macro shown in figure 13.17 is useful as an example, but in practice you'll probably want to incorporate the Find command as part of a larger macro. You'll see some examples later on in this section.

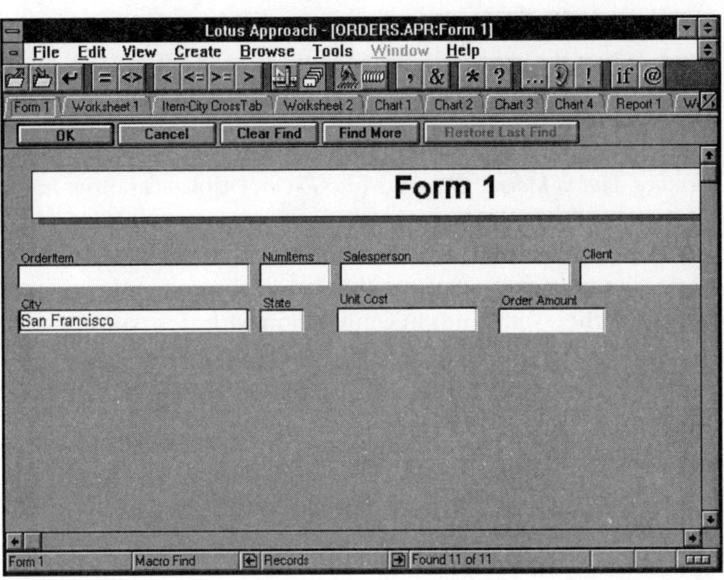

Fig. 13.18
Enter the find conditions you want to preset.

A Macro that Pauses for Input

Instead of presetting a group of find conditions within a macro, you can create a macro that pauses during execution, so that you can enter the conditions at that time. Figure 13.19 shows an example of this type of macro.

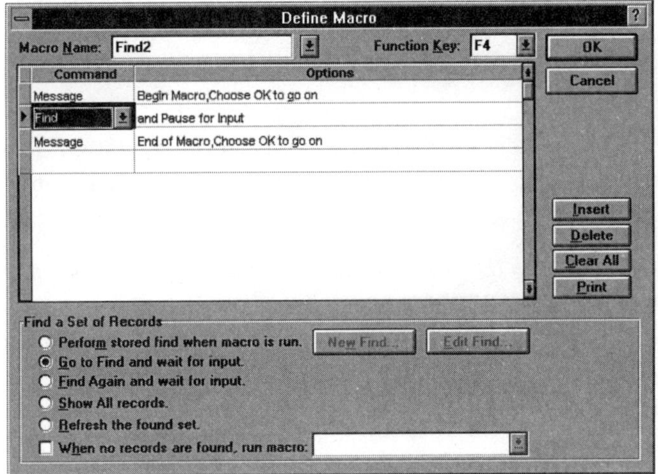

Fig. 13.19
This macro pauses for the user to input a set of find conditions.

Here's an explanation of the commands in this macro:

Message, Begin Macro, Choose OK to Go On. Displays a message for the user.

Find, And Pause for Input. Displays the Find dialog box, pausing for user input. When the user has finished entering find conditions, Approach finds and displays all records matching the find conditions, then resumes the macro.

Message, End of Macro, Choose OK to Go On. Displays another message for the user.

The message commands here are for illustration purposes only. In practice, you would use other commands in conjunction with this type of Find command.

Modifying a Group of Records—(1)

A common database operation involves modifying a particular group of records within a database. For instance, you might want to delete them or modify the contents of specific fields. As an example, suppose that you have hired a replacement salesperson to cover the San Francisco territory. To reflect this change in your Orders file, you'll need to change the SALESPERSON field for those records dealing with clients in San Francisco.

Note

This is the first of two different example macros for accomplishing the same operation, namely, modifying the San Francisco records to reflect a new salesperson. These macros illustrate an important point: there's usually more than one way to write a macro to perform a particular set of operations.

Figure 13.20 shows how a macro can accomplish this operation. This is a looping macro, similar to the one described earlier. Here's a synopsis of the commands it uses:

Set, Salesperson = IF(City='San Francisco', 'Caparelli', Salesperson). This rather complicated command conditionally changes the value of the SALESPERSON field for the current record. The command includes the built-in function IF(*Condition, Value 1, Value 2*), which has the following meaning:

IF: the value of *Condition* is true, then use the value *Value 1.*

OTHERWISE: use the value *Value 2.*

In the current context, the *Set, Salesperson...* command has the following meaning: If the value of the CITY field for the current record is "San Francisco," then set the SALESPERSON field to "Caparelli" (the new salesperson); otherwise, set the Salesperson field to itself—in other words, don't change it.

Records, Next. Go to the next record in the current database file.

Run, Replace1. Run this macro again.

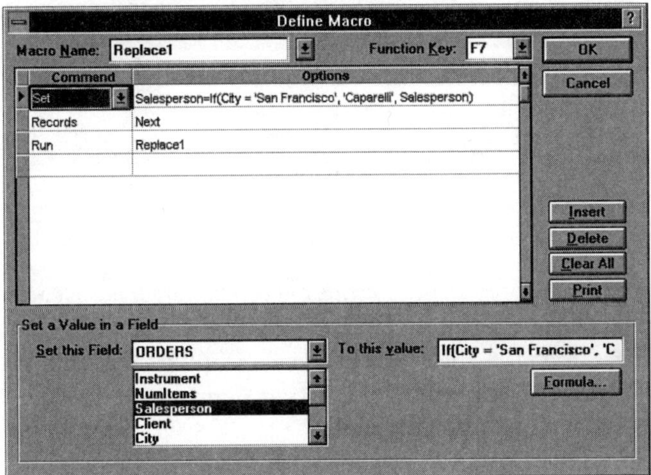

Fig. 13.20
You can use this macro to modify a particular set of records.

As in the previous looping example, before running this macro you would click the first record in the file. Or you could create a second macro, similar to the Go To Top macro described earlier, which would jump to the top of the file and then run the Replace1 macro.

Modifying a Group of Records—(2)

The previous example illustrated a macro that used the built-in conditional IF() function to modify a particular group of records. Figure 13.21 shows another approach to the problem.

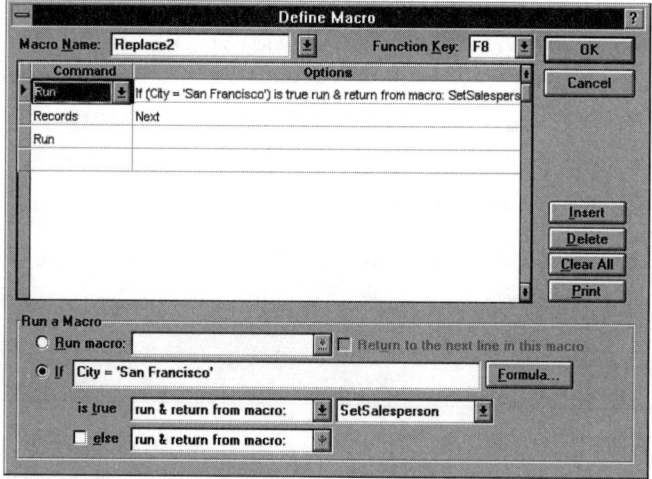

Fig. 13.21 Another macro for modifying a particular group of records.

Here's an explanation of the commands:

Run, IF(City='San Francisco') is true run & return from macro: SetSalesperson. This is a new variation on the Run command. When this command executes, the macro SetSalesperson will be run only if the value of the CITY field in the current record is "San Francisco."

The purpose of the SetSalesperson macro is to change the value of the SALESPERSON field, as shown below.

Records, Next. Jumps to the next record in the current database file.

Run, Replace2. Runs the current macro again, thus creating a loop that will process every record in the file (provided you move to the first record before running this macro).

The SetSalesperson macro is a separate macro you must create before building the Replace2 macro. Its only purpose is to modify the value of the SALESPERSON field in the current record. Figure 13.22 shows this one-command macro.

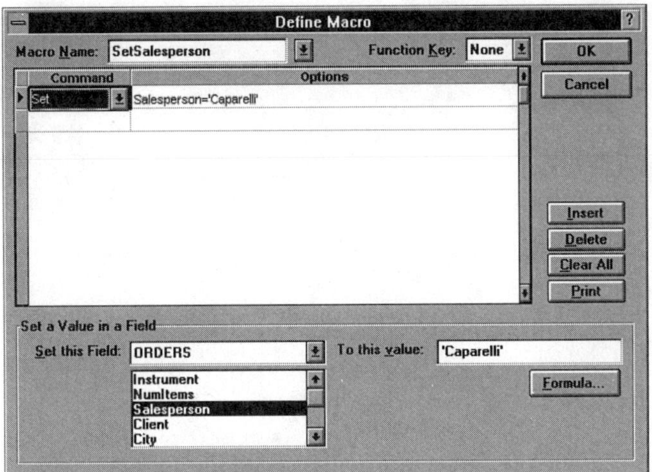

Fig. 13.22
This macro, used in the Replace2 macro, replaces the value of the SALESPERSON field for the current record.

Using Macros to Create a Multi-Page Data-Entry Form

Suppose you want to create a new data-entry form, but there isn't enough room on the screen for all the field objects you want to include. (Remember that each Approach form can occupy no more than one screen.)

To solve this dilemma, you can create a second form to display the remaining fields. As far as Approach is concerned, this second form is completely unrelated to the first one; only you know that there's a logical connection between the two. Whenever you enter new records or modify existing ones, you can switch from one form to the other as needed.

To simplify the process of switching back and forth between the two forms, you can use macros linked to command buttons on the forms. To switch from one form to the other, you simply click the appropriate button on either form.

To illustrate how this works, figure 13.23 shows the two screens that make up the complete data-entry form for a Customers database file. For the user's convenience, the two forms are labeled Page 1 and Page 2.

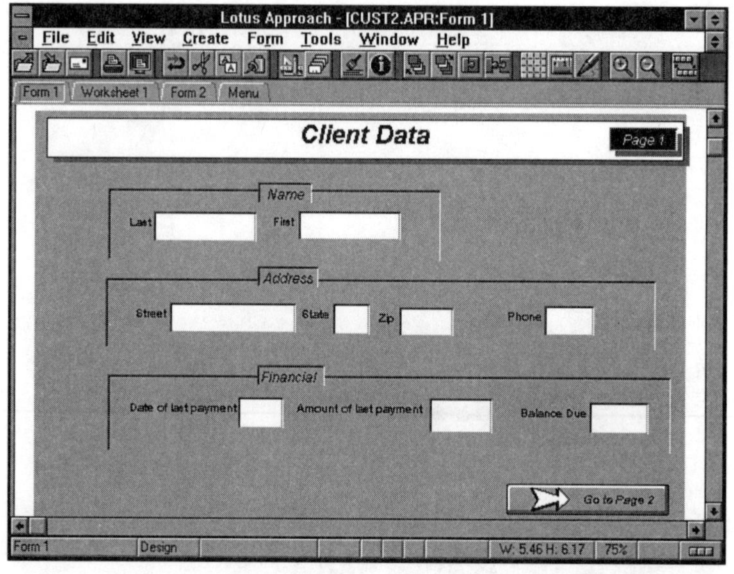

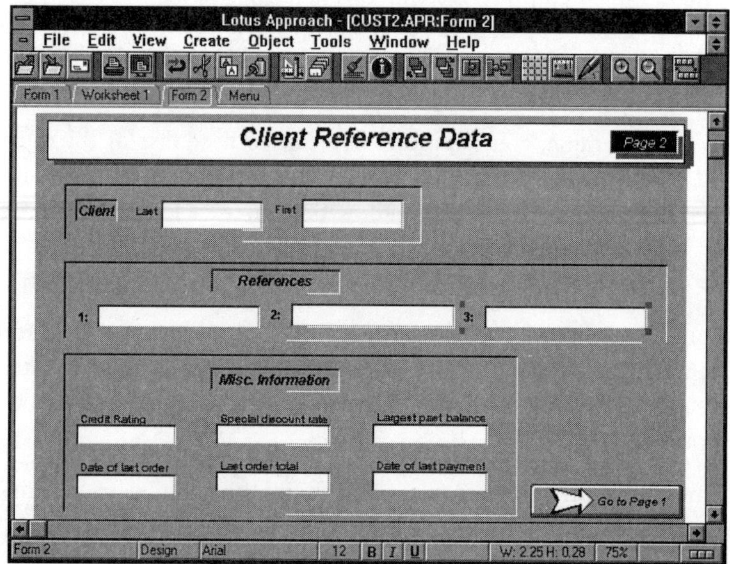

Fig. 13.23
A macro allows you to jump to a second screen for further data entry.

Notice that the bottom of the first screen displays a macro button labeled Go To Page 2. This button is attached to a macro whose only purpose is to switch to the other page. Consequently, when you click this macro button, the macro switches to page 2. Similarly, the second screen displays a macro button that, when clicked, switches to the first page.

Here's an outline of the steps you follow to create this two-page data-entry form—including the macro buttons:

1. Create the two separate forms, naming them Form 1 and Form 2 (or other names if you wish). Set up each form with the fields you want.
2. Create a new macro, assigning it the name "Go To Form 2," and consisting of the following single command: *View, Switch to Form 2.*
3. Create another new macro, giving it the name "Go To Form 1," and consisting of the following single command: *View, Switch to Form 1.*
4. Switch to Design mode in Form 1.

5. Create a macro button, placing it somewhere convenient on the form. Place the text "Go To Page 2" on the button.
6. Attach the macro "Go To Form 2" to this new macro button.
7. Switch to Form 2.
8. Create a macro button, placing it somewhere convenient on this form. Place the text "Go To Page 1" on the button.
9. Attach the macro "Go To Form 1" to this macro button.

Creating a Master Menu Form

Using the techniques described in this chapter, you can easily create an impressive Approach form that acts as a "main menu" to other forms and reports. You—or the staff in your office—can then use this menu to perform various operations. You can even automate Approach to display this menu each time a user opens the Approach file of interest.

Figure 13.24 illustrates this type of menu, which is labeled "Welcome to the Customers Database" and consists primarily of a group of macro buttons. Each button is attached to a macro that performs a particular operation or set of operations. For instance, clicking the first button would run a macro that switches to a data-entry form for adding new records.

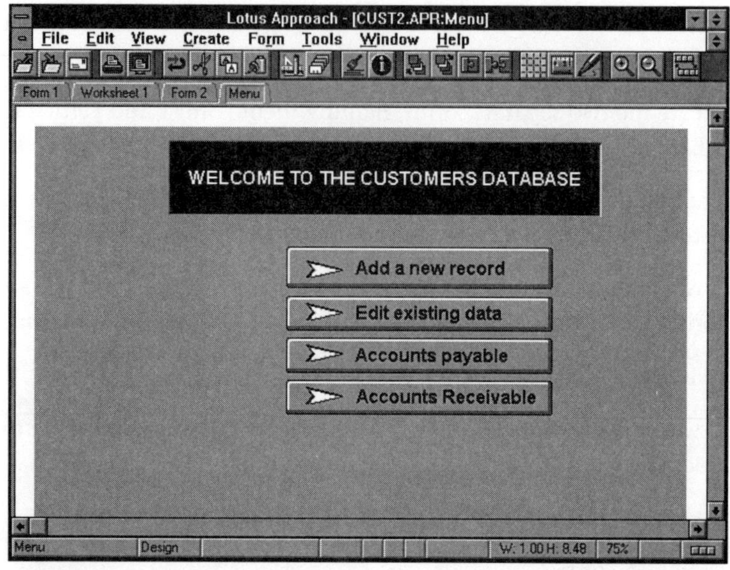

Fig. 13.24
Use this menu form to select other database activities.

The arrow on each macro button in figure 13.24 is not actually part of the button, even though it appears to be so. Instead, the arrow is a graphics object imported from a separate software package and positioned directly on top of the button.

Here are a few tips you might want to incorporate into your own menus:

- You can spruce up your menus by tastefully adding text and graphic objects. If you have access to a clip-art software package, browse through it for images that you might want to use.

- Using the technique described in this section, you can create a set of multi-tier menus. The main menu would contain a set of buttons, each of which would lead to a secondary menu. The options there could lead either to other menus or to specific views and tasks.

- You can have Approach automatically display a menu each time you open a particular database file. To accomplish this, create a new macro as part of that file, naming the macro Open. This macro should consist of the single command *View, Switch to Menu,* where *Menu* is the name of the form containing the main menu for the database file. Because the name of the macro is Open, it will automatically run each time you open the Approach file, thereby displaying the main menu for the database.

From Here...

This chapter has presented the basic tools you can use to create and run your own macros. Using the techniques described in this chapter, you can use macros to automate and simplify your work with Approach. Many other chapters can expand your knowledge of parts of Approach you can use with macros. Refer to the following chapters in this book for more information:

- Chapter 4, "Enhancing Data Input Forms," describes how to add graphics and text objects to your forms.
- Chapter 6, "Finding Records," explains how to search for groups of records.
- Chapter 11, "Performing Advanced Finds," describes advanced query operations that lend themselves to automation.
- Chapter 12, "Creating Advanced Reports," describes techniques for creating reports you can then control with macros.

Part III

Getting the Most from Approach

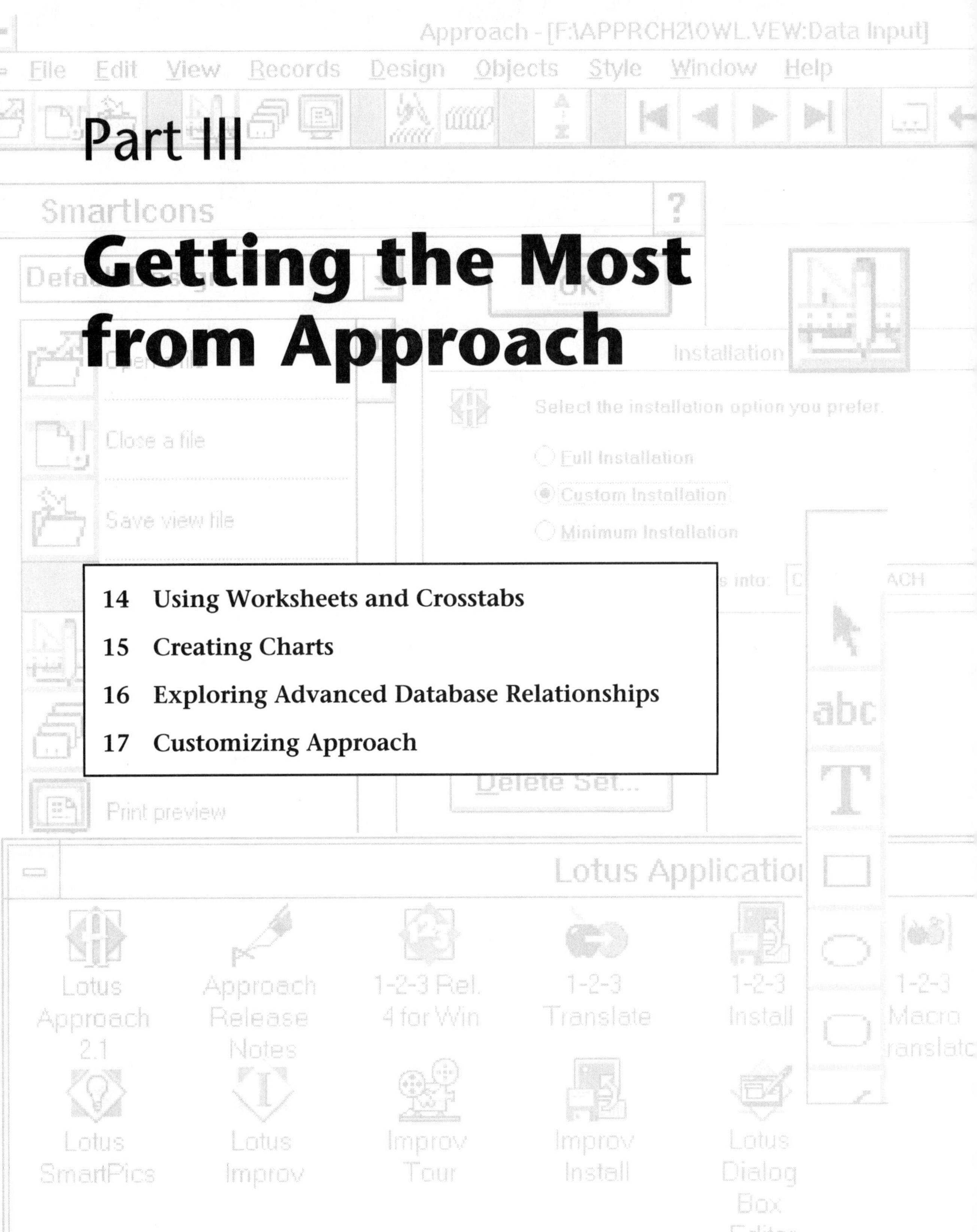

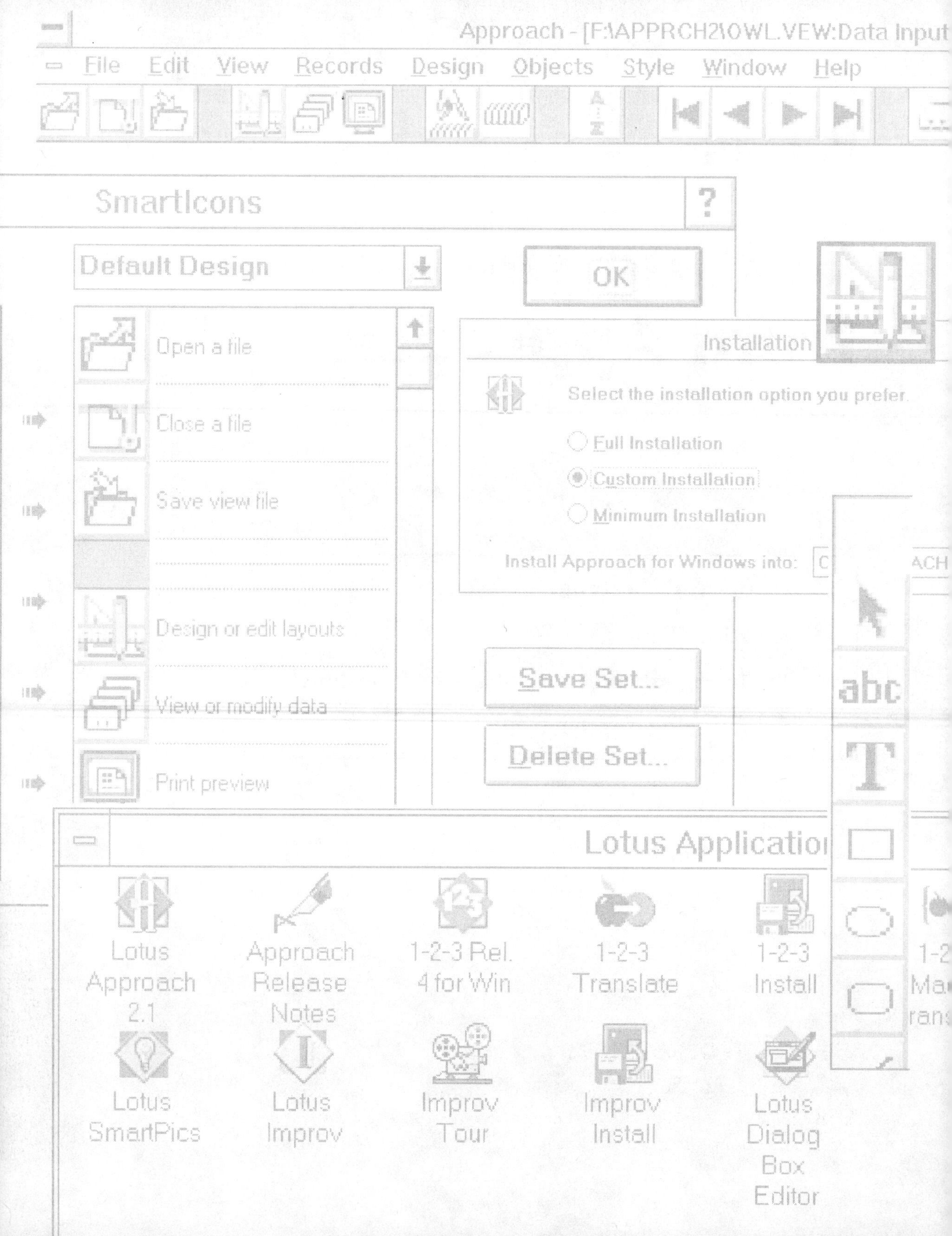
Approach - [F:\APPRCH2\OWL.VEW:Data Input
File Edit View Records Design Objects Style Window Help
SmartIcons
Default Design
OK
Open a file
Close a file
Save view file
Design or edit layouts
View or modify data
Print preview
Installation
Select the installation option you prefer.
Full Installation
Custom Installation
Minimum Installation
Install Approach for Windows into:
Save Set...
Delete Set...
abc
T
Lotus Application
Lotus Approach 2.1
Approach Release Notes
1-2-3 Rel. 4 for Win
1-2-3 Translate
1-2-3 Install
Lotus SmartPics
Lotus Improv
Improv Tour
Improv Install
Lotus Dialog Box Editor

Chapter 14

Using Worksheets and Crosstabs

While looking at a record in a form view is often best, Approach worksheets and crosstabs allow you to see the "bigger picture" of your database. Using worksheets, you can display and edit information in a convenient tabular format. A crosstab view also appears in tabular format, but unlike a worksheet, it displays summary information, rather than data from individual records.

In this chapter, you learn how to:

- Create a worksheet
- Select the data to be used in a worksheet
- Customize the worksheet's appearance
- Add, edit, or delete data from a worksheet view
- Create a crosstab view
- Adjust crosstab row height and appearance
- Add and delete crosstab fields
- Add and delete summary rows and columns

Using Worksheets

The Approach worksheet view gives you a two-dimensional, columnar picture of the information in your database. Each row in a worksheet displays the information from a single record, and each column contains values for a single field. Worksheets are very handy because they can display a large amount of database information on the screen.

> **Note**
>
> The examples in this chapter are based on the Orders database shown in figure 14.1.

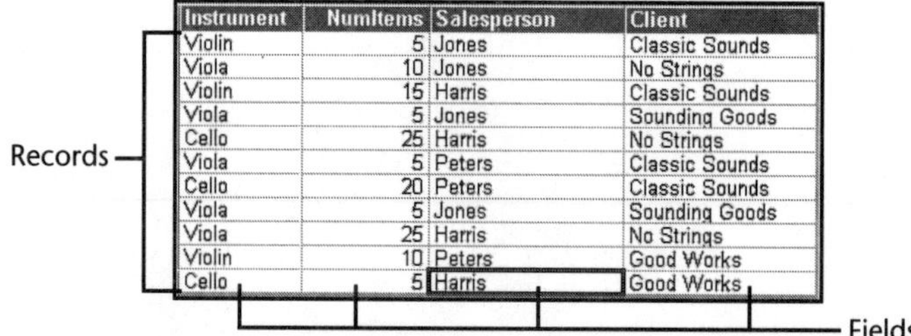

Instrument	NumItems	Salesperson	Client
Violin	5	Jones	Classic Sounds
Viola	10	Jones	No Strings
Violin	15	Harris	Classic Sounds
Viola	5	Jones	Sounding Goods
Cello	25	Harris	No Strings
Viola	5	Peters	Classic Sounds
Cello	20	Peters	Classic Sounds
Viola	5	Jones	Sounding Goods
Viola	25	Harris	No Strings
Violin	10	Peters	Good Works
Cello	5	Harris	Good Works

Fig. 14.1 A worksheet displays a columnar view of a database.

Figure 14.1 shows an example of a worksheet. The data displayed in this worksheet are sales figures from an Orders database for an instrument dealer. Each record in this database represents a single order placed by a customer. The database fields that are displayed in the worksheet are the following:

Field	Contents
Instrument	Type of instrument sold
NumItems	Number of instruments sold in this order
Salesperson	Name of salesperson making the sale
Client	Name of client purchasing the instruments

The top row of a worksheet contains column labels, which by default are the names of the fields. You can modify these labels to be more descriptive. Each of the remaining rows in a worksheet shows the information from a single record.

A worksheet is particularly useful for working with data on-screen because it offers a number of techniques for easily selecting the data you want to view. For example, you can quickly add a new field to a worksheet, simply by dragging and dropping the name of the field onto the screen. Similarly, you can easily delete a field from a worksheet by dragging the column out of the worksheet.

Because a worksheet displays a relatively large amount of data at one time, it is a convenient platform for browsing and editing. Moreover, you can split the screen into either two or four panes, each of which can display a different part of a worksheet. This can be extremely useful when working with large worksheets.

Approach allows you to display worksheet data sorted by the values of one or more fields. Using standard searching operations, you can display any desired subset of records. Also, you can use a worksheet as a platform for editing, adding, and deleting records.

Note

Each time you use Approach to create a new database, a new worksheet named Worksheet 1 is automatically created, which contains every field in the database.

You can create as many different types of worksheets for a database as you wish, each with its own group of fields. After creating a worksheet, you can customize its appearance by adjusting row and column dimensions, by assigning custom colors to the background and border of different groups of cells, and by formatting the data that's displayed on the worksheet.

You can use a worksheet to browse through a database. You can also edit the contents of the database by adding, deleting, and modifying records.

Creating a New Worksheet

To create a new worksheet, specify the names of the fields you want to be included. Approach automatically assigns a name—something like Worksheet 1—to the worksheet, and it assigns the field names as column labels. However, you can modify these names later if you wish.

To create a new worksheet, follow these steps:

1. Open the **C**reate menu and choose **W**orksheet. The Worksheet Assistant dialog box appears (see fig. 14.2).

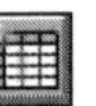

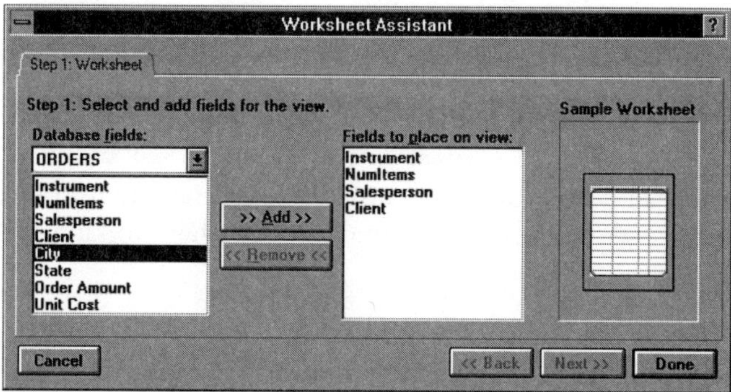

Fig. 14.2
Select the fields to appear in the new worksheet.

The list of fields labeled Database **F**ields shows the fields in the current database. The list on the right, labeled Fields to **P**lace on View, displays the fields you select to be part of the worksheet.

2. Choose the fields you want to appear in the worksheet. To copy a field from the list labeled Database **F**ields to the list labeled Fields to **P**lace on View, either double-click the field, or click it once and then click the **A**dd button.

3. If you change your mind while working with this dialog box, you can delete a field from the list on the right either by double-clicking it, or by clicking it once and then clicking the **R**emove button.

4. When you have finished selecting the fields, click the Done button. Approach creates and displays the new worksheet, switching to Browse mode.

Elements of a Worksheet

Each worksheet contains various standard elements, shown in figure 14.3. These worksheet elements include the following:

Column labels (also called headers) — Each column is headed by a label. Initially, Approach uses field names for these labels; however, you can change these labels to be more descriptive.

Column gutter — This narrow horizontal band contains all of the column labels.

Row gutter — This is a narrow vertical band at the left edge of the worksheet. This is where you click to select an entire row.

Row marker This marker appears next to the row containing the cell or cells currently selected. If more than one row is selected, the marker appears next to the top-most of the selected rows.

Pane dividers You can use these markers to divide the screen into two or four *worksheet panes* for viewing different parts of the worksheet simultaneously.

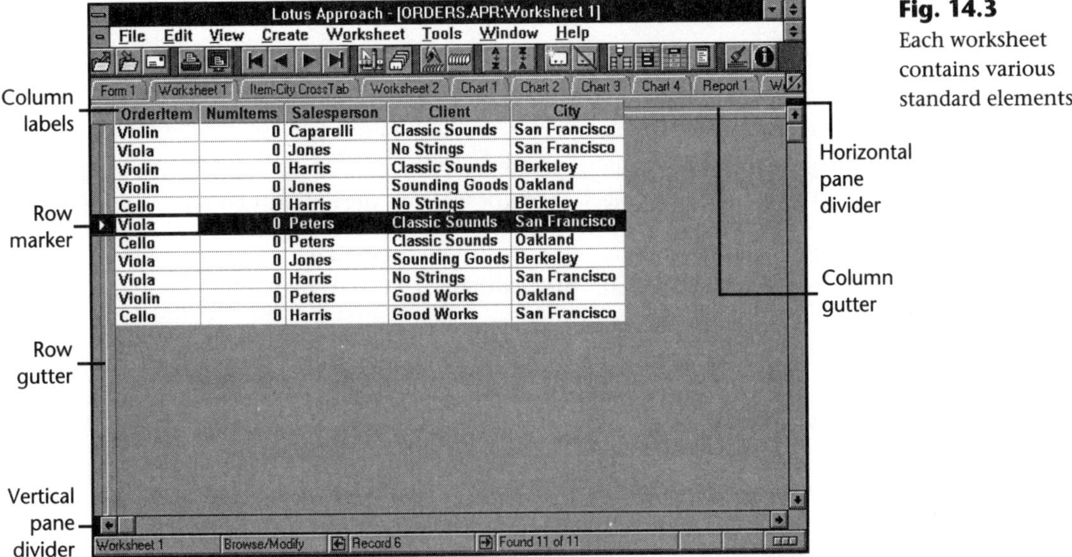

Fig. 14.3
Each worksheet contains various standard elements.

Basic Worksheet Operations

You can perform many different operations on the cells and column labels of a worksheet, including the following:

- Customize the background color and borders of the selected cells and labels
- Customize the font, alignment, and format of the selected cells and labels
- Copy the selected cells and labels to the Windows Clipboard

To enhance your ability to manipulate a worksheet, you can display either two or four worksheet panes, each of which can contain a separate view of the worksheet. You can resize the panes and navigate within each pane independently by using the associated horizontal and vertical scroll bars.

Note

When creating or using a worksheet, there are two reasons for switching to Design mode. First, some of Approach's functions work only in Design mode, and you might as well save yourself the trouble of having to switch back and forth between Browse and Design modes. The second reason is that you must be in Design mode if you're using a password with a worksheet. (You can use passwords to limit access to your database and Approach files.)

Selecting Cells and Labels

To perform any type of operation on a group of cells or labels, you must first select them. You can select individual cells or labels, groups of cells, one or more rows, or one or more columns—with or without the labels. You can also select the entire worksheet—with or without the column labels.

When you select a single cell, it becomes outlined with a heavy border. When you select a group of cells, the left-most cell is outlined and the rest are highlighted, as shown in figure 14.4.

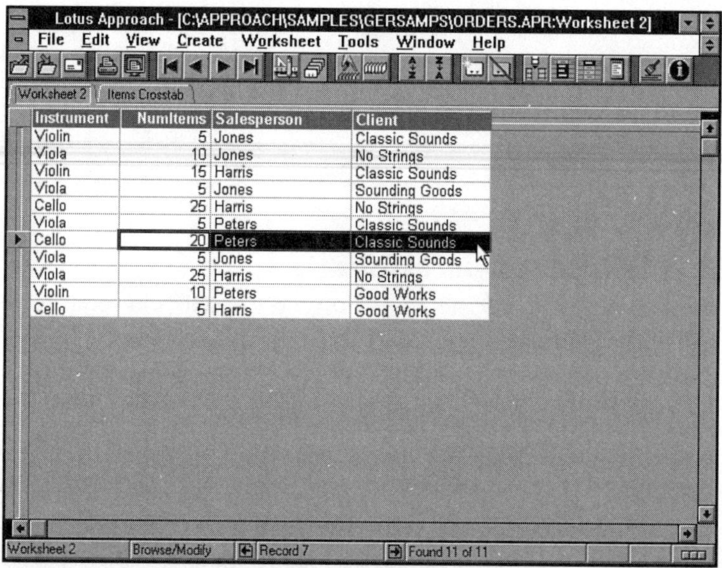

Fig. 14.4
Use the mouse to select a group of adjacent cells.

Table 14.1 lists the operations you can use for selecting various combinations of cells and labels.

Table 14.1 Selecting Cells and Labels in a Worksheet

To Select	Operation
A single cell	Click the cell with the mouse, or use the Tab and Shift+Tab keys to move from one cell to another.
A group of adjacent cells	Use the mouse to click the first cell, then hold the left mouse button down and drag the mouse left, right, up, or down to select the other cells you want.
An entire row of cells	Position the mouse cursor near the left end of the row, so that its shape changes to a right arrow , then click the mouse button (see fig. 14.5). When the row is selected, the row marker appears.
Two or more adjacent rows	Position the mouse cursor near the left end of the row, so that its shape changes to a right arrow. Then hold down the left mouse button and drag the mouse cursor up or down to select the other rows.
An entire column of cells, including the column label	Click the label for that column (see fig. 14.6).
A column of cells, not including the column label	Click the label for that column, then click the Select Column Cells icon. 
A column label	Click the label, then click the Select Label icon; or click the label twice. 
Two or more adjacent columns	Select the label for the first column, then hold down the mouse button and drag the mouse cursor across the labels for the other columns. If you want to exclude the labels from the selection, click the Select Column Cells icon.
Two or more adjacent column labels	Select those columns, then click the Select Label icon.
The entire worksheet, including labels	Click the upper-left corner of the worksheet.
All the column labels	Click twice in the upper-left corner of the worksheet.

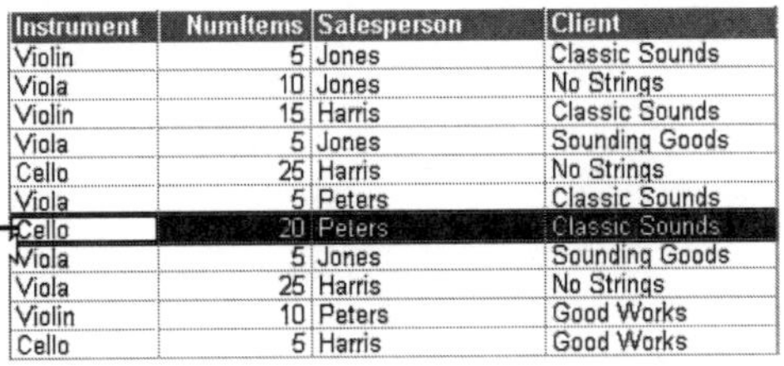

Instrument	NumItems	Salesperson	Client
Violin	5	Jones	Classic Sounds
Viola	10	Jones	No Strings
Violin	15	Harris	Classic Sounds
Viola	5	Jones	Sounding Goods
Cello	25	Harris	No Strings
Viola	5	Peters	Classic Sounds
Cello	20	Peters	Classic Sounds
Viola	5	Jones	Sounding Goods
Viola	25	Harris	No Strings
Violin	10	Peters	Good Works
Cello	5	Harris	Good Works

Row gutter

Fig. 14.5
To select a row of cells, click in the row gutter.

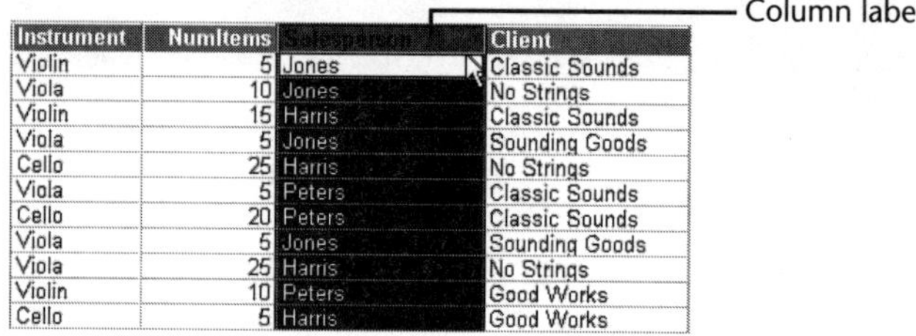

Instrument	NumItems	Salesperson	Client
Violin	5	Jones	Classic Sounds
Viola	10	Jones	No Strings
Violin	15	Harris	Classic Sounds
Viola	5	Jones	Sounding Goods
Cello	25	Harris	No Strings
Viola	5	Peters	Classic Sounds
Cello	20	Peters	Classic Sounds
Viola	5	Jones	Sounding Goods
Viola	25	Harris	No Strings
Violin	10	Peters	Good Works
Cello	5	Harris	Good Works

Fig. 14.6
To select a column of cells, click the column label.

Using Multiple Panes

When working with large worksheets, you probably won't be able to see all the data at once. However, you can display two different views of a worksheet, each in its own pane, and with the panes arranged either vertically or horizontally. You can then scroll each view somewhat independently, using the horizontal scroll bar and the two sets of vertical scroll bars.

You can also display four views of a worksheet, each in its own pane (see fig. 14.7). In this situation, Approach supplies four sets of scroll bars—two vertical and two horizontal, which you can use to scroll within each of the four panes.

If the same cells are shown in two or more different panes, and if you select those cells in either pane, they are also shown as selected in the other panes. Similarly, when you make a change to the worksheet in any pane, that change is reflected automatically in the other panes.

To display two panes arranged horizontally, drag down the horizontal pane divider, which is located at the top of the vertical elevator bar (see fig. 14.3). Or, to display two panes arranged vertically, drag the vertical pane divider (located at the left end of the horizontal scroll bar) to the right.

To display four panes, as shown in figure 14.7, use both the vertical and horizontal pane dividers. To readjust the size of the panes, use the mouse to reposition either the pane dividers or the divider bars separating the panes. You can also resize all four panes at the same time by dragging the intersection of the two divider bars.

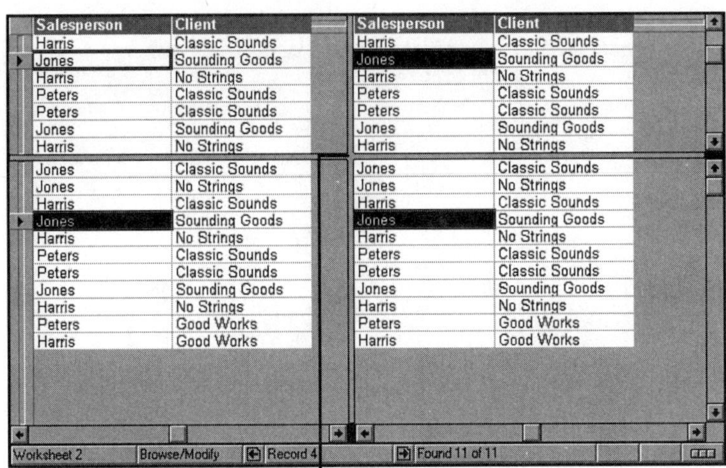

Fig. 14.7
You can simultaneously display four different parts of a worksheet.

Selecting the Data to Appear in a Worksheet

When you first create a new worksheet, you select the fields to be included. However, later you can modify the worksheet by adding new fields, deleting those you no longer need, or by rearranging and resizing the columns within the worksheet. You can also add new columns for displaying calculations that are based on the information in the database.

Adding New Fields

To add a new field, you begin by displaying the Add Field dialog box (see fig. 14.8). You can use this box to select the new fields for the worksheet.

To add one or more fields to a worksheet, follow these steps:

1. Display the Add Field dialog box by clicking the icon labeled Show Add Field Dialog, or by opening the W**o**rksheet menu and choosing **A**dd Field. The Add Field dialog box appears.

2. In the Add Field dialog box, click the name of the new field, then drag it onto the worksheet. As you drag the field name, a dark vertical line appears to the left of where the new field will appear (see fig. 14.8). If necessary, you can reposition the field later.

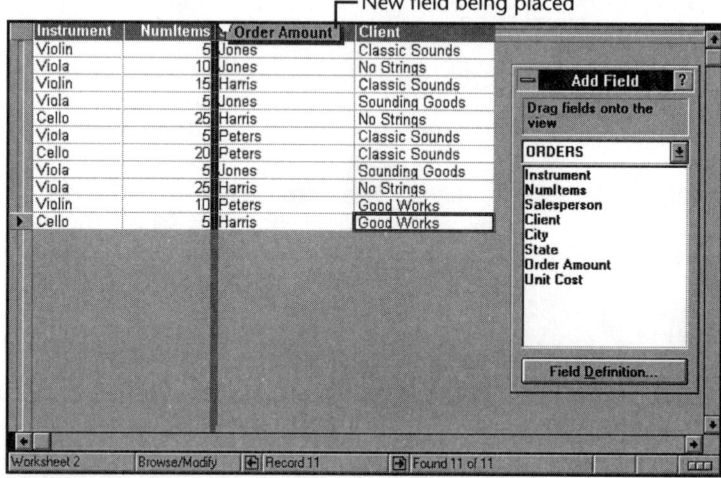

Fig. 14.8
Insert a new field by dragging its name onto the worksheet.

Deleting Fields

To delete a field from a worksheet:

1. Click the label for that column, then release the mouse button.

2. When the mouse cursor changes to the shape of a hand, click the column label again, hold down the button, and begin dragging the hand up. As you do, the hand changes to the shape of a wedge, as shown in figure 14.9. Continue dragging the icon up and off the worksheet.

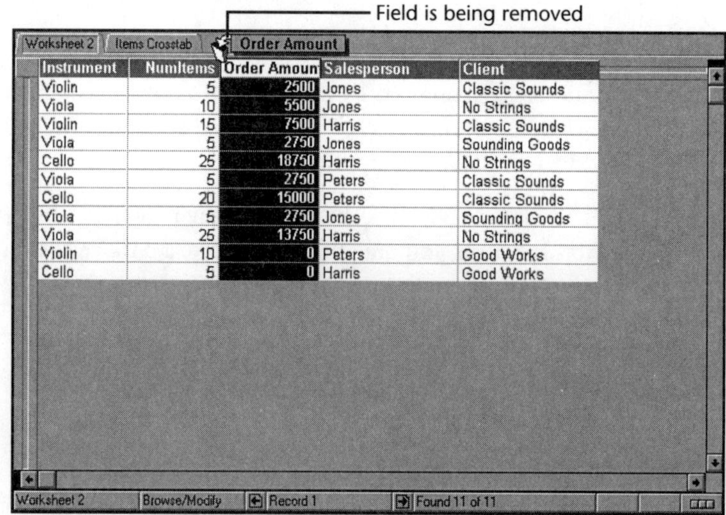

Fig. 14.9
Use the mouse to drag a field off the worksheet.

Rearranging the Fields

When you create a new worksheet, the columns are arranged in the order in which you originally selected the corresponding fields. However, you can easily rearrange the columns at any time.

To move a column from one position to another:

1. Click the label for that column, then release the mouse button.
2. When the mouse cursor changes to the shape of a hand, click the column label again, hold down the button, and drag the column left or right to the new position on the worksheet.

Inserting Special Calculations

You can enhance your worksheets by including special calculations based on values in the database. For example, suppose a worksheet contains the fields NUMBEROFITEMSSOLD and PRICEPERITEM. You can insert a special column that displays the product of these two fields.

Adding a special calculation to a worksheet requires two steps. First you create a new blank column where you want the calculations to appear; then you insert a formula into that column. Approach automatically applies the formula to every record in the worksheet.

When building a calculation, you can use any of Approach's built-in functions, or you can use standard arithmetic operators to create simple calculations.

Note

Approach contains a large repertoire of useful built-in functions. To review these functions, display the Formula dialog box, shown in figure 14.10. Open the Worksheet menu and choose Add Field, click the Field Definition button, click the Options button, and then click the Formula button.

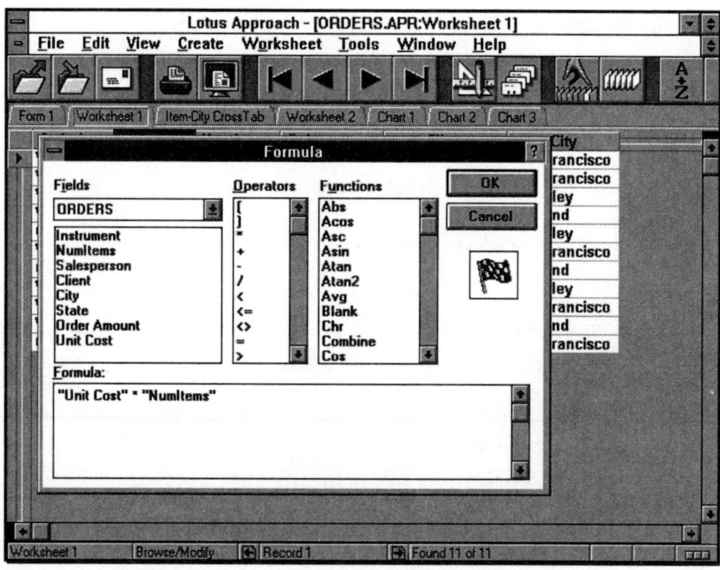

Fig. 14.10
Use the Formula dialog box to add a calculated field to your worksheet.

To insert a formula into a new column, follow these steps:

1. Select the column that's just to the left of where you want to insert the new column.

2. Open the W**o**rksheet menu and choose Add **C**olumn. The new column is created, and the Formula dialog box appears (see fig. 14.10).

3. In the bottom box, enter the formula you want to use. To use one of Approach's built-in functions, type the function exactly as it appears in the Functions list box. For example, to display the LASTNAME field values in all uppercase, you would enter the formula **Upper(LastName)**.

4. Click OK. Approach calculates the formula for every record in the worksheet and displays the results in the column.

Customizing the Worksheet Appearance

Approach offers a great deal of flexibility in customizing the appearance of your worksheets. You can:

- Adjust row and column sizes
- Edit column labels
- Customize cell background and border colors
- Control the formatting of cell contents

Adjusting Row and Column Sizes

You can adjust the width of individual columns. This might be necessary, for example, to accommodate extra-long data values. You can also control row heights. For instance, this might be necessary to accommodate text whose font size you have increased. Any change you make to the height of a row is automatically applied to every row in the worksheet.

To change the width of an individual column:

1. Click the column gutter at the right edge of the column you want to adjust, until the mouse cursor takes the shape of a double arrow (see fig. 14.11).

2. Holding down the mouse button, drag the mouse right or left to resize the column.

3. Release the button when the column is the size you want.

Tip
To insert extra space between columns, insert a blank column and adjust its width.

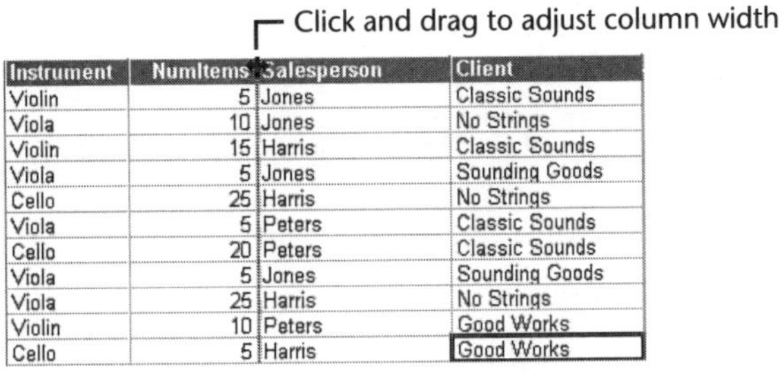

Click and drag to adjust column width

Instrument	NumItems	Salesperson	Client
Violin	5	Jones	Classic Sounds
Viola	10	Jones	No Strings
Violin	15	Harris	Classic Sounds
Viola	5	Jones	Sounding Goods
Cello	25	Harris	No Strings
Viola	5	Peters	Classic Sounds
Cello	20	Peters	Classic Sounds
Viola	5	Jones	Sounding Goods
Viola	25	Harris	No Strings
Violin	10	Peters	Good Works
Cello	5	Harris	Good Works

Fig. 14.11
You can adjust individual column widths.

To adjust the row height:

1. Click the row gutter at the bottom of any row, until the mouse cursor takes the shape of a double arrow.

2. Holding down the mouse button, drag the mouse up or down to resize the row.

3. Release the button when the row is the size you want.

Caution

If you reduce the row height too much, the entire worksheet disappears! If this happens, move the mouse cursor to the upper-left corner of the worksheet, at the top of the row gutter. When the cursor changes to a double arrow, drag it down approximately one-half inch. The worksheet reappears, and you can readjust the row heights—this time more carefully.

Changing Column Labels

When you create a new worksheet, Approach assigns field names to the column labels. However, you can change any of these labels to improve the clarity of the worksheet.

To modify a label:

1. Click the label you want to edit three times. The entire label is highlighted, and the text cursor appears.
2. To enter an entirely new label, just begin typing—the original label is replaced by whatever you enter. Or, you can click the label a fourth time to position the text cursor. You can then use the standard keystrokes for editing.

Customizing the Cell Appearance

Tip
You can customize one or more groups of columns, but you can't customize individual rows or cells.

You can customize the appearance of a table so that different columns and labels stand out in different ways. For instance, you can alternate the background colors of different columns, or assign special fonts to the labels.

You can customize any of the following groups of cells:

- A single column
- A group of columns
- One or more column labels
- The entire worksheet

To customize one or more columns, either with or without their labels, you must first select the cells; then you can apply any of the changes described in the following sections.

Displaying the Info Box

Using the Info Box, you can customize the cells that are currently selected. Unlike many other dialog boxes, you can switch back and forth between the Info Box and the regular Approach window. This means that you leave the Info Box on the screen while you select columns for customizing, then immediately switch back to the Info Box to make your changes.

You can use any of the following methods to display the Info Box:

- Click the Info Box icon.
- Open the W**o**rksheet menu and choose **S**tyle & Properties.

- Press Ctrl+E.
- Click anywhere on the worksheet with the right mouse button. Then choose Style & Properties from the temporary menu that appears.

The contents of the Info Box depends on which part of the worksheet is currently highlighted. For example, if an entire column is highlighted, the Info Box looks like the one shown in figure 14.12. On the other hand, if only a single cell is highlighted, the Info Box looks like the one shown in figure 14.13.

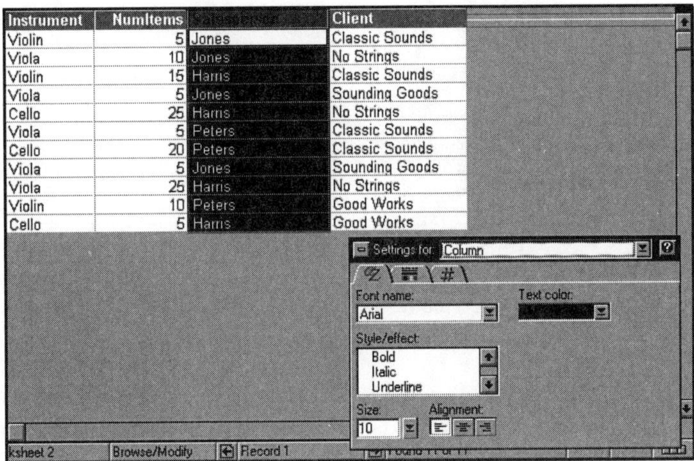

Fig. 14.12
The Info Box when one or more columns is highlighted.

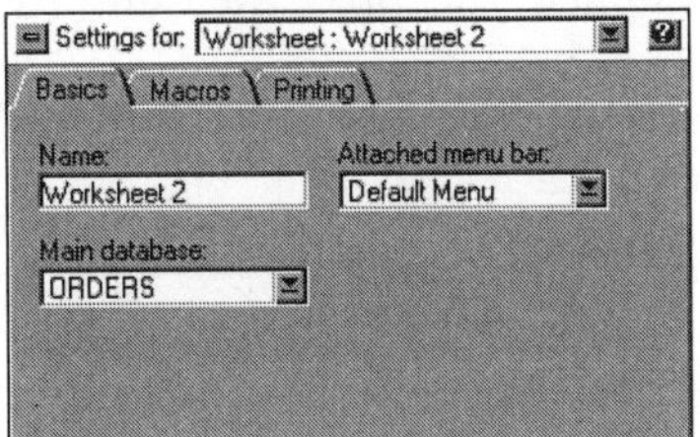

Fig. 14.13
The Info Box when a single cell is highlighted.

Tip
The options described in this and the following two sections are not available for single cells, single rows, or groups of rows.

To make a selection from the Info Box, follow these steps:

- Select the group of cells you want to customize.
- Click the appropriate tab at the top of the Info Box.
- Make your choices from the options that appear.

Cell Fill and Border Colors

To choose colors for the cell fill and borders, follow these steps:

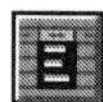

1. Click the column label to select the entire column. If you want to exclude the column label from your changes, click the Select Column Cells icon.

2. Click the middle tab at the top of the Info Box (see fig. 14.14).

3. Select your choices for cell fill and border colors.

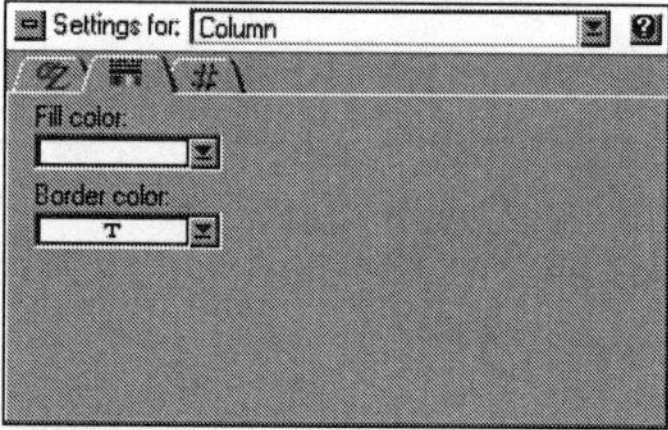

Fig. 14.14
Use this section of the Info Box to customize cell colors and borders.

Font, Color, and Alignment

You can control the appearance of data within one or more columns by adjusting their font, style, color, and alignment. To make these changes:

1. Click the column label to select the entire column. If you want to exclude the column label from your changes, click the Select Column Cells icon.

2. Click the left-most tab at the top of the Info Box (see fig. 14.15).

3. Select your choices for font, style, color, and alignment.

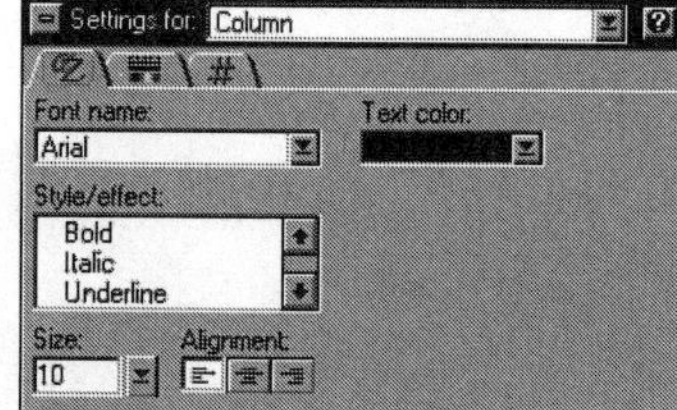

Fig. 14.15
Use this part of the Info Box to control the appearance of text.

Data Formatting

You can control the format of the data in a worksheet. The options available to you depend on whether you're formatting text, numeric, date, or time information.

To format the data in all the cells of one or more columns, follow these steps:

1. Select the entire column or columns, then exclude the column labels.
2. Click the right-most tab at the top of the Info Box (see fig. 14.16).
3. In the drop-down list box labeled Format Type, select the type of data displayed in the column.
4. A new set of list boxes appears, depending on the type of data you select. Using these list boxes, select the type of formatting you want.

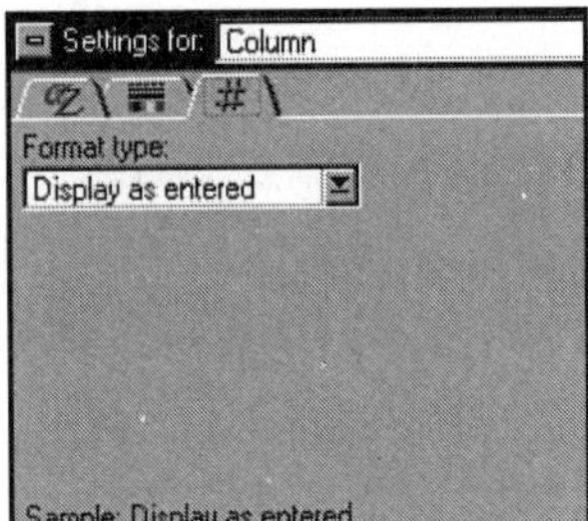

Fig. 14.16
Use the Info Box to control how text is formatted.

Customizing the Worksheet Settings

Several worksheet *settings* are associated with each worksheet, and you can adjust these settings to control various aspects of the worksheet. These settings include the following:

- The worksheet name
- Parameters that control how a worksheet appears when printed
- Macros that execute when you select or deselect a worksheet

These settings are all accessible via the Info Box for the worksheet, which you can display by using any of the methods described earlier. When the Info Box appears on your screen, click any single worksheet cell—except a column label—and the Info Box changes to look like figure 14.17.

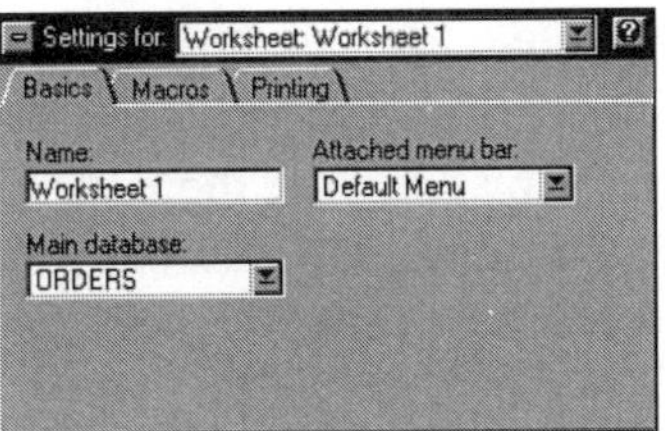

Fig. 14.17
Use this Info Box to choose the worksheet settings.

To change a worksheet name, click the left-most tab at the top of the Info Box, click the Name text box, then enter the new name.

You can attach two macros that will execute whenever you switch to or from a worksheet. To specify these macros, click the middle tab of the Info Box, pull down each of the macro lists and make your selection. Note that you can select an existing macro, or you can define a macro on the spot by clicking the Define Macro button in the Info Box.

You can control certain aspects of how a worksheet appears when printed. To make these selections, click the right-most tab of the Info Box, then choose the print options you want.

Manipulating Worksheet Records

Because a worksheet can display large amounts of data, it can sometimes be a handy view for editing database information. Using a worksheet, you can:

- Edit existing data
- Add and delete records
- Select subsets of records for display in a worksheet
- Arrange the order in which the records are displayed
- Copy information from the worksheet to the Clipboard

Editing Data

To edit an individual data value in a worksheet, follow these steps:

1. Double-click the cell.
2. When the text cursor appears, make any editing changes you wish.
3. To record your edits to the database, either press Enter or click anywhere outside the cell; or to restore the original cell value, press Esc.

Adding and Deleting Records

Because a worksheet offers a handy view into your data, you may prefer to use it as a vehicle for adding and deleting records. Of course, when you add new records you can insert values only for those fields displayed in the worksheet. This isn't a serious restriction, because you can easily add new fields to the worksheet—even on a temporary basis.

Adding Records

To add one or more new records, follow these steps:

1. Click the Create a New Record icon. Approach inserts a blank line at the bottom of the worksheet and moves the text cursor to the left-most cell there.

2. Enter the data values for the new record. To move from one cell to the next, use either the Tab key or the mouse.

If you press Tab when the cursor is positioned in the last cell of the new record, Approach automatically creates another blank line and tabs to its left-most cell, where you can begin adding another record.

Deleting Records

> **Caution**
>
> You can easily delete a large number of records with a single operation. Be careful to select only those records you want to delete.

To delete one or more records, follow these steps:

1. Select the record you want to delete by clicking next to it in the row gutter. To select multiple adjacent records, drag the mouse cursor down after the first record is highlighted (see fig. 14.18).

Instrument	NumItems	Salesperson	Client
Violin	5	Jones	Classic Sounds
Viola	10	Jones	No Strings
Violin	15	Harris	Classic Sounds
Viola	5	Jones	Sounding Goods
Cello	25	Harris	No Strings
Viola	5	Peters	Classic Sounds
Cello	20	Peters	Classic Sounds
Viola	5	Jones	Sounding Goods
Viola	25	Harris	No Strings
Violin	10	Peters	Good Works
Cello	5	Harris	Good Works

Records to be deleted

Fig. 14.18
Use the mouse to select records for deletion.

2. To delete the selected records, do one of the following:

   - Click the Delete Current Record icon.
   - Open the **E**dit menu and choose Cu**t**.
   - Open the W**o**rksheet menu and choose **D**elete **S**elected Records.

After asking you for verification, Approach deletes the records you selected.

> **Note**
>
> You can't delete selected groups of cells in a worksheet. You can delete only entire records. You can, however, erase the contents of individual cells.

Finding and Sorting Records

Using standard Approach commands, you can sort the order in which the records appear in a worksheet. You can also use Find commands to select subsets of records for display.

To sort the records displayed in a worksheet, open the W**o**rksheet menu and choose Sor**t**. The steps for performing these operations have been described elsewhere in this book and are not repeated here.

To display a subset of the records in the database, follow these steps:

1. Open the W**o**rksheet menu and choose **F**ind **F**ind command. Approach displays a blank line on the worksheet (see fig. 14.19).
2. Enter the search criteria for specifying the records you want to display.
3. Click OK.

Approach finds and displays only those records matching your search criteria.

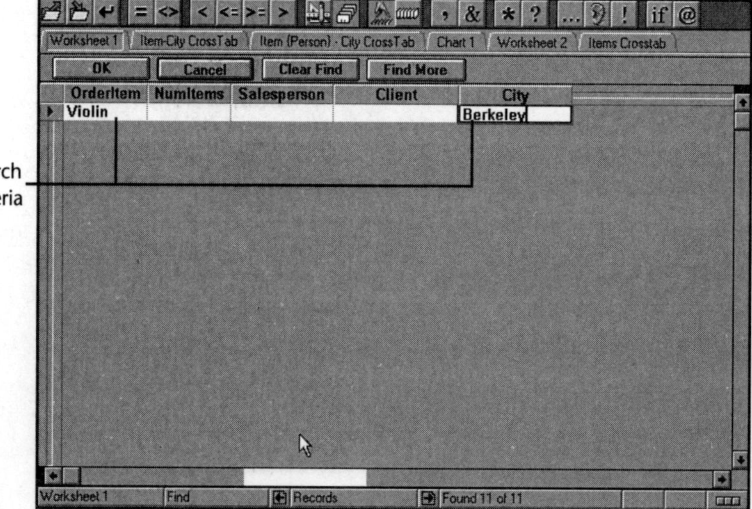

Fig. 14.19
Enter the search criteria for selecting a subset of records.

Copying Data to the Clipboard

You can copy part or all of a worksheet to the Clipboard. From there, you can then paste, link, or embed the information into a document in another application, as follows:

- As tab-delimited values, with a hard return inserted at each end-of-record. This format would be useful, for example, for pasting into an Ami Pro document or a 1-2-3 spreadsheet.
- As a graphic in Windows Metafile (WMF) format. For instance, you can paste a group of cells into a frame within an Ami Pro document, where it can then be manipulated as an ordinary graphic.
- As an embedded or linked OLE object.

To copy part or all of a worksheet, follow these steps:

1. Select the cell or cells you want to copy. To select the entire worksheet, click the upper-left corner of the worksheet, at the intersection of the row and column gutters.
2. Open the **E**dit menu and choose **C**opy. Approach copies the selected information to the Clipboard.

Using Crosstabs

A crosstab, which is short for *cross-tabulation worksheet,* is a special type of worksheet in which you can display summary information from a database. A crosstab can display summaries based on one, two, or several fields; and the crosstab calculations can be sums, numbers, averages, or other statistical measures.

Figure 14.20 shows a simple type of crosstab for the Orders database described earlier in this chapter. This crosstab summarizes the sales information from the database, categorized by the different values found in the INSTRUMENT field. The left-most column lists the different instruments sold (cello, viola, and violin), and the numbers in the second column are the total number of each type sold. The top row lists the name of the *summary field,* NUMITEMS, which is used in calculating these totals.

	NumItems
Cello	50
Viola	50
Violin	30
Total	130

Fig. 14.20
A crosstab view summarizes database information over a single field.

A crosstab view is an extremely flexible tool for analyzing database information. For instance, if you're not quite satisfied with the type of summary information displayed by a crosstab, you can easily modify it to display other summary information by adding and deleting fields.

Unlike a worksheet, a crosstab displays summary information about a database, rather than showing individual database values. Crosstabs are useful because they can condense a great deal of information into a small amount of space. For example, if a musical instrument dealer is doing a yearly budget, he may want to know the total yearly sales of each instrument type; but he won't care about the details of each sale, such as who bought which instruments.

A crosstab can summarize information either by number, average, or other statistical measures. You can create a crosstab to display summary information based on the values in one, two, or even three or more fields. Approach's intuitive interface makes it easy to create these different types of crosstabs. Moreover, you can change a crosstab as you work with it, so that you can quickly and easily see a variety of different perspectives on a database.

Crosstab Examples

The data from the Orders database illustrates some of the different types of crosstabs you can create. In this particular database, each record represents an order placed by a customer for a certain number of instruments of a particular type.

Figure 14.21 shows a common type of crosstab, based on the values in three fields:

INSTRUMENT: The type of instrument sold in any particular order.

NUMITEMS: The number of instruments sold in each order.

CITY: The city in which a customer does business.

	Berkeley	Oakland	San Francisco	Total
	NumItems	NumItems	NumItems	NumItems
Cello	25	20	5	50
Viola	5	5	40	50
Violin	15	10	5	30
Total	45	35	50	130

Fig. 14.21
This crosstab summarizes instrument sales by instrument type and city.

This crosstab shows the total number of instruments sold, categorized both by instrument type and city. The types of instruments are shown in the left-most column; and the city names are listed in the top row. The NUMITEMS field furnishes the numeric data for the body of the crosstab. A glance at this data indicates that 25 cellos have been sold to customers in Berkeley, and 20 to customers in Oakland.

Notice that the second row down from the top shows the name of the field used in performing the summary calculations, NUMITEMS, in this example. This is called the *summary calculations label.*

Figure 14.20 shows a more condensed type of crosstab, which summarizes total instrument sales broken down only by instrument type. Again, the NUMITEMS field furnishes the numeric data for the summary values in the body of the crosstab.

You can create a crosstab that summarizes information based on several fields. For instance, the crosstab in figure 14.22 shows summary information on instrument sales, broken down by instrument, city, and also by salesperson. This crosstab shows that five violins were sold in San Francisco by a salesperson named Jones.

		Berkeley	Oakland	San Francisco	Total
		No. of Items	No. of Items	No. of Items	No. of Items
Cello	Harris	25		5	30
	Jones				
	Peters		20		20
Viola	Harris			25	25
	Jones	5	5	10	20
	Peters			5	5
Violin	Harris	15			15
	Jones			5	5
	Peters		10		10
Total		45	35	50	130

Fig. 14.22
This crosstab summarizes instrument sales by instrument type, city, and salesperson.

Creating a Crosstab

The same basic steps are used for creating all types of crosstabs. You choose the fields from which the summary information is to be drawn, and you select the type of crosstab calculation you want. Approach automatically assigns a name like Crosstab 1 to the new crosstab, but you can change the name later to something more specific.

To create a new crosstab, follow these steps:

1. Open the **C**reate menu and choose Cross**t**ab. Approach displays the Crosstab Assistant dialog box, as shown in figure 14.23.

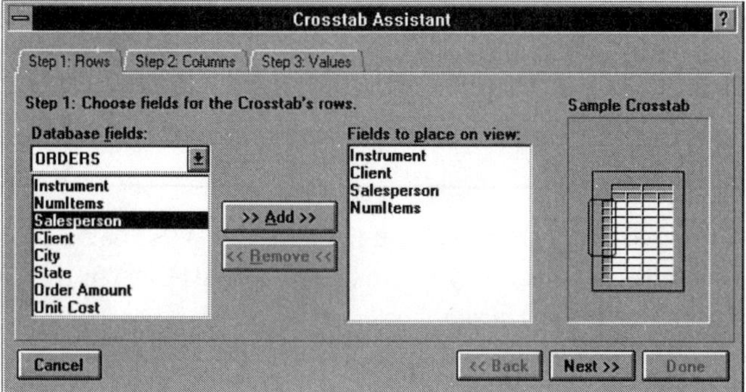

Fig. 14.23
Use the Crosstab Assistant to select the fields for a new crosstab.

> **Note**
>
> At each step in using the Crosstab Assistant, the diagram at the right side of the dialog box illustrates which items you're currently selecting.

2. Make sure the Step 1: Rows tab is selected.

3. Select the field (or fields) you want to use for the rows of the crosstab. For example, for the crosstab shown in figure 14.20 you would select the INSTRUMENT field.

4. Click either the Step 2: Columns tab at the top or the Next button.

5. Choose the field (or fields) for the columns of the crosstab. For example, for the crosstab in figure 14.21 you would choose the CITY field.

6. Click either the Step 3: Values tab at the top or the Next button.

7. Select the field to be used as the basis of the crosstab summary calculations.

8. From the drop-down list at the top, select the type of summary calculation you want performed. This calculation is applied to the field you selected in step 7. For instance, for the crosstab in figure 14.20 you would choose the Sum function.

9. Click the Done button. Approach creates and displays the new crosstab.

Standard Operations with Crosstabs

Most of the operations available with worksheets are also available with crosstabs, including the following:

- Customizing the background and border colors of all the cells in a column
- Adjusting the font, alignment, and color of the text in the cells of a column
- Adjusting the width of individual columns
- Customizing the appearance of individual row and column labels
- Creating multiple panes for viewing up to four different parts of a crosstab
- Changing the name of the crosstab
- Assigning macros to the crosstab
- Setting parameters for printing a crosstab

Because of their nature, crosstabs do not lend themselves to some operations that are available with worksheets. These include the following:

- You can't edit the row or column labels, because they represent actual data values in the database.
- You can't edit the values in the body of a crosstab, because they are the results of summary calculations.
- You can't change the order of data appearing in either the rows or column. Approach automatically sorts these items alphabetically.

You can perform a variety of operations on crosstabs that are not available to worksheets or any other type of view. These are described in the following sections.

Special Crosstab Operations

Because of the unique qualities of crosstabs, Approach offers several crosstab operations that give you a great deal of flexibility. For example, you can change the height of individual rows, and you can customize groups of cells on a row-by-row basis. You can also edit the label that defines the type of information that's summarized in a crosstab.

You can add and delete fields in a crosstab, however, these operations have entirely different meanings compared to the equivalent operations with worksheets.

Adjusting Row Height and Appearance

As with worksheets, you must first select the group of crosstab cells you want to customize. You can use nearly all of the operations listed in Table 14.1 for selecting various parts of a crosstab. However, there are a few differences, which are listed in Table 14.2.

Table 14.2 Special Operations for Selecting Cells and Labels in a Crosstab

To Select	Operation
The entire crosstab, including labels	Click the upper-left corner of the crosstab, at the intersection of the row and column gutters.
All the row and column labels (both of the top two rows of column labels)	Click twice in the upper-left corner of the crosstab.
The main body of the crosstab, and also the column labels in the second row	Click anywhere on the second row.
All the labels in the second row	Click twice anywhere on the second row.

You can adjust the height of individual rows, as follows:

1. Click the row gutter on the bottom border of the row, until the cursor changes to a double arrow, as shown in figure 14.24.

2. Drag the cursor up or down to resize the row.

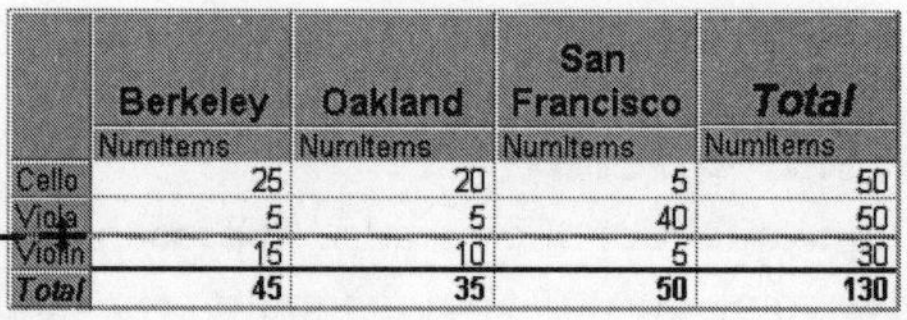

	Berkeley	Oakland	San Francisco	Total
	NumItems	NumItems	NumItems	NumItems
Cello	25	20	5	50
Viola	5	5	40	50
Violin	15	10	5	30
Total	45	35	50	130

Click and drag to adjust row height

Fig. 14.24 You can adjust the height of individual rows of a crosstab.

To clarify the nature of the crosstab calculation, you can edit the summary calculations labels in the second row. To change these labels, click three times anywhere on the second row, then make your changes. Note that these labels are identical for all columns, so when you make a change to any label, that change is automatically reflected in all the remaining ones.

Adding and Deleting Fields

You can easily change the basic meaning of a crosstab by adding and deleting fields. When you add a new field, Approach recalculates the entire crosstab, calculating new summary information based on the values in the new field, as well as by those of the original fields.

Adding a New Field

You can drag a field name either to the left edge of the crosstab or to the top, depending on how you want the new crosstab to appear. As you position the name, a black placement bar appears, indicating where the new field values will appear. The crosstab shown in figure 14.25 summarizes sales information by salesperson and city. In figure 14.26 the INSTRUMENT field name is positioned to the right of the SALESPERSON field values. When the INSTRUMENT field is added to the crosstab, Approach calculates new summary information based on the fields SALESPERSON, CITY, and INSTRUMENT, as shown in figure 14.27.

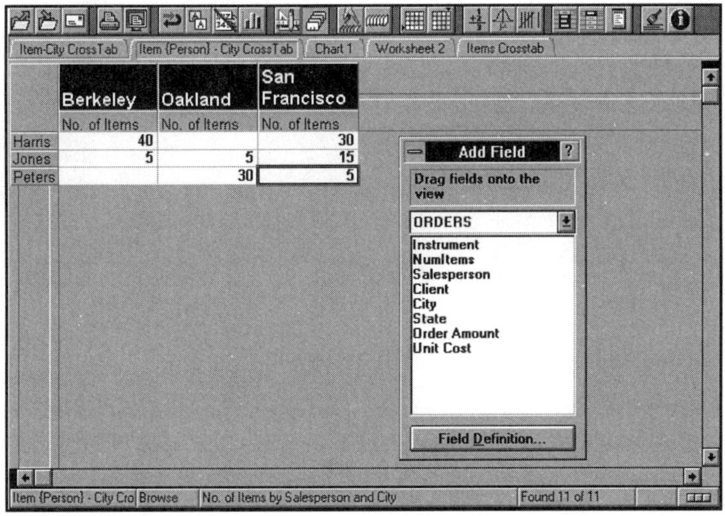

Fig. 14.25
A crosstab based on values in the SALESPERSON and CITY fields.

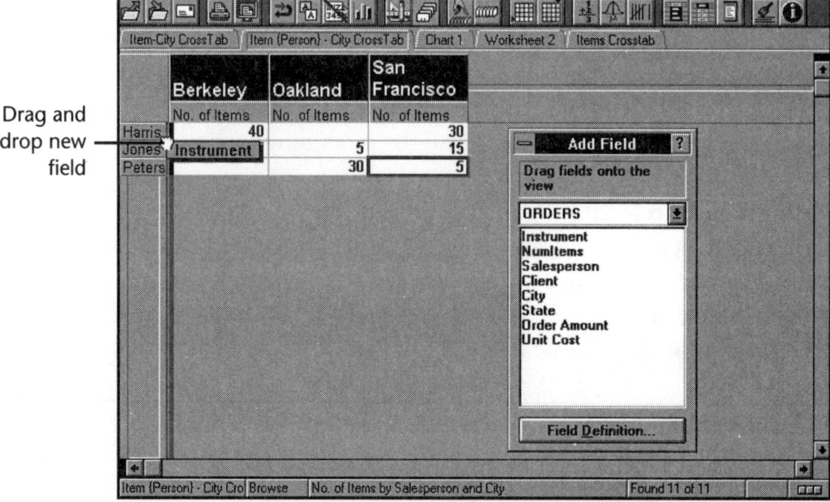

Fig. 14.26
Inserting a new field.

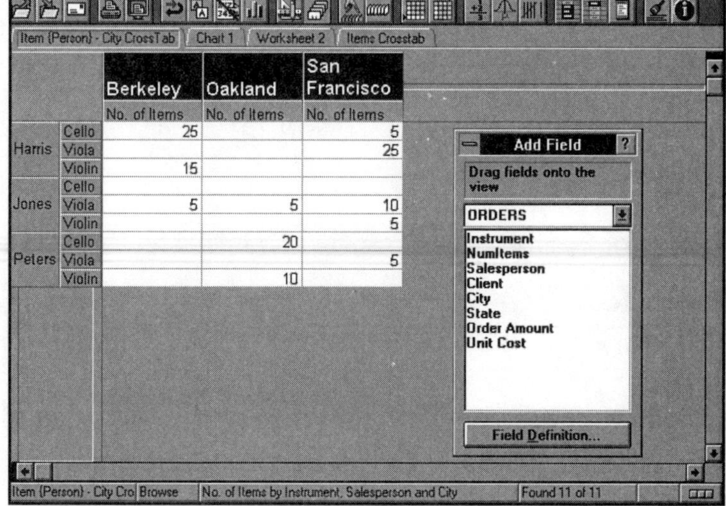

Fig. 14.27
The new crosstab, based on values in the fields SALESPERSON, CITY, and INSTRUMENT.

To add a new field to a crosstab, follow these steps:

1. Display the Add Field dialog box. To accomplish this, either click the Add Field icon or open the **C**rosstab menu and choose **A**dd Field.

2. To add a new field, drag its name from the Add Field dialog box onto the crosstab.

Note that when you add a new field to a crosstab, the resulting summary information is exactly the same regardless of where you place the new field. However, the exact placement order of this information depends on where you place the new field name.

Deleting a Field

Deleting a field from a crosstab has exactly the opposite effect from adding a field. Approach automatically recalculates the summary information, based on the remaining fields.

To delete a field from a crosstab, follow these steps:

1. Click anywhere on the row or column of values for that field.
2. When the cursor changes to the shape of a hand, click again in the same place and drag the field name up and off the crosstab.

Approach redisplays the new crosstab, basing the new calculations on the remaining fields.

Adding and Deleting Summary Rows and Columns

Each time you create a new crosstab, Approach automatically inserts summary columns and rows. For example, in the crosstab shown in figure 14.21, the far right column lists the total number of each type of instrument sold. If you prefer not to have these totals displayed, you can delete either the row, the column, or both.

To delete either the row or column of totals, click the row or column label, then release the mouse button. When the mouse cursor changes to a hand, drag the row or column away from the crosstab.

If you later change your mind, you can redisplay either or both the row and column totals, by opening the C**r**osstab menu and choosing S**u**mmarize Rows or Summarize **C**olumns. The corresponding totals row or column is added to the crosstab.

From Here...

Worksheets and crosstabs are powerful tools you can use when working with databases. Worksheets allow you to view and edit information in columnar format, whereas crosstabs offer a convenient mechanism for viewing summary information from all or part of a database file.

You can enhance the usefulness of worksheets and crosstabs by using other Approach features, such as charting, finding, and sorting groups of records. For more information, refer to the following chapters in this book:

- Chapter 5, "Working with Your Data," contains information about sorting groups of records.
- Chapter 6, "Finding Records," describes how to find selected groups of records.
- Chapter 15, "Creating Charts," tells you how to create graphical charts that let you visually analyze your data.

Chapter 15

Creating Charts

Using Approach's charting feature, you can create a wide variety of charts to enhance your tables. Each chart you create is stored as a separate view, and you can easily retrieve any particular one by selecting its name.

In this chapter, you learn how to:

- Distinguish between different types of charts
- Create a new chart
- Modify existing charts
- Customize a chart with legends, titles, and axes information
- Enhance charts with other text and graphics objects
- Adjust chart parameters, such as name, position, and background

Most of the charts shown in this chapter are based on sales figures from an Orders database for a musical instrument dealer. In this database, each record represents a single order placed by a customer. Each order is for a number of instruments of a single type (such as violins). Table 15.1 shows the data used for generating these charts. The fields in this table have the following meaning:

Field	Contents
INSTRUMENT	Type of instrument sold
NUMITEMS	Number of instruments sold
SALESPERSON	Name of salesperson making sale
CLIENT	Name of person or company purchasing instruments

Table 15.1 Sample Data

Instrument	NumItems	Salesperson	Client
Violin	5	Jones	Classic Sounds
Viola	5	Jones	No Strings
Violin	15	Harris	Classic Sounds
Violin	5	Jones	Sounding Goods
Cello	5	Harris	No Strings
Viola	8	Peters	Classic Sounds San Francisco
Cello	3	Peters	Classic Sounds Oakland
Viola	5	Jones	Sounding Goods Berkeley
Viola	5	Harris	No Strings San Francisco
Violin	5	Peters	Good Works Oakland
Cello	2	Harris	Good Works San Francisco

Using Charts

When creating a new chart, you can choose from a wide variety of types, including bar charts, pie charts, and many others. For each chart type, Approach offers a wide range of features you can customize, such as 3-dimensional effects, titles, legends, and many others. This section shows samples of the more commonly used types of charts you can create with Approach. These samples are representative only, because there are so many options available for each chart type.

Using Bar Charts

Bar charts are one of the most popular formats for displaying different types of information. Typically, the x-axis of a bar chart displays the different values stored in a field, while the values on the y-axis represent totals for those values.

For example, figure 15.1 illustrates a bar chart showing a breakdown of instrument sales. Here, the x-axis lists the different types of instruments, while the y-axis shows total number of each type sold. This bar chart offers a good visual representation of the relative sales numbers.

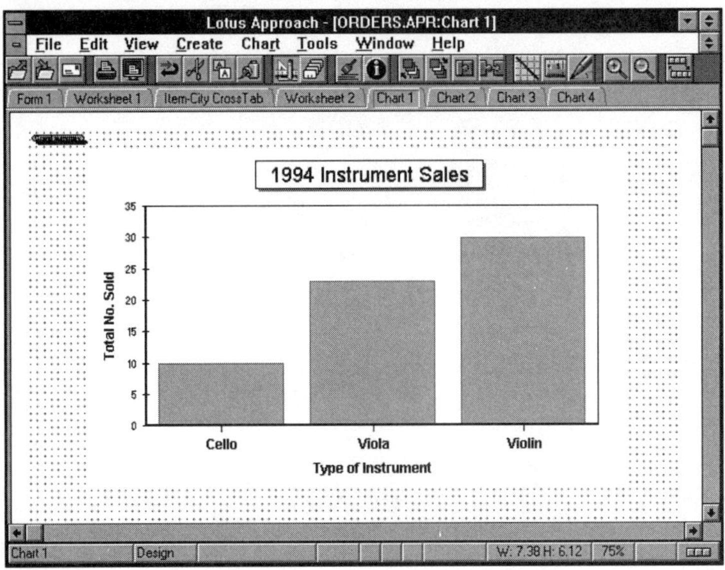

Fig. 15.1
A two-dimensional bar chart displays relative amounts.

You can enhance the appearance of bar charts by including special effects, such as depth and grid lines. When these modifications are applied to the bar chart in figure 15.1, the result is shown in figure 15.2. These enhancements—as well as many others—are available with most of Approach's chart types.

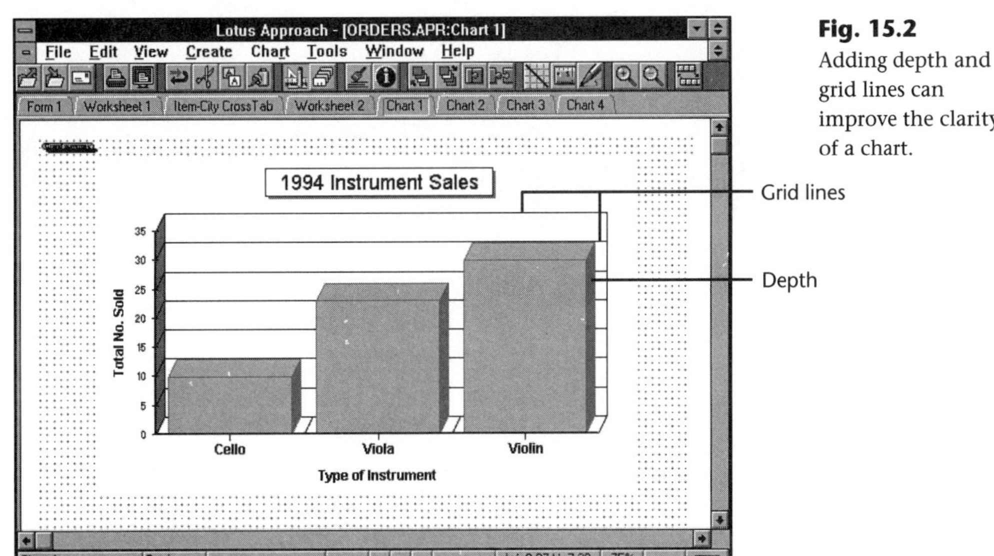

Fig. 15.2
Adding depth and grid lines can improve the clarity of a chart.

A bar chart is also a convenient tool for displaying values from more than one series of data. (A *series* is a subset of data within a database.) Using the data in Table 15.1 as an example, you can break down the total instrument sales by individual salesperson, so that the sales for each salesperson is a separate series. The result is the chart shown in figure 15.3.

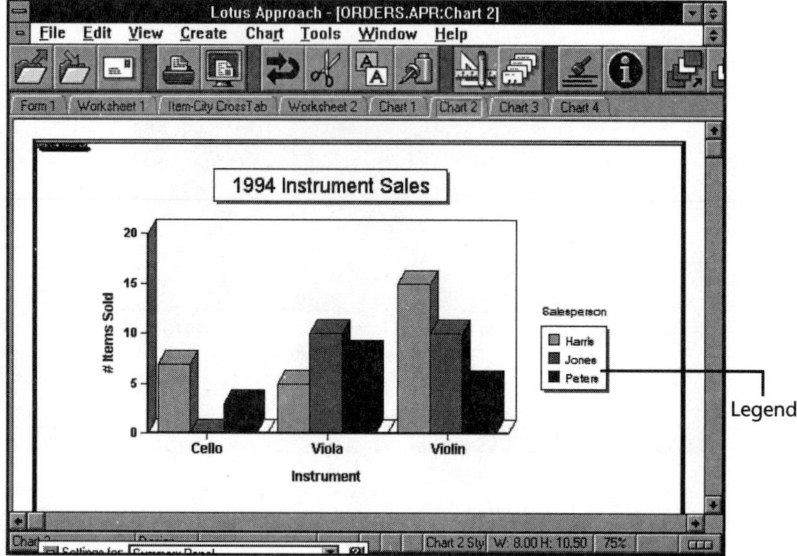

Fig. 15.3
Use a bar chart to display several series of values.

Note that figure 15.3 contains a legend, which serves to identify the different series included in the chart. You can optionally include a legend with most types of charts. Like other chart features, you can customize the appearance of the legend.

Another variation on the bar chart is the 3-dimensional perspective variety, such as the one shown in figure 15.4. Notice how this chart differs from the one shown in figure 15.3, even though both are drawn in three dimensions.

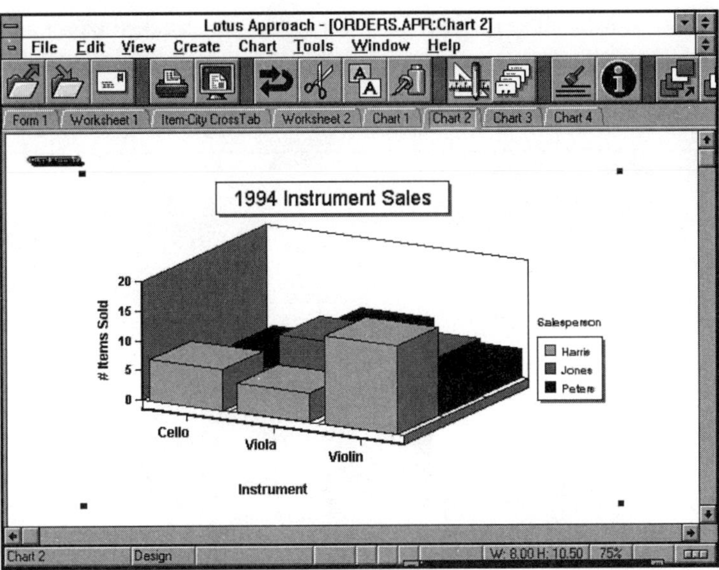

Fig. 15.4
A 3-dimensional chart gives a new perspective to data.

Figure 15.5 shows a type of bar chart in which the bars are drawn horizontally instead of vertically. There is no particular advantage in using a horizontal bar chart as opposed to a vertical one. The type you use is a matter of personal preference—either yours or your boss's.

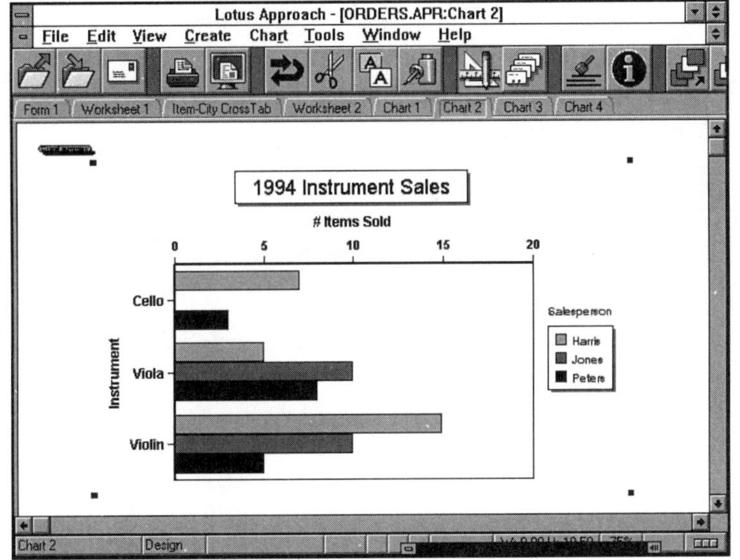

Fig. 15.5
Information can be displayed horizontally instead of vertically.

Figure 15.6 shows still another type of bar chart—the stacked bar chart. Here, the values for different series are placed directly on top of each other. This type of chart allows you to directly see various totals.

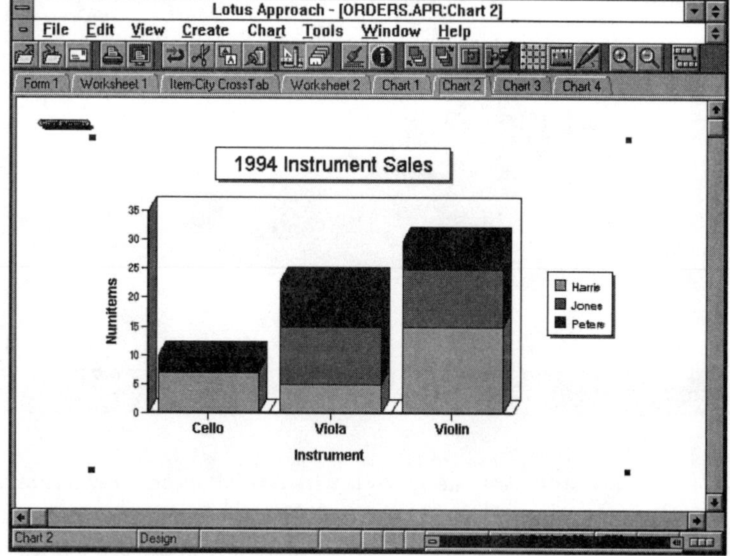

Fig. 15.6
A stacked bar chart offers another type of view.

Using Pie Charts

Pie charts are extremely popular, possibly because they remind us of food. Nevertheless, they do offer a unique way of displaying a single series of data, as shown in figure 15.7. An exploded pie chart, like the one in figure 15.8, adds a particularly dramatic touch.

A pie chart can display the information from only one series of data. For example, a pie chart can illustrate the total number of each type of instrument sold, but it can't display the total number of each type of instrument sold by each salesperson.

The legend shown in figure 15.7 is optional. You can control its placement and appearance, as you can with legends for other types of charts.

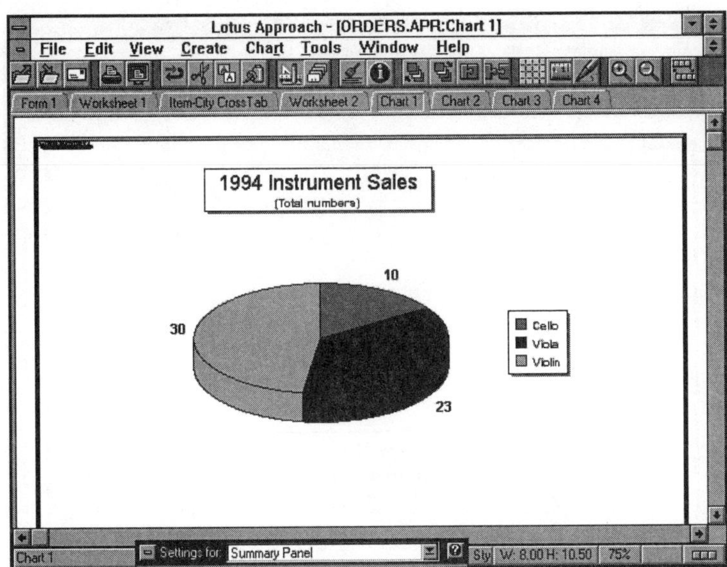

Fig. 15.7
A pie chart shows "slices" of your data.

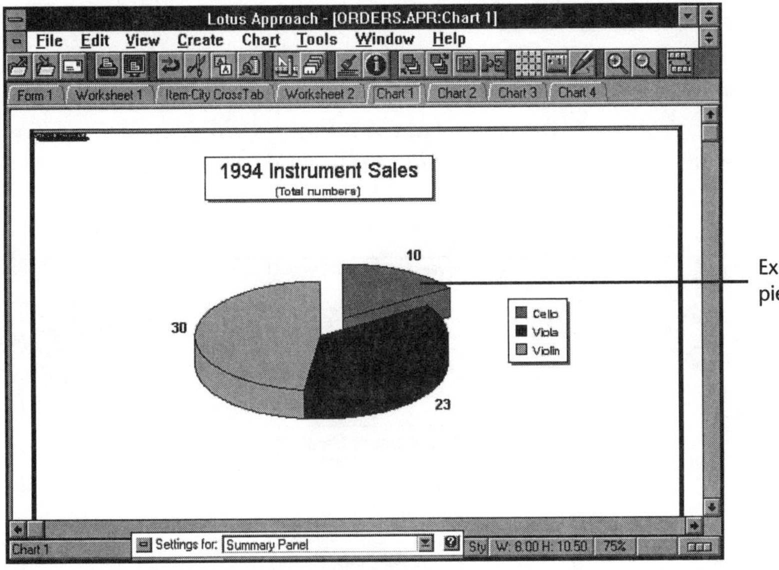

Fig. 15.8
An exploded pie chart can draw your attention to a single slice.

Using Line and Scatter Charts

Although not quite as striking as 3-dimensional bar or pie charts, *line charts* (also called x-y charts) and *scatter charts* are alternative ways of displaying relative values. Figures 15.9 shows an example of a line chart. A scatter chart is simply a line chart without the solid lines connecting the individual points.

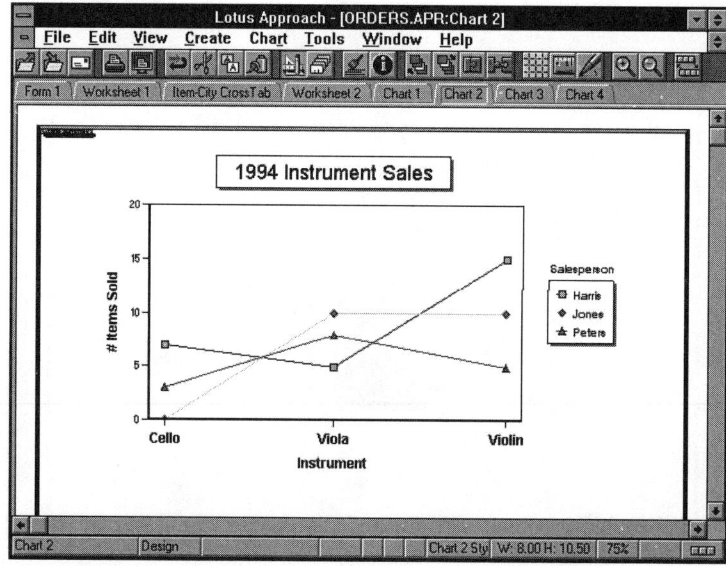

Fig. 15.9
A line chart shows relative values.

Using Area Charts

An *area chart*, such as the one shown in figure 15.10, is effective in portraying a change of values with respect to time or another variable. The advantage of using an area chart is that you can use it to show cumulative totals. For example, the vertical heights on the chart in figure 15.10 show total sales for each instrument type.

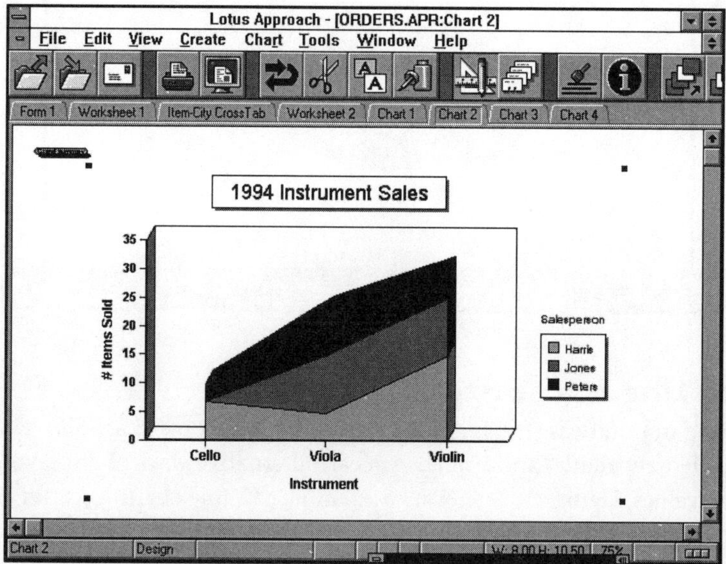

Fig. 15.10
An area chart stacks items for a cumulative total.

Creating a New Chart

There are two basic ways in which you can create a chart. The standard method is to use the Chart Assistant, which guides you through the steps for selecting the various chart elements. Alternatively, you can have Approach automatically create a chart directly from a crosstab view.

The first step in creating a new chart is to select the records you want to include by using standard Find commands. If you skip this step, Approach will automatically use all records in the current database.

After choosing the records to be charted, you can set up the basic format for the new chart. This includes the type of chart, the style and layout, and the fields to be plotted. Approach will then display the chart on-screen. If you wish, you can then customize the chart by using the wide variety of tools at your disposal.

Selecting the Data You Want to Chart

To chart a subset of records from a database, you must specify them as follows:

Tip
If you want to chart every record in a database, skip the steps below.

1. Switch to any convenient form, worksheet, or report for the table you want to chart.
2. If you select a report or a form view, switch to Browse or Preview mode.
3. Using a Find command, enter a query to specify the records you want to use.

4. Create the chart, as described in the following sections.

Suppose you select one of your worksheets in step 1 above. You would open the W**o**rksheet menu and then choose **F**ind **F**ind. Finally, type a query to specify which records you wanted.

Note

For more information on finding records, see Chapter 6.

Choosing the Chart Options

Note

A *series* is a subset of data for a particular field value. For example, if you create a chart showing company sales by salesperson, there will be a separate series of data for each salesperson.

After you have selected the records to be plotted, you can then create the chart. Choose the type of chart you want, the fields to be displayed on the x- and y-axes, and—if you plan to chart more than one series—the field to be used for isolating the different series. You can also override the default name supplied by Approach for the chart and select your own.

Note

When you create a new chart, you're limited to bar, line, area, and pie chart types. Later, when the chart is displayed on the screen, you can switch to one of the many other types of available charts.

Follow these steps to create a new chart:

1. Open the **C**reate menu and choose **C**hart. Approach then displays the Chart Assistant dialog box (see fig. 15.11).

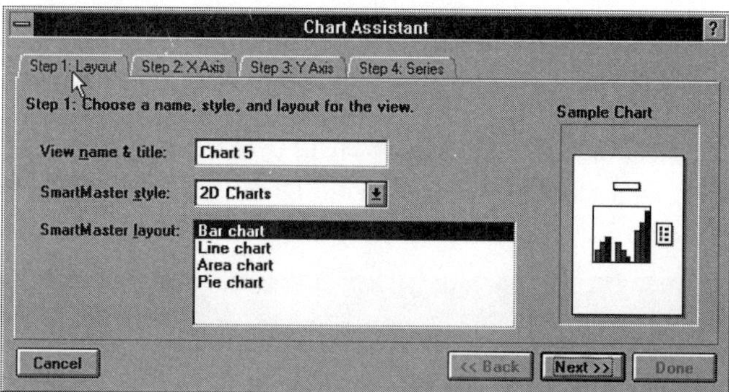

Fig. 15.11
Choose the basic layout features for the chart.

2. Make sure that left tab at the top of the Assistant is selected (the one labeled "Step 1: Layout"). Then fill in the options as shown in figure 15.11. At each step, the Sample Chart display on the right indicates which part of the chart you are currently choosing.

Note

If you select "pie" as the type of chart, the Step 2: X Axis tab at the top changes to "Pie Fields." Also, if you're creating a pie chart, skip to step 8 after you complete step 3.

3. Click the tab at the top labeled "Step 2: X Axis" or click the Next button.
4. When the next display appears select the field whose values you want to appear on the x-axis (see fig. 15.12).

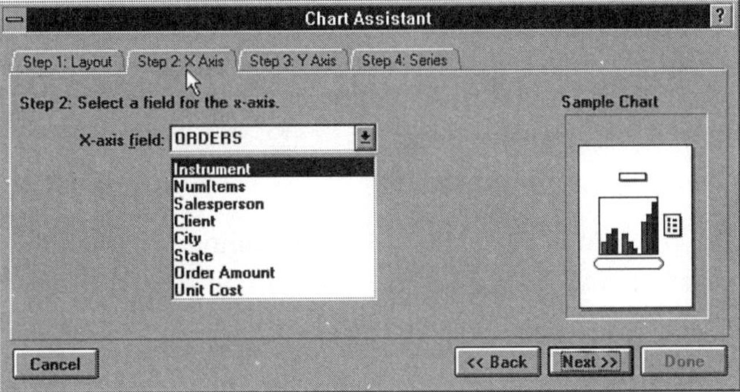

Fig. 15.12 Choose the field whose values will be displayed on the x-axis of the new chart.

5. Click either the Next button or the tab at the top labeled "Step 3: Y Axis." The screen then switches to the display shown in figure 15.13.

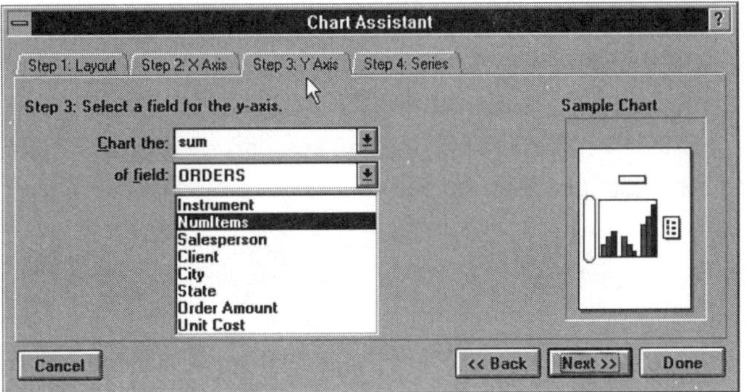

Fig. 15.13 Choose the field whose values will appear on the y-axis of the new chart.

6. Select the field whose values you want to appear on the y-axis.

7. Choose the type of calculation you want performed on the field you selected in step 6 (the most common selection is *Sum)*.

8. Click the top tab labeled "Step 4: Series" or click the Next button and you'll see the screen shown in figure 15.14. (If you plan to display only one series of values on the new chart, skip this step.)

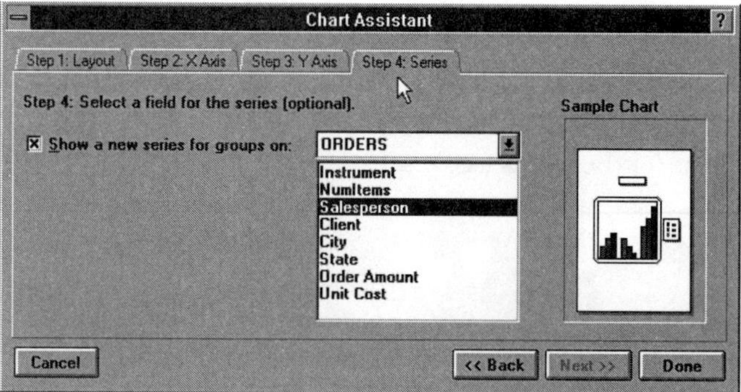

Fig. 15.14
Select the field that specifies the different series.

9. Choose the field whose values are to determine the different series in the chart. For example, if you select the SALESPERSON field, each individual name in this field will be the basis of a different series.

10. Click the Done button. Approach displays the new chart on your screen.

Creating an Instant Chart

If you're working with a crosstab view, you can bypass the steps described earlier for creating a new chart and let Approach automatically use the crosstab layout to create a vertical bar chart for you. This type of chart is called an *instant chart* because Approach automatically makes all the choices necessary to create the chart. If necessary, you can modify the chart by using the procedures described later in this chapter.

Note

For more information on crosstabs, see Chapter 14.

Suppose you're working with a simple crosstab based on the values of two fields, such as the one shown in figure 15.15. This crosstab lists the sum of the field NUMITEMS over all records for the various types of instruments. If you create an instant chart from this crosstab, it will be similar to the one shown in figure 15.16.

	NumItems
Cello	10
Viola	23
Violin	30
Total	**63**

Fig. 15.15
A simple crosstab.

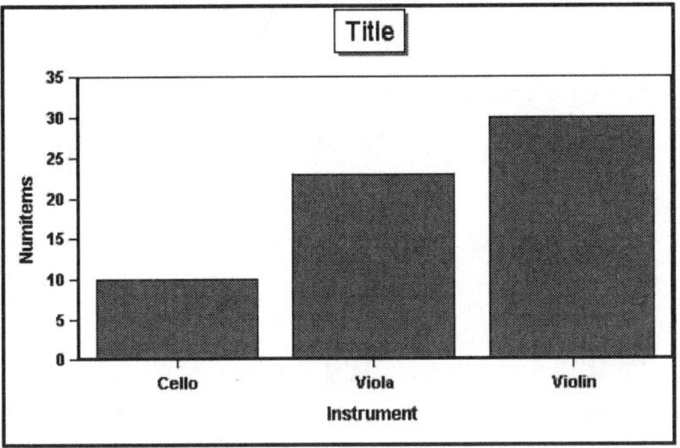

Fig. 15.16
You can have Approach automatically create an instant chart from a simple crosstab.

Similarly, a chart created from a crosstab based on three fields will be a bar chart showing several series of data. The field values in the first column of the crosstab will be displayed on the x-axis of the chart, while the field values displayed in the first row of the crosstab will furnish the values for the different series.

To create an instant chart from a crosstab, first select that crosstab as the current view, and then either click the Chart Crosstab icon or open the C**r**osstab menu and choose Char**t** Crosstab. Approach generates and displays the chart.

> **Note**
>
> When a new chart appears on-screen, the Drawing Tools also appear. To avoid this, open the **T**ools menu and choose **P**references, and deselect the Drawing Tools option. The next time you start up Approach, the Drawing Tools icons will not automatically appear.

Modifying an Existing Chart

Note

You can view a chart in either Preview or Design mode. To make any changes to a chart, however, you must be in Design mode. Furthermore, you must make sure the option Show Data in the View menu is selected.

Because you can modify just about any part of any chart, you have enormous control over its appearance. Here are some of the types of changes you can make:

- *Chart data.* You can change the fields whose values are displayed in a chart.
- *Chart type.* With a simple mouse click, you can change a chart from one type to another. For instance, you can easily switch from a bar chart to a pie, area, or other type of chart.
- *Chart layout.* The layout of a chart refers to whether or not a grid and/or legend are displayed with a chart.
- *Chart elements.* Each chart contains a variety of different bits and pieces, such as a title, legend, labels, and many other items. You can modify the appearance of these elements, and in many cases, you can also control their position.

Changing the Data in a Chart

When you create a chart, you select the fields whose values are to be displayed. If necessary, you can modify the chart later by selecting different fields. You can even change a chart that displays a single data series, so that it displays multiple series.

To select a different set of data to be displayed by the chart that's currently displayed, complete the following steps:

1. Open the Chart menu and choose Chart Data Source. The Chart Data Source Assistant dialog box appears (see fig. 15.17).

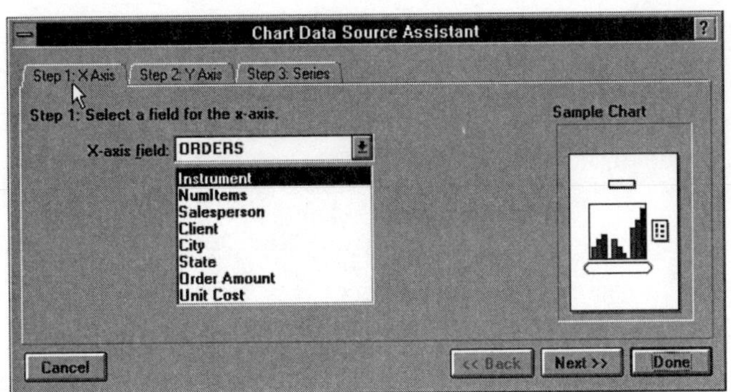

Fig. 15.17
Use the Chart Data Source Assistant dialog box to select a different data set for a chart.

2. Choose the new fields for the x-axis and y-axis.
3. To display multiple series, click the tab labeled "Step 3: Series"; then choose the field whose values will define the different series.
4. After making your selections, click the Done button. Approach will then recalculate and display the modified chart.

Tip
Using the Chart Data Source Assistant dialog box is nearly identical to using the Chart Assistant. However, the labels of the top tabs are arranged somewhat differently.

Using the Chart Info Box

To make most changes to a chart, you use its Info Box from the Design mode. As with other parts of Approach, the contents of the displayed Info Box depends on what you select on-screen. When the Info Box is displayed, you can switch back and forth between it and the regular Approach window; you can leave the Info Box on-screen while you select different parts of a chart for customizing, then immediately switch back to the Info Box to make your changes.

You can display the Info Box for a chart using any of the following methods:

- Click the Info Box icon.
- Open the Cha**r**t menu and select **S**tyle & Properties.
- Press Ctrl+E.
- Double-click anywhere on the chart.

The contents of the Info Box changes, depending on which part of a chart you've selected. However, its basic appearance remains the same, similar to that shown in figure 15.18.

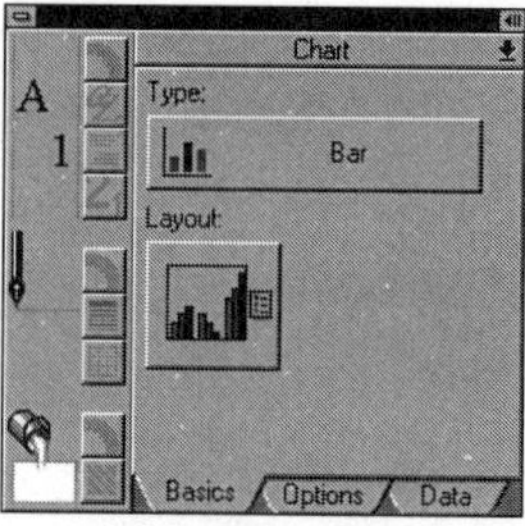

Fig. 15.18
Customize a chart by using its Info Box in Design mode.

To select which part of a chart you want to modify, pull down the list box at the top, as shown in figure 15.19, then make your selection. You can also double-click directly on the chart item you want to modify, in which case the Info Box will automatically display the appropriate options for you to modify.

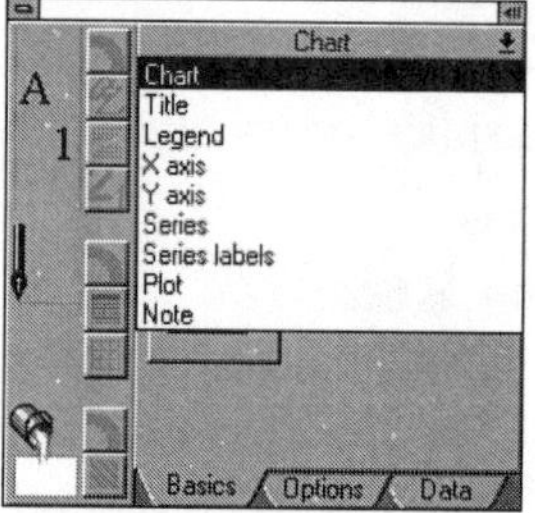

Fig. 15.19
Select the chart element you want to customize.

The left part of the Info Box contains various options for modifying colors, lines, and text attributes. Each of these elements remains dim unless it applies to the chart item you've currently selected. The bottom of the Info Box shows various tabs, which you can select to display other options.

> **Note**
>
> When working with the Info Box, the Summary Panel Info Box may sometimes appear, often caused by clicking outside the chart area. Double-clicking this Info Box's control box to delete it doesn't help much because it will continue to reappear. You can drag the Summary Panel Info Box down as far as it will go, so that it's nearly invisible.

Making Changes to Text, Lines, and Closed Objects

You can use the Info Box to customize the appearance of various text and line items on a chart. You can also select different fill colors for enclosed objects, such as bars.

Modifying Text

Note

When the Info Box for a chart is displayed, you can select an entire text element by clicking it once—its four handles will then appear. In some cases, you can select just part of a text element by double-clicking it and then highlighting the text you want to customize.

By changing the typeface, size, attributes, alignment, and numeric formatting, you can change the appearance of any text element on a chart. To make these adjustments to a text element, select that element and then use the top four buttons on the upper-left part of the Info Box.

Caution

Do not try to delete a text element by using the Del or Backspace key—or by opening the Edit menu and selecting Cut. If you do, the entire chart will disappear. Here's why: if you look closely, any chart you're working with is always selected. You can see this by noticing that its four selection handles are visible. When you press the Del or Backspace key, anything that's selected is deleted—in this case, the entire chart!

To change the font and attribute of the text you've selected, click the second button from the top, then make your selections from the Font dialog box that appears (see fig. 15.20).

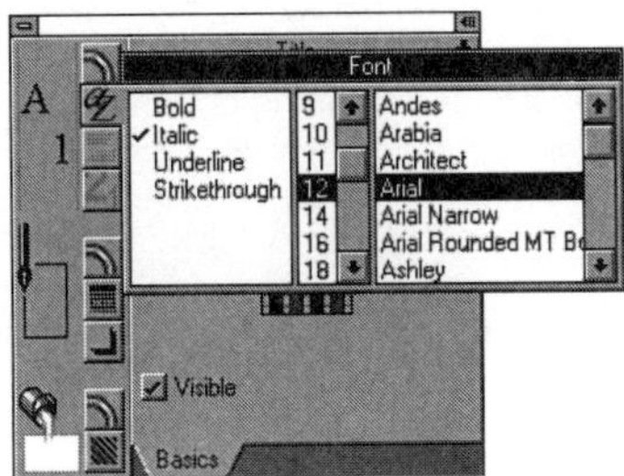

Fig. 15.20
You can customize text fonts and attributes.

To change the color of the selected text, click the top button, then select the color you want (see fig. 15.21).

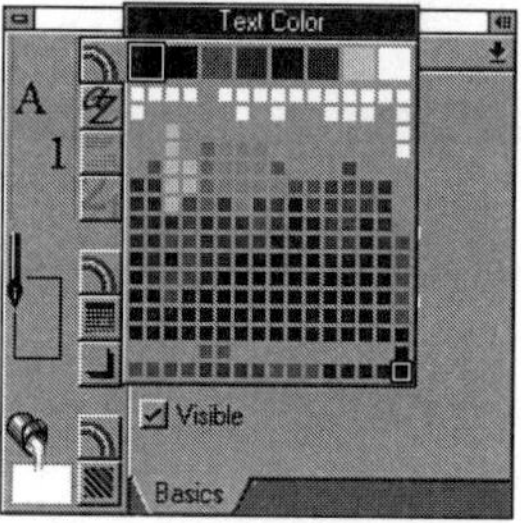

Fig. 15.21
You also can customize text colors.

To customize the format for numeric information, click the fourth button from the top. Then make your selections from the displayed options (see figure 15.22). These options are described in the following table.

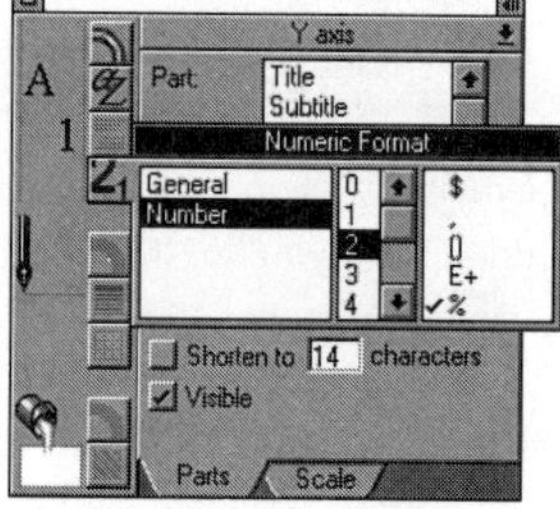

Fig. 15.22
You can format numeric text with these options.

Tip
These options are not available for non-numeric information.

Option	Description
General	Lets Approach automatically format the numbers. If you select this option, you can't choose any of the others described below.
Number	Use the remaining options to apply custom formatting.
# decimal places	From the middle column, choose the number of decimal places to apply.
$	Inserts a dollar sign before each number.
,	Insert commas as thousands separators, as needed.
()	Use parentheses to surround negative numbers.
E+	Use normalized exponential formatting for all numbers.
%	Express number as a percent.

Modifying Lines

Many components of a chart, such as the x- and y-axes, contain straight lines. Using the fifth and sixth buttons (down from the top) on the left side of the Info Box, you can customize the color and style of these lines.

- To customize the color of a line you've selected, click the top button in this group (see fig. 15.23), and then select the color you want.

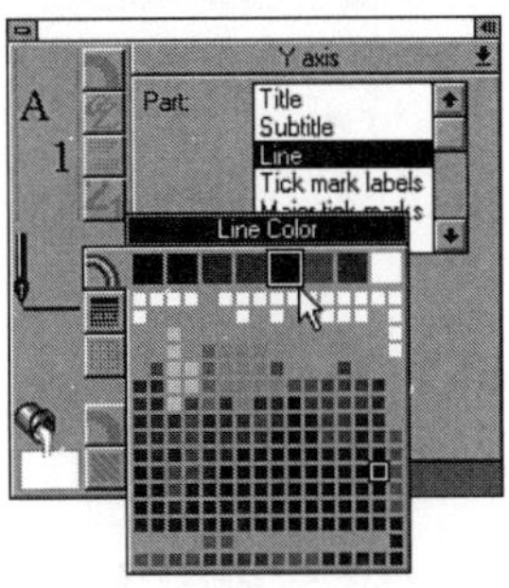

Fig. 15.23
Use these options to customize the color of a line.

- To customize the style of a line, click the middle button in this group (see fig. 15.24), and then select the style you want.

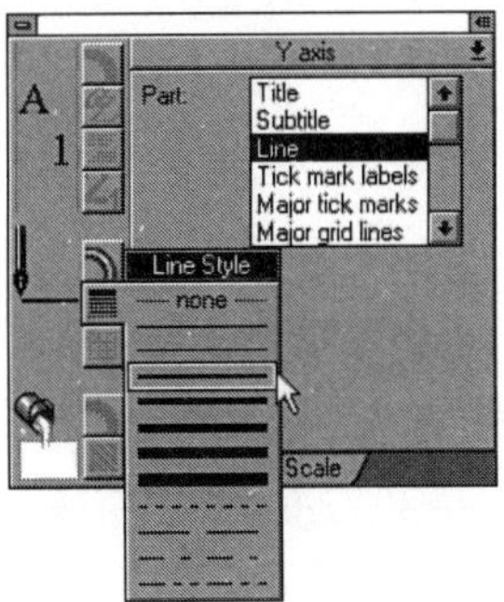

Fig. 15.24
Use these options to customize the style of a line.

Modifying Fill Colors

Many chart elements consist of closed areas, such as bars and pie wedges, and you can customize these areas by applying fill colors and patterns. To make these changes, you use the bottom two buttons on the left side of the Info Box, as shown in figure 15.25.

Fig. 15.25
Choose a color and fill pattern for the selected area.

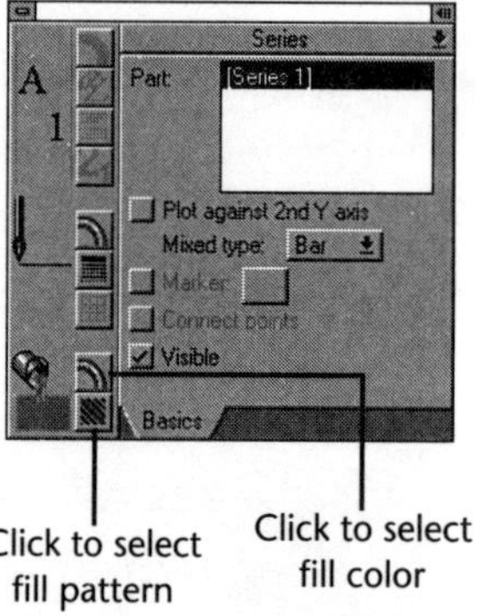

To select a color for a selected area, click the top button in this group, then select the color you want. To select a fill pattern, click the bottom button in this group, then select the pattern.

Modifying the Chart Type and Layout

When you create a new chart, you must choose one of the four basic types: line, bar, area, or pie. However, you can later change the chart type, choosing from a wide variety. You can also change the layout of a chart, which specifies the inclusion and placement of the following items:

- Legend
- Major grid lines
- Placement of various labels

To change the type of a chart, as well as its layout, follow these steps:

1. Make sure the chart is displayed on-screen and that you're in Design mode.
2. Pull down the list box at the top of the Info Box.
3. Select Chart from the drop-down list.
4. To choose a new chart type, click the large button directly under the Type label. When the display of available types appears, make your selection (see fig. 15.26).

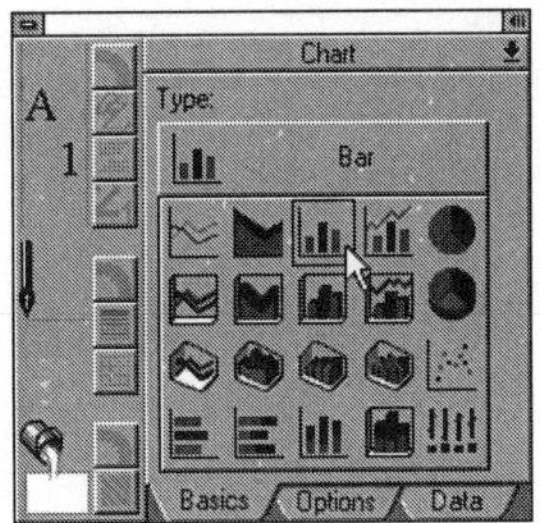

Fig. 15.26
Select the type of chart you want.

5. To choose a layout for the chart, click Layout in the Info Box. Make your selection from the list that appears (see fig. 15.27).

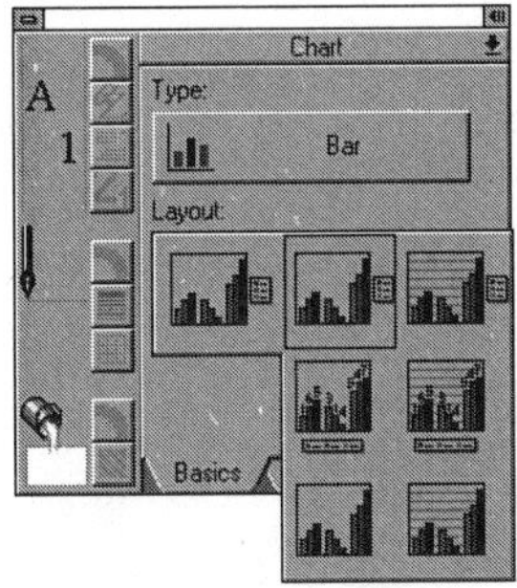

Fig. 15.27
Select the type of layout for your chosen chart.

Customizing the Chart Elements

Each type of chart has its own set of elements, and you can customize most of them. This section describes how to customize the elements that are common to most chart types. Figure 15.28 shows the standard elements:

- The *chart title* is a heading for the chart.
- The *legend* identifies the series when a chart contains more than one series.
- *X-axis* and *y-axis components* (including titles, lines, tick marks, and labels) identify and quantify the information being charted.

To help you learn how to customize the various types of charts, we'll go through the basic steps for each of the above types of elements. If you become familiar with these operations, you should then be able to customize any part of any chart.

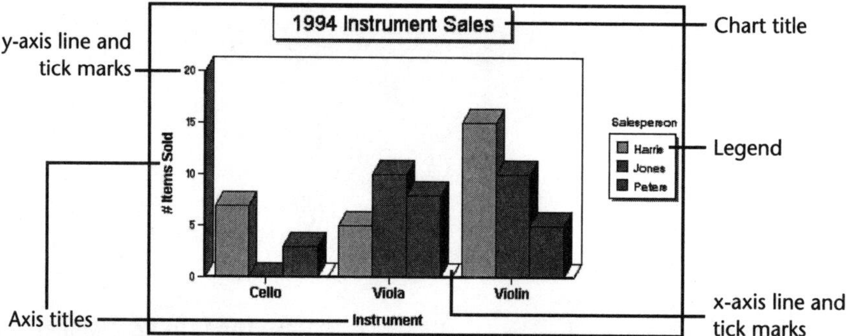

Fig. 15.28
Many elements are common to most charts.

To customize part of a chart, you must first display the Info Box, using any of the methods described earlier. Then, to select the part you want to change, you can do either of the following:

- Click the top drop-down list box (see fig. 15.19) and select the element containing the part you want to customize.
- Click directly on the part of the chart you want to customize.

When you select the element you want—using either of the above—the entire right section of the Info Box changes, displaying options specific to that element. In some cases this could include a list, from which you select the particular part of the element you want to customize.

For some elements, several tabs may become visible at the bottom of the Info Box, offering other options.

Adding a Chart Title

When Approach creates a new chart, it automatically affixes a title at the top. You can do the following to customize this title:

- Edit the text of the title.
- Customize the background, line, frame, and shadow of the title box.
- Change the font, style, and color of the text.
- Change the position of the title.
- Add a second title line.

To customize a title, select it by clicking it so that the Info Box appears as shown in figure 15.29. (You can also pull down the list box at the top of the Info Box, and then click Title.) To modify the title, follow these steps:

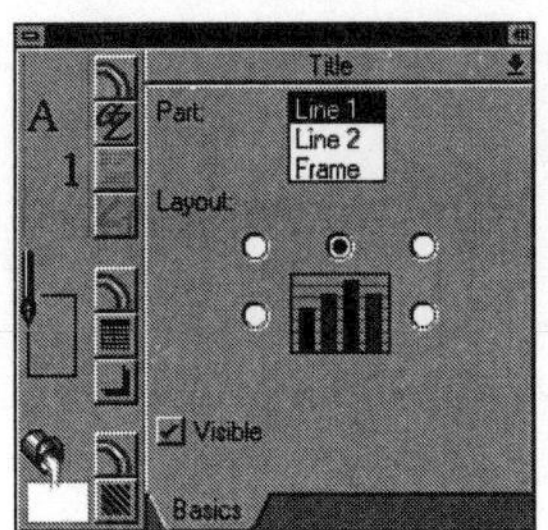

Fig. 15.29
You can customize a chart's title.

1. To edit the text in the title, double-click anywhere in the text and then make your changes.

2. To add a second line to the title, click the option labeled "Line 2" in the Info Box. When the new line appears in the title, double-click it, and then enter the text you want.

3. To change the font or color of the title, use the two buttons in the upper-left corner of the Info Box.

4. To modify the background color and fill pattern of the frame around the title, use the two bottom buttons.

5. To change the shadow of the title frame, use the third button up from the bottom.

6. To change the color and style of the line around the title frame, use the fifth and sixth buttons from the top.

7. To change the position of title on the page, click your choice in the Info Box. You can then click and drag the title to fine-tune its location.

8. To resize the title frame, click it so that the eight outer handles become visible (or, you can click the Frame option in the Info Box). Click and drag any of the handles in or out to resize the frame.

9. To remove the title from the chart, deselect the Visible option in the Info Box.

Tip
You can click the Visible checkbox to display or hide many of the chart elements. To delete a particular element from the chart, click it and then deselect the Visible option in the Info Box.

Adding a Legend

If a chart contains a legend, you can customize it in the following ways:

- Change its position with respect to the chart.
- Edit any part of the legend text.
- Change the font, style, and color of the legend text.

- Customize the frame surrounding the legend, including its size, color, and shadow.

To customize a legend, first select it so that the Info Box appears, as shown in figure 15.30. (Alternatively, you can select Legend from the pull-down list box at the top of the Info Box.) You can then use the various Info Box options to make your changes.

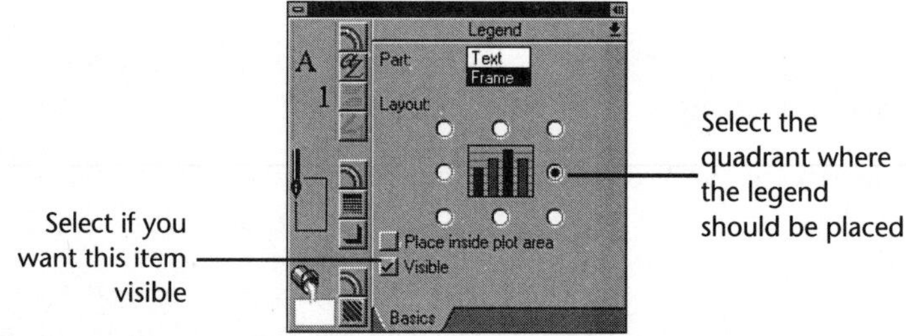

Fig. 15.30 Use these options to customize a chart legend.

Inserting a Note

You can insert a one- or two-line note at the bottom of a chart. You can customize this note, using the same types of options available for the chart title and legend.

To create a note, follow these steps:

1. Pull down the list box at the top of the Info Box, then select the Note option.
2. Make sure the Visible option is selected.
3. In the list box labeled Part, select "Line 1." A new line appears below the chart, and the Info Box takes on the appearance shown in figure 15.31.

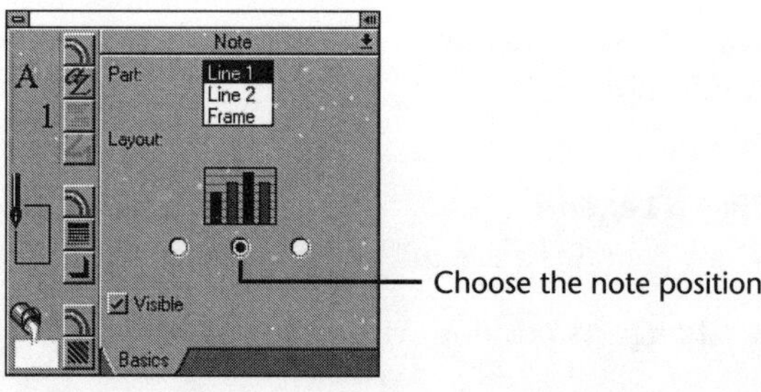

Fig. 15.31 You can create and customize a note for a chart.

4. Double-click the new note, then enter the text you want.

5. To customize the appearance of the note text, use the two top-left buttons of the Info Box.

6. To add a second line to the note, click the "Line 2" option in the Info Box. Then, double-click the new line and enter the text you want.

7. To customize the frame surrounding the note, use the five lower-left buttons of the Info Box.

8. To reposition the note horizontally, click it once and then drag it to where you want it. Alternatively, you can click one of the three radio buttons under the Layout option in the Info Box.

Tip
You can't change the vertical position of a note.

Customizing the X- and Y-Axes

With the exception of pie charts, all other chart types use x- and y-axes. Each axis includes the following parts, which you can individually customize:

- Title and subtitle
- Axis line
- Tick marks
- Labels for data values on the axis
- Range and scale for the axis data values
- Major grid lines

Tip
You can hide all the components of the axis by deselecting the Visible option in the Info Box.

To customize the components of either the x-axis or y-axis, select it from the pull-down list at the top of the Info Box. Alternatively, you can click any part of the axis you want to modify. The Info Box will then take on the appearance shown in figure 15.32.

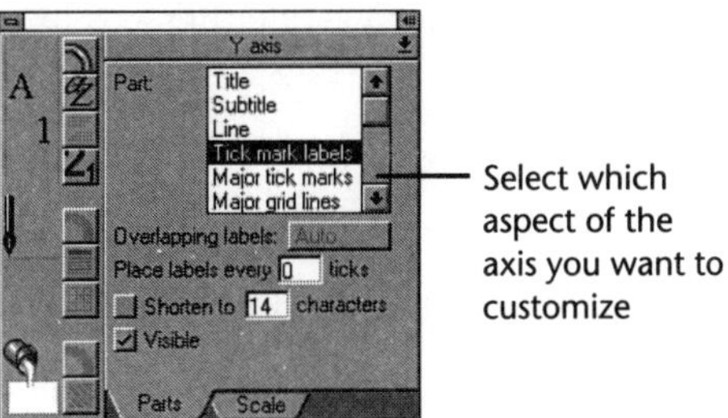

Fig. 15.32
Use these options to customize either axis of a chart.

Tip

You can't directly change the position of the axis title. To do so indirectly, deselect the Visible option for the title, then insert a text object wherever you want it.

Adding Title and Subtitles

Approach sets the title for each axis to the name of the field whose values are shown on that axis. You can edit this title by double-clicking it and then making your changes.

You can also add a subtitle to each axis, as follows:

1. Click Subtitle in the list box labeled Part.
2. Click the Manual option in the Info Box.
3. Pull down the Layout list (below the Manual option), then choose the location for the subtitle: either under or adjacent to the main axis title.
4. When the new subtitle appears, double-click it and then enter the text for it.

Note

You can customize the appearance of axis titles and subtitles using the techniques described earlier for other text elements (such as the chart title and legend).

Adding an Axis Line, Tick Marks, and a Scale

You can customize the following items on an axis:

- Color and style of the main axis lines
- Tick marks
- Range and scaling of data values
- Grid lines

To customize the color and style of either axis line, complete the following steps:

1. Pull down the list box at the top of the Info Box and select either "X axis" or "Y axis."
2. Select the Line option in the list box labeled Part.
3. To customize the color and style of the line, use the fifth and sixth buttons down from the top-left corner of the Info Box.

You can adjust the characteristics of the tick marks on either axis. Follow these steps:

1. Pull down the Part list box and click the Major Tick Marks option.
2. To customize the color and style of the tick marks, use the fifth and sixth buttons from the top-left corner of the Info Box.
3. To adjust the position of the tick marks relative to the axis, select a radio button under the Layout option.

> **Note**
>
> The scale options apply to an axis only if it displays numeric values.

You also have a great deal of control over the range and scaling of the data values displayed on an axis. To adjust these options, follow these steps:

1. In the top drop-down list box, select the axis you want to customize.
2. Click the Scale tab at the bottom of the Info Box, which then changes to the display shown in figure 15.33.

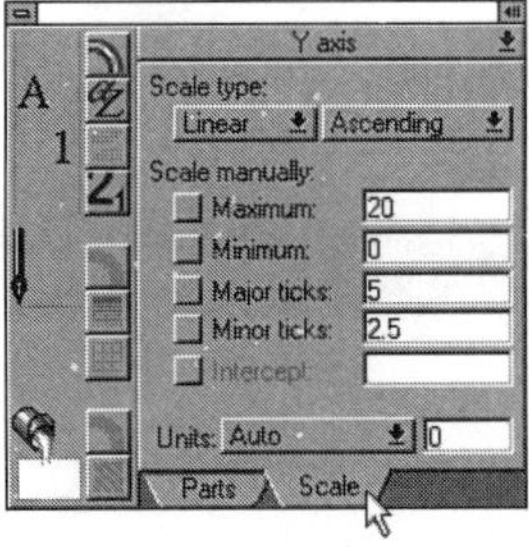

Fig. 15.33
You can customize the range and scale of a chart.

3. To select the type of scale you want (*linear* or *log, ascending* or *descending*), make your selections from the Scale Type drop-down list boxes.
4. To manually set the upper and lower limits and the position of the tick marks, make your selections for the Scale Manually options.
5. To manually set a multiplication factor for the data values displayed on the axis, pull down the list box labeled Units, then make your selection. For example, if you select Thousands, Approach will multiply every value on the axis by 0.001.

Adding Grid Lines

Grid lines can help you to read and interpret various types of charts, and you can optionally display grid lines for most chart types—pies being the notable exception.

When you display horizontal or vertical grid lines on a chart, they appear at the positions of the major tick marks on the corresponding axis. You can display these grid lines even if you hide these tick marks.

Here's how to display and customize either the vertical or horizontal grid lines for a chart:

1. Pull down the list box at the top of the Info Box.
2. Select either the x- or y-axis.
3. In the Part list box, click the Major Grid Lines option.
4. Select the Visible option. The grid lines will then appear at the same positions as the major tick marks on the axis, as shown in figure 15.34.

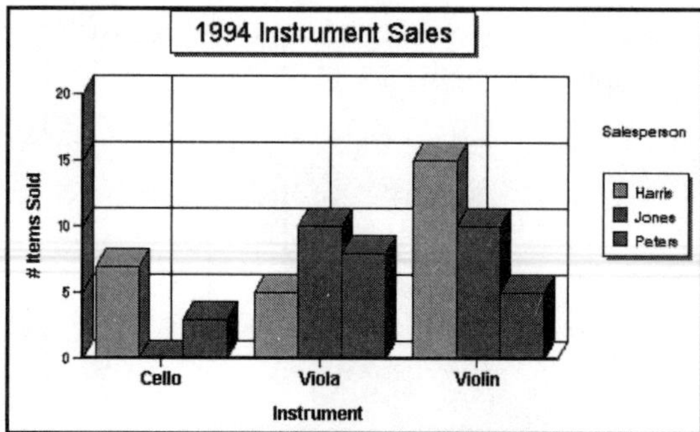

Fig. 15.34 Grid lines help you compare values.

5. To adjust the line color and style of the grid lines, use the fifth and sixth buttons from the top-left corner of the Info Box.

Deleting a Chart

You can easily delete a chart that's no longer of use to you. To accomplish this, use virtually the same steps you would for deleting any other type of view.

To delete a chart, follow these steps:

1. Display the chart you want to delete. The easiest way to accomplish this is to click the tab for that chart in the upper part of the Approach

window. You can also pop up the list of views for the current Approach file—in the lower-left corner of the status bar—and then click the name of the chart.

2. Pull down the **E**dit menu and choose D**e**lete Chart.

3. When Approach asks you to verify your deletion, choose **Y**es.

Enhancing a Chart with Text and Graphics

You can liven up your chart by inserting various text and graphics elements. For instance, you could add special text labels (in addition to those available as standard chart features), or you could insert a company logo. Figure 15.35 shows a chart containing both of these types of elements.

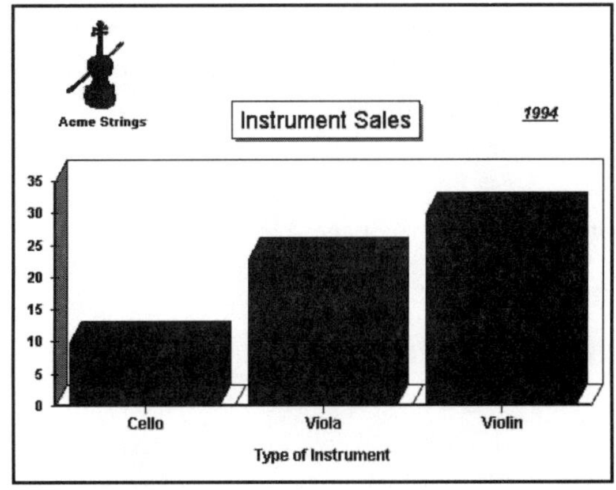

Fig. 15.35
You can place text and graphics objects on a chart.

You can add the following types of objects to a chart:

- Text objects
- Circles and ellipses
- Squares and rectangles
- Graphics images from other files
- Macro buttons

To add any of these elements, use the same techniques you would use for adding them to other types of Approach views. Suppose you want to add a special title to a chart, such as the "1994" object shown in figure 15.35. To insert this title as a text object, you could use the following steps:

1. Open the **C**reate menu and choose Dr**a**wing, and then choose **T**ext.
2. Click approximately where you want the text object to appear on the chart. An empty text object will then appear in this position.
3. Type in the text for the new label.
4. To customize the text, display its Info Box: Choose Cha**r**t **S**tyle & Properties; then click the text object. Make your customizing selections in the Info Box.
5. To deselect the text object, click anywhere outside of it.

Adjusting Chart Parameters

In addition to customizing the various bits and pieces that make up a chart, you can also adjust several parameters that affect the overall chart. These parameters include the following:

- Chart name
- Position of the chart on the page
- Background color
- Macros associated with the chart
- Printing the chart

Tip
You must be in Design mode in order to change the name of a chart.

Changing the Chart Name

When you create a new chart, Approach automatically assigns it a name like Chart 1, Chart 2, and so on. You can change it to a more descriptive name. To accomplish this, double-click the chart name on the tab at the top of the chart window then type in the new name (see fig. 15.36).

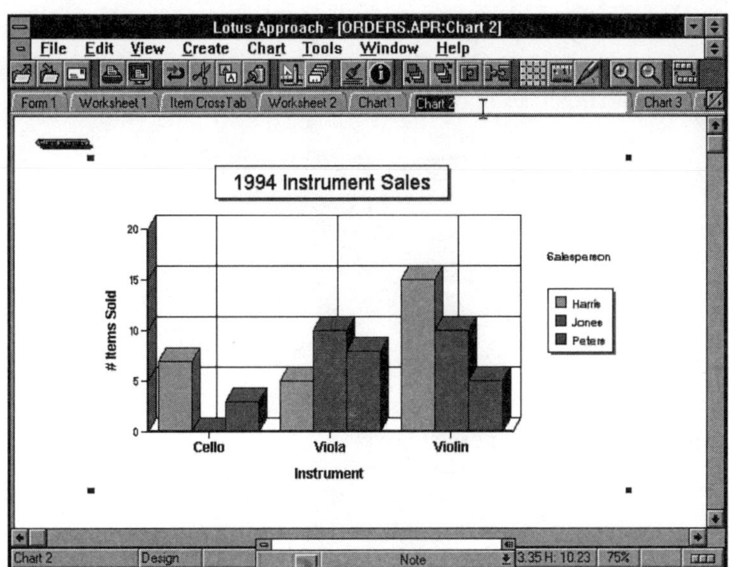

Fig. 15.36
Double-click to change a chart's name.

Adjusting the Chart Position

Each chart occupies an entire page on-screen—or when printed—and you can reposition the chart anywhere on that page. To accomplish this, follow these steps:

1. Click several times on the Zoom Out icon until the entire page is displayed on your screen.

2. Click anywhere off the Zoom Out icon.
3. Click anywhere within the chart handles.
4. Holding the mouse button down, reposition the chart where you want it on the page.

Changing the Background Color

You can adjust the color of the page that serves as a background for a chart. To accomplish this, follow these steps:

1. Click anywhere on the chart, so that the four chart handles appear.

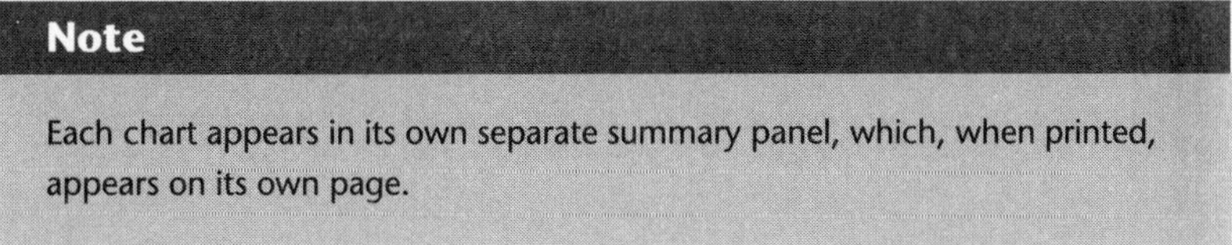

Note

Each chart appears in its own separate summary panel, which, when printed, appears on its own page.

2. Double-click anywhere *outside* the chart handles. You'll then see the Summary Panel Info Box. Click the far-left tab so that the Info Box appears as shown in figure 15.37.

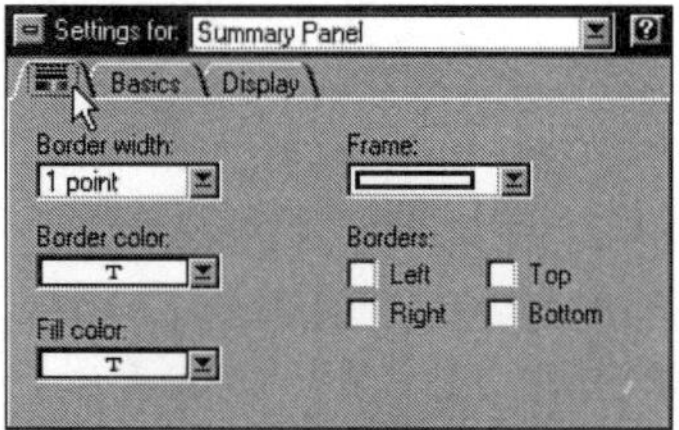

Fig. 15.37 Use this Info Box to select a background color.

3. Pull down the Fill Color list box.
4. Click the color you want as the chart background.

> **Caution**
>
> Be sure not to double-click the control box for either the chart or for the Approach window. If you do, Windows will attempt to exit either from the chart or from Approach itself.

5. To remove this Info Box from the screen, double-click its control box in the upper-left corner.

Associating Macros with a Chart

You can associate a pair of macros with each chart—one to execute when you display the chart, and the other when you exit from the chart. To make your selections for the current chart, follow these steps:

1. Double-click anywhere outside the chart area defined by its four handles.
2. When the Info Box appears, pull down the top list box, then choose the Chart option.
3. Click the top tab labeled Macros. The Info Box appears as shown in figure 15.38.

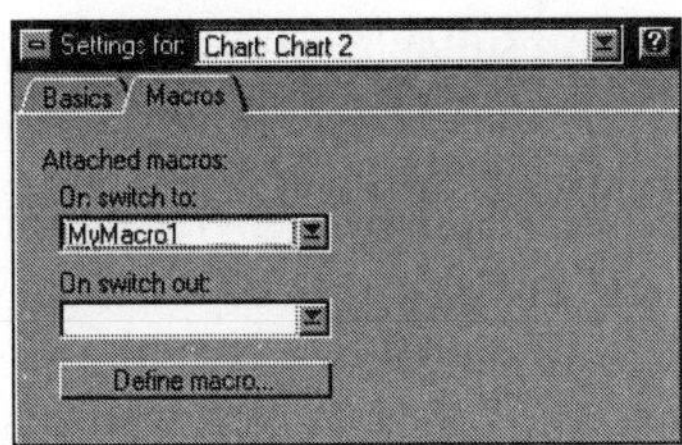

Fig. 15.38
Select macros to associate with a chart.

4. In the pull-down On Switch To list box, choose the macro you want to run each time you display the current chart.

5. In the pull-down On Switch Out list box, choose the macro you want to run each time you exit from the chart.

Steps 4 and 5 above assume that you have already created the macros you plan to use with the current chart. This is not an absolute requirement, because you can create one or both macros from within the Info Box. For each macro you want to create, click the Define Macro button, then follow the normal procedure for creating macros.

Printing a Chart

Printing a chart is usually quite straightforward, involving only a few steps:

1. Open the **F**ile menu and choose **P**rint.

2. Select the print options you want.

3. Click OK to start printing.

Depending on your printer, the output colors will strongly resemble those on-screen. If you have a color printer, the colors will probably be pretty close, although you can experiment a bit with Approach's wide range of colors to get just the output you want.

If you're using a black-and-white printer, each chart will be printed in various shades of gray. Depending on the type of printer, you will be pleasantly or unpleasantly surprised with the output. However, by experimenting with the various colors offered by Approach, you should be able to select tones that produce pleasing printouts.

Here are a few tips to follow when printing charts:

- For black-and-white printers, consider restricting the colors for the various chart elements to different shades of gray. This will simplify your experimentation to find suitable print colors, although it will somewhat deaden the images on your color monitor.

- To minimize the print time while generating experimental printouts—which can be considerable for most types of charts—use the lowest possible resolution available for your printer. For example, for HP LaserJet printers, you can use the Print Quality option on the Print dialog box to select 75 or 150 dpi (dots per inch). Then, when you've established the color scheme you want for your printouts, switch back to the printer's highest resolution.

- Some charts may look better when printed in landscape orientation. To switch to landscape, pull down the **F**ile menu, choose the Print Se**t**up option, then choose the **L**andscape option.

From Here...

This chapter has focused on using charts, which is one of Approach's most sophisticated methods for displaying stored information. Using the tools described in the chapter, you can create a wide variety of different chart types. You can also customize your charts in many different ways.

To learn about other important areas relevant to database management, refer to the following chapters in this book:

- Chapter 14, "Using Worksheets and Crosstabs," describes how to create crosstabs, which simplify creating charts.

- Chapter 16, "Exploring Advanced Database Relationships," explains the basics of using databases consisting of multiple tables. Using the information in this chapter, you'll be able to create a single chart containing information from several related tables.

Chapter 16

Exploring Advanced Database Relationships

Up to this point we've used Approach for one-to-one, many-to-one, and one-to-many relationships. In this chapter, we'll look at the remaining relational database case: a many-to-many relationship.

In this chapter, you learn how to:

- Recognize a many-to-many relationship
- Resolve many-to-many database dilemmas
- Use Approach to create a many-to-many relationship
- Join many-to-many relational databases
- Design forms for many-to-many relationships

Describing a Many-to-Many Relationship

Relational databases work well as long as the records in the joined databases are related by either a one-to-one, many-to-one, or a one-to-many relationship. With these types of relationships, a single linking field stored in the related database provides the linking information. However, relational technology can't handle tables related in a many-to-many relationship, which occurs when one record in Table A is related to many records in Table B and one record in Table B is related to many records in Table A. A common many-to-many relationship occurs between purchase orders and part numbers. One purchase order can include many part numbers and any part number can appear in multiple purchase orders (see fig. 16.1). With such relationships, you cannot document the relationship with a single linking field.

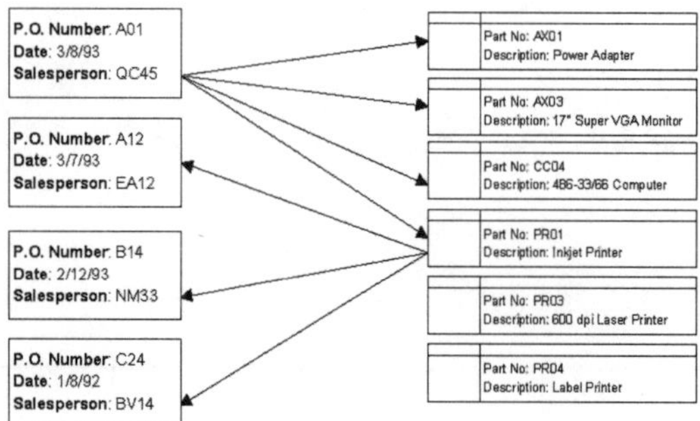

Fig. 16.1
Purchase orders and part numbers are one common many-to-many relationship.

Resolving a Many-to-Many Relationship

To properly maintain a many-to-many relationship, you must add another table to your application. This intermediate table connects each of the original many-to-many tables in a one-to-many relationship. Thus, the intermediate table must contain at least two fields: a field to link relationally to the first database, and a field to link relationally to the second database. In database jargon, you are "resolving a many to many." Each main database contains one or more fields, sometimes called *key fields*, which uniquely identify a record in the main database. You must then link the intermediate tables to the key field(s) in each main database. The intermediate table can also contain information specific to the relationship between the two main databases. Figure 16.2 illustrates how the intermediate table connects two many-to-many tables.

By using the Purchase Orders/Part Numbers model, for example, you can add a new intermediate database called Line Items. The Line Items database relates the Purchase Order database to the Part Number database as follows:

- Purchase Order-to-Line Items relationship:

  Each purchase order can contain multiple line items.

  Each line item can refer to only a single purchase order number.

- Part Number-to-Line Items relationship:

  A part number can be used by multiple line items.

  Each line item can use a single part number.

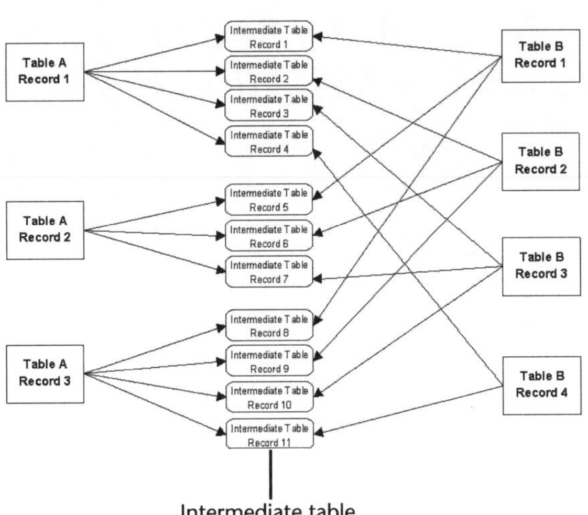

Fig. 16.2
An intermediate database resolves a many-to-many relationship into two one-to-many relationships.

The Line Items table shows one record for each occurrence of a particular part number on a particular purchase order. The key field in the Purchase Order database (for example, P.O. Number) relationally links the Line Items database to the Purchase Order table. The key field in the Part Number database (for example, Part Number) relationally links the Line Items table to the Part Numbers database.

Note

A Line Items database record can also contain other information, such as the quantity of each part ordered on the purchase order. Including such information in the Line Items table makes sense, because it refers to a particular part number on a particular purchase order.

Figure 16.3 shows how this example might look.

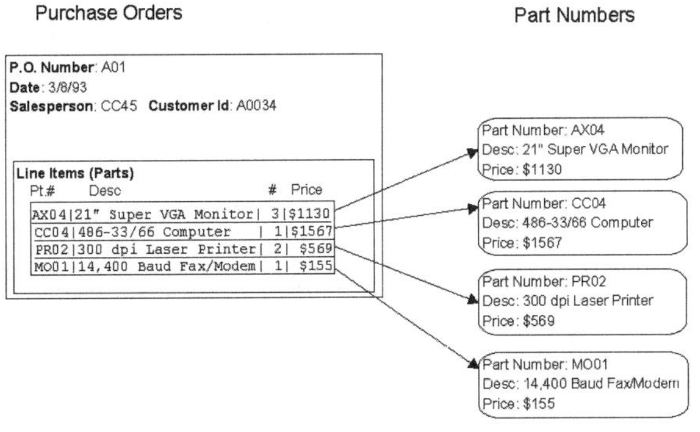

Fig. 16.3
The Purchase Orders database and the Part Numbers database can be related through the Line Items database.

Using Approach to Set Up a Many-to-Many Relationship

Once you understand that the problem you are dealing with is a many-to-many relationship, you can create the proper databases in Approach for this relationship.

To set up an application that links a many-to-many database through an intermediate one-to-many database, you must perform three steps:

1. Create three databases.
2. Relationally link the databases.
3. Build the forms.

Creating the Databases

Begin setting up a many-to-many environment by creating three databases. First, you build the two main databases which have the many-to-many relationship (the Purchase Order and Part Number databases). Then, you build the intermediate database to connect them (the Line Items database) as shown in figure 16.3.

If Owl Publishing decides to sell computers and accessories, for example, the company needs three databases to keep track of its business:

- A Purchase Orders database to store purchase order information
- A Part Number database to store part number information
- A Line Items database to relate the Purchase Orders database to the Part Number database

Building the Purchase Orders Database

To build the Purchase Orders database, follow these steps:

1. Open the **F**ile menu and choose **N**ew to open the New dialog box.
2. Type **PURCHORD** in the File **N**ame text box.
3. Click OK. The Creating New Database dialog box appears.
4. Use the field definitions in the following table for the PURCHORD database. Type the name of the field in the Field Name column, choose the field type from the Data Type drop-down list, and enter the size in the Size column (if necessary).

Field Name	Data Type	Size
PO_NUM	Text	10
SALES_ID	Text	10
DATE	Date	
CUST_ID	Text	10

5. Click OK in the Creating New Database dialog box to create the database and open the default form (see fig. 16.4).

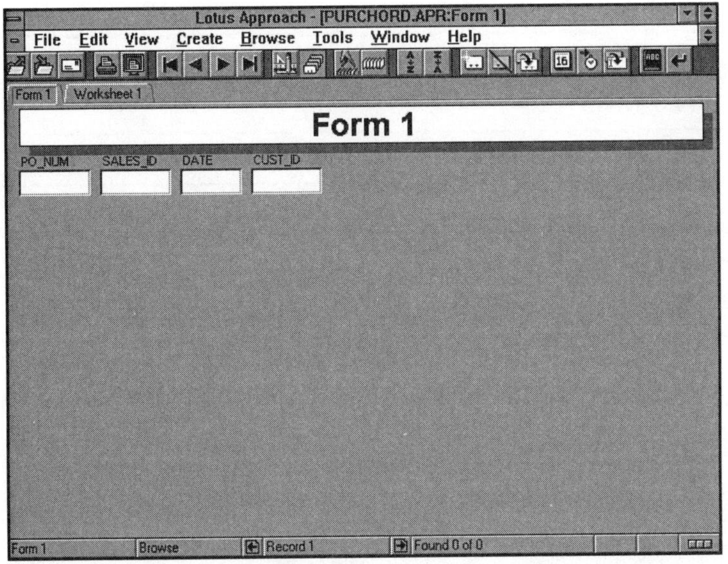

Fig. 16.4
The PURCHORD form is the first form you need in creating a many-to-many relationship.

6. Switch to Design mode and open the form's Info Box by selecting Form Style & Properties.

7. Type **Purchase Orders** into the Form Name text box in the Basics panel.

8. Select the form header text by clicking it twice. Change the default text by highlighting the default text ("Form 1") and typing **Purchase Orders**.

9. Open the File menu and choose Save Approach File. The Save Approach File dialog box appears.

10. Keep the default name for the Approach file. Click OK to save the Approach file.

Building the Part Number Database

Now you need to create a Part Number database to store part number information. Follow these steps:

1. Open the **F**ile menu and choose **N**ew. The New dialog box appears.
2. Type **PARTNUM** in the File **N**ame text box.
3. Click OK to open the Creating New Database dialog box.
4. Use the field definitions in the following table for the PARTNUM database. Type the name of the field in the Field Name column, choose the field type from the Data Type drop-down list, and enter the size in the Size column (if necessary).

Field Name	Data Type	Size
PART_NUM	Text	10
SHIP_WT	Numeric	4
INSTOCK	Numeric	4
DESCRIPT	Text	30
PRICE	Numeric	10.2

5. Click OK in the Creating New Database dialog box to create the database and open the default form (see fig. 16.5).

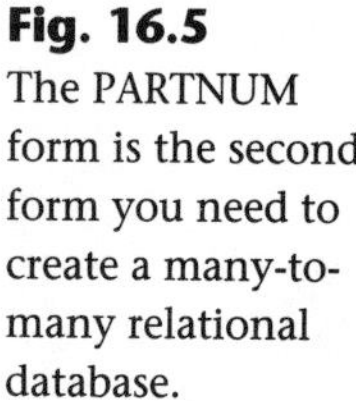

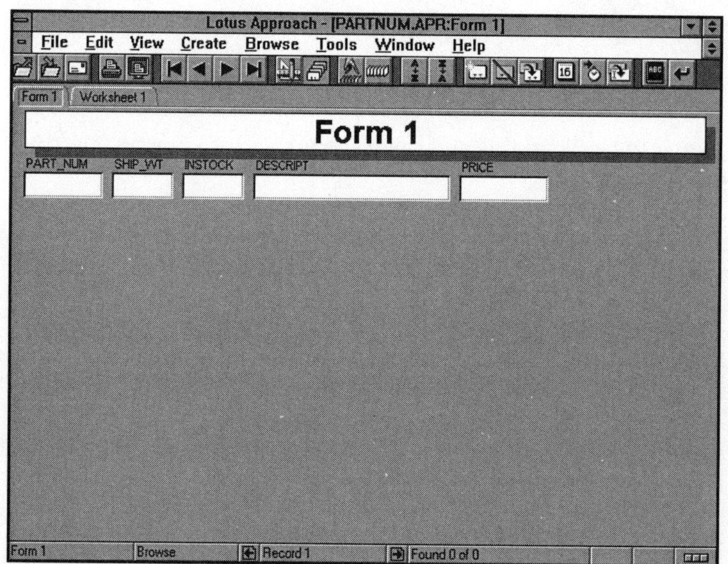

Fig. 16.5
The PARTNUM form is the second form you need to create a many-to-many relational database.

6. Enter the following records into the PARTNUM database.

PART_NUM	SHIP_WT	INSTOCK	DESCRIPT	PRICE
AX01	2	15	Power adapter	12.5
AX02	65	12	14" Super VGA monitor	439
AX03	69	7	17" Super VGA monitor	903
AX04	102	2	21" Super VGA monitor	1130
CC01	45	23	386-40 computer	888
CC02	40	13	486-25 computer	906
CC03	46	12	486-33 computer	1250
CC04	47	10	486-33/66 computer	1567
MO01	3	3	14,400 baud fax/ modem	155
MO02	3	9	9600/9600 fax/ modem	129
PR01	14	4	Inkjet printer	359
PR02	34	4	300 dpi laser printer	569
PR03	45	4	600 dpi laser printer	1599
PR04	2	4	Label printer	249

7. Switch to Design mode and open the form's Info Box by selecting Fo**r**m **S**tyle & Properties.

8. Type **Part Numbers** into the Form Name text box in the Basics panel.

9. Select the form header text by clicking it twice. Change the default text by highlighting the default text ("Form 1") and typing **Part Numbers**.

10. Open the **F**ile menu and choose **S**ave Approach File. The Save Approach File dialog box appears.

11. Keep the default name for the Approach file. Click OK to save Approach file.

12. Choose **C**lose from the **F**ile menu to close the PARTNUM form.

Building the Line Items Database

Lastly, you need to create a Line Items database, which you will use to relate the Purchase Orders in the PURCHORD database to the part numbers in the PARTNUM database. Follow these steps:

1. Open the **F**ile menu and choose **N**ew. The New dialog box appears.
2. Type **LINEITEM** in the File **N**ame text box.
3. Click OK. The Creating New Database dialog box appears.
4. Use the field definitions in the following table for the LINEITEM database. Type the name of the field in the Field Name column, choose the field type from the Data Type drop-down list, and enter the size in the Size column (if necessary).

Field Name	Data Type	Size
PO_NUM	Text	10
PART_NUM	Text	10
COLOR	Text	10
QUANTITY	Numeric	4

5. Click OK in the Creating New Database dialog box to create the database and open the default form (see fig. 16.6).

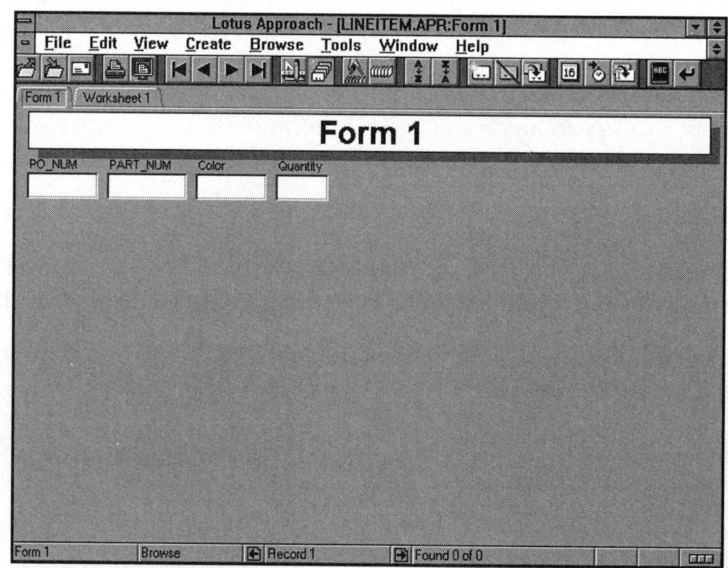

Fig. 16.6
The LINEITEM form ties the PURCHORD database to the PARTNUM database.

6. Switch to Design mode and open the form's Info Box by selecting Fo**r**m **S**tyle & Properties.

7. Type **Line Items** into the Form Name text box in the Basics panel.

8. Select the form header text by clicking it twice. Change the default text by highlighting the default text ("Form 1") and typing **Line Items**.

9. Open the **F**ile menu and choose **S**ave Approach File. The Save Approach File dialog box appears.

10. Keep the default name for the Approach file. Click OK to save Approach file.

11. Close the LINEITEM file by choosing **C**lose from the **F**ile menu.

Joining the Databases

Joining the three databases establishes the relational links between them. A join is specific to a single Approach file. For these steps all of the joins are done in the PURCHORD Approach file. Join the databases in the following order:

1. Join the first many database to the intermediate database (that is, join the Purchase Order database to the Line Items database). Set the join options so that

   - If no matching record exists in the intermediate database, Approach creates a record automatically.

   - If you delete a record in the main database, Approach deletes all matching intermediate database records.

2. Join the intermediate database to the second many database (that is, join the Line Item database to the Part Number database).

In the Owl Publishing example, follow these steps to join the Purchase Order, Line Item, and Part Number databases together:

1. If the PURCHORD view file is not open, open it by choosing **O**pen from the **F**ile menu. Select PURCHORD.APR from the Open dialog box, and then click OK.

2. Open the **C**reate menu and click **J**oin. The Join dialog box appears.

3. Choose **O**pen. The Open dialog box appears.

4. Select LINEITEM from the database file list and then click OK. The LINEITEM database appears in the Join dialog box. Change directories or file types in the Open dialog box, if needed.

5. Select the PO_NUM field in the PURCHORDER database box.

6. Select the PO_NUM field in the LINEITEM database box.

7. Click **J**oin. A join line appears between the PURCHORDER and LINEITEM database boxes.

8. Click the Op**t**ions button to open the Relational Options dialog box.

9. Check both Insert checkboxes and the Delete checkbox (see fig. 16.7). Make sure no other checkboxes are selected, and then click OK to close the Relational Options dialog box.

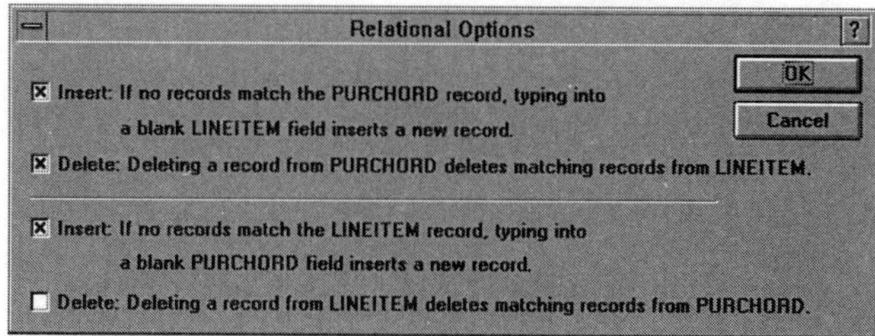

Fig. 16.7
Set your options for the relationship between PURCHORD and LINEITEM.

10. Click **O**pen in the Join dialog box. The Open dialog box appears.

11. Select PARTNUM from the database files and then click OK to close the Open dialog box. The PARTNUM database appears in the Join dialog box. Change the directory or file type in the Open dialog box, if necessary.

12. Select the PART_NUM field in the LINEITEM database box.

13. Select the PART_NUM field in the PARTNUM database box.

14. Click **J**oin. A join line appears between the LINEITEM and PARTNUM database boxes. The Join dialog box should now look like figure 16.8.

15. Click OK to create the joins.

16. Save the Approach file by opening the **F**ile menu and choosing **S**ave Approach File.

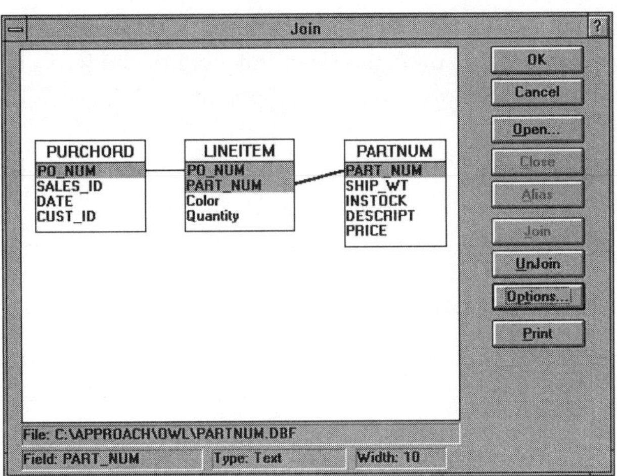

Fig. 16.8
Link PURCHORD to PARTNUM through the LINEITEM database.

Designing the Forms

Although you can enter the records into each database in the Approach file on separate forms, creating a single form for most of the information is usually best. Building this type of form by using repeating panels is very straightforward.

Ordinarily, you have greater interest in one of the two main databases (PURCHORD and PARTNUM). In the Purchase Order application, for example, you use the purchase order form (main database is PURCHORD) most often. But you can create a Part Number form (main database is PARTNUM) within the same Approach file to add new part numbers.

To create a form that displays information from one of the main databases as well as the intermediate database, add a repeating panel from the intermediate database (LINEITEM) to the form based on a main database (PURCHORD). (See Chapter 9 for more information about repeating panels.)

> **Note**
>
> Because of the relational link, information stored in the other main database (PARTNUM) can be displayed in the repeating panel based on the intermediate database (LINEITEM). You can display a part's price (the PRICE field in the PARTNUM database) in the repeating panel on the Purchase Orders form, for example.

Owl Publishing wants to create a Purchase Orders form. From this form, the company can set up new purchase orders and add line items, each referencing an individual part number to the purchase order. To build this form, follow these steps:

1. If the PURCHORD Approach file is not open, open it by choosing **O**pen from the **F**ile menu. Select PURCHORD.APR from the Open dialog box and then click OK.

2. Switch to Design mode.
3. Open the **C**reate menu and choose **F**orm. In the Form Assistant, type **Line Items** in the View **N**ame & Title text box. Select "Standard" from the SmartMaster **L**ayout list.
4. Click the Next button. Select the LINEITEM database and **A**dd all the fields in the LINEITEM database to the Fields to **P**lace on View list. Select **D**one to create the Line Items form.
5. Open the **C**reate menu and choose **F**orm. In the Form Assistant, type **Parts** in the View **N**ame & Title text box. Select "Standard" from the SmartMaster **L**ayout list.
6. Click the Next button. Select the PARTNUM database and **A**dd all the fields in the PARTNUM database to the Fields to **P**lace on View list. Select **D**one to create the Parts form.
7. Switch to the Purchase Orders form, if necessary. Open the **C**reate menu and choose Repeating **P**anel. The Add Repeating Panel dialog box opens.
8. Choose the LINEITEM database from the database list. This will be the main database for the repeating panel.
9. Select PART_NUM, QUANTITY, and COLOR from the Da**t**abase Fields box.
10. Choose **A**dd or double-click each field to move the selected fields to the **F**ields to Place in Panel list.
11. Click OK. A repeating panel appears on the Purchase Orders form.

12. Use the Text tool in the Drawing toolbar to place headings above the repeating panel (see fig. 16.9).

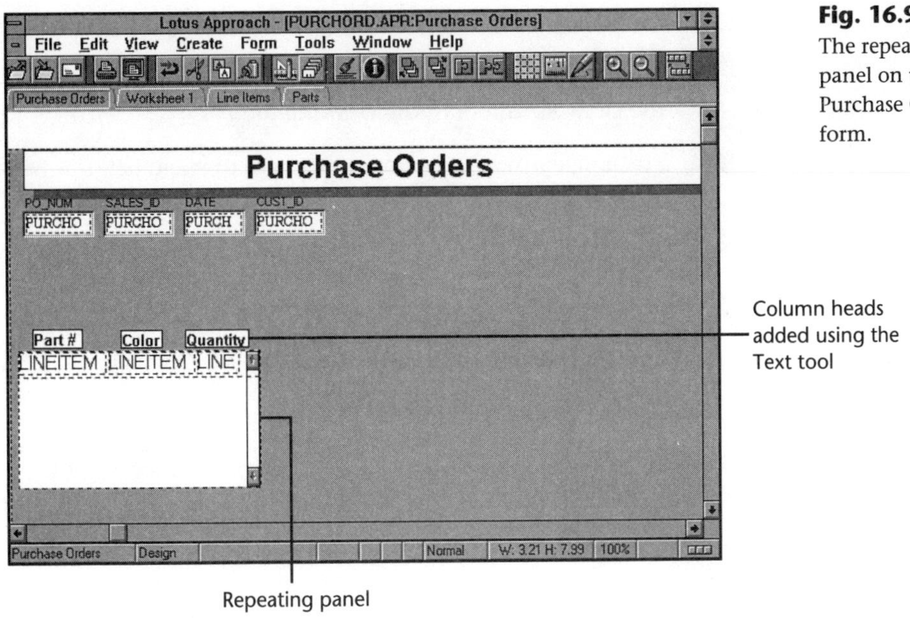

Fig. 16.9
The repeating panel on the Purchase Orders form.

To ensure that you enter only valid part numbers in the repeating panel, follow these steps:

1. Switch to Design mode, if necessary. Select the PARTNUM field in the repeating panel on the Purchase Orders form.
2. Open the **C**reate menu and choose Field **D**efinition. The Field Definition dialog box appears.
3. Click the **O**ptions button to expand the Field Definition dialog box and display the Default Value and Validation panels. Select the Validation tab to display the Validation panel.
4. Check the I**n** Field checkbox.
5. Select the PARTNUM database from the drop-down list.
6. Select the PART_NUM field from the list box.
7. Click OK to close the Field Definition dialog box.

To make room for more fields in the field bar, click the repeating panel. A gray box appears around the field bar. Resize the field bar to the right to make the repeating panel larger.

To add the PRICE field from the PARTNUM database to the repeating panel, follow these steps:

1. Click the Draw Field tool in the Drawing toolbar.
2. Drag a rectangle inside the empty portion of the field bar. If it is not already visible, the field Info Box appears.
3. Select the PARTNUM database from the drop-down list of databases.
4. Select the PRICE field from the Field list box.
5. Make sure no Borders options are checked in the Colors panel.
6. In the Label panel, make sure the Label position is set to No Label.
7. Drag the sizing handles for the PRICE field so that they are entirely contained within the field bar of the repeating panel.

8. Use the Text tool in the Drawing toolbar to create a heading for the PRICE field.
9. Select the PRICE field in the repeating panel.
10. Switch to the format (#) panel in the Info Box. Select Numeric from the Format type drop-down list.
11. Select Currency with Decimals from the Current format drop-down list.

12. Switch to Browse mode and view the Purchase Orders form. The PRICE field now appears in the repeating panel (see fig. 16.10).

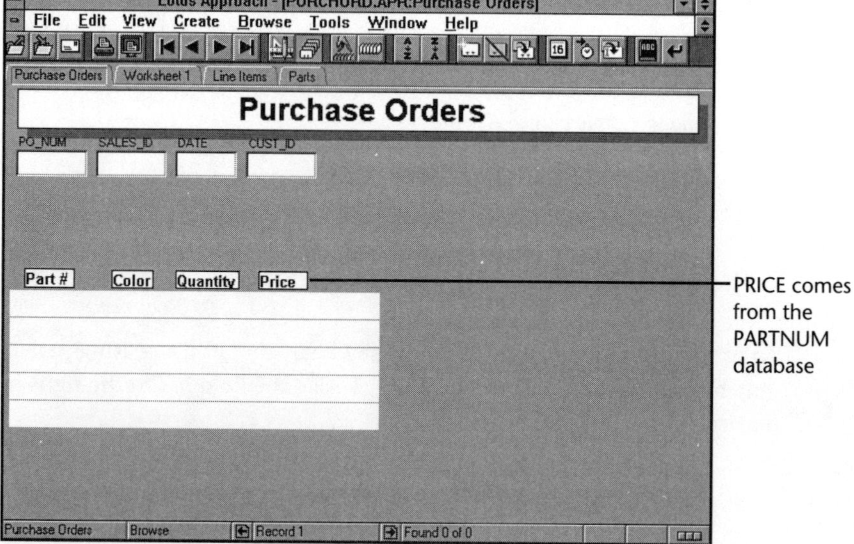

Fig. 16.10
The repeating panel displays the PRICE field from the PARTNUM database.

Returning to the Owl Publishing example, let's say you want to calculate the total for each line in the repeating panel on the Purchase Orders form. To do this, follow these steps:

1. Switch to Design mode.

2. If the repeating panel is not large enough for another field, enlarge the panel by clicking the field bar and then dragging the right border.
3. Choose the Draw Field tool in the Drawing toolbar.

4. Drag a rectangle inside the field bar of the repeating panel. If it isn't already visible, the field Info Box appears.
5. Click the Field Definition button. The Field Definition dialog box appears.
6. Scroll down to an empty line and type **LineTotal** in the Field Name column. Select Calculated as the data type. The Field Definition dialog box expands to display the Define Formula panel.
7. Type **PARTNUM.PRICE*LINEITEM.QUANTITY** in the **F**ormula text box. You can also select the databases and click the field in the Fie**l**ds list box.
8. Click OK to close the Field Definition dialog box.
9. In the Colors panel of the Info Box, make sure no Borders options are checked. In the Label panel, set the Label position to No Label.
10. Drag the sizing handles for the LineTotal field so that the field is completely within the field bar of the repeating panel.
11. Use the Text tool in the Drawing toolbar to create a heading for the LineTotal field.

12. Select the LineTotal field in the repeating panel.
13. Switch to the format (#) panel in the Info Box. Select Numeric from the Format Type drop-down list.
14. Select Currency with Decimals from the Current Format drop-down list.
15. Switch to Browse mode to view the Purchase Orders form. The LineTotal field now appears in the repeating panel (see fig. 16.11).

Fig. 16.11
The repeating panel with the LineTotal field from the PARTNUM database.

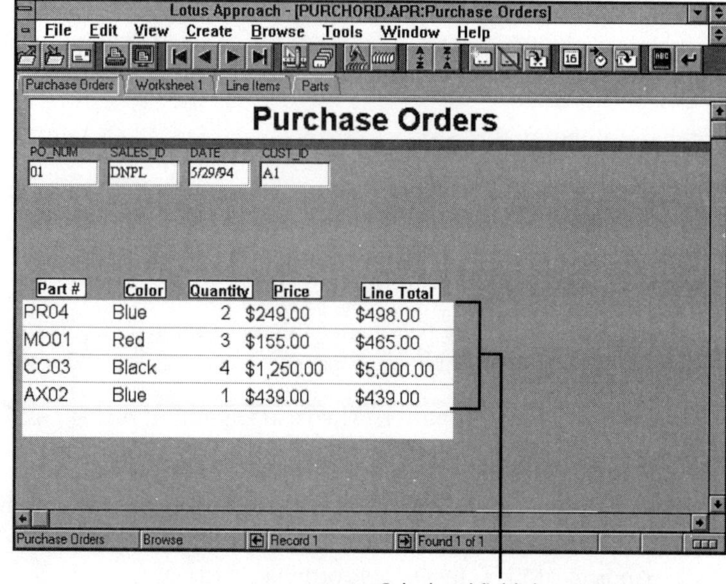

Calculated field determines total for each line

Owl Publishing also needs a field that totals the amount of each purchase order. To do this, follow these steps:

1. Switch to Design mode.

2. Click the Draw Field tool in the Drawing toolbar.
3. Drag a rectangle near the repeating panel. If it isn't already visible, the field Info Box appears.
4. Click the Field Definition button. The Field Definition dialog box appears.
5. Scroll down to an empty line in the Field Definition dialog box. Type **Total** in the Field Name column and select Calculated as the data type. The Field Definition dialog box expands to display the Define Formula panels.
6. Type **SSUM(LineTotal)** in the **F**ormula text box.
7. Click the Define Summary tab to switch to the Define Summary panel. Choose Summary Of All Records In LINEITEM from the **S**ummarize On drop-down list.
8. Click OK to close the Field Definition dialog box.

9. The Total field should still be selected. Switch to the Label panel in the field's Info Box. Change the Label text to **Order Total** by highlighting the Label text and typing the new value.

10. Switch to the format (#) panel. Select Numeric from the Format type drop-down list. Choose Currency with Decimals in the Current Format drop-down list.

11. Switch to Browse mode to view the Purchase Orders form. The Total field displays the total amount of the purchase order (see fig. 16.12).

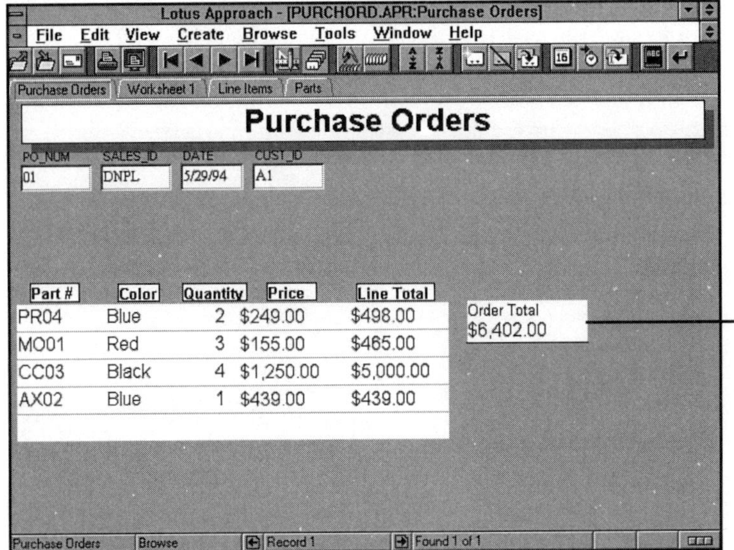

Fig. 16.12
The Total field displays the total amount of the purchase order.

The Owl Publishing employees assigned to fill out the Purchase Orders form are having trouble with the PART_NUM field in the repeating panel. If they type in a part number that doesn't exist, Approach refuses to accept the value. Adding a drop-down list that displays only the available parts corrects the problem. To create such a list, follow these steps:

1. Switch to Design mode. Move to the Purchase Orders form, if necessary.

2. Double-click the PART_NUM field in the repeating panel. If it wasn't already visible, the Info Box for the LINEITEM.PART_NUM field appears.

3. Select the Data Entry Type drop-down list on the Basics panel.

4. Click the Define List button to open the Drop-Down List dialog box.

III

Getting the Most...

5. Choose the **C**reate List Automatically from Field Data radio button.
6. Select the PARTNUM database from the drop-down list of databases. Choose PART_NUM from **F**ield to Create List From.
7. Check the **S**how Description Field checkbox.
8. Select the DESCRIPT field from the PARTNUM database.
9. Click OK to close the Drop-Down List dialog box.

10. Switch to Browse mode and choose the PART_NUM field in the repeating panel. A list of part descriptions appears. When you select a description, its part number is entered into the LINEITEM.PART_NUM field in the repeating panel (see figs. 16.13 and 16.14).

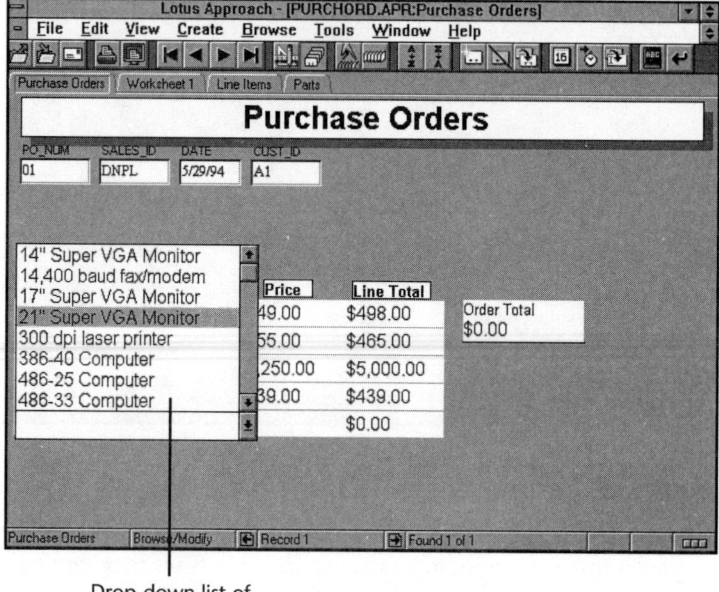

Fig. 16.13 Choosing the PART_NUM field in the repeating panel displays a list of product descriptions.

Owl Publishing wants to transfer from any line in the repeating panel to the PARTNUM record for that line. The company then can make inventory adjustments and so forth. To do so, follow the steps on the next page.

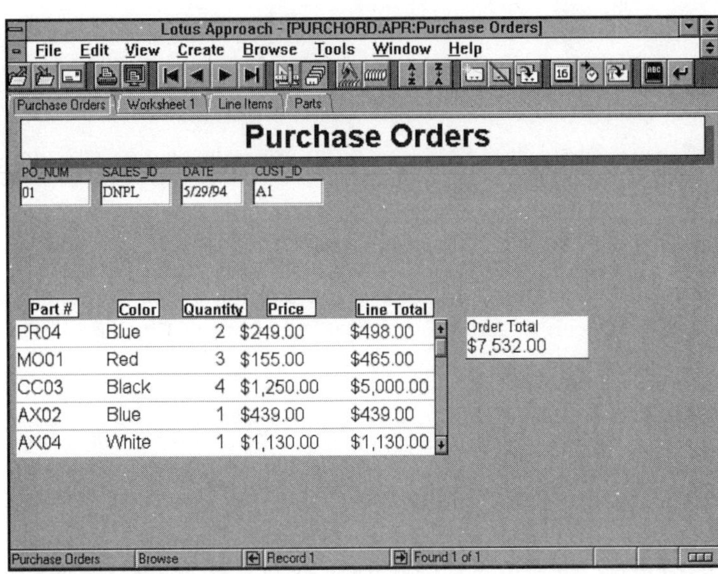

Fig. 16.14
Select a description to place the associated part number into the LINEITEM. PART_NUM field.

1. Switch to Design mode.
2. Open the **T**ools menu and choose **M**acros to open the Macros dialog box. Choose **N**ew. The Define Macro dialog box opens.
3. Type **Go To Part Number** in the Macro **N**ame text box.
4. On the first line in the Options section, select the **View** command from the Command column drop-down list.
5. Choose **Parts** from the list of available forms and reports in the Switch, Show, or Hide Views section near the bottom of the Define Macro dialog box.
6. Click the Command column on the second line of the Options section. Choose **Records** from the drop-down list.
7. Choose C**u**rrent Record in the Go To, Hide, Duplicate, or Create a Record section.
8. Click OK to close the Define Macro dialog box. Choose **D**one to close the Macros dialog box.
9. Click the Button tool from the Drawing toolbar.

10. Drag a rectangle in an empty section of the repeating panel's field bar. (Resize the field bar, if there are no empty sections.) If it wasn't already visible, the Button Info Box appears.

11. In the Macros panel of the Button Info Box, select Go to Part Number from the On Clicked drop-down list.

12. Switch to the Basics panel. Type **Part #** in the Button text box.

13. Switch to Browse mode and click a button on a line in the repeating panel. Approach switches to the PARTNUM record for that line (see figs. 16.15 and 16.16).

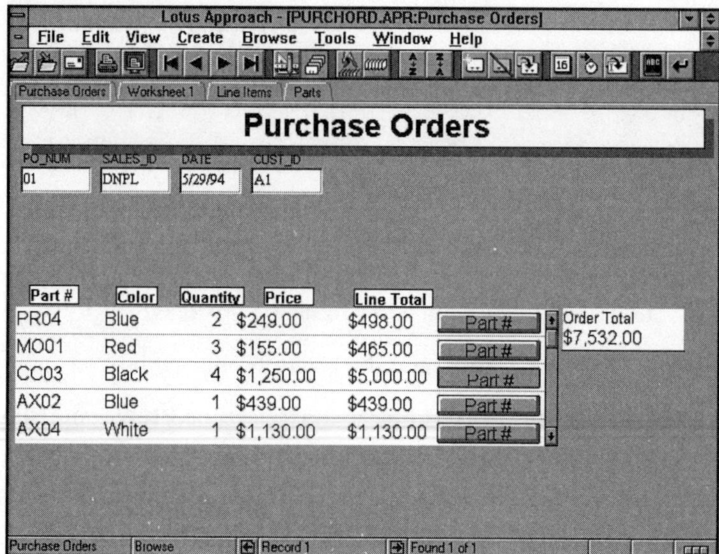

Fig. 16.15
Click a button for a record in the repeating panel.

Owl Publishing wants to determine which purchase orders include a certain part number. The company can then determine who is affected when a part is unavailable. Follow the steps on the next page.

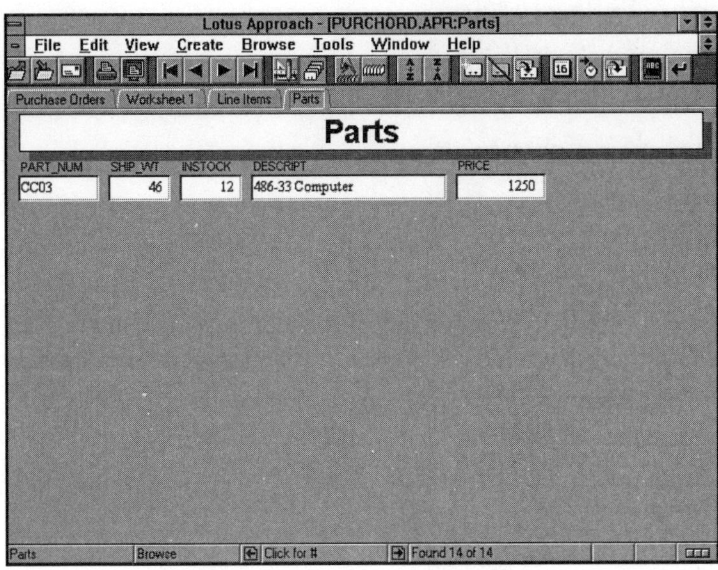

Fig. 16.16
You are transferred to that record in the PARTNUM form.

1. Switch to Design mode.
2. Select the Parts form from the tabs or the status line.
3. Open the **C**reate menu and choose Repeating **P**anel. The Add Repeating Panel dialog box appears.
4. Choose LINEITEM from the Database list.
5. Choose PO_NUM, COLOR, and QUANTITY from the field list.
6. Choose **A**dd to move the chosen fields from the Da**t**abase Fields box to the **F**ields to Place in Panel list or double-click each field.
7. Click OK in the Add Repeating Panel dialog box.
8. Use the Text tool in the Drawing toolbar to create headings for the repeating panel (see fig. 16.17).

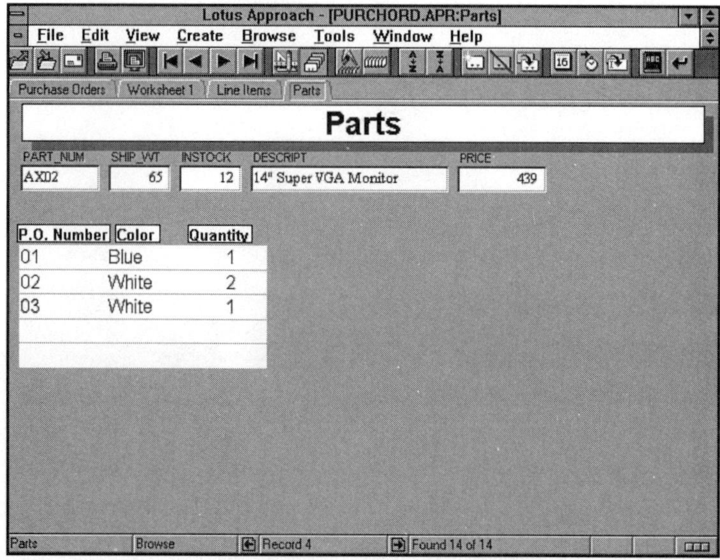

Fig. 16.17
A repeating panel on the Part Number form shows which purchase orders contain a particular part.

> **Note**
>
> Change the information in the repeating panel only on the Purchase Orders form. To keep users from changing the information in the repeating panel on the part number, open the Info Box, click each field in the panel, and then check the Read Only checkbox in the Basics panel.

The PURCHORD database contains a CUST_ID field to identify the customer of the purchase order. You can create a CUSTOMER database with name and address information for all your customers. The CUSTOMER database also contains a CUST_ID field to link it to the PURCHORD database (see fig. 16.18).

If you place the name and address fields from the CUSTOMER database on the Purchase Orders form, the customer information is displayed when you fill in the PURCHORD CUST_ID field on the Purchase Orders form (see fig. 16.19).

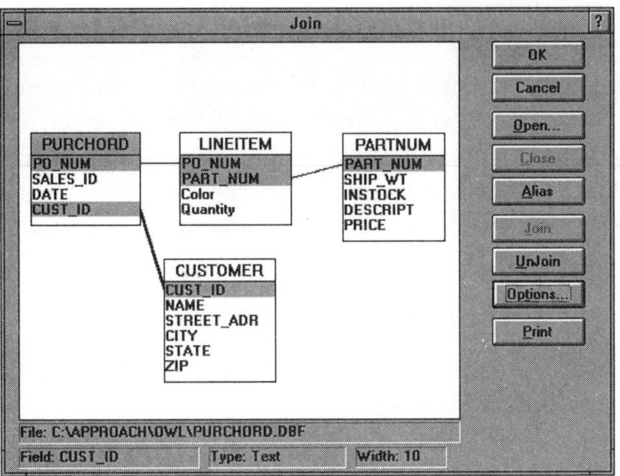

Fig. 16.18
The Join dialog box links PURCHORD to CUSTOMER.

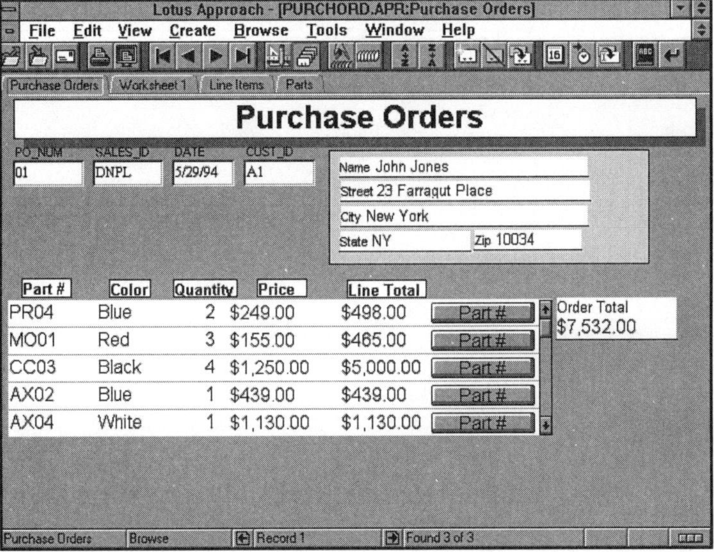

Fig. 16.19
The Purchase Orders form can display customer information from the CUSTOMER database.

From Here...

This chapter gives you a brief introduction into some of the more powerful uses of Approach. After you work with databases for a short time, you'll see how most problems can be broken down into one-to-many or many-to-many cases. Once these cases are defined, you can use the techniques learned in this chapter and throughout this book to create useful forms and reports using Lotus Approach.

For more information, refer to the following chapters in this book:

- Chapter 8, "Understanding Relational Databases," discusses how relational databases are formed and used.
- Chapter 9, "Designing Advanced Forms," shows you how to create forms that display information from several databases.
- Chapter 12, "Creating Advanced Reports," tells you how to develop reports that take full advantage of relational databases.

Chapter 17

Customizing Approach

Approach offers you several different ways to customize the program. This is helpful not only for setting personal preferences, but also when developing database applications for others.

Customization is more than changing how the screen looks. It can also affect how the data is displayed and how you work in designing a database.

In this chapter, you learn how to:

- Customize the SmartIcon toolbar
- Create custom menus
- Change the display defaults
- Configure Approach's phone dialer to work with your modem
- Set up preferences for specific database types

Customizing the SmartIcon Bar

Approach enables you to customize the appearance of the SmartIcon toolbar. You can add icons to or remove icons from the current SmartIcon bar to better suit your needs. You can also change the position of the SmartIcon bar on-screen and change the size of the displayed icons. You can choose to display help balloons either automatically or by clicking the right mouse button.

You can use the new design to replace an existing SmartIcon bar or to create a new SmartIcon bar. If you customize a SmartIcon bar associated with a mode (for example, the Browse SmartIcon bar), Approach displays the customized version of the SmartIcon bar when you switch to that mode.

To modify the SmartIcon bar, you must switch to the mode (Browse, Design, Find, or Preview) and view type (Form, Report, Mailing Label, Form Letter, Worksheet, or Crosstab) for which you want to modify the SmartIcon bar. Approach keeps separate SmartIcon files for different combinations of modes and view types. Open the **T**ools menu and choose Smart**I**cons to view the SmartIcons dialog box (see fig. 17.1).

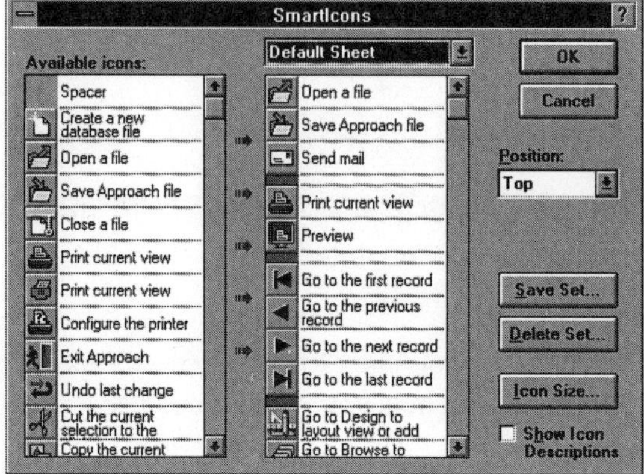

Fig. 17.1
The SmartIcons dialog box shows the default toolbar for a worksheet.

Approach displays the set names of existing SmartIcon files in a drop-down list box near the top center of the SmartIcons dialog box. The default is the set name of the currently open SmartIcon bar. If you want to modify a different SmartIcon bar, select the set name you want to use from this list.

> **Note**
>
> Approach gives you the choice of only those SmartIcons that work in the current mode and view type. If you are in Browse mode on a form, for example, you may select only Browse-mode SmartIcons. If you want to modify a SmartIcon file for another mode or view type (for example, Design, Preview, Find, Worksheet, or Crosstab), you must switch to that mode before choosing SmartIcons from the Tools menu.

Tip
Approach has several different default SmartIcon bars, each specific to a certain mode or type of view.

Approach loads the file and displays the list of icons on the selected SmartIcon bar in the list box near the center of the dialog box. On the left side of the SmartIcons dialog box is a list box that displays all the SmartIcons that you can place on the currently selected SmartIcon bar. This list includes only those SmartIcons appropriate for the mode and view type of the selected

SmartIcon bar. The following sections explain how to use these list boxes and customize the SmartIcon settings.

Tip
The Spacer SmartIcon allows you to add a space on the SmartIcon bar. This space can graphically separate groups of related SmartIcons.

Adding Icons to a SmartIcon Bar

To add an icon to the SmartIcon bar, use the mouse to select the icon you want to add from the list of available icons on the left side of the SmartIcons dialog box. Drag the icon to the list of icons toward the center of the dialog box, then release the mouse button. Approach inserts the new icon into the list.

Note

You can modify the SmartIcon bar only by using the mouse. The keyboard cannot be used.

If you drop the new icon on top of an existing icon, the existing icon (and all icons below it) move down to make room for the new icon. To add an icon to the end of the list, scroll down the list until the empty space at the end is visible. Drop the new icon into the empty space.

Removing Icons

To remove an icon from the SmartIcon bar, use the mouse to select the icon you want to remove from the list of icons in the center of the SmartIcons dialog box. Drag the icon anywhere outside the list and release the mouse button. The SmartIcon disappears from the list.

Tip
You don't need to save the current icon set to save changes to the help balloons. The changes are saved when you click OK in the SmartIcons dialog box.

Using Icon Description Balloons

The SmartIcons dialog box has a checkbox for S**h**ow Icon Descriptions. When turned on, this setting provides a help balloon when the mouse pointer is placed over a SmartIcon (see fig. 17.2). The checkbox controls all SmartIcon bars, not just the one currently in use. When the checkbox setting is off, the help balloons are still available by clicking the SmartIcons with the right mouse button.

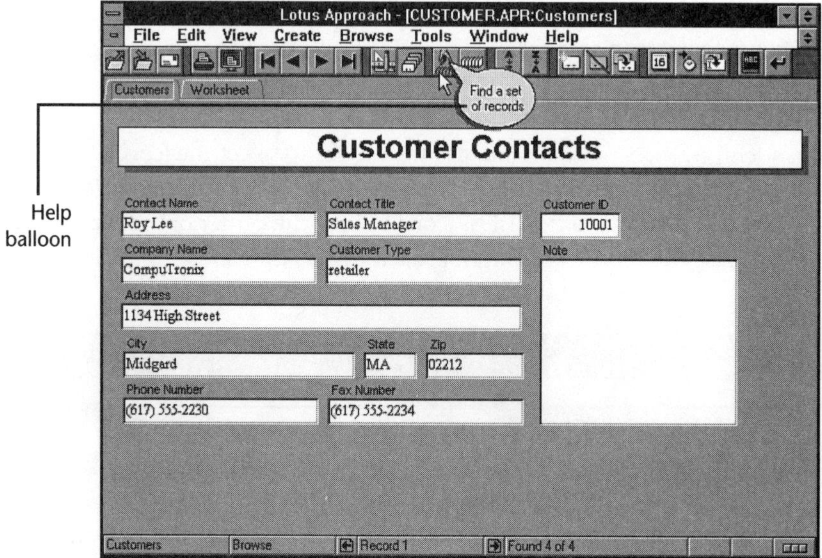

Fig. 17.2
Help balloons provide descriptions for the SmartIcons.

Saving Changes to the SmartIcon Bar

The changes you make to the SmartIcon bar normally last only through the current session of Approach. To make the changes permanent, you must save them by clicking the **S**ave Set button in the SmartIcons dialog box. The Save Set of SmartIcons dialog box appears (see fig. 17.3).

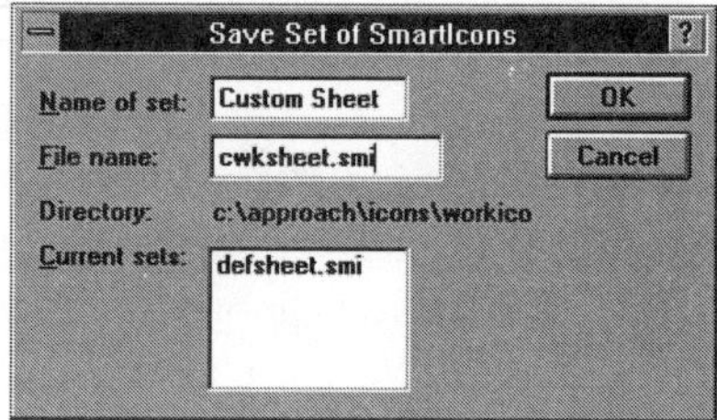

Fig. 17.3
When finished, you can save your custom set of SmartIcons.

To replace an existing SmartIcon set with a custom set, follow these steps:

1. By default, the file name for the SmartIcon set you are working with appears in the **F**ile Name text box. If you want to replace a different SmartIcon set file, select the file you want to replace from the **C**urrent Sets list near the bottom of the dialog box. The description of that file appears in the **N**ame of Set text box.

2. Click OK. In the dialog box that appears, confirm that you want to overwrite the file.

3. Click OK to save the changes.

To create a new SmartIcon set and save the changes in a file, follow these steps:

1. Type a new set name into the **N**ame of Set text box. The set name must be unique, otherwise Approach will refuse to accept it when you click OK.
2. Type a new file name into the **F**ile Name text box.
3. Click OK to save the new file.

Renaming a SmartIcon Set

Approach enables you to replace the name of the SmartIcon set with a different name. To do so, follow these steps:

1. Open the SmartIcons dialog box by opening the **T**ools menu and choosing Smart**I**cons.

2. Open the file by selecting its set name from the drop-down list in the SmartIcons dialog box.
3. Choose **S**ave Set. The Save Set of SmartIcons dialog box appears.
4. Change the name in the **N**ame of Set text box.
5. Retype the file name of the existing file in the **F**ile Name text box.
6. Click OK. Approach displays a dialog box warning you that the file name exists.
7. Click OK to save the changes.

Deleting a SmartIcon Set

Approach enables you to delete a SmartIcon file. To do so, follow these steps:

1. Open the SmartIcons dialog box by opening the **T**ools menu and choosing Smart**I**cons.

2. Choose **D**elete Set in the SmartIcons dialog box. The Delete Sets dialog box opens.
3. Select the set name for the SmartIcon bar you want to delete.
4. Click OK to delete the set. Approach doesn't ask you to confirm the deletion.

Changing the Icon Size

Approach can display icons on the SmartIcon bar in two sizes: medium and large. As you may expect, the large icons take up more room, so fewer of them can fit on the SmartIcon bar. The graphics are somewhat more detailed, however. To change the size of the displayed icons, choose **I**con Size in the SmartIcons dialog box. In the Icon Size dialog box, choose the size you want and then click OK.

Changing the Position of the SmartIcon Bar

You can put the SmartIcon at the top of the screen (the default position), at the bottom, or against the left or right sides. You can also place the SmartIcon bar in its own window.

To reposition the SmartIcon bar, select the position from the **P**osition drop-down list in the SmartIcons dialog box (see fig. 17.4). Choose the Floating, Left, Top, Right, or Bottom option in the drop-down list. If you change the SmartIcon bar position, Approach displays the SmartIcon bar in the new position in all modes.

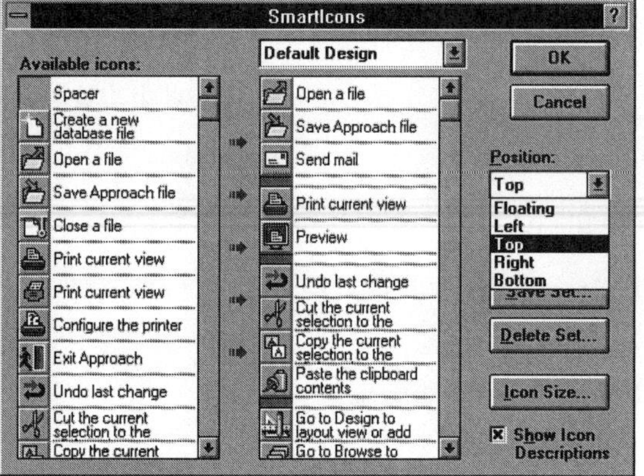

Fig. 17.4
Select where the SmartIcon bar is placed using the Position drop-down list.

Using a Floating SmartIcon Bar

Select the Floating option to place the SmartIcon bar in a window. When you place the SmartIcon bar in a window, you have much more flexibility in determining its position and size. You can also display a larger number of icons than you can with a standard SmartIcon bar.

To reposition this window, move the mouse pointer anywhere in the window, hold down the left mouse button, and drag the window to its new location. To resize the window, drag the window borders until you establish the new size. You can't stretch the window to a size larger than what is necessary to display the icons, but you can shrink the window so that some icons aren't displayed.

To close the floating SmartIcon window, click the close box in the upper-left corner. Hiding the SmartIcon window in one mode leaves it visible in other modes. You can redisplay a hidden SmartIcon window by selecting the SmartIcon set you want from the status bar button, or you can redisplay the SmartIcon window by opening the **V**iew menu and choosing Show **S**martIcons.

Customizing Menus

Customized menus allow a view or set of views to access only a certain set of menus selections. Each view can have its own custom menu. A custom menu can be used for each view in an Approach file, or a combination of menus can be used in an Approach file.

Custom menus are especially useful when defining a database application. A user's actions can be controlled by restricting which menu items are available on different views. If a task isn't in a menu, it's not available by SmartIcon either, even if the SmartIcon is present.

Caution

If a menu item isn't available in the current menu, the SmartIcon that performs the same task, if present, won't work.

Customized menus are available for Browse, Preview and Find modes, but not for Design mode. Menu selections that are not applicable in a certain mode, such as the Actual Size menu item in Browse mode, will be dimmed.

Defining and Editing Customized Menu

Customized menus are defined or modified in Design mode only. Open the **T**ools menu and choose **C**ustomize Menus to display the Customize Menus dialog box (see fig. 17.5).

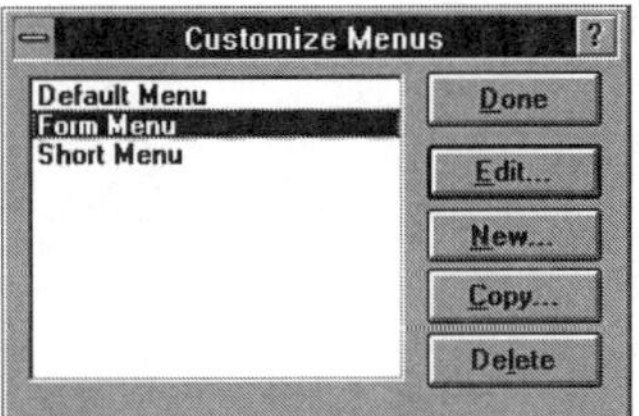

Fig. 17.5 You can design several custom menus.

The Customize Menus dialog box lists all of the currently defined menus. It has a series of buttons for creating and maintaining customized menus:

- **D**one closes the Customize Menus dialog box.
- **E**dit allows you to change the currently selected set. The Default Menu and Short Menu can't be edited.
- **N**ew starts a new customized menu.
- **C**opy copies the currently selected menu.
- De**l**ete removes the selected custom menu. The Default Menu and Short Menu can't be deleted.

Open the **E**dit menu and choose **N**ew or **C**opy to open the Define Custom Menu Bar dialog box (see fig. 17.6). Use this dialog box to define or modify custom menus.

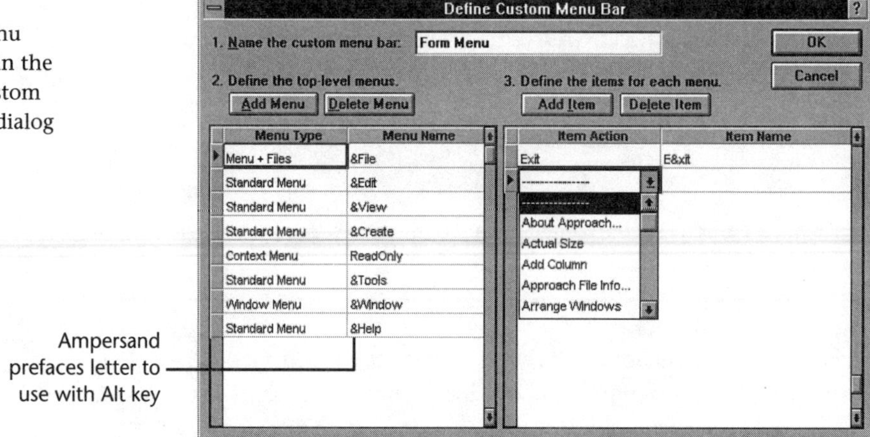

Fig. 17.6
Define menu selections in the Define Custom Menu Bar dialog box.

There are three sections in the Define Custom Menu Bar dialog box. The first is the name of the menu. When you create a new menu, Approach will give the menu a default name. You can either keep this name or give the menu a new, unique name.

The second section of the dialog box, the listings in the box on the left, is the top-level menu item. There are six types of top-level menus:

- The Standard Menu displays the menu items defined in the box on the right side of the dialog box.

- The Menu+Files Menu displays the menu items defined in the box on the right side of the dialog box and, at the bottom of the menu, lists the five most recently opened Approach files.
- The Window Menu displays the menu items defined in the box on the right side of the dialog box and a list of the currently open Approach files.
- The Context Menu varies by the view type and current mode. The Context Menu can't be modified.
- The Macro List Menu contains all macros defined to display in a menu. It can't include any other types of menu items.
- The View List Menu contains only those views defined to display in Browse mode. It can't include any other types of menu items.

Tip
The Context menus can't be edited. Items that appear in the context-sensitive menus can be included on other menus.

Note

The Macro List and View List menu types don't display any menu items. If you need a menu that combines macros, views, and standard menu items, use one of the menu types that can include items. Defined views and macros show up in the Item Action list for inclusion on other menus.

The Menu Type is listed in the left column. A new type can be selected by clicking the menu type box and then choosing the desired type from a drop-down list or by typing the first letter of the menu type. The text for the Menu Type cannot be edited.

The Menu Name—what is actually displayed in the menu bar—is the second column of items in this section. The name can be modified for all menu types except the Context menu. The menu name can have an accelerator, which allows it to be accessed with an Alt+key combination. To define an accelerator, use the ampersand (&) before the letter that will be underlined. For example, &File displays as **F**ile, and can be accessed by selecting Alt+F.

Menus are added or removed by clicking the **A**dd Menu and **D**elete Menu buttons. The current menu, either for editing or deleting, is the one with the triangle selection pointer in the box to the left. When a top-level menu is removed, so are all of its related items.

The third section of the Define Custom Menu Bar dialog box is where the individual menu items are defined for each top-level menu. The items displayed in this section are for the currently selected menu item (see fig. 17.7).

For the menu types that can't be edited or can't have commands added, Context, Macro List, and View List, this area will be empty and the Add **I**tem and De**l**ete Item buttons will be dimmed.

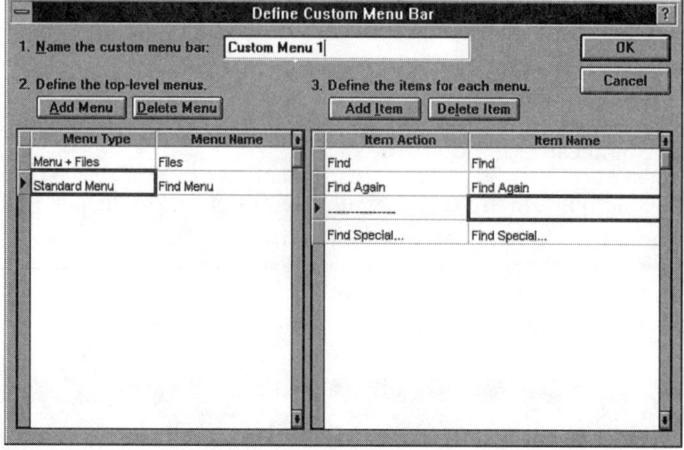

Fig. 17.7
The menu items on the right are for the Custom Find Menu.

Tip
The spacer, a dashed line that separates sections within a menu, is included as a Menu Item. Use it to keep similar menu choices together.

Menu items are added in the same way as the menu names. Use the Add **I**tem button to add a new line. The items are selected from a drop-down list. This list also includes all currently defined Macros and Views. Once an Item Action is selected, the corresponding Item Name section is filled in with the default name. The Item Actions can't be edited, but the Item Names can. Again, an accelerator can be added with the use of the ampersand, such as &Paste for **P**aste. The current item can be removed by clicking the De**l**ete Item button.

> **Caution**
>
> It is possible to add more menu items than can be displayed in the current resolution. In this case, the menus will not scroll to reveal the items that are defined but not displayed. If you're developing menus for others, check the menus in VGA resolution to guarantee that all items will be accessible.

Creating a Customized Menu from an Existing Menu

If you'd like a customized menu that's similar to the existing menu, the easiest way to create the new menu is to modify an existing menu bar. For example, you might want a menu similar to the Approach Default Menu. To define a customized menu bar based on an existing menu, follow these steps:

Note

These steps are presented sequentially, but editing does not have to follow this exact order.

1. Open the **T**ools menu and choose **C**ustomize Menus.
2. With the mouse, select the menu you wish to duplicate and click the **C**opy button.
3. The Define Custom Menu Bar dialog box opens. Change the menu name if you wish.
4. To remove any existing top-level menus that won't be needed, select the Menu Type box and click the **D**elete Menu button.
5. Add any new top-level menus by clicking the **A**dd Menu button. Choose the menu type from the drop down-list if it's different from the Standard Menu default.
6. Edit any menu names if you want to rename any top-level menus.
7. Select the top-level menu for which you'd like to edit the items. The selected menu will have a triangle to the left of its menu type.
8. Remove any unwanted menu items from the current menu by selecting the item and clicking the De**l**ete Item button. The selected item will have a triangle to the left of its Item Action.
9. Add any new items by clicking the Add **I**tem button, and then choose the desired Item Action from the drop-down list.
10. Edit the Item Name, if you want to rename an item.
11. Reorder any menu items by dragging and dropping in the Menu Items list (see fig. 17.8). Select an item by clicking the selection triangle to the right of the item name; the cursor will be a hand. Drag the item up or down in the list. The hand cursor is attached to a box, which represents the item, and a dark line appears to show where the item would be inserted when dropped. To drop an item into a new position, release the mouse button.

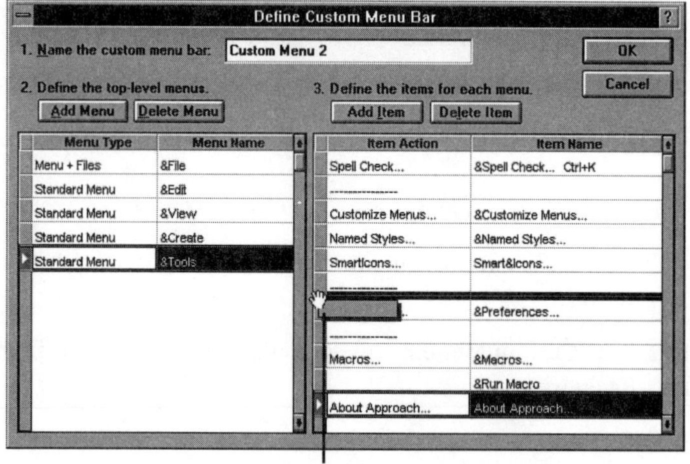

Fig. 17.8
Using drag and drop to change the order of items in a menu.

12. Reorder any top-level menus using the same drag-and-drop method. Select the menu, and then move it up or down in the list and drop it into its new position.

Creating a New Customized Menu

A custom menu can also be created from the ground up, rather than using an existing menu as a guide. This is often easier for short menus or menus that won't follow the standard Approach default menu structure. To create a new menu, follow these steps:

> **Note**
>
> These steps are presented sequentially, but editing does not have to follow this exact order.

1. Open the **T**ools menu and choose **C**ustomize Menus.
2. Click the **N**ew button.
3. The Define Custom Menu Bar dialog box opens. Change the menu name, if you wish.
4. Add any new top-level menus by clicking the **A**dd Menu button. Choose the menu type from the drop-down list if it's different from the default of Standard Menu.
5. Edit any menu names if you want to rename any top-level menus.

6. Select the top-level menu for which you'd like to edit the items. The selected menu will have a triangle to the left of its menu type.

7. Add any new items by choosing the Add **I**tem button, and then by choosing the desired Item Action from the drop-down list.

8. Edit the Item Name, if you want to rename an item.

9. Reorder any menu items by dragging and dropping in the Menu Items list. Select an item by clicking the selection triangle to the right of the item name; the cursor will be a hand. Drag the item up or down in the list. The hand cursor is attached to a box, which represents the item, and a dark line appears to show where the item would be inserted when dropped. To drop an item into a new position, release the mouse button.

10. Reorder any top-level menus by the same drag-and-drop method. Select the menu, and then move it up or down in the list and drop it into its new position.

11. If you need to remove any top-level menus, select the menu and click the **D**elete Menu button.

12. If you need to remove any menu items, select the menu item and click the De**l**ete Item button.

Editing an Existing Customized Menu

Editing an existing customized menu is very similar to creating a new menu by copying an existing menu. Follow these steps:

1. Switch to Design mode.

2. Open the **T**ools menu and choose **C**ustomize Menus.

3. Select the customized menu you want to edit by clicking it with the mouse.

4. Click the **E**dit button.

From this point you can continue from step 3 in the earlier section, "Creating a Customized Menu from an Existing Menu."

Duplicating a Customized Menu

To make a duplicate of a defined customized menu, follow these steps:

1. Switch to Design mode.

2. Open the **T**ools menu and choose **C**ustomize Menus.
3. Select the customized menu that you want to duplicate by clicking it with the mouse.
4. Click the **C**opy button.
5. If you want to edit the new menu, select it and click the **E**dit button.
6. Click **D**one to close the Customize Menus dialog box.

Attaching a Customized Menu to a View

A customized menu is attached to a view through the Info Box. The menu is attached in Design mode, but it is only used in Browse, Preview, or Find mode.

Because menus are attached to views, you must attach a custom menu to each view individually. If you duplicate a view with a custom menu, though, the custom menu will be attached to the duplicate.

> **Caution**
>
> Customized menus are only used in Browse mode. The menu bar will not change immediately after attaching a customized menu in Design mode. To view a customized menu bar, attach the menu and switch to Browse or Preview mode.

To attach a customized menu to a view, follow these steps:

1. Switch to Design mode and move to the view to which you want to attach the customized menu.
2. Define the customized menu, if it's not already defined.

3. Open the Info Box. The Info Box needs to be set for the view type, such as Form or Worksheet.
4. The Attached Menu Bar list appears on the Basics tab of the Info Box. Choose the menu bar that you want attached to the current view from this list (see fig. 17.9).

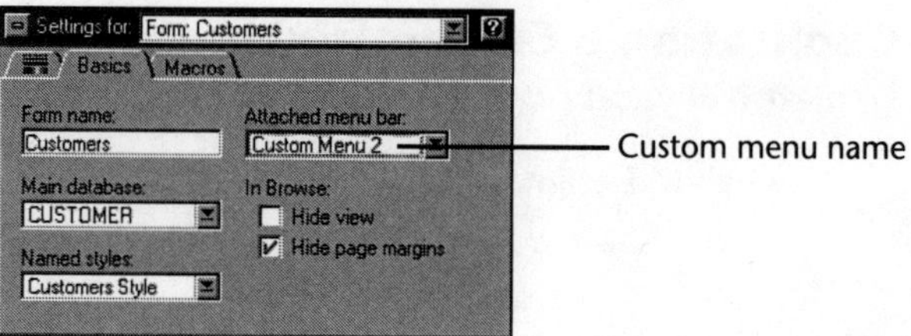

Fig. 17.9
The Info Box for a view lists the attached custom menu name.

5. Switch from Design mode to Browse or Preview mode to view the Custom Menu bar (see fig. 17.10). Remember, if a menu item isn't present in the view's current menu, the corresponding SmartIcon won't work either.

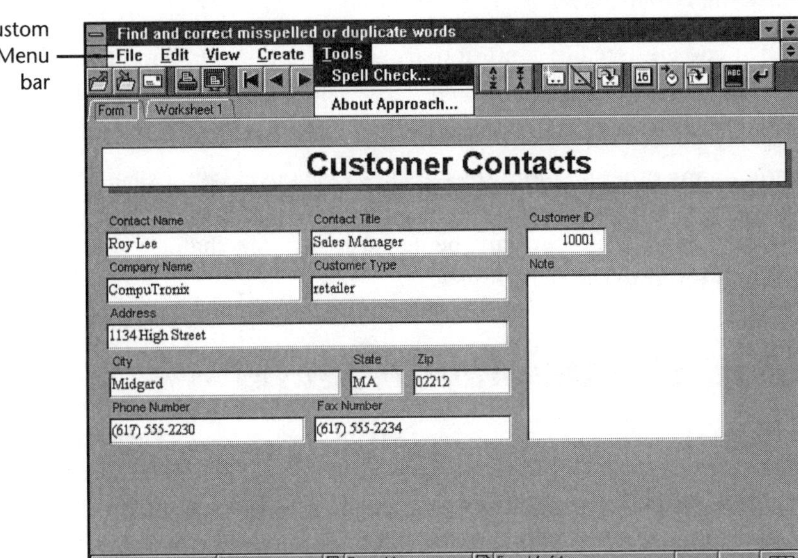

Fig. 17.10
A form showing the selections on an attached customized menu.

Removing a Customized Menu from a View

Customized menus are attached to a view through the Info Box. The menus can only be attached or modified in Design mode.

To remove a customized menu from a view, follow these steps:

1. Switch to Design mode and move to the view from where you want to remove the customized menu.

2. Open the Info Box. The Info Box needs to be set for the view type, such as Form or Worksheet.

3. The Attached Menu Bar list appears on the Basics tab of the Info Box. Choose the Default Menu to return to the Approach default for this view.

Deleting a Customized Menu

Customized menus can only be deleted in Design mode. To delete a customized menu, follow these steps:

Tip
The Display tab sets permanent defaults for an Approach file. This differs from setting the options with menu commands or SmartIcons, which are just for the current session.

1. Open the **T**ools menu and choose **C**ustomize Menus.
2. Select the customized menu that you want deleted by clicking it with the mouse.
3. Click the De**l**ete button.
4. When you are asked to confirm that you do want to permanently delete the menu, choose **Y**es. If you choose **N**o, you cancel the delete. With either choice you return to the Customize Menus dialog box.
5. Perform any other modifications or click **D**one to close the dialog box.

If you delete a menu that's currently being used, any view that it was attached to will revert to the Default menu.

Setting the Display Defaults

Approach allows each user to customize his or her own working environment. This includes what the working window will look like, what tools will be available in Design mode, and the settings chosen for default views. These display defaults are set on the Display tab in the Preferences dialog box (see fig. 17.11). This dialog box can be opened in any mode except Find. To open the dialog box, open the **T**ools menu and choose **P**references.

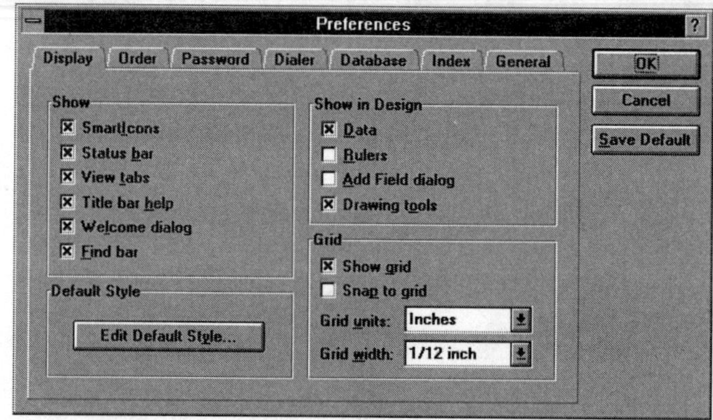

Fig. 17.11
Use the settings on the Display tab to adjust your working environment.

General Screen Item Defaults

The Show section of the Display tab affects items in the Approach main window (see fig. 17.12).

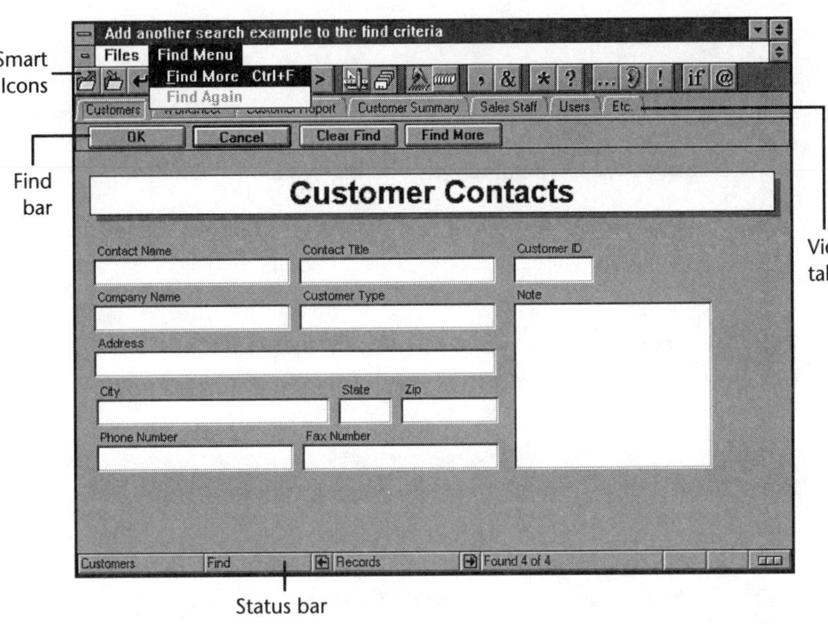

Fig. 17.12
Some of the items controlled by the Show section of the Display tab.

Each of these items is either turned on, if there's a check in the box next to the item, or off, if the box is empty. These settings can be just for the current Approach file. Or, if you adjust a setting and click the **S**ave Default button, this setting will also become the default for new Approach files.

These items are controlled in the Show section:

- *Smart**I**cons*. This turns the SmartIcons on or off for the Approach file for all modes. Any other open Approach files still have the use of SmartIcons.

  By contrast, opening the **V**iew menu and choosing Show **S**martIcons turns the SmartIcons on or off for all currently open Approach files.

- *Status **B**ar*. This selection adjusts the status bar for all currently open Approach files, the same as opening the **V**iew menu and choosing Show Stat**u**s Bar.

- *View **T**abs*. An Approach file's view tabs are either displayed or not, depending on this setting. To turn tabs off for individual views, use the In Browse Hide View checkbox in the view's Info Box.

- *Title Bar **H**elp*. Title Bar Help displays a help message for the selected menu item. This is different from the help balloons that are available for SmartIcons.

- *Welcome Dialog.* The Welcome dialog box, when enabled, appears whenever you start Approach or close all Approach files in an Approach session. The Welcome dialog box allows you to quickly open your most recently opened files, create a new file from a template, and have access to the standard File Open and New dialog boxes.
- *Find Bar.* When this is on, the Find toolbar is displayed whenever you're in Find mode.

Design Screen Items

The Design Screen Items adjust various tools that are available to most views in Design mode (see fig. 17.13).

> **Note**
>
> Worksheets and crosstabs are slightly different than other view types in the tools available. Because they don't allow added objects or free-form design, the Drawing Tools palette and Rulers aren't available on either view type. Also, worksheets and crosstabs are the only view types that can have the Add Field dialog box and Info Box active in Browse mode.

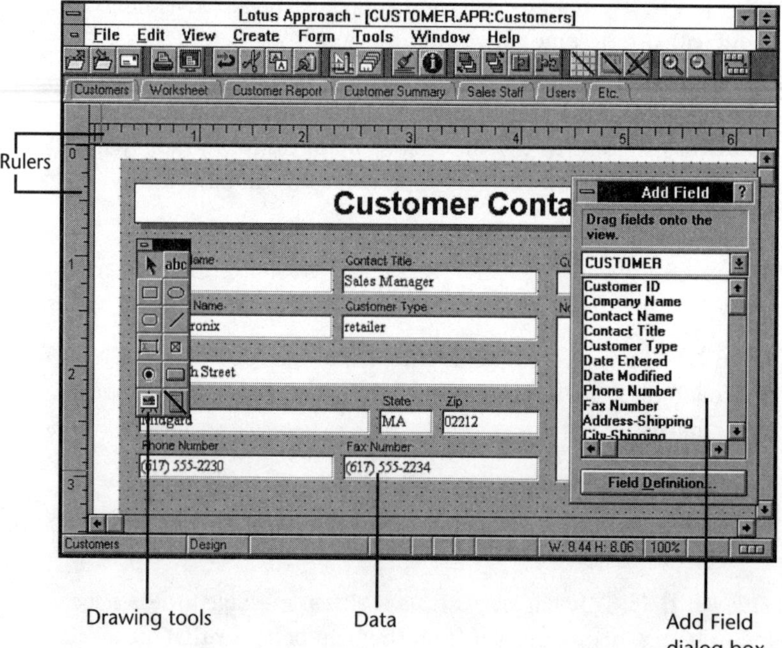

Fig. 17.13
A form in Design mode with items controlled by the Show in Design section of the Display tab.

Each of these items is either turned on, if there's a check in the box next to the item, or off, if the box is empty. These settings can be just for the current Approach file. Or, if you adjust a setting and click the **S**ave Default button, this setting will also become the default for new Approach files.

The Show in Design section controls the following:

- ***D**ata.* When the data checkbox is on, then data will be showing when you're in Design mode. The setting is saved in the file, but it can be changed temporarily by opening the **V**iew menu and choosing S**h**ow Data.
- ***R**ulers.* This controls whether or not rulers will be on by default in Design mode. The setting can be changed temporarily by opening the **V**iew menu and choosing Show **R**uler, or pressing Ctrl+J.
- ***A**dd Field Dialog.* The Add Field dialog box is a quick way to add new fields to a view, or to get into Field **D**efinition to define new fields. The Add Field dialog box can be closed temporarily by double-clicking the system menu in the dialog box's upper-left hand corner, or by the Context menu's current Add Field section.
- *Drawing T**o**ols.* The drawing tools are a floating palette of SmartIcons that are used for creating objects in Design mode. They can be removed temporarily by opening the **V**iew menu and choosing Show Dra**w**ing Tools, or pressing Ctrl+L.

Grid Defaults

The grid is a series of points at a certain interval (see fig. 17.14). It's available when you're in Design mode for all views except worksheets and crosstabs. The grid can be used either as a general guide, or, with the snap-to-grid setting, items can be easily aligned to various grid points. The grid interval can be set by the user in either inches or centimeters.

These are the grid settings:

- *Show **G**rid.* When this checkbox is on, the grid will be displayed when you're in Design mode. The grid is displayed as a series of dots. This setting can be temporarily overridden by opening the **V**iew menu and choosing Show Gr**i**d.
- *Sna**p** to Grid.* This setting is on when the box is checked. The "snap to" refers to how objects behave when being moved across the grid. The

III

Getting the Most...

objects are attracted to grid points, and seem to "snap" to a point when moved close to one. The grid does not have to be showing for objects to snap to the grid. Snapping to the grid can be temporarily overridden by opening the **V**iew menu and choosing Snap to **G**rid, or pressing Ctrl+Y.

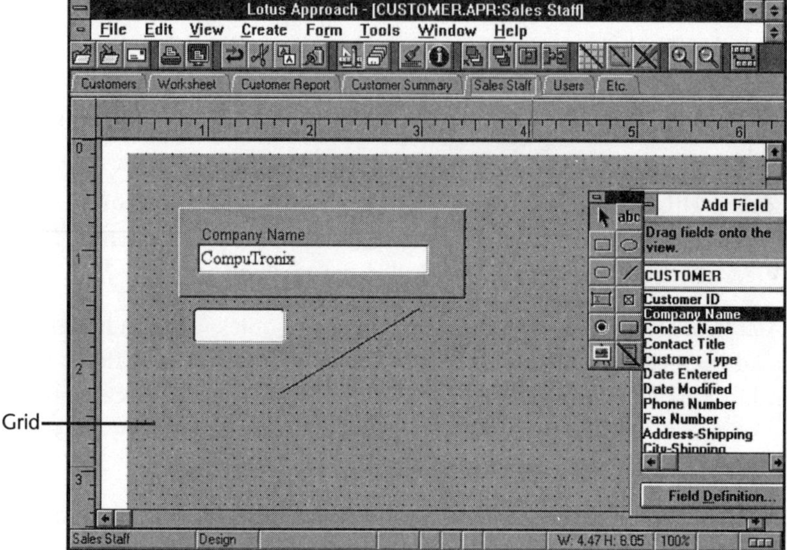

Fig. 17.14
Use the grid to align Design objects.

- *Grid **U**nits.* This setting is chosen from a drop-down list, and is in either inches or centimeters.
- *Grid **W**idth.* The widths available are also chosen from a list and depend on which units of measurements are used. The grid settings for inches are from 1/16 to 1/2 of an inch. The grid settings for centimeters are from 0.1 to 1 centimeter.

Default Style

The Edit Default St**y**le button in the Style section of the Preferences display tab allows you to set what will be used by the Assistants as the default for any view. The following attributes can be set:

- Font
- Lines and Color
- Label
- Picture
- Background

Working with this section is the same as when creating a named style. (For more information on named styles, see Chapter 3.)

The default style is saved with the Approach file. If you click the **S**ave Default button, this default style gets used for all new Approach files.

Phone Dialer Options

The Dialer tab in the Preferences dialog box sets default options for the autodialer (see fig. 17.15). These defaults are either for the current Approach file, or, if you click the **S**ave Default button, are available to all Approach files. To open the dialog box, open the **T**ools menu and choose **P**references.

Tip
Dialing is only available as a macro command.

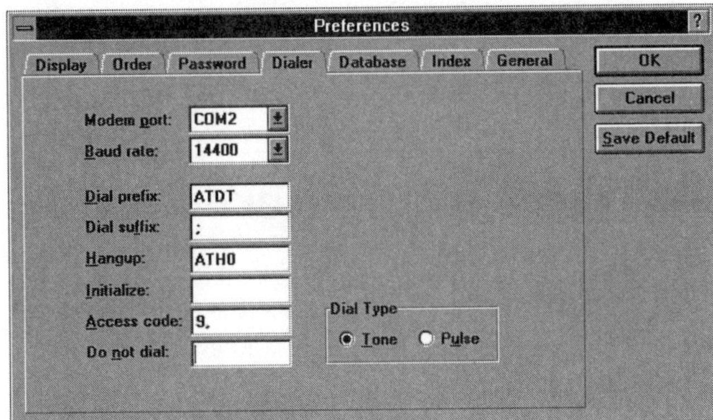

Fig. 17.15
You can configure your modem to dial for you from the Dialer tab of the Preferences dialog box.

These are the settings on the Dialer tab:

- *Modem **P**ort.* Use this drop-down list to select the communications port used by your modem.
- ***B**aud Rate.* Select the highest baud rate your modem can use in this drop-down list.
- ***D**ial Prefix.* This is the command sent to the modem before the number is dialed. Unless you know you need a different prefix, leave this setting at the default (ATDT). This sends a command to your modem telling it to dial using tones, rather than pulse.
- *Dial Su**f**fix.* This command is sent after the number is dialed.
- ***H**angup.* This command tells the modem to hang up the phone.

- *Initialize.* If your modem uses a certain initialization string, it needs to be typed into this box. Consult your modem manual for the proper string.
- *Access Code.* The access code is used if you need to dial a number, such as a 9, to get to an outside line. The comma is placed in there to pause while you're connecting to the outside line. If the pause time isn't long enough, add another comma.
- *Do **N**ot Dial.* Use this for the local area code or any other numbers or characters that might be in the field you're dialing from that you don't want the phone to dial.
- *Dial Type.* This is either **T**one or P**u**lse, depending on what your phone lines can use. Most telephones will use Tone. If you need to use Pulse, set the Dial Prefix to ATDP. This command sets the modem to use pulse dialing, rather than tone.

General Working Preferences

The General tab in the Preferences dialog box contains items that customize how you'd like Approach to act in various situations (see fig. 17.16). All items are controlled by checkboxes, checked for on and empty for off. If you click the **S**ave Default button, the settings are saved as defaults. Otherwise, they're just for the current file. To open the dialog box, open the **T**ools menu and choose **P**references.

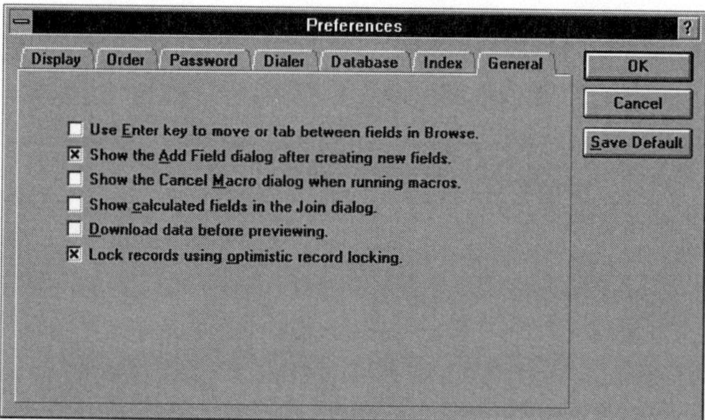

Fig. 17.16
Adjust your working preferences in the General tab of the Preferences dialog box.

These are the General tab settings:

- *Use **E**nter Key to Move or Tab Between Fields in Browse.* This is a user preference that will let you use Enter to move between fields when entering data rather than tabbing between fields.
- *Show the **A**dd Field Dialog After Creating New Fields.* If this setting is on, any time you use the Field Definition dialog box and define a new field or fields, you'll automatically be given the option to add the new fields from the Add Field dialog box to the current view. Then, if you close the Add Field dialog box, it brings up a dialog box with the option to change to Browse mode or remain in Design mode.
- *Show the Cancel **M**acro Dialog When Running Macros.* The Cancel Macro dialog box is a visual clue that a macro is running. It also has a Cancel button. Whether or not this button is displayed, macros can always be canceled by clicking the Escape key.
- *Show **C**alculated Fields in the Join Dialog.* This setting only affects datafile types that allow joins on calculated fields.
- ***D**ownload Data Before Previewing.* Downloading data is most useful when working in a shared-file environment or with SQL or ODBC data. The current set of data is downloaded to your local drive. This means that you don't have to worry about updates from other users or server access time while working with the downloaded set.
- *Lock Records Using **O**ptimistic Record Locking.* This setting is for users working in a multi-user environment, and should be the set to the same value for all users at the same site. Optimistic record locking allows multiple users to edit the same record. If two users are viewing a record and both users try to save changes, the second one attempting the save will get a warning that the record has been modified since they received the data. If this setting is off, the first person to use a record can edit data; all other users can view the record but can't edit it.

Database Preferences

Database preferences vary by the datafile type that is the currently opened file. In order to set the preferences for a certain file type, a file of that type needs to be the current file. For example, to set the preferences for the Paradox file types, you'll need to open a Paradox file. This is the same for the SQL or ODBC tables. To display the Preferences dialog box, open the **T**ools menu and choose **P**references.

Case Sensitivity on Paradox Files

The Paradox Case Sensitivity settings are found on the Database tab on the Preferences dialog box when a Paradox file is the current file (see fig. 17.17).

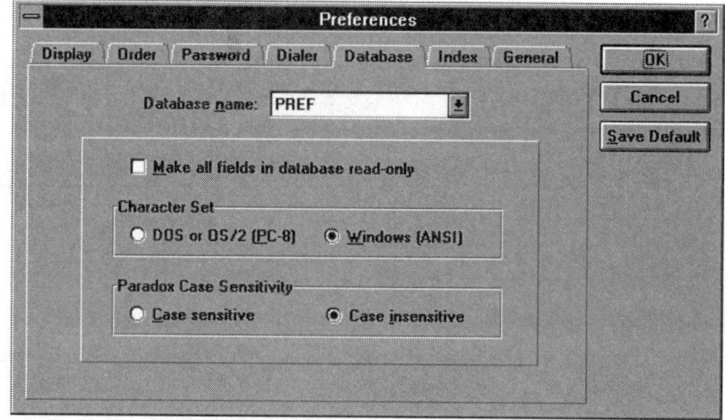

Fig. 17.17
The Case Sensitivity settings for Paradox are on the Database tab when a Paradox file is open.

Tip
Paradox 3.5 files are always case sensitive.

These settings are for Paradox 4.X and Paradox for Windows files only. Click the radio button for either **C**ase Sensitive or Case **I**nsensitive searches and indexes. After clicking OK to close the Preferences dialog box, a warning dialog box appears to inform you to close and reopen the file for the new case sensitivity setting.

Including SQL System Tables

The SQL and ODBC file types have a different Database tab in Preferences (see fig. 17.18). In the SQL Database, preferences is a checkbox for whether or not system tables are displayed. If the box is checked, the system tables are displayed; if the box is unchecked, they are not displayed.

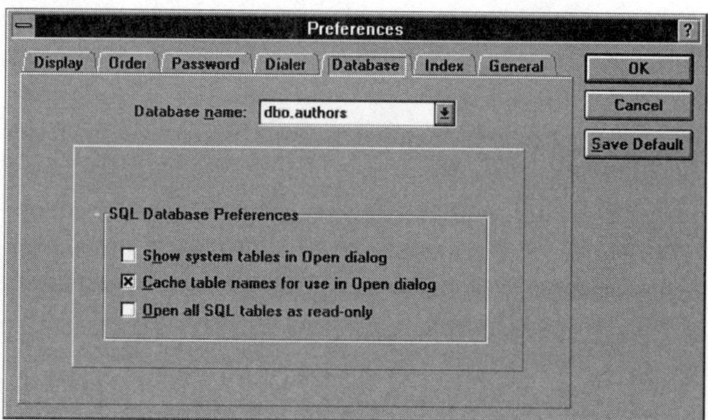

Fig. 17.18
Database preference settings for SQL tables.

Caching SQL Tables

The Database tab in Preferences also has a setting that allows the user to cache SQL table names in a session. When the names are cached they're stored locally, and a list of tables don't need to be generated from the server every time a dialog box—such as Open or New, which contain a list of the tables—is opened.

> **Caution**
>
> When table names are cached they don't get updated as you and other users insert or delete tables in the database. The table names at the beginning of the next session will reflect any changes.

From Here...

In this chapter, you learned how you can use the customization options in Approach to develop database applications. To learn more about automating your application through macros, refer to the following chapter in this book:

- Chapter 13, "Automating Your Work," shows how Approach macros can be used for most tasks, including navigating through different views, finding records, and printing reports.

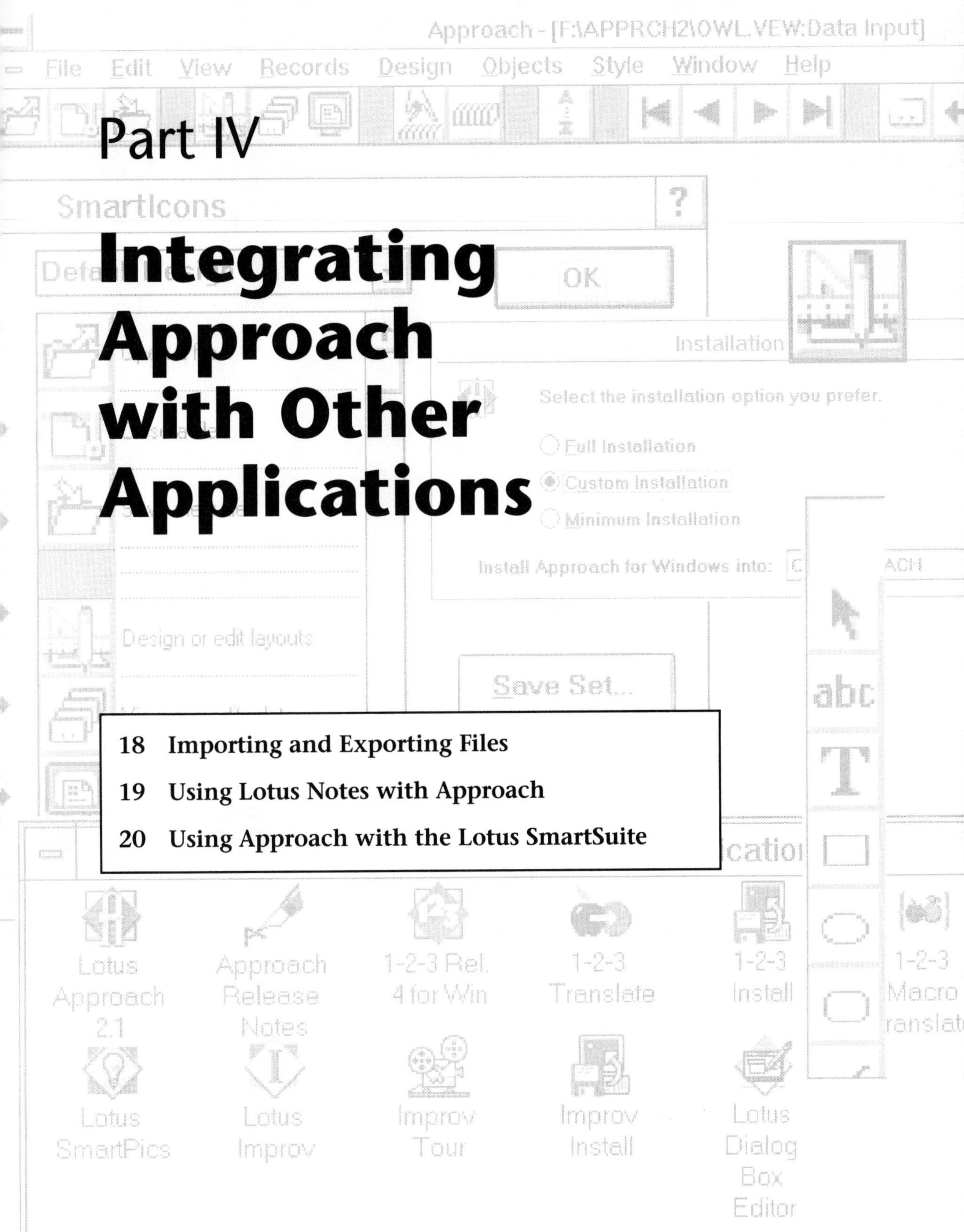

Part IV

Integrating Approach with Other Applications

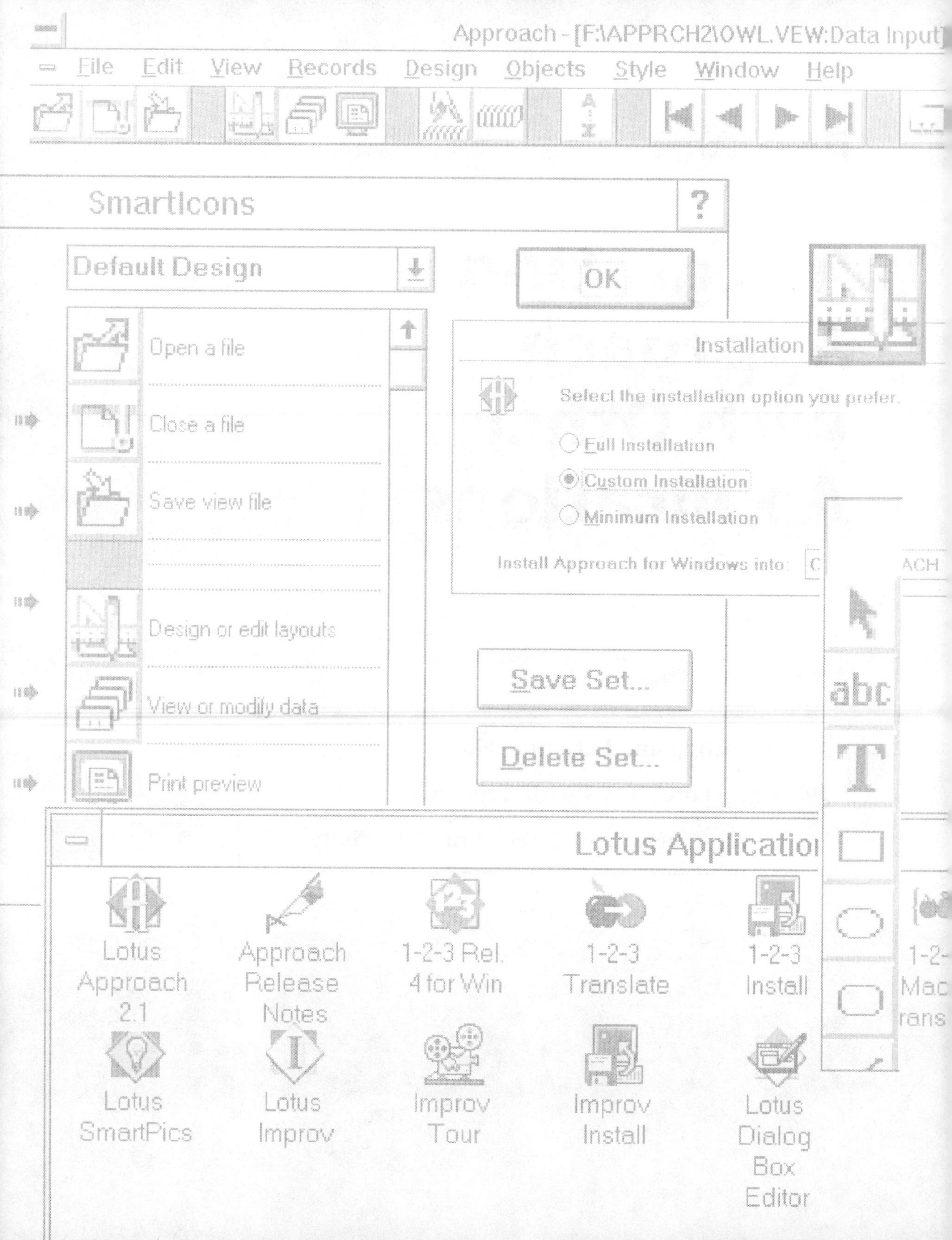
Approach - [F:\APPRCH2\OWL.VEW:Data Input]
File Edit View Records Design Objects Style Window Help
SmartIcons
Default Design
OK
Open a file
Close a file
Save view file
Design or edit layouts
View or modify data
Print preview
Save Set...
Delete Set...
Installation
Select the installation option you prefer.
Full Installation
Custom Installation
Minimum Installation
Install Approach for Windows into:
abc
T
Lotus Applicatio
Lotus Approach 2.1
Approach Release Notes
1-2-3 Rel. 4 for Win
1-2-3 Translate
1-2-3 Install
Lotus SmartPics
Lotus Improv
Improv Tour
Improv Install
Lotus Dialog Box Editor

Chapter 18

Importing and Exporting Files

Using Approach, you can import and export information in a variety of different data formats. With this flexibility, you can sort, store, and update information selectively. Importing and exporting also enables you to move information into and out of non-database formats to exchange data with applications that use a proprietary format.

Similar to sharing data, you can also share views that are already created by importing an Approach file. Views can also be inserted into other applications by using Approach as an OLE server.

In this chapter, you learn how to:

- Import data into Approach from another database
- Import data into Approach from a text file
- Import data into Approach from a spreadsheet
- Export data from Approach to other databases
- Export data from Approach to text files
- Export data from Approach to a spreadsheet
- Import other data from other Approach files
- Create Approach OLE Server Objects for use in other applications

Importing Data

Importing information into Approach enables you to use Approach's powerful database tools to view and modify the data.

Approach enables you to specify the fields from which information is imported and the fields in the open database to which that information is sent. It also has the capability to use Import to append information to the end of a file, update existing records, or a combination of both.

Using the Import Setup Dialog Box

The Import Setup dialog box is used to map which fields in the destination database will be used to receive data from the source database. It also lets you browse through the records that are being imported so you don't have to guess which field might have the data that goes into another field. This is especially helpful for data coming from a spreadsheet or text file that doesn't have predefined field names. The Import Setup dialog box also shows the number of records contained in the source file (see fig. 18.1).

Fig. 18.1
The Import Setup dialog box maps imported data to existing data.

The fields in the source database are listed on the left side of the Import Setup dialog box. The destination database name and its fields are listed on the right. The destination fields can be moved up or down to match the proper source field. In order to map the source and destination field together, they need to be positioned across from each other. The Previous and Next buttons in the lower-left corner of the dialog box (represented by a left-facing caret and right-facing caret, respectively) are used to browse the data in the source file.

The Import Setup dialog box is also used to set the merge or update options for the data from the source file. The imported data can complete the following tasks:

- *Add Imported Data as New Records.* Append to the end of the destination file as new records.
- *Use Imported Data to Update Existing Records.* Update only existing records in the destination file that match specified criteria.
- *Use Imported Data to Update and Add to Existing Records.* Update existing records that match specified criteria and append as new any records that don't match.

When using an import option that merges records, the Import Setup dialog box changes to allow you to set criteria for matches (see fig. 18.2). This criteria should be something unique, such as an employee number or a combination of name and telephone number. Because the contents fields that are marked unique will remain the same—or else there would be no match—they don't need to be mapped (with an arrow) in Import Setup.

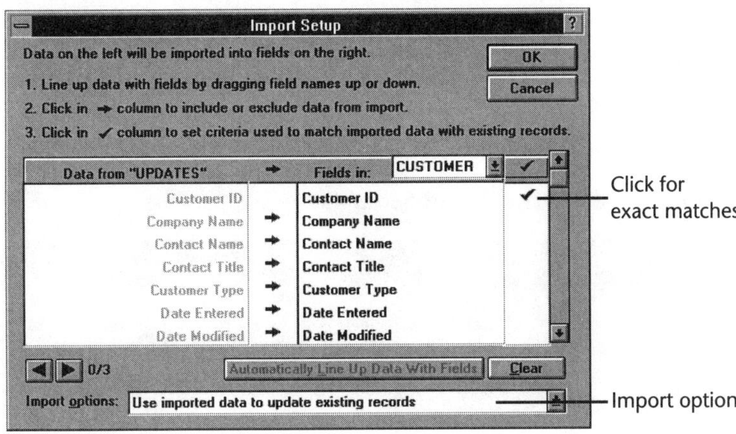

Fig. 18.2
This import updates records that exactly match the Customer ID field.

To import data, updating only those records that match an exact criteria, follow these steps:

1. Open the database into which you want to import data; this database is now known as the destination database.
2. Switch to Browse mode.

3. Open the **F**ile menu and choose **I**mport Data. The Import Data dialog box appears (see fig. 18.3).

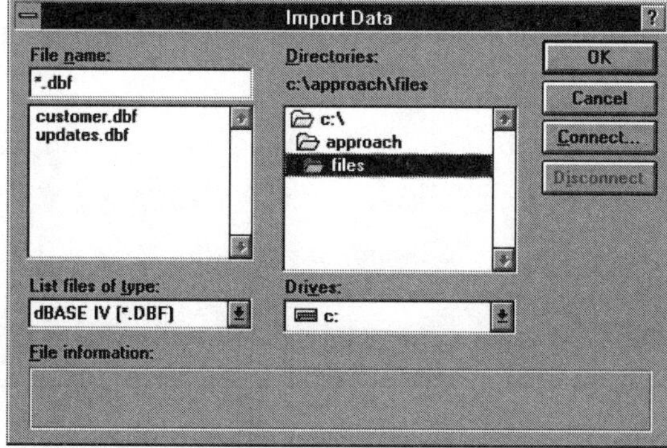

Fig. 18.3 The Import Data dialog box is used to select the file from which you are importing.

4. Select the type of file you're importing from in the List Files of **T**ype drop-down list. If you're importing from a text or spreadsheet file, another dialog box may appear for information specific to that type. Refer to the section specific to importing that file type for more information.

5. Use the Dri**v**es drop-down list and the **D**irectories list box to select the drive and directory that contain the file you want to import.

6. Select the file you want to import from—the source database—in the file list box.

7. Click OK. The Import Setup dialog box appears.

Note

If a field in the source database and a field in the destination database have the same name, Approach maps them automatically. These mapped fields have arrows between them when the Import Setup dialog box opens.

8. If the current Approach file contains multiple joined databases, select the destination database from the drop-down list of databases.

Caution

If your Approach file contains joined databases, you can only import information into one database at a time. Changing which database you're importing into erases any mappings you've established.

9. Set the Import **O**ptions to use imported data to match existing records. The dialog box changes to the one that allows you to set a matching criteria.

10. Move the destination fields up or down, if necessary, to line them up with the proper fields from the source database. To move a destination field, click the field so it's selected. The cursor changes to include up and down arrows to show that the field can be moved. Drag the field to the new position and release. The field you dragged switches places with another field (see fig. 18.4).

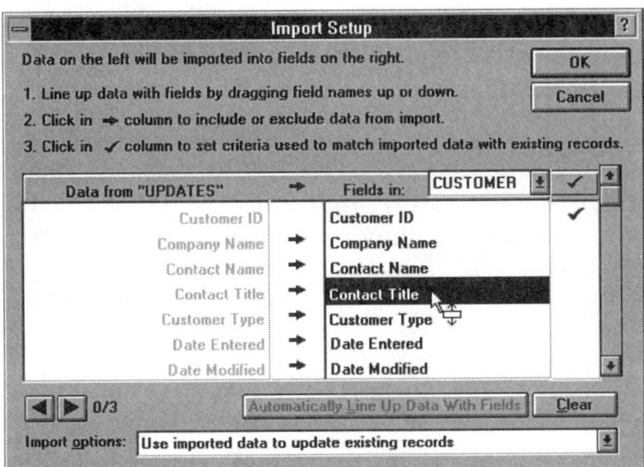

Fig. 18.4
Drag the destination fields up or down to align with source fields.

Note

Calculated and variable fields aren't displayed in the Import Setup dialog box because they're a part of the Approach file, not stored in a database file.

11. Once a set of source and destination fields are lined up properly, click the check column between them for an arrow to show that the two are mapped to each other.

Caution

Only the destination fields in Import Setup that have an arrow from a source field will receive data. If there are more fields in either the source or destination file shown in the Import Setup dialog box, use the scroll bar to scroll through the fields and check that all fields which should be receiving data are properly set.

Note

The two mapped fields should have the same field type. If they do not, Approach does not import the value in the source field into the destination database. The exception to this rule is that you can import any field type into a text-type field.

It's also important that the field lengths are similar, or at least that the destination field has a greater length. If the destination field is shorter than the source field, the incoming data is truncated to the length of the destination field.

12. Repeat step 10 for every field you want to map. Be sure to scroll the list if the Source or Destination Field list contains more fields than are shown in the list.

Note

If you need to unmap a pair of fields, click the arrow to turn it off. To clear all set mappings, click the **C**lear button. To redo all automatic mappings (based on name), click the Automatically **L**ine Up Data With Fields button.

13. Click OK in the Import Setup dialog box.

Approach imports the fields from the selected database, merging matching records into the destination database. Because you're not adding any records that don't match, the record counter should remain the same.

Tip
If you're going to create a new Approach database from an existing dBASE, Paradox, or FoxPro file, open the file directly. Use the Import Setup dialog box to update or consolidate information.

Importing Data from a Specific File Type

Since Approach covers a wide range of file types, some additional information may be necessary when importing from specific file types.

Importing Data from Another Database

Approach is able to directly access information in dBASE-, Paradox-, and FoxPro-format databases. You can import information stored in any of these formats into an open database in Approach. This capability is very useful if you have similar information stored in several different databases. For example, you can have multiple databases with customer information. Approach enables you to consolidate these files into a single file. You can do this even if the files are of different database formats.

Importing Data from a Text File

You can import information from a delimited or fixed-width text file. Because many programs can export data to a text file, you may find it useful to import the information from the text file if Approach is unable to directly read the database format from which you want to import data.

> **Note**
>
> If you're starting a new database from a text file, there's no need to create a database and then import the data. Open the **F**ile menu and choose **O**pen. You can select the text file type in the Open dialog box. Approach will open the file and convert it to a database for you.

Importing Data from a Delimited Text File

A delimited text file must have a special format before you can import its contents into a destination database. Each line (ending with a Carriage Return/Line Feed combination) is treated as a single record. Within the line, special characters called *delimiters* separate "fields." Commas are often used as delimiters, although you can use any character as a delimiter. In the following example, the text file "database" has one record per line, and "fields" are "comma-delimited":

```
"George","Smith","45 A Street","Carmichael","CA","90569"
"Joseph","Jordan","1290 Fortune Street","Lansing", "MI","59067"
"Fred","Grossman","67709 Chadworth Ave","New York","NY","10089"
"Gavin","39023 Palm Drive","Palm Springs","CA","96890"
```

In a delimited text file, fields that contain returns or the delimiter character can be imported if the entire field is enclosed in double quotes. Fields that are enclosed in double quotes should begin immediately after the delimiter, or the double quotes will be interpreted as a character in the field.

Fields that are not enclosed in double quotes should import correctly even without double quotes as long as the delimiter or a carriage return is not contained in the field.

> **Note**
>
> The text file should have the same number of fields on every line. If information in one of the fields is missing, you must indicate the presence of the missing field with a delimiter. In the preceding example, because the first field is missing from the last line, you need to add the leading comma on the last line. The comma indicates the end of the first (missing) field. If the missing field is in the record, rather than at the beginning, two commas are used to indicate the missing field.

When you choose delimited text as the file type in the Import Data dialog box, the Text File Options dialog box opens (see fig. 18.5).

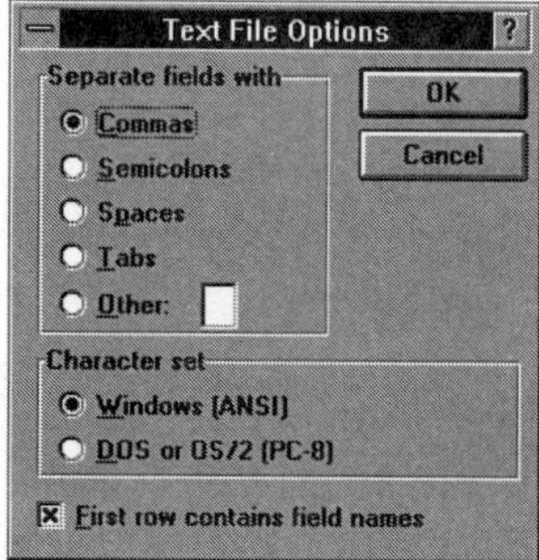

Fig. 18.5
The Text File Options dialog box contains settings specific to delimited text files.

Set the file options as necessary in the Text File Options dialog box:

- Use the Separate Fields With section of the dialog box to set the delimiter. If the delimiter is not listed, type it in the text box next to **O**ther.
- Select the proper character set (**W**indows or **D**OS) for the file. This is especially important if the file you're importing from has international characters.
- Check the box if the first row contains field names. Generally, you don't want to import the field names with the data.

Click OK to proceed to the Import Setup dialog box. Refer to "Using the Import Setup Dialog Box" at the beginning of this chapter for instructions.

Importing Data from a Fixed-Width Text File

A fixed-width text file has a certain number of spaces for each field. From these widths you know where each field starts and ends. Because you already know the position of each field, there are no delimiters. The preceding delimited file data might be stored in a fixed-width file, as follows:

```
George  Smith        45 A Street        Carmichael    CA90569
Joseph  Jordan     1290 Fortune Street  Lansing       MI59067
Fred    Grossman  67709 Chadworth Ave   New York      NY10089
        Gavin     39023 Palm Drive      Palm Springs  CA96890
```

For this file, the first field is 8 characters wide, the second is 10 characters, and so on. It's important to know where each file begins and ends in a fixed-width text database. If this information isn't correct, odds are that the data imported won't be, either.

Fixed-width text files have their own Fixed Length Text File Setup dialog box to describe where each field begins or ends (see fig. 18.6). In this figure, the information for the first field has been entered. Approach has used the starting point and width to fill in the starting point for the second field. Any fields for import need to be defined in this dialog box.

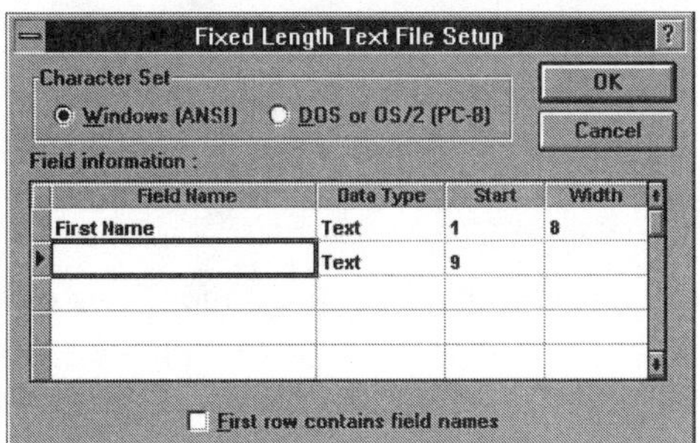

Fig. 18.6 Use the Fixed Length Text File Setup dialog box to describe field width and placement.

For each fixed-width field, you're able to do several tasks:

- Select the proper character set (**W**indows or **D**OS) for the file. This is especially important if the file you're importing from has international characters.
- Type in a field name, data type, starting position, and width.
- Check the box if the first row contains field names. Generally, you don't want to import the field names with the data.

Once all the fields are defined, click OK to proceed to the Import Setup dialog box. Refer to "Using the Import Setup Dialog Box" at the beginning of this chapter for instructions.

Importing Data from a Spreadsheet

Because spreadsheets such as Lotus 1-2-3 for Windows or Microsoft Excel have rudimentary database capabilities, a significant amount of data that should be stored in databases is instead stored in spreadsheets. In addition, spreadsheets display data in a format that many people are comfortable with: a table. In the table, each column in the spreadsheet is treated as a field, and each row is a record. Spreadsheets have limited database capabilities, however. You may want to import data from a spreadsheet into Approach to make use of Approach's extensive database capabilities.

Note

If you're starting a new database from a spreadsheet file, there's no need to create a database and then import the data. Open the **F**ile menu and choose **O**pen. Within the Open dialog box you're able to select the spreadsheet file type. Approach will open the file and convert it to a database for you.

A spreadsheet file must follow a special format before you can import its contents into an open database. Each row must be one record, and each column must be a field.

After you choose the spreadsheet file in the Import Data dialog box, a second dialog box opens, asking you to select a range for import (see fig. 18.7). This dialog box shows a list of named ranges and spreadsheets that contain data. In the Select Range dialog box you can also tell Approach to skip the first row of data that contains field names.

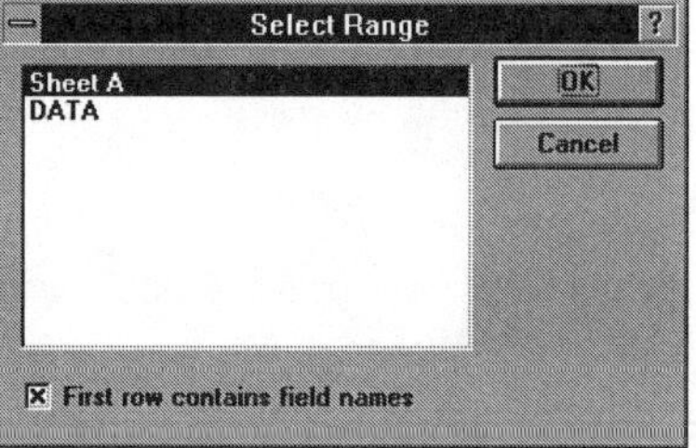

Fig. 18.7
Use the Select Range dialog box to choose the sheet or named range you want to import.

Note

You don't need to delete blank rows in a spreadsheet before you import data from that spreadsheet—Approach doesn't import the blank rows.

After selecting the range for import, click OK to proceed with the Import Setup dialog box. Refer to "Using the Import Setup Dialog Box" at the beginning of this chapter for instructions.

Note

In Excel, a column can hold a date and a time (such as 2/24/93 9:46pm). If a column in the Excel file is formatted in this manner, Approach lists that column twice in the Fields to Map list box—once as a date field, and once as a time field (for example, for column A, A DATE and A TIME).

Exporting Data

Approach enables you to export information to the following types of files:

- Other databases
- Text files
- Spreadsheets

Exporting data into other files enables you to work with your data outside of Approach. For example, you can work with text-file data in a word processor, or use the sophisticated mathematical functions of a spreadsheet in an exported spreadsheet-format file.

Exporting data also enables you to change the order in which the records are stored, choose a subset of your data, or both.

> **Note**
>
> Non-summary calculated fields and variable fields can be exported. They become standard database fields and contain their value at export in each record.

Limiting Exported Records

You may find it useful to perform a find before exporting records. If you perform a find, Approach exports only those records from the current found set. To perform a find before exporting, follow these steps:

1. Switch to Browse mode.
2. Select the view you want to use to create the find by selecting its tab or by clicking the view name from the pop-up list in the status bar.
3. Click the Find SmartIcon.

4. Type the find criteria on the form.
5. Press Enter to execute the find and create the found set.

Ordering Exported Records

Tip
If you want to perform both a find and a sort for the exported data, do the find first and then the sort.

Approach exports records from the currently open database in their current sort order. Thus, when exporting records, you may find it helpful to sort the records in the currently open database before performing the export. The records appear in the destination file in the order in which they are sorted.

Note

If you've used the Order tab in the **T**ools **P**references dialog box to set a default sort order on your database, the records are exported in that order.

To perform a sort before exporting records, follow these steps:

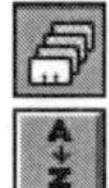

1. Switch to Browse mode.
2. Open the **B**rowse menu and choose Sor**t**. You can also press Ctrl+T, or, if it's present, click the Define Sort SmartIcon. The Sort dialog box appears.
3. Select the database you want to sort from the drop-down list under the Database **F**ields option name.
4. In the Database **F**ields list box, select the field you want to sort.

Caution

You can sort on a summary field, but you cannot export a summary field.

5. Click **A**dd or double-click the selected field to move the field to the Fields to **S**ort On list box. Adjust the sort direction, asc**e**nding or **d**escending, if needed.
6. Repeat steps 4 and 5 as needed. You can select fields from multiple databases if the Approach file contains joined databases.
7. Click OK in the Sort dialog box to perform the sort.

Using the Export Data Dialog Box

Approach enables you to export information from the currently open database or databases to a new file. This process is useful if you want to create a new file that has the following:

- Records stored in a specific order. Exporting records is the only way to reorder your records physically, although opening the **T**ools menu and choosing **P**references enables you to set a permanent display order on the database.
- Only a subset of the records in the currently open database.

> **Note**
>
> See the earlier sections, "Limiting Exported Records" and "Ordering Exported Records," for more information about using the Exporting Data dialog box.

To export information from an open database to a new file, follow these steps:

1. Open the database from which you want to export information.
2. Switch to Browse mode.

3. If desired, perform a sort or find on the records in the open database. If you want to perform both a sort and a find, do the find first.
4. Open the **F**ile menu and choose **E**xport Data. The Export Data dialog box appears (see fig. 18.8).

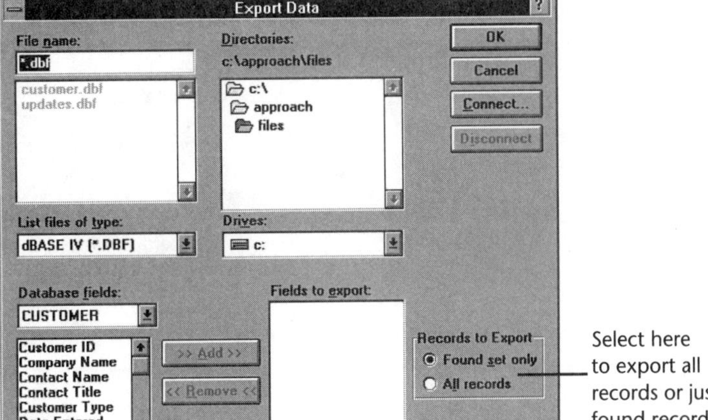

Fig. 18.8
Set file export options in the Export Data dialog box.

5. Select the export database file type from the List Files of **T**ype drop-down list.

Tip
If you have sorted ALL the records, you must select the Found **S**et Only radio button or the destination file will not have sorted records.

Tip
You can export fields from more than one database.

6. Use the Dri**v**es drop-down list and the **D**irectories list box to select the drive and directory in which you want to store the exported file.
7. Type the name of the export file in the File **N**ame text box.
8. Select the fields to export. If the current Approach file contains multiple joined databases, select the database from which you want to export fields from the list of databases. The fields in the selected database appear in the Database **F**ields list box.
9. Select a field in the Database **F**ields list box. The order in which you select fields determines their order in the new database.
10. Click **A**dd or double-click the selected field to move the field to the Fields to **E**xport list box.

Note

To remove a field from the Fields to **E**xport list box, select the field and click **R**emove or double-click the field.

11. Repeat steps 8–10 for all databases and fields you want to export.
12. Select one of the following options from the Records to Export section of the Export Data dialog box:

Button	Description
A**l**l Records	Exports all records in the currently open database. Records are exported in their true order in the database even if a default sort order has been set.
Found **S**et Only	Available only if you perform a find or a sort before starting the export. If you select this option, records are exported in their current or default sort order, and only records in the found set are exported.

13. Click OK in the Export Data dialog box.

Approach creates a new database with the selected fields and exports the selected records to this database.

Exporting Data to Another Database

Choose the database type you'll be exporting to in the List Files of **T**ype list box in the Export Data dialog box. The database type that you export to does not have to be the same type that you're exporting from. For example, you can use export to create a Paradox file from a dBASE file.

> **Note**
>
> If the export database is a Paradox database, the Choose Key Field dialog box appears. Choose one or more of the fields from the list of fields to be the key field. You can also choose **A**dd Key Field to have Approach create a serial key field.

Exporting Data to a Text File

Approach enables you to export information from the currently open database to a text file. This capability is handy if you want to move the information to a word processor or another application that can't read database-format files. As with import, the exported text file can be either delimited or fixed length.

Exporting Data to a Delimited Text File

To export the currently open database to a delimited text file, follow these steps:

1. Open the database from which you want to export information.
2. Switch to Browse mode.

3. If you want, perform a sort or find on the records in the open database.
4. Open the **F**ile menu and choose **E**xport Data. The Export Data dialog box appears.

5. Select the delimited text file type from the List Files of **T**ype drop-down list.
6. Use the Dri**v**es drop-down list and the **D**irectories list box to select the drive and directory in which you want to store the exported file.
7. Choose the field to export. This is covered in more detail in the earlier section, "Using the Export Data Dialog Box."
8. Select the A**l**l Records or Found **S**et Only option from the Records to Export section of the Export Data dialog box.

9. Click OK in the Export Data dialog box. The Text File Options dialog box appears (see fig. 18.5).

10. Choose a delimiter. If you choose the **O**ther button, type the delimiter character into the text box to the right of the **O**ther button.

11. Choose one of the following Character Set options to select the character set for the text file:

    Choose the **W**indows (ANSI) option if you are exporting to a Windows text file.

    Choose the **D**OS or OS/2 (PC-8) option if you are exporting to a DOS or OS/2 application.

12. Choose whether or not the first row of the exported file will contain field names.

13. Click OK in the Text File Options dialog box.

Approach creates the new delimited text file with the selected fields and exports the selected records to that file. Each record in the database appears as one line in the text file. Each field in the database becomes a portion of a line, separated from the next "field" by the delimiter character.

Note

Fields will be exported with double quotes at the beginning and end of the field. Returns in the field remain intact.

Exporting Data to a Fixed-Length File

In a fixed-length text file, each field has a specific starting and ending point. For example, a FIRST NAME field might be defined as 10 characters. In the text file, it would start at position 1 and end at position 10. The next field would start in the position that immediately follows (position 11).

To export data to a fixed-length text file, set up the Export Data dialog box as described in the earlier section, "Using the Export Data Dialog Box." For this example, however, select fixed-length text in the List Files of **T**ype drop-down list.

Click OK on the Export Data dialog box to bring up the Fixed Length Text File Setup dialog box. In this dialog box you can do the following:

- Set the character set, **W**indows or **D**OS.

- Adjust the field widths, if necessary.
- Choose whether or not the first row contains field names in the exported file.

Exporting Data to a Spreadsheet

Approach enables you to export data to a spreadsheet. After you store data in a spreadsheet, you can use the spreadsheet's powerful mathematical functions to manipulate the data.

To export data to a spreadsheet, choose the desired type in the List Files of **T**ype drop-down list in the Export Data dialog box, set export options as desired, and click OK.

Importing an Approach File

An Approach file (*.apr) contains information about all the views, forms, reports, form letters, mailing labels, worksheets, crosstabs, charts, macros, calculated fields and variable fields defined within it. You can import an Approach file into the currently open Approach file. This enables you to use the views, macros, and calculated and variable fields in the imported Approach file to display the information in the currently open Approach file.

Tip
Importing an Approach file, as opposed to importing a database, does not affect the data that's stored in the database in any way.

When you import an Approach file, you map which database fields will be displayed by which field objects in the imported Approach file. If no field in the current database is a mapped field in the imported Approach file, that field object won't display anything wherever it appears. Any macros or calculations that refer to that unmapped field won't run or evaluate.

To import an Approach file, follow these steps:

1. Open the database into which you want to import the Approach file. This is the destination file.
2. Switch to Design mode.

3. Open the **F**ile menu and choose **I**mport Approach File. The Import Approach File dialog box appears (see fig. 18.9).
4. Use the Dri**v**es drop-down list and the **D**irectories list box to select the drive and directory that contain the file you want to import.
5. Still in the Import Approach file dialog box, select the Approach file you want to import from, the source file, in the File **N**ame list box.

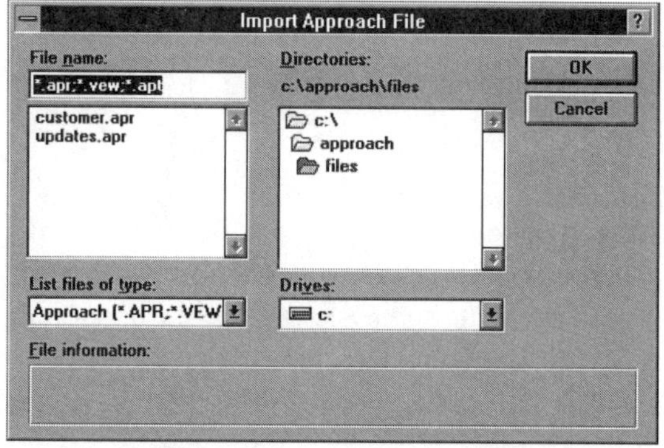

Fig. 18.9
Choose an Approach file to import from the Import Approach File dialog box.

6. Click OK. The Import Approach File Setup dialog box appears (see fig. 18.10).

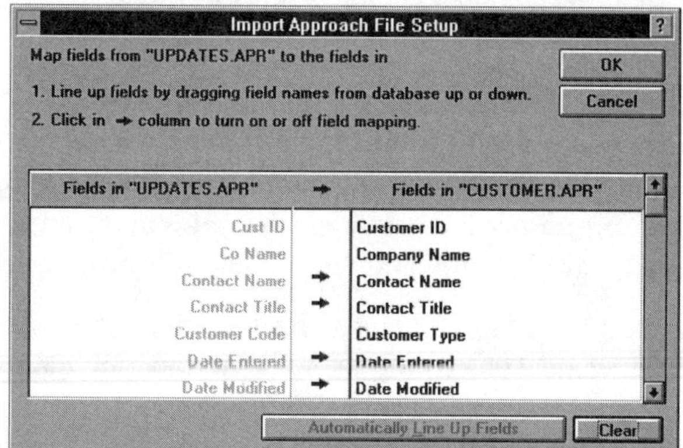

Fig. 18.10
The Import Approach File Setup dialog box is used to map existing fields to those in the imported Approach file.

7. Use the Import Approach File Setup dialog box to map the fields in the import Approach file to the fields in the open Approach file.

> **Note**
>
> If the current Approach file contains multiple joined databases, all fields are listed by FILENAME:FIELDNAME. This is different from importing data because the Approach file needs to know what field to display for each field referenced in the Approach file. Also, because you're not importing data, all fields including calculated and variable fields show up in the destination Approach file.

8. Any fields that match by name will be mapped automatically. To unmap those fields, click the arrow between the two fields.

9. Adjust any field in the destination file, if necessary, so it is directly across from the field to which it will be mapped. To move a destination field, click the field so it is selected. The cursor changes to show that the field can be moved. Drag the field to the new position and release. The field you dragged switches places with the field whose position it was in.

10. To map the two selected fields, click the arrow column between the two fields so an arrow appears between them.

11. Repeat steps 7–10 for every field you want to map. In order for a pair of source and destination fields to be mapped, they must have an arrow between them.

Note

If you need to unmap a pair of fields, click the arrow between a pair of fields. To clear all field mappings, click the **C**lear button. To redo all automatic mappings—those based on matching names—click the Automatically **L**ine Up Data With Fields button.

12. Click OK in the Import Approach File Setup dialog box. Approach imports the source Approach file into the destination file. All the views, macros, and calculated and variable fields in the source Approach file are available for use in the destination Approach file.

Caution

Any fields that aren't mapped when the Approach file is imported appear as NO FIELD REFERENCE in Design mode with Show Data mode turned off. With Show Data mode turned on, the unmapped fields are blank. Use the Info Box to assign database fields to these unmapped fields if you want to use them.

Creating Approach Objects for Other Applications

Approach is an OLE Server. This means that Approach has the ability to create objects that can be linked or embedded into other applications (called a *container application*). An object can then be activated, giving you access to an Approach view or application.

An OLE link means that other applications can have access to an .apr file. When that object is activated, the linked objects are updated to reflect any changes to the original file. An embedded file exists only in the object in which it was created. Either a linked or embedded Approach object can have access to data. It might be helpful to link a commonly used crosstab into a word processing document, for example, so that the crosstab can be activated and printed whenever the document is used.

Tip
Approach must be installed on your machine to activate an Approach object.

The default OLE object in Approach, such as a form object, is an object with a link to its original database. In order for it to use that data, the database has to be present.

If the database is no longer present, or if the object is activated on a machine that doesn't have access to the database, the Approach file displays a message that the file can't be found and asks if you would like to open a different file. At this point you can choose to open the object with a different file or cancel.

An option with an Approach object is to include data within the object. With this option, the person who'll be using the object doesn't need the original database present to view or use the data. Of course, at this point there's no longer a link back to the original data source, so any changes made to this copy will not be reflected in the original.

An Approach object with data is stored as an Approach Transfer file (*.apt). An Approach Transfer file is limited to using existing views and data. To get a fully modifiable copy of the view(s) and data, you can open the **F**ile menu and choose Save **A**s to create a fully functional Approach file (*.apr) with databases.

Creating an Approach OLE Object in Approach

An Approach object created within Approach has two options for including views—the current view, and all views in the Approach file.

Tip
Copy View appears at the same spot as the standard Copy command in the Edit menu.

For either of these two options, there are also five options for including data:

- All databases
- Found set
- Current record
- Blank databases
- No databases

To create an Approach object within Approach, follow these steps:

1. Switch to Browse mode.

2. Open the **E**dit menu and choose **C**opy View. This opens the Copy View to Clipboard dialog box (see fig. 18.11).

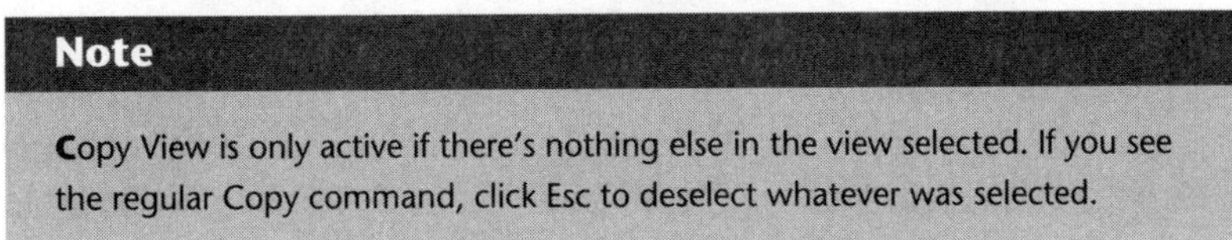

Note

Copy View is only active if there's nothing else in the view selected. If you see the regular Copy command, click Esc to deselect whatever was selected.

Fig. 18.11
Use the Copy View to Clipboard dialog box in Approach to create OLE objects.

3. Switch to the application where you wish to link or embed the Approach object.

4. In the application where you wish to paste the object, open the **E**dit menu and choose Paste **S**pecial. The Paste Special dialog box appears, listing the options for pasting in the Approach object (see fig. 18.12).

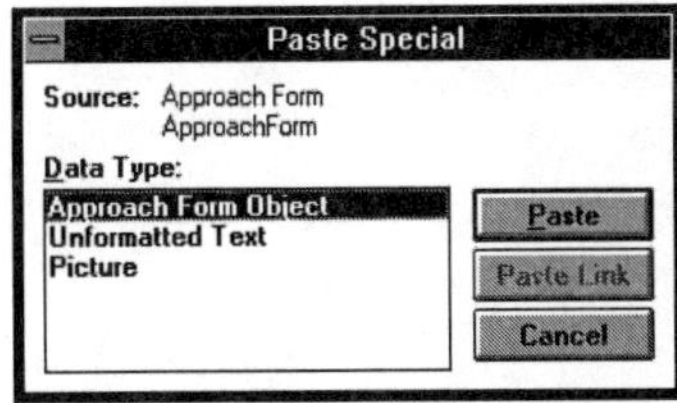

Fig. 18.12
Use the Paste Special dialog box to add an Approach object to a client application.

5. Select the desired option and select **P**aste or Paste Link. Click OK. The object is inserted into the container application (see fig. 18.13).

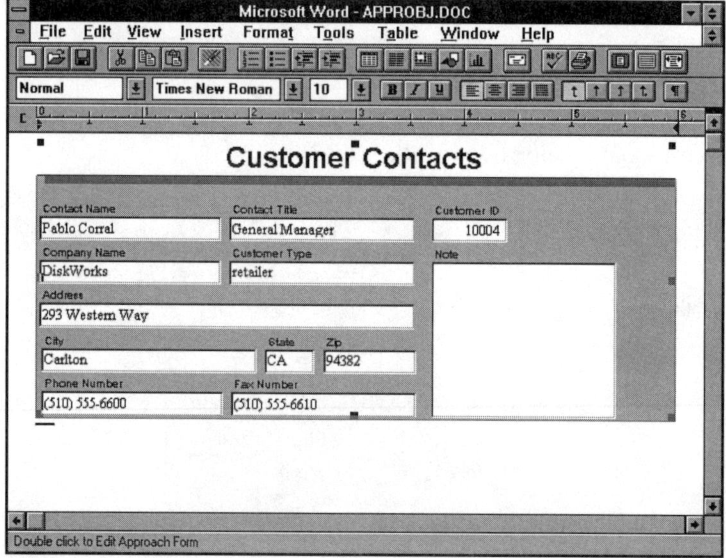

Fig. 18.13
An Approach Form Object is embedded into a Word for Windows document.

To activate the Approach object, double-click it. You can also select the object, open the **E**dit menu, and choose Edit Approach O**b**ject from the bottom of the menu.

Creating an Approach OLE Object in Another Application

To create an Approach OLE object within a container application, follow these steps:

1. Start by opening the application. From the **I**nsert menu, choose **O**bject. The Insert Object dialog box appears, listing all server applications currently installed on your machine (see fig. 18.14).

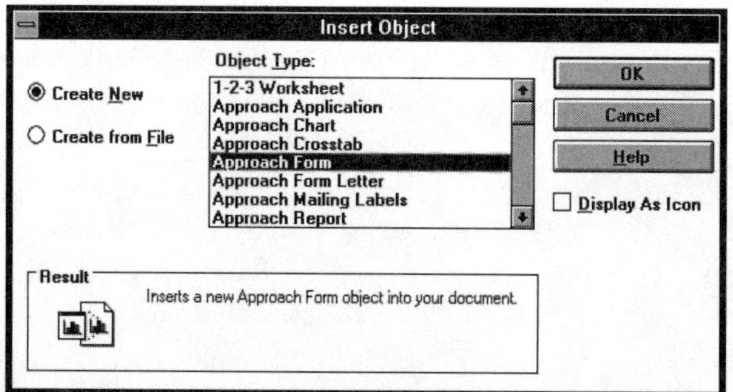

Fig. 18.14
The Insert Object dialog box lists possible object types.

Note

The list of objects that can be created will vary depending on what software is installed on your machine. Don't be surprised if your list or your dialog box looks different from the figure.

2. Select the Approach object of your choice, such as an Approach Form Object. Click OK. This brings up the standard Approach Open dialog box (see fig. 18.15).

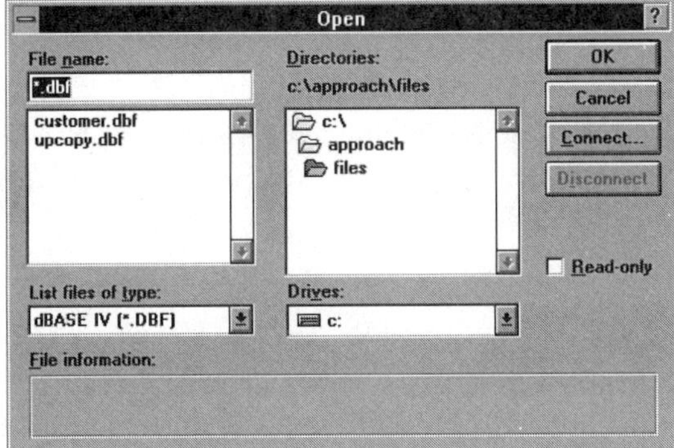

Fig. 18.15
Creating an Approach object starts by opening the database file.

3. Select the type of file you're using as the database for the object from the List Files of **T**ype drop-down list.

4. Use the Dri**v**es drop-down list and the **D**irectories list box to select the drive and directory that contain the file you want to import.

5. Select the file you want to use and click OK.

6. Here you get the Approach Assistant that's used to create the type of object selected. Since the object in this example is an Approach Form Object, the Approach Form Assistant dialog box opens (see fig. 18.16).

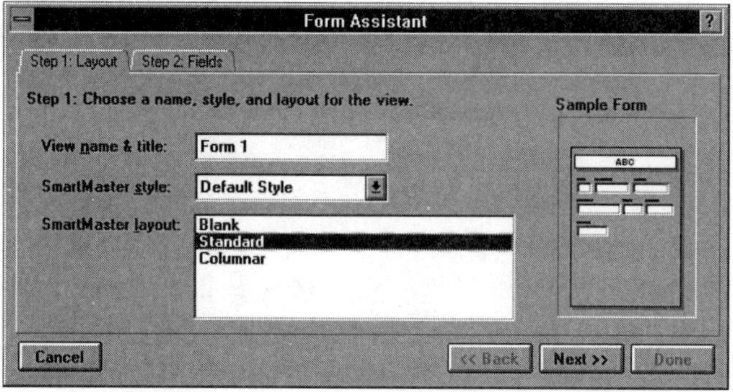

Fig. 18.16 Use the Approach Form Assistant dialog box to create an Approach Form Object.

7. Use the Assistant to create the form or whichever object you've selected.

To activate the Approach object, double-click it. You can also select the object, open the **E**dit menu, and choose Edit Approach O**b**ject from the bottom of the menu.

From Here...

As you've learned, much of Approach's versatility lies in its ability to interchange data between different formats. This ability is fully highlighted when doing imports and exports.

By importing Approach files, you can use stored views, macros, and calculated and variable fields from within a different Approach file—so there's no need to recreate all of the work it took to create the original.

With Approach's OLE capabilities, you can have Approach access your data from within any application that can serve as an OLE client.

To learn more about using Approach with Lotus Notes and other applications in the Lotus SmartSuite, refer to the following chapters in this book:

- Chapter 19, "Using Lotus Notes with Approach," teaches you how to share data in a workgroup using Lotus Notes electronic mail. You also learn how to use Approach as a data entry and reporting tool for Notes data.

- Chapter 20, "Using Approach with the Lotus SmartSuite," describes how Approach can be used as an OLE client or server for the other applications in the SmartSuite. It can also be used to display, enter, or report on Lotus 1-2-3 spreadsheet data.

Chapter 19

Using Lotus Notes with Approach

Beginning with version 3.0, Lotus Approach is tightly integrated with the workgroup software Lotus Notes. While Approach is a powerful database program, *Notes* is a document-based groupware system. You can easily share information across an entire Notes network to keep various parts of a business working together as a group.

Using both programs allows you to combine the groupware abilities of Notes with the data-storing features of Approach.

In this chapter, you learn how to:

- Open a Lotus Notes local and server database from Approach
- Change Notes database information from Approach
- Use Notes F/X and Approach to share information
- Send NotesMail from Approach
- Create a new replica database on your local machine from Approach
- Update a local replica copy database from Approach

Combining Lotus Approach and Notes

There are many ways to share data between Lotus Approach and Lotus Notes. For example, Approach can access views and forms in a Notes database. You can create new views, advanced forms, and summary reports in Approach with information stored in Notes. Approach can also be used to add, modify, or delete Notes records.

Notes F/X is a feature of Lotus products that allows you to connect information from another application directly with Lotus Notes. Similar to Object Linking and Embedding (OLE), F/X is more powerful, easy to use, and yields more direct access to shared bits of data.

Compatible with Notes F/X, Lotus Approach allows you to directly share fields of information with Lotus Notes databases without opening Approach. This bidirectional link between Approach and Notes allows you to modify information from either program and automatically reflect those changes through Notes F/X.

NotesMail, an integrated feature of Approach, can also be sent to other users. You can send both a snapshot of your current screen and your Approach application files to one or many users. In addition, Approach lets you route your NotesMail messages to users in a specified order.

Further integration with Lotus Notes permits Approach to replicate Notes databases. Using built-in commands, Approach users can create and update replica copies of databases from your Notes network onto your local machine.

Approach also allows you to create reports from Notes data. While accessing Notes databases, you can take advantage of advanced Approach Report creation functions. Now you can create summary reports, mailing labels, and form letters with the ease of Approach.

Accessing Lotus Notes Databases

You can easily access Notes databases from Approach. Whether the database is on your local machine or a distant server, Approach runs well on Notes databases. Approach will even prompt you to perform a login if you need to connect to a remote server.

Using Approach, you can view and modify information in Notes databases. Approach permits you to open views and forms in a Notes file. When you open a Notes view, the view is in *read-only* format. You can create reports and worksheets from the information, but you cannot modify the data in the Notes database.

When you open a Notes form, you can change Notes information. Approach treats each Notes document as a record and lets you directly access the database information. From Approach you can add, modify, and delete database records and have those changes directly saved in your Notes database.

Opening a Local Notes Database

From Approach, you can easily access a local Notes database by following these steps:

1. Open the **F**ile menu and choose **O**pen, or press Ctrl+O. The Open dialog box appears (see fig. 19.1).

2. Scroll through the List Files of **T**ype choices and select Lotus Notes—Local(*).

3. Scroll through the Dri**v**es and **D**irectories list boxes until you locate the Notes database you want to access.

4. Select the database and click OK.

5. All the forms and views in the database appear in the Files dialog box. Select a form or view to access and click OK to open it.

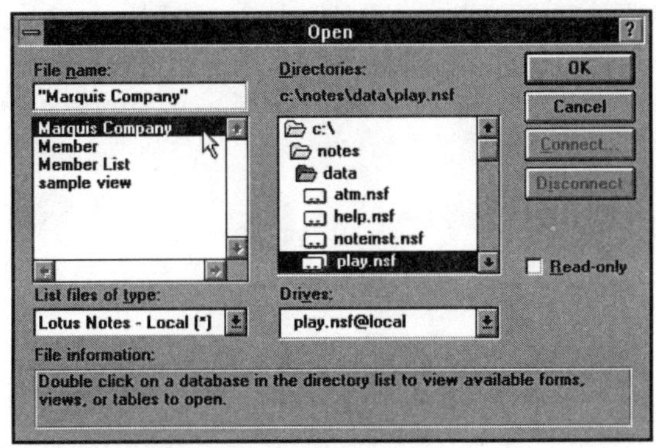

Fig. 19.1
As you open a Notes database, a selection of all the views and forms appears in the Files dialog box.

Opening a Notes Database from a Server

To open a Notes database from a server, follow these steps:

1. Open the **F**ile menu and choose **O**pen, or press Ctrl+O. The Open dialog box appears.

2. Scroll through the List Files of **T**ype choices and select Lotus Notes—Server(*).

3. Scroll through the Servers dialog box to identify the server to which you want to connect. Approach prompts you for your Notes user password and then opens a connection with that server. If necessary, Approach will prompt Notes to call and connect to a selected Notes server.

4. Scroll through the **D**irectories list box, select the database, and click OK.

> **Note**
>
> To open a Notes database, you must have reader access, which permits you to open a Lotus Notes database without making changes to existing documents.

5. All the forms and views in the database appear in the Files dialog box. Select a form or view to access and click OK to open it.

Changing Notes Data from Approach

Once you open a form in a Notes database, you can modify the database records from Approach. In Browse mode, Approach displays the Notes fields on an Approach form. You can scroll through the records (Notes documents) by using the arrows at the bottom of the Approach screen.

> **Note**
>
> You can set Notes forms to be read-only. From Approach, open the **T**ools menu and choose **P**references. Select the Database tab to bring up database access information. Make sure that the Open All Notes Forms as Read Only checkbox is selected, and save your changes.

To modify a record from Approach, click the field you want to update and type your changes. Your modifications will immediately be reflected in the Notes database.

To add a new record to the Notes database, open the **B**rowse menu and choose N**e**w Record, or press Ctrl+N. An empty database record appears. Once you fill out the fields, the record is immediately accessible in the Notes database because you are directly accessing it. This command is similar to composing a document in Notes.

To delete a record from the Notes database, choose the record you want to delete and select De**l**ete Record from the **B**rowse menu, or press Ctrl+Delete. Using the arrows at the bottom of the Approach screen, scroll through the Notes records until you reach the entry you want to delete. Again, this change immediately affects the Notes database because you are directly accessing it.

Any modifications you make from Approach on a Notes database are reflected to other users of the Notes database. Notes users will be prompted to update their views if they are accessing a database that is being changed at the same time.

Using Notes F/X

Notes F/X is an advanced feature that integrates Windows products with Lotus Notes. Windows OLE (Object Linking and Embedding) enables you to insert a file in a Notes document, and creates a link between Notes and the inserted application. F/X enables you to read and modify actual fields from a file inserted into a Notes document. Through F/X, Windows applications can bidirectionally share fields of information from Notes. This integrated feature allows information to easily be shared from a variety of applications.

Approach 3.0 is Notes F/X enabled. From Approach, you can define special fields that can be accessed directly from Lotus Notes. When you insert an Approach object into a Notes document, you can also read and modify the specifically defined F/X fields. These fields of information can be automatically updated in Approach if they are changed from Notes.

In Approach, all variable fields can be F/X enabled. Whether the variable field is a number, time, or Boolean value, those fields can be shared with Lotus Notes.

Enabling Approach Fields for Notes F/X

Once you have created your variable fields in Approach, you must enable them to be F/X available. Notes can read your variable fields from Approach whether or not they are enabled, and changes you make in Approach will also be linked to Notes documents. However if you want the changes you make in Notes to be reflected in Approach, you must enable the bidirectional link for the desired fields.

Follow these steps to enable the bidirectional Notes F/X links for Approach variable fields:

1. After you have created the variable fields for F/X to enable, open the **F**ile menu and choose Approach **F**ile Info.

2. In the Variable **F**ields dialog box, highlight the variable field(s) that you want to enable by selecting them with your mouse button (see fig. 19.2).

3. Click OK to save your changes and enable your fields for F/X.

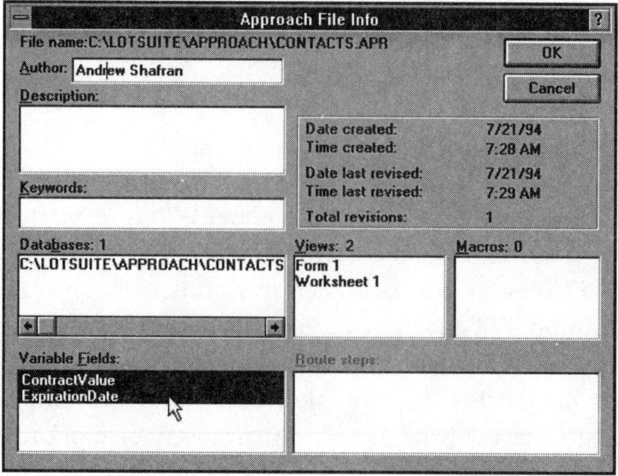

Fig. 19.2
Select the variable fields that you want enabled for F/X.

Accessing Approach Fields from Notes

Once your Approach variable fields are F/X enabled, you are ready to access them from Notes. To inherit information from Approach, you must have field names in your Notes documents that exactly correspond with the variable field names in Approach. Follow these steps:

1. Create or modify a Notes form and place the correct field names on your form.

> **Note**
>
> To create or modify a Notes form, open the **D**esign menu and choose **F**orms. From the Design Forms dialog box, select the form you want to edit and click the **E**dit button, or click **N**ew to create a new form.

2. From an Approach database with variable fields, open the **E**dit menu and choose **C**opy View to copy your view to the Windows Clipboard.

> **Caution**
>
> If you open the **E**dit menu and choose **P**aste from your Notes menu, Notes pastes a linked copy of your Approach application in the Notes form, but your Notes fields are not F/X enabled.

3. From your Notes form, open the **E**dit menu and choose Paste **S**pecial to bring up the Paste Special dialog box (see fig. 19.3).

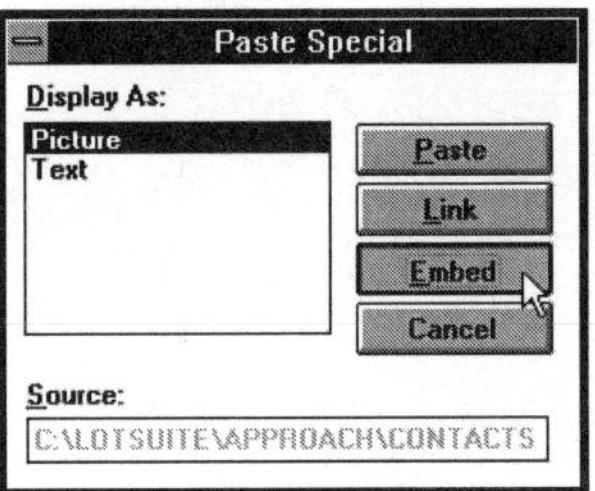

Fig. 19.3
Select Embed from the Paste Special dialog box to insert the Approach application from the Windows Clipboard.

4. Click **E**mbed to create a link between Notes and Approach (see fig. 19.4).

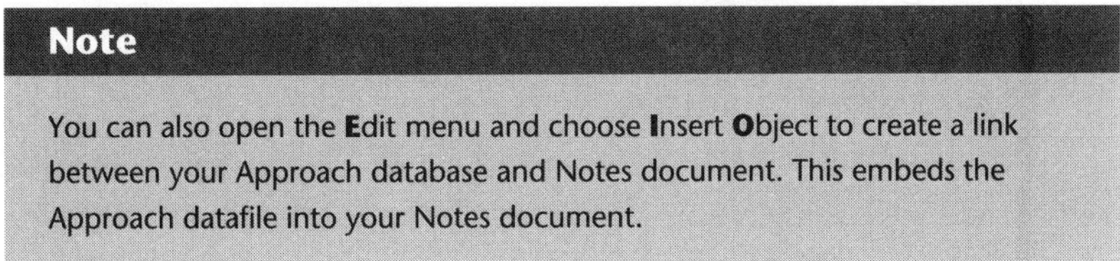

Note

You can also open the **E**dit menu and choose **I**nsert **O**bject to create a link between your Approach database and Notes document. This embeds the Approach datafile into your Notes document.

5. Open the **D**esign menu and choose Form **A**ttributes, making sure that the **S**tore Form in the Document checkbox is selected. Click OK to exit the Form Attributes dialog box and save the changes.

6. Save your Notes form.

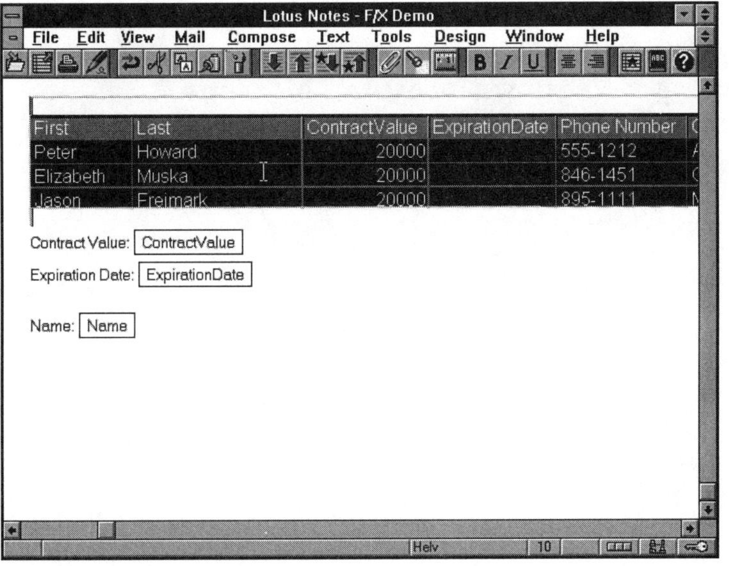

Fig. 19.4
Select the embedded object to open Approach with the embedded data.

Your Notes form is now linked to the embedded Approach application. Approach and Notes update their shared fields of information when you compose new documents with that form, and edit existing documents with the Approach application embedded inside of it.

Sending NotesMail

Electronic mail, or *e-mail*, has become a staple in communication. You can use e-mail to send messages back and forth to colleagues, friends, and business associates. Approach makes it easy for you to share your database information by letting you send e-mail directly from the menu bar. Approach messages can contain any combination of text, snapshots of current information, or actual Approach database files.

With Notes installed, Approach allows you to use the powerful document routing and addressing capabilities of Notes to communicate. You can use the Notes Name & Address Books to address your messages, or enter your own specific mail addresses. Approach even has a document routing feature that lets you route a single message from user to user in a specified order.

You even get the advanced security features of signing and encrypting your mail messages to ensure that your data is not compromised en route to the recipient. In short, built-in electronic mail functionality allows you to communicate with other Notes and Approach users in a safe, quick, and easy fashion.

Sending a Regular NotesMail Message from Approach

You can send e-mail messages to your associates directly from Approach. Working with Lotus Notes, Approach lets you type, address, and send your message.

To create and send an e-mail message from Approach, follow these steps:

1. With no databases currently open, open the **F**ile menu and choose Send Mail from the Notes menu bar.

2. Approach invokes Lotus Notes and prompts you for your User ID password. Type in your password (Notes is case sensitive) and click OK to bring up the Send dialog box.

3. Enter the desired recipients in the **T**o field, and select whether you want Notes to send a message to all of the recipients or one at a time in

the drop-down dialog box. You can also use the **A**ddress button to access your Notes Name & Address Book to look up recipients. Enter a subject and message text to be included with the message.

4. Check the Sign and/or Encrypt checkboxes to provide additional message security through Notes.

> **Note**
>
> When you check the Sign or Encrypt checkboxes, make sure that your recipients are in your Notes domain or have your decoding key to decrypt and verify your message upon arrival.

5. Click OK to send the message.

Sending an Approach File or View through NotesMail

In addition to sending regular e-mail messages from Approach, you can send snapshots of Approach screens and actual database files.

To send an Approach screen snapshot or file, follow these steps:

1. Open the **F**ile menu and choose Send Mail from the Notes menu bar. The Send Mail dialog box appears on-screen (see fig. 19.5).

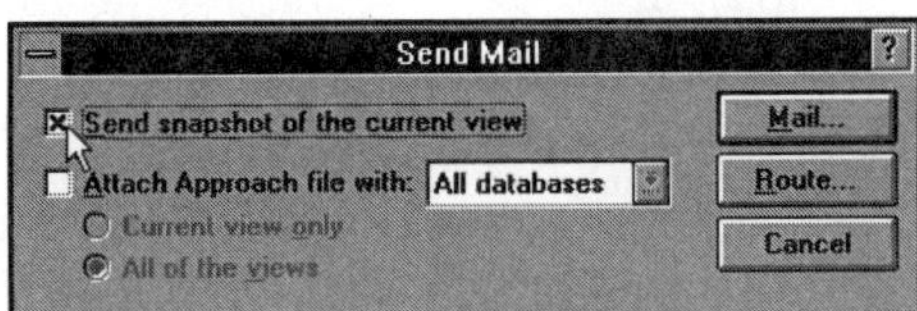

Fig. 19.5
Use the Send Mail dialog box to select the file and database information you want to send in your Notes message.

2. From this dialog box you can select whether you wish to send a snapshot of the current view (the current Approach screen), an actual Approach file, or both. If you choose to send a file, you can tell Approach to include only the current view or all the views in the database.

3. After selecting the data you wish to send, Approach requests your Notes user password. Approach then invokes the NotesMail capabilities and brings up the Send dialog box.

Tip
The Message field can only contain the maximum field length of 254 characters.

4. Enter the desired recipients in the **T**o field. Select whether you want Notes to send a message to all of the recipients or one recipient at a time in the drop-down dialog box. You can also use the **A**ddress button to access your Notes Name & Address Book to look up recipients. Enter a subject and message text to be included with the message.

5. Click the Options button if you want to change the mail priority of the Notes message or receive a receipt upon the message delivery (see fig. 19.6).

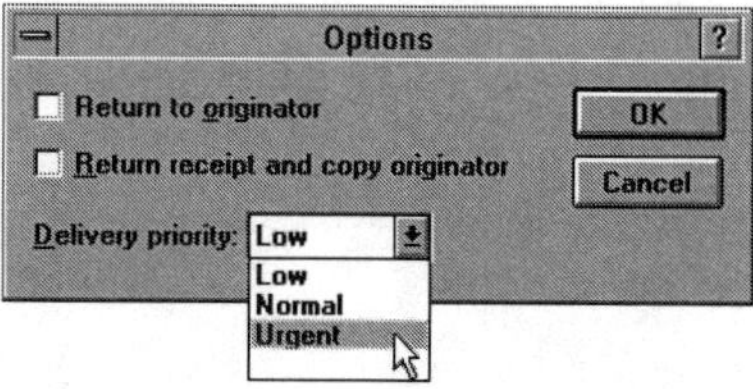

Fig. 19.6
Select the mail options and priority you want your NotesMail message to have.

6. Click OK to send the message.

Replicating Lotus Notes Databases

In Notes, replication enables many copies of the same database to be spread throughout the entire Notes network. When one copy of the database is modified, that change is replicated to all of the other copies. Replication is a scheduled event for most Notes servers. All changes to a replicated database are sent, and all updates are accounted for when two Notes servers talk to each other.

This process lets users of various Notes servers access the same updated information. Not only is it useful but also necessary for everyone in your Notes domain to have up-to-date information.

Through Approach, you can take advantage of this advanced information-sharing feature. Using built-in commands, Approach can create and update Notes databases. You can create a new local replica copy of a server-based database to make it easier to access the information from Approach. In addition, you can run replication update commands to ensure that your data is current. To run the special replication commands, Approach must use customized menus for each database.

This feature allows you to create powerful Approach applications on your local machine by using up-to-date information found in Notes databases.

Customizing Approach for Notes Replication

Although Notes replication features are built into Approach 3.0, they are only accessible through special customized menus. These menus have to be created specifically for each Approach application with which you want to use Notes replication.

Customizing Approach is simply a matter of creating a new menu accessible to you in Browse mode. Once the customized menu is created, you can quickly switch back and forth from the standard Approach menus to your customized ones.

Creating Your Customized Menu

To create a simple customized menu that lets you replicate Notes databases, follow these steps:

1. Open the Approach application with which you want to have replication functionality, and switch to Design mode.

2. Open the **T**ools menu and choose **C**ustomize Menus. The Customize Menus dialog box appears.

3. Click the **N**ew button to create a new customized menu and bring up the Define Custom Menu Bar dialog box.

4. Name your new custom menu, and select Standard Menu from the Menu Type drop-down box (see fig. 19.7).

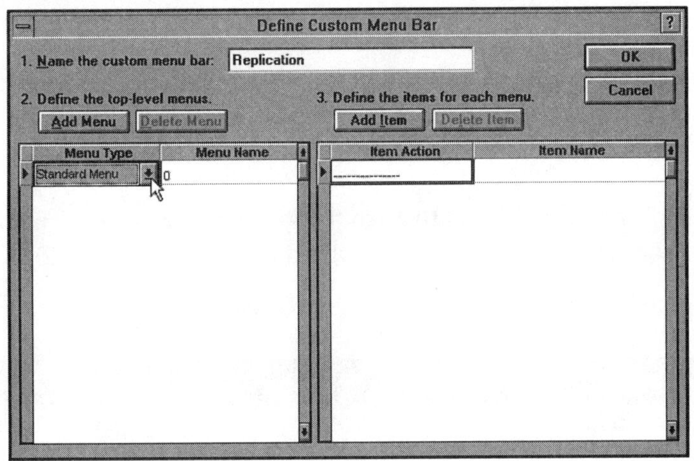

Fig. 19.7
Select the menu type for your customized replication menu bar.

5. Press Tab and enter a menu name.

6. Click the Item Action drop-down box and select Notes, New Notes Replica. Repeat the selection for the item below that and select Notes, Replicate with Notes Server (see fig. 19.8).

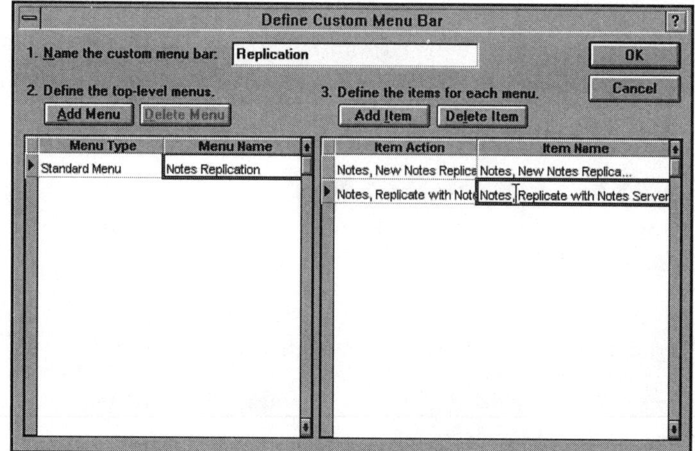

Fig. 19.8
Insert the menu items for your customized replication menu.

7. Click OK to save your new customized menu.

Accessing Your Customized Menu

Once your customized menu is complete, you can access it by following these steps:

1. Make sure you are accessing a worksheet in Design mode.
2. Open the W**o**rksheet menu and choose **S**tyle & Properties. The Settings dialog box appears.
3. Use your mouse to scroll through the Attached Menu Bar drop-down list and select your customized replication menu (see fig. 19.9).

4. Switch to Browse mode to view your new customized menu.

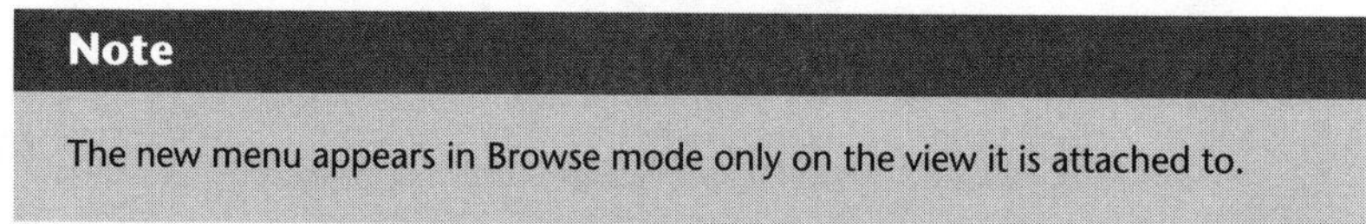

Note

The new menu appears in Browse mode only on the view it is attached to.

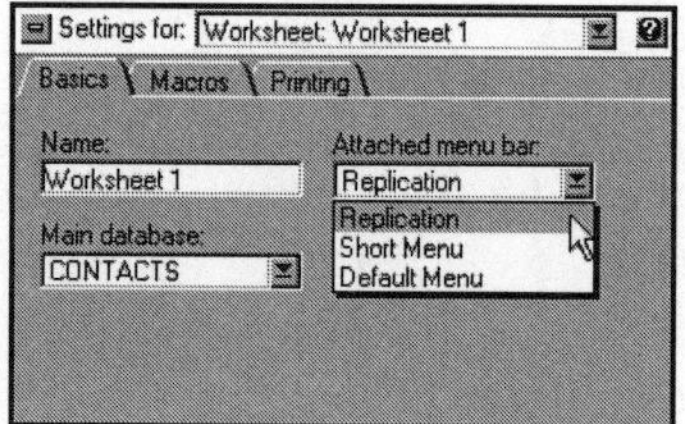

Fig. 19.9
Use your mouse to select the new attached menu from the Attached Menu Bar drop-down list.

Creating a New Notes Replica Database

Once you have created your customized Approach menu, you can take advantage of Notes replication features. From Approach you can access a Notes server and create a new copy of a database on your local machine.

To create a local replica of a Notes database, follow these steps:

1. Open the Notes customized menu and choose the New Notes Replica command.
2. Select the Server, database file name, and enter the new local file name in the correct fields. Check the **O**nly Replicate Documents Saved in the Last 90 Days checkbox if you want your local database to only replicate recent documents from the Notes Server. You can change the number of days to any value you wish (see fig. 19.10).
3. Click the New button to create the new replica. Your new replicated database is now in your Notes Data directory.

> **Note**
>
> Your local database isn't automatically updated if the replica copy on the server is modified. You must run a manual replication update for the local and server copies of the database to exchange modifications to the database.

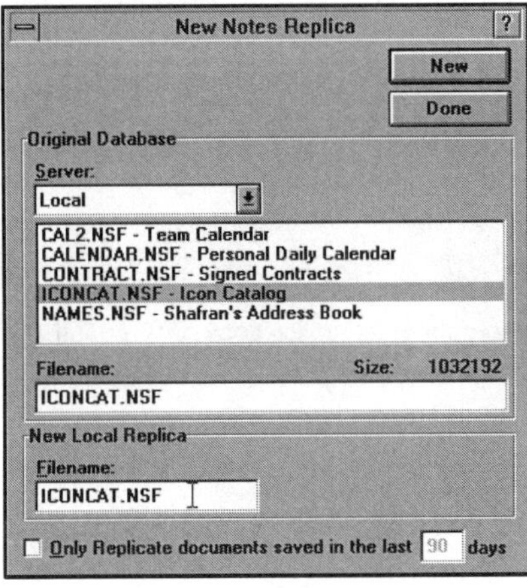

Fig. 19.10
Select the server and database from which to replicate, and the file name of the new local replica database.

Updating a Notes Replica Database

While Lotus Notes automatically updates replicated copies of a database on all of its servers, it does not update replica databases on local machines.

To update a local replica database, you must manually replicate it to a Notes Server. Approach is also able to manually run your Notes replication. Using the customized Approach menu, you can choose which database to replicate, and which replication updates are made.

To update your local copy of a replicated Notes database, follow these steps:

1. Open the customized Notes menu and choose Replicate with Notes Server.

2. Type the file name of the local Notes database to be replicated in the Replicate with Notes Server dialog box.

3. Select the replication options that you want to enable (see fig. 19.11), as described in the following table.

Exchange Document Read Marks	Exchanges information between the server and local databases on which documents you have already read
Receive Documents from Server	Enables local database to receive new and updated documents from the server database
Send **D**ocuments to Server	Enables local database to send new and updated documents to the server database for replication throughout the entire Notes network
Replicate Database **T**emplates	Enables design and template changes to update local database

4. Click OK to begin replication with the Notes server.

Caution

Any changes you make to your local replica copy of this database will be replicated to all of the copies of this database throughout your Notes network if you select Send Documents to Server.

Fig. 19.11
Enter your local database name and select your desired replication options.

From Here...

Using Lotus Notes and Approach together combines the data-storing power of Approach with the document management capabilities of Lotus Notes. In this chapter, you learned how to use the two programs to send mail and replicate databases, and how you can use Approach for increased flexibility with Lotus Notes databases.

For more information on these topics, refer to the following chapters in this book:

Chapter 17, "Customizing Approach," shows you how to modify Approach defaults to fit your specifications.

Chapter 20, "Using Approach with the Lotus SmartSuite," covers full integration with the entire Lotus SmartSuite. From using the Windows Clipboard to OLE, you can share data from the applications in the SmartSuite directly with Approach.

Chapter 20

Using Approach with the Lotus SmartSuite

The Windows environment makes it easy to use many different applications together. The built-in Windows features of the Clipboard and Object Linking and Embedding (OLE) can instantly share text, graphs, charts, pictures, and data files from one application to another.

In this chapter, you learn how to:

- Use the Windows Clipboard to copy or cut data from one Lotus application to another
- Use Object Linking and Embedding (OLE) to link information from either Lotus 1-2-3 or Ami Pro to Approach
- Update OLE-linked information
- Embed a Freelance picture into Approach or embed an Approach database into Ami Pro
- Create an Approach report directly from Lotus 1-2-3 data
- Open a named Lotus 1-2-3 range from Approach

Sharing Data with Approach

The entire Lotus SmartSuite and nearly all Windows applications permit you to take advantage of certain data-sharing techniques. For example, if you want to send a company letter, you can create your logo in Freelance, include a performance chart from Lotus 1-2-3, and type your letter in Ami Pro. All three pieces of your letter could be created in their respective applications and linked together for a complete printout. By integrating with Ami Pro, 1-2-3, and Freelance, Approach lets you easily take advantage of Windows Clipboard and OLE.

Using the Clipboard, you can directly cut text and images from one application and paste them into Approach. For example, you can create your company logo using Freelance and paste it directly onto your Approach company invoices. In addition, the entire Lotus SmartSuite allows you to copy direct information into Approach.

OLE is an advanced tool that lets you share data from different applications and modify that information from the original program. Embedding your company logo into an Approach invoice allows you to store the logo in the actual Approach form. You can then access Freelance directly from the embedded logo, make changes to it, and have those changes saved in the Approach form. Linking data into Approach is a similar process except the data is not stored in the actual form.

With 1-2-3, Approach also provides extra functionality. Installing Approach 3.0 adds additional menu commands to 1-2-3 that let you directly access some of Approach's powerful database features. From 1-2-3 you can directly create Approach forms, reports, crosstabs, and mailing labels. Approach even lets you access tabled 1-2-3 information as a database type.

This chapter teaches you how to share data between the Lotus SmartSuite group of applications. Using built-in Windows functionality and advanced Approach features, you can easily share data between all of your Windows applications.

Using the Clipboard

The Windows Clipboard is the broadest and easiest way to share information between two separate applications. All Windows programs support the Clipboard for interapplication data copying. Using the **E**dit **C**opy and **E**dit Cu**t** commands, you can place data from virtually any application into the Clipboard. The Clipboard can hold text, graphics, tables, charts, and bitmaps. The only limitation to what the Clipboard can hold is your personal computer's available memory.

Once you copy your data in the Clipboard, you can view it, save it, or use the information in another Windows application. To view or save the data in the Clipboard, open the Clipboard Viewer from your Windows Program Manager. To use the information in a different application, simply switch to your application and choose **P**aste from the **E**dit menu. The material stored in the Clipboard is pasted onto your screen.

The information in your application is a duplicate of the information you copied to the Clipboard. There are no links between the original and duplicate text. Changes made to the text in one application are not reflected in the text in the other.

Copying and Pasting Information from Freelance to Approach

It's easy to use the Clipboard and make a copy of desired information. To copy a logo from Freelance into an Approach application, follow these steps:

1. Open the Freelance file that contains the logo you want to copy.

2. Select the logo using the Freelance Pointer tool.

3. From Freelance, open the **E**dit menu and choose **C**opy or press Ctrl+C (see fig. 20.1). This copies the logo to the Windows Clipboard.

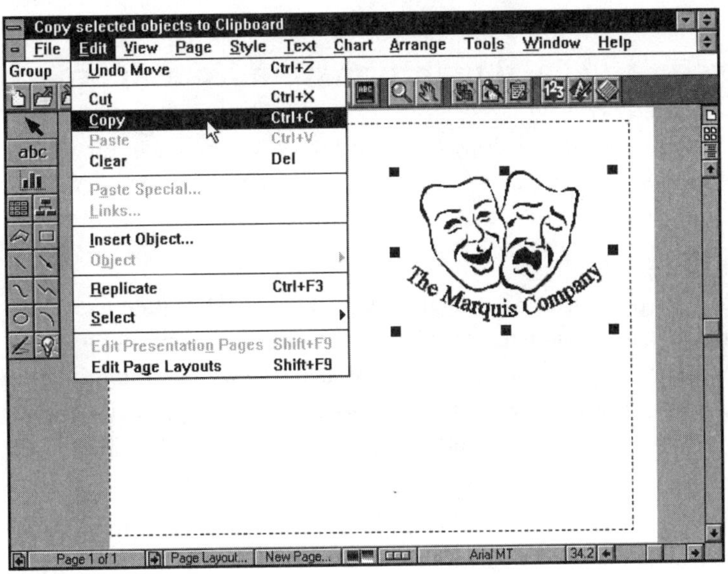

Fig. 20.1
After selecting the logo, copy it to the Windows Clipboard.

4. Open the Approach file that you want to paste the logo into and make sure you're in Design mode.

5. Open the **E**dit menu and choose **P**aste or press Ctrl+V. This pastes the logo from the Windows Clipboard (see fig. 20.2).

6. Use your mouse to resize and move the logo on your Approach form.

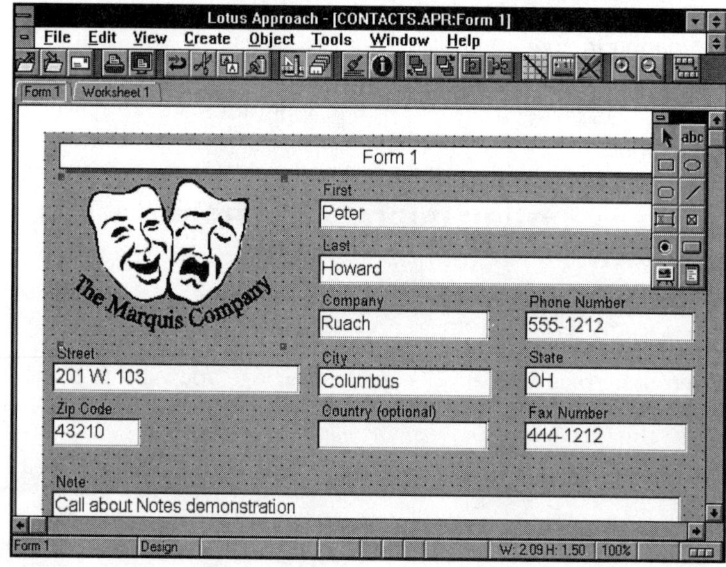

Fig. 20.2
Paste the logo onto your Approach form and resize it to fit the page.

Copying and Pasting Information from Approach to Lotus 1-2-3

You can also use the Windows Clipboard to paste Approach information into other SmartSuite applications. For example, when you paste an Approach form into Ami Pro, you get an image of the form framed by an Ami Pro image box.

In addition, pasting an Approach view into Lotus 1-2-3 offers extra benefits. Approach views include forms, reports, mailing labels, charts, crosstabs, form letters, and worksheets. Since both Approach's views and 1-2-3's worksheets are in column format, you can paste Approach information directly into 1-2-3 columns. This benefit allows you to transfer database information into spreadsheet format to easily make graphs and charts.

To copy an Approach view into a 1-2-3 spreadsheet, follow these steps:

1. Open the Approach application and access the worksheet you want to copy from.

2. Open the **E**dit menu and choose Select **A**ll from the Approach menu to highlight the entire view.

3. Open the **E**dit menu and choose **C**opy View from the Approach menu, or press Ctrl+C (see fig. 20.3).

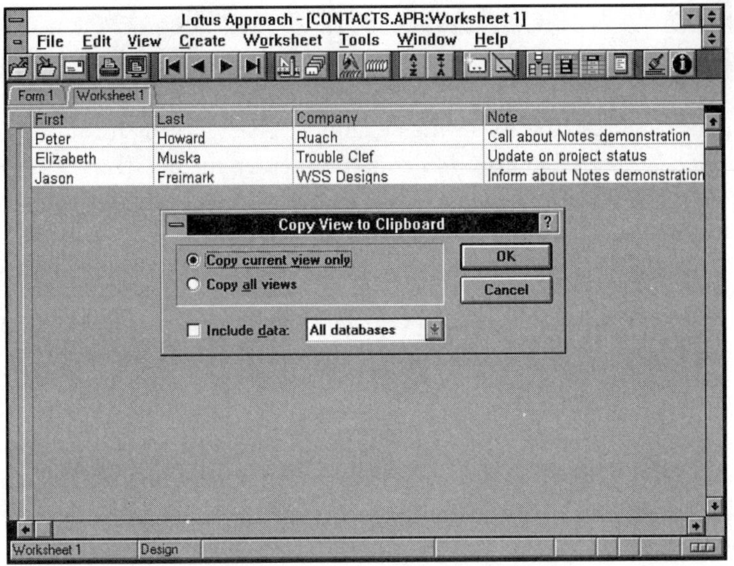

Fig. 20.3
After choosing Copy View, copy only the current view to the Windows Clipboard.

4. Select the Copy Current **V**iew Only radio button and click OK to copy the current view into the Windows Clipboard.
5. Open the 1-2-3 worksheet into which you want to paste the view.
6. Open the **E**dit menu and choose **P**aste from the 1-2-3 menu to paste the Approach view from the Windows Clipboard into the 1-2-3 columnized format (see fig. 20.4).

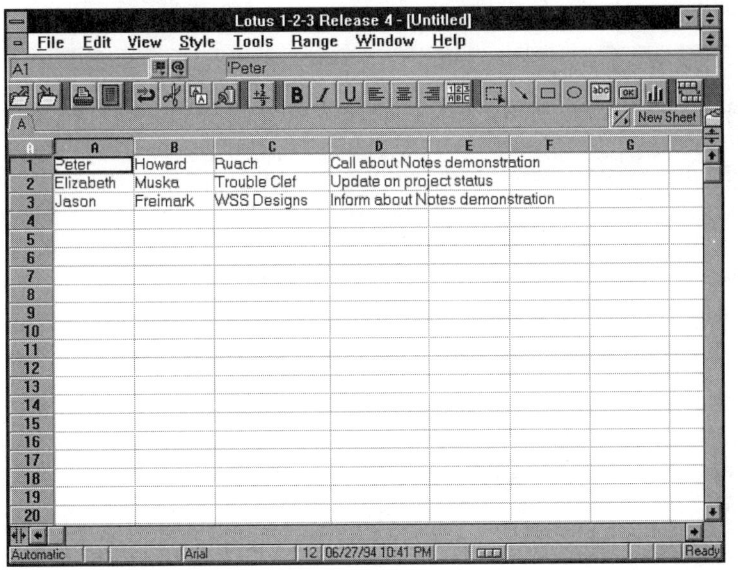

Fig. 20.4
Paste the Approach data directly into 1-2-3 columnized format.

Using Object Linking and Embedding (OLE)

While the Clipboard allows a wide flexibility of data sharing through Windows applications, OLE takes that concept one step further. Using OLE, you can share data from one application to another, and modify the inserted information using the original Windows program.

Linking and embedding are similar concepts, but there is an important difference between the two commands. Linking creates an image of data from one application into another, while embedding actually stores the original information in the indicated file.

For example, you can link the logo you created in Freelance to an Approach application form. To change the logo in the future, you can simply change the Freelance file instead of repasting an updated logo into Approach. In this example, there is an actual link placed in Approach connecting it to the Freelance file containing the logo. This link is regularly updated and the changes made to the Freelance file are updated automatically in Approach.

You can also access Freelance directly from Approach to make data modifications even easier.

Caution

For links to keep working, linked files must be kept in their original locations. These linked files can be numerous and difficult to track. Also, information is automatically updated in the linked files without your control.

Linked objects are primarily useful if you have data that might change in the future. Such changes would automatically change the linked applications to provide the most current information. It's also beneficial to link your applications together if you have many programs that use the same information. This saves you time and maintains continuity in your files. For example, if your logo is used in Approach, Ami Pro, and 1-2-3 for various reports and letters, it's easier to change the logo in one file and have those changes reflected in all your applications.

Embedding also enables you to share information between Windows applications. When you copy Windows data using embedding, the information is directly copied to the indicated program file. While linking stores a connection to a file, embedding stores the actual datafile (logo in this case) in the

Approach form. There is no established link to the original information. Any changes made to the original file are not reflected in the embedded information.

However, you can still make changes to the embedded data. Because all the information is stored in the indicated form, you can automatically open Freelance from Approach. The embedded information appears in Freelance where changes can be made. These changes are saved directly into the Approach form.

Embedding is particularly useful when you need to move files from one machine to another. Embedding information into Approach gives you the flexibility to decide when information is updated (links can update automatically). Also, you use only one file to store information from multiple applications, which allows you to move the file to different computers. One drawback to embedding is the increased size of the file containing the embedded data.

Linking Data with Approach

Linking data between applications is an important part of application communication. By linking two applications, changes made in one will be automatically reflected in the destination application.

Linking 1-2-3 Information into Approach

To create a link in Approach from 1-2-3 data, follow these steps:

Tip
You can also paste into a PicturePlus field while in Browse mode.

1. Open the 1-2-3 file you want to link to Approach.
2. Using the pointer, highlight the cells you want to place into Approach.
3. Open the **E**dit menu and choose **C**opy from the menu bar to copy the 1-2-3 information to the Windows Clipboard.
4. Open your Approach application and switch to Design mode on a form.
5. Open the **E**dit menu and choose Paste **S**pecial from the Approach menu to bring up the Paste Special dialog box.

6. Select Paste **L**ink to create a link to the original 1-2-3 document and then click OK (see fig. 20.5).
7. Your linked data should now appear in your Approach form (see fig. 20.6).

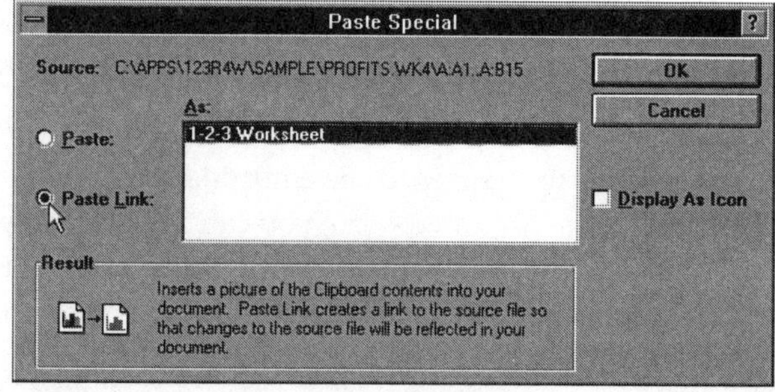

Fig. 20.5
Select Paste Link to create a link between the 1-2-3 file and Approach.

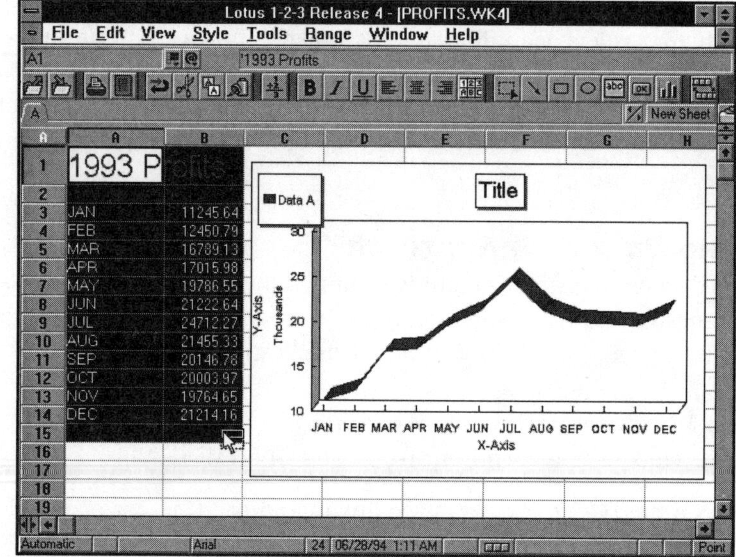

Fig. 20.6
Select the 1-2-3 cells that you want to link to Approach.

Tip
In Approach, the mouse pointer transforms into a hand when it is positioned over linked or embedded information.

Updating Linked Information

You can easily update your linked 1-2-3 information from Approach. Through Approach you can start 1-2-3, modify your information, and have those changes reflected in your original form.

To update your linked 1-2-3 information from Approach, follow these steps:

1. Open your Approach application with 1-2-3 data linked to it. Make sure you're in Design mode or accessing a picture plus field.

2. Double-click the 1-2-3 linked data to open 1-2-3 for Windows with your linked file.

3. Make the appropriate changes in 1-2-3.

4. Save and exit 1-2-3 for Windows, and notice the updated information in Approach.

Linking Approach Data to Ami Pro

Not only can you link SmartSuite files to Approach, but you can link your Approach databases to other Lotus applications. For example, you can link an Approach worksheet to Ami Pro to include as data in a letter you are sending. By linking the information to Ami Pro, if you add, modify, or delete records, your Ami Pro link will reflect the most current Approach information.

To create an Approach link in Ami Pro, follow these steps:

1. Open your Approach application, and select the worksheet you want to link to Ami Pro.

2. Open the **E**dit menu and choose Select **A**ll from the Approach menu to highlight the entire view.

3. Open the **E**dit menu and choose **C**opy View from the Approach menu bar to copy the current worksheet into the Windows Clipboard.

4. Open the Ami Pro document into which you want to link the Approach data.

5. Open the **E**dit menu and choose Paste **L**ink to paste the Approach link into Ami Pro (see fig. 20.7). The information automatically appears in an Ami Pro frame.

6. Size the frame to use in your Ami Pro letter.

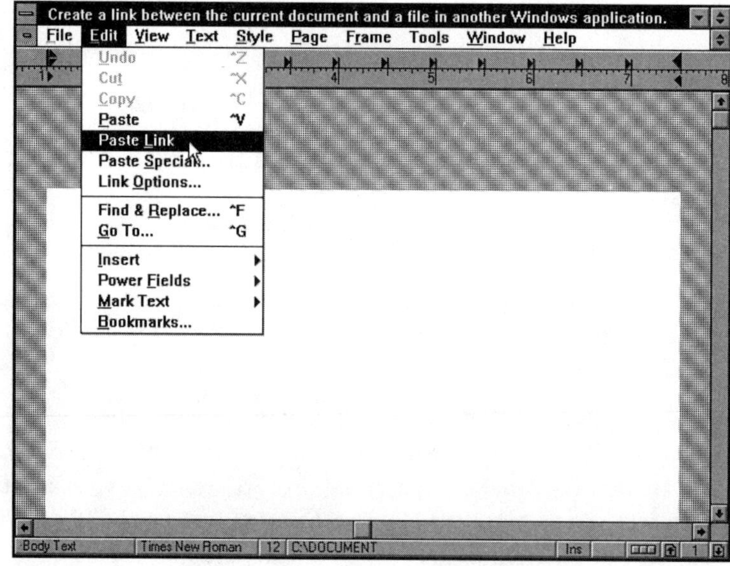

Fig. 20.7
Select Paste Link from Ami Pro to create an OLE Link from Approach and to insert the information.

Updating Approach Links

Once you create a link between Approach and another application, that connection is saved with the Approach file. The default settings for creating a link ensure that updates to the linked file automatically occur.

Sometimes you need to change the link options, however. If your linked Freelance file moves and you want Approach to keep the link active to the new location, you will want to change the Link Source file. Sometimes you will not want Approach to automatically update linked files, or even break the link between the applications entirely.

You can easily accomplish these goals through Approach by using the built-in Links command. From this dialog box, you can change the default link update status, change the link source file, or completely break the link.

To make these changes, open your Approach file with the linked document in it and make sure you are in Design mode. Open the **E**dit menu and choose L**i**nks from the Approach menu to bring up the Links dialog box (see fig. 20.8).

Sometimes you don't want Approach to automatically update from your linked document. If you're making multiple modifications to your company logo and using Approach at the same time, you may want to disable the automatic link update command until all of your changes are finished. This helps ease the load off your computer's memory because Approach will not constantly update the files linked to it. To disable the automatic link update command, first access the Links dialog box and then select the link you want to modify. Click the **M**anual radio button to have Approach update your linked documents at your manual command. Of course, the link is still maintained, and you can switch it back to automatic update any time in the future.

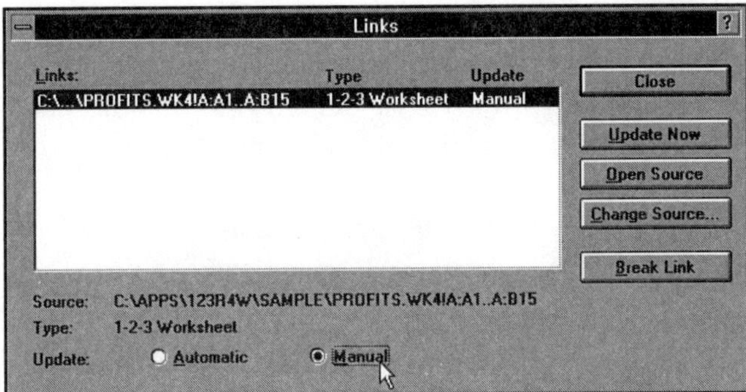

Fig. 20.8
Click the Manual button to disable the automatic link updates from Approach.

After switching the link update mode from **A**utomatic to **M**anual, you must manually refresh Approach to reflect updated linked information. By clicking the **U**pdate Now button from the Links dialog box, Approach updates your selected link.

If you want to make changes to a linked document, you can click the **O**pen Source button from the Links dialog box. This command opens the application using the linked data. You can also double-click the linked information directly from Approach to open the original application.

Sometimes you may need to update the actual link between Approach and the datafile. If you reorganize your hard drive or place a file on a server, you need to inform Approach of the new location. You can perform this command by clicking the **C**hange Source button from the Links dialog box. Approach then allows you to scan through your hard drive and select a different file to link to.

Caution

If you change an Approach link to an incorrect file, you lose the ability to update that information automatically. Change the link source again to the correct file to regain Object Linking update capabilities.

Tip
To make your linked changes permanent, you must save your Approach file. If you accidentally update or break a link or change the source to the wrong file, you can revert to your last saved version.

Finally, sometimes you may want to break your link between Approach and the other application permanently. By breaking the link, you still retain the data image in your Approach file. Any changes made to the linked file will not update your Approach file. To break your link, select **B**reak Link from the Approach Link dialog box.

Embedding Data into Approach

Object embedding allows you to directly store application data in an Approach file. By embedding the data, you can move your Approach files to different machines without worrying about links to other files and can still make changes to the data using the original application.

Embedding a Freelance Picture into Approach

To embed a Freelance file into Approach, follow these steps:

1. Create your Freelance logo or presentation.

2. Open the **V**iew menu and choose **P**age Sorter from the Freelance menu bar to view all of your Freelance slides.

> **Note**
>
> You must be in Page Sorter mode to embed a Freelance presentation into Approach. If you select a symbol and try to copy it into the Clipboard, Approach does not recognize it as a specific Freelance file, and the image pasted is not an embedded file.

3. Open the **E**dit menu and choose **C**opy or press Ctrl+C to copy the presentation into the Clipboard.

4. Open the Lotus Approach file into which you want to place the embedded presentation and enter Design mode.

5. Open the **E**dit menu and choose P**a**ste Special to bring up the Paste Special dialog box (see fig. 20.9).

6. Make sure that the **P**aste radio button is selected and click OK. The Freelance presentation is embedded into Approach.

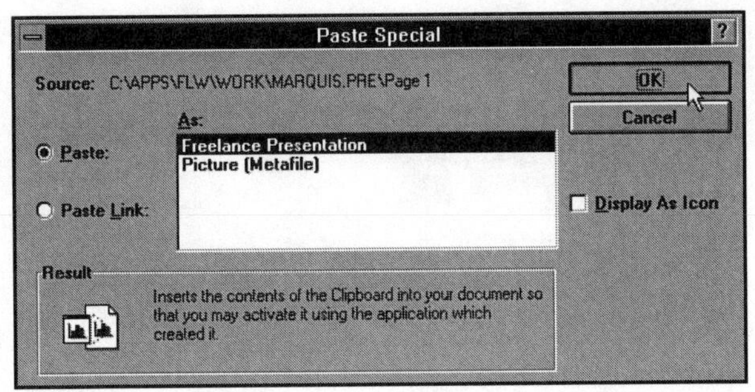

Fig. 20.9
Choose Paste Special to embed the Freelance presentation into Approach.

Embedding an Approach File into Ami Pro

You can also embed Approach data into the other SmartSuite applications. To embed an Approach view into an Ami Pro document, follow these steps:

Tip
Ami Pro automatically creates a frame when the file is embedded into it. You can resize this frame using your mouse to make it easier to use in your document.

1. Open the Approach file that you want to embed and access a worksheet.
2. Open the **E**dit menu and choose Select **A**ll from the Approach menu to highlight the entire view.
3. Open the **E**dit menu and choose Copy View from the Approach menu bar, or press Ctrl+C.
4. Select Copy This **V**iew Only to copy your current view into the Clipboard.
5. Open an Ami Pro document and choose Paste **S**pecial from the **E**dit menu.
6. Choose the OLE Embed file type from the **F**ormats list box to embed the Approach view into Ami Pro (see fig. 20.10).

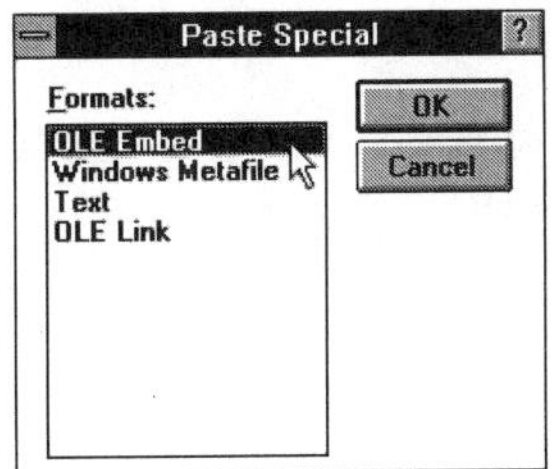

Fig. 20.10
Choose the OLE Embed file type to embed an Approach document into Ami Pro.

7. Double-click the object to open Approach with the embedded data in it (see fig. 20.11).

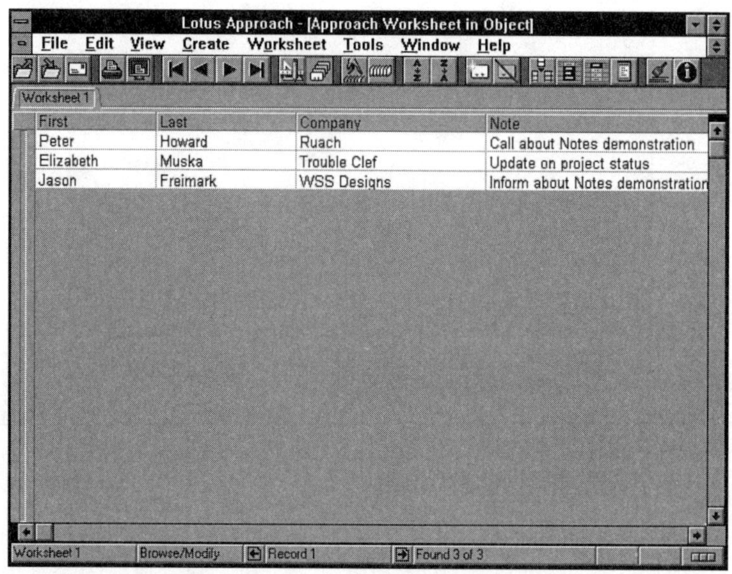

Fig. 20.11
Notice the title of the Approach screen when you access an embedded object.

Advanced Integration with Lotus 1-2-3

Besides using the Windows Clipboard and OLE features, Approach also provides additional built-in functionality for Lotus 1-2-3 users.

During installation, if Approach detects 1-2-3 on your system, extra menu commands are added to 1-2-3. These new commands allow you to use Approach's Form Assistant, Report Assistant, Crosstab Assistant, and Mailing List Assistant features from 1-2-3. To access these commands, open the **T**ools menu and choose Data**b**ase from 1-2-3.

Select the 1-2-3 information you want to use with your mouse, and run one of these new commands. Approach is automatically started, and you can create new forms, reports, crosstabs, and mailing lists with 1-2-3 data. When you finish using Approach, the new object is automatically embedded into your 1-2-3 spreadsheet.

In addition, you can also open named 1-2-3 ranges directly from Approach. By using these named ranges, you can load data into your spreadsheet directly from Approach.

Creating a Report Directly from 1-2-3 Data

Use one of the new 1-2-3 commands installed with Approach to create a report directly from your spreadsheet data. Select the columns you want to use to create a report, and then open Approach's Report Assistant from 1-2-3. Add the fields you want, and let Approach create a complete report for you!

To create a sample report from 1-2-3 information, follow these steps:

1. Create your 1-2-3 spreadsheet. Ensure that each column is named. This name is used by Approach as a field name.
2. Using your mouse, select the cells from which you want to create your report.

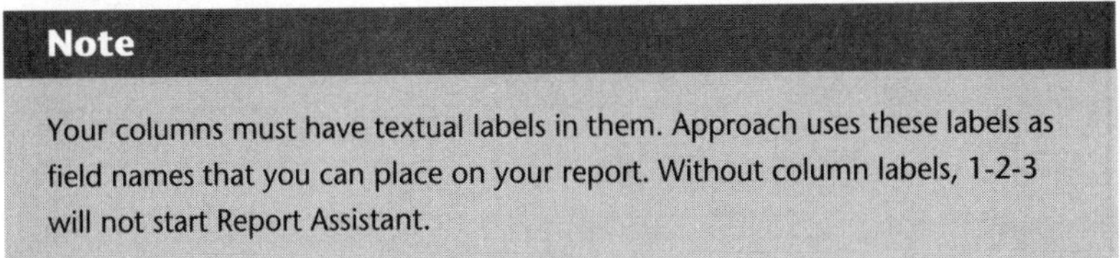

Note

Your columns must have textual labels in them. Approach uses these labels as field names that you can place on your report. Without column labels, 1-2-3 will not start Report Assistant.

3. From the 1-2-3 menu bar, open the **T**ools menu and choose Data**b**ase, R**e**port from the 1-2-3 menu bar to start Approach and access the Report Assistant dialog box (see fig. 20.12).

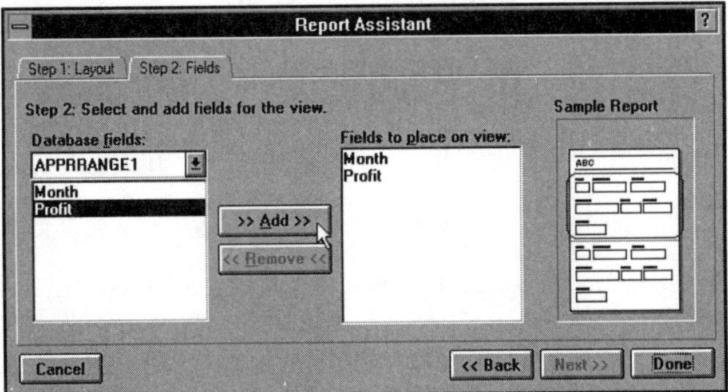

Fig. 20.12
Choose the 1-2-3 columns you want to place in your Approach report.

4. Select the report type you want to use, add the desired fields to your report form, and click the Done button. Approach automatically creates the report for you (see fig. 20.13).
5. Once you exit Approach, an embedded file icon appears in 1-2-3. You can double-click this icon to access your newly created report.

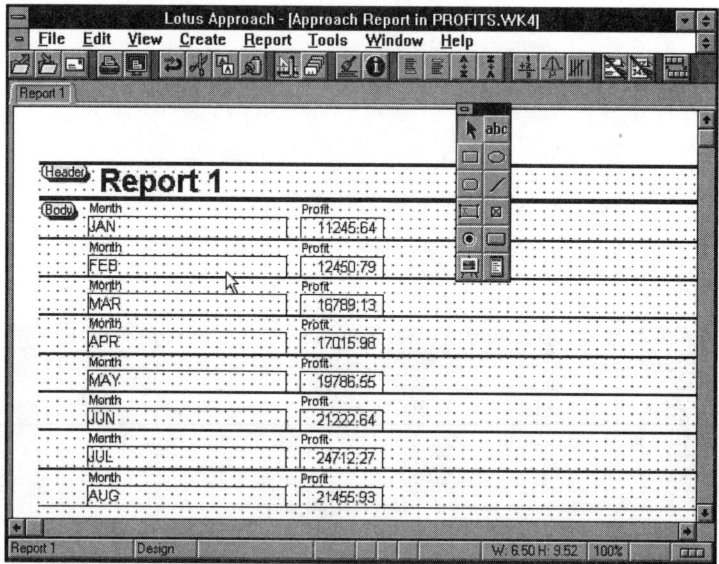

Fig. 20.13 Your newly created report appears in Approach.

Opening a Named 1-2-3 Range from Approach

Approach also lets you open a named 1-2-3 range. You can easily set up a named range in your 1-2-3 spreadsheet to open under Approach. Select the cells that you want in the named 1-2-3 range, use 1-2-3 to name the range, and then you can open the document from Approach.

To create and open a named 1-2-3 range from Approach, follow these steps:

1. Open your 1-2-3 spreadsheet.

2. Use your mouse to select the cells you want to be included in the named range.

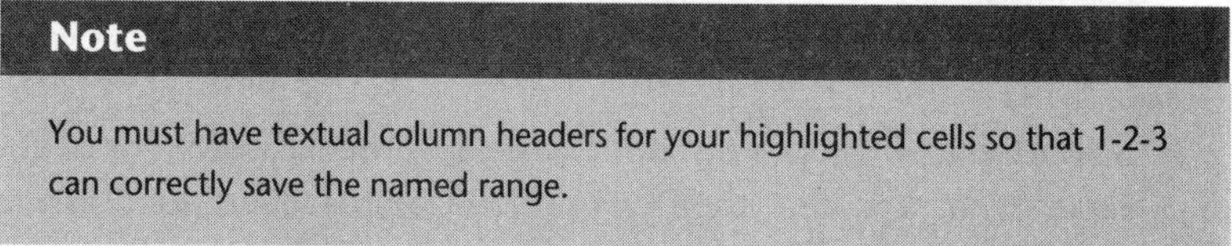

Note

You must have textual column headers for your highlighted cells so that 1-2-3 can correctly save the named range.

3. From 1-2-3, open the Name menu and choose Range. Enter an appropriate name for your data range.

4. Start Approach and open the **F**ile menu and choose **O**pen, or press Ctrl+O.

5. Scroll through the Filetypes dialog box and select 1-2-3 Ranges.

6. Your 1-2-3 document automatically appears and you can open the list of named ranges in that file. Select the named range and click OK (see fig. 20.14).

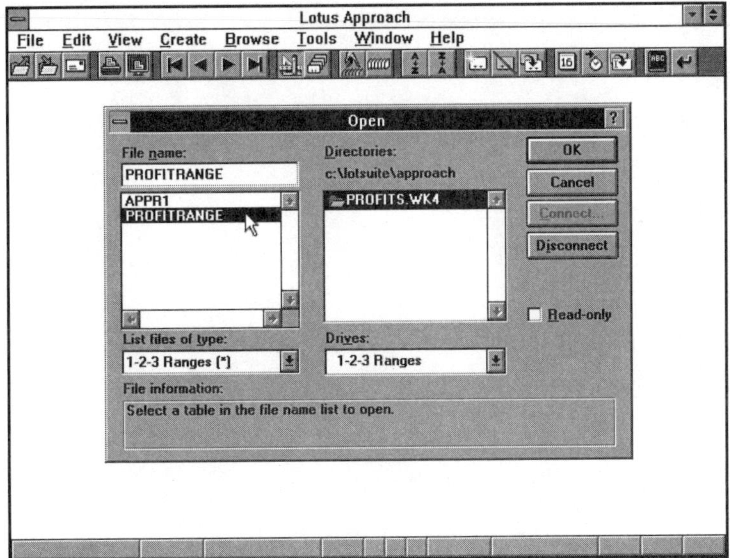

Fig. 20.14
Select 1-2-3 Ranges from the file types and then highlight the named range that you want Approach to open.

From Here...

In this chapter, you learned how to integrate the Lotus SmartSuite with Approach 3.0. Using the Windows Clipboard, you can copy data back and forth between multiple applications. Object Linking and Embedding gives you the advanced flexibility to share and update information. You can update and link graphics, text and spreadsheets into Approach files, and modify them using their original application.

In addition, you learned how to use additional integration between 1-2-3 and Approach. Approach can directly access 1-2-3 data and create powerful reports, forms, and mailing lists with a few clicks of the mouse. To learn more about using Approach with OLE, refer to the following chapters in this book:

- Chapter 18, "Importing and Exporting Files," also describes how OLE works.

- Chapter 19, "Using Lotus Notes with Approach," teaches you how to share data in a workgroup using Lotus Notes electronic mail. You also learn how to use Approach as a data entry and reporting tool for Notes data.

Index

Symbols

A

B

D

E

F

G

H

I

M

N

P

Q–R

S

T

U

V

W

X-Y-Z